W9-AWA-006

Dynamic Scheduling®
With Microsoft® Project 2010
The Book by and for Professionals

Rodolfo Ambriz, PMP, PMI-SP, PMI-RMP, MCTS, MCITP
Managing Director, IIL Mexico and Microsoft EPM Division
International Institute for Learning, Inc.

John White, MA, PMP, MCT, MCP, MCTS, MCITP
Director, Microsoft EPM Curriculum & Course Development
International Institute for Learning, Inc.

Published jointly by J. Ross Publishing and International Institute for Learning, Inc.

Copyright © 2011 by International Institute for Learning, Inc.

ISBN 978-1-60427-061-7

Printed and bound in the U.S.A. Printed on acid-free paper.

10 9 8 7 6 5 4 3 2 1

Library of Congress Cataloging-in-Publication Data

Ambriz, Rodolfo.
Dynamic scheduling with Microsoft Project 2010 : the book by and for professionals / by Rodolfo Ambriz and John White.
    p. cm.
Includes bibliographical references and index.
ISBN 978-1-60427-061-7 (pbk. : alk. paper) 1. Microsoft Project. 2. Project management--Computer programs. I. White, John, 1960- II. Title.
HD69.P75A483 2011
658.4'04028553--dc22

        2011007767

This publication contains information obtained from authentic and highly regarded sources. Reprinted material is used with permission, and sources are indicated. Reasonable effort has been made to publish reliable data and information, but the author and the publisher cannot assume responsibility for the validity of all materials or for the consequences of their use.

All rights reserved. Neither this publication nor any part thereof may be reproduced, stored in a retrieval system or transmitted in any form or by any means, electronic, mechanical, photocopying, recording or otherwise, without the prior written permission of the publisher. "PMI", "PMP", "PgMP", and "OPM3" are marks or registered marks of the Project Management Institute, which are registered in the United States and other countries. PMI does not endore or otherwise sponsor this publication.

The copyright owner's consent does not extend to copying for general distribution for promotion, for creating new works, or for resale. Specific permission must be obtained from J. Ross Publishing for such purposes.

Direct all inquiries to:

J. Ross Publishing, Inc., 5765 N. Andrews Way, Ft. Lauderdale, Florida 33309, USA.
Phone: (954) 727-9333
Fax: (561) 892-0700
Web: www.jrosspub.com

A Message from E. LaVerne Johnson
CEO, President and Founder - International Institute for Learning, Inc.

 As we round out the first decade of the 21st century, the global financial situation remains tenuous. Organizations continue to try to do more with less, and there is an increased demand for higher-level skills in Project and Program Management, Business Analysis, Risk Management, Strategic Leadership, Information Technology and Lean Six Sigma.

While many economists are hopeful that we will see some signs of recovery in the near future, the job market remains more competitive than ever. Building on your knowledge and "polishing your edge" are now not only critical to success, they are critical to survival.

So congratulations on taking this next step in your learning process and career! I'm confident that this book will help you master new skills to apply to your endeavors and strengthen those you already have. We hope that at the conclusion of this book, you feel an active desire and readiness to use what you've learned to benefit yourself and your workplace.

I would like to dedicate this book to all of the forward-thinking individuals who have worked to further project management as a recognized and critical discipline. International Institute for Learning, Inc. (IIL) is actively engaged in the advocacy of the project management profession and we commend those professionals who seek to advance their own skills and abilities, as well as those of entire organizations and communities. They seek to do this in order to increase their collective knowledge and capabilities, to advance constructive change and to have their organizations operate more adeptly and efficiently.

Our hope in writing this book was to inspire those in the project management profession to not only better understand and apply underlying project management principles and techniques in their day-to-day jobs, but to challenge them to break away from the common mindset and develop new and improved ideas.

I'd also like to acknowledge all those individuals who played a role in creating this book – from the initial release of the book on up to each new edition we publish. Your hard work and dedication have helped to create a resource that has truly become an industry standard. I recognize that the success of any collaborative effort is only as good as the sum of the contributions of all of those involved. From the original team members who had the vision to create such a powerful book, to those who have helped refine it over time, I am grateful to all of you for making this an indispensable reference to those who work throughout the project management community.

With kind regards,

E. LaVerne Johnson

E. LaVerne Johnson
Founder, President and Chief Executive Officer
International Institute for Learning, Inc.

International Institute for Learning, Inc. (IIL)

With operating companies all over the world and clients in 200 countries, IIL is a global leader in training, consulting, coaching and customized course development. Our core competencies include: Project, Program and Portfolio Management; Microsoft® Project and Project Server; Business Analysis; Lean Six Sigma; PRINCE2®; ITIL®; Leadership and Interpersonal Skills.

Using our proprietary Many Methods of Learning™, IIL delivers innovative, effective and consistent training solutions through a variety of learning approaches, including Traditional Classroom, Virtual Classroom, simulation training and interactive, on-demand learning. Now in our twenty-first year of doing business, we are proud to be the learning solution provider of choice for many top global companies.

IIL and Microsoft: a Rich History

IIL is a Microsoft Partner and has the Gold Competency in project and Portfolio Management from Microsoft. We are dedicated to providing individuals, teams and companies with the training they need to successfully manage projects and programs using the Microsoft Project and Project Server solutions.

Since 1998, IIL has been offering "Belt" certification for Microsoft Project. Since that time, we have trained more than 20,000 people in Microsoft Project and Project Server. IIL also helped Microsoft develop its own certification program for the 2007 versions of Project and Project Server, which consisted of three credential exams. In addition, Microsoft selected IIL to develop the Microsoft Official Curriculum (MOC) for the 2007 certification and to participate in the 2010 Project certification development.

What Sets Us Apart

Three key values define the IIL brand and guide us in all that we do: **Intelligence**, **Integrity** and **Innovation**. We pride ourselves in creating customer loyalty and building relationships that endure, and a large percentage of our clients are multi-year repeat customers. Strengths that have earned us our reputation as a frontrunner in the learning industry include:

➤ We believe that learning must yield practical, quantifiable benefits to have value, which is why all of our courses integrate training approaches that are easy to understand and assimilate. Our curriculum is designed to engage your critical thinking skills and give you real-world knowledge that you can take back and apply in your work environment.

➤ IIL program evaluations point overwhelmingly to the excellence of our trainers. We hold our staff to the highest standards of professionalism, and their expert facilitation skills complement extensive industry and classroom experience.

➤ To cater to diverse learning styles and preferences, we use Many Methods of Learning™ to deliver our courses and programs. These methods include traditional classroom, virtual classroom, simulation training and interactive, on-demand learning. Choose the approach that best aligns with your needs and your schedule.

➤ Our wide global reach gives you the opportunity to leverage the power of our wholly-owned network of IIL companies, strategically located all over the world. We have deep experience working in different languages, cultures, countries and industries and are proud that many top global companies have selected us as their learning solution partner.

Beyond Training Courses

Because we believe in a holistic approach to learning, we offer our clients all the key building blocks they need to achieve excellence in vital project processes, including:

➤ **Assessment tools** such as the Kerzner Project Management Maturity Model (KPM3) and our 360° Project Management Competency Assessment (360° PMCA™)

➤ **Needs analysis** to define gaps and to address the organizational and process changes needed to fill them

➤ **Measurement of efficiency and productivity performance** including changes in team behavior, return on investment for training and development initiatives, and specific key performance yardsticks in project management, Lean Six Sigma and Business Analysis

➤ **Group coaching and individual mentoring** to assure that classroom lessons are actually put into practice and integrated into the daily work flow

➤ **Process development and improvement** through direct, hands-on support or knowledge management solutions such as our Unified Project Management® Methodology (UPMM™), which assures enterprise-wide consistency and quality in project, program and portfolio management implementation

For more information about IIL or to download a copy of our Learning Catalog, please visit www.iil.com, or email learning@iil.com.

Download Resource Center

Downloadable Resources at
www.jrosspub.com

Free value-added materials available from the Download Resource Center at:

www.jrosspub.com

At J. Ross Publishing we are committed to providing today's professional with practical, hands-on tools that enhance the learning experience and give readers an opportunity to apply what they have learned. That is why we offer free ancillary materials available for download on this book and all participating Web Added Value™ publications. These online resources may include interactive versions of material that appears in the book or supplemental templates, worksheets, models, plans, case studies, proposals, spreadsheets and assessment tools, among other things. Whenever you see the WAV™ symbol in any of our publications, it means bonus materials accompany the book and are available from the WAV *Web Added Value* Download Resource Center at www.jrosspub.com.

Downloads available to all readers of *Dynamic Scheduling® with Microsoft® Project 2010* consist of solution files for the case study exercises included in Appendix 1, filters to check the quality of your own schedules, references, and a glossary of terms. There is also a solution's manual for instructors that contains answers to the remaining questions in this book.

This Training Material is MICROSOFT CERTIFICATION EXAM VALIDATED!

Microsoft Certification Training Validation authenticates and verifies that this material aligns with the topics identified in the external Microsoft Objective Domain. Only a select few can display the official Microsoft Project 2010 Validation seal. This sought-after accolade also certifies that this material prepares the user for the new Microsoft Project 2010 certification exam 70-178.

Short Table of Contents

Long Table of Contents

What's New in This Edition

➤ The content of the book has been aligned with the *PMBOK® Guide – Fourth Edition* published by PMI®.

➤ The text has been updated to reflect the 2010 release of Microsoft Project:

▶ The new Project 2010 features are discussed throughout and marked with a "2010" icon to make them easy to find.

▶ All of the screenshots were replaced to reflect Microsoft 's makeover of the Project 2010 interface with the new Fluent User™ interface (Ribbon).

➤ We've added more IIL best practices throughout the book, based on our extensive experience as project management practitioners and teachers. They are identified with a star icon and reflect the authors' consensus about an approach, method or technique that we believe will provide you with the best results.

➤ In this edition we assume that most readers are now using either Windows 7, Vista or XP. All of the screen shots were made in Windows 7; there may be some slight differences for users of other operating systems, but they shouldn't be troublesome.

➤ The concepts in the book are aligned with the Objective Domains of the Microsoft Project 2010 Certification exam 70-178.

▶ These objective domains are:

▸ **Initializing Project 2010**

▸ **Creating a Task-Based Schedule**

▸ **Managing Resources and Assignments**

▸ **Tracking and Analyzing a Project**

▸ **Communicating Project Information**

Foreword by Dr. Harold Kerzner

As the project management environment increases in complexity, project scheduling tools have become, quite simply, indispensable. The rapid rate of change in economic conditions as well as the need to compete in a global marketplace have forced us to rethink the way we schedule projects.

Being able to compete, and be successful at it, requires the taking of risks. And the rate at which we respond to these risks could very well dictate our competitive posture. The days of project teams working from paper charts hung on the war room walls are gone. Expecting the schedule that is prepared at project initiation to be the same schedule that we have at project completion is wishful thinking. Simply stated, the factors of risk, competitiveness, global competition and possibly the need for several breakthroughs in technology are making standard scheduling techniques outdated and unable to keep up with the needs of the business. We need the dynamic project models that only scheduling software can support: models that manage complexity, identify slippages, and support alternative scenarios — fast.

Fortunately, as the complexity of our environment has increased, so has the robustness and agility of project scheduling software tools. However, this increased functionality comes at a price: a steeper learning curve, making expert instruction in tool use a critical component of our scheduling efforts.

I believe there are a number of features that distinguish the instruction offered in this book from that offered by others in the field.

First, there is the skillful integration of project management theory with practical instructions on the use of the software. A solid understanding of project management principles is key to effectively harnessing the capacity Project 2010 offers. This book addresses both the principles of effective project management and the techniques for implementing those principles using Project 2010.

Another important feature of this book is its emphasis on dynamic modeling. There is thorough instruction on how to create a dynamic model in Project 2010 during project planning so that as change occurs during project execution, the schedule can be easily kept up to date and the true impact of changes quickly identified and addressed. Used properly, a dynamic model in Project 2010 will help keep your projects on course.

Other distinguishing features of this book are tools that readers can use to evaluate their own schedules: macros, filters and a full array of best practices for using Project 2010.

In terms of the Project Management Maturity Model I've introduced, this book creates a common language (Level 1) that will help you establish common processes for project scheduling (Level 2). The best practices described in the book will help you move toward a singular methodology (Level 3). Then, once your organization recognizes and uses the singular methodology, you can perform benchmarking on a continuous basis (Level 4), and finally, you can evaluate the results and enhance the processes defined in Level 3, applying a continuous improvement (Level 5) with each new edition.

The IIL authors who contributed to this edition are expert project management practitioners and experienced teachers of the software. They were able to draw on literally thousands of hours spent with both real life projects and students in the classroom. Their combined experience and wisdom will provide you with the insights you need to manage your projects more effectively.

Harold Kerzner, Ph.D., MS Engineering, MBA
Senior Executive Director, International Institute for Learning, Inc.

Acknowledgments

First, we want to thank you, our reader, for purchasing this book. You had many choices when it comes to Project 2010 books, and we thank you for selecting ours. We hope you'll find it worthwhile.

We would like to thank our co-authors: **Francisco Ambriz**, PMP; **Anson Caliste**, PMP; **Mario Landa**, PMP; **Cindy Lewis**, PMP, and **Ed Lively**, PMP, who provided direct input to chapters throughout the book and added invaluable technical insights based on best practices garnered from their classrooms and clients. A special thanks also goes to **Luis M. Arroyo**, PMP, who helped with the chapter on Earned Value Management.

We thank our editor **Jane Davenport**, PMP, for her expertise and finesse with the English language and for helping to ensure that we covered all necessary topics in a cohesive and meaningful manner.

Rafael Ruiz, PMP, your work creating and editing the macros and filters that accompany the text added an invaluable layer of authenticity to the book.

We also give an extra special thanks to **Illeana Galipienzo** who was instrumental in managing the team – from the people and the process to the screenshots, graphics, and overall morale.

We also want to give a special thanks to **John Winter**, Vice President, Global Learning Solutions, IIL, for his guidance and learning expertise; and to **Steve Osborn**, Chief Operations Officer, IIL for always being there to remove the roadblocks that got in the way of completing this book. We could not have done it without either of you!

Kristen Zekunde, as our production manager and creative director, your insight and technical expertise led the way for an amazing end product: you were the creative light that guided us.

Alejandro Acevedo, PMP; **Guillermo Ambriz**; **Andres Cuevas**, PMP; **Julio Diaz**, PMP; and **Alfonso Hernández**, your contribution of screenshots and graphics, as well as your technical review, will help readers comprehend even the most complex subjects. **Jorge Fernandez**, your always timely IT support was invaluable.

Heather Nolan, you served as more than just our graphic artist: you made magic out of our screen shots and brought our vision to life. **Christa Kirby**, we thank you for your expertise and input on global communications. Finally, special thanks to **Vonno A. Ambriz** for your cartoons, which helped us laugh about some frustrating common situations in our professional lives.

To each of our team members, we want to add a final thank you for your willingness to simply jump in and do whatever needed to be done. You maintained a true team spirit of collaboration throughout the process which made working on this project a pleasure. This project could have never come off without your expertise, patience, assistance, and professionalism.

Our thanks would not be complete without the acknowledgement of the leadership of **E. LaVerne Johnson**, President and CEO of IIL. Her amazing insights and entrepreneurial spirit are what guide each of us at IIL every day. She was a driving force behind the creation of this book and her dedication to the project management industry will continue to position IIL as a leader in the marketplace.

Finally, it is our wish that as you read each chapter, you're inspired to go farther and deeper with Project 2010, whether it's becoming a Subject Matter Expert for your department, leading your PMO with Project best practices, or even becoming Certified in Project 2010. And we hope that in turn, you'll be inspired to share your knowledge and skills with your colleagues

You are our most important critic and commentator. We value your opinion and want to know what we're doing right, what we could do better, and in what other areas you'd like to see us publish. Please e-mail us your thoughts at dynamicscheduling@iil.com.

In closing, we believe we did what we set out to do. We created a powerful book that will serve as an indispensible tool for project managers who wish to garner as much support from Project 2010 as was intended by the tool.

Again, our sincere thanks to all those involved and to those about to embark on the journey towards successful project outcomes.

Rodolfo Ambriz, PMP, PMI-SP, PMI-RMP, MCTS, MCITP
Managing Director, IIL Mexico and Microsoft EPM Division
International Institute for Learning, Inc.

John White, MA, PMP, MCT, MCP, MCTS, MCITP
Director, Microsoft EPM Curriculum & Course Development
International Institute for Learning, Inc.

Introduction

Microsoft® Project 2010

Microsoft Project helps you plan and control your projects. It can help you create Gantt charts, network diagrams, resource histograms and budgets. It will provide reports tailored to your needs and help you to determine and depict the progress of your project. The strengths of the software include:

➤ Ease of use for both novice and power users

➤ Flexibility in scheduling and re-scheduling

➤ A powerful reporting feature: you can extract almost any information from the project database and present it in concise reports

Project 2010 is a powerful tool and, like other tools, to use it proficiently requires knowledge and skill. The software is not a magic bean that will grow a successful project by itself. Experience has taught us that a successful project results from the combination of executive support, competent project management, a committed team and the right tools.

 In the 2003 and 2007 release, Microsoft Office Project was part of the Office family. Now, in the 2010 release, Microsoft Project 2010 is in its own separate category, but still retains all of the Office family features.

What's New in Microsoft Project 2010?

Previous versions of Microsoft Project included basic features for creating and managing schedules: they helped you do task creation, resource management, assignment development, progress tracking, and reporting. Project 2010 offers several new and enhanced features that help you improve your schedule control with greater flexibility and ease.

New in Project Standard 2010

➤ Fluent User Interface

Project 2010 has the same interface used in Microsoft Office 2010. The traditional menus and toolbars have been replaced by the Ribbon, a device that shows commands organized into sets of tabs. The tabs display the commands that are most relevant for each of the task areas in the application.

The Ribbon allows you to work more efficiently with new, intuitive graphical menus. The tabs are task oriented and contain contextual menu groupings that reveal the main features. You can easily customize the tabs to display your own menu options.

Also included in the interface is the new Backstage view; you can access it by clicking the File tab on the Ribbon. Think of the Backstage view as a one-stop graphical destination for managing your project files. It contains the same commands that were available on the File menu in earlier versions, as well as the Project Options.

The new interface improves the way you find the most commonly used commands: right-click over any item in a view such as a bar, table cell, or chart, and a list of commonly used commands will be displayed in a Shortcut Menu. There is also an optional Mini-Toolbar that contains additional shortcuts.

▶ The Shortcut Menu is the menu that appears when you right-click an item. It's displayed below the Mini-Toolbar.

▶ The Mini-Toolbar is the little toolbar that appears when you right-click an item. It's displayed above the Short-cut menu.

The Quick Access Toolbar is the command section at the top-left of the Ribbon that can be customized to enable one-click access to commands, regardless of how you customized the Ribbon. You can quickly and easily add the commands you use the most by right-clicking on the Ribbon and selecting *Customize Quick Access Toolbar*. You can also customize the Quick Access Toolbar so it's displayed below the Ribbon.

Most of the keyboard shortcuts used for navigation in Project 2007 still work in Project 2010. But now, the Ribbon tabs and commands have new keyboard shortcuts. These are called KeyTips and show up when you press the ALT key.

For example, if you are in the Task tab of the Ribbon, you can press the ALT key and then press *W* to switch to the View tab or press *U* to go to the Resource tab. You can then select specific KeyTips to drill down deeper into the specific commands on the Ribbon.

Notice the Status Bar, which displays project status information at the very bottom of the Project window. It has three main sections:

▶ Status Items: Located in the lower left-hand corner of the project window, this section reports status on the properties of the project. Here, you can see what Mode the project is in (Enter or Ready Mode), if a Filter is applied and if new Tasks are Manually or Automatically Scheduled. You can also see the connection state to Project Server and if an AutoFilter is applied.

▶ Temporary Pool: This section reports on any temporary actions that are taking place with the project, for example if your project is being saved or published.

▶ Quick View Switching and Zoom: This section allows you to quickly switch from one view to another view and to zoom in or zoom out the timescale. The View Icons from left to right are Gantt Chart, Task Usage, Team Planner, and Resource Sheet. The Zoom Slider is located in the bottom right-hand corner of the project window and allows you to quickly zoom a time-phased graphic or table, instead of clicking the old zoom icons (magnified lens).

➤ Excel-like features

In Project 2010 the table cells have some features similar to Excel cells. Caution: you can't manage your data the same way you do table cells in Excel; the cells/columns in Project represent the different fields we have in the tool.

The new Excel-like features are:

▸ You can add columns in a dynamic way without having to select the data type; just enter data and the appropriate field type is selected

▸ Text (entered in the name fields) is automatically wrapped and rows are automatically adjusted when you adjust column width

▸ Data entry includes the auto-complete feature, displaying a list of previously used values to select from

▸ Columns have auto filtering to display only relevant data that you can use to analyze results

▸ The cells' color and text formats can be modified easily

▸ Text can be entered in cells with different field formats. For instance, in a task duration cell, you can enter *TBD*, or in a milestone start date *Go ask Nate* as a reminder that further information is needed.

▸ The Format Painter icon lets you quickly copy formatting from one section of text to other sections.

➤ User-controlled Scheduling

Project 2010 has new features that allow you to improve schedule planning and control. The main new features are:

▸ Manual Scheduling. This is one of the major changes in how to schedule projects using the tool. Now, it is possible to manually schedule tasks with preliminary information. These manual tasks don't automatically adjust task dates and durations, and it's possible to change to auto scheduled mode any time you decide.

▸ Top-down Summary Tasks. You can easily create high-level schedules using manually scheduled top-down summary tasks and later break them into detail tasks. If the roll-up dates and durations do not exactly match, you can review the gaps and make the right decisions and adjustments. This is excellent for rolling wave planning.

➤ Compare Projects

This improved feature now allows you to compare information in project tables, Gantt bars and graphical images between versions, and clearly identify project differences.

➤ Placeholder tasks

Placeholder tasks let you create a plan by using task names only. You can enter any combination of start date, finish date, and duration and fill in the rest later.

➤ Timeline View

The Timeline view is a graphical display of the timeline of your project. You can easily adjust and configure it to suit your needs, for example, add selected tasks and milestones.

With the timeline, you can easily create an executive summary that conveys the big picture, or use it for on-the-spot reporting or presentations. It's easy to print or share the timeline: simply copy and paste it into any Office application, or send it in an email with its formatting retained.

➤ Improved collaboration and compatibility

Many people are involved in a real project environment, making efficient sharing of information a must. Project 2010 has new, improved support for information sharing.

▸ Enhanced copy & paste. Now you can copy and paste content to any Office application, keeping formatting, outline levels, and column headers. You can also create a task list in Excel or Word and then paste it into Project without having to reformat it.

▸ Create PDF/XPS Documents. Project 2010 can save projects in a PDF or XPS fixed format.

▸ Backwards compatibility. As with any new version, Project 2010 is compatible with previous versions of Microsoft Project (of course, with reduced functionality where new features are lost). In addition, you can create files in Project 2010 and later convert them to previous versions (Project 2007, 2000-2003 and 98); again, new features may cause some issues with earlier versions.

➤ Other improvements

With the new fluent user interface mentioned at the beginning of this section you'll find a lot of easy-to-use icons, lists and commands that make scheduling simple and friendly. Here are some enhancements that have captured our attention:

▸ Task Inspector. This feature replaces the Task Driver Pane of the previous version. With the Task Inspector you can review factors that affect a task: it can show warnings, suggestions and ignored problems, and you can also make certain task updates.

▸ Gantt Chart look and style. The Gantt Chart appearance reflects new features (manual tasks, warnings, etc.), and there is a new Gantt Chart Tools context-sensitive tab in the Ribbon for Gantt chart. This includes icons for different groups of features for modifying the Gantt Chart content and appearance. There are similar new groups in the Ribbon for Calendar Tools, Timeline Tools, Resource Form Tools, etc. These tabs appear shaded every time you change the view.

▸ One-click critical path, slack and late tasks. Another enhancement in Gantt Chart Tools are three checkboxes that allow you to show critical tasks in red, a line to represent slack, and/or late tasks in black.

- ▶ Highlighting. On the View tab, there is a Highlight list where you can select a filter criteria to highlight information in the view.

- ▶ Subprojects. On the Project tab you will find an Insert Subproject button that allows you to easily manage previously created subprojects within a master project.

New in Project Professional 2010

Here are the new and enhanced features specific to Project Professional 2010:

➤ Inactive Tasks

You can now mark tasks as inactivate and leave them in the project; you can also activate them later or use their information as part of actual data. In Project Professional 2010 it's possible to perform what-if analysis using both inactive and active tasks.

➤ The Team Planner

This is a great new feature for managing your resources. It's a resource schedule view with new interacting features. In summary, with the team planner view you can:

- ▶ See at a glance where your resources are assigned, who is over-allocated, and which tasks are unassigned or unscheduled.

- ▶ Drag and drop tasks to change assignments, or drag unassigned resources to tasks to make planning more efficient. You can also use team planner to solve resource over-allocations manually.

- ▶ Level over-allocated resources automatically on a task-by-task basis using Task Inspector and see the results instantly.

- ▶ Be visually alerted to potential resource allocation issues as you update your progress.

➤ Enhanced Collaboration

Project Professional 2010 supports easy information sharing. The Backstage view contains new sharing options, including:

- ▶ Publish the project in Project Server 2010 (if a Project Server connection is available)

- ▶ Import from, convert, or automatically synchronize scheduled tasks to a Microsoft SharePoint Foundation 2010 task list

- ▶ Save, share, publish, and manage Project Professional 2010 files in SharePoint Foundation 2010

- ▶ Connect Project Professional 2010 with Project Server 2010 and use all the features of a fully integrated enterprise project management (EPM) solution

Discontinued features in Project 2010

Here are the features and functionality that have been discontinued in Project 2010:

➤ Custom Forms. You can't create custom forms or use any that were created in previous versions; instead you can now use Visual Basic for Applications (VBA) to create custom forms.

➤ Task splitting by double-clicking on the Split Task button. Double-clicking on Split Task in previous versions allowed you to split a task several times with just one click of the Split Task icon. In Project 2010 you can single-click on the button to enable task splitting one time.

➤ Resource availability graphs. It's not possible to view resource availability graphs on the Assign Resources dialog box without temporarily assigning the resource to a task. You can only graph one resource at a time. The Team Planner, described in the previous section, is now the way to view, assign, modify, and fix issues with resource allocation.

➤ Project Guide. This was removed in Project 2010. Instead, you can find features for setting up new projects in the Ribbon, neatly organized by tabs.

 Custom Project Guides created for older versions of Project can be migrated to Project 2010.

➤ Add-ins and sample macros. Project 2010 doesn't include add-ins and sample macros. There are two add-ins now incorporated into the program: Adjust Dates and Compare Project Versions.

 Macros created for older versions of Project can be programmed to work with this version.

➤ PERT Analysis. You are no longer able to provide an optimistic, expected, and most likely value and have the three-point estimating formula applied to generate the duration estimate.

 This can still be done in Excel and the information can be copied over, or you can create custom fields and add formulas as needed as a work-around to calculate PERT in your project.

➤ Standard Templates: Now, standard project templates are available on-line from Office.com.

Is This Book for You?

The first edition of this book was written for Project 2000. This fifth edition retains the main characteristic that differentiates this book from other books written on Project 2010: it not only shows you how to use the Project 2010 software, but also provides real life insights and experiences from the IIL authors who are both expert project management practitioners and experienced teachers of the software. The book teaches you how to **manage** projects using Project 2010, instead of teaching you only how to click on features.

This book is intended for the following target groups:

➤ **Project managers who use Project 2010 on a day-to-day basis**
This book is aimed at the novice to intermediate user of Project 2010, but we're confident that advanced users will find it worthwhile as well, particularly if they mentor other users.

➤ **People who schedule and manage mainly single projects**
This book is aimed at people who manage a single project at a time with Project 2010. We have included a section on Master Schedules in the Appendix that will be helpful for those involved in program management, but we will not delve deeply into multi-project management issues.

This book is used as the course book in the Project Orange Belt 2010: Managing Projects with Microsoft Project 2010 course at the International Institute for Learning (IIL). (For our other Project 2010 courses, see IIL's Microsoft Project and Project Server 2010 Curriculum later in this chapter.)

➤ **Students and Professors at colleges and universities**
For effective delivery of college courses, we've included:
  ▶ Review questions for self-evaluation of understanding
  ▶ Start to finish exercises on an office relocation project
  ▶ Trouble shooting exercises drawn from real-life technical support
  ▶ Case studies drawn from our consulting experiences

All readers have access to the Web Added Value (**WAV**) files for this book, which include solutions for the office relocation exercises.

What You Will Find in This Book

At IIL, we've asked thousands of our course participants what features they use, why they use them and how. We've captured the insights we've gained in this book and cover the features that will benefit you most in practice. We'll present the Project 2010 features that will help you create effective schedules, and create them efficiently.

Many people have asked us for a good process to follow for creating schedules. The structure of the book matches the order of steps we recommend: it's as simple as following the Short Table of Contents. The book is aimed at the busy, practicing project manager who needs to get up to speed quickly with Project 2010.

This book is entirely based on and aligned with the *PMBOK® Guide – Fourth Edition*, published by PMI®. It is also aligned with other related PMI standards: *Practice Standard for Scheduling, Practice Standard for Work Breakdown Structures – Second Edition, and Practice Standard for Earned Value Management*. We recommend that you read these standards first or at least keep them nearby, as we won't explain the *PMBOK® Guide* and other PMI Standards concepts, but simply refer to them.

You may use this book as a preparation guide for passing the Microsoft Project 2010 Certification exam 70-178: *Microsoft Project 2010, Managing Projects*. We'll cover the following major objectives:

> Initializing Project 2010
> Creating a Task-Based Schedule
> Managing Resources and Assignments
> Tracking and Analyzing a Project
> Communicating Project Information

On the Microsoft website you will find more detailed information about the exam and how to register.

This book has an attitude. It is not a complete description of the features of Project 2010. We will recommend certain features and we'll argue against using some others. An important criterion we use for our recommendations is that the schedule you build with Project 2010 should be a good representation of your project.

In our opinion, a good schedule is a valid, dynamic model of the project:

> A *model* is a deliberate but smart simplification of the complex reality of the project.
> A model is *valid* if it reflects the reality of your project and provides reliable forecasts.
> A *dynamic* model updates itself when a change is entered. When one change happens in your project, ideally you should have to update only one field in the model to have a new, valid representation of your project. Changes happen often during project execution – a very busy time. Therefore, a dynamic model is a tremendous help during project execution because it helps you keep your project schedule current and useful. Hence the title of this book: *Dynamic Scheduling® with Microsoft® Project 2010*.

Static schedules do not maintain themselves. Some features in Project 2010 are nice to have, but create schedules that require a lot of maintenance. Therefore, we don't recommend features that continue to need attention from you. We have found the judicious application of features to be critical in effectively using Project 2010 and thousands of our students have helped determine which are the most beneficial.

In this book we will cover **one** main edition of Project 2010 currently in use: Project Professional 2010 used in the default configuration for the standalone tool.

What You Won't Find in This Book

> We won't provide an explanation of all of the features in Project 2010. We have made a careful selection of features that will benefit users most when managing a single project. This book is not a complete reference on Project 2010.

> We also won't provide explanations of all there is to know about Project Server. This book will only cover the basics of working with Project Server that project managers need to know. (IIL does offer classes on Project Server. See IIL's Microsoft Project and Project Server 2010 Curriculum later in this chapter.)

About the Authors

The Lead Authors

Rodolfo Ambriz (Civil Engineer, PMP, PMI-RMP, PMI-SP, MCTS, MCITP) is Managing Director of IIL Mexico, S.A. de C.V., responsible for corporate business in Latin America. He has extensive experience in project management methodologies, consulting and training, mostly in large to very large projects in Mexico, as well as in other Latin American countries. He is Past President of the PMI® Mexico Chapter, Past Director of the PMI® Latin America Regional Advocacy Committee, PMI Global *PMBOK® Guide* Spanish translation committee member, speaker and panelist in various PMI Global Congresses, Author of *Dynamic Scheduling® with Microsoft® Office Project 2007*, contributor and writer of articles for MPUG and allPM, and a REP Advisory Group Member. He is also a professor at La Salle University in Mexico City.

John White (MA, PMP, MCT, MCP, MCTS, MCITP) is Director, Microsoft EPM Curriculum & Course Development at IIL. He has over 20 years of insurance, airline, healthcare, military and technology information systems implementation and project management experience, and has trained hundreds of project managers and team members in Microsoft Project, Microsoft Project Server, Project Web Apps, and Portfolio Analysis. He has also customized Microsoft Project 2010 and 2007 course requirements into training curriculums to meet specific corporate needs and is co-author of *Dynamic Scheduling® with Microsoft® Office Project 2007*. He is an active member of the Phoenix, Minnesota, Chicago, and New York PMI® Chapters, the Chicago MPUG Chapter, and is past Vice President of PMI® Chicagoland Chapter and speaker at the PMI Global Congress and Microsoft Project Conferences.

The Contributing Authors

Francisco Ambriz-Cuevas (PMP, TPM) is Project Director of IIL Mexico, S.A. de C.V. in charge of coordinating activities, internal office management, and training and consulting for clients in both Mexico and Latin America. He has acquired his experience in the consulting area working with multi-national companies from the oil industry, manufacturing, as well as federal and local governments; he is also knowledgeable in the implementation of project management offices. He has taught courses on various project management topics and Microsoft Project and Project Server, as well as being a guest lecturer in Latin America and Spain.

Anson Caliste (MBA, PMP, MCT, MCITP) is a Consultant and Trainer with IIL. He has nearly 20 years of IT and project management experience and has managed projects or consulted with clients across North America, Europe and the Caribbean. He has also implemented project management offices and enterprise project management systems for companies in the financial, technology, education and energy sectors. As a trainer, he has conducted numerous sessions in Microsoft Project and general project management in both traditional and on-line settings.

Mario Landa (Civil Engineer, PMP, MCTS, MCITP) is Project Director in charge of implementing all IIL Mexico efforts with clients who need to use and customize Microsoft Office Project, as well as head of the IT Department and an instructor. He has vast experience helping key clients in Mexico, Spain, Venezuela and the United States use and customize Microsoft applications, as well as in-depth experience providing services and solutions in project management using key performance indicators. His areas of expertise include development of the Microsoft Official Curriculum, risk analysis for the oil industry, and support in the establishment of project management offices.

Cindy Lewis (MBA, PMP, PMI-SP, MCT, MCITP) has more than 18 years of experience with Microsoft Project and has been a featured speaker on Project at the Microsoft Project Conference and at PMI's Global Congress. Cindy is known for her work on Microsoft Official Curriculum (MOC) courseware and was selected by Microsoft as a Subject Matter Expert (SME). Her background covers a wide range of industries including: IT, medical, education, architecture/engineering/design build, and food service distribution. Cindy contributes articles and time to professional organizations including allPM, MPUG, and the Western Michigan Chapter of PMI.

Ed Lively (MBA, PMP, MCT, MCTS, MCITP) is a Senior Consultant and Trainer with IIL. In addition to project management, Ed has over 20 years experience in finance, banking, publishing, technology and consulting. He has managed the deployment of Microsoft Project Server and has established/managed several project management offices. Ed has delivered training in Microsoft Project and project management throughout the United States, Canada, Australia, Japan, Scotland, South Africa, Singapore and Trinidad. He also trains in Microsoft Project Server and Project Web Apps and is a member of PMI and MPUG, and is co-author of *Dynamic Scheduling® with Microsoft® Office Project 2007*.

The Authors' Perspective on Scheduling

In our years of consulting and training project managers, we've identified a number of common problems with the way that Microsoft Project is implemented.

➤ Schedules Need a Logical, Hierarchical Structure

Some large schedules we've seen don't have a work breakdown structure (WBS). All of the tasks are on the first (and only) indentation level.

Imagine trying to make sense of this book if it didn't have a hierarchy of sections, chapters and paragraphs. Organizations which don't use logical and hierarchical work breakdown structures create schedules that are difficult to explain to anyone who isn't interested in detail activities (like many executives).

➤ All Dependencies Need to be Identified

Many schedules created by experienced project managers turn out to have only a few dependencies (links between tasks). Not surprisingly, those schedules have many schedule constraints that anchor the tasks to specific dates. Constraints, however, make a schedule very rigid or static. Every time a change occurs, the entire schedule needs to be reviewed and updated. Isn't this reminiscent of the time when we made schedules on paper to hang on our walls? Such schedules are nice charts of the project, but are definitely not useful dynamic models of the project. Updating a static schedule is onerous, and project managers with static schedules inevitably stop updating early in the execution of their projects.

➤ Schedules Need the Right Level of Detail

Many organizations create schedules that are so complex it takes weeks to understand them. If the model of a project is as complex as the reality itself, it doesn't give you a better handle on that reality.

Modeling is, by definition, simplifying the reality to get a better handle on it. Too many project managers seem to forget this. If you can't explain your project schedule to your team, the schedule is simply too complex. If your team understands it, you get much more value from your schedule and scheduling efforts. If other stakeholders can also understand your schedule, even better.

➤ Include Resources in Your Schedule

Many project managers don't enter resources (e.g., people, equipment, materials) into Project 2010. Those who do, often don't check on whether the resources are over-allocated. A schedule without leveled resources may display agreeable finish dates, but it's doubtful they'll be realistic. When you enter resources into Project 2010 and level the workloads, it may become painfully clear that the promised dates are not feasible. If you notice that deadlines are often not accomplished in your organization, a lack of modeling resources may very well be the cause.

Any organization that shares its resources across projects but doesn't have a central, shared resource pool is also likely to suffer from missed deadlines. The cause is unidentified resource impacts across projects. Even though an individual schedule with leveled resources may show what appear to be realistic dates, once project execution starts and project managers start pulling each other's resources in order to meet deadlines, the individual schedules prove to be too optimistic. The total workload of the resources needs to be modeled across all of the projects that share resources.

➤ Apply Earned Value Management (EVM)

Earned Value Management (EVM) is an approach to measuring project performance based on comparing planned and actual progress related to scope, time and cost. We've run into a fair number of people who think that EVM is a complex technique that isn't worth the effort necessary to implement it. We believe that many of those may not know how to simplify the application of EVM with a tool like Project 2010. We have addressed this with the EVM chapter in this book.

EVM in Project 2010 will help you answer questions like: Are we ahead of or behind schedule? Under or over budget? What is the remaining work going to cost? When is the project going to finish? Having this information at hand will enable you to make the right decisions on a timely basis.

➤ Consolidate Schedules to Facilitate Management of Large Projects or Programs

Multiple projects performed simultaneously have become the norm, with projects logically related to each other and sharing resources. The ability to bring several subprojects into a single consolidated (master) schedule makes it much more practical to accomplish tasks like leveling when you use a shared resource pool, reporting on multiple projects and providing a big picture view of the work going on between several related projects.

➤ Don't Abandon Ship!

Many organizations invest in making schedules, but abandon them once project execution starts. The chance that a schedule will be abandoned increases with the complexity of the schedule, the lack of dependencies or an abundance of constraints. This book tries to address all of these problems.

➤ Consider Certification

The kinds of problems we've observed have led us to encourage people to consider becoming certified in Project. We've found that the process of pursuing certification can significantly elevate the skills of Project 2010 users and improve the accuracy of forecasts. For organizations this can mean more successful projects, more reasonable workloads, less burnout and more reliable long-term forecasts of resource needs. The cost of managing projects should decrease and the competitiveness of the organization should increase in the global marketplace.

Why Do We Need Dynamic Schedules?

A dynamic schedule is one that relies on a thorough definition of the relationships between tasks to determine scheduling and minimizes the use of hard deadlines. There are several reasons why we need schedules to be dynamic:

➤ Changes happen so frequently in projects that it's hard to keep up with them. If your schedule is static — it relies on hard deadline dates that you've entered — whenever you make a change to one task, you'll have to review every other task to see how it's affected. This is why static schedules quickly become outdated and ignored: they simply require too much time and effort to update.

With a dynamic schedule when you change one task, Project 2010 is able to update the other tasks based on the dependencies you've entered. Your updating efforts are manageable: you can keep your schedule alive and valid during project execution.

➤ Dynamic schedules make it possible to explore what-if scenarios in Project 2010. This is an enormous advantage when you're trying to fine-tune your schedule or adjust for slippages. If you've created a static schedule, the hard deadlines and constraints you've entered interfere with Project 2010's what-if capabilities: it's hard to assess the impact of proposed solutions.

➤ If you want to roll up subprojects into a master schedule, the subprojects need to be dynamic models. Otherwise, you'll spend too much time making changes in the master schedule. When dynamic models are rolled up, problems become visible in the master schedule and can easily be resolved by creating what-if scenarios.

➤ In order to do schedule simulation for quantitative risk analysis, you need dynamic models. Monte Carlo schedule simulation is essential to provide stakeholders with data to support contingency reserves and realistic forecasts.

We made an attempt to quantify the amount of time saved by working with a dynamic schedule instead of a static schedule. We calculated that for a 3 month project with 100 tasks, you would save about 50 hours of effort by using a dynamic schedule. We're sure you can find better ways to spend that time.

IIL's Microsoft® Project and Project Server 2010 Curriculum

IIL's Project "Belt" courses

With the launch of the Microsoft® 2010 version of Project and Project Server (EPM Solution), IIL is dedicated to providing organizations and practitioners with the training they need for the successful management of projects using the Microsoft Project and Project Server solutions. We keep our courseware aligned with the needs of the advancing project manager, as well as those of progressive organizations looking to be competitive in the global marketplace by increasing their project management maturity level and capabilities.

IIL's Project Belt courses prepare project managers for certification. Our series of Belt courses is progressive, with successful completion of one Belt course (or the equivalent) being a prerequisite to enrollment in the next level.

Project White Belt® 2010

Getting Started with Microsoft® Project 2010

Project White Belt 2010 earns you IIL's White Belt Certification and complements Project Orange Belt® in preparing you for the Microsoft Certified Technology Specialist (MCTS) credential. This course is designed for individuals relatively new to scheduling.

Project Orange Belt® 2010

Managing Projects with Microsoft® Project 2010

Project Orange Belt 2010 is an advanced course that will equip you with the knowledge and skills to build, maintain and control well-formed project plans in Microsoft Project 2010. This course also includes best practices and tips and tricks to use Project more effectively. The Orange Belt course fully prepares you for the new Project 2010 Microsoft Certified Technology Specialist (MCTS) exam.

Project Blue Belt® 2010

Managing Projects and Programs with Microsoft® Project Server 2010

Project Blue Belt 2010 is ideal for experienced portfolio managers, program managers, project managers and schedulers who are managing enterprise systems. Participants should be familiar with key enterprise project management concepts and terminology found in the *PMBOK® Guide – Fourth Edition, The Standard for Program Management – Second Edition and The Standard for Portfolio Management – Second Edition.* The Blue Belt course earns you IIL's Blue Belt certification and teaches you how to initiate, plan, execute, monitor and control enterprise projects using the Project Server 2010 Enterprise tool.

Project Black Belt® 2010

Managing Projects, Programs and Portfolios with Microsoft® Project Server 2010

Project Black Belt 2010 addresses the management of complex projects and programs using Project Server 2010 and Project Professional 2010. You'll learn to configure and customize the enterprise project management (EPM) solution according to your organization's requirements. The Black Belt course requires you to apply project management methodology and experience to the management of projects and program schedules in a Microsoft Enterprise Project Management (EPM) environment, and successful completion of the course earns you IIL's Black Belt certification. Substantial hands-on experience in Microsoft Project Professional 2010, Project Server 2010 and Project Web App is recommended for anyone wishing to participate in this course.

Microsoft EPM Role-Based Courses

Many organizations request customized onsite training to support the deployment of Microsoft Project Server 2010. IIL has developed a series of role-based courses that can easily be adapted to the specific needs of a company, depending on its existing business processes and the course configuration chosen. Typically, these courses will be delivered onsite or in dedicated Virtual Classroom sessions.

➤ **Microsoft EPM for Project Managers:** This course is designed to offer project managers the information needed to effectively build, optimize and update schedules in the enterprise environment using Microsoft® Project 2010 and Project Web App.

➤ **Microsoft EPM for Team Members:** In this course project team members will learn how to directly interact with Project Web App in order to view and update project tasks.

➤ **Microsoft EPM for Resource Managers:** This course covers the necessary elements for effective resource management in both Project Web App and Microsoft® Project 2010.

➤ **Microsoft EPM for Executives:** This course offers business and PMO executives information they need to effectively support the adoption of the Microsoft EPM solution within their organizations. It will also equip them with the knowledge and skills to view, analyze and respond to project, program and portfolio health indicators.

Microsoft® Project and Project Server 2010 Certifications

What are the Certifications?

IIL Project Belt courses prepare you to earn the following professional certifications:

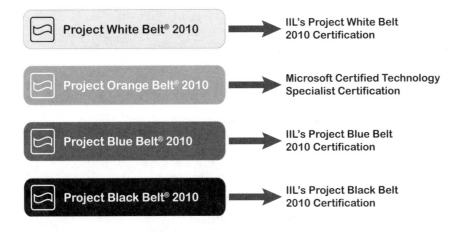

What are the Benefits of Certification?

Professional certification provides value to organizations as well as to individuals desiring to advance their skills and career opportunities within the field of project management. By validating a more comprehensive set of skills, these credentials give candidates and their hiring managers a reliable indicator of on-the-job performance.

IIL's Project Belt series of certifications is driven by customer demand for project management competencies that include practical and tool-specific capabilities. Certifications quantify proficiency in the use of Microsoft Project, Project Server and Portfolio Server 2010 to effectively initiate, plan, execute, monitor and control, and close projects, programs and portfolios.

Why Choose IIL for Your Microsoft® Project Training?

➤ IIL has a strict instructor qualification process, which includes all of the following:

  ▸ Instructors must have hands-on experience managing projects and demonstrate this with a best practices schedule
  ▸ Instructors must hold the Project Management Professional (PMP®) designation awarded by PMI®
  ▸ Instructors must demonstrate expertise in training, which includes completing our Train-the-Trainer program
  ▸ Instructors must hold the relevant certification for any course they will be teaching; in fact, most of our instructors are certified at a level above that which they are teaching

➤ IIL has led the Microsoft Project training industry by providing recognized professional certifications in Microsoft Project and Project Server. To date, we have trained more than 20,000 individuals through our Belt programs.

➤ IIL offers a rare blend of project management methodology training aligned with PMI's standards within our Microsoft® Project Belt curriculum.

➤ IIL is a Microsoft Partner with the Microsoft Gold Project and Portfolio Management competency. We provide customized training and consulting solutions to help organizations enhance their project management capabilities using the Microsoft Enterprise Project Management Solution.

Please Give Us Your Feedback

If you have any questions or if you would like to discuss any recommendations we make in this book, we would love to hear your feedback. Please don't hesitate to contact us at dynamicscheduling@iil.com.

Thank you for the time you are about to invest in reading this book. We hope you will find it well worth the effort!

Rodolfo Ambriz, PMP, PMI-RMP, PMI-SP, MCTS, MCITP
Managing Director, IIL Mexico and Microsoft EPM Division,
International Institute for Learning, Inc.

John White, MA, PMP, MCT, MCP, MCTS, MCITP
Director of Microsoft EPM Curriculum and Course Development
International Institute for Learning, Inc.

dynamicscheduling@iil.com
www.iil.com

About This Book

Learning Objectives

After reading this book you will be able to:

➤ Apply the basic project management principles outlined in PMI's *PMBOK® Guide – Fourth Edition* to the planning, executing, monitoring and controlling, and closing of your Project 2010 schedules

➤ Consider concepts from other PMI Standards such as the *Practice Standard for Scheduling*, the *Practice Standard for Work Breakdown Structures - Second Edition*, and the *Practice Standard for Earned Value Management*

➤ Understand that a project schedule is a model of a real world project and be able to recognize and analyze the pulling forces of a project

➤ Create a valid and dynamic model of your own project:
  ▸ Choose effective settings for options
  ▸ Create the project calendar
  ▸ Enter tasks, estimates, dependencies, constraints, resources and assignments

➤ Optimize your schedule in order to meet deadlines and budget restrictions, while keeping the workloads of your resources within their available limits

➤ Efficiently update your schedule during project execution so that you can continuously forecast the project cost and finish date

➤ Create standard reports, custom views and Visual Reports for your project that meet the needs of stakeholders

➤ Implement Earned Value Management with Project 2010

➤ Build and maintain consolidated schedules

➤ Assess how well you've implemented the best practices of scheduling, established by IIL based on our research of thousands of real-life schedules

➤ Understand new features of Project Professional 2010

In general, you should feel very comfortable with Project 2010 and have a good understanding of how the tool functions and behaves. This knowledge will enable you to efficiently and effectively manage your project(s).

Outline of This Book

First you initiate a project, then you plan it, and while you execute it, you monitor and control it. At the end, you close it out. This is an iterative or repeating cycle: over the life of the project things change and you need to cycle back and re-plan.

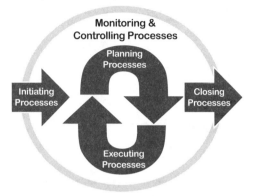

The illustration shows these five process groups as defined by the Project Management Institute (PMI) in the *PMBOK® Guide – Fourth Edition*.

We've used the five process groups to structure this book. In fact, we treat the creation of the project plan as a mini-project in itself, and we have mapped all steps for creating a schedule with Project 2010 to the five process groups.

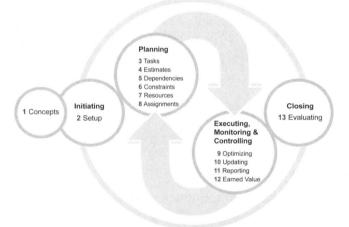

The result can be seen in this illustration that provides an overview of the contents of the book. Each balloon represents a chapter, as well as a step in the process of creating and managing a project using Project 2010. We recommend you use these same sequential steps when you model your own project with Project 2010.

Let's take a closer look at each step.

Concepts of Project Management (Chapter 1)

To use Project 2010 effectively, it's important to understand the project management concepts and processes that the tool supports. In this chapter, we explain basic concepts of project management and provide a conceptual framework for the project management business process. While this isn't a book on project management theory, throughout the book we'll provide as much background information as you need to utilize Project 2010 effectively, starting in chapter 1 with a high level overview of projects on your desktop.

Initiating

This is where we initiate the project.

Getting Started with Project 2010 (Chapter 2)

This chapter will help you become familiar with the Project 2010 interface. We'll discuss file management, templates and views. Then we'll guide you through the steps of creating a new project, including naming the project and entering the project start or finish date. We'll pay particular attention to the default settings in Project 2010, because some important options need to be set before tasks are entered. We'll also create the project calendar.

Planning

During the planning phase, we'll develop and enter all of the schedule data into Project 2010. This phase requires most of the effort needed to create a schedule. There are six types of data that Project 2010 needs to create a schedule, as discussed in the next six chapters.

Tasks (Chapter 3)

Tasks answer the question: *What needs to be done?* The task list is developed from the deliverables that together with the tasks form the work breakdown structure (WBS). We'll discuss techniques for ensuring that your task list is complete, well organized and reflects an appropriate level of detail. Then we'll cover how to enter the structured task list in Project 2010, and how to reorganize the task list by indenting, outdenting, moving and copying tasks.

Estimates (Chapter 4)

An estimate answers the question: *How long will the task take?* There are many factors to consider when estimating. We'll provide a process to clarify the estimating process and help you understand how Project 2010 can assist you when you have complete or even incomplete information about an estimate. We'll also discuss factors that can lead to inconsistent or biased estimates and suggest techniques for handling these difficulties.

Dependencies (Chapter 5)

Dependencies deal with the question: *In what sequence do the tasks have to be done, and how will the tasks affect each other?* Dependencies are the logical cause-and-effect relationships between tasks and they are critical for creating dynamic schedules. By entering dependencies instead of hard dates, you can build a very powerful, dynamic model of your project. If you change the duration of one task, Project 2010 will reschedule all affected dependent tasks. The core secrets of dynamic schedules will be revealed in this chapter.

Constraints (Chapter 6)

Constraints are the answer to the question: *What limitations are imposed on the schedule?* Constraints are dates that are imposed or promised on the project. Constraints can also be used for restricting Project 2010's freedom to move task bars around in the timescale, if practical circumstances require this. In addition to constraints, we will also discuss deadlines and task calendars.

Resources (Chapter 7)

Resources answer the question: *Who will do the work?* Resources can be people, facilities, machines, materials, or costs. In this chapter, we'll describe these types of resources, plus how to create a budget-based resource. We'll explore how to enter resources in Project 2010.

Assignments (Chapter 8)

Assignments answer the question: *Who does what?* This chapter focuses on assigning human, material and cost resources. We'll explain the formula that Project 2010 uses to recalculate data when you make or change assignments, and help you understand and predict Project 2010's behavior. We'll also explore the cost side of managing projects. The goal of this chapter is to make sure Project 2010 works for you instead of you working for Project 2010. If you've found in the past that Project 2010 doesn't do what you want it to do, make sure you read this chapter.

Executing, Monitoring and Controlling

During these phases of the project, many cycles will be made through the next three project management activities of optimizing, reporting and updating. Delivering a project involves many cycles of making progress (updating), monitoring the progress (reporting) and taking corrective actions (optimizing).

Optimizing (Chapter 9)

The first draft of your schedule rarely meets your time, resource and cost constraints. You may need to make changes to stay within the deadline, the budget or the availability of resources; applying these changes is called optimizing the schedule.

We'll present three different approaches for optimizing schedules: optimizing for time; optimizing for time and cost; and optimizing for time, cost and resources. We'll also discuss using the Critical Path Method to optimize logic-constrained schedules and the Resource-Critical Path to optimize resource-constrained schedules by leveling workloads.

Updating (Chapter 10)

Once your project schedule is approved, you set a baseline schedule against which you track your progress. You need to update your schedule on a regular basis in order to identify variances that have occurred on the project and to adjust your forecasts for the remainder of the project. An updated schedule shows the actual performance compared to the baseline.

Reporting (Chapter 11)

In this chapter, we'll show you how to use Project 2010 to communicate with your stakeholders, for example, to tell team members what to deliver, and when.

We'll discuss Project 2010's standard reports, how to customize views to create additional reports, and how to use the Visual Reports feature that generates PivotTables, PivotCharts and PivotDiagrams for Microsoft® Office Excel and Microsoft® Visio.

We'll also cover using filtering, grouping and formatting to create reports targeted for specific purposes and stakeholders.

Earned Value Management (Chapter 12)

While you are optimizing, updating, tracking, and controlling your project; you may want to analyze project progress to get a good estimate of current status. Earned Value Management (EVM) analysis helps you with this and evaluates cost and work estimates on the project. EVM is concerned with measuring the value that you have earned on the project, based on the work planned and the work actually completed. This analysis is conducted by comparing captured baseline information to actual information.

EVM helps you evaluate the effectiveness of the plan, analyze progress, review trends, propose forecasts and define any corrective action that may be needed to meet your project goals.

Closing

Evaluating (Chapter 13)

It's important to take some time to look back on a project to see what went well, what went wrong and to analyze why. In this chapter, we'll discuss how to evaluate your project.

The purpose of project evaluation is to help you conduct better projects in the future. Only by learning from the past can we become better prepared for the future.

Summary (Chapter 14)

In this chapter, you'll find a handy reference summary of the scheduling guidelines for creating valid and dynamic schedules. These reflect the results of our search for best practices in thousands of real life schedules.

End of Chapter Review Questions

At the end of each chapter we've included review questions to help you consolidate the knowledge you gained in the chapter. These questions review both the theoretical concepts and techniques covered in the chapter. Most answers can be found literally in the text of the book itself.

Appendix 1: Case Studies

Appendix 1 provides structured practice using Project 2010 to help you solidify what you've learned throughout the book. We've organized the material by chapter and recommend that you do each set of exercises immediately after reading the related chapter.

You'll find the following types of practice:

➤ A hands-on exercise where you are the project manager responsible for an office move of about 100 co-workers to a new location that you have yet to find. The exercises will take you through scheduling of the project from initiating to closing. You can compare your results to a model schedule available for download at www.jrosspub.com.

➤ Troubleshooting exercises which are based on situations we've encountered over many years of reviewing and certifying Project schedules. The exercises will help you understand some of the pitfalls people commonly encounter using Project 2010 and can help you prepare for providing technical support to other Project 2010 users.

➤ Case studies to give you additional practice in the Dynamic Scheduling techniques.

Appendix 2: Consolidated Master Schedules

This appendix describes how you can use Project 2010 to manage multiple projects in the context of a consolidated project schedule. You can use a consolidated schedule to bring separate schedules together for managing, reporting, analyzing, and/or leveling shared resources.

We'll take you through the process of embedding project schedules into a consolidated schedule, and show you how to create cross project dependencies, level multiple projects, and create a shared resource pool. We'll also discuss some of the issues involved in creating consolidated schedules.

Conventions in This Book

Symbols and Typeface

	Best Practice	This icon identifies the practices and techniques that we've found to be the most valuable in our years of experience in the project management field.
	Tip	The light bulb highlights a tip or recommendation that may help you use Project 2010 more efficiently. Many tips are time savers.
	Caution	Project 2010 is a robust, complicated program. We use exclamation points to highlight warnings that may help you avoid potential problems, unexpected results or loss of data in Project 2010.
	New Feature	The 2010 icon indicates a new feature in the Project 2010 release. New features apply to both the Project 2010 Standard and the Project 2010 Professional editions, unless otherwise noted in the text.
	Note	Notes simply contain additional information.
File		Words in bold type are words that can be found on your screen in Project 2010 — either as a menu item or as a label or phrase in a dialog box.
Quotes		Italicized words are literal references. These can be quotes from people, or literal data you need to enter into Project 2010.
<file name>		Any text enclosed between smaller than (<) and greater than (>) signs is text that should not be taken literally, because it refers to other things. For example, < file name> refers to the name of a project file with which you are currently working.

Word Choice and Step Formulation

➤ For the Microsoft® Fluent™ User Interface (hereafter referred to as the Ribbon) tabs, we use the verb choose as in:
On the **File** tab (of the Ribbon), in the Microsoft® Office Backstage™ view, (hereafter referred to as **Backstage** view), choose **Options**.

We assume you use the **Ribbon** tabs in their default layout. If you can't find icons that we refer to, consider resetting the tabs to their default appearance: on the **File** tab, click ⌈ Options... ⌋, then in the **Project Options** dialog box, click **Customize Ribbon** 🔧, and then in **Customization**: click **Reset** 🔄 and select **Reset all Customizations**.

➤ For tab pages in dialog boxes we use the verb *click* with the name of the tab as in:
Click **Advanced** (in **Task Information** dialog box).

➤ For shortcut key combinations on your keyboard we use the verbs *hold* and *press*:

  ▸ For a single keystroke: Press ⌊F2⌋.

  ▸ For two keystrokes: Hold down ⌊Alt⌋ and press ⌊F1⌋.

  ▸ For three keystrokes: Hold down ⌊Alt⌋ + ⌊Shift⌋ and press ⌊→⌋.

➤ For entering text with your keyboard into named fields we use *type* or *enter* as in:
Type in a *file name* of your choice in the field **File Name**.

➤ KeyTips are keyboard shortcuts that let you quickly perform tasks on the Ribbon without using the mouse:

  ▸ Press the ⌊Alt⌋ key to display KeyTips over the available features

  ▸ Press the keystroke letter that appears over the feature you want

  ▸ Additional KeyTips may appear depending on which feature you select

  ▸ Continue to press the letters of the commands that you want to use. You may first need to press the letter of the group, then the letter of the command within that group.

  ▸ Press the ⌊Alt⌋ to cancel and hide KeyTips

➤ For check boxes we use the verb select or clear as in:
Select ☑ **New tasks are effort driven**
Clear ☐ **New tasks are effort driven**

➤ For radio buttons we use the verb select as in:
Select ⦿ On.

Screenshots and Illustrations

Most illustrations in the book only show a small portion of a larger schedule. This allowed us to keep the illustrations concise and to the point.

The screen shots that we used are from Microsoft® Project Professional 2010, and the operating system is Microsoft® Windows 7. Depending on whether you use Project Professional or Project Standard, what you see on the screen may vary slightly from our screenshots. Some items displayed in the Ribbon, tabs, and dialog boxes (dealing primarily with collaboration capabilities) will be "grayed" in Project Professional unless you are connected to Project Server. In Project Standard, these items simply won't exist. If you are using an operating system other than Windows 7, your computer screen may also look different. These differences should not hinder your ability to understand the concepts offered in the book or to perform the techniques presented.

We've annotated most of the screenshots with blue lines and callouts, so you can easily find the option or field referred to in the text. The annotations sometimes contain extra tips, so we suggest you take the time to read them.

Cartoons

The cartoons in each chapter depict project management scenarios related to topics covered in the chapter and will help us to laugh about some common frustrating situations in our professional lives. Special thanks to Vonno A. Ambriz for your cartoons.

Chapter 1: Concepts of Project Management

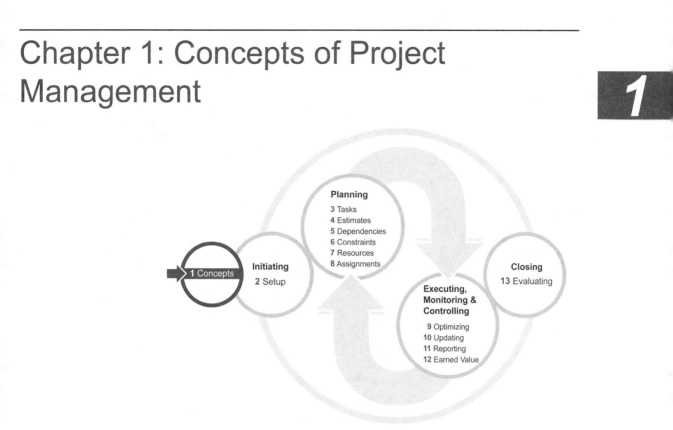

To use Project 2010 effectively, you'll want to understand the project management concepts and processes that the tool supports. In this chapter we'll look at the big picture of project management. We'll discuss what project management is and where it fits in the enterprise and in the context of programs and portfolios.

After reading this chapter you'll be able to:

➤ Define what a project, program and portfolio of projects are and describe how they relate to one another in the context of Enterprise Project Management
➤ Describe the critical role of projects and programs in an enterprise
➤ Describe the basic principles and processes for managing individual projects and dynamic project scheduling
➤ Describe the advantages of a dynamic model over a static chart

I think I should start learning about **dynamic models**...

Overview

In this chapter, we'll define what projects and project management are, position project management in the context of the multi-project enterprise and finally focus in on the principles and processes for managing individual projects.

This book deals primarily with managing a single project but we do address some issues related to multiple projects. This is because we rarely perform a project in a vacuum: multiple projects performed simultaneously have become the norm. Some projects are logically related to one another, while others may be related only because they share resources and occur within the same organization.

Project 2010 provides features and functions that help you manage multiple projects and we'll point those out throughout the book. However to fully address multi-project management, you'll need Project Server, the software that enables multiple users to effectively collaborate on projects.

What is Project Management?

"Project management (PM) is the application of knowledge, skills, tools and techniques to project activities to meet project requirements. Project management is accomplished through the application and integration of the project management process groups: initiating, planning, executing, monitoring and controlling, and closing."[1]

The project management process is effective when projects are aligned with the organization's strategy, completed to the satisfaction of the client and sponsor, and produced on time and within schedule.

Why Project Management

Projects are critical to the success of any organization: they are how an organization gets new things done. But projects are often poorly managed and the costs of this mismanagement are high. They include projects that are late, over budget, produce substandard products, don't satisfy stakeholders and don't align with the organization's business strategy.

Projects are by nature complex: they involve people and variables that make it impossible to follow a simplistic cookbook approach and to predict outcomes with complete accuracy. We need project management to manage dynamic and complex efforts to achieve objectives within a project's competing demands of scope, time, cost, quality, resources and risk.

Completing projects efficiently and effectively provides a competitive edge and enables an organization to improve the way it serves its clients, stakeholders and employees. Project management improves the likelihood that projects will be completed successfully.

What is a Project?

"A project is a *temporary endeavor undertaken to create a unique product, service or result.*"[2]

Projects are the means for making all changes (new and improved products and processes, mergers and acquisitions, etc.) in any organization. They represent a significant expenditure of money and critical resources. Projects are critical factors in meeting strategic goals and objectives.

Some organizations have projects as their core operations, like construction, aerospace and consulting companies. There are full-time project managers in these companies. In other organizations, projects are often used to implement changes (like relocations and reorganizations) or for creating new systems (such as information and financial systems). These organizations may also have professional project managers, but many projects may be managed by occasional or incidental project managers. The line manager of today often has one or more projects in progress.

Examples of Projects

Here is a list of some common project types with examples. Each may have a wide range of complexity, cost, duration and criticality.

---

1 —— *PMBOK® Guide – Fourth Edition*, PMI, 2008, p. 6.
2 Ibid., 5.

> Organizational change projects: implementing a new methodology or relocating an office
> Regulation implementation projects: meeting new environmental or reporting requirements
> Event projects: conducting a conference or making a presentation to investors
> New product development: developing a new pharmaceutical drug
> Information systems projects: developing new software or maintaining existing software
> Construction projects: designing and constructing buildings or roads
> Education projects: developing new courseware or conducting workshops

A Word About Small Projects

There is a tendency to downplay the importance of small projects to justify not bringing project management principles into play. Small projects are as important as any, particularly because there are so many of them and they may be critical to business operations.

The formality of project management must be scaled to the size, complexity and setting of the project to be managed. The fact that a project is small may seem to indicate less of a need for formality. However, when there is a dynamic flow of many small projects, as in a maintenance environment, you may in fact need greater formality.

Some small projects are complex and critical. For example, when a condenser needs to be replaced in a coal-fueled power plant (a project that is small in the context of major facilities projects), it can require that operations be suspended for several weeks. The potential for this "small" project to fall off track has huge financial consequences and therefore a need for greater formality.

Every project needs to be managed carefully.

Enterprise Project Management (EPM)

Project management is a process designed to improve project performance. Before we look at the principles of managing a single project, it's important to understand the context within which projects exist.

Enterprise Project Management (EPM) or Organizational Project Management (OPM) is the higher-level process within which project management fits. EPM improves organizational performance by linking project work, along with operational work, to organizational strategy.

EPM addresses the multi-project environment of an organization and the relationships between projects, programs, portfolios of projects, resources and the organization's strategies, goals and objectives, across all the organization units.

1

EPM is made up of three complex processes: project, program and portfolio management, as described below. In addition, it includes the continuous improvement of the overall PM process and the way it relates to other business processes like quality management, engagement management and new product development.

Components of EPM

As we said earlier, project management is "the application of knowledge, skills, tools and techniques to project activities to meet project requirements."[3]   The focus of PM is the individual project, where the detailed action of PM is defining scope, estimating, scheduling, executing, controlling, etc.   Projects deliver results.

Program and portfolio management are different: they focus on strategic thinking, optimizing resources and prioritizing, coordinating and facilitating multiple projects.

➤ **Portfolio Management**
Portfolio management is "the centralized management of one or more portfolios, which includes identifying, prioritizing, authorizing, managing and controlling projects, programs, and other related work, to achieve specific strategic business objectives."[4]

A project portfolio is a collection of projects, programs and/or other portfolios. There may be multiple portfolios of projects which roll up into a complete enterprise wide portfolio.

Portfolio managers and decision makers prioritize among projects within portfolios and select those which will best support the organization's objectives by effectively utilizing resources in a way that is aligned with the organization's strategy.

➤ **Program Management**
Program management is "the centralized, coordinated management of a program to achieve the program's strategic objectives and benefits."[5]   It is the coordinated application of marketing, strategic planning, project management, and general management to meet program objectives.

A Program is "a group of related projects managed in a coordinated way to obtain benefits and control not available from managing them individually. Programs may include elements of related work outside of the scope of the discrete projects in the program"[6]   The related work may be operational and include product or customer support activities.

---

3   Ibid., 37.
4   ———— *The Standard for Portfolio Management – Second Edition*, PMI, 2008, p. 138.
5   ———— *The Standard for Program Management – Second Edition*, PMI, 2008, p. 312.
6   Ibid.

Programs deliver benefits that cannot be delivered in the context of individual projects and portfolios and their management assures that the right projects are done to satisfy organizational strategy.

EPM Process Model

The graphic of the EPM process model below shows EPM as a process that combines governance, portfolio, program and multi-project management, as well as individual project management. Portfolio management is a critical component that relies on the effective performance of project and program management and at the same time drives their performance. The whole EPM process is supported by collaboration and consultative support, relationship management, organizational change management, coaching, knowledge transfer, etc.

You can see the following steps in the diagram:

➤ Step 1.0, Originating, is a bridge between portfolio and program management and individual project initiation. It is where requests for projects arise, are evaluated and decisions are made as to which will be proposed as project possibilities. Originating is really a part of portfolio management and governance.

➤ Steps 2.0 through 6.0, Initiating through Closing, represent the management process for a single project.

➤ Step 7.0 addresses the way the overall process is continuously improved based on lessons learned from individual projects, best practices and new PM tools.

The "Gates" in the diagram are decision checkpoints at major points in a project's life. At the gates, portfolio management and individual project management meet. Decisions regarding the continuation of the project are made.

EPM Process Model[7]

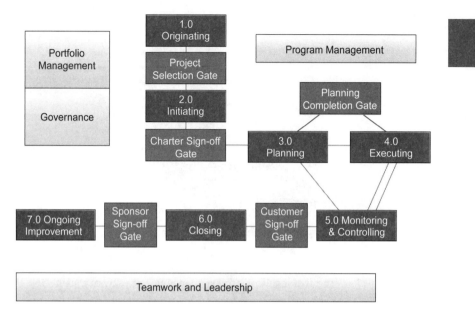

Strategic Planning for Project Management

"Strategic planning for project management is the development of a standard methodology for project management, a methodology that can be used over and over again, and that will produce a high likelihood of achieving the project's objectives."

In every organization, there is a desire to achieve excellence in project management: to reach success in projects by obtaining the benefits that were initially expected.

To achieve excellence in project management, you need to have the foundation of a project management maturity model (PMMM) in place. There are many models that the organization can use. We present the following PMMM graphic that represents an industry-validated model.

---

7   IIL's Unified Project Management Methodology Model™ (UPMM™)

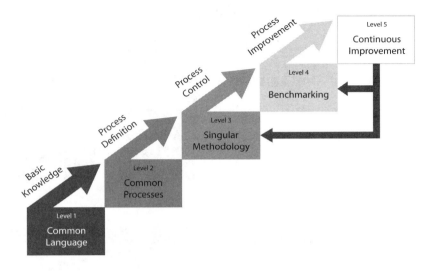

The five levels of project management maturity, using the PMMM by Harold Kerzner[8], are:

➤ Level 1 – Common Language: The organization recognizes the importance of project management and the need for a common project management language and terminology.

➤ Level 2 – Common Processes: The organization recognizes the need for common processes that can be repeated and also recognizes the application and support of project management principles to other organizational processes.

➤ Level 3 – Singular Methodology: The organization recognizes the synergistic effect of combining all corporate methodologies into a singular methodology.

➤ Level 4 – Benchmarking: The organization recognizes that process improvement is necessary to maintain a competitive advantage and that benchmarking must be performed on a continuous basis to achieve this.

➤ Level 5 – Continuous Improvement: The organization evaluates the results from benchmarking and enhances the processes defined in Level 3.

Any project management singular methodology, as mentioned in Level 3, needs to include sound scheduling processes. This is the main objective of this book. A sound scheduling methodology will not cover all project management processes, but will help you cover the majority of them.

---

8   Kerzner, Harold, *Using the Project Management Maturity Model: Strategic Planning for Project Management, Second Ed.*, New Jersey: Wiley, 2005, p. 16.

1

Managing Individual Projects

As we have said, the focus of this book is on how to use Project 2010 to manage individual projects. To do this, you need a solid understanding of the basic principles of project management and how to adapt and apply them to specific project situations.

Areas of Knowledge

According to the *PMBOK® Guide – Fourth Edition* published by PMI® there are nine areas of knowledge that must be addressed to manage any project:

Adapted from
PMBOK® Guide — Fourth Edition

Where Project 2010 Fits

As a stand-alone tool, Project 2010 is most helpful in managing time (schedule development and control), cost (budget development and control), and resources (the availability and workloads of the people, machines and other resources). It helps in managing scope (what is to be accomplished) to the extent that it reflects the work activities to be performed.

Project 2010 also provides features that help to manage communication among project stakeholders. Reports of project status, progress and predicted outcomes can be produced, emails can be triggered, etc.

Project Server 2010 can be of even greater help to the project manager in managing communication, risk and other areas. Program management and portfolio management are also covered, thanks to Project Server 2010.

Project Demands

Every project is a response to a request for some outcome (deliverable) within a stated time and cost. The requester wants a new or changed product, process, or event in a certain amount of time and for a desired cost.

During the project life-cycle, the project may be pulled by many forces that compete against one another and can make strong demands upon it. These are commonly referred to as the competing demands and include: scope, time, cost, quality, resources and risk. These competing demands are initially client- and sponsor-driven. Then, through negotiation, they are turned into a realistic plan that considers other demands on the project, such as the size and complexity of the deliverables, the size and complexity of the project team, the availability and capacity of the human and other resources, reliance on other projects, cultural and legal restrictions, and risk and uncertainty regarding any and all factors that influence project performance.

In the end, the scope must be able to be delivered within time and cost demands, given real-world conditions. It should be noted that scope drives the time and cost of the project but is in turn influenced by the time and cost demands. For example, when time is the most critical demand on the project, scope may be reshaped to accommodate getting something meaningful delivered within time parameters. The refined scope would then, among other factors, drive the time and cost required to deliver. The project manager must also consider quality and any risks that may occur and how all of this impacts the project.

Balance Flexibility and Discipline

Discipline promotes best practices and a broader perspective, and supports continuous improvement. Further, it helps the organization comply with regulatory and due diligence constraints.

However, flexibility is essential to provide people the autonomy and support they need to creatively navigate the intricacies of the organization while meeting objectives effectively and efficiently.

A balance between flexibility and discipline is needed to create a dynamic project management process that meets the needs of complex organizations in fast-paced environments.

Over-discipline can lead to unnecessary costs, delays, frustration and poor products. Over-flexibility can lead to the same results. The nature of the project and its environment should drive the degrees of discipline and flexibility needed and the forms they take. Project planning includes decisions regarding the way procedures and approaches will address discipline and flexibility.

The PM Process

The *PMBOK® Guide – Fourth Edition* defines PM as a process with five process groups: Initiating, Planning, Executing, Monitoring and Controlling, and Closing.

The illustration below graphically represents these process groups and their complex interrelationships. [9]

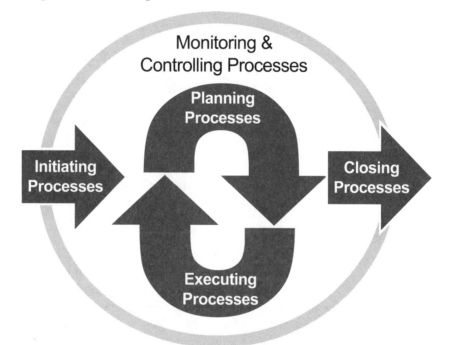

The process groups are defined in detail below. The following explains the relationships among the process groups, which are iterative and non-linear:

➤ Initiating is typically thought to be the first step in any process; however, there is need for planning *before* initiating any project. Further, there are decision points in some projects at which initiating is revisited.

➤ Planning continues throughout the life of the project. It overlaps with initiating to provide cost, time and resource information for use in decision making. Planning also provides the baseline for controlling the project.

➤ Monitoring and Controlling provide information for refining the plan.

➤ Executing provides the deliverables as well as the data for use in Monitoring and Controlling.

➤ Closing is a process that begins well before the project ends and influences future projects.

---

9   Adapted from *PMBOK® Guide – Fourth Edition*, PMI, 2008, p. 40.

The next sections will briefly describe the five process groups. The planning process group is covered in more depth than the others, as it is the central process and a principle focus of this book.

Initiating

Initiating results in a project that (1) has been authorized by people who have the responsibility to decide which projects are to be funded and (2) can begin to use money and resources to execute the project. Authorization often extends up to a checkpoint at which the project will be reevaluated.

To initiate a project, decision makers use information regarding project scope, time and cost. These "triple constraints" plus others like resource availability, risk, and market and regulatory issues, are the factors to consider when initiating a project. This implies that planning must begin prior to project authorization. Early estimates can be made with a fairly wide range of possible variance. This applies the principle of managing expectations by acknowledging uncertainty and risk.

During initiating, potential project stakeholders are identified and may take part in providing supporting information to be used in decision making.

Planning

Planning is arguably the most central and critical part of project management.

Planning results in a project plan that is the baseline for directing and controlling project performance. The plan is a model of the project and since projects are dynamic the plan must also be dynamic. Planning begins as soon as anyone begins to describe the project and continues throughout the project's life. Planning is the opportunity to learn about the needs and character of the participants and identify optimum ways to fulfill their needs. It is the means for managing expectations and acknowledging and reducing risk.

Planning is part of the "real work." The value of planning was impressively demonstrated in a project some years back: a project team coordinated equipment and multiple suppliers to build a real house that met stringent building codes in only three hours. The only way this was possible was to do a significant amount of planning beforehand to minimize chance and make sure everything went perfectly. Of course, over-planning and expecting the plan to be rigidly followed is as ineffective as not planning. The plan is a useful guide as opposed to a set of orders to be followed.

Planning can be done with a wide variety of levels of detail and formality. It consists of the following activities:

➤ Identify scope — objectives and requirements
➤ Agree on the approach
➤ Identify and describe the activities
➤ Estimate and schedule the work (this includes addressing risk and uncertainty)

➤ Optimize the plan

➤ Adjust as needed and throughout the project cycle to keep the plan up-to-date to truly reflect the project's real-world situation

These planning activities are not performed in a simple sequence. Each step's outcome is influenced by the outcomes of previous steps and may influence those outcomes as well. Optimizing the schedule might require adjustments to the objectives and requirements. Planning is a complex, iterative process.

Risk and uncertainty are realities. To manage them, you should include allowances for contingency, issues and changes. State your assumptions. Clearly communicate the degree of uncertainty.

Planning is done throughout the life of a project. Rolling wave planning (as illustrated in chapter 4) is an approach that recognizes the uncertainty that is faced by many project managers. In rolling wave planning, a high-level plan is developed for the whole project and the next phase of work is planned in greater detail. At the completion of that phase, the overall plan is reviewed and possibly refined, and a detailed plan for the next phase is created. This rolling wave approach is used to give project stakeholders increasingly accurate estimates and schedules as more becomes known about the project and its requirements.

Identify scope — objectives and requirements

The more people know about what they expect to receive or deliver, the more likely it is they will be satisfied. Objectives and requirements define what's expected. They answer questions like:

➤ What are the overall intent and major outcomes of the project?

➤ What is the underlying reason for performing the project (e.g., save money, make more money, improve service to customers)?

➤ What is the desired outcome (the product), when is it desired and what are the cost expectations and limitations?

➤ What are the specific behavioral and functional requirements?

Objectives and requirements drive the project and form the basis for determining whether the project was successful. They are progressively elaborated starting with a relatively abstract definition and proceeding to greater degrees of detail and specification as the project unfolds.

Agree Upon the Approach

It is essential to forge agreements among the stakeholders early in the life of the project. Establish guidelines, standards and procedures scaled to the needs of the project. Get agreement on how communication, procurement, issues and change control, and quality control will be handled. This will help avoid confusion during the project and promote best practices that increase effectiveness and efficiency. Avoid bureaucracy and seek the right balance between flexibility and discipline. The use of Project 2010 to manage this area of planning is covered in chapter 3.

| Identify and Describe Activities and Deliverables | Identify all of the project's outcomes or deliverables and the work required to deliver them. The work breakdown structure (WBS) is "a deliverable-oriented hierarchical decomposition of the work to be executed by the project team to accomplish the project objectives and create the required deliverables, with each descending level of the WBS representing an increasingly detailed definition of the project work. The WBS organizes and defines the total scope of the project and represents the work specified in the current approved project scope statement ."[10] |

Taking a layered or hierarchical approach enables planners to more accurately identify all of the work that needs to be done and manage it at different levels of detail. The WBS also becomes a focal point for project cost accounting and for assigning responsibility and accountability. It is the base for estimating and scheduling.

Project 2010 is designed to automate work breakdown structures. Chapter 3, Entering Tasks, will explore the WBS and how it is used in Project 2010.

Estimate and Schedule the Work

When you estimate you are attempting to predict a project's effort, cost and duration. Scheduling brings together the availability of resources and their numbers and capability; the activities to be done, including their sequence, estimated labor and other costs; the environmental conditions and the calendar. The output of scheduling is a time line predicting when tasks will be performed, resources will be needed and deliverables will be delivered. The estimated cost of the project can be calculated and a budget created based on the schedule. You should estimate based on past experience and at an appropriate level of detail.

Dynamic scheduling recognizes and accepts that change is inevitable. It is based on a systematic linking of project activities to one another and to resources so that change in one part of the model can be easily analyzed to determine its impact elsewhere.

Sequencing or linking is a critical part of scheduling. Analyze the dependencies among activities to determine which activities must be done serially and which can be done in parallel. For example, if an activity is completed late and other activities are delayed waiting for the results of the first activity, there is a ripple effect through the project. Chapter 5 addresses dependencies.

Will resources be available? Planning requires realistic assessment as to whether the staff and other resources will be available at the right time. Resource availability and capability directly affect the schedule. Assess the likelihood of resources being what, when and where you expect them to be. Chapters 7 and 8 address resource-related aspects of scheduling.

---

10 ———— *PMBOK® Guide – Fourth Edition*, PMI, 2008, p. 116.

The project manager is responsible for keeping the project plan up to date and realistic. A dynamic schedule allows Project 2010 to minimize the work required and to give stakeholders the ability to assess risks and impacts. Further, it enables planners and managers to play "what if" games to explore alternatives so as to come up with the optimal schedule.

Unfortunately, project management tools do not estimate or sequence project activities. That is why chapters 3 – 8 are all titled "Entering …" People enter estimates, resources and dependencies. Chapter 6 addresses deadlines, constraints and task calendars.

The use of Project 2010 to manage this area of planning is covered in chapters 4 through 8.

Optimize

Scheduling is modeling. A model is a simplification of reality that enables modelers to optimize the reality without spending undo time, effort and money. Dynamic scheduling, as described in this book, is predicated on the idea that a schedule is only truly useful if it is kept up-to-date and allows for change. A dynamic model allows the schedulers to come up with multiple alternatives and to optimize the plan.

Optimize to come to the right combination of product quality, cost and time, given resource and other constraints. Get agreement with the client and/or sponsor about priorities and trade-offs. This means that the project's outcome, target date, budget, available resources, tools, techniques and the project environment may all be adjusted to find a realistic and optimum plan to achieve objectives. Pushing back and justifying why you may have to say no is part of the process to manage expectations and ensure project success.

Chapter 9 addresses how to optimize the schedule using Project 2010.

Keep the Plan up to Date

Planning continues throughout the project's life and should always accurately reflect the project in its current state. The plan is a baseline for determining if expectations are being met and for identifying action needed to keep the project on track.

Dynamic scheduling using Project 2010 enables project managers to assess the impact of changes, compare the current plan for the rest of the project against the baseline plan and change the baseline if necessary.

Chapter 10 addresses updating the schedule to keep it up to date.

Executing

Planning is where most of the management is. Executing is where 90% of the action is. Project activities are performed, deliverables are produced and data is created. You can use Project 2010 to capture time and cost data and provide a repository for performance data such as the amount of effort expended to complete a task. Another important aspect of executing is to manage and document project issues and changes.

Chapter 11 addresses reporting on the schedule and monitoring project progress.

Monitoring and Controlling

In Monitoring and Controlling you take the project performance data and compare it to the plan to determine whether expectations are being met, changes are needed to the plan, or corrective action is needed.

You can use reports of the project's status compared with the planned schedule and budget as a baseline to monitor progress.

Remember, the process is iterative: as the project progresses there may be variance from the original plan and there certainly will be more information available for validating assumptions. You need to go back into planning to refine the plan so as to make it more realistic. Further, planning is performed at key points in the project to make more refined short term estimates and to re-estimate out to the end of the project.

Chapter 12 on Earned Value Management and parts of other chapters address how to use Project 2010 to monitor and control your projects.

Monitoring and Controlling is not limited to the budget and schedule. You should also assess the quality of the product and the relationships among the project stakeholders, and plan and take any necessary corrective action.

Closing

Projects MUST end. They end when they are cancelled or when they achieve their objectives and deliver the end product. Closing includes the processes that formally terminate a project and transfer the completed product to those who will support, use, manage or maintain it for its life. Formal termination includes archiving project documents, closing out cost accounts and contracts, and obtaining formal acceptance of the project results.

Closing also includes the review and evaluation of the project's performance and the identification of lessons learned. In large, complex projects, Closing processes may also occur at the end of key project phases.

Dynamic Scheduling

We use the term "Dynamic Scheduling" in the title of this book; we present here a brief explanation about why we schedule and what we consider a dynamic schedule.

Why Do We Schedule?

There are many reasons for preparing project schedules. Here are four reasons which require varying levels of challenge and detail:

➤ **Sell**

You can use schedules to sell upper management or a client on undertaking a new project.

Project 2010 schedules support this type of selling with the Timeline View graphic with the main dates, or by making the timing of milestones visible in a high-level Gantt chart. Schedules built for this purpose often look very slick.

Selling requires the least detail in your schedule, but requires a high level of knowledge and experience about the situation, because you must present a realistic prediction without a deep analysis of details. The expected result would be that you get the contract or project authorization.

➤ **Delegate**

Once your project is authorized, you need a more detailed schedule to delegate the work.

With Project 2010, you can develop this from the high-level schedules you used for authorization or selling purposes. Create your work breakdown structure and use the details from it to generate activities to assign to team members or subcontractors. Use your schedule to communicate commitments: everybody will know what to do and when to do it, and you'll also have a budget of your project. The expected result is a plan with commitments agreed upon and the project baseline set.

➤ **Track**

In order to track your project, you enter the current status regularly into your Project 2010 schedule and compare the progress against the previously defined baseline. The output of tracking is a status report that shows how far the project has progressed.

Tracking allows you to report to stakeholders what has been accomplished in the project and provides a history that allows you to learn from past mistakes. If you use Earned Value Management for tracking, you will also obtain variances and performance indexes, which are the basis for trend analysis and forecasting.

> **Forecast**
> You can use Project 2010 to model your project to forecast the finish date and the total cost. You have to create the schedule in such a way that it immediately shows what impact actual events have on the project finish date and cost as you enter progress information.
>
> Forecasting provides answers for questions such as: When will deliverables be available? On what dates will individual resources be needed? When will the project be done? What will the project cost? If the answers to these questions aren't acceptable according to your commitments, you will need to apply corrective actions and replan the remaining activities. If this is not possible, you will need to renegotiate the main objectives or maybe even look at some trade-offs between them.

In order to use your schedule for the four purposes described above, you will need to prepare your Project 2010 schedule model for the initial planning phases. We will provide you with all the guidelines to help you set up a dynamic schedule that will give you this predictive power.

Static Chart or Dynamic Model?

Your project schedule is a model: a simplification of a reality. We use models because we can build a model at a fraction of the cost of building the reality. Models let us simplify complex realities so we can manage them to make decisions. But it's crucial to represent that reality in a way that helps us make the right decisions.

A static chart is one that requires you to do all of the updating. A dynamic model updates itself: when you enter change in one part of the project, other parts are automatically updated.

As a project manager, you should make it your goal to create a dynamic model of your project situation, not just draw a static chart that will look impressive hanging on your wall. The advantages of a dynamic model are:

> A dynamic model is easier to update
> A static schedule might initially represent a good model of the real project timeline and costs, but in a fast-changing environment, a static schedule will soon be obsolete. The re-work to build a new static model can be huge and you're likely to miss some important progress updates which could result in wrong decisions for the future.
>
> A dynamic schedule is a living document and should be kept alive until the project's ends. If a schedule model is not or cannot be kept easily up-to-date, it is not a dynamic schedule.

> A dynamic model is responsive
> In order for schedules to be easily kept up-to-date, they need to be responsive. A responsive model updates itself as much as it can. Schedules

can do this if they were created with as many dependencies as needed and as few fixed dates (constraints or manually scheduled tasks in Project 2010) as possible. A dynamic schedule uses all of Project 2010's automatic updating features to keep it updated as you enter information on progress.

➤ A dynamic model has predictive power
Schedules need to show the latest forecasts of the finish date and the final expenses of the project. Only then can a schedule truly be a powerful decision-support system for the project manager and key stakeholders. This requires that the model use empirical, actual data that is translated into forecasts using algorithms. To complement these algorithms, it is necessary for the project manager to use trend analysis. And most importantly, corrective actions need to be taken if the project deviates from the original objectives. A dynamic schedule will allow all of these.

Another advantage a dynamic model has over a static chart is that you can use a dynamic model to develop different scenarios to analyze other possible situations and then implement what could be a better option.

➤ A dynamic model is easily accessible online and in real time
In order to keep the project team working together and aligned, all information from the dynamic schedule model needs to be easily accessible to everyone. This is essential in order for good decisions and corrective actions to be made in a timely manner.

The project manager is responsible for making the schedule readily available. The traditional solution is to deliver reports at different levels of detail following pre-established reporting periods. The other option is to have all of the information online and in a real time, using the advantages of Project Server 2010 and SharePoint Server 2010. With this solution, you'll have the powerful and dynamic features of Project 2010 accessible through a user-friendly interface that executives and team members can use to keep their fingers on the pulse of their portfolio, programs and projects.

In the chapters that follow, we will show you how to create a model of your project—one that meets all the criteria of a dynamic schedule we just described.

Recap

In this chapter we have defined terms and set a conceptual foundation for what project management is: what its basic principles are and what process groups make up the overall process of managing a project.

The remainder of the book addresses the use of Project 2010 in planning, executing, monitoring and controlling, and closing a project. The book is centered on the concept of dynamic scheduling.

Former US President and Military General Dwight D. Eisenhower once said, "In preparing for battle, I have always found that plans are useless, but planning is indispensable." In the time in which he lived (1890–1969), most project plans were static in nature and "dead" as soon as they were written. A plan that can't be or isn't updated is of limited use. Clearly, President Eisenhower was a very knowledgeable project manager.

With the advent of computers and with Project 2010, we can create plans that are alive and dynamic. In Project 2010, the project schedule is a model that shows the most current status and allows predictions based on the combination of dependency and resource linkages. This easy to update electronic model of your project allows you to make forecasts at any time during the life of the project, adjusting for the inevitable changes.

Such a dynamic model is a powerful tool for project managers. Maybe if President Eisenhower were still alive, he'd say: *"In preparing for the global marketplace, I have found that planning is indispensable and dynamic models are a critical success factor."*

But planning by itself is not enough. We must apply the principles of project management throughout the project management process groups, from initiating to closing, and we must do it with full awareness of the enterprise and environmental conditions that influence our projects.

The remainder of this book addresses the way that Project 2010 can be used to enable effective scheduling and budgeting, as well as project control, through dynamic scheduling.

Review Questions

1. What is a project and what makes it different from other kinds of work?

2. Are there organizations that never have any projects?

3. Are there organizations that only have projects?

4. What is the difference between project management, program management and portfolio management?

5. What are the PM knowledge areas according to the *PMBOK® Guide – Fourth Edition* from PMI®?

6. What are the competing demands in project management and why are they important?

7. What is the rolling wave approach to project planning?

8. What are the six activities of project planning and are they always done in sequence?

9. What advantages does a dynamic model have over a static chart?

Chapter 2: Getting Started with Project 2010

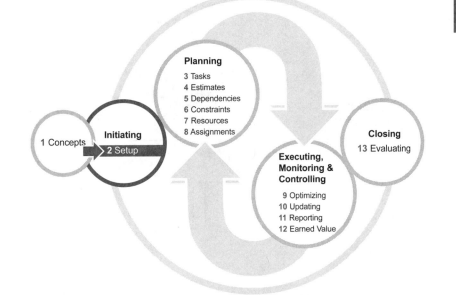

Now that we've reviewed the terminology and basic concepts of project management, we're ready to explore the Project 2010 application interface and set up a new project.

After reading this chapter you will be able to:

➤ Describe the basic functions Project 2010 performs
➤ Discuss the differences/benefits of the task scheduling modes in Project 2010
➤ Identify the components of the Enterprise Project Management (EPM) tools
➤ Navigate the Project 2010 interface
➤ Identify where Project 2010 stores data
➤ Identify and select among the Project 2010 views
➤ Select and use a project template
➤ Set up a new project and choose the appropriate options
➤ Create a Project Calendar
➤ Identify and describe best practices for setting up new project schedules

Okay, I know I have everything I need but I just don't know how to swim!

Project Management Software	In any project, you need to answer these seven questions to provide the basic information you need for scheduling:

	Question	Used to define
1.	*What needs to be done?*	Deliverables and Tasks
2.	*How long will it take?*	Duration Estimates or Work Estimates
3.	*In what order?*	Dependencies
4.	*When must it happen?*	Constraints
5.	*Who is going to do it?*	Resources and Assignments
6.	***When will it happen?***	Start and Finish Dates
7.	***How much will it cost?***	Total Cost of the Task or Deliverable

Project 2010 helps you record, manage, maintain and even create the data that answers these questions.

➤ You enter the answers to the first five questions

➤ Project 2010 computes the last two bolded questions (and allows you to adjust them, if needed)

➤ Project 2010 stores the data, organizes it and reports on it

You typically enter the answers to the first five questions. However, it is a best practice and beneficial to you to let Project 2010 assist you in accurately answering questions 6 and 7. Lets look at questions 6 and 7 below:

6. When will it happen?

You can enter start and finish dates for auto scheduled tasks using Project 2010. However, this usually results in your task dates being bound or constrained in one way or another. As we will discuss later in the chapter, we recommend that you let Project calculate Start and Finish dates for your auto scheduled tasks so that you can reap the benefits of a dynamic schedule. With the manually scheduled tasks, you can enter as much information about the task as you have to get started with planning. Once you have all the needed information about the task, you can make the task auto scheduled and let the powerful scheduling engine of Project 2010 calculate your Start and Finish dates for you.

7. How much will it cost?

Project 2010 can capture and calculate costs in a variety of ways. You can enter costs that are Fixed or generated by Cost resources directly into your schedule. However, another advantage of using project management software is its ability to quickly calculate variable costs – i.e. costs that are rate, time or consumption based. By simply setting up standard rates for Work resources and assigning them to tasks, Project 2010 can calculate costs of items in your project. You can also track costs related to items that are consumed in the project, (like lumber, paper, or cement). Here, you can set up Material resources to track these individual items on a task by task basis. Lastly, you can track your current budgets using Budget resources. We will discuss how Project 2010 calculates costs in Chapter 7 – Assigning Resources.

Project 2010 reduces the effort needed to manage project management processes. It serves as a project management information system, maintaining information on the project, its tasks, resources, dependencies, estimates, costs, etc. Dynamic scheduling (as described in this book) helps you use Project 2010 not only for creating your schedule, but also for keeping it up-to-date and reporting on status vis-à-vis the plan.

In Project 2010, you now have the ability to specify the "task mode" of specific tasks to be automatically scheduled or manually scheduled. With manually scheduled tasks, you are responsible for entering and maintaining Start and Finish dates of the tasks. For more Dynamic Schedules, however, we recommend you set your tasks to be automatically scheduled. This way, Project 2010 can **compute** start and finish dates based on duration estimates, resource dependencies and logical dependencies. A schedule with dependencies is flexible; the tool knows how to update the other tasks automatically when preceding tasks are changed, or when resource availabilities change. That said, we don't want to give the impression that once you set up a dynamic schedule with dependencies, the tool does all the work. It does not.

For example, the tool doesn't know much about the relationship among project stakeholders or about the project environment. In its standalone form, the tool doesn't know about other projects and how changes in those projects may affect your project. Changes in resources can have effects that can't be interpreted by the tool to accurately recalculate finish dates unless you enter durations, assignments and revised effort estimates. Further, based on the cause of slippage and on the corrective action to be taken, you must enter revised tasks, estimates, dependencies, constraints and resources to enable Project 2010 to re-compute start and finish dates.

 Project 2010 now has the capability to schedule tasks automatically (as with previous versions of the application) or manually. When manually scheduled, the Start and Finish dates of tasks do NOT move when other linked or related tasks are moved. Manually scheduled tasks are ideal for placeholders you can use as you wait for approval or further information about a task.

 Manually scheduled tasks are not to be confused with Inactive tasks – which are also new to Project 2010. Inactive tasks are visible within the project schedule but the information is not counted toward project or summary task totals.

 If you use manually scheduled tasks in your project schedule, changes in resources or tasks will not affect these tasks' start and finish dates in the schedule.

Based on the resource cost rates, effort estimates and assignments you enter, the software calculates the total cost, per deliverable, per level of detail in the work breakdown structure (WBS) and for the whole project. If you enter actual effort data, actual costs can be compared to planned costs.

Project 2010 does efficient reporting. The software is a database in that you can pull data from the database to focus on any task or deliverable at any level of summary, any period or any resource you want. You can customize reports to show cost, schedule and other data and to compare actual against planned progress.

Enterprise PM Tools

Individual projects don't exist in a vacuum. Project 2010 Professional is one component of a larger system.

While Project 2010 Professional can be used on its own, (as with Project 2010 Standard), it is much more powerful in the context of an enterprise solution that makes use of the power of servers and the Web by weaving together a number of products: Microsoft Project Professional 2010, Project Server 2010, Project Web Apps (PWA), Microsoft Windows Server 2008, Microsoft SharePoint Server 2010, and the rest of the Microsoft Office 2010 suite. There are also add-on tools that help to manage knowledge and perform other functions such as assessing risk through Monte Carlo Simulation.

Working together, these tools enable functions such as:
- ➤ Automatic notification of project events to relevant stakeholders
- ➤ Management of multiple projects with shared resource pools
- ➤ Aggregate reporting and analysis of multiple projects in portfolios and programs
- ➤ Risk and issues management
- ➤ The ability to integrate document and deliverables management with project management

Microsoft Project 2010 Standard and Professional

Project 2010 comes in two editions: Microsoft Project 2010 Standard and Microsoft Project 2010 Professional. The Professional edition can connect to a Project Server database which provides the capability to implement EPM. There are other differences in functionality between the Professional and Standard editions of Project 2010 that were discussed in the Introduction chapter of this book.

There are also differences between using Project 2010 Professional with Project Server, and using either Project 2010 Standard or Professional without Project Server. We will use the term *Project 2010* or *Project 2010 standalone* when addressing functions that are the same in both the Standard and Professional versions used by themselves. We will use Project 2010 Professional to explain features that are only included in this edition. In this book, we will concentrate on Project 2010 in the standalone configuration.

Working with Files in Project 2010

File Types

Project 2010 can store its data in various types of files. Two commonly used file types that are native to the application are:

➤ Regular Project files (extension **.mpp** for Microsoft Project Plan)

➤ Template files (extension **.mpt** for Microsoft Project Template)

Template files are similar to project files, but with an added protection against accidental changes: when you open a template, you work with a copy of the template. The original template stays unchanged.

Project templates can be used to store layouts, settings and information that you want to use for multiple projects. Each time you start a new project you start with a copy of the template, which you can adjust as needed for the specific project.

Project files (.mpp) and project template files (.mpt) can both contain:

➤ **Data**: tasks, estimates, dependencies, constraints, resources, assignments

➤ **Objects**: views, reports, tables, filters, calendars, groups, maps, fields, groups and modules (Visual Basic for Applications [VBA])

➤ **Project-specific options**: these relate to the project only and are stored in the individual project. You can easily recognize which options are project specific (local) in the **Project Options** dialog. (To view this, on the **File** tab, in the **Backstage** view, choose the **Options** tab, and then select the specific tab for the functions you want to set to be project specific.) Where the section heading has the suffix "_____ **options for this project**:" *<name of current file>*, the option is local and stored with the project. We will discuss the **Project Options** dialog later in the chapter.

There is a default template file for Project 2010 called Global.mpt which contains default objects—like views, tables and filters that you use for reporting purposes. The Global.mpt is always open when Project 2010 is running. The main difference between the Global.mpt template and other project template files is that the Global.mpt cannot contain schedule data like tasks and dependencies.

 You can view the available objects in the Global.mpt in the **Organizer**. We will talk more about the **Organizer** in the Backstage – Info section, later in this chapter.

Backwards
Compatibility

Project 2010 is compatible with previous versions of Microsoft Project.

You can use Project 2010 to create mpp files compatible with previous versions of Project (2000-2003 and 2007). When you do this, however, features which are specific and new to Project 2010 will be lost. You can also use Project 2010 to open and edit files created in older versions of Project. These files will be opened in Project 2010 in a reduced-functionality mode.

Items created using features that are unique to Project 2010, such as manually scheduled tasks and top-down summary tasks, may not appear as expected when viewed with Project 2007.

Working with Schedules from Project 2010 Standalone

When you use Project 2010 in standalone mode, (not connected to Project Server), the projects are stored as separate files on your file directory system. When you use Project Server, the projects are stored in one SQL Server database.

Project 2010
as a Relational
Database
Application

At first glance, the Project 2010 application with its columns and rows bears a striking resemblance to a spreadsheet application. However, instead of seeing it as a spreadsheet, we suggest you think of Project 2010 as an application to access a relational database.

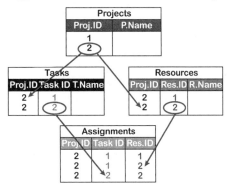

A relational database has several different tables that are related to each other through fields they have in common. In Project 2010, these common fields are the **ID** fields.[1] You can see this in the illustration. The tasks and assignments tables have what is called a one-to-many relationship, since one task can be assigned to multiple resources. Similarly for resources, one resource can be assigned to multiple tasks. It is the one-to-many relationships in the data that are hard to manage within a spreadsheet application.

There are three reasons for seeing Project 2010 as a relational database application:

1. **There are four types of data.**

---

1 In fact, the **Unique ID** field contains the unique identifiers, because the **ID** values are just row numbers that constantly change when items are inserted or moved.

There are four distinct types of data, or data entities, in the database: projects, tasks, resources and assignments. In a spreadsheet table, you typically monitor only one type of data.

2. **The data have one-to-many relationships.**

The data entities are related and have one-to-many relationships between them.

3. **Each data entity has its own table.**
   ▶ Projects can be found in the projects table
   ▶ Tasks can be found in the task table that can be seen in any of the task views
   ▶ Resources are stored in the resource table and can be seen in the resource views
   ▶ Assignments are in their own table as well. Assignments can be found in between the tasks in the **Task Usage** view or in between the resources in the **Resource Usage** view.

Project Server 2010 users store their projects in SQL Server as the relational database instead of in .mpp files. In a relational database, you can see each data entity in its own table. The (simplified) data model for the Project Server database is shown in the illustration on the previous page. A multi-project database like Project Server has an extra table at the top that contains all projects. The Projects table is where Project Server stores all the project level data, like project name, project manager and project start and finish date, for all projects in the database.

The Project 2010 Interface

The Ribbon **2010** Project 2010 has adopted the concept of the Ribbon, which was first introduced with the release of the 2007 version of Microsoft Office. With the Ribbon, options are no longer listed under dropdown menus. Instead, related commands are placed together in groups and displayed in a series of topic-specific tabs across the top of the project window/screen. For example, when you click on the Task tab, you will see commands that relate to manipulating tasks such as copy, paste, link and indent/outdent. The commands themselves are organized into logical groups such as **Clipboard**, **Font** and **Schedule**.

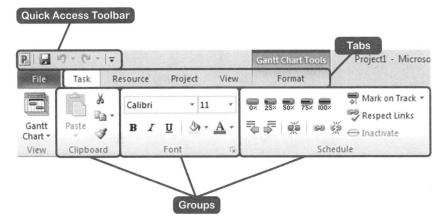

To choose a command from the Ribbon, just click on it with the primary mouse button. If there is a small down arrow next to the command or option, click on the arrow to show a dropdown list of additional options. Click on the ▼ at the lower right hand corner of a group of commands to open a dialog box/window of options.

The **Format** tab of the Ribbon is context sensitive and shows different options depending on the current Project view you are working in.

Customize the Ribbon You can customize the appearance of the Ribbon by adding or removing tabs, groups or commands. You will not be able to add new commands to the pre-defined groups but you can create your own groups either within the standard tabs or on your own custom tab.

1. Right-click on any section of the **Ribbon** and select **Customize the Ribbon**. The **Project Options** dialog box will open.

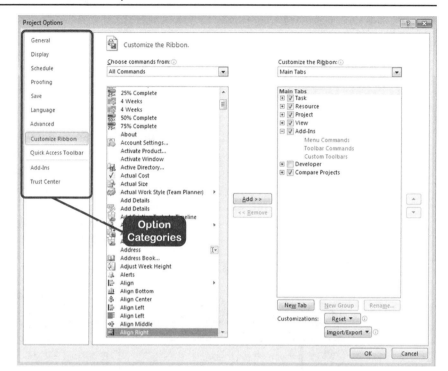

2. On the right hand side of **Project Options**, click on **New Tab**. Two new rows will be added to the window on the right, one showing **New Tab (Custom)** and a second indented below it showing **New Group (Custom)**.

3. Click on **New Tab (Custom)** then **Rename** to give the tab a more meaningful display name.

4. Click on **New Group (Custom)**, then **Rename**, to give the group a more meaningful name.

5. If you want to create a group in one of the pre-defined tabs, select the tab where you want to add the command, then click the **New Group** button.

 If you need to re-position your custom group or tab, select the group or tab and use the (Up/Down) arrows.

6. To add a command to your custom group, in the **Choose commands** from dropdown, select **All Commands** then scroll to find the command you want.

7. Select the command on the left and the custom group on the right, then click Add >> .

 You can only add commands to custom groups.

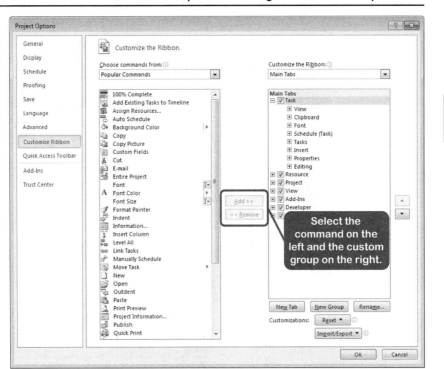

2

The Quick Access Toolbar

In addition to the Ribbon, Microsoft Project 2010 presents you with the Quick Access Toolbar. This toolbar can be displayed either above or below the Ribbon. You can use the toolbar to run the commands you use most often.

You can customize the items on the Quick Access toolbar. To do this, click the {Arrow} at the end of the toolbar and select **More Commands**. The **Project Options** dialog (as seen below), will open.

Commands can also be added directly from the Ribbon to the Quick Access Toolbar. Right-click on the command in the Ribbon then select **Add to Quick Access Toolbar**.

To remove a command from the Quick Access Toolbar, right-click on the command, then select **Remove from Quick Access Toolbar**.

You can display the Quick Access Toolbar beneath the Ribbon. To do this, click the down-arrow to the right-end of the Quick Access Toolbar and select **Show Below the Ribbon**.

The Backstage View

Backstage is another new feature of Project 2010. You can use the Backstage view to perform most file-related functions such as Open, Save, Save As, Print and Close. You can also use the Backstage view to manage your Project Server connections and to access the Project Options dialog, which was found in the Tools menu in previous versions of Project.

To get to the Backstage view, click on the **File** tab to the left end of the Ribbon.

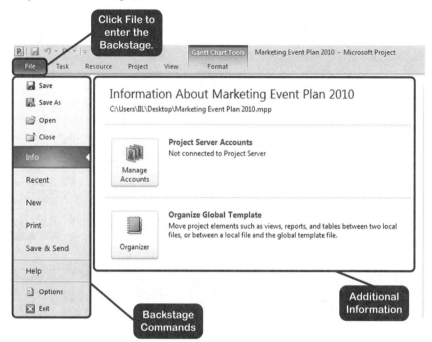

Saving Changes in an Existing .mpp File

1. On the **File** tab, in the **Backstage** view, click 💾 OR on the **Quick Access Toolbar,** click 💾.

2. If your file exists already, the file on your hard disk will be updated with the changes. If the file does not exist, the **Save As** dialog will appear automatically. (See below).

Saving a New File with Project 2010

1. If you save a schedule for the first time or if you opened the file read-only and then save it, you are prompted for a file name in the **Save As** dialog:

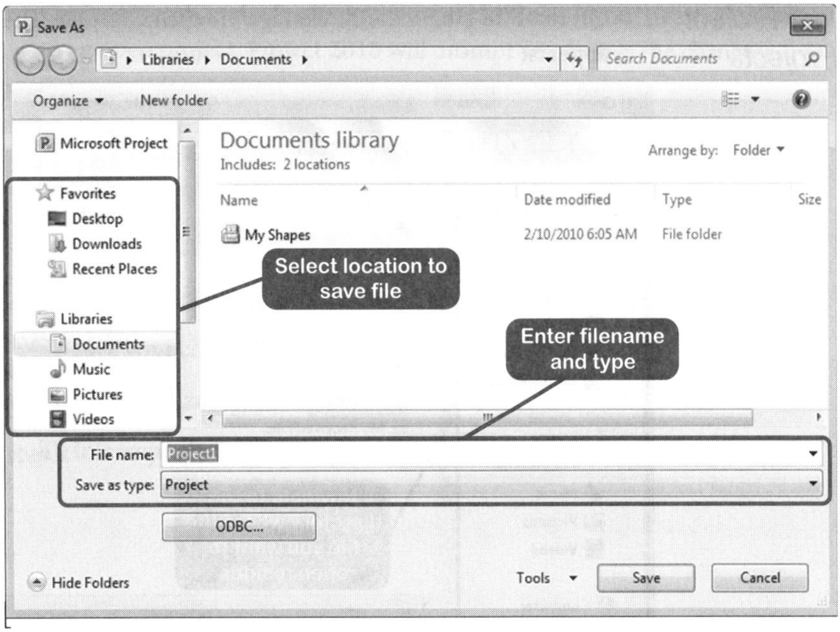

2. Click [Save]. Each project file will be saved with the extension **.mpp** by default.

Saving an .mpp File in a New Directory or with a New Name

1. On the **File** tab, in the **Backstage** view, click [P] **Save As**. The **Save As** dialog (as shown above) appears.

2. Select the drive and directory then enter the new name in the **File name** dropdown at the bottom of the window.

3. Click [Save].

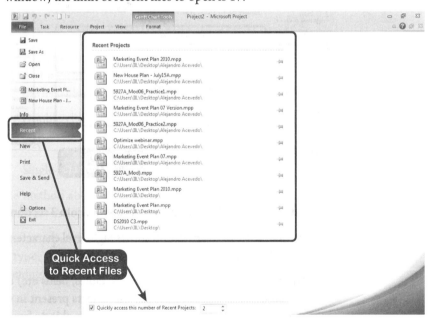

You can use the **Manage Accounts** button to control access to project information stored in Project Server. Project Server 2010 is beyond the scope of this book.

Backstage –
Recent

The **Recent** command in the **Backstage** view gives you links to the files you worked with recently in Project 2010. You can also display the recently open file list on the left pane with the other commands by placing a check in the ☐ Quickly access this number of Recent Projects: 4 ⊕ checkbox at the lower left of the Project window; the limit of recent files to open is 17.

Backstage – New   You can use the **New** button to create new blank projects or projects based on templates stored locally or online. Project 2010 also makes it easy to create projects from Excel workbooks and Windows SharePoint task lists.

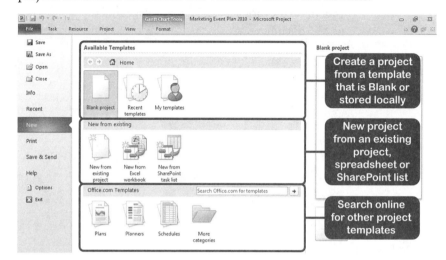

Backstage – Print   The **Print** command in the **Backstage** view provides a single place to prepare your project file for printing. We will discuss each of the printing options in depth in chapter 11 Reporting.

Backstage – Save & Send

The options under the **Save & Send** command make it easy for you to send your project information to stakeholders. You can send your entire project schedule as an attachment or have tasks sent to Outlook or SharePoint. You can also save your file in the format of a different version of Project 2010 or create a static PDF or XPS document. We discuss sharing project information in chapter 11.

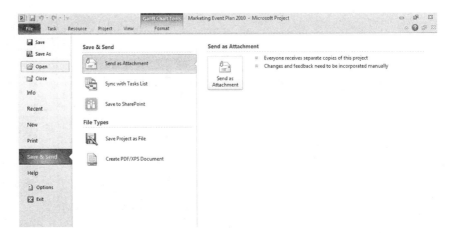

Backstage – Help

The options in the **Help** command in the Backstage view make it easy for you to search for help on Project 2010 and general Microsoft Office topics. You can search Help and How To topics and even link directly to official Microsoft sites to get the latest information and updates.

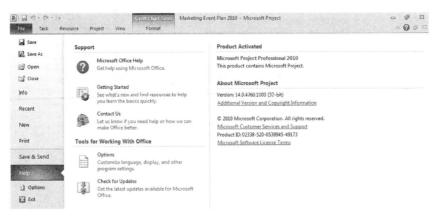

Backstage – Options

When you use Project 2010, you can set many options that affect how the application behaves on your computer or for a specific project file. We'll discuss the Project **Options** as we go through the life-cycle of your project throughout this book.

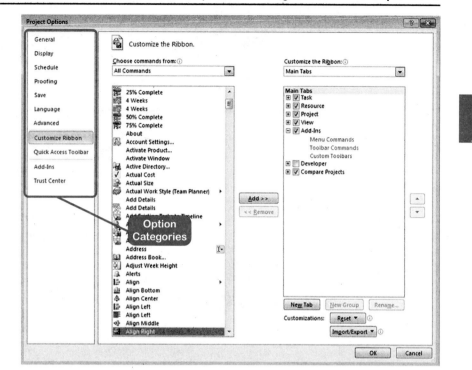

Backstage – Exit

Use the **Exit** command to quit Project 2010. The application will attempt to close all project windows. If an opened project has been modified but not saved, you will be prompted to save before the project and the Project 2010 application are closed.

The Project 2010 Main Screen

In addition to the Ribbon, Backstage, and Quick Access Toolbar, Project 2010 has many different screen areas that appear when they are needed. In order to follow our procedural steps, you have to know the names of the parts of the screen, as labeled in this screenshot:

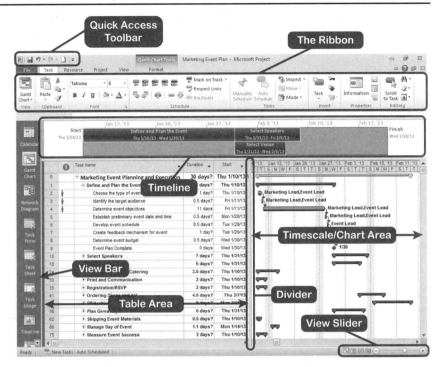

 Project 2010 includes a **Timeline** view that you can use to get a concise view of your entire project schedule. You can add or remove tasks from the Timeline and have it displayed at the top of your other Project 2010 views. The Timeline can also be printed or copied to presentations and reports. We will discuss the Timeline as a view later in this chapter.

Table and Timescale

The main portion of the screen in the illustration is divided into two sections. The left area is referred to as the Table or Spreadsheet. This area shows a subset of task, resource or assignment information in an arrangement of rows and columns. You can determine which columns (data fields) are displayed by inserting or hiding columns as necessary. The right side of the screen is referred to as the Chart Area or Timescale. This area features a timephased view of the project. The view can be adjusted to show different time periods. You can adjust the relative size of the Table and Chart areas by dragging the vertical divider to the left or right, and the relative size of Timeline and Gantt Chart views by dragging the horizontal divider up or down.

 Adding new columns quickly to the table area has been greatly simplified in Project 2010. To do this, click the ⎡ **Add New Column** ▾ ⎤ heading at the right end of a Table area. Then, type or select the name of column you wish to add from the column drop-down.

The View Bar

The **View Bar** lets you switch from one view to another. It appears along the left side of the Project 2010 window and contains icons representing the different views. If the View Bar is visible and you want to hide it, right-click on the bar and select View Bar from the list (to remove the check mark). The View Bar will now be replaced by a single strip showing the name of the current view. To display the View Bar again, right-click on the strip and select View Bar.

Scroll Bars

The scroll bar consists of three parts:

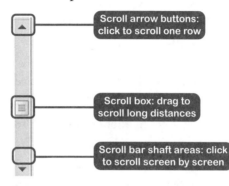

As you are dragging the timescale scroll boxes, you will see a yellow feedback box pop up that tells you where you will be if you stop scrolling. The vertical scroll box shows the ID number of the task you are browsing to:

ID: 6
Name: Develop event schedule

The horizontal scroll box tells you the date you are traveling to:

Thu 1/24/13

Zoom Slider

New to Project 2010 is the **Zoom Slider**. You can use the view slider to adjust the view of the project's timescale. Move the Slider's cursor to the left to Zoom Out and see a higher-level timeframe of the project, such as years or months. Move the Slider to the right to Zoom in and view the finer time details of the project schedule. You can find the Zoom slider on the lower right hand corner of the screen on the Status bar. The Slider only works on the Gantt Chart, Network Diagram, Calendar and all graph views.

Mouse or Touchpad: Right-Clicks and Double-Clicks

For those who are right-handed, the right mouse button or right touchpad click button under your middle finger can pop up shortcut menus that relate to a particular screen area. For example, in the stylized version of a Gantt Chart in the illustration, you can right-click on all of the labeled locations to call up shortcut menus. You can do this in other views, as well.

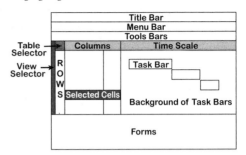

Alternatively, you can double-click with the left mouse button or left touchpad click button in these places; this will display a dialog box for the most likely shortcut for that area.

Moving Around in a Project

In addition to the Ribbon, you can also use the keyboard to move around in Project 2010. When you press the [Alt] key, KeyTips pop up next to each of the commands available in the Ribbon and the current view. The tips tell you which keys you can use to execute the command you want.

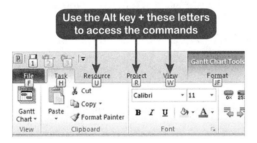

The table below shows some of the more popular commands and shortcuts. The following convention is used: [Alt] + [→] means hold down [Alt] and press [→].

Move to	By keyboard	By mouse
Next row	[Enter ↵] or [↓]	Click
Next column	[Tab] or [→]	Click
Next minor time unit in the timescale, or Previous	[Alt] + [→] [Alt] + [←]	Click the arrow button [▶] on the scroll bar of the timescale, or click [◀]

Move to	By keyboard	By mouse
Next screen in timescale	Alt + Page Up or Alt + Page Dn	Click to the left or right of the scroll box in the horizontal scroll bar
The start date of the project	Alt + Home	Left align the scroll box in the horizontal scroll bar
The end date of the project	Alt + End	Right align the scroll box in the horizontal scroll bar
The first task of the project	Control + Home	Drag the vertical scroll box to the top
The last task of the project	Alt + End	Drag the vertical scroll box to the bottom
A specific task and task bar, resource or date	F5 or Control + F	On the **Task** tab, in the **Editing** group, click **Find**
The other view in a split window	F6	Click in the other view to make it active
Move the timescale to a task bar	Control + Shift + F5	On the **Task** tab, in the **Editing** group, click **Scroll to Task**.

Moving Around in a Dialog Box

The following convention is used: Alt + Tab means hold down Alt and press Tab.

Action	By keyboard	By mouse
Move to next field in a dialog box, or	Tab	Click in the field
Move to previous field	Shift + Tab	
Move to any field in a form	Alt + press underlined letter of the field name	Click in the field
Increase or decrease value in a field	Alt + ↑ or Alt + ↓	Use the spin button
While the tab label is selected, move to the next tab in the direction of the arrow	Control + → Control + ←	Click on the tab

Selecting Data

The following convention is used in the table: [Alt] + [Tab] means hold down [Alt] and press [Tab].

Select	By keyboard	By mouse
An entire row or record (task or resource)	[Shift] + [Space]	Click on a row heading
An entire column	[Control] + [Space]	Click on a column heading

When you select an entire row as explained in the previous table, ALL the fields of a task are selected, even if they are not visible. It is important to select a task in its entirety before moving or copying it.

Project 2010 Views

The view of a project is a predefined layout that presents the project from a certain perspective. The views allow you to enter or edit data, review or report on your project. Certain views are more appropriate for performing certain functions.

View	Shows
Calendar	Tasks are shown as bars on a calendar
Gantt Chart	The tasks over time, plus Table columns and Timeline View
Network Diagram	The network of dependencies between tasks (dependencies are shown as arrows)
Resource Sheet	The Table area with resource information
Resource Usage	Resources with their assigned tasks, with the workloads or cost over time
Resource Form	Information about a single resource
Resource Graph	The workloads for resources in a bar chart format
Task Usage	Tasks with their assigned resources and the effort or cost over time
Task Sheet	The Table area with task information
Team Planner	Resources with their assigned tasks, shown graphically over time (**only in Project 2010 Professional**)
Timeline	Graphical representation showing selected tasks relative to each other over time
Tracking Gantt	The original (baseline) schedule versus the most recently revised schedule

Calendar View

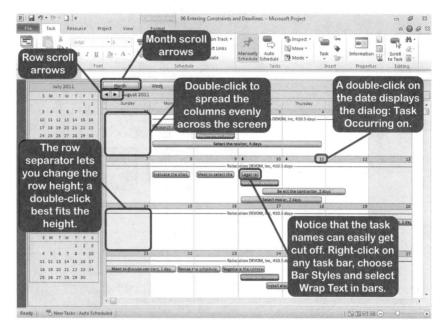

To see the **Calendar** view, on the **View** tab, in the **Task Views** group, click OR click on the View Bar.

 Perhaps the greatest value of the Calendar view is that it shows the schedule in a familiar format similar to a conventional wall calendar. We recommend you use the Calendar view to communicate to-do lists to team members (unless you use Project Server). You can create a calendar view for a specific resource by applying a filter. To do this, on the **View** tab, in the **Data** group, click the **Filter** down-arrow, **Using Resource...**

Notice that the **Calendar** view is different from the **Project Calendar**. The **Calendar** view, like the **Gantt Chart**, displays task bars, whereas the **Project Calendar** is used to define the working times and holidays.

To See All Tasks on a Day

The Calendar view is not suitable for showing the entire schedule. As you can see in the next two screenshots, not all task bars always show within a day because of the limited height of the day box. If there is too little room vertically, Project 2010 displays a ↓ in the date heading:

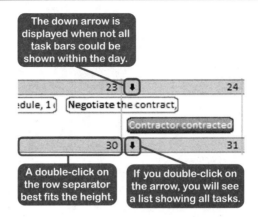

The down arrow is displayed when not all task bars could be shown within the day.

A double-click on the row separator best fits the height.

If you double-click on the arrow, you will see a list showing all tasks.

To display all of the tasks occurring on a day, click on the down arrow; a list showing all the tasks on that day appears:

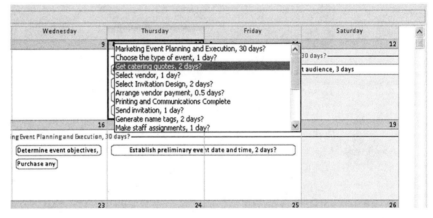

 To show all the task bars on any day, position your mouse pointer on any of the horizontal grid lines and double-click when you see the mouse pointer ✛.

To Create
Tasks

 Creating new tasks in the Calendar view is not recommended, because the new tasks end up at the end of the task list. You will still have to move them to the right place in the work breakdown structure (task list) in the Gantt Chart. We recommend that you enter tasks in the Gantt Chart view. (If you insist, you can create new tasks in the Calendar view by going to the **Task** tab, **Insert** group, and clicking on Insert. Once the new task is inserted in the calendar view, you can drag the shape of a new task bar onto the date where you want it. Double-click on it to give it a task name. Notice that the task will have a constraint that is visible on the Advanced tab, and you should replace it with appropriate dependencies.)

**To Edit the
Data of a Task**

1. Double-click on a task bar; the **Task Information** dialog appears:

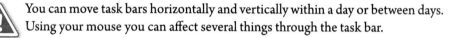

2. Make the changes, and click [OK].

**To Move
Task Bars**

You can move task bars horizontally and vertically within a day or between days. Using your mouse you can affect several things through the task bar.

1. If you click in the middle of the task bar and drag to the next task bar you can create a finish-to-start dependency.

2. If you click on the outline edge of the task and drag to another period in the calendar, you can reschedule the task (this places a Start No Earlier Than constraint on the task).

3. If you click on the end of the task bar and drag horizontally you can increase/decrease the duration of the task.

Unless you stay within the same day, you are creating Start No Earlier Than constraints on the tasks. Constraints are undesirable in schedules, since they make schedules less dynamic. We recommend you show restraint using constraints. There is a full discussion of constraints in chapter 6.

Gantt Chart

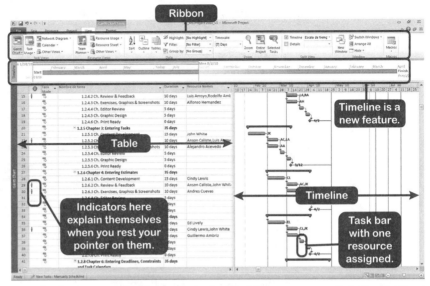

To apply the view, on the **View** tab, in the **Task Views** group, click **Gantt Chart**
OR click in the **View Bar**.

The Gantt Chart shows tasks over time with the duration of each task reflected in
the length of its task bar. The Gantt Chart also shows the list of deliverables and
tasks, which is commonly referred to as the work breakdown structure (WBS).
The WBS typically has a logical hierarchy of summary tasks with detail tasks
indented beneath them. The WBS/task list is discussed in detail in chapter 3.

 Notice that most items in the schedule explain themselves in a screen tip that
pops up when you rest your mouse pointer over them. For example:

➤ The icons in the **Indicators** 🛈 column explain problems in the schedule

➤ If the task name is cut off, you can pop up the complete name

➤ The timescale time units will display the year you are in

➤ The task bars inform you of the type of task (summary, detail, milestone)
and the deadline, task name, start, finish and duration

➤ The dependency arrows show which two tasks are linked by the dependency
and if there is lag

 The Gantt Chart is one of the best views to use when creating or modifying tasks
in your project. Because it's useful, we recommend that you provide some brief
training on it to your team members who aren't familiar with it.

To See More Table or Timescale

You can change the amount of the table you see on the left of the screen and the length of the timescale on the right of your screen. Revealing more of one will show you less of the other. You do this by pointing to the divider line between the table and the timescale. When you see the mouse pointer change to a ◀▐▶, click and hold down to drag it to the desired position.

 If you double-click on the divider, it will jump to the nearest split between two columns. This allows you to clean up the look of the view.

Collapsing and Expanding Levels

The task list or WBS on the left side of the Gantt Chart view can be structured to show summary tasks and detail tasks (as described in chapter 3). To collapse or expand levels:

➤ Click the minus button ⊟ next to a summary task name to hide its detail tasks

OR

press [Alt] + [Shift] + [–].

➤ Click the plus button ⊞ of a summary task to reveal its detail tasks

OR

press [Alt] + [Shift] + [+].

Zooming the Timescale

To zoom the timescale into smaller time units to see the details: on the **View** tab, in the **Zoom** group, click the **Zoom down-arrow**, **Zoom In** 🔍. When zoomed in, you can move the timescale to the show the task bar of the selected task using the **Scroll to task** tool 🔍 on the **Task** tab, in the **Editing** group.

To zoom the timescale out to larger time units in order to get an overview, on the **View** tab, in the **Zoom** group, click the **Zoom down arrow**, **Zoom Out**.

If you put the horizontal scroll box of the timescale at the extreme left on the scroll bar, you will always see the start date of the project. You can also press [Alt] + [Home] on the keyboard.

 You can also zoom the timescale using the Zoom Slider ⊖――▽――⊕ on the lower right of the screen. Drag the slider to the right to zoom in on the timescale and to the left to zoom out.

 To fit the entire project duration within the timescale so you always see task bars when you are paging up or down, on the **View** tab, in the **Zoom** group, click **Entire Project** 🔍.

The Ribbon in Project 2010 includes a Timescale dropdown that you use to adjust how you see your project. This dropdown is in the **Zoom** group of the **View** tab.

Finding the Task Bars

If there are tasks in your project but you don't see any task bars in the Gantt timescale, the timescale is just displaying a time period when no tasks happen to be scheduled.

If you hold down the primary mouse button on the scroll box in the horizontal scroll bar, it will tell you the exact date. It will include the year you currently have on your screen, which is handy in case the timescale does not reveal the year.

 To quickly see the task bar of a task, click on the task and then, on the **Task** tab, in the **Editing** group, click **Scroll to task** .

Network Diagram

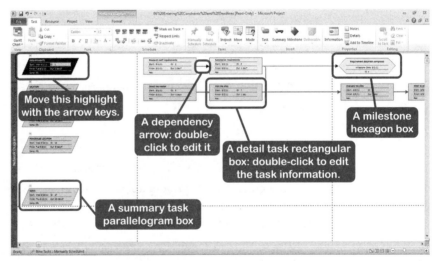

To apply the view: On the **View** tab, in the **Task Views** group, click **Network Diagram** OR click on the View Bar.

The **Network Diagram** shows the network of dependencies between tasks, with the dependencies depicted as arrows.

When you enter this view for the first time, you often don't see many dependencies, in which case you need to zoom out to see more boxes and arrows. When you zoom out far, the text becomes illegible. If you rest the mouse pointer on a task box, a screen tip pops up that allows you to read the task data. An example of such a screen tip is:

Get catering quotes	
Start: Thu 1/10/13	ID: 25
Finish: Fri 1/11/13	Dur: 2 days?
Res: Event Team	

To zoom back in, use **Zoom In** under the **View** tab or use the **Zoom Slider**.

By default, the Network Diagram displays the different types of tasks in boxes with distinct shapes:

➤ Summary tasks in a parallelogram

➤ Detail tasks in a rectangle

➤ Milestones in a hexagon

We'll learn more about each of these in chapter 3.

The critical tasks (discussed in chapter 9) have a red border instead of the (default) blue.

 The **Network Diagram** view is typically used to check the logic in the network. To follow the logic, just use the arrow keys on your keyboard to move the highlight from task to task. If the text is too small, keep your eyes on the entry bar which will show the name of the task.

As we'll discuss in chapter 5, you can easily add and delete dependencies in this view.

Task Usage

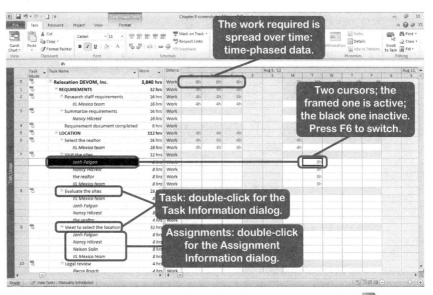

To apply the view: On the **View** tab, in the **Task Views** group, click ⬜ OR click ⬜ on the **View Bar**.

The **Task Usage** view shows the assignments in between the tasks. You can differentiate the assignments from tasks by the lack of ID numbers and the italicized text on the assignments.

The **Task Usage** and Resource Usage views are the only views that display the assignments as separate line items.

The timescale on the right of your screen shows how Project 2010 schedules the tasks and assignments. It shows the detailed numbers behind the task bars of the Gantt Chart. This view helps in understanding the Gantt Chart and troubleshooting it, if needed.

If you zoom in or zoom out, Project 2010 immediately calculates the totals for the new time unit. This allows you to create interesting management reports by month, for example.

You can report on the spread of the effort or cost across the life of the project with this view: a time-phased budget by activity or deliverable.

Tracking Gantt

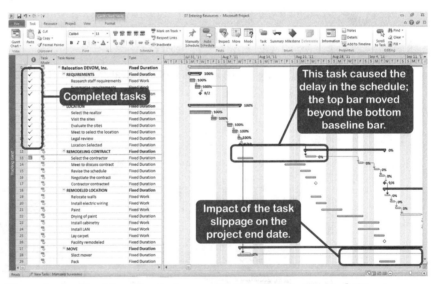

To apply the **Tracking Gantt** view on the **View** tab, in the **Task Views** group, click the **Gantt Chart** down-arrow, **Tracking Gantt** OR click the icon on the **View Bar**.

You can use the Tracking Gantt view during project execution to track your progress against your original schedule (the baseline). In this view all task bars are split into two halves: a top half that represents the current schedule and a bottom half for the baseline. If you don't have a baseline in your schedule, it only shows the thin top task bars for the current schedule.

Resource Graph

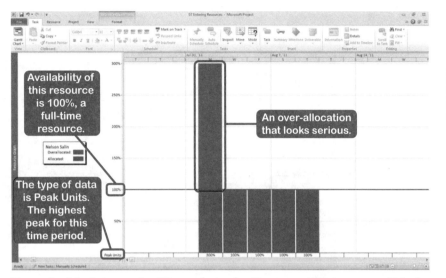

To apply the view: on the **View** tab, in the **Resource Views** group, click the **Other Views** down-arrow, **Resource Graph**. You can also click on the **View Bar**.

The **Resource Graph** shows bar charts of the workload over time for one resource at a time. This view is also called a workload histogram. By pressing [Page Dn] or by using the bottom left horizontal scroll bar you can browse from resource to resource. If you don't see any bars in the timescale pane, hold down [Alt] and press [Home] to jump to the project start date. If you still don't see any, zoom out using the **Zoom Slider** or the **Zoom** options in the **View** tab.

Notice that the Resource Graph shows Peak Units by default. Peak units means that if you zoom out and go from days to weeks, the highest daily bar will be shown as the peak for the week. This helps you find any over-allocation. However, the more you zoom out, the more pessimistic the depiction of the workload becomes; if you are double-booked during only a one hour meeting task, the entire quarter will depict you as double-booked. You can change from displaying peak units by using the **Graph** pulldown, in the **Data** group on the **Format** tab. If you select **Work** from the **Graph** pulldown OR right-click in the **chart** area and choose **Work** from the pop-up menu, you will see the "real" totals of the work hours charted for the time period shown.

Resource Sheet

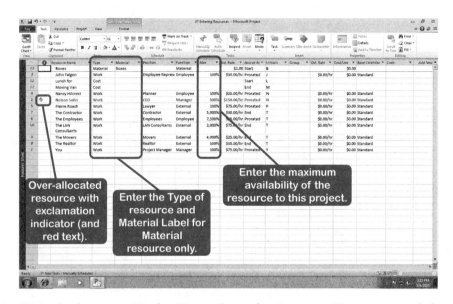

Over-allocated resource with exclamation indicator (and red text).

Enter the Type of resource and Material Label for Material resource only.

Enter the maximum availability of the resource to this project.

To apply the view: On the **View** tab, in the **Resource Views** group, click **Resource Sheet** 🔳 OR click 🔳 on the **View Bar.**

The **Resource Sheet** is used to enter the resources needed in a project. Resources can be human resources, facilities, machines, materials or cost resources.

Important fields in the Resource Sheet are:

➤ Name: Name of the resource.
➤ Type:
  ▶ Material: a material resource that is consumed on tasks
  ▶ Work: equipment or human resources that work on tasks
  ▶ Cost: cost items incurred in the performance of a task
➤ Max Units: The maximum units represents the maximum availability of the resource to the project expressed as a percentage (default) or in decimals depending on the setting in the Schedule section of Project Options. For example, a full-time individual would either be "100%" available (percentage) or be shown as "1" (decimals).

Resource Usage

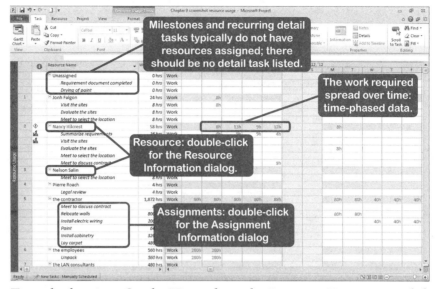

To apply the view: On the **View** tab, in the **Resource Views** group, click **Resource Usage**, OR click 🔲 on the **View Bar**.

The **Resource Usage** view shows the amounts of work or cost over time. As in the Task Usage view, this view shows the assignments as separate line items. You can differentiate the assignments from resources by the lack of ID numbers and the italicized text on the assignments.

This view allows you to analyze workloads and resolve any over-allocations.

*Timeline
View*

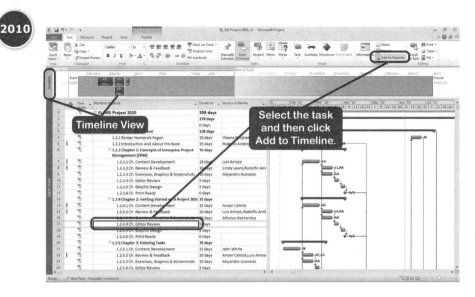

To display the Timeline: On the View tab, in the **Split View** group, select the **Timeline** checkbox OR click the 🖳 icon on the **View Bar.**

The **Timeline** is a compact and concise view that can provide a high level view of the entire or selected parts of the project. You can easily copy the timeline to share in an e-mail or presentation.

Not all project tasks show in the **Timeline** view. You must explicitly add the task for it to appear in the view. To add a task to the Timeline, select the task in the Table area, then, on the **Task** tab, in the **Properties** group, click **Add to Timeline** 🖳. You can also add the task to the Timeline by selecting the option in the **General** tab of the **Task Information** dialog for the task, or by right-clicking on the task and selecting **Add to Timeline** from the dropdown list. (You can even drag and drop tasks from the table to build your timeline. To do this, click on the task ID, grab the task with your mouse and then drag and drop the task to the timeline).

Team Planner

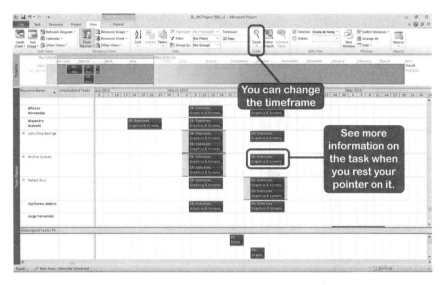

 The **Team Planner** view is only available in Project 2010 Professional. It gives a graphical representation of each resource's assignments along a timeline. It is one of the new viewing features to assist Project and Resource Managers in understanding where overallocations might exist within the team.

To apply the **Team Planner** view: On the **View** tab, in the **Resource View** group, click **Team Planner** OR click **Team Planner** in the **View Bar**.

You can use the zoom commands in the View tab of the **Ribbon** or the **Zoom Slider** to adjust the timeframe shown on the right hand side of the screen.

You can also mouse over the specific assignments to get more information.

Resource Form

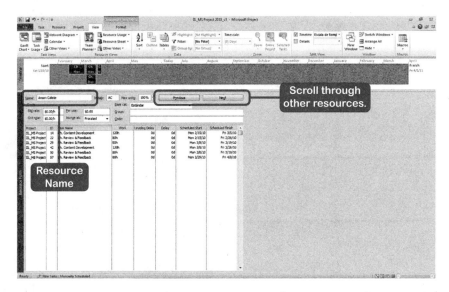

The **Resource Form** is used to view resource and assignment information for a single resource at a time. It is similar to the **Task Form** view that existed in previous versions of Project and provides a quick and easy way to view and update information about a specific resource.

To access the Resource Form: On the **View** tab, in the **Resource View** group, click the **Other Views** down-arrow, **Resource Form**, or click **Resource Form** on the **View Bar**.

You can use the **Next** and **Previous** buttons to scroll through for other resources.

Navigating the Views

To Switch Views

You can select views by using the **View Bar** or view options on the Ribbon. The **View Bar** is usually visible along the left side of the screen. If the **View Bar** is not displayed, right-click on the thin blue bar at the left of your screen and select the **View Bar** (or the required view) from the pop-up menu.

You can also switch views using the commands in the Ribbon. On the **View** tab, there are groups representing **Task Views** and **Resource Views**. The most commonly used of each type of these views is always visible as icons in the groups. If the view you want is not shown as a command icon, click on the down-arrow next to any view and select **More Views**. The **More Views** dialog will open showing all available views.

Single View Versus Combination View

A single view is a one-view screen; the views shown on the previous pages are single views. A combination view is a screen with two views, one on the top and one on the bottom.

The bottom view only shows information pertaining to the tasks (or resources) selected in the top view. This interaction between top and bottom view can be very useful for data entry with a sheet view in the top and a form view in the bottom. Form views allow you to enter detail information.

The **Task Entry** view is a combination view with the **Gantt Chart** in the top and the **Task Form** in the bottom, as in the next screenshot:

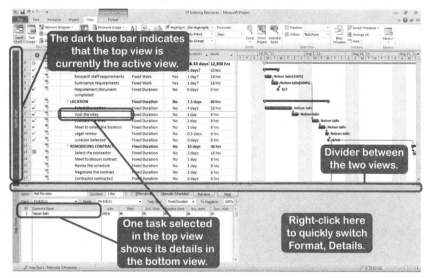

The **Task Entry** view allows you to enter detailed information on tasks. You can enter resource assignments and predecessors. The task you select in the top Gantt Chart view is shown in detail in the bottom Task Form view. The top and bottom views interact; whatever you select in the top is shown in more detail in the bottom.

This makes combination views well suited for analysis of schedules. For example, with a task view in the top and a resource view in the bottom (or vice versa), you can check assignments.

With a resource view in the top and a task view in the bottom you can check over-allocations. An example of this is shown below in the **Resource Allocation** view. To get to this view: On the **View** tab, in the **Resource Views** group, click the **Other Views** down-arrow, **More Views**. The **More Views** dialog will open. Click **Resource Allocation**, then **Apply**.

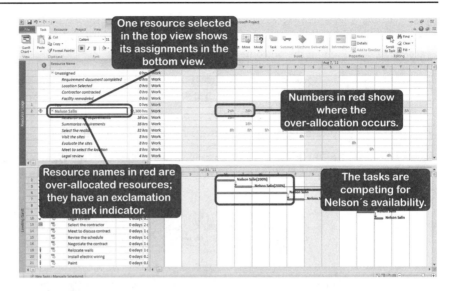

The **Resource Allocation** view has the **Resource Usage** in the top view and the **Leveling Gantt** view in the bottom. This combination view allows you to analyze and resolve over-allocations. The interaction between the top and bottom view is such that the assignments on the task selected in the top view are shown in detail in the bottom.

To Create a Combination View

You can click the **Timeline** checkbox in **View** tab, **Split View** group to create a combination view that shows the Timeline in the top view of the screen. To change the top section of your new combination view, click on the **Timeline** down-arrow, **More Views**. The **More Views** dialog will open. Select the new view you want at the top then click **Apply**.

To create a combination view by adding a new view to the lower section on the **View** tab, in the **Split View**, click the **Details** down-arrow, **More Views**. Select the view you wish to have at the bottom of your Combination view, then click **Apply**.

You can also create a combination view by pointing with the tip of the mouse pointer to the sliding window handle at the bottom right of your screen (the tiny little horizontal bar under the scroll down button).

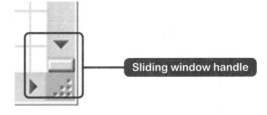

Sliding window handle

The mouse pointer will become a double-headed arrow ⭥. Drag it up or double-click on it to display the bottom view. You now have two views on the screen, one in the top and one in the bottom.

You can change the size of each view by pointing to the divider line between the views; the mouse pointer should change to ┿. Hold down and drag when you see this mouse pointer. To move the cursor between the views, press ⌷ or click in the other view.

 You can drag both the horizontal border and the vertical dividers at the same time. Put your mouse pointer on the intersection between the two divider lines:

You should see the mouse pointer ⤢. Drag both dividers to the sizes of the views you need.

To Switch Back to a Single View

Drag the view divider line to the top or bottom (depending on which view you want to keep) using the mouse pointer ⭥.

OR

Double-click on the view divider when you see the mouse pointer ⭥ to keep the top section of the view.

OR

On the **View** tab, **Split View** group, clear the **Details** or **Timeline**.

Using Help

Project Help Task Pane

1. On the **File** tab, in the **Backstage** view, click **Help** to reveal the different **Help** options available in Project 2010.

2. Click on the ❓ icon and the **Project Help** task pane appears:

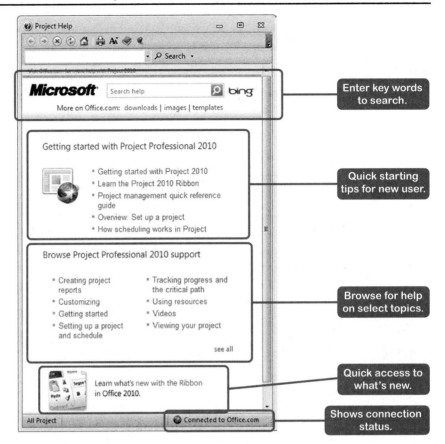

3. In the **Project Help** task pane, enter keywords for your search. More words usually give more accurate results (and the shortest list to dig through). Microsoft recommends entering between 2 and 7 keywords. Click on **Search** or hit the Enter key.

4. The search results will be displayed in the same window. Click one of the help topics listed; Each of the help topics is a hyperlink. When clicked, the link will display information about the topic you searched for. If you did not find what you need, you can enter different keywords in the search text area or you can use the Back Arrow at the top left of the window to return to the list of search results.

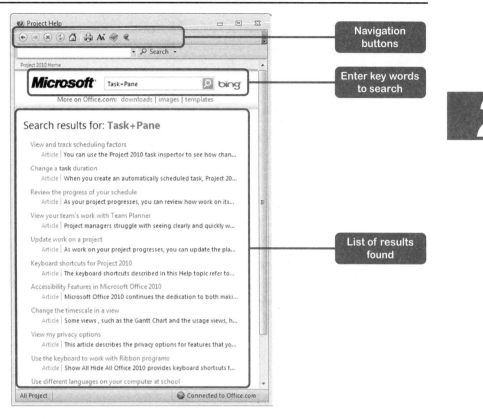

5.   To close the help panes, click the Close button ⊠.

 If you are connected to the internet, you can have the search engine browse online content by setting the connection status on the lower right corner of the screen:

Connection Status:

✓ Show content from Office.com

Show content only from this computer

❓ Explain these options...

Help on Fields   Position your mouse pointer over a column heading and a screen tip giving a brief description of the field will pop up. If you do not see the pop ups, check the **Screen Tip Style** setting in the **General** section of the **Project Options** dialog.

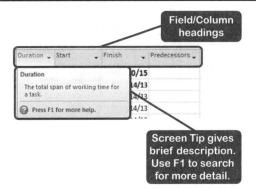

*Help with
Scheduling:
Planning Wizard*

The Planning Wizard can help you find your way around Project 2010. The Wizard searches for ambiguity, and if it finds it, provides you with choices to resolve the problem.

We recommend keeping the Planning Wizard turned on. If you start to get annoyed with a particular type of message, select ☑ **Don't tell me about this again** at the bottom left of the dialog:

There are three categories of Planning Wizard messages and each time you select **Don't tell me about this again**, that message in the category will be turned off. When all the messages in a category have been turned off, the category will be turned off as well. To turn the messages back on: On the **File** tab, in the **Backstage** view, click on **Options**, **Advanced**. Select the **Advice from Planning Wizard** checkboxes.

We recommend that you turn on **all** of the **Planning Wizard** options to assist you with scheduling.

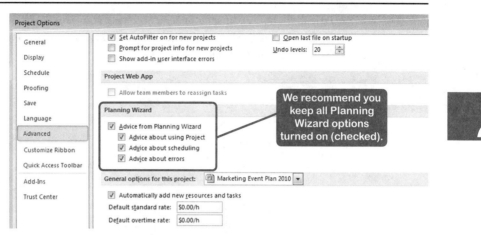

Help When Making Changes: Smart Tags

Whenever you see a small graphical tag appear to the left of where you have made changes to a schedule, you are given additional choices. These pop-ups are called Smart Tags. Smart Tags ask for clarification when you do something that may produce unintended side effects. Depending on the situation, different Smart Tag graphics appear:

Graphic	Appears when
✗	You press ⌊Delete⌋ on a task name
◈	You change the duration, OR You change the work, OR You change the units, OR You add a resource to a task, or remove one, OR You change the start or finish date

An example of the choices you get when you increase a duration and click the Smart Tag button is:

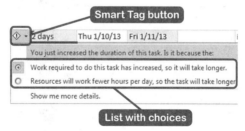

Help with Tasks: Task Inspector

You can use the **Task Inspector** view to quickly get a look at the factors that are affecting a task. The Task Inspector will show you if there are constraints, Task Calendars or special Resource Calendars applied to the selected task.

To launch the Task Inspector select the task you want to review, then on the **Task** tab in the **Tasks** group, click 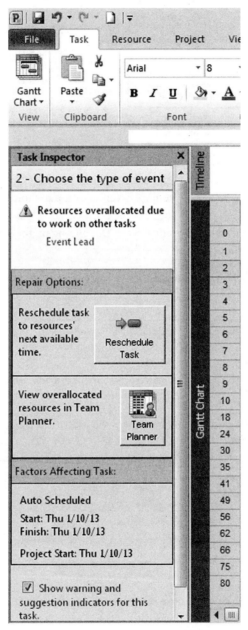. The **Task Inspector Pane** will open to the left, next to the **View Bar**.

Getting Help from Microsoft

The Help area of Backstage gives you convenient links to official Microsoft sites where you can get assistance using Project 2010:

➤ Click **Getting Started** to open a page that has information about the newest features of Project 2010

➤ Click **Contact Us** to go to the Microsoft Support page where you can type a question for a Microsoft Automated Customer Support Agent

➤ Click **Check for Updates** to download the latest updates (patches, services packs) from Microsoft

2

Technical Specifications and Support

For information on the specifications of your system, on the **File** tab, in the **Backstage** view, click **Help**, then **Additional Version and Copyright Information**. The **About Microsoft Office Project** window will open. You'll see which version or release of Microsoft Project 2010 you are using as well as copyright and license information. Other options here are:

➤ Click System Info... to get the technical specifications of your computer system.

➤ Click Tech Support... to get contact information on how to reach technical support people on the telephone.

Setting Up a New Project Schedule

Now that you are familiar with the Project 2010 interface you are ready to set up a new project. Setting up the project results in either a project that has no tasks or one that has tasks derived from a project template. Once the project is set up you are ready to enter and/or edit the tasks that make up the project.

The standard steps for setting up a new project schedule are:

➤ Create new project schedule from the ground up OR base your project on a project template. Project 2010 lets you create new project schedules by importing Excel spreadsheets and SharePoint lists (this will be discussed in more detail in chapter 3 – Entering Tasks).

➤ Describe the project in the dialog boxes:
  ▶ Project Information
  ▶ Properties

➤ Set the options. Options to consider are:
  ▶ Date format
  ▶ Schedule Options
  ▶ Advanced Options
  ▶ Level Resources…
  ▶ Undo levels

➤ Set the Project Calendar (Change Working Time). Use the Exceptions or Work Week tabs to decide:
  ▶ Normal working hours and working business days
  ▶ Exceptions like holidays or non-working times
  ▶ Any special alternate work weeks

Creating a New Project Schedule

Project 2010 provides you with many different options to create new project files.

These include:
➤ Blank Project – you add all task, resource and project information
➤ Recent templates – if you previously created a project from a local or online template
➤ My Templates – personal templates you created and saved
➤ New from existing project – if your new project is similar to another one
➤ New from Excel Workbook – you can import basic task information from Excel
➤ New from SharePoint task list – if you want to now manage your SharePoint task list using Project 2010
➤ Office.com templates – available for download if you are online

To access these options and to create a new file, on the **File** tab, in the **Backstage** view, click **New**. The screen below is displayed.

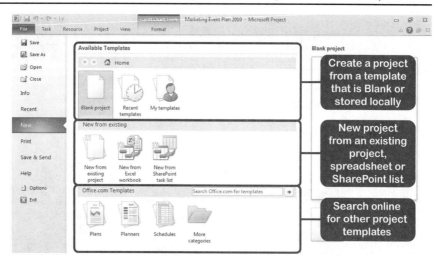

You can also create new projects using templates posted online using any of the options in the **Office.com Templates** section. This section provides you with search capability so you will be able find templates for the type of project you are looking for.

 If you use an existing project file (with company information already in it) as the basis for a new project file, you should make sure you remove any residual information such as the **Author**, **Manager**, **Company** and **Last Saved by**. To clear these fields check the checkbox **Remove personal information from file properties on save**. You can find this checkbox on the **File** tab, in the **Backstage** view. Click **Options**, **Trust Center**, **Trust Center Settings**, **Privacy Options** tab.

 If you use an existing project file as the basis for a new project file, adjust the dates to reflect the new start date. To do this on the **Project** tab, in the **Schedule** group, click **Move Project**. The **Move Project** dialog will open. Enter the date required in **New project start date**.

Describing the Project

One of the first things you should do is to set up basic parameters that define your specific project:

1. On the **Project** tab, in the **Properties** group, click **Project Information**. The **Project Information** dialog appears:

2. Enter the basic project information in this dialog. There are two choices in the list **Schedule from**:

   ▶ **Project Start Date** (forward scheduling): Enter the **Start Date** and Project 2010 will schedule all tasks As Soon As Possible (ASAP) after the project start date. After you have entered all the data, Project 2010 will show what the earliest finish date will be for the project.

   ▶ **Project Finish Date** (backward scheduling): Enter the **Finish Date** and Project 2010 will schedule all tasks As Late As Possible (ALAP) working backward from the project finish date. After you have entered all the data, Project 2010 will show what the target start date of the project should be.

   The choice you make depends on which you're most certain of: the start date or the finish date for your project. Neither approach will prevent the common occurrence that the initial schedule is too long. You usually have to squeeze the project into a time box that is available for the project. This makes the choice between entering the start or the finish date less important, and most people leave it to the default: scheduling from the project start date forward. Click [OK].

3. On the **File** tab, in the **Backstage** view, click on **Info**.

4. On the right pane, click **Project Information**, **Advanced Properties**. The **Properties** dialog appears.

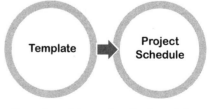

5. Click the tab **Summary** and enter:
   - The name of the project in the field **Title**
   - Your name as the **Author** and/or **Manager**
   - The project objective or a description of the final project product in the **Comments** field. Try to come up with a single sentence that captures the essence of your project.

6. Click [OK].

 We recommend that you enter as much information as possible concerning **Title**, **Subject**, **Author**, **Manager**, and **Company** in the **Properties** dialog. The entries you make can be used in the headers and footers of reports you create. They save time, particularly since when you change an entry, all of your reports will be updated automatically.

Creating a New Schedule from a Project Template

Project templates are useful as a jumpstart for your project plan. They store layouts, settings and information that you want to use for multiple projects. Each time you start a new project you start with a copy of the template, which you can adjust as needed for the specific project.

Templates can be created centrally by your project office to promote consistent work breakdown structures, common project

Open template copies the template

options, standard reports, shared Project Calendars and standard resource names.

 Templates are protected from accidental changes. When you open a template, Project 2010 copies it; you never open the template itself. When saving the template, you will always be asked for a (new) file name or schedule name. Template files have the extension **.mpt**.

Using a Project Template

1. On the **File** tab, in the **Backstage** view, click **New**. The options to create a new project will be displayed.

2. Click on **My Templates**. The **New** dialog box (as seen below) will open showing templates you created and saved locally, as well as those you previously downloaded from *Office.com*.

New			✕
Personal Templates			
Local Template	ProdEvalPo...		Preview
			Preview not available.
		OK	Cancel

3. Double-click on a template OR select a template and click [OK]; a copy of the template opens. It appears with the project-specific options and project calendar set. There may also be tasks, dependencies, estimates, generic resources and assignments, as well as custom views and reports.

4. If you want to use a template stored online, use the options in **Office.com Templates**. Click on a category or type the type of template you are searching for in the search text box, then click the start searching arrow.

Setting the Options

The way Project 2010 operates is controlled by the settings in Project Options. The steps to change the options are:

1. On the **File** tab, in the **Backstage** view, click **Options**. The **Project Options** dialog appears.

2. Select the category of options you want to work with from the left pane.

3. Set the options.

4. Click [OK] to accept the changes and close the dialog.

    There are two types of options:
    ▶   Global options that are in effect for all projects
    ▶   Project-specific options that affect the active project only. You can recognize these because they start with a section divider showing the name of the project schedule. These options are stored in the project file (.mpp) or in the schedule (Project Server database).

Setting the Date Order

The date order (ddmmyy or mmddyy) cannot be set inside Project 2010. You have to set it in the Windows Control Panel. If you do this, it will affect the date order in all of your Windows applications.

1. If you are using Windows 7, click 🪟 and choose **Control Panel**. Click

    🔵 Clock, Language, and Region
       Change keyboards or other input methods
       Change display language

    . The **Region and Language** dialog box opens. Click the

Format tab and in the **Short Date:** [M/d/yyyy ▾] dropdown, select the required date format. Click [OK].

OR

2. In Windows Vista , click 🪟 and choose **Control Panel**. Click
   🗺 Clock, Language, and Region
   Change keyboards or other input methods
   Change display language   OR

   In Windows 2000 and Windows XP, click [🎆 start] and choose Settings, Control Panel. Click 🌐 Regional and Language Options .

3. Click the tab **Date** and select the date order from the list: **Short Date Format** [M/d/yyyy ▾]. (NOTE: International date format is "d/M/yyyy".)

4. Click [OK]. All lists in Project 2010 that provide choices for date formats will now show items in the date order you chose in the Control Panel.

Options for a New Project 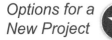 Set scheduling options as described below to match your organization standards **before** you enter any tasks.

This table indicates the most important options we recommend you review at this point. Typically, at the start of each chapter, we will discuss the options most relevant to that chapter.

Project Options	Recommended Choices
General	**Set the Options on the General tab:**
	☑ **Tasks will always honor their constraint dates** We recommend you keep this option on to make sure your schedule observes the few real and hard constraint dates that you may have in it. (We'll cover this in a minute.)
	Screen Tip style: [Show feature descriptions in ScreenTips ▾] When you set this ScreenTip style, you will get the most possible information about an object when you position the mouse ove the object.
	Date Format: [Jan 28 '09 ▾] To avoid confusion about dates in international projects, a date format should be chosen with the month spelled out, i.e., 31 Jan. '13. Americans will interpret a date like 7-8-2013 as July 8, 2013. Most of the rest of the world will interpret it as August 7, 2013.
	User Name: [_____] Enter your name. (If you are connected to Project Server, it will be filled in already.)

Project Options	Recommended Choices
Display	**Set the Options on the Display tab:**
	Currency: USD ▼ Use the dropdown to select the currency you want to use for your project costs. Project 2010 will fill in the appropriate Symbol for the selected currency.
Schedule	**Set the Options on the Schedule tab:**
	Hours per day: 8 ⏫ Project 2010 uses this number to convert days that are entered in the Duration and Work fields into hours. This number should represent the hours worked by a full-time equivalent employee.
	Hours per week: 40 ⏫ Project 2010 uses this number to convert weeks into hours. If this number does not reflect your situation, the schedule will not be accurate. It should correspond to the Hours per Day setting.
	Days per month: 20 ⏫ Project 2010 uses this number to convert months into days. This number should reflect your situation.
	☑ **Show scheduling messages**: will give helpful messages when it notices a problem in the schedule.
	Calculate project after each edit: will ensure that you see the effect of changes immediately. We recommend that you leave this setting ◉ on unless schedule performance becomes a concern.
Advanced	**Set the Options on the Advanced tab:**
	☑ **Advice from Planning Wizard**. This is most useful for novice users. You may want to clear the check box once you are more experienced with Project 2010.

 Do not use a fiscal calendar if your schedule will be shared with anyone outside of your organization as it can create confusion when reading the Gantt Chart.

You have to decide on the **Calendar** option **Hours per Day** before entering any tasks into the schedule and it can't be changed without re-entering all durations. You have to specify how many work hours a workday has. Project 2010 uses this setting to convert between time units (the time unit conversion factor). For example, if the **Hours per Day** is set to 8 hours and you enter a duration of 5 days, Project 2010 knows this equals 40 hours (8 * 5). If you then change the **Hours per Day** setting to 7 hours per day, Project 2010 changes the duration to 5.71 days (= 5 * 8 / 7). You must consider this option before entering any tasks. If you start with the wrong number, Project 2010 will interpret the durations you enter incorrectly which may result in a schedule that is too optimistic or pessimistic.

There is one way to keep the current durations without having to re-enter all durations again when you change the **Hours per Day** setting. Before changing the **Hours per Day**, copy all durations to one of the extra fields (**Text1** for example), change the **Hours per Day**, and then copy the durations from the **Text1** field back into the **Duration** field. Make sure you have the task field **Type** set to **Fixed Units** for all tasks.

Leveling Option: Automatic or Manual

Workload leveling involves changing a schedule so that the workloads of the resources are within their availability at any given time. In the illustration, you can see that on the left Harry has to work full-time on two tasks that are scheduled in parallel. It causes a workload that exceeds his availability of 100%, which is called an over-allocation. The over-allocation was solved on the right by delaying the task *Read y* until after *Read x*.

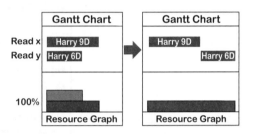

Delaying tasks is something Project 2010 can help you with; it is called automatic leveling. There are other ways to level the workloads which we'll talk about in chapter 9 on Optimizing. These can result in a shorter schedule, but require more effort from you.

We recommend that you use manual leveling at this time. If you select automatic leveling, Project 2010 will constantly make changes to your schedule as it tries to keep the workloads leveled. When you've read chapter 9 on optimizing schedules, we will generate some scenarios using the leveling features in Project 2010 and discuss this dialog box in more detail. We will also explain methods to level the workloads yourself.

1. On the **Resource** tab, in the **Level** group, click **Leveling Options**. The **Resource Leveling** dialog appears:

Resource Leveling

Leveling calculations

○ Automatic   ● Manual

Look for overallocations on a Day by Day ▾ basis

☑ Clear leveling values before leveling

Leveling range for 'Marketing Event Plan.mpp'

● Level entire project

○ Level   From: Thu 1/10/13 ▾

To: Wed 2/20/13 ▾

Resolving overallocations

Leveling order: Standard ▾

☐ Level only within available slack

☑ Leveling can adjust individual assignments on a task

☑ Leveling can create splits in remaining work

☐ Level resources with the proposed booking type

☑ Level manually scheduled tasks

[Help] [Clear Leveling...] [Level All] [OK] [Cancel]

2. In **Leveling calculations**, select ● **Manual**. This will allow you to level the workloads only when you are ready for it. Leveling is discussed in detail in Chapter 9.

Setting the Project Calendar

In Project 2010, you select a base calendar from which to develop your Project Calendar. The base calendar is based upon your organization-wide working hours, working days, and non-working days. The three base calendars that come with Project 2010 are Standard, Night Shift, and 24 Hours.

The **Change Working Time** dialog, which can be found on the Project tab of the Ribbon, allows you to modify the Project Calendar to model the work week.

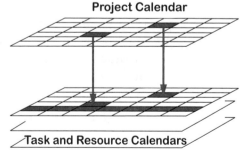

Project Calendar

Task and Resource Calendars

The default Project Calendar is called Standard. Working time for the Standard calendar is set to Monday through Friday, 8:00 A.M. until 5:00 P.M., with one hour off for lunch between 12:00 P.M. and 1:00 P.M. each working day. You can change these defaults to correspond to your organization's working times.

On the Project Calendar you indicate:

➤ Business days and standard working hours
Which days are working days and what are the working hours in a regular work week?

➤ Calendar exceptions (national and corporate holidays)
What days are nonworking days (weekends, holidays, etc.) throughout the year?

➤ Alternate work weeks
Do some weeks require a special schedule to get a specific phase completed in time?

Set the Project Calendar with standard business days, working hours, calendar exceptions and any alternate work weeks **before** entering task information.

In addition to the Project Calendar there are:

➤ Task calendars
These can be used to schedule individual tasks. For example, outdoor construction tasks can only take place when the weather permits, and a Task Calendar could be created for all tasks affected by winter weather. Task calendars are covered in chapter 6.

➤ Resource calendars
These can be used as calendars for individual people or groups of people. A Resource Calendar for an individual typically contains individual working days and vacations; sometimes the working hours are individualized as well. These are covered in chapter 7.

We recommend that where possible you create a new Resource Calendar for large groups of resources, not individual resources. For example, if you had international resources or 2nd shift resources working on a project, you would create a Resource Calendar for the group, instead of creating a new calendar for each International resource or each resource on the 2nd shift.

The business days, working hours, calendar exceptions like national and corporate holidays, and any specific alternate work weeks of the Project Calendar will be transferred to all Resource Calendars.

Project 2010 allows you to provide the name for each holiday or exception day and gives you the option to make an exception recurring. The recurring feature works like a recurring appointment in Outlook and allows you to set the recurrence on a specific day or in a specific pattern.

For example, a holiday could occur on the fourth day of each month or could occur on the first Monday of every month. This feature can save you considerable time because you do not have to scroll month to month and year to year to add all of the exception days.

Notice the tabs below on the **Change Working Time** dialog window:

Change Working Time

For calendar: Standard (Project Calendar) ▼   Create New Calendar ...

Calendar 'Standard' is a base calendar.

Legend:

- [ ] Working
- [ ] Nonworking
- [31] Edited working hours

On this calendar:

- [31] Exception day
- [31] Nondefault work week

Click on a day to see its working times:

September 2012

S	M	T	W	Th	F	S
						1
2	3	4	5	6	7	8
9	10	11	12	13	14	15
16	17	18	19	20	21	22
23	24	25	26	27	28	29
30						

September 3, 2012 is nonworking.

Based on:

Exception 'Labor Day' on calendar 'Standard'.

Exceptions | Work Weeks

	Name	Start	Finish	
1	Labor Day	9/3/2012	9/3/2012	
2	Columbus Day	10/8/2012	10/8/2012	
3	Veterans Day	11/12/2012	11/12/2012	

Details...
Delete

Help   Options...   OK   Cancel

➤ **Exceptions**: Regularly scheduled working day on which work will not occur, which includes exceptions to the normal working time. An example would be company holidays.

➤ **Work Weeks**: Includes alternate work weeks specified for a certain period of time. An example would be an accelerated work week for a construction company to get the job done before a major snow storm arrives.

The changes you make on the Project Calendar apply to every task and every resource in the project (unless you have overwritten those settings in the Task or Resource Calendars). At this point, we will only edit the Project Calendar; later we will create Task calendars and Resource Calendars, which override the Project Calendar.

In summary, the Project Calendar has two functions:

➤ It is a time-saving device to change all Task and Resource Calendars.

➤ It is used to schedule tasks that don't have a Task Calendar or resources assigned.

Hours per Day Option versus Working Time

The following is very confusing to many people. If you change the number of hours per day in the Project Options (via the Backstage), Project 2010 does not automatically update the working times in the Project Calendar. Project 2010 uses the hours per day option for conversion purposes only. When you enter a duration of 1w, it will convert it to hours. If the setting in the Project Options is 40h/w, then it knows that 1w = 40h.

In the Project Calendar, you can indicate the regular working hours for a full-time resource. Project 2010 uses these settings to schedule the 40 hours of effort

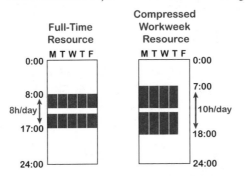

within the working hours. 40 hours of effort for a full-time resource will take 5 business days (Monday–Friday). 40 hours of effort for a compressed workweek resource who works 10 hours a day will only need 4 business days (see the illustration). The conclusion is that the Hours per Day setting in the Project Options dialog needs to be aligned manually with the working hours in the Project Calendar.

Make sure the hours per day and per week in the Standard calendar match the calendar options settings in the Project Options.

Enter Business Days with Standard Working Days & Hours

1. On the **Project** tab, in the **Properties** group, click **Change Working Time**. The **Change Working Time** dialog box opens.

Change Working Time

For calendar: Standard (Project Calendar) ▾   Create New Calendar ...

Calendar 'Standard' is a base calendar.

> Select the calendar to change.

Legend: Click on a day to see its working times:

| | Working |

September 2012 — September 3, 2012 is nonworking.

	S	M	T	W	Th	F	S
							1
	2	**3**	4	5	6	7	8
	9	10	11	12	13	14	15
	16	17	18	19	20	21	22
	23	24	25	26	27	28	29
	30						

| | Nonworking |
| **31** | Edited working hours |

On this calendar:

| **31** | Exception day |
| **31** | Nondefault work week |

Based on:
Exception 'Labor Day' on cal... 'Standard'.

> On the Work Weeks tab, select "Default" to select the business days in every week of every month in every year.

Exceptions | Work Weeks

	Name	Start	Finish
1	Labor Day	9/3/2012	9/3/2012
2	Columbus Day	10/8/2012	10/8/2012
3	Veterans Day	11/12/2012	11/12/2012

Details...
Delete

> After selecting Default, click on "Details" to set the working hours.

Help   Options...   OK   Cancel

2. From the: **For:** For calendar: Standard (Project Calendar) ▾ dropdown at the top of the dialog, select **Standard (Project Calendar)**.

3. To specify the normal business work week for working days and working hours in the Standard Project base calendar, select the **Work Weeks** tab near the middle of the **Change Working Time** dialog box. If you have a Monday to Friday work week, you can select the workdays of the week by selecting the **Default** row on the **Work Weeks** tab and then clicking on the Details button to open the **Details** for the **Default** dialog box.

Details for '[Default]'

Set working time for this work week

Select day(s):
- ⦿ Use Project default times for these days.
- ○ Set days to nonworking time.
- ○ Set day(s) to these specific working times:

| Sunday |
| Monday |
| Tuesday |
| Wednesday |
| Thursday |
| Friday |
| Saturday |

From	To

Help   OK   Cancel

Notice that when you select any Monday through Friday, the default is set for all weekdays as working days with working hours of **8:00 AM-12:00 PM** and **1:00 PM-5:00 PM**.

It is here, in the **Details** dialog box, that you can change these normal default working times.

4. You have three choices in the **Set working time for this work week** buttons above the **From/To** table:
   ▶ Use Project default times for these days
   ▶ Set days to nonworking time
   ▶ Set day(s) to these specific working times

5. Select the specific days that you want to change in the table. (Select consecutive days by left clicking the mouse and dragging downward, or select nonadjacent days by holding down the [Control] key and selecting the other days needed.)

6. To set these days as nonworking time, select **Set days to nonworking time**. To change the working times of a working day(s) or to change a nonworking day to a working day, select **Set day(s) to these specific working times.**

7. In the **From/To** table, enter the start and finish working times. (Click into the next lower blank cell when completed to make sure your start and finish times are entered.)

8. Click [OK] at the bottom of the **Details** dialog box and then click [OK] in the **Change Working Time** dialog box.

9. Make sure you also click [Options...] to adjust the time unit conversion factors.

Enter Alternate Work Weeks with Specific Working Hours

Sometimes you need to set up an alternate work week to reflect changed work schedules for the week(s). (For example, your team might be working on an accelerated testing schedule before a server installation.) In this situation, you could set up an alternate work week to reflect the accelerated work week.

1. On the **Project** tab, in the **Properties** group, click **Change Working Time**. The **Change Working Time** dialog box opens.

2. From the For: For calendar: [Standard (Project Calendar) ▾] dropdown, select **Standard (Project Calendar)**.

3. If you did not set the hours per day in **Project Options**, do this first by clicking [Options...] to adjust the time unit conversion factors. Upon clicking [OK] you will be returned to this dialog.

4. Click the **Work Weeks** tab near the middle of the **Change Working Time** dialog box.

5. In the **Work Weeks** tab, click the blank row under the **Default** row. In the **Name** column for the new Work Week, type in the name for the alternate work week. For example, *Server Set-up/Test Week*.

6. Click in the **Start** field and enter the date when the alternate working times should start.

7. On the same row, click in the **Finish** field and enter the date that when the alternate working times should end.

8. With the same new row selected, click the **Details** button.

9. In the **Select Day(s)** box, click the days of the week you want to change. Select consecutive days by clicking the mouse and dragging downward, or select nonadjacent days by holding down the [Control] key and selecting each day you need. To set these days as nonworking time, select **Set days to nonworking time**.

10. To change the working times of the specified alternate work week, select the day(s) in the **Select** day (s) table and select **Set day(s) to these specific working times**. Next, in the **From/To** table, enter the start and finish working times. (Hint: Click into the next lower blank cell when completed to make sure your start and finish times are accepted.)

11. Click [OK] at the bottom of the **Details** dialog box and then click [OK] in the **Change Working Time** dialog box.

One-Time & Recurring Calendar Exceptions

Entering One-Time Calendar Exceptions

Sometimes you need to record exceptions such as holidays on the Project Calendar. These can be either one-time only (e.g., a corporate picnic) or recurring (e.g., New Year's Day). In Project 2010, you can set up these exceptions.

1. On the **Project** tab, in the **Properties** group, click **Change Working Time**. The **Change Working Time** dialog box opens.

2. From the **For:** [For calendar: Standard (Project Calendar) ▾] dropdown, select **Standard (Project Calendar)**.

3. If you did not set the hours per day in **Project Options**, do this first by clicking [Options...] to adjust the time unit conversion factors. Upon clicking [OK] you will be returned to this dialog.

4. On the **Change Working Time** dialog box, click the day in the calendar whose working times you want to change. The working times for that day will be displayed.

5. Next, select the **Exceptions** tab and select the next available blank row in the **Name** column. Enter the name of the calendar exception and press

[Tab]. The start and finish dates are entered, defaulting to the date that you clicked in the calendar. You can change this date now, if needed. Notice that to the right of the calendar it says that the date is **nonworking**.

6. Click on **Details** to open the detail dialog box. Notice that the default changes to a non-working day for the date that you selected.

7. If the exception is a change other than to a non-working day, you can change this in the **Details** dialog box. If you want to change working time to something other than the default, you can select **Non-default Working Time**, then change the times in the **From/To** boxes as needed.

8. Click [OK] at the bottom of the **Details** dialog box and then click [OK] in the **Change Working Time** dialog box.

Entering "Recurring" Calendar Exceptions

1. On the **Project** tab, in the **Properties** group, click **Change Working Time**. The **Change Working Time** dialog box opens.

2. From the **For:** For calendar: [Standard (Project Calendar) ▾] dropdown, select **Standard (Project Calendar)**.

3. If you did not set the hours per day in **Project Options**, do this first by clicking [Options...] to adjust the time unit conversion factors. Upon clicking [OK] you will be returned to this dialog.

4. On the **Change Working Time** dialog box, click the day in the calendar whose working times you want to change. The working times for that day will be displayed.

5. Next, select the **Exceptions** tab and select the next available blank row in the **Name** column. Enter the name of the calendar exception and press [Tab]. The start and finish dates are entered, defaulting to the date that you clicked in the calendar. You can change this date now, if needed. Notice that to the right of the calendar it says that the date is **nonworking**.

6. Click on **Details** to open the detail dialog box. Notice that the default changes to a non-working day for the date that you selected.

7. If the exception is a change other than to a non-working day, you can change this in the **Details** dialog box. If you want to change working time to something other than the default, you can select **Non-default Working Time**, then change the times in the **From/To** boxes as needed.

8. Under the **Recurrence Pattern** selection heading, select if the calendar exception will take place daily, weekly, monthly, or yearly. To the right of that selection, enter the frequency or interval for which the exception will take place.

9. Under the **Range of Recurrence** select the **Start date** for the recurrence. Then either:

   ▶ Select **End after** and enter the number of times the recurring exception is to take place

   OR

   ▶ Select **End by** and specify the date when the recurring exception will end.

10. Click [OK] at the bottom of the **Details** dialog box and then click [OK] in the **Change Working Time** dialog box.

 Create recurring corporate holidays on the Project Calendar and set the dates into the future by a couple of years. This will help in not having to remember to add corporate holidays every year into your Project Calendar.

 Calendar working days and working times set in the standard Project Calendar are carried over to the Resource Calendars and the Task Calendars. However, if the Project Calendar is changed after Resource Calendars are created, the changes will show up automatically in Resource Calendars, but not in Task Calendars.

Mark nonworking days which apply to almost everyone, such as national and company holidays, in the Project Calendar. Use Resource Calendars to override the Project Calendar and set nonworking days to working days for any resources who are exceptions.

The calendar information is saved in the project schedule. To distribute a Project Calendar to your colleagues, you have to transfer them via the Organizer.

Checks on Setting Up a Project

Here are some checks to verify that you used best practices when setting up your project:

➤ Does the Comments field in the Project Properties (**File**, **Info**, **File Properties**, **Advanced Properties**) contain a succinct description of the objective or final product of the project?

The description is visible as a Note on the project summary task. You need to have some background information on the project to properly evaluate the schedule.

➤ Do the working hours as specified in the Project Calendar through Change Working Time, correspond to the Hours per day conversion values set in the Project Options (**File, Options**)?

For example, working times of 8:00 AM-12:00 PM and 1:00 PM-5:00 PM are consistent with 8 hours per day and 40 hours per week. If the settings are inconsistent, your forecasts are either too optimistic or too pessimistic. Also, you might see decimals in the task durations.

The quickest way to check consistency is by launching the **Change Working Time** window from the **Project** tab of the Ribbon. The button Options... will take you directly to the **Project Options**.

 When you first create your project, set all of the project options to match your organization's standards and your personal selections before entering tasks. On the **Backstage** view click the **File** tab, then click **Options** to review all the settings.

Review Questions

1. Does Project 2010 function more like Microsoft Office Excel or Microsoft Office Access? Why?

2. What is the function of the *Global.mpt* file?

3. In which situations would you recommend the use of project templates?

4. Which view would you use for:

Task	Recommended View
Entering tasks?	
Entering resources?	
Entering assignments?	
Checking the network logic?	
Viewing workloads?	
Recording To-do lists?	

5. Why would you use a split view (combination view) in Project 2010?

6. What steps do you recommend as a process for creating a new project schedule?

7. How do the **Hours per day** setting in the Project Options and the working hours in **Change Working Time** of the Standard (Project) Calendar) relate to each other?

8. How can you change the default calendar, i.e., how can you edit the Standard Project Calendar in *Global.mpt file*?

9. What functions are on the Backstage view? What functions are on the Ribbon? What functions are on the Quick Access Toolbar? Can you customize the Ribbon and the Quick Access Toolbar?

Additional Practice   For experience working with the features you've learned about in this chapter, we strongly suggest that you do the additional exercises for this chapter that are included in Appendix 1.

Chapter 3: Entering Tasks

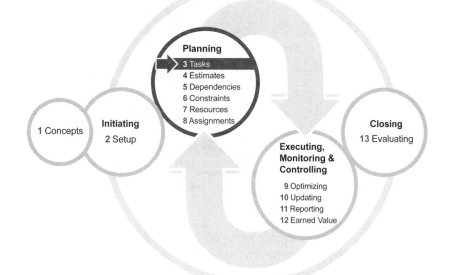

We've finished the Setup process and are ready to begin the Planning Processes. In this chapter we'll focus on the first process: defining tasks and entering them in Project 2010.

After reading this chapter you will be able to:

➤ Define what a work breakdown structure (WBS) is
➤ Discuss the benefits of a WBS and its importance as the foundation of the project schedule
➤ Establish an appropriate level of detail for your WBS
➤ Write effective summary tasks, detail tasks and milestones
➤ In Project 2010 you will be able to:
  ▸ Create and change an indented WBS
  ▸ Create summary tasks, detail tasks, and milestone tasks
  ▸ Create tasks using the new user-controlled scheduling feature
  ▸ Edit, copy and move tasks
  ▸ Check the WBS of the project schedule using scheduling best practices
  ▸ Import tasks to the WBS from Microsoft Excel and Microsoft Outlook
  ▸ Import and Export tasks to/from SharePoint 2010

DO IT YOURSELF
1. Open the box.
2. Assemble the pieces.
3. You're finished!

The Planning Processes

The planning processes are performed in an iterative cycle: you revisit them repeatedly throughout the project in order to refine and optimize your schedule. The key processes are:

➤ Define and enter the **tasks** needed to complete the project

➤ Identify the **Task Mode** – manual or auto-scheduled – for each task or for the whole project

➤ **Estimate** the time needed to complete each task

➤ Identify **dependencies** between tasks

➤ Identify task **constraints**

➤ Identify the **resources** needed to get the tasks done

➤ Make staff **assignments** to get the work done

➤ **Refine** as you go to optimize the schedule and manage client expectations

2010 **User-controlled Scheduling** means that you can now either schedule your tasks manually, controlling the start and finish dates, or automatically, as in prior versions of Project, having the powerful scheduling engine schedule the task's start and finish dates for you. We will talk more about this later.

We'll start with the process of defining tasks and entering them in Project 2010.

The Work Breakdown Structure

Before you enter tasks in Project 2010, you need to decide what your project tasks are. The starting point for this is to develop a WBS.

We strongly suggest that you start by creating a WBS and use that as the basis for creating your schedule.

According to PMI, a WBS is "a deliverable-oriented hierarchical decomposition of the work to be executed by the project team to accomplish the project objectives and create the required deliverables".[1]

Whew! Let's look at a couple of the key phrases of this definition.

A WBS is "Deliverable-Oriented"

A deliverable is "any unique and verifiable product, result, or capability to perform a service that must be produced to complete a process, phase or project."[2]

Deliverables are the products the project is going to produce: both final deliverables that you hand off to your client, (e.g., a completed computer program, building, or relocation) and interim deliverables that your stakeholders use during the project (e.g., a weekly status report).

The WBS should cover 100% of your project's scope and capture all of your key deliverables.

It is generally accepted project management practice that work that is not in the WBS is not within the scope of the project.

You need to establish this understanding early with your project stakeholders: if the client requests a deliverable during project execution that is not in the WBS, it is out of scope and must be negotiated under the project's change control procedures as an addition to the project.

The work described in the WBS is also the basis for estimating, scheduling, and assigning responsibilities on the project. It is the means for tying project objectives and requirements to the work required to deliver them.

A WBS is a "Hierarchical Decomposition"

When we say that a WBS is a hierarchical decomposition, it simply means that your WBS should break down (decompose) your primary deliverables into smaller, more manageable parts and that this decomposition should be organized in a logical (hierarchical) way.

---

1   ———*PMBOK® Guide – Fourth Edition*, PMI, 2008, p. 116.
2   Ibid, p. 432.

Shown below is a portion of a simplified WBS:

Software Implementation
1. Project Management
2. Software
   2.1 Software Requirements
   2.2 Initial Software Design
   2.3 Final Software Design
   2.4 Software Development
   2.5 Software Delivery
3. Hardware
   3.1 Hardware Requirements
   3.2 Initial Hardware Design
   3.3 Final Hardware Design
   3.4 Hardware Acquisition
   3.5 Hardware Installation
4. User Documentation
   4.1 Documentation Requirements
   4.2 Documentation
   4.3 Approved User Documentation
5. Training
   5.1 Training Requirements
   5.2 Training Materials
   5.3 Approved Training Materials
6. Testing
   6.1 Test Plan
   6.2 Test Cases
   6.3 System Test
   6.4 User Acceptance Test
7. Go Live

As you can see, the sample WBS:

➤ Contains the project deliverables (e.g., "2.1 Software Requirements", "2.2 Initial Software Design" and "2.3 Final Software Design" are all deliverables)

➤ Has deliverables decomposed into smaller parts

➤ Is organized in a logical manner to identify the work required to produce the deliverables

Organizing Your WBS

There are many ways to organize your WBS, e.g. by key deliverables, physical components, chronological phases in the project life cycle, functional specialties, or in a program by project and sub-project.

In our sample WBS above, we organized the WBS by deliverable. Here's the same WBS, organized by phases—requirements phase, design phase, etc.

Software Implementation
1. Project Management
2. Requirements
   2.1 Software Requirements
   2.2 Hardware Requirements
   2.3 Documentation Requirements
   2.4 Training Requirements
3. Design
   3.1 Initial Software Design
   3.2 Final Software Design
   3.3 Initial Hardware Design
   3.4 Final Hardware Design
4. Construction
   4.1 Software Development
   4.2 Hardware Installation
   4.3 Documentation
   4.4 Training Materials
5. Testing
   5.1 Test Plan
   5.2 Test Cases
   5.3 System Test
   5.4 Approved User Documentation
   5.5 Approved Training Materials
   5.6 User Acceptance Test
6. Go Live

Notice that both examples contain the same deliverables.

 Regardless of how you organize your WBS, it should be deliverable-oriented, i.e., it should explicitly state all of the key deliverables for your project.

According to PMI, a WBS with phases and activities only and no deliverables is not a WBS! Every phase, activity or task must have one or more deliverables.

Including deliverables in your WBS makes sense:

➤ The WBS should be an elaboration of the deliverables promised in the project's scope statement. A deliverable-oriented WBS makes it easier to track work back to the scope statement.

➤ Because many of your deliverables are the key products you'll be delivering to your client, your client will find it easier to understand a deliverable-oriented WBS.

➤ Deliverables are often tangible and easily understood when making team assignments. Imagine that you were made responsible for either "researching requirements" (an activity) or for delivering the "list of requirements" (a deliverable) for a project. The latter is a concrete deliverable; it is verifiable and therefore creates a firmer commitment.

➤ A deliverable-oriented grouping enables you to get useful reports from Project 2010, like an effort or cost by deliverable report.

➤ Once you identify and describe deliverables, it is easier to identify, estimate and schedule the activities needed to create those deliverables.

Our definition of a deliverable includes the phrase: a deliverable is "any **unique and verifiable** product, result, or capability".[3] By describing each deliverable identified in the WBS, you create verifiability in the project: you clarify what you are going to produce each step of the way. When you ask your client to sign off on the WBS and the definition of deliverables, you have established how task and project completions will be verified. This practice of identifying and describing deliverables early in the project will decrease misunderstandings that can become fatal if not surfaced until near the end (when they typically result in nasty disputes or litigation).

You may not be used to thinking in terms of deliverables, and it can take practice to learn to identify them. However, it's important to put some effort into this. After all, if you can't define the deliverables, how will you and your stakeholders ever agree upon what needs to be done? It's a common view that if you can't identify the deliverables for a project, you don't **have** a project.

Phases in the WBS

Often the WBS is organized by phases—distinct periods in the life of a project such as requirements, analysis and development. If you organize by phase, it's important to identify the deliverables for each phase. For example, the requirements phase may produce requirements definition, the analysis phase designs, and the development phase software modules. These interim deliverables are necessary in many projects to enable a controlled process with checkpoints between phases.

While phases can establish a chronology for the project, it's important to note that the focus during WBS development should be on identifying, defining and decomposing deliverables; not on sequencing and scheduling. This comes later.

 Chronological breakdowns in your WBS can make it harder to manage iterative (repeating) processes.

Iterative processes are common in projects, often as a result of the progressive elaboration of project requirements and designs as the product is developed. For

---

3   Ibid.

example, you might create a requirements document during the requirements phase, refine it in the analysis phase, and finalize it in the development phase. If your WBS is organized by chronological phases, work on your requirements document will be scattered across all three phases, making it more difficult to track progress on the deliverable, a finalized requirements document. In a deliverable-oriented WBS the work on the requirements document will all be listed in a single section and you can add activities with ease.

 The bottom line: there are times when organizing your WBS by phase makes perfect sense. We recommend that in large projects you consider using a combination of phases and deliverables in your WBS. Just make sure that if you do use phases in your WBS, you've also captured all your deliverables.

Indented List or Organization Chart Format?

You can build your WBS either as an indented list or in a format similar to an organization chart, with the summary tasks—generally the largest or most important deliverables—toward the top and the detail tasks underneath.

The next illustration shows a WBS for an aircraft manufacturer in chart format.

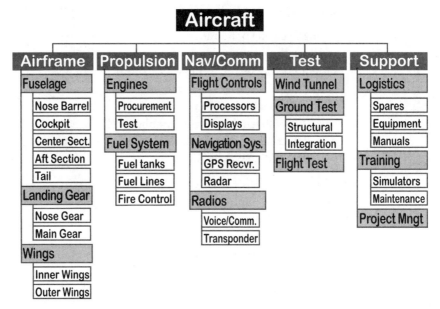

WBS - Chart **WBS - List**

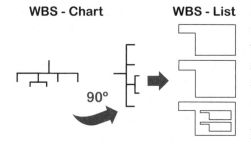

If you create your WBS as a chart (rather than an indented list), you'll need to convert it to an indented list in order to enter it into Project 2010. You do this by simply rotating your chart 90 degrees and then indenting the lower levels.

Many people find the graphic format easy to read and understand because it enables them to see relationships among the elements more clearly. While Project 2010 doesn't support this view, add-on tools are available which do.

Using the Project 2010 Visual Report feature, it is possible to export the WBS to Microsoft Visio 2010. (See chapter 11 to learn more about Visual Reports.)

How to Create your WBS

Your WBS is not a static document. As you proceed through your project, you'll gain information and experience which will help you improve the quality and specificity of your WBS, and you should flesh out your WBS accordingly.

An ideal starting point for creating your WBS is the scope statement, which should list the key deliverables for the project. Analyze the scope statement carefully to make sure you understand both the stated and any implied deliverables. Then use these to form the basis for building your WBS.

It can also be useful to base your WBS on the WBS from another, similar project, or on a template. Many organizations have developed internal standards and templates to help promote WBS consistency and quality.

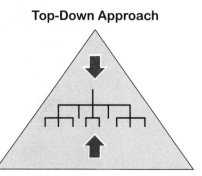

Two common methods for developing the WBS are:

➤ **Top-down**: You list the deliverables first and then identify all the tasks needed to accomplish the deliverables.

➤ **Bottom-up**: You brainstorm about all of the tasks and then group them under their deliverables. Each deliverable becomes a summary task.

While the two approaches can lead to the same result, experienced project managers usually find it more efficient and effective to take the top-down approach. The top-down approach also lends itself well to the use of models and templates to assist less experienced project managers in developing a WBS.

 We suggest that you have your project team help construct the WBS. For example, you can assign the breakdown of an activity or deliverable at any level of the WBS to the responsible person for decomposition.

Your team members are the people who will be doing the work and they usually bring a different perspective that is valuable to capture. Having the team help develop the WBS also promotes team members' understanding of and buy-in to the project.

Naming and Describing Deliverables

Deliverables should create both measurability and verifiability in the project plan.

We find that most plans can be greatly improved in this respect. Describing deliverables as specifically as possible is a critical factor in aligning the expectations of your project stakeholders.

You should define each deliverable in terms of its form, content, behavioral characteristics and level of quality. This includes using a name that as much as possible captures the meaning of the deliverable.

The following are examples of deliverables that we came across in real life schedules and our suggestions for tighter naming. In our view, the renamed, right-hand column deliverables would be easier to verify on completion:

Ambiguously named deliverable	Verifiable, measurable deliverable
Closing	Customer approval of the project product
Subcontracting	Signed contract
Moving to new location	Operational, new location
Higher revenue	30% increase in revenue marketing
Renovation	Renovated facility
Planning	Project plan
Material procurement	Procured construction materials
Prototype development	Developed prototype
Training	300 trained application users
Staff	50 newly hired staff members
Implementation	New workstations operational for entire team

We recommend that when naming tasks and milestones you use nouns or gerunds.[4] Whenever possible use a term that names the deliverable to be produced.

Milestones should make clear exactly what event is to have occurred at the milestone.

An important advantage of using nouns in task and milestone names is that they focus you on the deliverables of the project, rather than on the process. You may find it helpful to add adjectives if they clarify or improve the measurability of deliverables, for example, "draft report" or "final report."

More important than the exact naming conventions you use are that:

➤ Every task at every level **must** have one or more deliverables

➤ You are consistent in your naming conventions

➤ Your WBS and Project 2010 task list read coherently so they can be understood as a story of how the project will unfold.

You will probably use your WBS as a primary communication tool for your project. The clearer and more consistent it is, the simpler it will be for your stakeholders to understand and participate in your project.

If you find yourself explaining your WBS all the time, it is not (yet) a good communication piece. Ideally, a WBS should be self-explanatory. If needed, provide a legend of abbreviations with it. The WBS should enable readers to see the big picture and then drill down to the details without losing track of the big picture.

The WBS Dictionary

The WBS dictionary is "a document that describes each component in the work breakdown structure (WBS). For each WBS component, the WBS dictionary includes a brief definition of the scope or statement of work, defined deliverable(s), a list of associated activities, and a list of milestones. Other information may include: responsible organization, start and end dates, resources required, an estimate of cost, charge number, contract information, quality requirements, and technical references to facilitate performance of the work."[5]

While in small simple projects this may be overkill, the more complex the project the more necessary it is to have a complete description of the work to be done and the deliverables. In Project 2010, the task description for each task represents the WBS dictionary entry for the task.

---

4   In English, gerunds are verbs that are used as nouns. For example, in the phrase "We're training the staff" the word "training" is used as a verb. In the phrase "We're going to conduct training" the word "training" is used as a gerund.

5   ———*PMBOK® Guide – Fourth Edition*, PMI, 2008, p. 453.

The Right Level of Detail

One of the biggest challenges in creating a WBS is decomposing it to an appropriate level of detail. The WBS should have neither too little detail nor too much! A logical structure with an appropriate level of detail is key to tracking work throughout the project.

On average, you'll want each summary task to have detail tasks that describe the entire scope of the summary task. This helps to make the meaning of the summary task more easily understood by readers and makes the task manager's job easier. The specific number of detail tasks that fall under summary tasks should be appropriate to effectively manage the project and it's deliverables.[6]

3

In the illustration, we've indicated the right level of detail for this project with the bold lines of the chart. Notice that they are not consistently on one level in the WBS. If it makes sense to break down one deliverable into more levels than another, you should do this.

Too Little Detail?

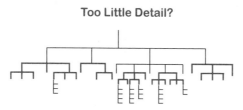

Too Much Detail?

Adding levels generally improves the accuracy of the estimates; however with too much detail, you'll create a schedule that's a real chore to update during project execution. Validating that you've found the right level of detail in your WBS and project schedule will help you keep your schedule alive during project execution. Use the following guidelines to validate your WBS.

Too Little Detail?

If your answer to any of the following questions is no, you may need to add detail to your WBS:

➤ Is it clear how the deliverable will be created and what the activities involved are?

➤ Do these activities correspond to meeting the acceptance criteria for the deliverable?

➤ Can I estimate the duration, effort and cost of the detail tasks?

➤ Can I find the dependencies between the tasks?
Dependencies are links between tasks that capture how they affect each other. (For example, you have to obtain equipment before you can install it; the second task is dependent on completion of the first.) Dependencies will be discussed in chapter 5.

➤ Can I assign the detail task to somebody?
If you can't assign each detail task to an individual, you may have too little detail in the WBS. If you cannot assign the deliverables in large projects to

---

6   This concept is adapted from *The Practice Standard for Work Breakdown Structures – Second Edition*, PMI, 2006.

organizational departments, you may need to add components to those deliverables, or perhaps even to the detail tasks.

We will discuss estimating, dependencies and assignments in later chapters.

Too Many Tasks?   If your answer to any of the following questions is no, you may have too many tasks:

> Is this task necessary in the WBS?
> If it's not, get rid of it. Otherwise you'll have to spend time updating it during the project.

> Is this task merely a reminder to myself?
> A WBS is not meant to be a personal reminder system. A WBS is supposed to capture tasks with significant effort involved. You can enter reminders in the **Notes** field using the task **Notes** [icon] on the **Task** tab. In the **Properties** group, click **Notes**.

> Is this task a to-do list item or a real task that will take significant effort?
> If the items do not take much time or effort, you have not created a WBS, but a to-do list. To-do list items are what you list at the start of the day to organize your work for that day. They may represent steps to be taken to perform an activity (for example, call Fred to discuss the design idea; set up a log in on the client's website). To-do items can be entered in the **Notes** field using task **Notes** [icon] as described above.

> Is this task an acceptance criterion?
> Acceptance criteria are part of the WBS dictionary and are typically captured in a checklist format in the **Notes** field, (using task **Notes** [icon] as described above). The task name could then read *complete checklist*.

> Will I continue to update all these detail tasks when I am busy during project execution?
> If you think you may not be able to update all the tasks during the execution phase, this is the time to roll them up into a higher-level task.

 We recommend keeping your schedule lean and mean! Only by doing so will you be able to keep it alive as a forecasting model during the hectic execution phase of the project. Lean and mean means your schedule has the right level of detail, is deliverable-oriented and is realistically related to the way the work will be done.

Task Duration Considerations   We won't cover estimating durations for WBS tasks until the next chapter, but there are two duration considerations you'll want to consider when defining the level of detail in your WBS: reporting periods and the 1% – 10% guideline. Both are applied to work packages: a unit of work that will be used in controlling the project.

> **Reporting Period**

The reporting period is the time frame in which you report status on your project. For example, if your project manager wants you to report the status on your project every week, your reporting period is one week. Reporting periods can vary from one project to another, depending on the project's complexity and communication needs. As a general rule, the duration of your detail tasks should not be longer than one reporting period, or in this example, one week .

This allows you to ask your team members at status time the very pointed question: Is this task done now, or are we still working on it? As a project manager, you know that if a task is still in progress in two consecutive status meetings, there may be a bigger problem that requires your immediate attention.

What to do if a task takes longer than a reporting period? If possible, break the task down so that there are two or more sub tasks that fit within reporting periods. For those tasks that you can't or choose not to break down, you can monitor their progress in other ways, (see Earned Value Management in chapter 12). Remember, in the end you can only rely on the receipt of a deliverable as proof that a task is done. The amount of effort expended or time passed does not indicate accomplishment.

> **The 1% – 10% Rule**

The 1% – 10% guideline suggests that the duration of any detail task should be between 1% of the project duration and 10% of the project duration.

For example, if you have a project that will take about 60 business days the minimum duration is 1% of 60 or 0.6 day, which you could round to half a day. Detail tasks should not last less than half a day (unless the project or part of it requires very tight control). If they are smaller, you could logically bring them together into larger tasks. The maximum is 10% of 60 or 6 days; let's round it to one week. Detail tasks would be no more than one week in duration.

The 1% – 10% rule should be applied to detail level tasks or work packages, and may not be appropriate for:

▶   Summary tasks
▶   Level of effort tasks
▶   Recurring detail tasks
▶   Milestones
▶   Rolling wave planning

The 1% – 10% rule may not be appropriate when using rolling wave planning for the entire project schedule, since you are not detailing the whole WBS at one time. You may want to apply rolling wave planning to the individual periods or to the "planning window" of the schedule, but take note that this may not be a true representation of the overall project duration. We will talk more about rolling wave planning in chapter 4.

It can be helpful to blend the 1% – 10% guideline with the reporting period guideline. But neither should be used as an absolute rule: there will be instances where they just don't provide the level of control that you need. For example, if in a very large project, tasks at the 10% level were to take a month in duration, it would be wise to break the tasks down further to enable more precise control and estimating.

Why Is the Right Level of Detail and Structure Important?

The rationale behind finding the right level of detail is to create enough checkpoints for monitoring and controlling the progress of the project and to enable estimating and scheduling.

In project management, we need feedback loops to control a project. A feedback loop is the communication between the project team members, the project manager, the client and sponsor, and other stakeholders.

The project manager assigns tasks and the plan tells performers what they need to deliver and by when. Performers tell the project manager how much time and effort they have spent, what deliverables they have produced, what issues and changes have come up, and what obstacles need to be cleared. The project manager (with an electronic assist from Project 2010) summarizes and interprets the analysis of the data. The project manager communicates to all of the project stakeholders the project's progress against the plan and needs for corrective action.

If the WBS is structured so that it's easy to understand at all levels of detail, the sponsor and client can see the big picture and be confident that they are getting the true picture of the project scope; they can go into detail as they see fit. Detail level data from performers can be automatically summarized for reporting and control at multiple levels.

The right level of detail and its use in reporting enable effective control. The diagram below shows the relationship between the recognition of the need for corrective action, taking the corrective action, and the ability to see its results.

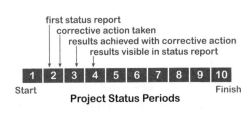

Project Status Periods

The first status report normally becomes available halfway through the second status period. If the report shows a problem, a decision is made to take corrective action. If you take the corrective action in the rest of the **second** period, you may see the results appear in the **third** period. The report on the **third** period becomes available in the **fourth** period. So problems in the **first** period will be corrected visibly for the client or executives only in the **fourth** period—or even later, depending on the situation. There is always a delay in determining the problem, taking action and seeing the result of the action. If you have ten checkpoints, clients really only have six or so manage-points. You need, therefore, a number of reporting periods that enables catching problems as early as possible and being able to see the results of corrective action.

 Clients and executives tend to get nervous when you don't give them enough opportunities to know where you are and to make a difference in your project. As a result, they may start micro-managing you as the project manager.

 Of course, successful project managers don't depend on their own status reports to find out what is happening in their projects: they make sure they know the status of their projects at all times. They continually check up with their teams and communicate frequently on the work floor. In some projects there are brief daily meetings to report progress and raise issues and obstacles. This increases the number of feedback loops dramatically and thus the chance for successful completion of the project.

Characteristics of a Good WBS

When you're creating your WBS, keep these structural rules in mind:[7]

➤ Keep the most important items—your key deliverables—on the highest level. Make sure they represent the entire scope of the project.

➤ Under any WBS element, there should be at least two detail elements. If there is only one detail element, remove it and reword the summary level element as needed to incorporate it, or identify another element to fully describe the summary element.

➤ There should be no duplication or logical overlap between WBS elements. There can be an overlap in the schedule, which is a chronological overlap. But each deliverable or task should be shown once and only once on your WBS.

➤ Each group of detail elements should completely capture its summary element (top-down check).

Ask yourself: if we do all of the detail elements will we have completely accomplished the summary deliverable?

---

7   These checks have been adapted from *The Practice Standard for Work Breakdown Structures – Second Edition*, PMI, 2006.

> ➤ Each element should relate to its summary elements on all higher levels (bottom-up check).

 In an organization chart, the greater the scope of a function, the higher it is in the chart. The CEO function encompasses the entire organization while the direct reporting functions—business units, divisions, etc.—follow. The WBS works in the same way. The project as a whole breaks down into a few major deliverables or phases, and these break down into the work that is needed to deliver them. Each element of the work has its own deliverable(s).

However, a WBS should not follow the lines of an organization. Do not break down the project work by functional group. Eventually, the deliverables will be assigned to functional groups in the responsibility assignment matrix, but this is a later step. In your WBS, concentrate on breaking down work by deliverables and/or phases and activities.

Importance of the WBS

The WBS is the most important document in a project plan:

> ➤ Many key project management documents (e.g., your project schedule, your budget) need the WBS as input. This means that the quality of these documents rests in part on the quality of your WBS.

> ➤ The WBS serves as an important communication tool between the project manager and the stakeholders of the project, such as the sponsor, the customers, and the internal and external suppliers. Along with the scope statement, it is **the source** for defining what needs to be done on the project.

Working out a detailed WBS with your clients helps you manage their expectations and ensures a veritable meeting of the minds early in your project. Like all other parts of the plan, the WBS is subject to change as the project progresses. Time spent on your WBS is generally time well spent.

Note that a Work Breakdown Structure is not a project schedule. It only tells us what needs to be done, not how or when or by whom. These steps come later.

Entering WBS Tasks in Project 2010

Choosing the Options

Before you begin entering tasks, set the **Default task type** option and **Effort driven** options to match the majority of your tasks.

On the **File** tab, in the **Backstage View**, Click on **Options** and consider the following options:

Project Options	Recommended Choices
Schedule	**Set the Schedule Options on the Schedule tab:** **Current Project or All New Projects** 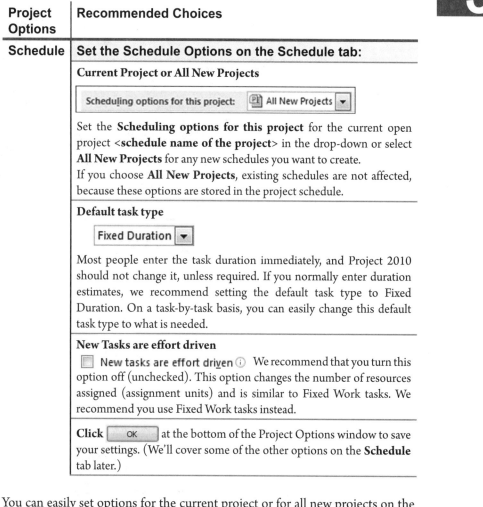 Scheduling options for this project: [PI] All New Projects [▼] Set the **Scheduling options for this project** for the current open project <**schedule name of the project**> in the drop-down or select **All New Projects** for any new schedules you want to create. If you choose **All New Projects**, existing schedules are not affected, because these options are stored in the project schedule. **Default task type** Fixed Duration [▼] Most people enter the task duration immediately, and Project 2010 should not change it, unless required. If you normally enter duration estimates, we recommend setting the default task type to Fixed Duration. On a task-by-task basis, you can easily change this default task type to what is needed. **New Tasks are effort driven** [☐] New tasks are effort driven ⓘ We recommend that you turn this option off (unchecked). This option changes the number of resources assigned (assignment units) and is similar to Fixed Work tasks. We recommend you use Fixed Work tasks instead. **Click** [OK] at the bottom of the Project Options window to save your settings. (We'll cover some of the other options on the **Schedule** tab later.)

 You can easily set options for the current project or for all new projects on the **Schedule** and **Advanced** tabs. Go to the **File** tab in the **Backstage** View and click on **Options**. Both the **Schedule** and **Advanced** tabs have sections that allow you to apply the settings that follow to the current project <current project name> or **All New Projects**.

Types of Tasks in Project 2010

You'll enter your WBS in Project 2010 as a series of tasks. It's important to remember that though Project 2010 terms its WBS elements as tasks, they can (and should!) include your deliverables as well as the tasks and activities needed to produce those deliverables. Remember, every task at any level of detail should have one or more well defined deliverables.

Project 2010 has a number of task types; including a project summary task, summary tasks, detail tasks and milestones. It's important to understand the difference between these components because each is treated differently in Project 2010.

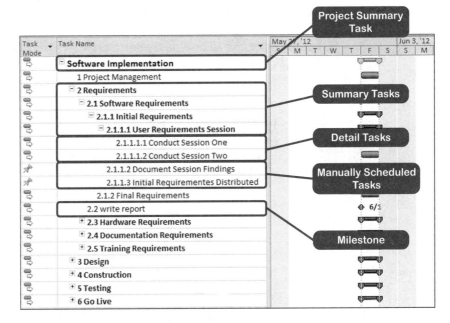

> ➤ **Project Summary Task**
>
> Each project has a single project summary task which represents a summary of the project. It is automatically generated by Project 2010 and shows totals for the entire project in all of its standard and customized fields. It also displays a bar in the timescale that represents the whole project.
>
> In the example above, *Software Implementation* is the project summary task.
>
> The project summary task may be hidden (the default) or displayed, as we'll see below. When displayed, it will always appear in row 0 and will display a bar in the timescale that represents the whole project.

> You cannot assign regular resources to the project summary task (row 0); only budget resources can be assigned here. It is also important to remember that they must be specifically identified as a budget resource when created, otherwise Project will not allow you to assign them to row 0. (For more

information, see chapter 7 on entering Resources and chapter 8 on entering Assignments.)

It is possible to assign a fixed cost to the project summary task, but we urge you not to do this. You will have much greater control of costs if you manage costs on a more detailed level of the project.

Always use the project summary task that Project 2010 automatically generates in row 0 to show the totals for the project. Avoid using a task you create yourself in row 1 that represents the project totals, because this task will not function in the same way as the automatically created project summary task on row 0.

By default, the project summary task (row 0) is turned off. To turn it back on for your current project or for all new projects go to the **File** tab and in the **Backstage** view, click on **Options**, **Advanced**. Under the **Display** options for this project section, check the box **Show Project Summary Task**. You can select this option for the current project <Current Project Name> that you have open, or for **All New Projects** going forward.

If you just wanted to display the project summary task for the current open project and not all new projects going forward, you can go to the **Task** tab in the **View** group, and click **Gantt Chart**. On the **Format** tab, in the **Show/Hide** group, click the **Project Summary Task** box.

➤ **Summary Tasks**

A summary task is any task that includes a lower level (or levels) of detail tasks.

In the example above, *2. Requirements, 2.1 Software Requirements* and *2.1.1 Initial Requirements* are summary tasks because they include lower levels of detail tasks. For example, the summary task *2. Requirements* includes **all** of the detail tasks indented beneath it.

Note, however, that the summary task *2.1.1 Initial Requirements* includes only the tasks **indented** beneath it. For example, the task *2.1.2 Final Requirements* is **not** part of the task *2.1.1. Initial Requirements.*

The top-level summary tasks are often the key deliverables or phases of your project—the components that you'll be delivering to your client. In the example above, Requirements and Equipment are two key deliverables for the project.

You generally do not assign costs, work or duration to summary tasks—unless you are entering budgets by assigning Budget Resources to the project summary task. Instead, it is usually better to allow Project 2010 to calculate these totals for the summary task based on its detail tasks. (That's why these are called summary tasks.) We'll cover more on this in later chapters.

The Project 2010 default settings are for summary tasks to show up in boldface with a "-" in front of the summary task name if all of the detail tasks are displayed, or a "+" in front of the summary task name if there are hidden detail tasks. The "+" in front of the task *2.1.2 Final Requirements* tells us that there are detail tasks associated with this summary task that currently aren't displayed.

In prior versions of Project, you would have to insert a new task or select a current task and then click "outdent" to make it a summary task, or highlight the tasks underneath it and click "indent". Now in Project 2010, you can directly insert summary tasks with just a click. To do this, on the **Task** tab, in the **View** group, click **Gantt Chart**. Select the task name just before where you want to insert the summary task, then on **Task** tab, in the **Insert** group, click **Summary** . Type the name of the summary task. Project will convert the task that is immediately below the inserted summary task to be a child task (a detail task under the parent summary task).

➤ **Detail Tasks**

A detail task is any task that doesn't have lower level subtasks (in other words, it's not a summary task). Detail tasks are the units of work for which duration estimates and resources must be assigned.

Detail tasks can be scheduled either manually or automatically, as we'll discuss later in this chapter.

In our example, the tasks *2.1.1.1.1 Conduct Session One* and *2.1.1.1.2 Conduct Session Two* are detail tasks because they don't have any lower level subtasks.

Each detail task belongs to the summary task under which it's indented. For example, *2.1.1.1.1 Conduct Session One* belongs to *2.1.1.1 User Requirements Session*.

➤ **Milestones**

A milestone is an event you define in your schedule; it might be an evaluation point or the completion of an important deliverable.

A milestone has a zero duration; it is a point in time, an event and not an activity.[8] You can insert milestones in your schedule wherever you think they'll be useful. As a general rule of thumb, we recommend you enter at least one milestone as the last item for each summary task. Most people

---

8   You can mark tasks with non-zero durations as "milestones" also. This creates hard-to-explain gaps between task bars in the timescale. We recommend you use lag on dependencies as described in chapter 5 instead.

3

indent the milestone on the same level as the detail tasks for the summary task.

You may fix the dates of milestones to set initial scheduling targets, but be careful not to make a schedule that looks like it will make a milestone target when the probability of doing so is small.

In our example, *2.2 Software Requirements Finalized* is a milestone for the *2. Software Requirements* task. We'll see later how to identify milestones in Project 2010.

 Unless you are using the new **Insert Summary Task** or **Insert Milestone Task** on the **Task** tab, **Insert** group of the **Ribbon**, Project 2010 doesn't always know whether you're creating a summary task, a detail task or a milestone. For example, a summary task doesn't become a summary task until you indent a detail task beneath it. So you enter all tasks into a field simply called **Task Name** (known in the database as the field **Task**). Remember that although the field is named **task**, you use it to enter not only tasks, but deliverables, phases and milestones as well.

 In prior versions of Project, you would have to insert a new task or select a current task and then set the duration field to zero (0) for it to become a Milestone task. Now in Project 2010, you can directly insert a Milestone task with just a click. To do this, on the **Task** tab, in the **View** group, click **Gantt Chart**. Select the task name prior to where you want to insert the Milestone task, then on the **Task** tab, in the **Insert** group, click **Milestone**. Type the name of the Milestone task.

Task Structure in Project 2010

If you analyze an indented list of tasks, you'll find that a standard module recurs: a summary task with its detail tasks and a milestone. These standard modules can even be nested inside one another, thus creating the next indentation level, as the illustration also shows. The indentation level is captured in the field **Outline Level**. The first level is outline level 1, the next indentation outline level 2, etc.

Build your plan in a modular way and use the following standard module of tasks. Your WBS will consist of several of these standard modules (with a varying number of detail tasks):

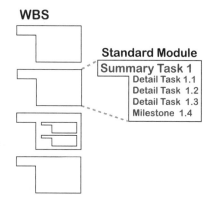

Standard Module		Example
Summary task	1	REPORT
Detail task	1.1	Data Gathered
Detail task	1.2	Data Categorized
Detail task	1.3	Report Written
Milestone	1.4	Report Ready

Entering Tasks

Project 2010 has two new scheduling enhancements to improve your control over your schedule: one is enhanced copy and paste and the other is user-controlled scheduling.

Enhanced copy and paste

At times you may want to create an initial task list in another Microsoft application (e.g., Word or Excel) and then decide to manage this list using the full, powerful and robust functionality of Project 2010. You can now copy and paste content between other Microsoft Office 2010 programs and Project 2010 and still retain its formatting, outline levels, and column headers. With two clicks of the mouse, you can then generate an instant report and copy it to other Microsoft Office programs. (We will talk more about this in chapter 11, Reporting).

User-controlled Scheduling: Manual vs Auto Scheduling

Project 2010 introduces a new major shift in how projects are scheduled. You can now schedule tasks automatically, using the same powerful and robust Project scheduling engine as before, or you can schedule tasks manually, keeping the task dates where you want them.

Manually scheduled tasks differ from automatically scheduled tasks in two key ways:

➤ In the past, you usually had to schedule a task by assigning duration estimates and resources, even though you might not have this information readily available. Now, with manually-scheduled tasks in Project 2010, you don't need to do this. You can provide high-level task information for the task without assigning duration estimates and resources. For example, you could enter "*TBD*" in the **Start Date** or "*Go ask Nate*" in the **Duration** field until you know the estimated duration and start date. This allows you to start planning your project right away without knowing all the information about the manually scheduled tasks up front.

➤ For manually-scheduled tasks, changes to the schedule (such as task dependencies and the project calendar) will no longer automatically adjust task dates. So manually-scheduled tasks will stay where you want them to stay in your project schedule.

 ➤ By default, new tasks are manually scheduled in Project 2010. If you want to schedule a specific task to be auto-scheduled, select the task, then on the **Task** tab, in the **Tasks** group, select **Auto Schedule**, or change the scheduling option for the specific task in the **Task Mode** column.

 ➤ If you want all of your new tasks to be automatically-scheduled, on the **File** tab, in the **Backstage** view, click on **Options**, **Schedule**. In the **Scheduling options for this project** section, select the current project <Current Project Name> that you have open, or select **All New Projects** for all projects going forward for the settings to be selected. In the **New tasks created** section, select either **Schedule on Project Start date** or **Schedule on Current Date** from the drop-down, depending on your preference.

Project managers who are used to automatic scheduling (the only choice available with past versions of Project) may prefer to turn manual scheduling off. For some projects, especially complicated ones, you may want Project's powerful scheduling engine to schedule and reschedule tasks for you.

Summary Tasks, Detail Tasks and Milestone Tasks

Now, we will discuss how to enter summary tasks, detail tasks and, milestones.

You can use either the **Gantt Chart** view or the **Network Diagram** view for entering tasks. You may find the **Gantt Chart** view more comfortable because you can see the levels of the breakdown structure shown through the indentation of the tasks and graphically in the chart. The farther indented to the right, the lower the level of the task.

To switch to the **Gantt Chart** view, on the **Task** tab, in the **View** group, click **Gantt Chart**, OR on the **View** tab, in the **Task Views** group, click **Gantt Chart**.

Displaying the Project Summary Task

As mentioned above, we recommend that you not enter a project summary task on row 1, but instead display the project summary task automatically generated by Project 2010 on row 0:

To display the **Project Summary** task:

1. On the **Task** tab, in the **View** group, click **Gantt Chart**.

   OR

   On the **View** tab in the **Task View** group, click **Gantt Chart**.

2. On the **Format** tab, in the **Show/Hide** group, click **Project Summary Task**. The project summary task will be displayed in row 0.

For summary tasks you only need to enter the name, since most of the other fields are calculated.

Entering Summary Tasks

1. On the **Task** tab, in the **View** group, click **Gantt Chart**.

2. Select the task name prior to where you want to insert the new summary task. On the **Task** tab, in the **Insert** group, click **Summary** 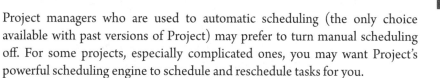. Notice

that a new summary task is inserted and the task you selected is now a "child task" of this new summary task.

3. Type the name of the summary task. The Summary task can be named with a noun. We recommend that you add an adjective with the noun, if it will help clarify acceptance criteria for the deliverable. If one adjective is not enough, use task **Notes** on the **Task** tab, **Properties** group to add more explicit acceptance criteria.

With the **Insert Summary Task** function, Project 2010 will convert the task that is immediately below the inserted summary task to be a "child" task. If necessary, adjust the indentation level as needed.

4. Press [Enter ↵] to go to the next task, which is automatically indented for you after creating the new summary task,

    OR

    You can insert new detail tasks. On the **Task** tab, in the **Insert** group, click **Task** and then select **Task** from the drop-down menu 🔲.

5. Adjust the other tasks as needed.

 We recommend that you type summary tasks in **UPPERCASE**. In dialog boxes where there is a drop-down list of tasks, indenting does not show, and putting the summary in uppercase allows you to more easily view a long list of tasks. It also helps you avoid linking to summary tasks (linking is covered chapter 5).

 The task name is normally the only thing you need to enter for summary tasks. In previous versions of Microsoft Project, a summary task would start summarizing only when tasks were indented beneath it on the next row. With the new version of Project, you can insert summary tasks with just a **click**. The Summary task will then get its characteristic task bar ▔▔▔▔▔▔.

Entering Detail Tasks

For detail tasks, you can just enter the task name or you can add in the duration estimate and other information (description of deliverables, hyperlinks to deliverables, notes, responsible parties, etc.) if that information is available. We will discuss adding these other elements in more detail in later chapters and strongly suggest that you read the chapter on estimating before you enter duration estimates.

 You can insert and attach documents or link deliverables to a task. To do this, insert the **Hyperlink** column and right-click on the **Hyperlink** cell for the task. Then you can add or edit the hyperlink text by clicking **Hyperlink** from the drop-down and then completing the **Text to display** box.

1. If you need to insert a new row for a detail task, click on any cell in the row before where you want to insert a new task.

2. On the **Task** tab, in the **Insert** group, click **Task** or right-click and select **Insert task** from the Short-Cut menu that appears.

3. Enter the **Task Name**; make it meaningful so users will fully understand the task at hand.

4. Press ⎰Tab⎱ to go to its **Duration** field. Enter an estimate and press ⎰Tab⎱.

   If necessary, indent it under its summary task by clicking **Indent** ⇛ to indent the task OR **Outdent** ⇚ to outdent the task on the **Task** tab in the **Schedule** group,

   OR

   You can right-click and select the **Indent** or **Outdent** icons commands from the **Mini-Toolbar** menu that appears.

 You may want to enter a task for which you don't yet have all the details. With the new manual scheduling feature of Project 2010, if you don't have a duration estimate, you can enter non-specific information such as "*Go ask Nate*" in the **Duration** field (until Nate provides the needed estimate). This allows you to create a high-level plan without knowing specific estimates for a task.

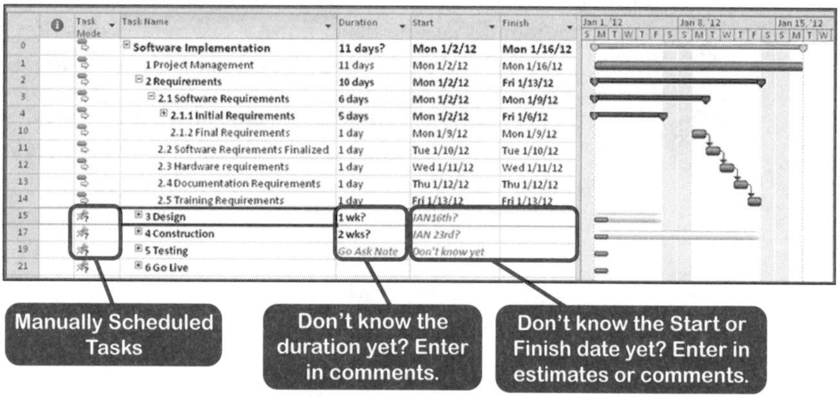

	�︎	Task Mode	Task Name	Duration	Start	Finish	Jan 1, '12 / Jan 8, '12 / Jan 15, '12
0			⊟ **Software Implementation**	11 days?	Mon 1/2/12	Mon 1/16/12	
1			1 Project Management	11 days	Mon 1/2/12	Mon 1/16/12	
2			⊟ 2 Requirements	10 days	Mon 1/2/12	Fri 1/13/12	
3			⊟ 2.1 Software Requirements	6 days	Mon 1/2/12	Mon 1/9/12	
4			⊞ 2.1.1 Initial Requirements	5 days	Mon 1/2/12	Fri 1/6/12	
10			2.1.2 Final Requirements	1 day	Mon 1/9/12	Mon 1/9/12	
11			2.2 Software Reqirements Finalized	1 day	Tue 1/10/12	Tue 1/10/12	
12			2.3 Hardware requirements	1 day	Wed 1/11/12	Wed 1/11/12	
13			2.4 Documentation Requirements	1 day	Thu 1/12/12	Thu 1/12/12	
14			2.5 Training Requirements	1 day	Fri 1/13/12	Fri 1/13/12	
15			⊞ 3 Design	1 wk?	JAN16th?		
17			⊞ 4 Construction	2 wks?	JAN 23rd?		
19			⊞ 5 Testing	Go Ask Note	Don't know yet		
21			⊞ 6 Go Live				

Manually Scheduled Tasks

Don't know the duration yet? Enter in comments.

Don't know the Start or Finish date yet? Enter in estimates or comments.

Entering Milestones

 The last task under a summary heading should be a milestone task that represents completion of everything within the summary. This way you can verify completion of the summary. We don't recommend assigning resources or the person responsible to the milestone task. Instead we recommend entering the person responsible for the milestone task in the **Milestone Note** field.

Inserting Milestone tasks:

1. To insert a milestone task, on the **Task** tab, in the **View** group, click **Gantt Chart**.

2. Select the task name prior to where you want to insert the Milestone task, then on the **Task** tab, in the **Insert** group, click **Milestone** ◆.

3. Enter the name of the milestone in the **Task Name** field.

4. The **Duration** of this milestone task is set to 0 (zero). This zero duration is what tells Project 2010 that you are entering a milestone, and two things happen: the field **Milestone** is toggled from **No** to **Yes** behind the screen, and a black diamond is inserted on the **Gantt Chart** timescale on the right of the screen if the task is auto-scheduled, (if the task is manually-scheduled, the diamond will be gray in color).

5. If necessary, adjust the indentation level to the same level as the detail tasks above it by using the **Indent** ⇛ and **Outdent** ⇚ tools on the Mini-Toolbar menu that appears when you right-click on the milestone.

The **Task Information** dialog box has a **Mark task as milestone** feature on the **Advanced tab**, but we recommend that you not use this feature. It creates confusion because the task will show the real duration in the Duration field, using this duration for all schedule calculations, and will show a milestone symbol (for example a black diamond) at the end of the task in the Gantt Chart. We recommend that you use a normal task with a duration other than zero to model activities and designate tasks with zero duration to model as milestones.

To open the **Task Information** dialog box, either double-click on the Task name; or select the task and on the **Task** tab, in the **Properties** group, select the **Information** icon ▱.

Use the Advanced tab

Task Information

General | Predecessors | Resources | **Advanced** | Notes | Custom Fields |

Name: Visit the sites   Duration: 0 days ☐ Estimated

Constrain task

Deadline: NA

Constraint type: As Soon As Possible ▼   Constraint date: Tue 8/7/12 ▼

Task type: Fixed Units ▼   ☐ Effort driven

Calendar: None ▼   ☐ Scheduling ignores resource calendars

WBS code: 2.2

Earned value method: % Complete ▼

☐ Mark task as milestone

Leave this box unchecked

Help   OK   Cancel

3

Creating a Hierarchical WBS in Project 2010

Now that you've entered some tasks, you'll want to use indenting and outdenting to create an outline in Project 2010 that reflects the structure of your WBS.

Outlining makes the plan easier to read and understand. It also generates extra aggregate information on the summary tasks. Project 2010 automatically calculates the duration, cost and work fields on the summary tasks. You can immediately see what a deliverable costs. For example, if your deliverables are software features, executives can now compare the efforts and costs associated with the various software features. This is invaluable if tough choices have to be made about which features will make it into a particular software release.

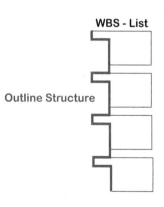

WBS - List

Outline Structure

Summary tasks can be collapsed to hide detail tasks or expanded to reveal them on an as-needed basis, providing just enough detail to perform your analysis or to focus your reports. If you collapse the summary tasks, you have the kind of overview that many executives prefer.

Indenting a Series of Detail Tasks

Select the detail tasks by dragging anywhere over them in the table.

To indent, right-click and select the **Indent** ⇛ icon command from the Mini-Toolbar menu that appears

OR

Hold down [Alt] + [Shift] and press [→].

After indenting, the summary task shows a duration that summarizes all its detail tasks.

Indenting a task cannot be done by inserting spaces in front of the task name. Project 2010 will not recognize this as a lower level subtask, even though it may look like one. Project 2010 also does not allow you to use the [Tab] key to create indentation, as you would in Word and PowerPoint.

Outdenting Tasks

1. Select the tasks by dragging over them in the spreadsheet.

2. To indent, right-click and select the **Outdent** ⇚ icon command from the Mini-Toolbar menu that appears.

   OR

   Hold down [Alt] + [Shift] and press [←].

Indenting and Outdenting by Dragging

You can also indent or outdent tasks by dragging them:

1. Select the tasks by dragging over them in the task table.

2. In the **Task Name** column, point to the first characters of the task name; the mouse pointer changes to a two-headed arrow: ↔. Before proceeding, make sure you see this arrow (and not the mouse pointer ✥).

3. Hold down and drag the task to the right for indenting or to the left for outdenting. A vertical gray line gives you feedback on which outline level it will end up on when you release the mouse. The higher the level, the greater the indentation.

4. Release the mouse button when the gray line appears at the right level of indentation.

To Hide and Re-display Detail Tasks

Click the minus ▬ button in front of the summary task name to hide its detail tasks.

OR

Select the summary task and hold down [Alt] + [Shift] and press [-].

The detail tasks can be displayed again by clicking the plus [+].

OR

Select the summary task and hold down [Alt] + [Shift] and press [+].

To Hide All Detail Tasks

On the **View** tab, in the **Data** group, click **Outline** and select **Outline Level 1** in the list.

OR

1. Click on the heading of any column; the entire column should be highlighted now.

2. On the **View** tab, in the Data group, click **Outline** and select **Hide Subtasks** ➖ in the list. You should now only see the first outline level.

To Reveal the Next Level

Click on the title of any column. On the **View** tab, in the **Data** group, click **Outline** and select + **Show Subtasks** in the list.

OR

On the **View** tab, in the **Data** group, click **Outline** and select the next **Outline Level** to be revealed.

To Reveal a Certain Level

On the **View** tab, in the **Data** group, click **Outline** and select the specific **Outline Level** you want to be revealed.

If you are not sure how Project 2010 counts the levels, insert the column **Outline Level** and study the numbers that Project 2010 displays. The left most level is level 1.

To Reveal All Levels

On the **View** tab, **Data** Group, click on **Outline** 🔲; a list is displayed with the available outline levels. Click the item ➕ **All Subtasks**.

What You Do to a Summary Task, You Do to it's Detail Tasks

It's critical to understand that what you do to a summary task affects all its detail tasks as well. If you delete a summary task, you are deleting its detail tasks as well. The same applies to cutting, copying and indenting.

Outline Numbers

As you enter and edit tasks, Project 2010 automatically assigns each task an **Outline Number**. You can choose to display or hide these numbers in the **Task Name** field:

1. On the **Task** tab, in the **View** group, click **Gantt Chart**. On the **Format** tab in the **Show/Hide** Group, select the **Outline Number** ☑ Outline Number check box.

2. You will now see the **Outline Code** for each task displayed before the task name in the **Task Name** field. Project 2010 will automatically adjust the

Outline Codes if you change the order or indent level of tasks by moving, inserting, deleting, indenting, etc.

WBS Codes

WBS Codes are stored in the **WBS** field. By default, they have the same numbers as Outline Codes.

To display **WBS Codes** you can insert a column in your table:

1. Right-click on the column heading to the right of where you want to insert the new column and select **Insert Column**.

2. Type or select **WBS** from the dropdown that appears.

3. The **WBS** field will be displayed.

Customized WBS Codes

You can't change the Outline Codes assigned by Project 2010. If you want to use a different numbering scheme, you can do this by customizing the WBS Code field.

1. On the **Project** tab, in the **Properties** group, click on **WBS** and select **Define Code**… from the list.

2. The **WBS Code Definition** dialog will be displayed.

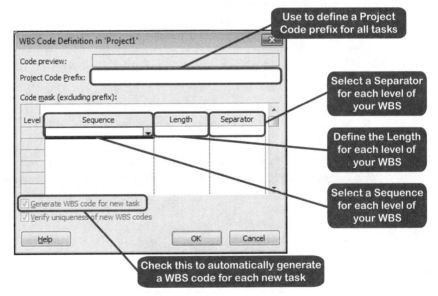

3. If you want a prefix to appear at the beginning of all of your tasks, enter it in **Project Code Prefix**.

 If you're creating task dependencies across projects, or creating consolidated or master projects, the Project Code Prefix is very useful in identifying the subproject.

4. Use the **Code mask** to define the **Sequence**, **Length**, and **Separator** for each level of your WBS:

   ▶ The **Sequence** can be: *Numbers (ordered), Uppercase Letters (ordered), Lowercase Letters (ordered) or Characters (unordered).*

   ▶ You can define any length for each level of your WBS code (if you choose *Any*, Project 2010 will allow any length up to 255 characters).

   ▶ Enter the character that you want to use to separate the WBS code levels. This separator is optional; the default is a period.

5. Check ☑ **Generate WBS code for new task** to have Project 2010 automatically generate a WBS code when you create a new task.

6. Check ☑ **Verify uniqueness of new WBS codes** to have Project 2010 warn you if you enter a WBS code that has already been used.

7. Click [OK].

To display your customized WBS codes:

1. Right-click on the column heading before which to insert the column **WBS**.

2. Type or select **WBS** from the list that appears.

Changing the WBS

Editing a Task Name

You can replace a task name by typing over it. If you need to make small editorial changes (correct a typo), you are better off editing the task name rather than replacing the entire name.

1. Press [F2]. The cursor will blink as a line in the cell, as in the following screenshot: [write report] .

   OR

   Click once in the field and, after one second, click another time and a blinking insertion point will appear in the cell: [write report]

   OR

   Click in the **entry bar** at the top of the screen; the cursor will blink as a vertical line: [✕✓ write report]

2. Move the cursor by clicking with the mouse or by using the **arrow keys** on the keyboard.

   OR

Press ⌂[Home] to jump to the start of the cell and [End] to jump back to the end.

OR

Hold down [Control] and press [←] to jump one word to the left, or [→] to jump to the right.

3. Make the changes.

4. Press [Enter ↵] to accept the changes and finish the editing. The red-cross and green-checkmark buttons ✕✔ in the entry bar should now disappear.

If Project 2010 seems stuck and does not allow you to click on menu items, chances are that you are still in the middle of an editing process and still in Edit Mode. Check if you see blinking insertion points or the red-cross and green-checkmark buttons ✕✔ in the entry bar. Press [Enter ↵] or click on another cell to finish the editing. Now you can proceed to the menu items again. You should return to Ready Mode.

Status Bar The Status Bar displays project status information.

You can view the **Status Bar** at the bottom of the Project 2010 window to see your project status information and the current mode: either **Ready**, **Edit**, or **Busy Mode**, will be displayed. See below:

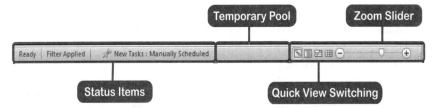

The **Status Bar** consists of three sections:

Status Items: Reports on the status on a property of the project. Now in Project 2010, you will be able to tell if a filter or AutoFilter has been applied and if new tasks are manually scheduled in this section. There are also additional status items that inform you about your connection state to Project Server.

Temporary Pool: Reports on temporary actions that are currently taking place in the project, for example, when the project is being saved or published.

Quick View Switching and Zoom: Allows you to quickly switch to another view and zoom in or zoom out on the timescale. The icons listed to the left of the Zoom Slider are **Gantt Chart**, **Task Usage**, **Team Planner**, and **Resource Sheet**.

Inserting Multiple Tasks

We already discussed how to insert one task; you press [Ins]. To insert multiple tasks:

1. Point to the row heading before which you wish to insert multiple tasks, click and drag down to highlight as many rows as you need inserted.

2. Press [Ins] and the number of rows you highlighted are inserted as blank rows.

 If you insert tasks between linked tasks, Project 2010 may set dependencies automatically if the **Autolink** option is turned on. On the **File** tab, in the **Backstage** view, click on **Options**. In the **Project Options** window select the **Schedule** tab to verify if the option **Autolink inserted or moved tasks** has a checkmark or not. Always check the dependencies after adding, copying or moving tasks (or turn **Autolink** off, if you don't want Project 2010 to think and link for you). See chapter 5 for more information on dependencies and links.

Deleting Tasks

To delete tasks that you don't need, follow these steps:

1. Select the tasks by dragging over their row headings (where you see their **ID** numbers).

2. Right-click on the selection and the **Shortcut Menu** appears, select **Delete Task**

   OR

   Press the **delete** key [Delete]

   OR

3. For auto-scheduled tasks, you can also click the task name instead of the row heading and then press the **delete** key. The delete indicator **Smart Tag** (an "X") appears in the Task's Indicator column.

 Smart Tags are indicators that contain drop-down option buttons to help you make certain adjustments to your project plan. Smart Tags list the action that you have just taken, plus any other possible actions suggested, to help avoid mistakes in uncertain situations. Smart Tags appear when you add, change, or remove resource assignments, change start or finish dates, change work, duration, or units, or delete auto-scheduled tasks or a **Resource** in the Name column.

4. Click on this Smart Tag (an "X") and you can now choose to either delete just the task name (**Only clear the contents of the Task Name Cell**) or the entire task (**Delete the entire task**) from the drop-down menu.

When deleting specific cells, the Smart Tag will only activate when the delete key is pressed for auto-scheduled tasks. Clicking the cell containing the task name on a manually scheduled task and pressing the delete key will delete the contents of the cell but will not bring up the Smart Tag.

5. If you delete only the task name, you can now enter the new task name into the cell, then press enter.

 Note that the [Delete] delete key deletes cells instead of entire rows just like in Excel (unless you selected row headings first). Also remember that when you delete a summary task you delete all of its subtasks.

Copying or Moving Tasks

For copying or moving tasks, it is important to select the entire task (including its fields that are hidden from view). Do this by clicking on its row heading (the first column with the ID numbers and the gray color).

 Clicking on the row heading ensures that you get the entire task row—all fields, including the ones that aren't displayed. It also ensures that you don't accidentally overwrite other tasks. In addition when you click a row number for a summary task, all subtasks are affected and will be copied or moved with it.

The gray color of the first column tells you that the column is locked, which means that:

➤ It will not scroll off the screen
➤ Its data cannot be edited
➤ You can select the entire task by clicking on it

 Some project managers use this locked first column to display the WBS-codes (field **WBS**) instead of the **ID** field. Other project managers lock the **Task Name** column to prevent task names from scrolling off of their screen.

 If the first column is not gray, you will have to lock the column first.

Locking the First Column of a Table

If the first column of the table is not locked, follow these steps:

1. On the **Task** tab, in the **View** group, click **Gantt Chart**. On the **View** tab, **Data** group, select **Tables: <name of the table>**, **More Tables**.

2. Click [Edit...].

3. Check ☑ **Lock first column**.

4. Click [OK] and then [Apply].

5. If you now click on a locked row heading, the whole row should be selected.

Copying Tasks

1. Select the tasks by clicking and dragging over the locked row headings by using the ➡ mouse pointer.

2. Release the mouse button when you have selected all tasks to copy; they are now highlighted.

3. Point to one of the selected row headings and the mouse pointer changes to ⬚. Hold down the [Control] key, and hold down the primary mouse button. The mouse pointer changes to ⬚ where the small plus sign indicates that you are copying. Drag the copied tasks to their new place.

   OR

   Select the row number of the row you want to copy. Right-click to display the **Shortcut Menu** and click **Copy** ⬚ from the list that appears.

   Select the row number where you want to place the copied row. Right-click to display the **Shortcut Menu** and click **Paste** ⬚ from the list that appears.

 To preserve dependencies when copying tasks, on the **File** tab, in the **Backstage** view, click on **Options**, **Schedule**. Clear the ☑ **Autolink inserted or moved tasks**. You should make a habit of checking the dependency links after adding, copying or moving tasks.

Moving Tasks

1. Select the tasks by dragging over locked row headings using the ➡ mouse pointer.

2. Release the mouse button; the tasks should now be highlighted.

3. Point to one of the selected row headings; you should now see this mouse pointer ⬚.

4. Click and hold the primary mouse button; you should now see a changed mouse pointer: ⬚ .

5. Drag the tasks to their new place; a horizontal gray line will indicate where the tasks will be placed when you release the mouse.

   OR

   Right-click on the row number of one of the selected tasks. Click **Cut** ⬚ on the **Shortcut menu** list that appears. The tasks are now temporarily stored in the clipboard.

6. Right-click on the row number where you want to insert the tasks you're moving. Click Paste ⬚ on the **Shortcut menu** list that appears on the **Clipboard** grouping of the **Task** tab on the **Ribbon**. Project 2010 creates new rows and inserts the moved tasks.

To preserve dependencies when moving tasks, on the **File** tab, in the **Backstage View**, click on **Options, Schedule**. Clear ☐ **Autolink inserted or moved tasks**. You should make a habit of checking the dependencies after adding, copying or moving tasks.

To Copy or Move a Summary Family

1. Select the summary task by clicking on its row heading.

2. Hold the ⌈Control⌉ key down to copy.

3. Hold down the primary mouse button and Project 2010 will immediately highlight all its detail tasks and move or copy them as well.

4. Drag the summary task and its subtasks to where you want it.

If you use the clipboard instead, the detail tasks will also be copied or moved.

Importing Tasks

When creating a task list, you may find it useful to import a list created in another program, such as Outlook or Excel. Importing is a time-saving technique that brings information from one software program into another.

In order for Project 2010 to import information in non-default file formats, you first need to allow non-default formats:

1. On the **File** tab, in the **Backstage** view, click on **Options, Trust Center**.

2. Click **Trust Center Settings** to reveal the **Trust Center** dialog then click on **Legacy Formats**.

3. Select one of the following options:

   Prompt when loading files with legacy or non default file format (**medium security**) or *Allow loading files with legacy or non default file formats* (**low security**).

4. Click ⌈ OK ⌉.

To import a file:

1. On the **File** tab, in the **Backstage** view, click on **Open**. The Project 2010 **import wizard** automatically opens when you attempt to open an alternative file format.

2. Specify the location of the file you want to import in the **Look in** menu.

3. Specify the file type (e.g., *Microsoft Excel Workbooks*), or select *All Files* from the **Files of Type** drop-down.

4. Select the file you want to import.

During the import process, Project 2010 will prompt you to match source fields with Project 2010 fields. This is called **mapping**. To simplify the mapping process, predefined maps contain a subset of all of the available fields in Project 2010. Mapping allows you to concentrate on a desired subject area and import only the related fields.

The Import Wizard is designed to work with fields created in the Excel (.xls or .xlsx) format.

Project 2010 also allows you to import from an Outlook task list. However, importing from Outlook generates static data. No link between data in Outlook and data in Project 2010 is created.

Importing and Exporting Tasks using SharePoint 2010

It is not within the scope of this book to address the functionality of SharePoint, (SharePoint Foundation 2010 or SharePoint Server 2010). However, we will address importing and exporting tasks between Project Professional 2010 and SharePoint 2010.

SharePoint Server 2010 offers tools to build business applications to better organize, store, share, and manage digital information within a company.

Importing Tasks from SharePoint 2010 to Project Professional 2010:

If your company has SharePoint installed, you can use SharePoint Foundation 2010 or SharePoint Server 2010 to share information within the enterprise. If you have a SharePoint task list in place, you can import these tasks into Project Professional 2010 to create your WBS, and you can do this without using Project Server 2010.

Exporting Tasks from Project Professional 2010 to SharePoint 2010:

If you are using Project Professional 2010, you can create a new project schedule and export it, saving and syncing the task list to SharePoint Foundation 2010 or SharePoint Server 2010.

After your project has been synced to a SharePoint list, any changes to the task list within Project Professional 2010 will be displayed in the task list on the SharePoint 2010 site, and vice versa.

Syncing more than 1,000 tasks between Project Professional 2010 and SharePoint 2010 is not recommended. If you want to sync more than 1,000 tasks, it is recommended that you use Microsoft Project Server 2010. Even if you have more than 100 tasks, we recommend Project Server 2010 because it is a better solution to manage collaboration.

How to Import a SharePoint Task List into Project

To import a list of tasks from SharePoint 2010 into Project Professional 2010:

1. In Project Professional 2010, click the **File** tab to open the **Backstage** view, click **New**, **New from SharePoint task list**. The **Import SharePoint Tasks List** dialog appears.

2. In the **Site URL** list, select or enter the URL name of the SharePoint site that contains the task list you want to use and then Click **Validate URL**.

3. In the **Tasks List**, select the name of the SharePoint task list you want.

4. Click [OK]

OR

1. In SharePoint 2010, from the SharePoint task list, on the **List Tools**, click **List** and on the **Connect & Export** group click **Open Schedule** button. Project Professional 2010 opens and the dialog window indicates the site you are opening.

2. Click [Yes]. The task list is available in Project Professional 2010 to edit.

Options to **Sync to Tasks Lists** are only available when Project 2010 is not connected to a Project Server.

How to Export and Synchronize Project Tasks to SharePoint

To export project tasks from Project Professional 2010 to SharePoint 2010.

1. In Project Professional 2010, click the **File** tab to open the **Backstage View** and click **Save & Send**.

2. Click **Sync with Tasks Lists**.

3. In the **Site URL** list, select or enter the URL address of the SharePoint site that contains the list that you want to sync to and then Click **Validate URL**.

4. In the **Select an existing tasks** list, select the name of the SharePoint task list to which you want the project tasks list to sync.

If you want to sync the Project task list with a new list in SharePoint, type a new name. A new task list will be created in SharePoint, and will become synced up with the one in Project.

5. Click **Sync**.

After the two task lists are synced, changes to one list will be reflected in the other. If changes are made to the two lists at the same time, a dialog box appears that prompts you to decide which version of the change you want to keep.

 After the two task lists are synced, you can go the SharePoint version of the task list from Project. Click the **File** tab, click **Info**. In the **Sync to Tasks Lists** section, click the link to the SharePoint site.

Checks on the WBS for Your Project

Here's a quick checklist you can use to evaluate your WBS in Project 2010:

➤ Are there deliverables in the WBS and are the deliverables complete, but lean?

➤ Does the WBS have a **logical hierarchy**?
  ▶ Is the WBS an indented list with multiple hierarchical levels instead of a long list without structure?
  ▶ Does each **summary task** have at least two subtasks?
  ▶ Is there any duplication or logical overlap between deliverables?
  ▶ Does each group of subtasks capture all the work of their summary task (top-down check)?
  ▶ Does each item **logically** relate to its summary tasks on all higher levels (bottom-up check)?
  ▶ Is the **Project Summary Task** (row 0) used instead of a physical project summary task?

➤ Are there enough milestones—roughly one for each summary task? You can check this by applying the standard filter **Milestones.**

➤ Does the WBS have the right level of detail?
  ▶ Is it clear how deliverables will be created and what the activities involved are?
  ▶ Is the WBS lean enough that you'll be able to update all detail tasks in the schedule during project execution?
➤ Is the WBS clear to all project stakeholders?

Review Questions

1. What is the definition of a WBS according to PMI's *PMBOK® Guide Fourth Edition*?

2. Why is the WBS an important project tool?

3. What is a deliverable and why is it important that your WBS be deliverable-oriented?

4. What are the differences between a to-do list and a WBS?

5. Why is using consistent naming conventions for your deliverables, activities and milestones important?

6. How do you know you have found the appropriate level of detail in your WBS? Why is finding the right level of detail important?

7. How has the copy and paste of tasks between Microsoft applications and Project 2010 gotten easier?

8. What is the difference between manually-scheduled tasks and auto-scheduled tasks in the schedule? What are some of the advantages that manually-scheduled tasks offer? What are some of the disadvantages?

9. Why would it be beneficial to export task lists to SharePoint 2010 with Project Professional 2010?

Additional Practice For experience working with the features you've learned about in this chapter, we strongly suggest that you do the additional exercises for this chapter that are included in Appendix 1.

Chapter 4: Entering Estimates

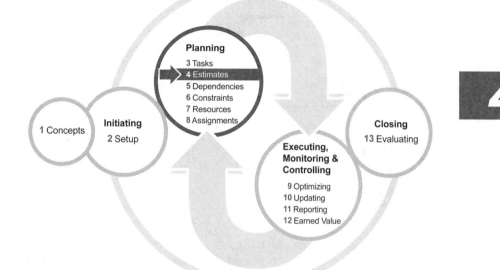

Now that we have the work breakdown structure including the activities (tasks) entered into our project schedule, our next step is to enter estimates: predictions for how much time each task will take to complete. Accurate estimates—estimates with a high probability of being actualized—are the goal.

After reading this chapter you will be able to:

➤ Discuss the human tendencies in estimating and techniques to handle them
➤ Discuss the practical difficulties in estimating and techniques to address them
➤ Apply the rolling wave approach
➤ Define the difference between pure and gross work time estimates
➤ Define buffers and discuss the tradeoffs between hiding them and leaving them visible in the schedule
➤ Employ a process for generating estimates
➤ Define duration and work/effort estimates
➤ Use Project 2010 to:
　▶ Enter activities with incomplete estimates
　▶ Enter duration and work estimates
　▶ Set the appropriate task type and effort-driven settings for specific estimates

Yes… after careful analysis, I think you and your team
should be able to finish this in four months!

> ▶ Describe Project 2010's scheduling formula and its importance when estimating (D * U = W)
> ▶ Differentiate between task bar style formats
> ▶ Create milestones, split tasks and recurring tasks
> ▶ Enter, move and copy data efficiently
> ▶ Check the estimates of your project schedule using best scheduling practices

"How do we estimate?" is the question we are asked most often in our project management courses. Estimating is one of the most difficult skills in project management. It is particularly difficult when you or your team:

➤ Have little or no experience with the work

➤ Have incomplete or nonexistent knowledge of deliverables and acceptance criteria

➤ Have to estimate for tasks with uncertain outcomes, like many research and development tasks

How can you know how much effort it will take to do something if you have never done it before or if you don't really know what you are to deliver? How can you map out the latter stages of a project if they depend entirely on the results of research you are currently conducting?

And if the work is to be performed by people you don't know, how can you estimate effort if you don't know their skill levels and capacities?

The Human Tendencies in Estimating

To answer these questions, let's start with exploring the human side of estimating.

People tend to:

> Not want to commit themselves when there is uncertainty
> Work better when they estimate their own work and are involved in setting their own deadlines
> Be overly optimistic about what they can do

It is accepted project management practice that the person who is most familiar with the work involved in an activity should make the estimate for that activity. In general, this is the person who will actually be doing the work.

Someone who hasn't performed a task before may naturally be reluctant to provide you with an estimate. Estimating is a skill, and the only way to acquire a skill is through practice. As a project manager, you should be a mentor for novice estimators: coach them through the process of making estimates and make sure they check the accuracy of their estimates after the work is done.

This is not only how your team will improve their estimating skills, it's also the process through which team members increase their sense of ownership of and commitment to their work. People are more likely to meet deadlines that they set for themselves.

Here are four common problems that you're likely to encounter in the estimating process:

> "I can't predict the future!' from team members
> "I am always off!" from team members
> "Can't you do it?" from executives and sales representatives
> "What is the date you'll be done?" from project managers

"I Can't Predict the Future!"

Team members often have difficulty coming up with estimates, particularly if they are new to estimating or to the types of tasks to which they're assigned.

As an experienced project manager, why not just supply the estimate yourself? Do this and if a task is late, you're likely to hear: "I never told you I'd have it done by that date; you came up with that yourself!" You really want to get estimates from your team members; they have to "own" them, and then own up to them.

Ask your team members to provide a range of estimates rather than a single estimate. Get three estimates: a most likely estimate, a pessimistic estimate and an optimistic estimate.

> ➤ The most likely estimate is the estimate that has a high probability of being accurate, given normal circumstances. Questions to solicit good "most likely" estimates might be: "What is the expected estimate?" or "To feel confident that you can accomplish the task, how long would it take you?"

> ➤ The pessimistic estimate answers the question, "How long would it take if more than the usual number of things went wrong?" Make sure your team understands that this is not the same as a worst case estimate. If you ask for a worst case estimate, people will tend to consider extreme and extremely unlikely situations (e.g., natural disasters).

> ➤ The third estimate is an optimistic estimate: "If many things go smoothly, how long would it take you?" or "What would be an aggressive estimate?"

Asking for more than one estimate gives you a better idea of what to expect. It forces the estimator to think about the assumptions he or she is making and to evaluate risks and uncertainties. It also helps you determine how much buffer you may want to apply to the duration estimate. Best of all, range estimates are much easier for people to make, particularly when you deal with people who want to get it right. A three-point estimate also allows you to do a PERT analysis, or apply a Monte Carlo simulation to the schedule. We will be discussing Monte Carlo in chapter 9. (Monte Carlo simulation is not done in Project 2010 except through the use of third-party software.) As we mentioned in the Introduction, PERT is no longer automatically calculated by Project 2010; however, you can use custom fields and create this formula if you desire (custom fields and formulas will be discussed in chapter 11).

When you ask someone for a range of estimates, also ask for the assumptions he is making for each point in the range. This will help you evaluate the validity of the estimate.

And finally, make it clear that you are not looking for a guarantee, just a good sense of how much time and effort will be required under different conditions.

Remember that estimates are not actuals. If a target date is not quite met, forgive the estimator and help her learn for the future by finding out why it wasn't met. Making errors is human, but not learning from them is truly regrettable.

"I Am Always Off!"   People are optimistic or pessimistic by nature, and this can greatly affect their estimating. Many estimating gurus have found that estimators tend to be more optimistic than pessimistic.

You may gain a rough insight into people's tendencies by studying their track records from previous projects. You can get a quick impression if you look in the **Actual Work** field and compare it to the **Baseline Work** field of a finished project. (Since the numbers are aggregated from all of the team member's tasks, the more estimates the person has made correctly, the more confidence you can have in a tendency to err.)

While this analysis may give you an idea about a person's estimating accuracy, the key to improving that accuracy is to find out what assumptions the person is making and what other causes of variance there might be.

A pattern of inaccuracy often indicates that the estimator is making unconscious assumptions that are consistently wrong. What are the assumptions? What are the habitual behaviors that cause the variance?

 People tend to be consistent in their tendency toward optimistic or pessimistic estimates until they see the **reasons** for their errors. Once you have learned the tendencies of your team members, you can look into making sure that they are aware of the assumptions they are using to arrive at their estimates.

"Can't You Do It?" We have seen organizations get stuck in scheduling a project when they use estimates produced by people other than the people who do the work. Examples of people who tend to produce these "estimates" are:

➤ Executives and upper management: "Can't you do it in two weeks?"
Project managers know the stress that occurs when executives impose their "estimates" on a project. You're put in a double bind position: you are in trouble if you do commit to their estimates and in trouble if you don't.

Estimates from executives should really be treated as targets, not as estimates. Enter these as deadlines in Project 2010 and then create a detailed schedule. If you sincerely feel the work cannot be done in the timeframe requested, report this back to the executive. With your detailed schedule in hand, you'll be able to make a clearer, stronger case for more rational deadlines. In short, push back and negotiate.

➤ Sales representatives: "The client gets what she wants."
Project managers know the disastrous effects that occur when salespeople present their own "estimates" to a client without consulting you. You cannot win in such a situation. These "estimates" are not estimates; they are commitments to please the client and win a sale, often at the project manager's and the team's expense.

➤ "PIT" estimating teams. Some larger companies have something like a "PIT" Team, or a "Project Initiation Team". These teams create all of the estimates for projects in the corporation and then hand them off to the project manager. Sometimes, they don't even know the team members or complexities of the tasks involved. Yet the project manager is expected to follow these estimates and deliver the project on time, usually without input.

Unknown Resources

During the planning phase it is often unclear whether enough resources will be available, who those resources will be, and whether they'll be available when needed.

Despite these uncertainties, you still need to make assumptions for planning purposes: otherwise, you can't develop a schedule. One common assumption project managers make is that resources will be available when they are needed. Of course, it is a good idea to discuss your resource needs with the resource manager, HR or your executives as a reality check on this assumption. Make the assumption loud, clear and explicit in the project plan, so no one's lack of memory will come back to haunt you.

If you don't know the names of your team members, enter them in terms of their roles. For example, instead of "Illeana", you simply enter "Purchasing Manager." This allows you to make your estimates, and enter resources and assignments as well. You can now produce a detailed schedule. Once you know the names of the individuals, there are simple techniques to update your schedule to reflect this.

Entering a role instead of an individual's name is an example of a generic resource. Generic resources are placeholders for specifically named resources. In Project 2010, you can define generic resources on the resource sheet by setting the field **Generic** to **Yes**. Although setting the field is not required, this allows you to generate views that display accumulated workload estimates which could be useful in staffing decisions. If you anticipate replacing the role with a specific resource name, we recommend you list generics that represent individuals instead of representing consolidated resources which are more difficult to replace.

Earlier we said that it is best to have the performer make the estimate. That is not always possible and if estimates are made before resources have been assigned, the estimates should be reviewed and accepted by the performer.

Unknown Experience and Skill Level

Even if you know who will be doing a particular job, you may not know much about that person's experience or skill levels. This creates a challenge for estimating because as the project manager you should look not only at the job, but also at who will do the job, since this has a significant impact on estimates and your schedule.

Unknown Learning Curves

Learning curve theory states that the time needed for performing a task will decrease with each repetition until it reaches an optimum pace. Learning curves are considerations both in estimating and in making resource assignments.

Because each project is by definition unique, some say that the effect of the learning curve in projects is limited. Still, learning plays an important role: because each project is new, participants have to be willing to learn.

Research and development projects and product development projects are prime examples in which learning plays a key role. There are some repetitive tasks in all projects, for example preparing status reports and time sheets and performing quality control. And in some projects, there is a lot of repetition. For example, in an implementation project, the same system might be installed in many different locations.

Together, the amount of learning and the lack of repetition in projects imply that resources hired on projects should be very fast learners. The ability to learn quickly is perhaps even the most important characteristic of good project resources.

Fast learners (B and C in the illustration on the left) have a learning curve that has a steep slope down. The second time they repeat something, the time needed goes down fast. Fast learners can also end up with a faster time per deliverable after many repetitions than slow learners (compare the horizontal dotted lines for A and B). However, it is not a

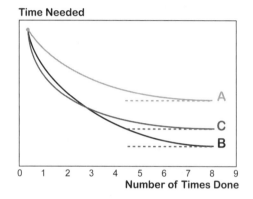

given that the fastest time possible per deliverable is eventually lower for fast learners. To see this, compare the horizontal lines for B and C.

Because of the lack of repetition in projects, the initial learning rate seems to be more important than the eventual fastest time per unit for most projects. We therefore recommend you that you try to retain people with a C learning curve—fast learners—for your projects. We also recommend that you manage the knowledge in your environment to enable the slower learners to be more productive more quickly.

An exception is implementation projects where there are many repetitions of the same activities (e.g., installing software in a number of locations). Here you probably want resources who have learning curve B instead of C, because B resources will eventually be the fastest, whereas C learners may become bored by frequent repetition.

So remember, look not only at the job, but also at who will do the job in order to produce a good estimate. How much repetition does the job have? Is the resource a slow or a fast learner? How can you maximize the learning by mixing fast and slow learners on an implementation team? You may have to make some assumptions about the learning rates of your resources. Make these assumptions explicit in your project plan. Otherwise you may end up with a slow learner (and be blamed for late delivery). In addition, if you don't document how you arrived at your estimates, you won't be able to learn from the discrepancies between your original plan and actual execution.

Living Document Approach

As we've seen, there are many unknowns in projects: events, resources, experience and skill levels, and learning curves. A common way to deal with these unknowns is to make assumptions and treat the project plan as a living document. An assumption is something you treat as true just for estimating purposes.

 We urge you to document the assumptions on which you base your estimates: if any of your assumptions change, you have a more supportable position for revising your estimate.

With the living document approach your detailed project plan is not finished and final until the project is closed. The project plan "lives": you keep reviewing your assumptions, and refining your task list, estimates and assignments during the entire project life. Rolling wave is one example of how the living document approach can be implemented.

 Note that most often, the high-level project plan does not change in a living document approach; the scope and quality requirements, the major deadlines and the budget may not change at all. The baseline may not change. Changes in the high-level project plan only happen through a formal approval process that typically involves your executives and clients. In the living document approach, changes happen at the lower levels of detail.

 Plan at a high level and later expand the estimate (rolling wave). For example, enter a manually scheduled summary task and an estimate for the summary until you are able to elaborate on the details. As the project continues, you can review the duration considering the detail tasks against the duration you have initially estimated for the manually scheduled summary task.

Pure Work Time or Gross Work Time?

Pure work time is working 100% of your time with 100% focus on the project task. Pure work time is 100% productive time without interruptions.

Gross work time includes time spent on things other than project tasks.

It's your job as project manager to make sure your team understands whether you want them to provide estimates expressed in pure work time or gross work time. Particularly if work is to be billed to a client, it has to be very clear what should and shouldn't be included in estimates.

People spend their time at work on three basic types of activities:

➤ Project tasks (pure work time for project planning purposes)

➤ Non-project, but work-related tasks, for example:
  ▸ Operational tasks
  ▸ Answering e-mails and phone calls that don't pertain to the project
  ▸ Blogging on the company website
  ▸ Company meetings (for example, on employee benefits)
  ▸ Professional development training (not project-related)
  ▸ Providing emotional or technical support for colleagues
  ▸ Introducing and training new staff
  ▸ Changing into the company uniform
  ▸ Troubleshooting and answering support calls (helpdesk)
  ▸ Debugging released versions of software applications (hot fixes, service packs)

➤ Non work-related activities (personal time), for example:
  ▸ Private telephone calls
  ▸ Chats with colleagues and other passers-by
  ▸ Daydreaming
  ▸ Visits to the washroom, water fountain, coffee pot and fridge
  ▸ Updating social networking sites
  ▸ Celebratory lunches for colleagues
  ▸ Sick leave
  ▸ Vacation days (this is a special case that can be captured separately in Project 2010 on the resource calendar)

All the listed items are included in gross work time. At IIL, our course participants tell us that only about 70% of gross work time is spent on project work (pure work time), although this percentage can vary significantly from industry to industry. If you don't take the difference between gross and pure work time into account, you'll underestimate the time needed to complete tasks and your projects will always be late. Therefore, it is important that you incorporate gross work time in your project schedule.

For gross working time, estimates should be entered in the schedule with gross working hours (typically 8:00 AM – 5:00 PM).

For pure work time working hours correspond to a shorter working day, for example, 8:00 AM –3:00 PM.

Let's say your normal workday has 8 hours. If you estimate that the productive hours are 70% of the hours worked, the working hours should be 70% * 8h = 5.6 hours, rounded to 5.5 hours (68.75%). Working hours that correspond to this are, for example, 9:00 AM –-12:00 PM and 1:00 PM – 3:30 PM. We prefer that you set working hours like these on the Project Calendar. You can set other working times, as long as the total number of hours adds up to 5.5.

It is important that:

➤ All team members estimate consistently in either pure work time or gross work time; you cannot use a mix of the two.

➤ Every estimator has the same understanding of what a "gross working time estimate" or "pure working time estimate" means. For example, some organizations include non-project, work-related time in "pure" working time estimates, though most exclude it.

➤ Whatever basis the team uses for estimates is also used for time sheets of actual hours. Otherwise, you can't compare your estimates to actuals.

 ➤ You consider whether you want the costs in your project to be calculated based upon pure work estimates or gross work estimates. The cost of pure work estimates may be lower than you want to report, since personal time is typically included in cost estimates to clients or executives. If you use pure work estimates, you may need to apply a multiplication factor to correct for this.

Of the thousands of schedules we've evaluated, an estimated 80% used gross working time estimates and gross working times on the Project Calendar. Particularly if you use your schedule for developing cost estimates, it is important to use the gross working time system. However, if your team members have a large portion of non-project work (like operations, maintenance and technical support), gross estimates may be too rough from a cost perspective. In that case, you may want to exclude these from the gross estimates and include the rest of the non-project work factors. Effort on the excluded tasks is tracked outside of the project and team members bill only time spent on included work.

Whenever you get or give a date forecast, ask questions like these to help determine the accuracy of the estimate:

➤ Is this estimate based on 100% fully focused work time or does it include the normal workday interruptions like e-mail and voice mail?

➤ Do you have other ongoing responsibilities that will take time as well, like providing technical support, help-desk duties, troubleshooting, other projects, attending meetings or training?

➤ Do you have any personal commitments or other work commitments that will take time out of your workday?

➤ Are there any gaps where you will have to wait for other tasks to deliver results you need?

> ➤ Is the effort estimate accurate?

> ➤ What are the unknowns and risks that might impact the ability to deliver?

Standardize your schedule on either pure or gross work time and ask your team to provide a specific type of estimate. This ensures a consistent schedule.

Project 2010 is set up by default to receive gross work time estimates based on 8 hours for a full workday, because the default working times are 8:00 AM – 12:00 PM and 1:00 PM – 5:00 PM.[2] If everybody estimates in gross work time based on 8 hours per day, you don't have to change the default settings in Project 2010; in any other case, you do have to make changes.

If you want to work with pure work time estimates, you have to do one of the following:

> ➤ You can adjust the working times for everybody in the **Project Calendar** by choosing **Change Working Time** 📅 on the **Project** tab. Here you simply shorten the working times. For example, if you believe that your resources are productive on project work for 75% of the day, you could change the working times to reflect 75% of an 8 hour day or 6 hours. This could be entered on the Project Calendar as: 9AM – 12PM and 1PM – 4PM.
> ➤ Another solution is to decrease everybody's availability from 100% to less than 100%. If you have found that people are productive 75% of their work time, you have to enter this as their availability in the Max Units field in the Resource Sheet (refer to chapter 7 for a discussion on setting resource availability).

Before we discuss techniques for entering estimates, it's important to cover a sometimes controversial issue that arises on almost every project: the appropriate use of buffers.

Buffers

For purposes of this discussion, we'll define buffers as additional time added to the project schedule to allow for unforeseen events. It's generally accepted project management practice that project managers who are responsible for meeting hard deadlines include a buffer in their projects in order to mitigate risk. Questions sometimes arise about whether and how these buffers should be communicated to project stakeholders. That is the focus of the following discussion.

Measure Planning and Performance?

Performance measurement involves not only the quality of the project's performance with respect to the plan, but also the quality of the planning itself. Both the baseline and the performance relative to the baseline are products of the project manager. For example, if a project manager deliberately pads his

---

2   Times are for the English USA version of Project 2010. Other international versions may have different default standard working times.

schedule by 50% and then boasts that he delivered his project in 30% less time, is this good performance or poor planning? We think the latter.

Executives can't measure performance by itself; they need to measure the quality of the planning as well. Executives need to be involved in the planning process to make sure they have a solid grasp of the project's baseline. With a good baseline, an executive can delegate the execution phase and measure the project's real performance with confidence.

Eliminate Hidden Time Buffers

When you optimize a schedule, you may find you have a healthy amount of time as a buffer to accomplish the deadline. This buffer helps compensate for risk. How to display the buffer can be a difficult choice. If you show the buffer, you may lose it. If you hide the buffer, you enter into a game of secrecy, and you may have to do double bookkeeping with your schedule. We recommend you consider the following:

➤ What is the dominant pulling force in the project?
Is the project driven by time, cost, quality or availability of resources? If time is the dominant force, everybody will be scrutinizing your schedule to find time. The more people who look for it, the less the chance you will succeed in keeping any buffer hidden.

➤ How mature is upper management in terms of project management?
Does management accept that as the project manager, you should own a buffer to meet the hard deadlines? It is generally accepted project management practice that project managers who are responsible for meeting hard deadlines own a buffer in their projects. However, upper management may not understand that the buffer is there as a legitimate assist for managing risk and may wish to remove it.

➤ If you are performing work for an external client, what type of contract do you have?
If you have a time and materials contract, the client will likely be looking over your shoulder, and you won't need a buffer at all. If the contract is a firm fixed price contract, you may need a buffer that you discuss with the client in terms of mitigating risks.

Methods That Have Been Used To Hide Buffers

We strongly support clearly showing buffers and educating everyone in what they mean and why they are important. The following are methods that have been used to hide buffers. Most of them are the opposite of the optimizing methods that will be discussed in chapter 9. They are ranked in order of ascending sophistication. The likelihood that a buffer will stay hidden from examining eyes increases as you move down the list:

1. **Overestimating lags**

   Lags are gaps between task bars of dependent tasks. They model waiting time that is out of your control, as when you are waiting to receive a construction permit. Some prefer to estimate these lags on the (very) safe side. However, they can easily be noticed in the Gantt Chart. This method is cost neutral.

2. **Inserting extra holidays in the Project Calendar**

   You can insert extra common holidays in the Project Calendar. The task bars that span these days will simply stretch. This can be noticed in the Gantt Chart by sharp analysts. This method is cost neutral.

3. **Decreasing the working hours in the Project Calendar**

   Resources are not focused and productive throughout an 8 hour workday. In the Project Calendar, start the business day later or finish it earlier. This may make the calendar inconsistent with the Hours per day setting in the Project Options dialog box. Durations may start to show decimals and will be obvious. This method is cost neutral.

4. **Ignoring the benefits of learning curves**

   If you have repetitive activities in your schedule, you will likely benefit from the decreasing learning time with every repetition. Your estimate should be lower with every repeat. If you ignore this effect of the learning curve, you are in fact keeping a buffer in your schedule. The cost of the project will be overstated with this method.

5. **Introducing ramp-up and wind-down factors**

   If your resources are involved in more than one project at a time, your resources will be less productive because of setting up and closing down work when moving from project to project. You can include this time in your estimates, which will also affect the cost.

6. **Introducing distraction factors for high-focus tasks**

   Certain tasks require full focus, but the world around will not stop spinning. Writing a report or a book is a situation in which most people need to concentrate fully and need consecutive, uninterrupted time.

7. **Introducing extra revision cycles**

   Every revision cycle has two tasks: *revise* and *modify*. For writing, you could add tasks like *edit* and *rewrite*. You might even get away with another cycle of re-edit and re-re-write, but you may want to call it something else. Inserting extra revision cycles increases the cost as well, but could have a positive impact on quality.

8. **Keeping maximum units of resources low**

   In a resource-constrained schedule you can influence the forecasted project end date by changing the availability of resources (Max Units). If you are not entirely sure how many you will receive, you can create a time buffer in your schedule if you keep the maximum units on the low and safe side. This will only affect the duration of the project, not the cost.

9. **Assigning one scarce expert to more tasks than needed**

If an expert is in great demand, he will likely drive the project finish date. If you assign him to more tasks than strictly needed, he will drive out the forecasted finish date even further, thus creating a time buffer for you. It is hard to argue with using the best resource on many tasks. If the expert is paid at a higher rate than other resources, you are also increasing the cost.

10. **Creating extra inconspicuous tasks**

One project manager confided that she adds the task F*ind alternative resources* in the task list wherever it is appropriate. Others that are hard to argue with are *Apply quality check* or *Update the project plan*. These extra tasks increase the cost as well.

11. **Padding the duration and work estimates**

As one project manager once put it, "To pad or not to pad" is similar to the Shakespearian "To be or not to be". However, if you start padding, you are entering into a culture of secrecy. Padding also increases cost.

12. **Not using overtime yet**

If you know you can count on your resources working some overtime, don't enter it into the schedule during the planning phase. Whenever your team members work a weekend, the 2 days will be pure gain. Be careful with this method if you pay a higher rate for overtime, since the planned cost of the project may be understated because it is based on regular rates. You may gain time but run over budget. Also, be aware of the impact on the team member who works too many overtime hours. This can affect quality, morale, and in the end have negative impacts on time and cost.

13. **Setting extra soft dependencies**

Soft dependencies are dependencies that are not absolutely needed, but can be defended with an argument such as: "We prefer to do it this way, because it has the following advantage ..." and you rationalize away. This method is cost neutral.

14. **Being pessimistic about material delivery dates**

When you are dependent upon receiving a shipment before you can do your work, you can create a delivery milestone on a date later than the date you were promised by the supplier. In this way you create some buffer on the performance of others on whom you depend. Now you face a new dilemma: Will you tell your supplier? This method is cost neutral.

15. Inserting extra holidays for your critical resources

Determine who the most critical resources are in your schedule and insert extra holidays in their resource calendars. This cannot be easily seen in the Gantt Chart and is a very sophisticated way of hiding buffer time. This method is cost neutral.

As you may have noticed, all these methods boil down to not fully optimizing your schedule. In our opinion you should not hide your buffers. Hiding buffers tends to obscure when resources will actually be needed and obscures the true return on investment in the project. We acknowledge that the practice takes place and we have discussed some of the methods employed. That said, let's move forward with our suggestions and reasons for making buffers visible.

Why You Should Make Buffers Visible

As we've stated, we strongly recommend that you keep the buffer you own visible in your schedule. There are several reasons for this:

➤ It is the professional thing to do, because it is generally accepted project management practice that when upper management asks project managers to commit to hard deadlines, project managers are allowed to own time buffers.

➤ Hiding time buffers from executives creates a culture of secrecy in projects. If the different levels of management stop communicating openly with each other, the situation worsens over time. Ideally, the time and money buffers should be on the table instead of under it. If a project manager habitually hides time buffers and an executive happens to find out, the executive may start cutting time off future schedules. In turn, the project manager will then hide bigger buffers in harder to find places. The executive may start slashing the schedules more, making arbitrary cuts. The situation deteriorates in a downward spiral. As consultants, we have witnessed organizations that continuously play this game, instead of conducting projects in an open and professional manner. If you think you can defend the buffer in your project successfully, we recommend you do that. Openness is greatly preferred over a culture of secrecy that can create a vicious downward spiral.

➤ Your team members will follow your example as the project manager and start hiding their buffers from you.
If you pad your schedule estimates, your team will almost certainly follow your lead and start padding the estimates and time sheets they give you. Like it or not, you are leading by example. This will make it impossible to come out ahead of schedule, and at best, you will finish on time. More likely, you will finish a little late every time, which is typical for a culture of secrecy that may have developed slowly over a long period within your organization. From a statistical point of view, it is abnormal if your projects always run a bit late. Statistically, it is normal if several projects run over and

several under, some much over and some much under. This is typical for a healthy organization where a culture of openness and integrity reigns.

➤ If project managers hide time money buffers, their organizations never get clarity on the true return on investment, true profit margins and true time-to-market gains. It's important to know how much you contributed as a project manager to the bottom line. That would be a point to talk about during your performance appraisal.

Defending Visible Buffers

There are several ways for project managers who want to be professionally responsible to defend buffers that are explicitly visible in the schedule:

➤ First make sure that you understand the appropriate use of buffers. Read up on risk mitigation and reserves (for example in the *PMBOK Guide – Fourth Edition*) so that you're prepared to defend your buffers.

➤ Then make sure that your executives understand what buffers are for and why they're needed. Talk to them about the uncertainty and risks (both known and unknown) that are a part of every project, and the setting aside of time reserves for protection.

➤ Draw a parallel between financial and time reserves: monetary budgets have financial reserves as a generally accepted budgeting practice. Why can't schedules have time reserves?

➤ Create a separate line item for the time buffer in the task list instead of leaving it as an undefined, gaping hole in your schedule. You can assign yourself as the resource, so it becomes clear to everybody that you own it (this also adds a buffer of effort and cost). Make sure this line item is dependent on the last tasks. Set the project end milestone as its sole successor.

➤ Name the time buffer line item *Time Contingency Reserve* which is a technical term that may lend weight to the idea that this is a formal item, which they may be less likely to question.

➤ Split a large buffer into smaller ones that you spread across your schedule. Visually, this will look more acceptable and it also allows you to tie the buffers to areas that are prone to more risk and need a buffer to protect the project's delivery date.

➤ Use a Monte Carlo simulation to demonstrate that you need a reasonable time buffer. You can use simulation to create a probability curve of project end dates. When you have the curve, you can decide which probability you feel comfortable with and find out what buffered end date results. This indicates how much time you need as a buffer. Or you can ask upper management with what level of confidence they feel comfortable and quote the corresponding date from the S-curve. You then add the buffer as a line item that makes the schedule extend to this date.

➤ If executives still try to cut your time buffer, you may respond in a number of ways. One way is simply to recognize that you have been open and honest about the risks and now your role is to do the best you can to manage your project to a successful completion.

Entering Estimates in Project 2010

Entering Activities with Incomplete Estimates

Getting started with estimating can be difficult when you are not able to gather all the information necessary to generate a valid estimate for a task. In this situation, you should create an unscheduled activity. This is done by switching the task mode to manually scheduled . In the **Task Mode** column of the desired task, simply select **manually scheduled** from the list. Next, enter the task name in the field **Name** and a note in the field **Duration**. For example, *tbd* or *Ask Amit*. You could also create an unscheduled activity by entering a note in the **Start** or **Finish** fields.

 Manually scheduled tasks display a push pin in the Task Mode column. If the task is missing either the duration, start, or finish information, you will see a push pin with a question mark in the Task Mode column.

The note you left in the duration field will provide a reminder to you that further planning will be required. Notice the task mode is set to manually scheduled. Both bottom-up and top-down planning support unscheduled activities. Top-down planning lets you create a summary task, a series of indented detail tasks and lets you provide a note in the summary task duration to indicate that perhaps your proposed project phase might be 10 weeks even through you have only entered the details to tasks within that phase for the first 2 weeks.

An unscheduled task or manually scheduled task is not driven by the scheduling engine.

 When using the rolling wave approach to planning your schedule, create unscheduled tasks to represent activities that will occur in the future and are difficult to plan until after the planning window has moved forward.

To switch the task mode back to auto scheduled, in the **Task Mode** column of the desired task, simply select **Auto Scheduled** from the list. Notice the fields where you entered notes are reset to default values.

Duration and Work Effort

Duration is the number of units of calendar time (e.g., business days) it will take to complete a task. Work effort is the number of resource units (e.g., person days) it will take to complete a task.

Here's an example of the difference between duration and work effort: If you have 3 carpenters working for 2 business days, the duration is 2 business days, and the work effort is 6 person days (3 carpenters x 2 business days).

As the project manager, you will most likely know either the duration estimate or the work estimate. You can make your estimates in terms of the duration of a task or the work effort required to perform a task. The duration is based upon the time for the task, which may include other factors like non-project work. The work effort is based solely on the deliverable and does not include non-project work.

Duration or Business Day Estimates Entered in the Duration Field

Task duration is typically expressed in business hours or in business days.

You enter a duration estimate in the field **Duration**. The default time unit for duration is days. By default, a business day has 8 hours in Project 2010, but you can change this on the **File** tab, in the **Backstage** View, click on ⊞ Options, **Schedule**.

Assuming the default of 8 hours per day, to enter a duration of five days (1 week), you could type any of the following:
- ➤ 5 days
- ➤ 5d
- ➤ 5
- ➤ 1w

Notice that while Project 2010 displays durations as days and not as business days, it will help you if you think of the duration as the number of business days (to distinguish them from calendar or elapsed days, which we'll cover below).

You cannot assign a duration to a summary task when it is auto scheduled. Instead, Project 2010 will calculate this based on the duration of its detail tasks. For example, suppose a summary task has two detail tasks scheduled in parallel. One task has a duration of 5 days, the other 8 days. The summary task would indicate a duration of 8 days—the duration of the longer task because the other is being performed at the same time.

In the Project Calendar you can find which days are working days and which are non-working days. Project 2010 uses the business days provided in the duration column to determine the finish dates on auto scheduled tasks and to create the Gantt bars for these tasks.

Work Effort or Person Day Estimates Entered in the Work Field

Work is the amount of effort applied directly to the task. It may also be referred to as person hours, or person days as it represents one person working full-time for one hour or one day. For example, if you have to write 20 pages of text and it takes you 2 hours per page, the total work or effort is 20 * 2 = 40 hours. This would also be the number of person hours because you are working on the task yourself. If you have help to perform this task (from someone working at the same pace), so that each of you would only have to write 10 pages, the total work would still be 40 hours because each person would be spending 20 hours on his/her section of the task.

 When we estimate the amount of Work, we are estimating the effort it would take one person to complete the task while working fulltime.

You enter a work effort estimate in the task-related field Work in Project 2010. (Refer to Preparing the Gantt Chart for instructions on how to insert the Work field later in this chapter.) The default time unit of the Work field is Hours. To enter effort of 16 hours on a task, you could type:

➤ 16 hours
➤ 16h
➤ 16
➤ 2d (Project 2010 will convert 2d into the default time unit of hours).

 Project 2010 displays work estimates in the Work field as hours and not as person hours.

Person hour estimates are needed to calculate the cost of the project. Each person hour applied needs to be multiplied by the appropriate rate to arrive at the cost.

Calendar Days: Elapsed Time

Another key concept to understand is the calendar day. Calendar days are the number of consecutive days or 24-hour periods, which could include Saturdays, Sundays or nonworking days. For example, if paint dries in 2 days, the number of calendar days is 2. The number of calendar days needed is not dependent on the working times, since paint dries during the night and weekend as well.

Calendar days are also known in Project 2010 as elapsed days. Project 2010 does not have a field that corresponds to elapsed days; however, you can easily modify the Duration field to indicate elapsed days.

A working day has 8 hours for most of us, whereas an elapsed day has 24 hours and may be either a working or nonworking day.

Examples where elapsed days are important include backing up a computer system or the drying of paint. At food companies, new products are shelved for months in order to test food preservation procedures. These months are elapsed months: they continue 24 hours and 7 days a week.

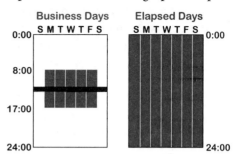

If you want to enter an elapsed duration in the Duration field, you have to specify the time unit as follows:

Time unit	Enter normally as	Enter in elapsed time as
Minutes	*m*	*em*
Hours	*h*	*eh*
Days	*d*	*ed*
Weeks	*w*	*ew*
Months	*mo*	*emo*

Instead of typing in "5d" to get 5 days, you have to enter "5ed" to get 5 elapsed days, which would always represent 5 consecutive days on the calendar.

In chapter 6 you'll learn that you can create Task Calendars for tasks that need to operate on a different schedule from your Project Calendar. However, we recommend that you use elapsed duration instead of creating a new calendar for a task that operates on a continuous basis through holidays and weekends, 24 hours a day. It's easier to create and very visible to others who view the schedule.

A separate issue is whether estimates should include waiting time, e.g., time spent waiting to receive a permit or approval. Many people include waiting times in their duration estimates. We recommend entering them as lags on dependencies (covered in chapter 5) or as separate tasks instead.

Duration * Units = Work (D*U=W)

Project 2010 uses the formula: Duration * Units = Work.
- ➤ Duration is how many business days you have to finish the job
- ➤ Units are how many resource units will do the work
- ➤ Work is how many person hours or days it will take

It's crucial to understand that you only have to enter two of these three variables. The formula is meant to make your life easier: when you provide two of three variables in the formula, Project 2010 will calculate the third one for you. However, if you are not aware of this formula, you can't predict how Project

2010 will behave, and your life will be not easier, but more difficult (refer to chapter 8 for a thorough discussion of these concepts).

 Enter either a duration or work estimate for a task, not both when tasks are auto scheduled. Entering both interferes with Project 2010's ability to calculate a third variable once resources are assigned.

What you estimate first is entirely up to you, but will typically depend on the task and the situation. If you first estimate the duration, you have a Fixed Duration task. This is quite common. In any situation you will have to estimate the first variable, decide on the second and let Project 2010 calculate the third. The result is that you will know the date the task will be done. For a detailed explanation of how Project 2010 calculates variables, refer to chapter 8 where we introduce the concept of units when we talk about assigning resources.

On the next pages we will discuss Fixed Work tasks and Fixed Duration tasks. The Fixed Units tasks are less common when planning a project, (you tend to know more about the duration or work of a task, rather than who is going to work on it), and we will postpone discussion of those. You need Fixed Units mostly when you make changes to assignments as we will see when we discuss resource assignments.

 If you don't intend to enter resources and assignments, but would like to see Gantt bars for each task, you will have to estimate the durations for all tasks, since Project 2010 needs durations to create the Gantt Chart!

An Estimating Example

Let's assume you want to repaint the interior of your house. You wonder on what date you could be done repainting the room; how many calendar days will this project take?

To begin by simply estimating the number of calendar days is a difficult process, so you start with estimating the number of business days (workdays) the job will take. Once you know the number of business days and on which day of the week you will start, you can convert the business days into actual days on the calendar.

Estimating in business days, however, may be difficult as well, because you may not know how many resources will be available. You take another step back and decide to focus on an effort estimate in person days. To estimate the effort (work), you realize you must look at parameters like the difference between the old and new color, the number of coats needed, area to be painted, and what you will do with the wallpaper. After you have decided all of those factors, you figure it will take, let's say, 10 person days (see the next illustration).

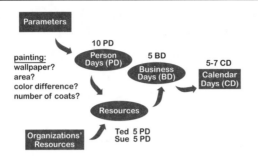

You still can't say how many business days this requires, because you have no firm commitments from family members or friends to help you. You ask around, and you find that your significant other is willing to help and that you are going to share the workload.

Each of you will contribute 5 person days of effort, so the 10 person days of effort can be delivered by 2 people in 5 business days. But, will it? Will there be extra time and effort because two people are working on the job. Will they argue, play, or chat? Will there be up front planning of who does what? But let's say it is 5 business days.

If you start on Monday and you decide not to work on the weekend, you can have your house painted by Friday (5 business days and 5 calendar days). However, if you start on Tuesday, you will be done on Monday of the next week (5 business days, but 7 calendar days). You now know what you wanted to know: the project end date.

The last conversion from business days to calendar days is elegantly taken care of by Project 2010. Once you have filled in the Project Calendar, you can count on the eager and rapid cooperation of Project 2010. The challenge in estimating with Project 2010 lies in solving the puzzle of person days, resource units and business days. We will present a process for solving this puzzle.

A Process for Estimating

Estimating: Types of Tasks

Eventually, Project 2010 needs to know the start date and the finish date of a task in order to fit it into the time line. To get to those dates, it needs to find out the number of calendar days a job will take, as shown in the illustration. You will find it too difficult to estimate the number of calendar days. You will immediately get bogged down with questions like: *When will we start this task? If we start it on a Monday, it will take 2 calendar days, but if we start*

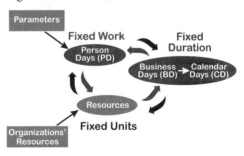

on a Friday, it will take 4 calendar days! You don't want to deal with those issues at this point. You should instead try to estimate the number of business days and have Project 2010 do the conversion from business days to calendar days. The software does an excellent job here once you have filled in the Project Calendar. (We filled it in when we set up the new project in chapter 2.)

In some situations, it is possible to estimate the number of business days (or business hours) directly, for example for tasks like *meeting*, *training* and *presentation*. For a meeting you set the duration to, let's say, 2 business hours. Activities like these do not shorten in duration when you add more resources to them; these are *Fixed Duration* tasks.

For many other tasks, it is impossible to estimate the number of business days without knowing how much effort it will take and how many resources are available to do the work. You have to step back in the process and estimate the amount of effort first in person hours or person days. Project 2010 calls effort Work.

In order to estimate the work (effort), you may find that you have to look at the parameters of the job. Each industry has its own metrics to refine the estimates of a job; this is known as parametric estimating, for example:

> The construction industry has quantity surveyors; they can tell exactly how much a brick wall will cost given the square footage and choice of brick.

> The software industry works with function points. Once software estimators know the number of function points of an application to be built, they can calculate their estimates. Dividing the function point total by 150 approximates the number of analysts, programmers and technicians they will need.

For each job there are relevant parameters to consider. You may have to ask the client to provide some of these; others come as a result of design work. With the parameters known it may be possible to compute the estimate by multiplying the number of units by a per unit effort estimate. For when there is no algorithm, or for more refined estimates, bottom-up, expert and analogous estimating are used.

Once you have determined the amount of work, you have to decide how many resources will be assigned to the job. After that, you can usually determine how many business days the task will take (duration).

Choosing the Options

Before you enter estimates, it's important to be aware of how Project 2010 treats them. On the **File** tab, in the **Backstage** view, click 🗊 **Options**. The **Project Options** dialog box appears. We recommend you set or accept the following options to alter Project 2010's behavior.

Project Options	Recommended Choices
Schedule	**Set the Options on the Schedule tab:**
	Duration is entered in: Choose the unit (e.g., *days*, *hours*) that fits the majority of your inputs. Project 2010 will use this as the default time unit for the **Duration** field. With the default duration time unit set to days, you can type in 5 instead of *5d* to get 5 days in the duration fields.
	Work is entered in: Choose the unit (e.g., days, hours) that fits the majority of your inputs. Project 2010 will use this as the default time unit for the **Work** field. It's important to note that the **Work** field, unlike the **Duration** field, will convert entries to the default time unit according to the hours per day value.
	Default task type: Most people enter the duration immediately, and Project 2010 should not change it, unless required. If you normally enter duration estimates rather than work (effort) estimates, we recommend setting the Default Task Type to Fixed Duration.
	☐ **New Tasks are effort driven** When turned on, this option can divide work based on the number of resources assigned; we recommend you turn it off when setting up your schedule. (Effort driven is discussed in greater detail in chapter 8.)
	☑ **Show that scheduled tasks have estimated durations** will add a question mark to the durations that you did not enter yourself.
	☑ **New scheduled tasks have estimated durations** will add a question mark to the durations of new tasks you may create.
	Scheduling Options for this project: All New Projects ▣ All New Projects ▾ Sets the options under this heading as the default settings for any new schedules you create. Any existing schedules are not affected, because these options are stored in the project schedules. To change the scheduling options for an existing schedule, make sure it is open first and then choose it from the **Scheduling Options for this project:** drop-down list.

Project Options	Recommended Choices
Advanced	**Set the Options on the Advanced tab:**
	Allow cell drag and drop
	This allows you to move or copy the selected cells, rows or columns by dragging. This option may be set for new or existing projects in **General Options for this Project**: drop-down list.
	Under the heading **Display options for this project**: you will find options for these items:
	Minutes, Hours, Days, Weeks, Months and **Years**
	This allows you to change the way time units are labeled in your project or all new projects. The shorter you make the label, the more space you save, so you may want to set them to the shortest label.

4

 It's a good idea to make sure the duration time unit is different than the work time unit (for example, use days for duration and hours for work). This makes it easier to avoid confusion (particularly in phone discussions).

 Make sure the **Effort Driven** field is displayed when working with task types on a task-by-task basis. The effort driven flag may not turn off when switching from fixed work to fixed duration and you may not get the results you were looking for.

Estimated Durations in Project 2010

 If you are not 100% sure of your duration estimate, you can mark it as an "estimated duration" by adding a question mark "?" to the duration entry. For example, enter "3 *day?*" in the duration field if you are not entirely sure of the 3-day estimate and plan to re-visit it shortly.

In its default settings, Project 2010 will fill in "1 day?" for the duration of newly created, auto scheduled tasks. Durations displayed with a question mark are referred to as 'estimated durations' by Project 2010. This is a reminder to you that you have estimated the duration and plan to come back with a more confident estimate, i.e., you have not filled in the duration; instead it has been filled in automatically for you.

To remove the question mark symbol for an individual task, simply double-click the task. The **Task Information** dialog box appears. On the **General** tab, clear the **Estimated** option.

If you type over the duration value with a new value, the question mark will also disappear.

This is a useful option if you only supply duration estimates in your project. But on the other-hand, if you supply a duration estimate for some tasks and a work estimate for other tasks, you may wish to disable the 'estimated duration' option since there is no similar option for the work field. Refer to the section Choosing the Options above for more information.

Preparing the Gantt Chart

	ⓘ	Task Mode	Task Name	Type	Effort Driven	Duration	Work
0	📝		Relocation DEVON, Inc.	Fixed Duration	No	1 day?	0 hrs
1			⊟ REQUIREMENTS	Fixed Duration	No	1 day?	0 hrs
2			Research staff requirements	Fixed Duration	No	1 day?	0 hrs
3			Summarize requirements	Fixed Duration	No	1 day?	0 hrs
4			Requirement document completed	Fixed Duration	No	1 day?	0 hrs
5			⊟ LOCATION	Fixed Duration	No	1 day?	0 hrs
6			Select the realtor	Fixed Duration	No	1 day?	0 hrs
7				Fixed Duration	No	1 day?	0 hrs

Manually Scheduled or Auto Scheduled

In order to be able to change the Type and the Effort Driven of the Task, it has to be in the Task Mode, Auto Schedule.

Fixed Units, Fixed Work or Fixed Duration

Yes or No

In order to use the Gantt Chart to enter estimates, we suggest you customize the Entry table to make the data entry process more efficient.

Let's prepare the Gantt Chart so we have the right fields to enter our estimates. The illustration above shows which fields we will insert. We recommend you insert them in the order shown. You typically have to insert the fields Type, Effort Driven and Work into the Entry table.

For now we need the following fields in the Entry table:
- ➤ **ID**: Generated automatically
- ➤ **Indicators**: Generated automatically
- ➤ **Task Mode**: To switch between manually scheduled or auto scheduled mode for a task
- ➤ **Task Name**: Note that the database name of this field is simply **Name**. You can see this if you double-click on the column heading
- ➤ **Type**: By setting the right task type, you tell Project 2010 to leave the estimate you entered alone. For example, if you estimate that a task will take 10 person days, you enter 10 days or 80 hours in the Work field and you set the task type to Fixed Work
- ➤ **Effort Driven**: By including this field, you can easily switch it to Yes or No
- ➤ **Duration**: To enter the duration for Fixed Duration tasks
- ➤ **Work**: To enter the effort for Fixed Work tasks

If you have the default **Entry table** displayed, you need to insert the fields **Type**, **Effort Driven** and **Work**:

1. On the **Task** tab, in the **View** group, click **Gantt Chart** .

2. Right-click on the **Duration** column heading and click **Insert Column**; the list of available fields/columns appears.

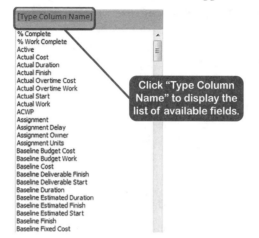

Click "Type Column Name" to display the list of available fields.

Select from the list **Type**. If you type the first characters of the field name, you will get to it more quickly; the list is very long.

3. Repeat steps 2 and 3 to insert the columns **Effort Driven** and **Work**.

4. You are now ready to enter duration and work estimates.

We recommend that you also hide the start and finish columns to avoid accidental entry in these columns.

1. Right-click on the **Start** column heading and select **Hide Column**.

2. Right-click on the **Finish** column heading and select **Hide Column**.

Entering a Duration Estimate for Fixed Duration Tasks

A fixed duration task is a task where the duration doesn't change if you change the number of resources assigned to it, or the working hours of those resources. Examples of fixed duration tasks might be status meetings, training, backing up computer systems or drying paint. Tasks tend to have a fixed duration when you assign many resources to them (a meeting, training) or none (backing up a computer system, drying of paint).

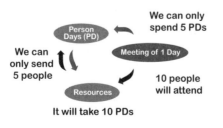

For Fixed Duration tasks, enter the duration first. A task such as a meeting is a prime example of a fixed duration task, because you decide the duration up front (it is more a matter of deciding than of estimating). Then you can decide who you will invite to the meeting and assign the number of units (people) (counterclockwise arrows in illustration). Once you have assigned the number of resource units, Project 2010 will calculate the total amount of work.

Sometimes you know the maximum number of person hours you are willing to spend in the meeting and you enter it as work (clockwise arrows in the illustration). In this case Project 2010 will calculate the number of resources needed (refer to chapter 8 for a discussion about providing multiple pieces of information and related calculations).

1. Enter the name of the task in the field **Task Name**.

2. Press [Tab]; the cursor moves to the field **Type**. (If you press [Enter ↵], the cursor will move down to the next task.)

3. Select from the task type list [Fixed Duration ▼] **Fixed Duration** and press [Tab] to move to the **Effort Driven** field.

4. Change **Effort Driven** to **No** (if you didn't switch the default to **No** in **Project Options**.) and press [Tab] to move to the **Duration** field.

5. Enter in the **Duration** field [1 day? ⬍] the number of business days you estimate the task will take. This will override the default duration of **1 day**? that Project 2010 had entered. You only need to enter the number and Project 2010 will append days. If you want to display a different time unit, for example hours, you have to type the time unit abbreviation as well (e.g., *2h*). Valid abbreviations for the time units are: "m" for minutes, "h" for hours, "d" for days, "w" for weeks and "mo" for months. Notice the "m" for minutes versus the "mo" for months.

6. Press [Enter ↵] and then [Home] to position the cursor for the next task.

When a task is set to Fixed Duration, Project 2010 will keep the value in the Duration field constant when Project 2010 applies the scheduling formula.

Entering a Work Estimate for Fixed Work Tasks

A fixed work task is one where the amount of effort is only dependent upon the parameters of the job, i.e., the technical specifications of the finished work, and not dependent upon the number of resources that you assign or the working times (calendars). For example, it might take 100 hours to create a specific design, regardless of whether you have one or more people working on it.

As in the house painting example, Once you determine the amount of work, often your next step will be to establish how many resources will do the job (clockwise arrows in the illustration). When you know the work and the number of resource units, Project 2010 will derive the number of business days (duration).

Once you know the amount of work (10 person days), you sometimes know in how many business days it needs to be done (counterclockwise arrows in the illustration). Let's say you have only 4 business days for the task (duration). From this, Project 2010 can derive for you the number of resources you need (2.5). Keep in mind that the algorithm used to calculate the number of resources may not take into consideration overhead or other factors that might change the effort estimate when resources are increased or decreased. You may have to adjust by changing the task to a fixed duration task (refer to chapter 8 for a discussion about providing multiple pieces of information and related calculations).

1. Enter the name of the task in the field **Task Name**.

2. Press $\boxed{\text{Tab}}$; the cursor moves to the field **Type**.

3. Select from the list $\boxed{\text{Fixed Work} \quad \blacktriangledown}$ the task type **Fixed Work**. Press $\boxed{\text{Tab}}$ repeatedly to reach the **Work** field. The field **Effort Driven** is set to **Yes** and cannot be changed for **Fixed Work** tasks.

4. Enter in the **Work** field $\boxed{\text{0 hrs} \quad \updownarrow}$ the number of person hours you estimate the task will take. You only need to enter the number and Project 2010 will append "**hrs**". If you want a different time unit, for example weeks, add the appropriate abbreviation: *m* for minutes, *h* for hours, *d* for days, *w* for weeks and *mo* for months. Notice the *m* for minutes versus the *mo* for months.

5. Review the parameters of the job, if needed. Press $\boxed{\text{Enter} \leftarrow}$ and then $\boxed{\text{Home}}$ to position the cursor for the next task.

 If you started with the wrong default task type, you can change all existing tasks at once by clicking on a column heading to select all tasks and clicking **Task Information** 📧 on the **Tasks** tab. Choose the **Advanced** tab, select the type you want from the **Task type** list, and select the ☐ **Effort Driven** option as required. If you want to turn off Effort Driven, make sure it is clear, not shaded. Click the box again if it is shaded (the check box has three states when multiple tasks are selected: on, off, and shaded for some on, others off). Click $\boxed{\text{OK}}$.

When a task is set to Fixed Work, Project 2010 will keep the value in the Work field constant when Project 2010 applies the scheduling formula.

Task Bars

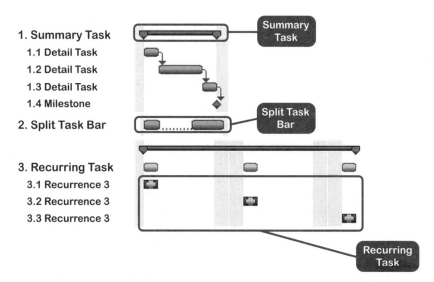

1. Summary Task
   1.1 Detail Task
   1.2 Detail Task
   1.3 Detail Task
   1.4 Milestone
2. Split Task Bar

3. Recurring Task
   3.1 Recurrence 3
   3.2 Recurrence 3
   3.3 Recurrence 3

As you enter tasks in the Gantt Chart view, you'll see durations appear as bars in the timescale. As you enter your estimates the bars will adjust to reflect the duration of the task. Each category of task has a different task bar style. (Bar style formatting is discussed in chapter 11).

➤ Summary task bar
A summary task bar has small shapes (pentagons by default) at its start and end points. The summary task bar summarizes all its detail tasks and milestones: it starts when its first detail task starts and it ends when its last detail task or milestone ends for auto scheduled tasks.

	ⓘ	Task Mode	Task Name	Duration	Start	Finish	Pred	08 Jan '12 S M T W T F	15 Jan '12 S S M T W T F
1		⚲	⊟ Summary Task	5 days	Mon 09/01/12	Fri 13/01/12			
2		⬎	Auto Scheduled Task	6 days	Mon 09/01/12	Mon 16/01/12			
3		⚲	Manual Task	5 days	Mon 09/01/12	Fri 13/01/12			
4		⚲	Manual Task - Duration Only	5 days					
5		⚲	Manual Task - No Finish		Mon 09/01/12	tbd			
6		⚲	Manual Task - No Start		tbd	Fri 13/01/12			

 By default, summary tasks are auto scheduled and are represented by the bars described above. However, with Project 2010, you can change the task mode for summary tasks to manually scheduled. This creates a manual summary rollup which is shown by a thin bar directly under the usual summary bar. The thin rollup bar extends or shortens depending on the earliest start and latest finish of the detailed sub tasks, and will be red as a warning sign if there is some conflict between the manual duration and the summary rollup duration.

➤ Detail task bar
A detail task bar is shown as a bar which represents its estimated duration. For auto-scheduled tasks, the bar is solid with rounded edges. If the task is manually scheduled, the shape of the bar reflects the known information provided: if only Duration is entered, the semi-transparent bar is shown; if a Start and Finish Date is also provided, the ends of the bar are shown as closed solid corners.

➤ Milestone diamond
A milestone appears as a diamond.

 Milestones typically have zero days duration, however, Project 2010 will allow you to set the Milestone flag for any task regardless of the duration (using the Mark as Milestone option in the Task Information dialog box). These tasks are also shown in the Gantt Chart as diamonds.

➤ Split task bars
A split task bar has multiple parts connected by dots. The work on a split task bar is scheduled to be interrupted and resumed at a later date.

 Even though the feature is called split "task," it is truly the bar that is split into multiple pieces, not the task itself. While the task remains on one line with the bar, the bar is split into multiple pieces visible on the Gantt Chart.

➤ Recurring task bars
Recurring task bars represent tasks that have multiple parts that occur at regular intervals throughout the project, as described below. They are set up in Project 2010 as summary tasks with detail tasks indented beneath.

Split and Recurring Tasks

In chapter 3 we discussed summary tasks, detail tasks and milestones. Two additional task types come into play when we consider task durations: split tasks and recurring tasks.

Split Tasks

Some tasks need to be split into multiple time periods. For example, when electricians wire a building, they have to come back to install the switch plates after the inspection. Or perhaps a resource has to interrupt work on a task to attend a one-day meeting. Splits are often not planned, but occur during project execution.

We discourage you from splitting tasks during the planning phase, since splits typically need frequent rescheduling and increase your schedule maintenance.

As we'll see in the next chapter you also can't set dependencies on the start or finish of a split to move it when the split task moves, which will also increase the time you spend on schedule maintenance.

 Instead of splitting task bars when you are planning your project, we recommend that you try to divide the task into multiple tasks and schedule each separately.

For example, instead of having a single task for the electricians wiring our building, simply split the task into two tasks: *pull cables* and *install switch plates* and set dependencies on these tasks. You can set a dependency from the activity *inspect electric wiring* to *install switch plates* task, and you have a fully dynamic model (as described in chapter 5.)

Where you must have a split task, you can add a second task bar to an existing one. You do this by drawing a second bar in the timescale to the right or to the left (but not before the project start date) of the existing task bar. Just click, hold down and drag to where you want the second part of the task bar.

To split an existing task bar into two parts:

1. Click **Split Task** 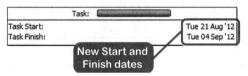 on the **Task** tab; a pop-up window appears with this mouse pointer **|▶**.

2. Point to a task bar and click and drag the split part to where you want the split to start. The new start and finish dates of this part appear in the pop-up window when you release the mouse:

3. Drop it where you want it by releasing the mouse button; the task bar is now split into two parts. Notice that the two parts are connected by dots:

 To remove a split, just drag the right-most part of the bar to the left and reconnect it to its original bar part. If you have split it multiple times and you want to reconnect the parts, just keep doing this.

Recurring Tasks

We recommend using recurring tasks for scheduling things you do regularly such as team status meetings, schedule updates, change request reviews and status reports.

Recurring tasks are in fact summary tasks with detail tasks indented beneath.

Choose **Task** tab, select from the list **Task;** the **Recurring Task** ; **Recurring Task Information** dialog appears:

Recurring Task Information

Task Name: Status Meetings   Duration: 1d

Recurrence pattern
- Daily
- Weekly
- Monthly
- Yearly

Recur every 1 week(s) on:

Sunday   Monday   Tuesday   Wednesday
Thursday   Friday   Saturday

Range of recurrence

Start: Mon 06 Aug '12   End after: 0 occurrences
End by: Fri 30 Nov '12

Calendar for scheduling this task

Calendar: None   Scheduling ignores resource calendars

Help   OK   Cancel

> With this dialog you can enter many recurring detail tasks at once that are summarized under the Task name you enter here.

1. Type the name in the **Task Name** field.

2. Type the duration for a single occurrence of the task in the Duration field or use its ⬍ to change the duration with pre-set increments.

3. Under **Recurrence Pattern** select the interval at which the task recurs. The dialog will change and present appropriate choices for the selected interval.

4. Under **Range of recurrence** choose the period or the number of occurrences. Click OK.

Some remarks about recurring tasks:

➤ Notice that the duration of the recurring summary task encompasses the entire period of its detail tasks for auto scheduled tasks.

➤ Project 2010 sets constraints on each recurring detail task that will keep it on its dates in the timescale. Even though we recommend against using constraints in schedules (described in chapter 6), there is nothing wrong with constraints on recurring detail tasks. They are a legitimate exception to the rule. Recurring detail tasks are typically not hooked up into the network of dependencies, and only scheduling constraints will keep them on the proper dates.

> ➤ If one occurrence accidentally falls on a non work day (as entered in the Project Calendar), Project 2010 will ask you what to do with it: drop it or move it to the next business day.

> ➤ You can set dependencies for recurring tasks, although in practice, we have found that project managers normally don't.

> ➤ Assigning resources to recurring tasks is okay, but Project 2010 will not level recurring tasks by default! (described in chapter 9).

Milestone Durations

To mark a task as a milestone, on the **Task** tab click **Information** ; choose the **Advanced** tab and then check the ☐ Mark task as milestone. However, if the task you've marked as a milestone has a duration, although Project 2010 will change the regular detail task bar into a diamond and shrink the task bar from 10 days to a 0 day diamond in the timescale, it keeps the 10 day duration in the spreadsheet. This means that when dependencies stem from the task, it looks like there is a gap between the milestone task and its linked task(s).

To avoid this we recommend that your milestone tasks have an estimated duration of 0.

Copying and Moving Data to Speed up the Entry of Estimates

Entering estimates can be a tedious job. Here are some ways to speed up estimate entry.

Several of the following techniques rely on using Project 2010's drag and drop feature. After your task list is finalized, you may want to disable drag and drop to avoid accidentally moving one task name on top of another. Do this by choosing the **File** tab; **Backstage** view appears. Choose ⊟ Options; **Project Options** dialog appears. Under the **Edit** heading, clear ☐ **Allow Cell Drag and Drop**.

Editing Fields for Multiple Tasks

1. Select the tasks by clicking on the first task, holding down ⌞Control⌟ and clicking on the next ones until they are all selected.

2. Click **Task Information** ⌹ on the **Task** tab

    OR

    hold down ⌞Shift⌟ and press ⌞F2⌟; the **Multiple Task Information** dialog appears:

Multiple Task Information

General | Predecessors | Resources | **Advanced** | Notes | Custom Fields

Name: _____ Duration: ___ ☐ Estimated

Constrain task

Deadline: _____ ▾

> Notice that with more than one task selected, the title of the dialog is Multiple task Information and that all the fields are blank.

Constraint type: _____ ▾ Constraint date: _____

Task type: _____ ▾ ☑ Effort driven

Calendar: _____ ▾ ☑ Scheduling ignores resource

WBS code: _____

Earned value method: _____ ▾

☐ Mark task as milestone

Some of the fields above are not editable because the task is Manually Scheduled.

> Gray check boxes mean that for some selected tasks the option may be on and for others off.

Help   OK   Cancel

3. Make the changes needed on each tab.

4. Click [OK]. The changes will be applied to all of the tasks you selected.

You can use the **Multiple Task Information** dialog for many purposes, including:

➤ Setting the duration of all milestones to zero on the tab **General** and clearing ☐ **Estimated** to make the question mark disappear.

➤ Changing the task type—for example from **Fixed Duration** to **Fixed Work**—on the **Advanced** tab in the field **Task type**. This shows up in the field **Type** in the spreadsheet.

➤ Assigning or adding a resource to multiple tasks on the tab **Resources**.

Copying with Fill Down

You use the fill down feature to duplicate the same value in multiple adjacent or nonadjacent cells.

1. Enter the value you want to copy in the top cell of the area you're going to fill.

2. Click and hold down on the top cell and drag down over all adjacent cells you want to fill.

OR

Hold down [Shift] and press [↓] to select all cells you wish to fill.

OR

Hold down [Control] and click on all nonadjacent cells to fill with the value.

3. Choose **Task** tab, select from the list **Fill** and then click **Down**.

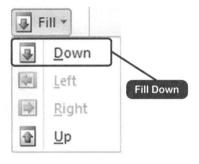

OR

Hold down [Control] and press [D].

You can use the fill down feature for various reasons including:

➤ Changing the constraint types for many tasks. To get rid of constraints, fill *As Soon As Possible* in the field Constraint Type.

➤ Setting the Level Assignments field for all detail recurring tasks to *Yes* to include them in the workload leveling.

➤ In the resource sheet you can fill down the department (field Group) for your resources.

Copying Values Using the Fill Handle

You use the fill handle feature to duplicate the same value in multiple adjacent cells.

1. Enter the value you wish to fill in the top or the bottom cell of the area to be filled.

2. Make sure you have the cell selected: at the bottom right of the cell you will see a fill handle:

3. Point to the fill handle; watch the mouse pointer:

4. When you see a crosshair mouse pointer, click and hold down, and then drag over the cells to be filled.

You can even enter a pattern of values in some cells: select the cells that define the pattern and drag the fill handle. Project 2010 will copy and repeat this same pattern as many times as you drag up or down. (Project 2010 does not work like Excel in this regard: Excel will increment values in the pattern, not repeat the same pattern.)

Copying, Moving or Clearing Cells

 Project 2010 will prevent you from copying or moving data to incompatible cells. For example, you can't copy dates into the duration field.

Copying Cells

1. Select the cells you want to copy and point to the border of the selected area. Make sure the mouse pointer changes from a plus sign ⊹ to a 🕏.

2. Hold down ⌊Control⌋ and drag the cells to their place.

You can't use copy and paste to copy one cell and paste it into many other cells like you can in Microsoft Office Excel. Project 2010 will only paste the value into the first cell of a copy-to range.

Moving Cells

1. Select the cells and point to the border of the selected area. Make sure the mouse pointer changes from a plus sign ⊹ to 🕏.

2. Click and drag the cells to their new place.

Clearing Cells

The ⌊Delete⌋ key clears the content from a cell. When you press ⌊Delete⌋ in the task name column, a smart tag ✗ will appear to ask if you want to delete the entire task.

OR

Select the cells (not the row heading or ID column—as this is a locked first column), right-click, and click **Clear Contents** from the short-cut menu.

 Properly clear a cell by pressing the delete key which will reset the value in the cell to its default. Warning: do not type in the default value. If you manually type in a value—even if it is the same as the default value—you impose a restriction on that cell that impacts calculations.

Clearing Rows

Select one or more rows to delete by selecting the rows first and then pressing ⌊Delete⌋.

Select multiple adjacent tasks by dragging over their row headings. Select non-adjacent tasks by holding down ⌊Control⌋ then clicking on tasks.

Moving a Column

1. Select the column by clicking on its column heading.

 Be sure to release the mouse button before doing the next step to indicate that you are done selecting columns.

2. Point the mouse on the selected column and click and drag to move it to its new location. Notice the T shape to help you position the column.

Copying a Column

1. Select the column by clicking on its column heading.

2. Click **Copy** on the **Task** tab in the **Clipboard** group, or right-click, and then click **Copy** from the short-cut menu.

3. Select the column into which you want to paste the data.

4. Click **Paste** on the **Task** tab or right-click and then click **Paste**.

Copying or Moving a Row

Click the ID number and then follow the same process as described above when copying or moving cells.

Copy or move an entire row by clicking the task ID number. This ensures that all data associated with the task gets copied with it.

Copying Between Projects

1. Open the project you want to copy from.

2. Select the tasks or resources by dragging over their ID numbers (the very first column) to select entire tasks or resources.

   OR

   Select non-adjacent tasks or resources by holding down [Control] and clicking on the ID-number of each task or resource.

3. Click **Copy** on the **Task** tab in the **Clipboard** group, or right-click, and then click **Copy** from the short-cut menu.

4. The data is now temporarily stored in the clipboard.

5. Open the project into which you want to copy.

6. Select the row before which you want to insert the data and click **Paste** on the **Task** tab in the **Clipboard** group, or right-click, and then click **Paste** from the short-cut menu.

Copying Cells Between Projects

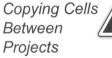

The steps are the same as the previous steps, except that you select cells instead of entire rows. If you do this, you have to be careful to paste the data into a blank area of the sheet; otherwise existing line items may be overridden. Choose **Undo** on the **Quick Access toolbar** if an accident occurs.

Copying Objects Between Projects

Objects are views, reports, calendars and other things that change the appearance of the data or affect the scheduling. You copy objects between projects using the Organizer.

If necessary, open the project that contains the object(s) you want to copy from and the project that you intend to copy to.

1. On the **File** tab, choose the **Backstage** view. Then choose **Info**, and click on the **Organizer** ; the **Organizer** dialog appears:

> **Selected object ready to be copied**

> **With the Organizer dialog, you can move objects between project files and/or the Global.mpt. Objects in the Global.mpt are visible in all your projects.**

> **Files between which the object will be copied.**

2. Click on the tab for the type of object you want to transfer.

3. From the lists at the bottom of the dialog select the schedule from which to copy the object and the schedule to copy to.

4. Select the object and click `Copy >>` to copy from left to right or `<< Copy` to copy from right to left.

5. Click `Close` or `Cancel` when done.

The organizer allows you to copy objects to other project schedules or to the global template *Global.mpt*. Any objects you put into the global template are visible in all your projects, unless they have the same name as other objects that are part of a particular project schedule.

With the organizer you can, for example:
➤ Make your Project Calendar available to other project managers
➤ Create a standard report and make it available to colleagues
➤ Share views, tables and filters

Copying an Entire Project

If you want to duplicate an entire project, open the project file you want to copy and then choose **File** tab; **Backstage** view appears. Choose **Save As** and save it under a different name.

If you try to duplicate a project by simply copying all of the project's rows and pasting then into a new schedule, you'll lose all the settings stored in Project Options.

Checking Estimates

Once you've gathered initial estimates, you'll want to perform some reasonability checks on them.

➤ Are the estimates reasonable given the work that needs to be performed? You will need some technical expertise and recorded past experience to verify if estimates are reasonable. If you don't have this technical expertise, you can:

   ▶ Review the schedules of previous, similar projects

   ▶ Ask team members with technical knowledge to peer review each others' estimates

   ▶ Ask a subject matter expert to review the estimates

➤ Did you include manually scheduled tasks for items where you are not able to provide a complete estimate?

➤ Was the rolling wave approach applied to activities in the future that you are only planning at a high level?

➤ Did your estimate for each task include a work or duration estimate and did you set the appropriate task type and effort-driven settings?

➤ Are the estimates that you collected consistent with the working hours entered in the Standard (Project Calendar)? For example, if you collected pure estimates did you reduce the hours per day to reflect purely productive hours per day, such as 5.5 or 6. If they are not consistent the schedule will be too long or too short.

➤ Do the durations of your estimates fall within the 1% – 10% rule (as discussed in chapter 3 and reviewed below)?

➤ Are the completion of deliverables of your project modeled as milestones with zero days duration.

➤ Did you include buffers to address schedule risk?

Once you have done your estimating and the other steps in the process (including assigning resources and setting dependencies), you can find the project duration easily by:

clicking **Project Information** 🖳 on the **Project tab** and clicking [Statistics...].

OR

viewing the **Duration** field of the project summary task. You can display the project summary task by choosing ☑ **Project Summary Task** on the **Format tab**. This task will appear at the top of the list as a task with ID number 0.

In chapter 3 we covered the 1% – 10% rule: the duration of any detail task should be between a minimum of 1% of the project duration (rounded) and a maximum of 10% of the project duration (rounded). Note that this rule is a guideline.

If you find a task that is longer than 10% of the project, you can split the task into multiple subtasks. Or if the assigned resources are working part-time on the task, you can increase their commitment to full-time, and the duration will decrease. This is more refinement to the WBS, discussed in chapter 3.

Notice that the 1% – 10% rule should only be applied to the durations and not to the work values (effort). If there are many part-time assignments or many multiple assignments per task, the boundaries for work estimates should be narrower or wider than for the duration. In general, the minimum and maximum values for work are harder to indicate, which is why we stayed away from that.

Review Questions

1. Why is estimating the duration of project activities difficult?

2. You are the project manager. While working with your team members on task estimates, someone makes one of the following statements. What would you say?

Statement	Your response
Your team member says: "I can't give you an estimate because I can't predict the future!"	
Your team member says: "Listen, we went over this already. I'm not going to give you any more estimates because my estimates are always off! My estimates don't help you anyway!"	
Your executive says: "You are one of our most experienced and best project managers. Can't you do this project in three weeks?"	

3. In your own words, what is the difference between Duration and Work?

4. What formula is working behind the screens of Project 2010 that relates Duration to Work?

5. What is the difference between a pure work time estimate and a gross work time estimate?

6. Somebody gives you an estimate of 100 person hours of effort for a task and says that the estimate assumes uninterrupted and fully focused work time. You just created a new project schedule that has all options set to the default settings in Project 2010.

   What other fields or dialog boxes would you have to change in order to get a valid finish date forecast for this task from Project 2010?

   In which field would you enter this estimate in Project 2010?

7. What are manually scheduled tasks? How can these be used in the rolling wave approach for estimating when some information is unavailable for future activities.

Additional Practice For experience working with the features you've learned about in this chapter, we strongly suggest that you do the additional exercises for this chapter that are included in Appendix 1.

Chapter 5: Entering Dependencies

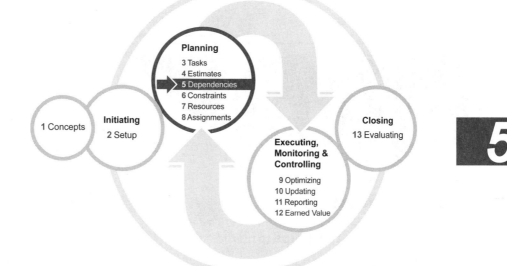

We have the tasks and the estimates entered into our project schedule and are ready to enter the dependencies. Dependencies are relationships between tasks.

After reading this chapter you will be able to:

➤ Describe what dependencies are and why they are important for dynamic schedules
➤ Enter dependencies into a Project 2010 schedule
➤ Choose the right type of dependency
➤ Determine if you need a lag or lead on a dependency, expressed in absolute or relative terms
➤ Set multiple predecessors or successors on a task
➤ Apply best practices for the network logic in project schedules
➤ Check whether the network logic of a schedule follows the best practices
➤ Apply dependencies to integrate new manually scheduled tasks in your network

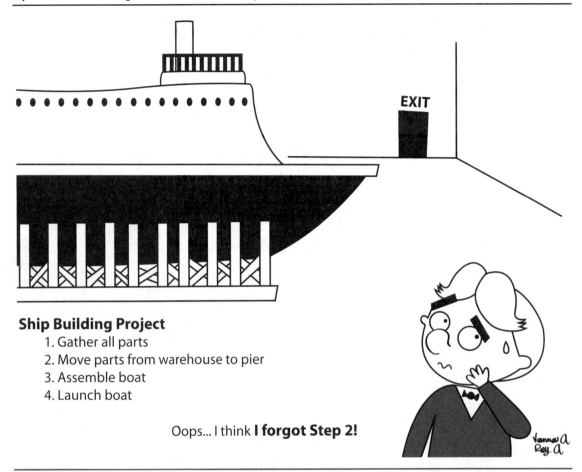

Ship Building Project
1. Gather all parts
2. Move parts from warehouse to pier
3. Assemble boat
4. Launch boat

Oops... I think **I forgot Step 2!**

Dependencies

The Principle of Dynamic Schedules

"Dynamic scheduling" isn't just a fancy marketing term. A dynamic schedule is one that can be kept up-to-date easily when you are busy during project execution.

Every time a change happens—and changes occur on every project—you need to change your schedule. If you have a static model—one where you haven't identified the relationships between tasks—you need to review **all** future tasks every time a change occurs to determine how that one change may impact the completion of other tasks. This is a formidable amount of analysis and schedule updating to manage for every change throughout the life of your project.

 Instead of a static schedule, you should create a dynamic schedule.

With a dynamic schedule, when **one** thing changes in your project, you only have to change one field in your Project 2010 model and the software will generate valid forecasts for all impacted tasks. This is the fundamental principle of dynamic schedules.

You will only come close to this ideal if your schedule meets the following requirements:

> You find and enter all the relationships between tasks that may impact your forecasts. These relationships are called "dependencies"; they are concerned with the order in which tasks are done, and are discussed in this chapter.

> You minimize the number of manually scheduled tasks and hard dates in your schedule. Hard dates or fixed dates may also be called schedule constraints in Project 2010. We'll discuss constraints in the next chapter.

 The simple truth is that you cannot create a valid schedule without knowing which tasks precede which other tasks. Dependency analysis is a MUST.

If you do an excellent job of defining dependencies, theoretically you don't even need to review the impact of a change on future tasks. Of course, in the practical world of complex projects, we use the tool as an aid but we always verify the end product.

The good news is that network logic—the logical dependencies between tasks—tends to stay the same during the entire project. So if you define the network logic well once during the planning phase, you'll be rewarded with a minimum of maintenance during the hectic days of project execution.

 New in Project 2010 is the ability to choose between auto scheduled and manually scheduled tasks. While this book is dedicated to the art of dynamic scheduling, there are situations in which creating a static schedule with manually scheduled tasks is useful. One such case involves schedules where there are few, if any, dependencies between tasks. For example, if a company has several locations that are independently hosting multiple events and you would like to schedule these events showing the dates each will occur. In this case, each event is independent of any other event and the addition, deletion or delaying of an event would not affect another event.

In Project 2010, the default scheduling mode for new tasks is manually scheduled. In manually scheduled mode the initial dependencies are honored, but any changes that affect linked tasks are not calculated immediately. Refer to chapter 4 for information about setting or changing the options for new schedules. This default behavior can be changed to Auto Schedule by clicking on the **File** tab, **Options**, **Schedule** and under **Scheduling Options for this project**: **New tasks created: Auto Scheduled**.

We recommend you set the default option for new tasks to auto scheduled when you are in a phase where you have enough information and detail about the tasks; otherwise we recommend that you leave this default setting to manually scheduled.

Other Options settings that can affect manual or auto scheduling behavior are:

➤ Update Manually Scheduled tasks when editing links
➤ Keep task on nearest working day when changing to Automatically Scheduled mode, and
➤ Selecting Off or On for the Calculate project after each edit radio buttons.

Switching from **Manual** to **Auto** scheduling (or vice-versa) can also be accomplished on the **Task** tab. The **Respect Links** icon serves as a recalculate button for your tasks with manually scheduled mode, or when the scheduling mode is set to manual.

As a reminder, the advantage of dynamically scheduling your project is primarily one of being able to respond to changes and updates that occur in the schedule. The project manager is responsible for keeping the project plan up-to-date and realistic. A dynamic schedule allows Project 2010 to minimize the work required and to give stakeholders the ability to assess risks and impacts. For example, edit one task, and all the dependent tasks are automatically updated. This feature can prevent you from missing a critical update and makes forecasting future impacts much easier and more time effective.

Note that when using the manual scheduling mode for a task, you cannot change the constraint type. By default, the constraint stays As Soon As Possible.

What Are Dependencies?

A dependency is a relationship between the start or finish of one task and the start or finish of another. With each dependency we need to define which task is driving the other.

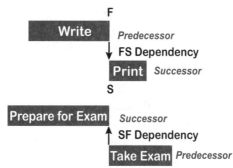

In the first example in the illustration, once writing is finished, printing is to begin. The task *Write* (predecessor) is driving the dependent task *Print* (successor) to begin. By defining a Finish-to-Start or FS dependency between the two tasks, when the finish date of Write changes, the start date of Print must move with it.

It's important to understand that the predecessor does not always come first chronologically. In the second illustrated example, the completion date of *Prepare for Exam* is driven by the start date of *Take Exam*. This means that if the start date for *Take Exam* changes, the finish date of *Prepare for Exam* must also change. This is a Start-to-Finish or SF dependency. (We'll discuss types of dependencies in more depth later in this chapter.)

So dependencies are relationships. From a scheduling perspective, think of the predecessor as the driving task (driver) and of the successor as the dependent or driven task (follower).

 In order to find the predecessor, ask "*Which task drives the scheduling of which other tasks?*" Then link the tasks to establish the predecessor/successor relationship that serves best to model the relationship.

The whole network of dependencies is also called the network logic. It shows the logical relationships among the tasks.

Why Should I Use Dependencies?

It's not necessary to indicate start and end dates when you work with Project 2010. In fact, we strongly recommend that you not enter start and finish dates, unless you want to intentionally create schedule constraints or manually scheduled tasks. You should let Project 2010 drive start and end dates based on the relationships (dependencies) you define between the tasks and the task durations.

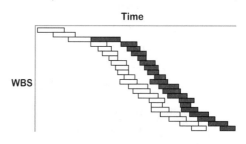

In the illustration, the duration of the third task was extended, and all the dependent tasks were immediately rescheduled by Project 2010 as a result.

If you didn't identify the dependencies in Project 2010, you would have to review and redo the future portion of the schedule by hand. Too often, early in the execution phase of the project as things start to change, the schedule is abandoned: the Gantt Chart is dumped in a drawer and never looked at again. There are companies that have never been able to keep any of their schedules alive during project execution. The linking of dependencies facilitates keeping the schedule up-to-date.

The great benefit from a dynamic schedule is the continuously valid forecasts of project end date and final cost. Without a dynamic schedule, running alternative schedule scenarios during planning and keeping the schedule up to date during execution become too tedious and time consuming to continue.

Choosing the Options

On the **File** tab, in the **Backstage** view click on **Options**, **Schedule**. Here are the options we recommend for setting dependencies.

Project Options	Recommended Choices
Schedule	**Set the Schedule Options for this Project:**
	☑ **Autolink inserted or moved tasks** With Autolink on, Project 2010 itself will set or break dependencies inside a chain of Finish-to-Start dependencies. It assumes that you want sequential dependencies for the tasks you inserted or moved inside a chain.

Autolink works inside a chain of sequentially dependent tasks. If you insert a task inside the chain as shown in the illustration, Project 2010 will immediately incorporate it in the chain of dependencies. It breaks one dependency (the one crossed out) and sets two new ones (the thick blue arrows).

If you move a task, it closes the chain by cutting two dependencies and creating one new one, and it incorporates the task in the chain of dependencies (cutting one dependency and creating two new ones) at the destination.

This is a time saver during planning and we recommend that you turn on **Autolink inserted or moved tasks** when planning your schedule.

During project execution you may want to turn off the **Autolink inserted or moved tasks** feature so that when you move around tasks doing "what-if scenarios", the tasks will not automatically link when they are inserted or moved. You can then get a clearer analysis of the task.

Types of Dependencies

You will be using mostly FS-dependencies that run from the finish (F) of the driver to the start (S) of the follower. The driver task (predecessor) can be linked from its start or from its finish. The follower task can be linked to its start or to its finish. This gives a total of four different possibilities and four types of dependencies. The dependencies are identified by these abbreviations: FS, SS, FF and SF, as shown in the illustration.

Here are examples of each type of dependency:

> **Finish-to-Start (FS)**: The finish of the predecessor determines the start of the successor.
>   ▸ The foundation must be poured before the walls are erected.
>   ▸ A report must be written before it is printed.

> **Start-to-Start (SS)**: The start of the predecessor determines the start of the successor.
>   ▸ When you pour concrete, you want to level it immediately before it cures. There is an SS link between the tasks *pour concrete* and *level concrete*.
>   ▸ Two days after the carpenters start to break out old drywalls and put up new ones, the electricians can start (SS plus 2 days).

> **Finish-to-Finish (FF)**: The finish of the predecessor determines the finish of the successor.
>   ▸ If you train people in using new software, you want the software installed just as they return to their workstations. There is an FF link between the tasks *train users* and *install application*.
>   ▸ Two days after the writing is finished, the editing will be finished. (FF plus 2 days).

> **Start-to-Finish (SF)**: The start of the predecessor determines the finish of the successor.
>   ▸ The fixed start date of an exam will force the preparation to end (whether or not you are ready!).

▶   A newspaper reporter must submit copy before the paper's deadline or the article will not be in tomorrow's edition.

Absolute Lead or Lag Time

Sometimes you want to separate a predecessor and successor by a defined amount of time. You do this by using lags or leads (negative lags).

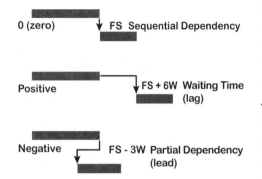

For example, you *apply for a building permit* (predecessor), and estimate that you'll have to wait 6 weeks from the time you apply before you can *dig the foundation* (successor).

To accommodate this, you add a lag to the dependency: a waiting time between the predecessor and the successor.

In this example, you'd have an FS dependency with a lag of 6 weeks between the tasks *apply for permit* and *dig the foundation*, as shown in the first example in the illustration.

The lag is expressed in business days just like the duration. Using a lag avoids calculating Work during this period (which is what would happen if you simply increased the duration of a task) and it always keeps the predecessor and successor separated by the amount of lag time you define.

The lag can be negative. A negative lag is called a lead, since the start of the successor will be earlier than the finish of the predecessor. In such a partial dependency, the follower (successor) is dependent upon the partial completion of its predecessor. As a result, the task bars overlap each other in time. For example, if you write a report, you might send the first half of the report to an editor, and then writing and editing would take place concurrently. This would be an FS dependency between *write report* and *edit report* with a lead of, say, 3 weeks, as shown in the second illustration.

Project 2010 only has one field called **Lag**, and you enter leads as negative lags, so in this case you would enter *FS-3W*.

Note that although in the previous illustration lag and lead are shown only on the FS dependency they can be applied to all other types of dependencies as well.

You can even enter the lag as an elapsed time and Project 2010 will schedule the follower accordingly. Elapsed time is 24 * 7 time (elapsed durations are scheduled 24 hours a day, 7 days a week, until finished). You can enter an **elapsed duration lag** by entering, for example, "**2ed**" instead of "**2d**" in the **Lag** field. If the driver finishes at the end of Friday, a lag of **2ed** will cause the FS follower to start on

Monday (weekend days count as elapsed days), whereas **2d** will make it start on Wednesday (Monday and Tuesday count as business days).

 Use lag or lead time to adjust the schedule for reality instead of putting in an inaccurate duration estimate.

 Put a note on a task that has lag or lead time to explain its purpose.

 Use absolute lag/lead time for values that won't change (fixed value).

Relative Lead or Lag Time

You can also express the amount of lead or lag as a percentage of the duration of the driver task (predecessor). The follower task is scheduled relative to the driver task.

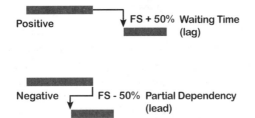

In the second illustration, we have two tasks: *write report* and *edit report*. After the first half of the report is written, we want to send it to the editor. We need an FS-50% dependency between *write report* and *edit report*.

With this feature it is possible to have a successor start halfway through the duration of the predecessor and to keep it at the halfway mark. It will stay at the halfway point even if the duration of the driver task is changed later on.

 Use relative lag/lead time when the amount of lead or lag time should adjust because of a change in the duration of the predecessor.

Multiple Predecessors and Successors

As the illustration shows, each task can have more than one predecessor and successor. This allows you to schedule several activities concurrently. Tasks that do not have a logical relationship generally should be scheduled in parallel. This creates a network of dependencies where some parallel tasks or chains of tasks will take longer than other shorter ones. An example of activities that might take place in

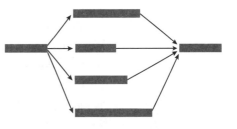

parallel is installing systems at several different sites.

Choosing the Right Type of Dependency

You may not always be certain about the type of dependency to use. In the Prepare for Exam/Take Exam example, whether to use a FS or SF dependency depends on the situation that is being modeled. If the situation allows you to postpone the exam when you are not finished preparing for it, the FS dependency is the best alternative because the schedule will be adjusted depending on a change in the duration of the preparation. An example is the PMP exam[1], which can be postponed if you are not ready to take it.

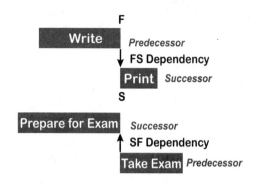

If you cannot postpone taking the exam, the Start-to-Finish dependency is the best choice. The moment an exam starts, the preparation will have to stop. This allows you to count backwards in preparing for the exam: *What is the latest date I have to start preparing for the exam so that everything will be fresh in my memory?*

You could argue that when you schedule backwards from the project finish date, the SF dependency should be the dependency you use most often. After all, in backward scheduling, the finish date drives every task in the project. However, Project 2010 does not change the default dependency to SF when you switch to backward scheduling. In forward scheduling, you will use the FS dependency most often, which is the default in Project 2010.

Steps for Choosing the Right Type of Dependency

Ask yourself the following questions, in the order shown, to help you choose the right dependency relationship:

1. **Which task drives the other?** or **What do you need in order to do this task and where does it come from?**
   To determine which task is the predecessor, first ask "**What do you need in order to do this task?**" Once you know what is needed, then ask "**Where does it come from?**" and finally, "**Which task drives the other task's dates?**" Then choose the dependency type that best models the actual situation.

People often ask themselves: "**What should be scheduled first or earliest?**" This question asks for the chronology of tasks, not the dependency. Remember, the predecessor task doesn't always come first: in an SF dependency the predecessor task is chronologically **later** than the successor.

---

1   PMP® stands for *Project Management Professional*, an accreditation of the Project Management Institute (PMI). See www.pmi.org for more information.

2. **Does the start or the finish of the predecessor drive the other task?**
This tells you whether you need a F or S for the predecessor end of the dependency.

3. **Does the predecessor drive the start or the finish of the successor?**
This tells you whether you need an F or S for the successor end of the dependency.

Once you know the answer to questions 2 and 3, you know the type of dependency you need: FS, SS, FF or SF.

4. **Should there be a gap or overlap between the two tasks?**
If your answer is **no**, you're ready with this dependency. If the answer is yes, continue with the next questions.

5. **Do you need a positive lag or a negative lag (lead)?**
A positive lag delays the successor in time and creates a gap in an FS-dependency. A negative lag (lead) schedules the successor earlier in time and creates an overlap in a FS-dependency.

6. **Is the lag an absolute number of days (weeks), or is the lag relative to the duration of the predecessor?**
   ▶ If absolute, ask: **Should it be in business days or in elapsed days?** Enter the number of business days (or weeks) including the time unit, for example *5d*, or *5ed* for elapsed days.
   ▶ If relative, enter a percentage in the **Lag** field, like *50%* or *-30%* (including the percent sign).

7. **How much should the lag or lead be?**
At this point you should know the complete dependency definition, for example *FS+50%*, *SS+3d*, or *FF+2ed*.

 Often dependencies follow the flow of data, information or deliverables (documents) that are passed between team members. For example, the detailed design document is passed on from the software architect to the software programmer. If you ask your team members to identify what they need from other people to do their tasks, you will slowly but surely identify all dependencies from the end of the network to the beginning.

Different Applications of Dependencies

Different situations need different applications of dependencies, including:

➤ Decision point dependencies
➤ Hard and soft dependencies
➤ External dependencies
➤ Resource dependencies
➤ Dynamic link dependencies

We'll discuss each of these in more detail.

Decision Point Dependencies

Decision points (also called gates or checkpoints) are important nodes (intersections) in the network of dependencies. If your schedule has decision points, you are using gate project management, also known as stage-gate project management (stage gates may also be known as phase-gates, quality-gates, toll-gates, etc.).

Gates are to dependencies as central stations are to railroads; many tracks come together and spring from them, as you can see in the illustration. All the deliverables that are needed for making the right decision are drivers (predecessors) for the decision point. All activities that rely upon the decision being made are followers of the decision point (dependent successors). What you will see in a schedule with decision points is that several sub-networks of dependencies are linked together at the decision points.

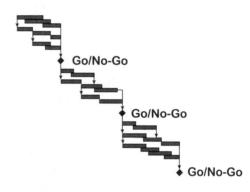

Hard and Soft Dependencies

Tasks with hard or mandatory dependencies (also referred to as logical dependencies) have to be done in an absolute sequence, while tasks with soft dependencies have a preferred sequence.

In hard dependencies there is a physical requirement that the predecessor must drive the successor. For example, you physically can't print a report until after the writing is finished. The finish of *Write* must precede the start of *Print*. (If you find another way to do this, let us know; you'll make the authors really happy.) Common sense and knowledge of your project tasks dictate when to create these hard dependencies.

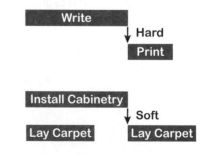

Soft or discretionary dependencies are a matter of preference. For example, the two tasks *Installing Cabinetry* and *Lay Carpet* are not necessarily dependent on each other. The project manager may prefer to set a dependency to make sure that the cabinetmakers do not spill glue that damages the new carpet. However, if he's in a time crunch, he could save time by doing both tasks in parallel.

There is no hard or soft dependency "setting" in Project 2010, but it's important to distinguish between the two so that you can quickly distinguish between tasks you may be able to shift (soft dependencies) and tasks you can't shift (hard dependencies).

 Note which tasks have soft dependencies for easy optimization later. If you remember where you created the soft dependencies, it will be easier to optimize the schedule later on. Because Project 2010 doesn't distinguish between hard and soft dependencies, it is a good practice to document the soft, discretionary dependencies in the **Notes** field. Double-click the affected task and enter notes on the **Notes** tab.

External Dependencies

External dependencies are dependencies where the successor task is dependent on a predecessor that is outside your control. For example:

➤ You need to receive materials from a supplier before you can construct something

➤ You need input from another department before you can complete a report

 We recommend that when you have an external dependency, you insert an extra milestone for the event with a **Start No Earlier Than** schedule constraint (constraints are covered in chapter 6). This is a simple technique that helps tell the entire story in the case of a slippage or, worse, a contract dispute.

In the illustration, if you don't have a milestone set if the cabinets arrive late, it appears to be simply a slipped start date on the task *Install Cabinetry*. Who is accountable for the slip in the schedule? The installers appear to be.

However, if you insert a milestone for the event in your schedule with a **Start No Earlier Than** schedule constraint, the constraint will keep the milestone on the date you've agreed to. Then create dependencies from the

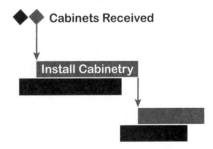

Cabinets Received

Install Cabinetry

milestone into your activities. Now if the cabinets arrive late, it's clear that this was beyond the control of the installers.

Resource Dependencies

Until now we've been discussing logical dependencies. Now let's talk about resource dependencies.

Resource dependencies force tasks to be sequenced to avoid work overloads. A resource dependency occurs when two tasks compete for the same resource. If you can't find another solution for the overload, one or both tasks have to be delayed in order to keep the workload reasonable for the resource. Of course, you could force the sequence by setting an extra logical dependency as shown in the illustration, but let's say the two tasks are really independent and could be done in any order. Harry could either read report *X* or *Y* first.

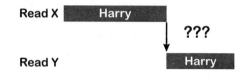

We don't think you should model resource dependencies by setting extra logical dependencies. What happens if you reassign one of Harry's tasks to Sam? Will you remember to take the logical dependency out again? (We added the question marks to the illustration for this reason.) You should at least write yourself a reminder in the **Note** field if you specifically set resource dependencies by creating extra logical dependencies.

 Do not create a link dependency because of a resource limitation. Project 2010 has special features to keep the workloads leveled and we suggest you use those features as described in chapter 9, Optimizing the Schedule.

Entering Dependency Logic

Project 2010 offers a variety of ways to enter dependencies into the schedule. We'll discuss entering dependencies in the Gantt Chart and Network Diagram views. In both views, the tools and forms work in a similar manner. For both views, we'll discuss using:

> The Planning Wizard
> The Link tool
> The mouse
> The Task Information dialog box
> The Task form

Entering Dependencies in the Gantt Chart

Using the Planning Wizard

Before you start, make sure the Planning Wizard is still on. On the **File** tab, in the **Backstage** view, click **Options**, **Advanced**. Select ☑ **Advice from the Planning Wizard** under **Planning Wizard**. Select the indented check boxes as well.

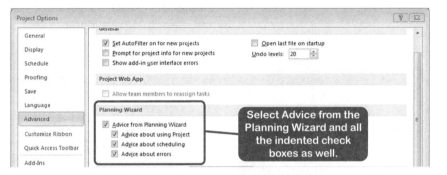

If you attempt to enter a date for a task, the Planning Wizard will suggest to you that this is not the best way to schedule this task and will instead remind you to implement the principle of dynamic scheduling by linking tasks.

You will get an "accidental" constraint of **Start No Earlier Than** when:

➤ You enter a start date into the field Start that immediately follows the finish date of a nearby task above or below it, or

➤ You drag a task bar after the task bar of a nearby task above or below. This can be a very quick method for linking tasks. Here are the steps:

Point to the middle of the task bar; make sure you see a four-headed arrow: ✛.

1. Click and hold down to drag the bar **horizontally** to where you want it scheduled. Make sure you see a horizontal two-headed arrow.

2. Look at the pop-up window to see what the new dates will be:

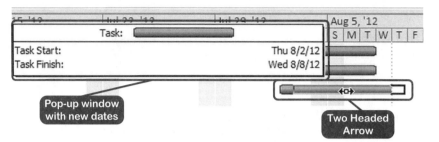

3. Release the mouse when the task bar is scheduled on the date you want, but this should be near the end of another nearby task bar that is above or below it. The following dialog will appear:

Planning Wizard

You moved 'Summarize requirements' just after 'Research staff requirements'.

The Planning Wizard encourages you to use network logic in your schedule.

You can:

◉ Link them. 'Summarize requirements' will always follow 'Research staff requirements'.

◯ Move 'Summarize requirements' without adding a link.

[OK] [Cancel] [Help]

☐ Don't tell me about this again.

4. Select ◉ **Link them** and click [OK].

Using the Link Tool

With the link tool you can create a waterfall of multiple **Finish-to-Start** dependencies with one click after selecting the tasks:

1. If the tasks you want to link are adjacent and in the order you want, simply select them by dragging over their task names. You can select more than two tasks.

OR

If the tasks are not adjacent or not in the order you want, select the driver (predecessor) first, hold down the Control key and click on the first follower (successor). You can click on the task name in the spreadsheet or on its task bar in the timescale. Click on as many tasks as you want to link. Make sure you select the tasks in the order in which you want the tasks linked (from driver to follower). Let go of the Control key when you have them all selected.

2. On the **Task** tab, in the **Schedule** group, click **Link Tasks** 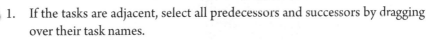 or hold down `Control` and press `F2`; the tasks are now Finish-to-Start dependent.

This method allows you to set Finish-to-Start dependencies only.

To Delete a Chain of Dependencies Between Tasks

1. If the tasks are adjacent, select all predecessors and successors by dragging over their task names.

   OR

   If the tasks are not adjacent, select the predecessor first and then hold down and click the successor. You can click on the task name or on the task bar, and you can click on more than two tasks that you want unlinked.

2. On the **Task** tab, in the **Schedule** group, click **Unlink Tasks** or hold down `Control` + `Shift` and press `F2`.

To Delete All Dependencies on one Task

On the **Task** tab, in the **Schedule** group, select the task and click **Unlink Tasks** .

Be careful: you can easily delete all dependencies in the entire schedule if you select all tasks first by clicking on any column heading and then click Unlink Tasks.

Using the Mouse

Using your mouse to draw dependencies is useful if you have many dependencies pointing up instead of down and also when you want to create parallel paths. Usually this works best when the dependencies are close together.

To Draw Dependencies

1. This method is easier if the task bars are wide. If necessary, On the **View** tab, on the zoom icon, in the **Zoom** group, click **Zoom In** to make the task bars wider/longer.

2. Point to the center of the predecessor task bar; make sure you see a four-headed arrow mouse pointer like. (Near the front of the task bar you will see another mouse pointer: and near the back:.)

3. Click and drag down, then drag vertically toward the successor task bar, making sure the mouse pointer now looks like. A pop-up window tells you between which two tasks you are about to set a Finish-to-Start dependency:

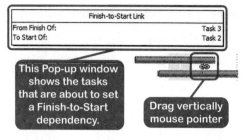

 Do not drag a task bar horizontally to try to link to another task in the Gantt Chart view.

If you drag horizontally, you are rescheduling the task bar and setting a schedule constraint that will make your schedule static instead of dynamic!

4. Release the mouse button inside the task bar of the successor. A dependency is set and shows up as an arrow. The task bar of the successor moves out to just after the finish date of the predecessor's task bar. A **Finish-to-Start** dependency is set:

 If you drag into the edge of the screen, the screen starts scrolling very fast in the Gantt Chart.

This method of setting dependencies allows you to set **Finish-to-Start** dependencies only, but you can use the next steps to change to another type of dependency.

To Edit or Delete a Dependency

1. Point with the tip of the arrow mouse pointer precisely to the dependency arrow you want to change, as in the next screenshot:

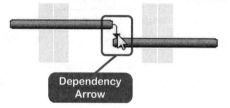

2. Dependency arrows can overlap each other, so wait one second until the feedback window pops up to confirm which dependency you are on.

3. If you have the proper dependency arrow selected, double-click and the **Task Dependency** dialog appears:

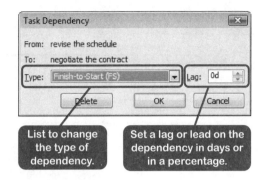

4. Select the type of dependency using the list **Type**

   Finish-to-Start (FS) ▼

   AND

   Enter a positive lag or a negative lag (lead) time, or if needed, a percent in the **Lag** field if you want to set a relative lag.

   OR

5. Click ☐ Delete ☐ to get rid of the dependency.

Using the Task Information Dialog

You may need to use this method if the predecessor and successor tasks are a screen or more apart.

1. Select the successor task.

2. On the **Task** tab, in the **Properties** group, click **Information** or hold down ☐ Shift ☐ and press ☐ F2 ☐; the **Task Information** dialog appears.

3. Click the **Predecessors** tab; the dialog should now look like this:

Task Information   [X]

General | Predecessors | Resources | Advanced | Notes | Custom Fields |

Name: | Visit the Sites   Duration: | 1 day |▲▼| ☐ Estimated

Predecessors:

5			
ID	Task Name	Type	Lag
5	Select the Realtor	Finish-to-Start (FS)	0d

> The Task Information dialog allows you to give the selected successor task one or more predecessors.

Help   OK   Cancel

4. Click in the **Task Name** field in an empty row and select the predecessor task from the list [▼].

    OR

    Enter the ID number of the predecessor in the **ID** field.

5. Select the type of dependency in the **Type** field.

6. Enter a positive lag or a negative lag (lead) time, if needed, or a percent in the **Lag** field if you want to set a relative lag. Click [OK] and the dependencies are entered into the schedule.

 This method allows you to assign multiple predecessors to one task. The next method allows you to set both multiple predecessors and successors to a task.

Using the Task Details Form

The Task Details form allows you to set multiple dependencies—both predecessors and successors—to a task at the same time. The Task Details form also lets you see the dependencies: the arrows in the Gantt timescale run on top of one another and the Task Details form shows you exactly how they run.

1. On the **Task** tab, in the **Properties** group, click on **Display Task Details** [Details]. The **Task Details** form appears in the bottom of the screen.

2. Click on the **Task Details** form (this will change the context-sensitive description above the **Format** tab) and choose the **Format** tab. In the **Details** group, click on **Predecessors & Successors** to view all dependencies of the selected task. Your screen should now look like this:

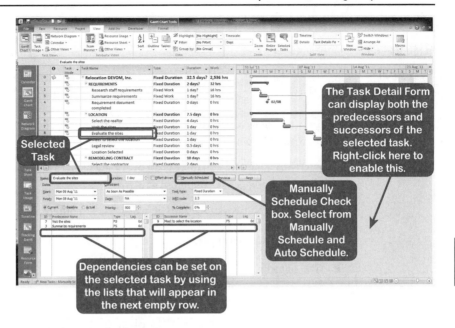

The Task Detail Form can display both the predecessors and successors of the selected task. Right-click here to enable this.

Selected Task

Manually Schedule Check box. Select from Manually Schedule and Auto Schedule.

Dependencies can be set on the selected task by using the lists that will appear in the next empty row.

3. Click in the field **Predecessor Name** or **Successor Name** in an empty row and use the list [‎   ⌄] to create the dependency.

OR

Type the ID number of the predecessor or successor task in the **ID** field.

4. Enter a positive lag or a negative lag (lead) time, if needed, or a percent in the **Lag** field if you want to set a relative lag.

5. Click [OK].

To delete a dependency on the Task Form, select the task name, and when it is highlighted press the [Delete] key on your keyboard. Then click [OK].

 To show predecessors and successors of a particular task in a graphical view you may want to use a combination Gantt Chart/Relationship Diagram view. On the **Task** tab, in the **View** group, click **Gantt Chart**. Next, choose **Display** to **Display Task Details** from the within the **Properties** grouping on the **Task** tab to turn on a combination view. In the lower pane, right-click the title **Task Details** form, click **More Views**. The **More Views** dialog box appears. Select **Relationship Diagram**, and then click **Apply**. You now see the entire chain, which makes checking the logic even easier.

Entering Dependencies in the Network Diagram

The Network Diagram

To apply the view, on the **Task** tab, in the **View** group, click on the **Gantt Chart** down-arrow, **Network Diagram**.

The Network Diagram can display an overview of all the dependencies you have set; the dependencies are depicted as arrows.

By default, the Network Diagram displays tasks in differently shaped nodes:

➤ Summary tasks in a parallelogram

➤ Detail tasks in a rectangle

➤ Milestones in a hexagon

The critical tasks have a red border instead of the (default) blue. The color and the shape of the nodes can be changed by choosing the **Format** tab, **Box Styles** within the **Format** grouping.

Using the Mouse to Set Dependencies

Once you've gained the overview and start to identify places where you are missing important links, you can create them right here in the Network Diagram.

1. Point to the center of the predecessor node and make sure the mouse pointer is a plus sign: ✚.

2. Click and hold down the primary mouse button, then drag towards the node of the successor; the mouse pointer should change to a 🔗. Even if the node is not visible, you can drag against the side of the screen, which will then start scrolling automatically.

3. Release the mouse button in the center of the successor node; an arrow appears and the dependency is set.

This method allows you to set FS dependencies only, but you can easily change the type by double-clicking on a dependency arrow.

 If you change the type of dependency from FS, the arrows will still look like you only have a FS dependency, however, the Link Labels option will display the true nature of the link.

 Do not release the mouse in an empty white space or drag in an empty white space in the Network Diagram view.

If you release the mouse button outside of the successor node, a new task is created! For those who like to build the task list and the network at the same time, this is a great feature. If this happens inadvertently, press ⌊Del⌋ right away, while the new task is still selected, to get rid of it.

Using the Link Button to Set Dependencies

When you use the **Link** button, select the tasks in the order in which you want to link them (select the predecessor first, then its successor, then the successor of the successor, etc.).

1. Hold down ⌊Control⌋ and click on all tasks to link.

   OR

   You can select multiple tasks quickly by dragging a box around them. As soon as you hold down the mouse, the mouse pointer will change to a ✛. When you drag, you are drawing a box with a gray border. Any tasks that you enclose in the box will be selected upon releasing the mouse button.

   You can even select another set of tasks by holding down ⌊Control⌋ before you drag again.

2. On the **Task** tab, in the **Schedule** group, click the **Link** ∞ button to link the tasks.

As in the Gantt Chart view, you can also set dependencies in the Network Diagram view using the Task Information dialog or the Task Details form. The steps are the same as for the Gantt Chart view.

To Edit or Delete a Dependency in the Network Diagram

1. Point with the tip of the mouse pointer to the dependency arrow you want to delete. The pointer should look like this: ⟶.

2. Double-click and the **Task Dependency** dialog appears:

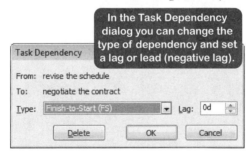

In the Task Dependency dialog you can change the type of dependency and set a lag or lead (negative lag).

3. To edit the dependency, change the **Type** of the dependency using the list

   Finish-to-Start (FS) ▾

   AND

   Enter a positive lag or a negative lag (lead) time, if needed, or a percent in the Lag field if you want to set a relative lag.

You delete a dependency by clicking [Delete] in the **Task Dependency dialog.**

When you delete a dependency arrow, all dependent tasks are rescheduled to their As Soon As Possible date under forward scheduling. They may zip all the way to the project start date and disappear from your screen. We recommend you create the new dependency first and then delete the old dependency to prevent nodes from disappearing from your screen.

Although you may change the dependency type, in the Network Diagram view it will still appear as a FS dependency. You can see the actual dependency type in the Gantt Chart view or by using the Link Labels button on the Format tab while viewing the Network Diagram.

Using the Network Diagram to Display the Schedule

The Network Diagram has an invisible grid, like a spreadsheet. When you press the arrow keys to move the cursor, they will only take you to the visible "cells" in the grid, the task nodes. If you leave the layout challenge to Project 2010, it uses this invisible grid:

1. Turn **Automatically position all boxes off.** If you have it on, the nodes are rearranged with every change you make. It is very difficult to check the logic in the network when the nodes keep jumping all over the place. We recommend turning this off. On the **Format** tab, in the **Format** group, click **Layout** 🔲. The **Layout** dialog box appears.

The Layout dialog allows you to change the layout of the boxes in the Network Diagram.

Layout

Position the boxes manually by dragging.

Layout Mode

○ Automatically position all boxes   ◉ Allow manual box positioning

Box Layout

Arrangement:	Top Down From Left	▼

Row:	Alignment:	Center	▼	Spacing:	40	⏶⏷	Height:	Best Fit	▼
Column:	Alignment:	Center	▼	Spacing:	60	⏶⏷	Width:	Best Fit	▼

☑ Show summary tasks   ☑ Adjust for page breaks
☑ Keep tasks with their summaries

Predefined automatic layouts

Link style

◉ Rectilinear   ○ Straight   ☑ Show arrows   ☐ Show link labels

Link color

◉ Noncritical links: [   ] ▼   Critical links: [   ] ▼
○ Match predecessor box border

Diagram Options

Background color: [   ] ▼   Background pattern: [   ] ▼

☑ Show page breaks   ☑ Hide all fields except ID
☑ Mark in-progress and completed

Check to see many task boxes in the diagram.

| Help | | OK | Cancel |

2.   Select ◉ **Allow manual box positioning** and click [OK].

3.   To see if the logic of the dependencies makes sense, use the arrow keys to follow a chain of dependencies. Click on the first task node in a chain and press [→] to follow the chain forward. When there is a split, press [→] once more to move into one path, and then you can switch between the chains by pressing [↓] OR press [←] to go backward and press [↓] or [↑] to switch chains.

4.   Use the methods discussed before to delete, add or modify dependencies, if necessary.

Gaining an Overview of the Network

Even a large screen can't display a large network in its entirety. In the past large networks were printed on plotters and hung like wallpaper. However, one of the points of this book is that we need to conserve our resources (natural and otherwise), and we have to find a way to see the entire network while keeping task details legible. Here are some tips for how to see more of a large network:

> ➤ Double-click on the active tab. This will temporarily remove the ribbon.
> ➤ If you have the window split, remove it: on the **Task** tab, in the **Properties** group, click on **Details** or point to the divider between the top and bottom view and double-click when you see the mouse pointer ⇳.
>> ▸ Adjust the level of detail by using the **Zoom Slider** ⊖──────◡──────⊕ located in the lower right-hand corner.

If you want to see data about a task while you are zoomed out, point the mouse pointer to a task node and a pop-up window will appear with the task data.

Select the contractor		
Start: 10/08/12	ID: 13	
Finish: 14/08/12	Dur: 2 days	
Res:		

To read and analyze the network while you are zoomed out, you can zoom back into the detail by clicking the **Collapse Boxes** button in the **Display** group on the **Format** tab. Project 2010 always keeps the selected task on the screen when toggling between hiding and displaying the fields. Toggling back and forth is perhaps the easiest way to analyze the network and this button allows you to do this.

Remember that you have to be in the **Network Diagram** view while selecting the **Format** tab in order for the correct formatting options to be presented for this topic.

Dependency Logic on Summary Tasks

There are advantages and disadvantages of setting dependencies on summary tasks.

Advantages of summary dependencies

> ➤ Setting dependencies on summary tasks seems easier and quicker

> ➤ Summary logic is high-level logic that executives sometimes like to see

> ➤ In certain situations, you can make do with one summary dependency instead of setting several dependencies on detail tasks. When detail tasks all start at the same time independently of each other, one dependency on their summary task makes sense. In the next screenshot, tasks 19 to 21 are all driven by the dependency on their summary task, 18.

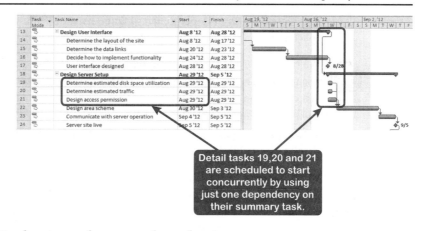

Detail tasks 19,20 and 21 are scheduled to start concurrently by using just one dependency on their summary task.

Disadvantages of summary dependencies

➤ It can be difficult to check whether the network of dependencies is complete. The check is simple if you only have dependencies between detail tasks: you just have to find the detail tasks and milestones without an entry in the predecessor or successor field. If you have logic both on summary tasks and detail tasks in parallel, you cannot perform this simple check any longer. Checking the logic then becomes a very painstaking and laborious process.

The critical path (the longest path in the network and therefore the one that sets the end date)[2] is more difficult to find when the dependencies run over detail tasks and summary tasks in parallel. When you follow the critical path, a critical detail task may not have any successor. It looks like the critical path stops, and you may not realize that the critical path continues through a dependency on the summary task. In the next screenshot, task 17 appears to be the end of the critical path, but it actually continues via the summary dependency to task 21:

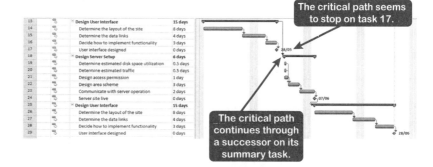

The critical path seems to stop on task 17.

The critical path continues through a successor on its summary task.

➤ On summary tasks, you can only set rough, high-level logic. High-level logic often does not allow you to create the tightest schedule possible.

---

2 See chapter 9 Optimizing the Schedule for more information on critical paths.

> ➤ Not all types of dependencies can be used on summary tasks; you cannot link FF or SF to summary tasks.

 We recommend that you not set dependencies (links) on summary tasks. Even though there seem to be some advantages to setting dependencies on summary tasks, they don't measure up against the disadvantages. Time gained with setting fewer dependencies is lost threefold when checking the logic and analyzing the critical path. We therefore recommend that you keep the dependency logic on detail tasks and milestones only.

Dependencies and Manually Scheduled Tasks

As we mentioned, you can set dependencies with manually scheduled tasks, but you need to consider that these tasks have different internal considerations.

First, when you enter a new manually scheduled task and its duration, you will have a duration only manually scheduled task with this format in your schedule:

2010 As you see in the above screenshot, we have new fields: **Scheduled Duration**, **Scheduled Start** and **Scheduled Finish**. These were added to manage new manually scheduled tasks. For manually scheduled tasks, these fields are the recommended duration, start or finish and are **read-only**. These are the equivalent of the **Duration**, **Start** and **Finish** fields for automatically scheduled tasks.

When you establish a dependency in a duration only manually scheduled task, the **Scheduled Start** and **Scheduled Finish** fields are copied to the **Start** and **Finish** fields:

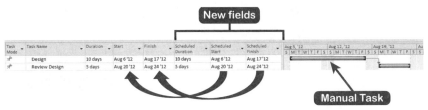

Note that manually scheduled tasks respect the dependency, in this case finish to start, when you first establish the dependency. But if you change something in a manually scheduled task, for example its duration, any predecessor tasks will

maintain the same previous dates and won't honor the new date as auto
scheduled tasks do:

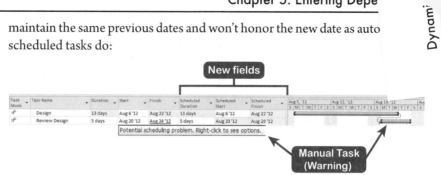

In the previous screenshot you can see that the predecessor manually scheduled
task, **Review Design**, doesn't honor the dependency, but gives you warning
signs about a potential scheduling problem (red squiggly line under the Finish
date and the dotted-line around the Gantt bar). You can also notice that fields
Scheduled Start and **Scheduled Finish** have the information that honor the
dependency, but the fields **Start** and **Finish** have the previous information. If
you want a manually scheduled task to honor the dependencies, you need to
select the task and click **Respect Links** , in the **Task** tab, **Schedule** group.
The **Scheduled Start** and **Scheduled Finish** will be copied to the **Start** and
Finish fields, and the bar will move to the new dates.

Checks on Dependencies

Now that you've entered dependencies, you need to check the network of
dependencies to determine if it will indeed give you the benefit that you created
it for in the first place: if you change one field (Work, Duration, Resources,
Constraints, or Dependencies in the schedule), is the rest of the schedule
updated automatically, so that you immediately have a valid schedule of your
project again? The schedule will update itself only if the answers to the following
questions are all yes:

➤ Is the network of dependencies complete?

➤ Is the network logic simple enough?

➤ Is the network free of circular dependencies?
A circular dependency exists where two tasks drive each other: task A drives
task B, but task B also drives task A. A schedule with circular dependencies
will not be dynamic, but entirely static: Project 2010 can't recalculate a
schedule as soon as a circular dependency is created. The application will
warn you if you try to create circularity in the logic within a single schedule.

 Do not create any circular dependency references within or between
projects.

➤ Does the logic of the network make sense?

➤ Are resource dependencies accounted for?

➤ Are manually-scheduled task warnings considered or resolved in your logic?

After all the previous checks are done, perform one more high level check to see if the resulting schedule actually makes sense.

You can check this best by showing only the first outline levels of the work breakdown structure and checking if the timing of the deliverables (or phases) makes sense on this high level, given business targets and experience with other similar projects. If you go to the **View** tab, in the **Data** group, and click on **Outline** ⊞ you can display **Outline level 2** or **Outline level 3** depending on the size of your project. Even though you may not be an expert in the field of this project, you can always pick up on common sense things like *design* scheduled before *construction*, *write* before *print*, etc.

If you followed our recommendations to minimize the number of constraints and set all dependencies, the start and finish dates of the tasks are driven by the network of dependencies. If the resulting schedule does not make sense, it's likely you've overlooked an essential dependency, estimated overly optimistic or overly pessimistic task durations, over or under allocated resources, etc.

The next screenshot shows a schedule that doesn't make sense from a common sense perspective: it looks like the *move* task starts too early. In this case the probable cause is a missing dependency in a schedule where all tasks are scheduled ASAP. However, if you expanded the move summary task it would become clear that the actual move takes place in the week of November 7 and all the essential logic seems to be there:

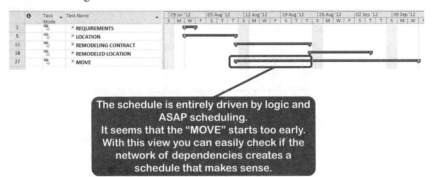

The schedule is entirely driven by logic and ASAP scheduling.
It seems that the "MOVE" starts too early.
With this view you can easily check if the network of dependencies creates a schedule that makes sense.

Is the Network of Dependencies Complete?

The network is complete if the task bars of all detail tasks and milestones are tied up at the end of the schedule. The network can have multiple starting points, but only one ending point. The critical path method is the most widely used technique to manage the time dimension of a project, and you must have only one ending point in the network for the critical path calculation to be correct in a single project.

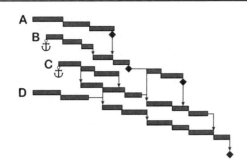

A typical network will look like the illustration. We do not require the network to start with just one starting point: we find that this can make the network unnecessarily complex and that it does not provide additional benefits.

However, when you have multiple starting points, check to see if the detail tasks (A, B, C and D in the illustration) have a missing predecessor. If they don't have a logical predecessor, you need to determine if they can indeed start on the project start date or if they need a Start No Earlier Than constraint (under forward scheduling). You can see that A and D start at the project start date, but B and C have a constraint (anchor), since they start later. B and C do not have a driver (predecessor) and may need one. Whenever there is a constraint, a predecessor may be implied: it may be an external predecessor (e.g., the delivery of something), a resource dependency, or a logical dependency on a task that is not explicitly included in the WBS.

 In the thousands of schedules we've evaluated in our curriculum, we found that about 50% had starting points in the network that should have had a predecessor. So, check your starting points carefully.

Why a Complete Network Is Important

 Make sure your network of dependencies is complete.

There are two reasons why you should complete the network logic in your schedule:

➤ If you forget to set dependencies, the schedule will not update itself properly when you make a change to it. It will not be a dynamic schedule. As we have said, having a dynamic schedule saves time and effort. When you enter changes based on planning scenarios or actual progress, the rest of the schedule is able to update itself automatically so that you quickly have a valid model of the project again.

➤ With an incomplete network you will most likely not have a meaningful critical path (as explained in chapter 9). Or worse, Project 2010 might lead you to think that tasks are critical that really aren't critical at all and you will monitor the wrong tasks closely. Project managers also need to see their critical tasks, because they harbor possibilities for shortening the project and bringing it in on time. In the thousands of schedules we've evaluated in our curriculum, we found that in about 50% of them, the project manager had not identified the real critical path. (The critical path is covered in detail in chapter 9.)

Checks on the Completeness of the Network	Remember that if you miss just one essential dependency, your critical path is wrong, your forecasts are not valid and your model is not dynamic. To check the completeness of your network, ask yourself the following questions:

> Is the logic set only on detail tasks and milestones?
> If dependencies run over summary tasks and detail tasks in parallel, it is too hard to check if the network is complete and too hard to trace and understand the critical path. Therefore, we recommend that you keep the logic on the detail tasks and milestones only. You can check if there are dependencies on summary tasks by applying the filter **04 IIL Summary Tasks with Dependencies**.[3]

> Are all the starts of the detail tasks linked to at least one other task or milestone? Exceptions are:
> ▶ Tasks that can start when the project starts or that are driven by external forces or deliveries rather than by hand-offs within the project.
> ▶ External delivery milestones with a Start No Earlier Than constraint date.
> ▶ Recurring tasks
> ▶ Overhead tasks
> ▶ Hammock tasks

You can verify if all starts are linked by applying the filter **05 IIL Detail Tasks without Predecessors**.[4] If you used SS or FF dependencies, the filter is not conclusive. There will be another check on those described below.

OR

On the **View** tab, in the **Data** group, click **Filter** down-arrow, ⑂ **Display AutoFilter**. In the **Predecessors** column heading, click the button ▾ and choose the blank item in the list. Now all tasks without an entry in the predecessor field will be displayed, including summary tasks (this is where the IIL filter is better). Notice that the column heading title appears in blue to remind you that an AutoFilter is in effect.

> Are all the ends of the detail tasks linked to at least one other task or milestone? Exceptions are:
> ▶ The project end milestone
> ▶ Recurring tasks
> ▶ Overhead tasks
> ▶ Hammock tasks

---

3 This filter can be found in the file *IIL Project 2010 Tools* available for download at www.jrosspub.com. Please click the link *WAV Download Resource Center* to enter the download site.
4 Ibid.

A loose end, hanger or dangling task is a detail task that does not have its finish tied to any other task. In any project there should only be one loose end, the project finish milestone.

You can verify if all ends are linked up by applying the filter **06 IIL Detail Tasks without Successors**.[5] If you used SS or FF dependencies, the filter is not conclusive. There will be another check on those described below.

OR

Display the **AutoFilter** buttons by clicking the **Filter** drop down arrow within the **Data** grouping on the **View** tab. In the **Successors** column heading, click the button ▾ and choose the blank item in the list. Now all tasks without an entry in the successor field will be displayed, including summary tasks (this is where the IIL filter is better). Notice that the column label appears in blue to remind you that an AutoFilter is in effect.

➤ Do you have SS and FF dependencies properly linked?
Project managers often forget to give every task a successor when they use SS or FF dependencies.

People often forget to set a dependency on the finish of the predecessor in an SS dependency (see the question marks in the illustration). The finish must also be linked, otherwise the predecessor could still continue even though the project is finished, since you have not linked it to anything. The check for detail tasks without successors won't find these loose ends. In the illustration, *Pour Concrete* has an SS successor, but its finish is not tied to any other task.

Pour Concrete ??? **SS** **Cure Concrete**

People also often forget to set a dependency on the start of the successor in an FF dependency (see the question marks in the illustration). The task *Train Users* has an FF predecessor, but its start is not linked

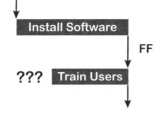

to any other task which means that you don't need to find a trainer or create course material for the task *Train Users*, which is just hard to believe. You are probably missing a link. Alternatively, the start date can be held in place by a schedule constraint.

Again, if you only check that each detail task has a successor, you will not find these loose ends. If you used SS or FF dependencies in your schedule, you should filter and display all those tasks with SS and FF dependencies and check on loose

5   Ibid.

ends manually. You can do this check by applying the filter **07 IIL Detail Tasks with SS or FF**.[6] Since the filter will display both the predecessor and successor tasks involved in the SS or FF dependency, you can check if they are hooked up properly to other tasks by revealing the Predecessors and Successors fields. What you should look for is:

➤ Does a task with SS in the **Successor** field also have an FS or FF successor that ties up its end?

➤ Does a task with FF in the **Predecessor** field also have an SS or FS predecessor that ties up its start?

If the answer to either question is **no**, you have found a missing link.

Make sure SS and FF links aren't missing a beginning or ending link.

➤ Are there tasks with an unreasonably large amount of total slack?
Total slack, as we'll discuss in chapter 9, is buffer time: the amount of time a task can be delayed without impacting an end date in the project. Check if the tasks with the most slack were expected to have a lot of slack. If not, you may have found missing logic. Even after you have given all detail tasks a successor, you should still apply this check, because even if each task has a successor, it does not guarantee that you haven't forgotten important links. Checking the **Total Slack** will actually lead you to where you forgot to set important dependencies in your model of the project.

➤ When a change is entered into the schedule, does it update the rest of the schedule automatically and appropriately through dependencies? Is the entire schedule still valid? Where the schedule is not valid, an essential dependency might be missing. If you have to check the entire schedule after each change, you don't have a dynamic model. Remember, the logic should be helpful especially during project execution when you update your schedule regularly.

Exceptions to the Rule of a Complete Network

Certain tasks do not need links:
➤ Summary tasks
➤ Recurring detail tasks like status meetings
➤ Overhead tasks like project management or quality control
➤ Hammock tasks that support a process

All other detail tasks and milestones (except the end of the project) need to have at least one successor. If you cannot find logical links to other detail tasks in your schedule, you should create a link to the project end milestone. If you don't have a project end milestone, you should create one even if this only serves the

---

6   Ibid.

purpose of hooking up all your loose ends. Certain tasks can only be linked to the project end milestone. Examples are:

➤ Tasks to inform other departments or organizations (not related to completing project deliverables).

➤ Tasks that create entirely independent parts of a system, which can easily and quickly be assembled without much effort. If it will take effort, you should definitely consider creating a detail task for assembling the final product.

Is the Network Logic Simple Enough?

 Make sure the network logic is logical and simple.

A network that is too complex to understand and maintain is not helpful in managing the project. Redundant dependencies clutter the view and make the network overly complicated. If the network is complicated, team members will not try to understand or use it. Many project managers fall prey to the following fallacy: *All tasks are related to each other, and I have to set dependencies everywhere I notice relationships.* While all tasks are related to each other (that is how you arrive at a complete network of dependencies), most tasks are only related **indirectly** to each other, i.e. via other tasks.

You only have to link the tasks that have a **direct** relationship.

The following questions will help you determine if the network is simple enough:

➤ Are there dependencies that leapfrog each other? Dependencies that skip over the back of multiple dependencies within a chain are redundant. These are the indirect relationships. Remove them.

➤ Are there dependencies that run in parallel on detail tasks and their summary tasks? If that is the case, keep the detail task dependency and remove the parallel dependency on the summary task.

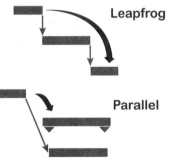

➤ Can you, as the project manager, explain the network to your project team? If you can't, the network is too complex.

If you can explain the network, you can immediately show a team member who else will be affected if his or her task slips. This is a very powerful method to motivate team members to deliver on time and to facilitate coordination within your team.

A clear network also allows you to do a quick impact analysis of suggestions made by executives. Imagine that your project sponsor on a software development project comes to you during the execution phase and asks: "What if we wait for the new release of this operating system?" or "What if we use this new line of more powerful computers?" With a simple network, you will be able to indicate the impacts very clearly by following the dependency arrows from the components that will be affected by such a change in direction. You may be able to stem some unwanted turbulence, or immediately negotiate for more time or money.

Limitations on Dependencies

There are some technical limitations when creating dependencies:

> **You can set only one link between two tasks**
> It is impossible to set more than one link between two tasks. You will receive the following error message:

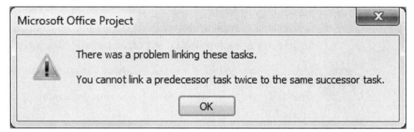

Therefore you can't hook up both the start and the finish of two tasks using an SS as well as an FF dependency. For example, you may have set a SS dependency between *relocate the drywall* and *wire the electricity*. If relocating the walls takes longer than planned, your model may show that the electricians finish earlier than the carpenters, which is unreasonable. If you could set a FF dependency between the same tasks, the problem would be solved. A workaround for this is to insert an extra milestone and run two FF dependencies to and from that milestone.

> **You cannot set links on all parts of a split task bar**
> You cannot set dependencies on all parts of a split task bar; you can only link to the start of the first part and from the finish of the last part. Therefore you cannot create very dynamic models with split task bars. This is the reason why we don't recommend using them when you are planning the project; you will see enough splits appear when you update during project execution.

> **You cannot link to the finish of a summary task**
> You cannot set a FF or SF dependency to a summary task as the successor, because the finish date of a summary task is always calculated. However, you

can link **from** the finish of the summary task. Remember, however, that we don't recommend logic on summary tasks.

➤ **Percentage lags only apply to the duration of the predecessor task**
You cannot set a lag that takes a percentage of the duration of the successor task; the percentages are always taken from the duration of the predecessor. So you cannot create a dependency that drives, for example, the halfway point of a successor.

A Special Topic: Dynamic Links

Another way to manage a different type of relationship in Project 2010 is with dynamic links. These links are useful in managing overhead tasks, hammock tasks, and for utilizing data from other applications.

Dynamic links are useful when the start, finish, duration or other task data affect elements of another task in the project schedule.

 Dynamic links tend to be easily broken and it is a good idea to attach a note to the linked tasks to document the link. This will assist in reestablishing a broken link.

To establish a dynamic link, you copy the cell of the driving task's information, and then paste a link into the cell of the driven task's information, by choosing **Paste Special**, and **Paste Link**. The linked cell updates itself automatically when the driving task's information changes and saves you the need to constantly adjust the affected task. Following are some of the uses for dynamic links, but before we get to them, here are some cautions:

 Dynamic links are good options to assist in modeling your schedule, but we recommend minimizing your use of them. Every time you enter a change in Project 2010, the dynamic links will be updated (if the calculation mode is set to automatic), and you will notice a blink in the screen. If you have a lot of dynamic links you will have an annoying number of blinks every time you update your schedule.

 You may have concerns with the displayed critical path and slack using dynamic links, because the critical path calculations use the logical dependencies.

 A dynamic link adds a constraint in your task (check the icon in the Indicators column), but it really isn't a constraint because it is updated according to the dynamically linked cells.

Overhead Tasks

Overhead tasks are tasks that are ongoing during the entire project, for example *project management*, *technical support* and *quality control*. You may think it isn't necessary to track these items in your schedule but they consume resources, create expenses and could have consequences to your project if you forget them, especially project management tasks. Overhead tasks are typically placed near the top of the project.

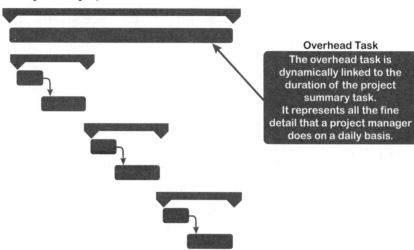

Overhead Task
The overhead task is dynamically linked to the duration of the project summary task.
It represents all the fine detail that a project manager does on a daily basis.

You can enter overhead tasks in one of two ways: as a long-duration task (long task bar), or as a recurring task (discussed in detail in chapter 4).

The long-duration task method is easier to maintain since the task bar automatically extends when the project extends, while the recurring task feature requires you to add additional occurrences and apply resource assignments to the new occurrences if the project extends. If you intend to solve resource over allocations in your project, the long-duration task has only one resource assignment that may need to be modified, while the recurring task has numerous resource assignments that may need to be modified. By default, recurring tasks are excluded from the Level Now function (chapter 9 includes a discussion on leveling options).

The dynamic link that is recommended for an overhead task is to copy the duration of the overall project summary task and Paste Special, Paste Link it to the duration of the overhead task.

As you have probably concluded, we recommend you enter overhead tasks as a long-duration task rather than a recurring task.

Typically the project manager performs many tasks that may be too brief and repetitive to include in the schedule (e.g., responding to voicemail and email, mentoring, communications, conflict resolution). These can be rolled into a single item called *Project Management* to account for the project manager's time and cost.

Hammock Tasks

A hammock task is also called a supporting task (envision the shape of a hammock) or a task that must occur sometime within a date range or must occur the entire length of a date range. An example of a hammock task could be the task *Project Management*, where the project manager is assigned to the task and manages the project on a daily basis during the life-cycle of the project. A hammock task is usually illustrated as a long-duration task just below a series of tasks. The tasks that represent the date range might be milestone tasks or regular tasks, but independently they do not equal the overall duration of the hammock task.

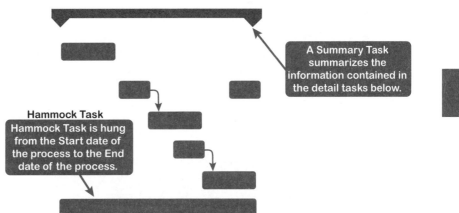

A Summary Task summarizes the information contained in the detail tasks below.

Hammock Task
Hammock Task is hung from the Start date of the process to the End date of the process.

The dynamic link that is recommended for a hammock task is to copy the Start Date from the first task and **Paste Special**, **Paste Link** it to the Start Date of the hammock task and then copy the Finish Date from the last task and **Paste Special**, **Paste Link** it to the Finish Date of the hammock task. The result is the overall duration of the hammock is calculated.

Often a hammock task is used to represent the length of time a series of tasks in a process will take. In this example, there are three tasks (A, B, C) that form a process. The hammock task D will start with the beginning of the process and end when the process ends.

➤ Tasks A (4 days), B (3 days) and C (8 days) are linked sequentially with Finish-to-Start logical dependencies. A, B and C represent the flow of work in the process.
➤ Task D is representative of the overall process. If we copy the start date of task A and then **Paste Special, Paste Link** into the start date of task D, then the these tasks are linked by start dates.
➤ To complete task D, we copy the finish date of task C and **Paste Special, Paste Link** into the finish date of task D.
➤ Note that the duration of task D is now 15 days (matching the duration of the process).

For the dynamic links to work properly, the hammock task <u>must not</u> be a Fixed Duration task type.

Now suppose that the duration of task B has been increased to 7 days. You will notice that task D will adjust its duration automatically to 19 days. The same will occur if you increase or reduce any of the tasks included in the process (group).

 We recommend placing the hammock task just **below** the process (group of tasks). This will allow you to update the tasks, top to bottom, and when you arrive at the hammock task, it will already be updated. During the tracking or updating cycle, just "update as scheduled".

 Do not link a predecessor task to the hammock since its position in the schedule and start date are already controlled by the dynamic link.

Review Questions

1. Why should a project manager set all the dependencies in her schedule?

2. How are dependencies handled in manually-scheduled tasks?

3. What is the difference between **Duration**, **Start** and **Finish** fields, versus **Scheduled Duration**, **Scheduled Start** and **Scheduled Finish** fields?

4. What are the criteria for a good and solid network of dependencies that creates an entirely dynamic schedule?

5. If you are dependent upon supplies to arrive for one deliverable in your project, what would you recommend in terms of scheduling this situation?

6. This chapter covered multiple ways of setting dependencies. Please name at least 4 of them.

7. Are the following valid entries in the lag field? Yes or no? Why?
   a. 5d
   b. –3d
   c. +30%
   d. +5ed

8. Should you allow logic on summary tasks? Why or why not?

9. How would you schedule ordering materials and receiving materials with a delivery time of 3 weeks? Would you use a Finish-to-Start dependency with a 3-week lag? Or would you split the task bar for 3 weeks? Explain your answer.

10. For each of the following situations determine:
    ▶ Which task is the predecessor and successor: A or B?
    ▶ What type of dependency you need: FS, SS, FF or SF?
    ▶ Whether you would add a lead or a lag to the dependency? If so, as a relative lag or absolute lag? And how much?

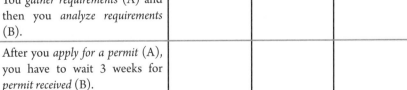

	Predecessor (A or B)	Type of Dependency	Add Lag? Relative/ absolute? How much?
You *gather requirements* (A) and then you *analyze requirements* (B).			
After you *apply for a permit* (A), you have to wait 3 weeks for *permit received* (B).			

	Predecessor (A or B)	Type of Dependency	Add Lag? Relative/ absolute? How much?
Halfway through *perform system analysis* (A) we typically *start programming code* (B).			
You have to *pour foundation* (A) and let the concrete dry before you *lay bricks* (B) to *erect the walls*.			
One day after the finish of *conduct courses* (A), *write evaluation report* (B) *has to be completed*.			
Prepare for the PMP exam (A) and *take the PMP exam (B)*.			

11. You have a task, *test unit*, with a 10-day duration, and you need to decide between using a FS-5d or a SS+5d dependency with this task as the predecessor. The FS-5d dependency will give the successor a different start date than the SS+5d when:
    a. The start date of test unit changes
    b. The finish date of test unit changes (while its start date stays the same)
    c. The duration of test unit changes
    d. The finish date or the duration of test unit changes

12. You have two tasks, *survey clients* and *summarize survey results*, and you need to decide between using a FS-30% or a SS+70% dependency between the two tasks. The FS-30% dependency will cause a different start date of the successor than the SS+70% dependency when:
    a. The start date of *survey clients* changes
    b. The finish date of *survey clients* changes (while its start date stays the same)
    c. The duration of *survey clients* changes
    d. None of the above will cause an impact between FS-30% and SS+70%

Additional Practice For experience working with the features you've learned about in this chapter, we strongly suggest that you do the additional exercises for this chapter that are included in Appendix 1.

Chapter 6: Entering Deadlines, Constraints and Task Calendars

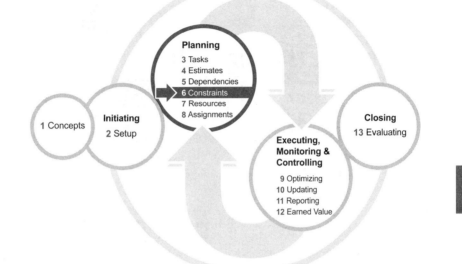

Your Gantt Chart is starting to take shape. There may be certain constraint dates or deadline dates that you have to add to your model to make it stay within the boundaries of the reality of your project. In this chapter we cover three features that capture specific dates: constraints, deadlines and Task Calendars.

After reading this chapter you will be able to:

➤ Describe the differences between constraints and deadlines
➤ Describe the different types of schedule constraints
➤ Discuss in which situations to use constraints or deadlines
➤ Choose the right type of constraint
➤ Enter schedule constraints and deadlines into your project model
➤ Describe the advantages and disadvantages of using constraints
➤ Describe the advantages and disadvantages of using deadlines
➤ Recognize when it's better to use Task Calendars than constraints
➤ Create a Task Calendar and restrict the scheduling of a task with it
➤ Use scheduling best practices to check your deadlines, constraints and Task Calendars

I'm happy to announce that the MEGA STADIUM
will be ready to open in two weeks!

MEGA
STADIUM

But Sir, the electrical and plumbing won't be
finished for two months!

Vanna a.

What Are Deadlines and Schedule Constraints?

Sometimes you need certain tasks to be scheduled on specific dates (e.g., if you are waiting on a resource and there is no logical predecessor task identified). There are two basic methods for identifying tasks to be started or completed on specific dates: using constraints or using deadlines.

➤ A constraint is a date that restricts Project 2010 in scheduling a task

As we'll see, there are various types of constraints you can set; all of them impact the scheduling of tasks in your project. For example, if you set a constraint that a task must start as soon as possible, Project 2010 will tend to pull related tasks towards earlier completion dates in your schedule.

This can restrict the dynamic nature with which tasks shift when you enter changes, create scheduling conflicts and require you to spend more time resolving these conflicts.

➤ A deadline is a date you commit to that does not restrict the scheduling of a task

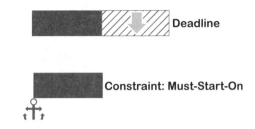

Fixing dates is a matter of putting a schedule constraint on the task. One option for this would be a Must Start On constraint for the task. A Must Start On is a hard constraint, and Project 2010 cannot reschedule tasks with hard constraints.

Deadline dates stay visible in the timescale as down-facing green arrows ⇩. When you miss a deadline date Project 2010 displays a visual indicator ◆ in the ⓘ **Indicators** column.

We recommend that you enter dates you are committed to as deadline dates rather than as constraint dates. Since deadlines don't restrict the scheduling, they don't cause the same kinds of scheduling conflicts as constraints, which can require continuous and immediate maintenance (as we'll see when we discuss the Planning Wizard warnings that scheduling conflicts cause). If tasks slip in the schedule, Project 2010 can adjust an unconstrained schedule to show the impact of the slippage on the target date. This ability to forecast in the schedule enables early responses instead of knee-jerk reactions at the last minute.

6

Deadlines

Although deadlines don't restrict scheduling, they do have an impact on the critical path. If you enter a deadline before the task's finish date, all of the predecessor tasks now show up as critical. This is due to the way Project calculates the backward pass. If you think about it, it makes sense because you are now missing a deadline and this creates negative slack (suggesting you do not have any time to spare). Constraints also behave this way.

Entering Deadlines

1. On the **Task** tab in the **View** group, click **Gantt Chart**.

2. Double-click on the task for which you want to set the deadline.

   OR

   Select the task for which you want to set a deadline then, on the **Task** tab, in the **Properties** group, click **Information** 🖳

   OR

   Hold down [Shift] and press [F2]. The **Task Information** dialog box appears.

3. Click the **Advanced** tab; the dialog box will appear:

Task Information

General | Predecessors | Resources | **Advanced** | Notes | Custom Fields

Name: Contractor contracted   Duration: 0 days   ☐ Estimated

Constrain task

Deadline: Wed Aug 29, '12 ▼

	August, 2012	
Su Mo Tu We Th Fr Sa		

Constraint type: As Soon As Possible   Fri 07 Sep '12 ▼

```
    Su  Mo  Tu  We  Th  Fr  Sa
    29  30  31   1   2   3   4
     5   6   7   8   9  10  11
    12  13  14  15  16  17  18
    19  20  21  22  23  24  25
    26  27  28  29  30  31   1
     2   3   4   5   6   7   8
```

Task type: Fixed Duration

Calendar: None

WBS code: 3.5

Earned value method: % Compl

☑ Mark task as milestone

> The Advanced tab allows setting a deadline date.

Help   OK   Cancel

4. Under **Constrain task**, type the deadline date in the **Deadline** field or use the pull-down calendar to click on a date.

5. Click [OK] and you will now see an arrow ⬇ in the timescale that represents the deadline date you entered. If you rest your mouse pointer on it, you will see its screen tip.

Enter your deadline in Project 2010 at least one day before the actual deadline. Since by default Project 2010 uses the end of the day on the deadline date you enter, if you have to be done before that date, enter the previous day as your deadline date.

You can move deadline dates by simply dragging the deadline arrow ⬇ in the timescale to a new date. You can start dragging as soon as you see the four-arrow mouse pointer ✥.

The symbol for a deadline ⬇ does not stand out in the timescale, particularly when there are many dependency arrows. We suggest you change it to a solid symbol and more striking color in the **Bar Styles** dialog box: on the **Format** tab, in the **Gantt Chart Style** group, click the **Format Bar Styles** down-arrow in the lower right hand corner.

To remove a deadline, simply delete the date from the **Deadline** field on the **Advanced** tab of the **Task Information** dialog box.

Managing Deadlines

You will not get automatic warning messages from Project 2010 if deadlines are overrun because of the slippage of a logical predecessor or the task taking longer than expected. What you do get is an exclamation icon ◆ in the **Indicators** column, which serves as a red flag that a deadline has been missed.

You can quickly display all tasks with deadlines by using one of the built-in filters. To do this:

On the **View** tab, in the **Data** group, click the **Filter** down-arrow, **More Filters**. The **More Filter** dialog box appears. Select **Tasks with Deadlines**, then **Apply**.

Press 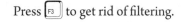 to get rid of filtering.

Constraints

Scheduling Regimes

Before discussing the types of constraints, we need to discuss the two basic scheduling regimes you can choose:

➤ **Forward Scheduling** from the project start date
You do forward scheduling if you entered the project start date and want the model to tell you the expected finish date for the project. Under forward scheduling, tasks are scheduled as soon as possible (ASAP) by default.

➤ **Backward Scheduling** from the project finish date
You schedule backward if you entered the project finish date and want to find out when to start the project to meet this date. Under backward scheduling tasks are scheduled As Late As Possible (ALAP) by default.

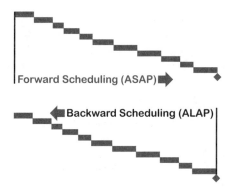

You can see whether you are using forward or backward scheduling by checking the **Schedule From** dropdown in the **Project Information** dialog box. To do this, on the **Project** tab, in the **Properties** group, click **Project Information**. If the value in **Schedule from** is **Project Start Date**, you're using forward scheduling. If the value is **Project Finish Date**, you're using backward scheduling.

If you change your scheduling regime, e.g., from forward to backward scheduling after you have entered tasks, the constraint for these tasks will stay ASAP; new tasks will be ALAP. Combining ASAP tasks with ALAP tasks in one schedule sometimes creates unexpected results.

Schedule Conflict

You will have a schedule conflict when Project 2010 can't find an acceptable and feasible schedule for you based on the input you've provided. For example, your schedule is currently 12 weeks long, but you have set a Finish No Later Than constraint for the project in week 11. Typically a schedule conflict occurs when a constraint date is not met. Project 2010 will immediately tell you when there is a schedule conflict with the message in one of the dialog boxes below.

> **Planning Wizard**   ✕
>
> This action will cause a scheduling conflict. Task 27 of 'Relocation Chapter 6' has a task constraint or is linked to a task that cannot move, and as a result the constraint or the link cannot be set.
>
> **This dialog appears immediately and repeatedly when you make a change that causes a schedule conflict.**
>
> You can:
>
> ⦿ Cancel. Avoid the scheduling conflict.
> ◯ Continue. Allow the scheduling conflict.
>
> [OK] [Cancel] [Help]
>
> ☐ Don't tell me about this again.

OR

> **Planning Wizard**   ✕
>
> You set a Finish No Later Than constraint on the task 'New location opened'. This could result in a scheduling conflict either now or later because this task has at least one other task linked to it.
>
> **This dialog provides some constructive hints on how to resolve the conflict.**
>
> You can:
>
> ⦿ Cancel. No constraint will be set on 'New location opened'.
> ◯ Continue, but avoid the conflict by using a Finish No Earlier Than constraint instead.
> ◯ Continue. A Finish No Later Than constraint will be set.
>
> [OK] [Cancel] [Help]
>
> ☐ Don't tell me about this again.

You are forced to deal with the scheduling conflict because one of the two dialog boxes will keep popping up (unless you check **Don't tell me about this again**).

To turn these notifications off:

1. On the **File** tab, in the **Backstage** view, click **Options**, **Advanced**.

2. In the **Planning Wizard** area, uncheck **Advice about Scheduling** and **Advice about Errors**.

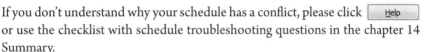

Selecting the Advice from Planning Wizard check boxes will ensure that you get warnings about making changes that affect constraint dates.

If you don't understand why your schedule has a conflict, please click [Help] or use the checklist with schedule troubleshooting questions in the chapter 14 Summary.

Types of Constraints

The eight types of constraints can be characterized as flexible; semi-flexible or inflexible:

Tendencies (Flexible) constraints
➤ As Soon As Possible (ASAP, the default under forward scheduling)
➤ As Late As Possible (ALAP, the default under backward scheduling)

One-sided (Semi-flexible) constraints
➤ Start No Earlier Than (SNET)
➤ Finish No Earlier Than (FNET)
➤ Start No Later Than (SNLT)
➤ Finish No Later Than (FNLT)

Rigid (Inflexible) constraints
➤ Must Start On (MSO)
➤ Must Finish On (MFO)

Tendencies (Flexible) Constraints

Project 2010 uses forward scheduling as its default regime and schedules tasks As Soon As Possible (ASAP). Project 2010 will pull task bars in the timescale as far to the left as the network of predecessors allows.

Even when the regime is ASAP, you can still schedule certain tasks As Late As Possible (ALAP). For example, in a move project you might schedule packing equipment ALAP. Training is another task that should generally take place as late as possible so that people remember what they've been taught when they need to use it. ALAP task bars will tend to go to the right in the timescale as much as the network of successors and constraints allows.

 Note that the one ALAP task tends to be stronger than it's ASAP successors, so check that the one ALAP task did not hijack the rest of your schedule.

Under backward scheduling, tasks are ALAP by default, but you can still change some tasks to ASAP scheduling.

 Even though ALAP and ASAP do not have a constraint date, their attempts to pull tasks earlier or later have a tremendous impact on the schedule and are in that sense "constraining".

 Manually scheduled tasks use ASAP or ALAP constraint types only. You must change the task to be auto-scheduled to take advantage of other constraint types.

One-Sided (Semi-Flexible) Constraints

Semi-flexible or one-sided constraints limit the movement of task bars to only one direction, either to the left (no earlier than) or to the right (no later than):

➤ Start No Earlier Than (SNET) and Finish No Earlier Than (FNET) constrain free movement of the task bars towards the left in the timescale: the start date (SNET) or finish date (FNET) cannot go to the left of the No Earlier Than date.

➤ Start No Later Than (SNLT) and Finish No Later Than (FNLT) constrain free movement of the task bars towards the right in the timescale: the start date (SNLT) or finish date (FNLT) cannot go to the right of the No Later Than date.

No Earlier Than Constraints

An example of a Start No Earlier Than (SNET) constraint is when raw materials will not be delivered until a certain date and you can start the activity for which you need the raw materials no earlier than the delivery date.

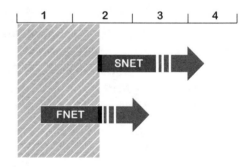

An example of a Finish No Earlier Than (FNET) is when you need a final approval for a deliverable. You know the approval can take place during the next board meeting planned on the first day of every month. You enter a FNET constraint on the first of the next month.

The No Earlier Than constraints are restricted from moving earlier in time (to the left in the timescale). They can be pushed to the right by the network without a limit. Under ASAP scheduling they will not be able to cause a schedule conflict; in other words, they are soft constraints under forward scheduling.

 Under backward scheduling, the project finish date is hard. As you enter dependencies you will see that the As Late As Possible (ALAP) task bars will be pushed out earlier in time (moving to the left in the timescale). They can be pushed to the left as far as the No Earlier Than date allows. If pushed any further, Project 2010 will alert you to a schedule conflict. No Earlier Than constraints are therefore said to be hard constraints under backward scheduling.

 A tiny little red dot in the icon in the **Indicators** column will tell you if a constraint is hard. If the dot is blue, it is a soft constraint.

No Later Than Constraints

An example of a Start No Later Than (SNLT) constraint might be the backing up of a computer system that can be scheduled at a later time, but would have to start no later than, let's say, midnight in order to be finished on time.

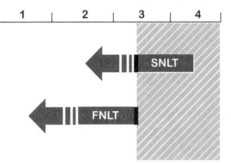

An example of a Finish No Later Than (FNLT) constraint is when you commit to deliver a report no later than March 13 and this date is a do-or-die date.

 In an instance such as this, we suggest you use both a deadline and a constraint. The deadline will give you an early warning before you miss the constraint (do-or-die) date.

The No Later Than constraints are restricted from moving beyond the date specified (moving to the right in a timescale view). They can be allowed earlier by the network all the way up to the start date of the project. Under ALAP scheduling these constraints will not be able to cause a schedule conflict. In other words, they are soft under backward scheduling.

 Under forward scheduling, the project start date is hard. As you enter dependencies, you will see that the As Soon As Possible (ASAP) task bars will be pushed out to the right in the timescale. They can be pushed out as far as the No Later Than constraint date allows. If pushed any further, Project 2010 will warn you that there is a schedule conflict. Therefore, No Later Than constraints are said to be hard constraints under forward scheduling.

A tiny little red dot in the icon in the **Indicators** column will tell you if a constraint is hard. If the dot is blue, it is a soft constraint.

Rigid (Inflexible) Constraints

The inflexible or rigid constraints—Must Start On (MSO) and Must Finish On (MFO)—fix <u>one end</u> of task bar to the date indicated and deny any free movement at that end. Constraints like these will severely affect your schedule.

Note that the unconstrained end of the task bar can still move in either direction when you revise the estimate.

Use a semi-flexible constraint instead of a rigid or inflexible constraint whenever possible. With a one-sided constraint, the constrained end of the task (Start or Finish) can still move in one direction, giving your schedule more flexibility than if the end was not allowed to move at all—as is the case with the rigid constraints.

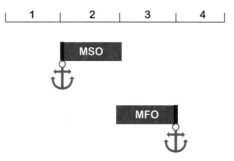

An example of a Must Start On (MSO) constraint is holding an important meeting that must start on January 9 at 9:00 AM.

An example of a Must Finish On (MFO) constraint is when you have a contractual date by which you must move out of an office space or pay a steep penalty.

Where you use an MSO constraint, the start will always be on the date indicated. With an MFO constraint, the finish will always be on the date specified. MSO and MFO constraints can easily cause schedule conflicts. These constraints are always hard constraints under both forward and backward scheduling. They should be used only when you absolutely need them to keep the schedule valid. Let's explore some situations.

When Might You Need Constraints?

Deadlines do not need a lot of maintenance while the project is running, but constraints do. Every time you have a change in your schedule, you may either have to update all the constraint dates downstream, or you will have to solve all the schedule conflicts. If you don't solve scheduling conflicts right away, Project 2010 will keep popping up messages until you do. Constraints require immediate attention when you may not have time. If a task doesn't have any constraints, its dependencies push it into place in the timescale.

 We recommend, therefore, that you enter only the constraints that are absolutely necessary. However, you can enter many deadlines in your schedule without many disadvantages.

Constraints should <u>not</u> be used to model temporary availability of resources. A better place to indicate temporary availability is through availability profiles. Constraints also should not be used to create a limited scheduling window for certain tasks, for example to force an office move task to the weekend. A better way to do that is through a Task Calendar (covered later in this chapter). Task calendars create a more dynamic model than constraints, because you can mark every weekend as a target for the move task. If one weekend cannot be met, the Task Calendar will force it to the next weekend and will update all dependent forecasts. With constraints you would be restricted to scheduling on one particular weekend.

Here are some situations where it may be appropriate to set constraints:

➤ External dependencies
We recommended that an external dependency be entered as an extra milestone and that the milestone be held in place by a Start No Earlier Than (SNET) constraint.

➤ Weather restrictions
For example, if you have to get road construction done before the rainy or winter season starts (or after it ends), a constraint can help. Later in this chapter we'll cover another feature called Task Calendars that we recommend you use to schedule in these situations.

➤ Group activities
Meetings, presentations, training or, in general, tasks that involve a group of people may require a set date. When the date is agreed upon, a constraint should be set on that date so Project 2010 does not move it off of its date. Often, you will use Must Start On or Must Finish On constraints here.

➤ Certain milestones (see the following section).

Types of Milestones

Milestones are used in a schedule to indicate events like decisions, approvals, target dates and ceremonies.

The type of constraint needed for a milestone will depend on the "hardness" of the milestone. The hardness of a milestone is the resistance you will experience in practice when you try to move its date.

➤ For soft dates, you can use the deadline feature instead of constraints
➤ For hard dates, use schedule constraints. The harder the date, the harder the constraint should be. The hardest constraints are MSO and MFO.

Here are the different types of milestones used in schedules, listed from soft to hard:

➤ Decision points

These are important events on which decisions about the remainder of the project are made. The decision can be:

▶ Go/No-go: A no-go decision will end the project. A go decision will authorize spending for the next phase.

▶ Go-left/Go-right: The how-to or direction is determined for the rest of the project. You will often find this type of milestone in R&D projects where the research findings determine the direction (the deliverables) for the rest of the project.

If there is a target date or a deadline for the decision point, we recommend using the deadline feature. The decision will typically not be taken until the required information is available. That is why these dates are often soft dates.

➤ Target dates

These are soft deadlines that are inserted to break up a long series of tasks. They focus the efforts on finishing a component of a deliverable. The project manager decides with the team where to insert these target dates. Teams may need several target dates on components of their deliverable in order to meet the deadline of the overall deliverable. Target dates are interim evaluation points; they function as reminders to keep everyone focused and on track. For target dates, we recommend the use of the deadline feature and no constraints.

➤ Do-or-die dates

These are hard deadlines (often contractual dates) by which you are committed to hand over a deliverable. These dates should be clear in the schedule at all times. We recommend you enter these into the schedule as deadlines as much as possible in order to keep the schedule dynamic. However, if one is a very hard contractual date (e.g., there is a huge penalty associated with missing the date), you could consider a Finish No Later Than (FNLT) constraint. This allows the task to float up to the constraint date and never pass it without immediately notifying you with a pop-up dialog.

➤ Deliveries

We recommend you enter the delivery dates of raw materials, supplies or client deliverables as separate milestones in the work breakdown structure. The delivery date you agreed upon with the vendor, supplier or client should be entered as an event milestone with a Start No Earlier Than (SNET) constraint.

➤ Ceremonies

Ceremonies are short official events to which many people are invited. If the duration of the ceremony is negligible, it can be entered as a milestone with a zero duration. An example might be the official ribbon cutting to open a new plant. The date of a ceremony is often hard, because ceremonies are public events. The schedule needs a Must Start On (MSO) constraint for these events. If the ceremony has a duration, it is no longer a milestone, but a task and will still need a constraint.

➤ Project end date
This is the delivery date for the project product. Meeting the project end date is always a challenge in project management. All the chains of dependencies come together in the project end milestone. A Must Finish On (MFO) or a Finish No Later Than (FNLT) constraint is often set on the project end date. You will immediately receive a scheduling conflict message when this date is in jeopardy. In many projects, a deadline date could do the trick as well. You will then only see the red exclamation icon appear in the column if the deadline is missed.

 When initially planning your schedule enter a milestone task as the last task at the bottom of your schedule with a deadline which represents the due date of your schedule. Then link all the tasks in the schedule to the milestone.

This is preferable to entering a constraint on your last task; it gives you the most flexibility in planning your schedule and you can visually see the date you are working towards.

Entering and Removing Constraints in Project 2010

Choosing the Options

To access the options, click the **File** tab on the Ribbon to enter the **Backstage** view, then click the **Options** button.

Project Options	Recommended Choices
Schedule	**Set the Schedule Options on the Schedule Tab:**
	☑ **Tasks will always honor their constraint dates** We recommend you keep this option on to make sure your schedule observes the few real and hard constraint dates that you may have in it. (We'll cover this in a minute.)

Entering Constraints

Just as with deadlines, if you have to be done before November 1, you have to enter October 31 as the constraint date. The constraint time will be at the end of the day on the date you enter. If you enter November 1 as the date, the task won't be scheduled to be done until 5:00 PM on November 1.

You can set constraint dates in a variety of ways:

➤ Use the Advanced tab on the Task Information dialog box

➤ Use the task fields Constraint Type and Constraint Date
➤ Drag task bars:
  This method will allow you to set only Start No Earlier Than (SNET) constraints under forward scheduling or Finish No Later Than (FNLT) constraints under backward scheduling.

➤ Enter dates:
  Under forward scheduling you can enter a start date that will set an SNET constraint, or you can enter a finish date that will set a Finish No Earlier Than (FNET) constraint. Under backward scheduling, entering a start date will create a Start No Later Than (SNLT) constraint; a finish date creates an FNLT constraint. (This is probably too much to remember!)

As is often the case in Project 2010, there are several ways to do the same thing. The last two ways are easy and quick, but require you to know and predict which constraints Project 2010 will set. Therefore, although we'll discuss all four methods below, we recommend using the first two.

*Setting
Constraints
Using the Task
Information Dialog*

We recommend you use either this method or the next method to set constraints.

1. Select the task.

2. On the **Task** tab, in the **Properties** group, click **Information** ▭▤ OR hold
   down [Shift⎵] and press [F2].

3. The **Task Information** dialog box appears. Click the **Advanced** tab; the
   dialog box should now look like this:

4. Select the type from the **Constraint type** pull-down list and select a date
   from the **Constraint date** drop-down calendar.

5. Click [OK].

*Setting
Constraints Using
the Task Fields*

With this method, you start by inserting two columns in your Gantt table.

1. First insert the field **Constraint Type** by right-clicking on the column
   heading before which you wish to insert and selecting **Insert Column**
   from the dropdown. When the new column list appears, type or select
   Constraint Type.

[Type Column Name]

% Complete
% Work Complete
Active
Actual Cost
Actual Duration
Actual Finish
Actual Overtime Cost
Actual Overtime Work
Actual Start
Actual Work
ACWP
Assignment
Assignment Delay
Assignment Owner
Assignment Units
Baseline Budget Cost
Baseline Budget Work
Baseline Cost
Baseline Deliverable Finish
Baseline Deliverable Start
Baseline Duration
Baseline Estimated Duration
Baseline Estimated Finish
Baseline Estimated Start
Baseline Finish
Baseline Fixed Cost

Type or select the name of the field you want to insert.

2. Repeat the step above to insert the field **Constraint Date** as well.

3. You can now enter any type of constraint in the Gantt table by selecting the type from the list in the field **Constraint type** Constraint type: | As Soon As Possible ▾ and picking the date from the drop-down calendar in **Constraint date** Constraint date: | Wed 15 Aug '12 ▾ .

Setting Constraints by Dragging Task Bars Horizontally

This method for setting constraints is often done accidentally and as mentioned earlier is not recommended since it requires you to predict the resulting constraint.

These steps assume that you drag the bar to the right, later in time.

1. Point to the middle of the task bar; make sure you see a four-headed arrow: ✥.

2. Click and hold down to drag the bar **horizontally** to where you want it scheduled. Make sure you see a horizontal two-headed arrow at this point ◄□►.

3. Look at the pop-up window to see what the new dates will be:

Task:	
Task Start:	Tue 18 Sep '12
Task Finish:	Fri 21 Sep '12

4. Release the mouse when the task bar is scheduled on the date you want. The Planning Wizard may prompt you to choose whether:

    ▶ You want to keep the link and set a constraint when you moved it away from its predecessor, or

    ▶ You want to set a link instead of a constraint when you moved it just behind another bar.

    Answer the prompt of the Planning Wizard and click [OK].

5. The task will now have a **Start No Earlier Than** constraint on it to keep it in its new place. (Under backward scheduling it will have a **Finish No Later Than** constraint.)

 If you drag **vertically**, you will see the mouse pointer , and you will be creating dependencies instead of constraints!

Setting Constraints by Entering Dates

 This method for setting constraints is often done accidentally and as mentioned earlier is not recommended since it requires you to predict the resulting constraint.

In the field **Start** you can pick a date from the drop-down calendar. By default, this creates a Start No Earlier Than (SNET) constraint on the task under forward scheduling, and it creates a Start No Later Than (SNLT) constraint under backward scheduling.

In the field **Finish**, you can pick a date from the drop-down calendar. By default, this creates a Finish No Earlier Than (FNET) constraint on the task under forward scheduling, but it creates a Finish No Later Than (FNLT) constraint under backward scheduling.

 Many people use the **Start** and **Finish** fields to schedule all their tasks. Most do not intend to create constraints, but are unaware that Project 2010 does exactly that. Their schedules become rigid and require a lot of work to maintain. If dependencies, resource constraints and calendars are used to drive the computation of dates instead, schedules require a lot less maintenance. We don't recommend using the **Start** and **Finish** fields at all for data entry. In addition, using them will require you to memorize what type of constraint will be set under both forward and backward scheduling.

*To Check All
the Scheduling
Constraints*

1. On the **View** tab, in the **Data** group, click the **Tables** down-arrow, **More Tables**. The **More Tables** dialog box appears:

> This dialog lists all the predefined tables, one of which is the Constraint Dates table.

More Tables

Tables: ⊙ Task ○ Resource

Baseline
Constraint Dates
Cost
Delay
Earned Value
Earned Value Cost Indicators
Earned Value Schedule Indicators
Entry
Export
Hyperlink
Rollup Table

New...
Edit...
Copy...
Organizer...

Apply   Cancel

2. Select the **Constraint Dates** table in the list.

3. Click [Apply]. You can now see the fields **Constraint Type** and **Constraint Dates** to check all constraints on the tasks.

4. You can apply a filter that displays all the tasks that have a constraint date. On the **View** tab, in the **Properties** group, click the **Filter** down-arrow, **More Filters**. The **More Filters** dialog box appears. Select **Tasks with Fixed Dates**, then **Apply**. When done, press [F3] to remove the filtering.

*To Remove
Constraints*

You can remove constraints one by one, but if you want to delete them quickly, you can use the fill-down feature to replace constraints with ASAP or ALAP. This is useful if you inadvertently entered dates in the Start and Finish fields without wanting the constraints that came with them.

1. To remove all constraints, click on a column heading in the **Gantt Chart** to select all tasks.
   On the **Task** tab, in the **Properties** group, click ▣. The **Multiple Task Information** dialog box appears.

2. On the **Advanced** tab in the dialog box, in the **Constraint Type** list, select the appropriate constraint type: **As Soon As Possible** under forward scheduling or **As Late As Possible** under backward scheduling.

3. Click [OK].

Make sure you don't remove real constraint dates that are necessary to keep your project schedule valid.

Limitations of Constraints

In dynamic scheduling practices, constraints have their limitations:

➤ Summary tasks can only accept FNLT and SNET constraints
Project 2010 does not allow other types of constraints on summary tasks, because summary tasks would not be summarizing their detail tasks any longer.

➤ You can set a **maximum of one constraint per task**
Sometimes it would be nice to set two constraints on a task, especially when the task has to be done within a window of opportunity. For example, you can only do a test when a specialized lab is available. You cannot model this window with constraints, because you can only set one constraint on a task.

You can, however, use the Task Calendar feature that allows you to create a calendar for the task that reflects all the windows of opportunity, essentially allowing you to set multiple constraints

 An alternate approach to modeling a task that occurs within a window of time is the Hammock task discussed in chapter 5.

 6

Task Calendars

By default, tasks are scheduled based on the Project Calendar. But Project 2010 also allows you to create Task Calendars that override the Project Calendar for individual tasks.

Here are some examples of when you might want to use Task Calendars:

➤ Create a winter weather Task Calendar to schedule all outdoor construction activities affected by winter weather, as shown in the illustration above.

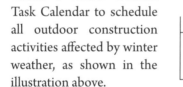

Construction

| | Fall | Winter | Spring | Summer |

➤ In a research and development project, you can use a Task Calendar to schedule testing only for the times when you can use the lab.

➤ Make sure that an office move takes place during a weekend instead of on weekdays

➤ Make sure that demolition activities take place during evening hours or on the weekend

 Create a Task Calendar when you want to force all of your resources on a specific task to work during a specific time.

 Task Calendars are good for tasks with or without resources assigned. If resources are assigned, the Resource Calendars and the Task Calendar may fight with each other, and if there are conflicts between the calendars, the following message will appear:

 Also, the **Indicators** ⓘ column will display the icon 📵 when there is an unresolved conflict between calendars. You cannot leave these conflicts unresolved.

The order of precedence between the calendars is:

1. Task Calendar

2. Resource Calendar

3. Project Calendar

 Task Calendars override Resource Calendars, which override the Project Calendar. There is a task field Ignore Resource Calendar, which when selected, means that even if a resource is unavailable during that time, the Task Calendar will take precedence over the resource's calendar and make the resource work.

Creating a New Task Calendar

1. On the **Project** tab, in the **Properties** group, click **Change Working Time**. The **Change Working Time** dialog box appears:

2. Select a base calendar that is closest to what you need for the new **Task Calendar** in the list: For `Standard (Project Calendar) ▾`.

3. Click the **Create New Calendar**... button; the **Create New Base Calendar** dialog box appears:

4. Enter a descriptive name for the new **Task Calendar** that reflects its settings and select either:

   ◉ **Create new base calendar**, or

◉ **Make a copy of** the calendar you selected under step 2.

5. Click [OK]; you have now created a new Task Calendar.

6. Enter any new task exceptions—like specific task holidays—into the **Task Calendar** by using the **Exceptions** tab on the **Change Working Time** dialog box. To do this:

   a. Enter the name of the exception on the first empty line under the name column in the **Change Working Time** dialog box.

   b. Select the **Start** and **Finish** of the exception in the next two columns.

   c. Click on **Details...** and in the **Details for** dialog box, select non-working times, decide the recurrence pattern, then decide the range of recurrence and click [OK].

7. Enter any new task working days or working times into the Task Calendar by using the **Work Weeks** tab on the **Change Working Time** dialog box.

   a. Select **Default** on the first line of the **Work Weeks** dialog box to select ALL Work Weeks for this task calendar, or select the first empty line under **Default** to select a specific alternate work week.

   b. If you did not select **Default**, enter the name of the specific alternate work week that you want to change under **Default** in the name column of the **Change Working Time** dialog box.

   c. Select the **Start** and **Finish** of the alternate work week in the next two columns.

   d. Click on **Details...** and in the **Details for** dialog box, select non-working or decide the working times, decide the recurrence pattern, then decide the range of recurrence and click [OK].

8. Now, all you need to do is to assign the calendar to the task.

Using a Task Calendar

1. Double-click on a task or select the task, then on the **Task** tab, in the **Properties**, group, select **Information** ▣. The **Task Information** dialog box appears.

   Click the **Advanced** tab, and select the **Task Calendar** from the **Calendar** dropdown. You can also check the option ☑ **Scheduling ignores Resource Calendars** here if that is your decision in case of conflicts.

   OR

   Right-click on the column heading before which you want to insert the **Task Calendar** column and choose **Insert Column** from the pop-up menu

OR

Click anywhere on the column before which you wish to insert the **Task Calendar** column, then on the **Format** tab, in the **Columns** group, click **Insert Column**.

2. Type or select **Task Calendar** from the list of field names that appears.

3. Click in the **Task Calendar** field `None ▾` of a task and select a **Task Calendar** from the list provided.

4. The task will now display a **Task Calendar** icon 📇 in the **Indicators** ⓘ column.

Checks on Deadlines, Constraints and Task Calendars

Here are some checks you can use to verify whether you've applied best practices in your use of deadlines and constraints in your dynamic model of the project:

➤ Is the project deadline date captured in the schedule?
It can be set using the Deadline date feature or the Constraint feature in Project 2010. The deadline or constraint date needs to be set on the project finish milestone. Whether you use a deadline or a constraint depends on how hard the project target finish date is.

➤ Are there as few as possible Task Calendars in the schedule?
As we discussed, Task Calendars have a very specific purpose and should only be used in those situations where needed.

➤ Does the schedule have as few schedule constraints as possible?
Constraints make the schedule rigid and jeopardize its dynamic nature. However, constraints are legitimate on:

▸ Recurring detail tasks like status meetings 1, status meetings 2, etc.

▸ External dependencies such as delivery of supplies or arrival of materials

▸ Activities that have to occur on an agreed-upon date, like presentations or training. In general these are activities in which a number of people are involved.

▸ Do-or-die-by dates, such as launches or opening dates of events for which marketing and advertising has already been done. Huge recurring sporting events which take place at set times in the calendar would also be good examples.

▸ Activities affected by weather conditions, e.g., in Canada asphalting streets starts no earlier than April 1st, because of the cold. You can also use the Task Calendars feature for these situations. Task Calendars would be a better way in the case of the multi-year planning of infrastructural works because unlike constraints, Task Calendars will push a job automatically out to the next year if it will no longer fit in the current year.

You can display all tasks that have constraints by applying the filter **10 IIL Constraints other than ASAP**.[1] The filter will not display recurring detail tasks. Recurring detail tasks have SNET constraints. This is because they are usually dependent on an established time rather on than another task.

---

1   This filter can be found in the file *IIL Project Tools* available for download at www.jrosspub.com. Please click the link *WAV Download Resource Center* to enter the download site.

Review Questions

1. What is the difference between how Project 2010 treats constraints and deadline dates?

2. What is the question to be answered from a project model that is scheduled forward? What about one that is scheduled backward?

3. Which of the following constraints can cause a scheduling conflict? In the next table, add a check mark in the cells where scheduling conflicts could occur:

	In a Forward Scheduled Project	In a Backward Scheduled Project
ASAP		
ALAP		
FNET		
FNLT		
MFO		
MSO		
SNET		
SNLT		

4. Would you set a constraint in the following situations? If so, which type of constraint? If you would recommend using a constraint, indicate the type in the table below.

Situation	Type of Constraint
You have a board meeting coming up on January 16 in which a go/no-go decision will be taken on the next stage of your project. The board expects certain reports to be ready.	
A vendor needs to deliver custom-made computers to you that you need for testing activities in your project (computers delivered).	
You have planned a "project burial" ceremony to close off your project. You have invited senior executives and other dignitaries for this special day.	
A testing lab is only available to your project from March 1 to March 15.	

5. Why would you want to minimize the number of constraint dates in your project model?

6. As a car manufacturer, you would like to use an outdoor test lab that consists of a 10 mile highway stretch on which different weather conditions can be simulated. The lab is fully booked, but there is a window of opportunity for your project from November 10-17 in 2012 or after April 1st in 2013. How would you model this in Project 2010?

Additional Practice For experience working with the features you've learned about in this chapter, we strongly suggest that you do the additional exercises for this chapter that are included in Appendix 1.

Chapter 7: Entering Resources

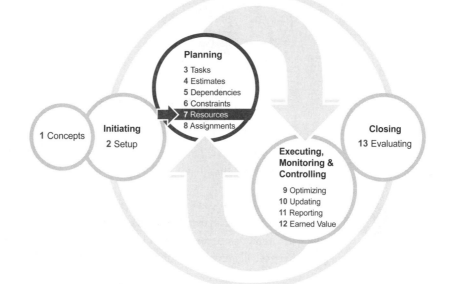

With the tasks, estimates, dependencies, constraints (and deadlines) entered, you now have a Gantt Chart that is a dynamic model of the project. You could stop here if resources, their workloads and costs are of little concern to you. Usually, however, resources are a significant constraint in the schedule and to make it truly dynamic, you should add resources and their assignments to your schedule. The result is called a resource-loaded schedule.

After reading this chapter you will be able to:

> Explain what resources are and when to add a resource to the project model
> Identify and describe the different types of resources: work, material, and cost
> Identify the important resource-related fields
> Enter resources into a schedule using your address book or manual data entry
> Enter the availability of different types of resources
> Create Resource Calendars
> Explain the cost features of Project 2010
> Check the list of resources against best scheduling practices

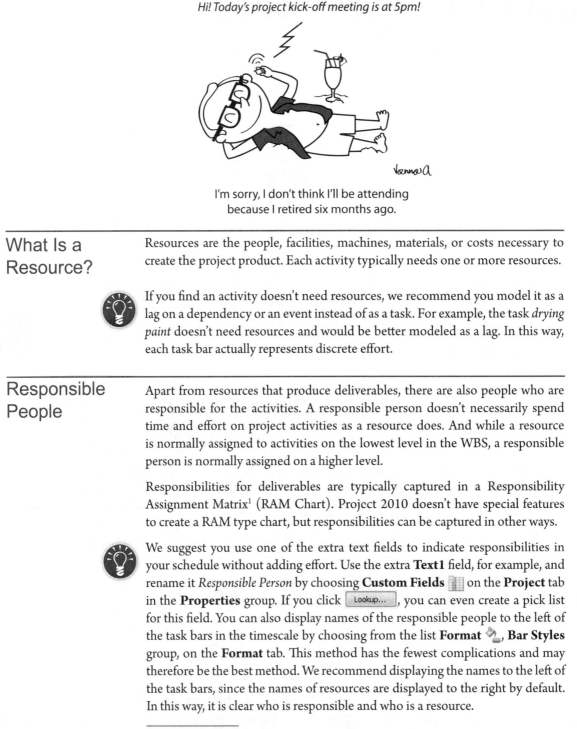

Hi! Today's project kick-off meeting is at 5pm!

I'm sorry, I don't think I'll be attending
because I retired six months ago.

What Is a Resource?

Resources are the people, facilities, machines, materials, or costs necessary to create the project product. Each activity typically needs one or more resources.

If you find an activity doesn't need resources, we recommend you model it as a lag on a dependency or an event instead of as a task. For example, the task *drying paint* doesn't need resources and would be better modeled as a lag. In this way, each task bar actually represents discrete effort.

Responsible People

Apart from resources that produce deliverables, there are also people who are responsible for the activities. A responsible person doesn't necessarily spend time and effort on project activities as a resource does. And while a resource is normally assigned to activities on the lowest level in the WBS, a responsible person is normally assigned on a higher level.

Responsibilities for deliverables are typically captured in a Responsibility Assignment Matrix[1] (RAM Chart). Project 2010 doesn't have special features to create a RAM type chart, but responsibilities can be captured in other ways.

We suggest you use one of the extra text fields to indicate responsibilities in your schedule without adding effort. Use the extra **Text1** field, for example, and rename it *Responsible Person* by choosing **Custom Fields** on the **Project** tab in the **Properties** group. If you click Lookup..., you can even create a pick list for this field. You can also display names of the responsible people to the left of the task bars in the timescale by choosing from the list **Format**, **Bar Styles** group, on the **Format** tab. This method has the fewest complications and may therefore be the best method. We recommend displaying the names to the left of the task bars, since the names of resources are displayed to the right by default. In this way, it is clear who is responsible and who is a resource.

---

1 ——–*PMBOK® Guide – Fourth Edition*, PMI, 2008, p. 221.

Project 2010 accommodates defining resources in the Resource Sheet and assigning resources in the Gantt Chart view. We will discuss defining the resources here in this chapter and assigning them in chapter 8.

When to Add a Resource

You should only enter a resource in the project model if you expect that resource to significantly affect the quality, duration or cost of the project. If not, you can keep your model leaner by leaving the resource out.

A resource that is easy to replace is not likely to affect your schedule. Resources that are scarce can. For example, resources will increase the duration of your project if they aren't available when you need them (e.g., backordered materials or delayed executive sign-offs).

In addition, over-allocating resources can affect the duration of your project. If human resources are assigned too many tasks, their workloads need to be leveled and leveling often leads to longer projects. If you find that limited resource availability affects the scheduling of tasks, you have a resource-constrained or resource-limited schedule.

Resources are the basis for project cost. To manage the cost of the project, you have to define the people, facilities, machines, materials, and their costs. While you may not be directly responsible for doing cost accounting, there is a growing trend to require clear accounting for project-related costs. If you are working with accountants, get their guidance about how to do the accounting in your project. You have a range of choices in Project 2010 regarding resources and their costs, from keeping it simple and not even including them to getting down into the detail of addressing the scheduling of people, machinery, equipment, facilities and other resources.

Choosing the Options

On the **File** tab, in the **Backstage** view, click **Options**. The **Project Options** dialog box appears.

We recommend that you used the following settings when adding resources.

Project Options	Recommended Choices
Advanced	**Set the Advanced Options on the Advanced Tab:**
	General options for this project: [📋 All New Projects ▾] This sets the options as the default setting for any new schedules you create. Existing schedules aren't affected, because the options are stored in the project schedule.
	☑ **Automatically add new resources and tasks** Lets you enter a new resource without having to answer a prompt asking if you really want to create the new resource.
	Default standard rate Enter your most commonly used rate. You'll then only have to enter rates for those resources where the rates are different from the default.
	Default overtime rate Enter a default rate to reduce the amount of typing you have to do.
Schedule	**Set the Schedule Options on the Schedule Tab:**
	Show assignment units as a: Percentage or Decimal Units of resources can be expressed as a percentage or in decimals in the **Max Units** field (availability) and in the assignment **Units** field (workload).
	For example, if you have a resource that is available half-time to your project you can enter this as 50% (percentage) or as 0.5 (decimal) in the **Max Units** field. For part-time resources, **Percentages** seem to make the most sense.
	On the other hand, if you'll be using 3 carpenters on your project, you could enter them as a group and enter either 300% (percentage) or 3 (decimal). For consolidated resources the **Decimals** seem easier to understand.
	This option is a global option and applies to all your projects, existing or new. You can switch the option at any time.

Types of Resources

Project 2010 distinguishes between three types of resources: work resources, material resources, and cost resources. These are the three choices in the resource field Type on the Resource Sheet view. We will also talk about a special budget resource, used for budget tracking and comparisons (Budget resources can also be work, material, or cost resources).

In practice, you will come across five different types of resources: human, facility, machinery/equipment, material, and cost.

Important questions for each type are:

➤ Should the resource add to the total amount of effort in the project?

➤ Should the resource be included in workload leveling?

➤ Does the resource have a time-related or a unit-related cost?

➤ Should Work, Material or Cost be chosen in the resource-related field Type?

➤ Should there be a Budget resource type associated with the resource?

We will discuss these questions for each type of resource:

➤ Human resources are people whose efforts should be added in the **Work** field. The total amount of work per week for each resource should be reasonable, which means it is within, or close to, weekly availability. If there are over-allocations, their workloads should be leveled.

Human effort costs money, and human resources should be given a standard rate, an overtime rate and a cost-per-use rate, if applicable. They generally have a time-related cost and the rate needs to be appended with /h (per hour), /w (per week), /mo (per month) or /y (per year).

➤ Facilities should not add to the total amount of effort of the project (work) and therefore we make them material resources.

The cost of facilities is typically time-related, e.g., a monthly rent. Facilities therefore need a standard rate per time unit, and perhaps a cost-per-use rate. Unfortunately, only work resources can have a time-related rate. If you want to calculate time-related cost, you could use a workaround that will be explained later in the section Entering Facility and Machine Costs.

 If you enter facilities as material resources, Project 2010 can't do leveling, so, for example, it can't prevent double reservations by leveling the workload of a conference room. You will have to keep an eye on the reservation of the facility yourself. You could enter the facility as a work resource to level its "workload", but this would start adding its "effort" to the amount of work in the project, which is not desirable.

➤ Machines are similar to facilities in terms of the points just made. Machines should not add to the effort of the project and should be entered as material resources.

Machines typically have a time-related cost and thus need a standard rate per time unit, but only work resources can have a time-related rate. We can use the workaround explained in the section Entering Facility and Machine Costs.

➤ Material resources are consumable resources such as desktop computers, electric cable, meeting room or concrete. They should not add to the amount of effort (work) of the project.

Materials don't have a capacity like humans or facilities and do not need to be leveled.

Materials do cost money and typically have a unit-related cost only. Materials should be entered as a material resource. The cost per unit should be entered in the Std. Rate field without a time unit.

➤ Cost resources are financial cost items that are specific to the task such as hotels, meals, airfare, and car rentals. Cost resources don't add to work and they don't affect the scheduling of a task. These resources contain financial cost items that are not related to costs associated to work and material resources assigned to the task.

➤ Budget resources are a special category of resources that are created specifically to list a budget category needed within a project. Budget resources can be work, material, or cost resources. Once the budget resource is created and assigned, the project work and/or project cost amounts can be rolled-up, tracked and compared to the budgeted amounts listed in the budget resource. It is important to remember that budget resources can be assigned only to the project summary task and must be specifically identified as a budget resource when created. Examples of budget resources are *EMPLOYEE-BUDGET*, *PAPER-BUDGET*, and *TRAVEL-BUDGET*.

Generic Resources

In the planning phase, if you don't know who is going to do a task, you can enter a resource under a generic name (e.g., junior programmer or senior programmer).

Not knowing the exact names of the individuals should not stop you from creating a resource-loaded schedule. Once you know who the people will be, you can easily reassign the tasks from the generic resources to real people. There are several easy ways to accomplish this. You can use the Generic field (see details in the Resource Fields section below).

Change the View to Enter Resources

On the **View** tab, in the **Resource Views** group, click **Resource Sheet** .

Check if the table **Entry** is active on the **View** tab, in **Data** group, in **Tables** down- arrow list.

You will find the following fields in the **Resource Sheet**:

Resource Fields

Indicator

This field will display indicators for a variety of situations. For example, if a resource is over-allocated, this column will show an ◈ icon.

Resource Name (required)

Note that the name of this field in the database is **Name**. This is where you enter the name of the resource.

Use a standard naming convention to prevent duplicating resources inadvertently. The convention should allow you to recognize and sort the resource names. We recommend using *last name - first name* when the list gets long.

Notice the use of a hyphen instead of a comma. The comma is used to separate multiple entries in a field. Project 2010 won't let you use a comma in the resource name field because it thinks you are trying to enter multiple resources in one row.[2]

What you type in the Name field will show up as the only name in the lists used for assigning resources, like the Assign Resources dialog. Therefore make sure that:

➤ Your resource names are easy to recognize
➤ Each resource name is unique

Make sure the same resource is not represented twice on the Resource Sheet, for example, William Smith and Bill Smith, or Thomas Charley and Charley Thomas.

Sort the resource list alphabetically.

1. On the **View** tab in the **Data** group, select the **Sort** down arrow ⬇.

2. From the drop down list select **Sort By...** ⬇ Sort By....

3. In the **Sort** dialog select **Name** from the **Sort By** drop down list, and check ☑ **Permanently renumber resources**.

4. Click the **Sort** button. The **Assign Resources** dialog sorts your resources.

Type (required)

The type of resource can be **Work** (default), **Material**, or **Cost**. Work resources are people. Material resources are facilities, equipment or materials. Cost resources are financial cost items that are specific to the task such as hotels, meals, airfare, and car rentals.

Material Label (optional)

You can enter a label (for a material resource only!) that will show up in several other views and reports. For example, the label *desktop computers* will show on the y-axis in the Resource Graph view to indicate the number of units needed

---

2   If you anticipate upgrading to Project Server, pick a resource naming convention that is consistent with your naming convention within Active Directory (if you use Active Directory for Windows authentication). This will facilitate importing legacy schedules into Project Server.

over time. In the timescale of the Gantt Chart, it will show up to the right of the task bars.

The label is particularly important for bulk resources to indicate the unit of measurement: the material label defines one unit for the bulk resource. For example, concrete is measured in *cubic feet* or *cubic meters*. When *500 units* of the bulk resource concrete are assigned, the material label will show up in the Gantt timescale as *500 cubic feet*.

Initials (optional)

In previous versions of Project this field was very useful, because you could assign resources to tasks by typing their initials, but now you can point and click to assign resources or even select more than one resource with the Assign Resources dialog. You may still find Initials to be useful for reporting.

Group (optional)

You can use this field for any group identifier you'd like. We suggest you use it to record something about each resource that you may want to report on or filter on later. For example if you use it for department name you could filter all tasks for a department or see totals for work and cost by department.

Note that the **Group** field and the group feature (**View** tab, in the **Data** group, click on the **Group by** as discussed in chapter 11) are two different things.

Max Units (required for Work resources)

This is the maximum availability of the resource to the project:

➤ Use 100% for a full-time resource in the Max Units field and 50% for a half-time resource
➤ For a consolidated resource the Max Units is the total number of team members on the team
➤ You won't be able to enter availability for material resources

Std. Rate (optional)

Enter the standard rate for regular work in this field (e.g., *10.50/h*, for someone who earns $10.50 per hour). You don't need a time unit for material resources; the rate will be calculated per unit of material you assign to the task. We'll discuss assigning in the next chapter.

You can use the following time units:

If you type	You will see	Which means
m	min	minutes
h	hr	hours
d	day	days
w	wk	weeks
mo	mon	months
y	yr	years

Ovt. Rate (optional)

Enter the rate for overtime work in this field. Do this only:

➤ If you will pay for overtime instead of compensating with extra time off, and

➤ If you will pay a higher rate than the standard rate.

Project 2010 expects you to indicate separately how many overtime hours are worked on each assignment; those hours will be charged against the overtime rate. Material resources can't have an overtime rate.

Cost/Use (optional)

Enter the cost-per-use rate that is paid each time the resource is used, which means on each task to which it is assigned. The cost is calculated as the Cost/Use rate times the number of units assigned.

Accrue At (optional)

Tab to the **Accrue at** field and a pull-down button appears. Select one of the following from the pull-down list to indicate when costs are incurred:

Accrue at	Incurs the Cost	Example
Start	As soon as the task starts.	*Actors*
Prorated	As the task progresses; the cost goes up with the **% Complete**.	*Employees*
End	As soon as the task finishes.	*Consultants*

 The accrual options only pertain to standard and overtime rates; the cost per use is always accrued at the start of the task.

Base Calendar (optional)

Select a Calendar from the list. The Base Calendar specifies the general working hours and working days for the resource. You can create new Base Calendars. You can also override the Base Calendar and set individual working hours in the Resource Calendar. Base Calendars are useful in international projects; you can base the resources working in the UK on a UK Base Calendar and the resources in the US on a US Base Calendar. Material resources cannot have a Base Calendar.

Code (optional)

Type an alphanumeric code, such as an accounting code. This is used to charge the expenses for the resource to a particular cost account. It can be useful for the finance department, but often the tasks or assignments, and not the resources, will be coded to charge to the cost accounts.

Budget (optional)

This field can be inserted in the Resource Sheet as a column which will display a *Yes* if the resource is designated as a budget resource and *No* if it's not. After the Budget resource is created (as covered later in this chapter), double click on the budget resource name to pull-up the **Resource Information** dialog box and in the **General** tab, click the check box **Budget** to indicate its role as a budget resource.

Generic (optional)

Use the Yes/No Generic field to mark a resource as a generic resource (e.g., a *carpenter* rather than a specific individual). You can use generic resources during initial planning and then replace them with individual names. Generic resources are very useful for longer term planning. This field can also be inserted in the Resource Sheet as a column if you want to set several resources as generic at one time.

Inactive (optional)

The Yes/No Inactive field indicates whether the resource is still active in the resource pool or is inactive and kept for historical purposes only. This file can be inserted in the Resource Sheet as a column if you want to make it easier for you to set this value for more than one resource.

Entering Resources

You can enter resources into the Resource Sheet in four ways:

➤ Use the shared resource pool. The resources in this pool are managed in a single .mpp file and stored in a central location. See Appendix 2 for a discussion of consolidated projects and shared resource pools.

➤ Download the resources from your Outlook address book.

➤ Use the Active Directory to download the resources.

➤ Key in the (rest of the) resources manually.

Downloading Human Resources from Your Address Book

If you're using Outlook for managing your contact information and address list, you may be able to download the resource names to Project from that list (so that you don't have to retype them). If you keep your addresses in another contact management application, you should be able to import them into Outlook 2010 by using the Import wizard in Outlook (on the **File** tab, select **Open**, then click on **Import**).

Once the contact information is in Outlook, you can then import it into Project:

1. On the **View** tab, in the **Resources View** group, click **Resource Sheet** 📇.

2. On the **Resource** tab, in the **Insert** group, click on the **Add Resources** down arrow 🖐. The Add Resources list is displayed:

The Address Book tool for downloading resources from your Outlook address book.

3. Click **Address Book** 📖 Address Book..., and the **Select Resources** dialog appears.

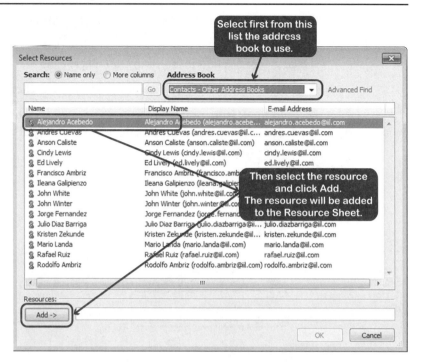

4. Select the address list from the **Address Book** drop down list: Contacts - Other Address Books ▾ and the names of the resources will be displayed.

5. In the **Search** field type in the first character(s) of the name of the person to add; the list scrolls alphabetically. Press the arrow keys up or down as needed to highlight the right resource. Press **Enter** or click Add -> or double-click on the resource name.

   The resource is now added to the list of people at the bottom of the screen that will be transferred into the Project 2010 Resource Sheet.

6. Repeat the previous step for all resources you would like to add.

7. Click OK ; the resources are now added to the end of the resource list. You can repeat this process at any time to pick up additional resource names from your address book. You may want to sort the list alphabetically again to make it easy to find resources.

Using the Active Directory to Download Resources

If you're using the Active Directory to download the resources for your users information, you may be able to download the resource names from that list (so that you don't have to retype them) using the following steps:

1. On the **View** tab, in the **Resources View** group, click **Resource Sheet** 📖.

2. On the **Resource** tab, in the **Insert** group, click on **Add Resources** down arrow 🖐. The Add Resources list is displayed:

The Active Directory tool for downloading resources from your Active Directory.

3. Click **Active Directory**… and the **Select Users** dialog appears.

4. In the **Enter the object names** to select space, type the object names that you want to find. You can search for multiple objects by separating each name with a semicolon. Use one of the following syntax examples:

   DisplayName (example: FirstName LastName), ObjectName (example: Computer1), UserName (example: User1), ObjectName@DomainName (example: User1@Domain1), DomainName\ObjectName (example: Domain1\User1)

5. Click **Check names.** The resource is now added to the list of people at the bottom of the screen that will be transferred into the Project 2010 **Resource Sheet**.

6. Repeat the previous step for all resources you would like to add.

7. Click [OK   ]; the resources are now added to the end of the resource list. You can repeat this process at any time to pick up additional resource names from your Active Directory. You may want to sort the list alphabetically again to make it easy to find resources.

Keying in Resources Manually

An easy way to enter data in certain cells is to click and drag over all cells in which you want to enter resource information. Multiple cells are selected with one cell still white, which is the input cell. Enter the data in this input cell and press the

[Tab] key to make the cursor move to the next cell until you have entered them all.

You can even select a nonadjacent series of cells by pressing and holding down the [Control] key while dragging.

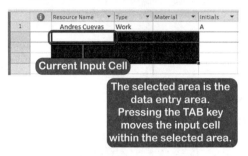

Here are more precise instructions for the different fields:

1. We recommend you customize the table first so that it has the right columns in the right order for entering data:

   ▶ Delete all columns you won't use by clicking on their column headings and pressing [Del] on your keyboard.

   ▶ Insert new fields by clicking on **Add New Column**, [Add New Column ▼]. A dropdown list appears with all the available fields. Select the field from the dropdown list.

   ▶ You can drag a column by its heading if you want to move it. First click the column heading and when you see the mouse pointer, drag the column to its desired place.

2. Enter the name of the resource in the field **Resource Name** and press:

   [↓] to go down (to the next row), or

   [Tab] to go to the right (to the next column).

3. If the resource is a material resource (facilities, machines or materials), change the field **Type** from **Work** to **Material** and enter the unit of measure in the field **Material Label** (for example *cubic yard* for the resource *concrete*).

   If you change the type of resource, you'll lose any rates you may have entered for the resource. This is because Work resources require a time-related rate, like *$50/h*, whereas Material resources need a per-unit cost, like *$150 per door*.

4. Make sure material resources have a material rate and material label. When that resource is used, Project 2010 will automatically calculate and display the correct representation of the material.

5. For work resources only, enter the availability on the Resource Calendar or in the field Max Units. Project 2010 assumes that the availability of material resources is unlimited.

6. Enter the cost rates in the fields **Std. Rate**, **Ovt. Rate** and **Cost/Use** and determine when the cost will be accrued by choosing **Start**, **Prorated** or **End** in **Accrue at**.

7. For cost resources, make sure that the resource **Type** field is set to **Cost**. Since Cost resources are task specific, **do not** enter in a cost for the cost resource until it is assigned to the task.

8. Enter the **Base Calendar** field and a list button ⯆ will appear. Select the appropriate Base Calendar for the resource from this list. Normally this would be **Standard** unless more Base Calendars were created. You can create other Base Calendars by choosing Project tab, **Change Working Time**... 🗓 and clicking the button **Create New Calendar**. For more detailed information see the "Base Calendars and Resource Calendars section" later in this chapter.

Entering Cost Resources

For cost resources, enter the name of the cost resource on the Resource Sheet and select Cost from the field Type. Examples of cost resources are hotels, meals, airfare, and car rentals. Cost resources are assigned to tasks just like work and material resources. For example, you assign the airfare cost resource to a task and enter in a cost of $500 for airfare for that task on the Resources tab in the Task Information 🔲 dialog box on the Task tab.

To enter costs for these resources select the task, then:

1. Click on the **Task Information** 🔲 icon on the **Task** tab.

2. Select the **Resources** tab.

3. Enter the specific cost for the selected cost resource in the **Cost** column.

4. Click ⬚ OK ⬚.

5. You can also enter in the cost for the cost resource in the Assign Resource dialog, when you first assign cost resources to the task. Click on the **Assign Resources icon** 🗟 on the **Resource** tab. Then select the cost resource and then enter the cost in the **Cost column** in the **Assign Resources** dialog.

Entering Budget Resources

1. Go to the **Resource Sheet** and type in the budget resource name, e.g., *TRAVEL-BUDGET*.

For budget resources, use all caps and include the word *BUDGET* in the name to help you identify them for assignments.

2. Select the type of resource, work, material, or cost budget resource, from the field **Type.**

3. Complete the **Material Label** field:

▶ For Work Budget Resources, designate the budget as the budgeted number of hours worked. Note that for Work resources, you are not able to enter a Material Label.

▶ For Cost Budget Resources, designate the budget as the budgeted cost amount. Note that for Cost resources, you are not able to enter a Material Label.

▶ For Material Budget Resources, designate the unit of measurement for the material. For example, for the *CEMENT-BUDGET* material budget resource, designate the material label as *Metric Tons* on the Resource Sheet. Now when you assign the Material Budget Resource to the project summary task, you will be able to enter in the budgeted work amount for this project, say *5000* metric tons of cement . You can now track and compare current usage to the budgeted amount: in the **Resource** or **Task Usage** view, insert and compare the **Budget Work** field to the **Work** field for the material resource.

4. You must specifically identify the budget resource as a budget resource by double-clicking on the budget resource name or clicking on the Information icon 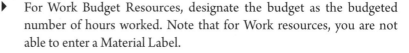 on the **Resource** tab and opening the **Resource Information** dialog box. Then on the General tab, check the box for **Budget** and click ⟨ OK ⟩.

 Entering budget amounts will be discussed in chapter 8 when we discuss resource assignments.

Base Calendars and Resource Calendars

A Resource Calendar is a Calendar for a specific individual. Initially each Resource Calendar will have the settings you entered in the Project Calendar. You can then adjust individual working times and vacations in a Resource Calendar, but you don't need to do this unless you expect the changes in availability to have a significant impact on the schedule.

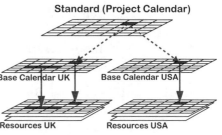

Apart from the Project Calendar, there can be one or more Base Calendars on which Resource Calendars can be based. For example, you will need Base Calendars if your team members are in different countries. You would create a Base Calendar for each country and then base each resource on his or her Country Calendar (see the illustration). If resources belong to different companies, you may also need multiple Base Calendars.

Creating a Base Calendar

The Standard Project Calendar is the default Base Calendar for all resources. You can create new Base Calendars (and new task Calendars) in the following way:

1. On **Project** tab, in the **Properties** group, click the **Change Working Time** ; the **Change Working Time** dialog appears:

    > **Change Working Time**
    >
    > For calendar: Standard (Project Calendar) ▼   [Create New Calendar ...]
    >
    > Calendar 'Standard' is a base calendar.
    >
    > Legend: Click on a day to see its working times:
    >
    > ☐ Working
    > ▨ Nonworking
    > 31 Edited working hours
    >
    > On this calendar:
    > 31 Exception day
    > 31 Nondefault work week
    >
    > April 2012
    >
    > | S | M | T | W | Th | F | S |
    > |---|---|---|---|----|---|---|
    > | 1 | 2 | 3 | 4 | 5 | 6 | 7 |
    > | 8 | 9 | 10 | 11 | 12 | 13 | 14 |
    > | 15 | 16 | 17 | 18 | 19 | 20 | 21 |
    > | 22 | 23 | 24 | 25 | 26 | 27 | 28 |
    > | 29 | 30 | | | | | |
    >
    > Based on:
    > Default work week on calendar 'Standard'.
    >
    > **To create a new base calendar, click on the "Create New Calendar" button.**
    >
    > Exceptions | Work Weeks
    >
    > | Name | Start | Finish | | [Details...] |
    > |------|-------|--------|--|------------|
    > | | | | | [Delete] |

2. Click on the **Create New Calendar** and the **Create New Base Calendar** dialog appears:

    > **Create New Base Calendar**
    >
    > Name: Copy of Standard
    >
    > ○ Create new base calendar
    > ◉ Make a copy of   Standard ▼   calendar
    >
    > [OK]   [Cancel]
    >
    > **Copy the standard project calendar as a starting point for the new base calendar.**

3. You can copy the standard Project Calendar as a starting point for the new Base Calendar. This is a onetime affair; the standard Calendar will not continue to be synchronized with the Base Calendar. (You'll see this if you look back at the illustration of Calendar relationships at the beginning of

this section and note the dotted arrows between the Project Calendar and the two Base Calendars. Also note the solid arrows that indicate that the standard Calendar does continue to update all the Resource Calendars.)

Enter the name of the new Calendar and select either ◉ **Create new Base Calendar** or ◉ **Make copy of Standard** and click [OK].

4. You are now back in the **Change Working Time** dialog, but with the newly created Base Calendar shown in the list **For Calendar**: at the top of the dialog.

   ▶ Enter the default working days and times for the new Base Calendar in the **Work Weeks** tab. Select [**Default**], then select the days, click on [Details...]. Then select **From/To** times in the table, and click [OK].

   ▶ Enter the holidays or non-working day exceptions in the **Exceptions** tab. Selecting the first blank cell, enter the exception name, e.g., *Spring Vacation*, then select the days on the **Start** and **Finish** columns, and click [OK].

You are now back in the **Resource Sheet** view (if not, please switch to this view). In the resource-related field **Base Calendar** you can select the new Base Calendar from the list and assign it to certain resources. The resources will then be based on the Calendar and Project 2010 will schedule their work accordingly.

Editing a Resource Calendar

The Resource Calendar will initially have the same working times and holidays as the Project Calendar (or Base Calendar if the resource was based on a Base Calendar). You can override these times and holidays on each individual Resource Calendar.

Project Calendar or Base Calendars

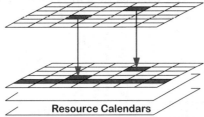

Resource Calendars

If someone takes a vacation, assignments will be delayed until the resource returns. The duration of the project will increase, and a poorly timed vacation can jeopardize deadlines. For these reasons it's important to model vacations in Project 2010. It's not a lot of work, so there's no good reason not to do it.

To edit a Resource Calendar you can:

Double click on a resource or click on a resource and click on the **Information** icon 🗐 on the **Resource** tab, and in the **Resource Information** dialog, click Change Working Time ... . This will allow you to edit one resource at a time.

OR

If you want to edit several Resource Calendars in a row:

1. Click on **Change Working Time** icon 🗒 on the **Project** tab; the **Change Working Time** dialog appears:

2. Select the resource for which to set the Calendar in the list **For Calendar:** Standard (Project Calendar) ▾ (If you don't find any resource names in this list, you have not entered the resources yet into your schedule.)

    Now you're ready to enter specific working days and hours for the resource.

3. If you put vacation time or unique hours on a resource's Calendar, add a "Note" to the resource on the Resource Sheet to help you remember. This saves you from having to scroll through the Resource Calendar, or print an exception report to find a resource's vacation or unique working hours information.

Entering Working Days and Hours for the Resource Calendar

1. To specify the normal business work week in the specified Resource Calendar, select the **Work Weeks** tab near the bottom of the **Change Working Time** dialog box. If you have a Monday to Friday workweek, you can select the workdays by selecting the **Default** row on the **Work Weeks**

tab and then clicking on [D̲etails...] to open the Details for the **Default** dialog box.

2. When you select any Monday through Friday, the default is set for all weekdays to working days with default working hours of **8:00 AM-12:00 PM** and **1:00 PM-5:00 PM**. It is here, in the **Details** dialog box, that you can change these default working times.

3. You have three choices in the **Set working time for this work week** buttons above the **From/To** times table:

▶ Use Project default times for these days

▶ Set days to nonworking time

▶ Set day(s) to these specific working times

4. In the **Details** dialog, select the specific days you want to change. Select consecutive days by clicking the mouse and dragging downward, or select nonadjacent days by holding down the [Control] key and selecting each day you need.

5. To set these days as nonworking time, select ◉ **Set days to nonworking time**.

6. To change the working times of a working day(s) or to change a nonworking day to a working day, select the day(s) in the table and select ◉ **Set day(s) to these specific working times**.

7. Next, in the **From/To** times table, enter the start and finish working times for the resource. Click into the next lower blank cell when completed to make sure your start and finish times are entered.

8. Click [OK] at the bottom of the **Details** dialog box and then click [OK] in the **Change Working Time** dialog box.

You're now ready to enter specific nonworking days or hours (exceptions), like vacations for the resource.

Entering Resource Calendar Exceptions

1. While still in the **Change Working Time** dialog box of the specific **Resource Calendar**, click the day in the **Calendar** whose working times you want to change. Notice that after clicking on a specific day, the working times information about that specific day is represented to the right.

2. Next, select the **Exceptions** tab and select the next available blank row in the **Name** column. Once selected, enter the name of the Calendar exception, like **Spring vacation** and press [Tab]. The start and finish dates are automatically entered, defaulting to the date that you clicked in the Calendar. You can change this date now, if needed, by editing the start and finish dates.

3. Click on **Details** to open the **Details** dialog box. Notice that the default changes to a non-working day for the date that you selected.

4. If the exception is a change other than to a non-working day, you can change this in the Details dialog box. For example, select ◉ **Working times**, then change the times in the **From/To** tables as needed.

5. Click [OK] at the bottom of the **Details** dialog box and then click [OK] in the **Change Working Time** dialog box.

 The task-related field Ignore Resource Calendar is by default set to No for all tasks. This field determines if Project 2010 will use the Resource Calendar when scheduling assignments. The field is useful when the task also has a task Calendar.

The task Calendar overrides the Resource Calendar. With the new field you can let Project 2010 know that you have resolved the conflict between the Resource Calendar and the task Calendar. If you leave it set to No, the Calendar conflict icon will stay visible in the Indicators ⓘ column. If you change it to Yes, it will go away. The schedule should stay the same.

The working hours in Resource Calendars can become very intricate and require a lot of data entry, such as when there are resources working day or night shifts in alternating weeks. You have to ask yourself if you would prefer to manage these shift resources as a consolidated resource instead of as individual resources. If you choose the latter option, your schedule might become very maintenance-hungry.

We don't recommend you model the exact working hours of individual resources. There seems to be little gain in that in terms of accuracy of the forecasts and a lot of effort to keep them up to date.

The Fixed Duration tasks will look at the Resource Calendars, but may extend the task duration and task bar when one of the assigned resources is not available. This surprises many people. Project 2010 does prompt you before extending a fixed duration.

The Max Units of a Resource

The maximum units (Max Units) of a resource define what percentage of a resource's work hours is available to the project. In the illustration you can see that Tom works 8 hours per day and if the Max Units is 50% there would be a steep over-allocation (blue).

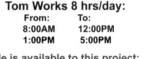

Tom Works 8 hrs/day:

From:	To:
8:00AM	12:00PM
1:00PM	5:00PM

He is available to this project:

If the Max Units is set to 100%, there is a small over-allocation. If it is 150% there is remaining availability. You can see that the percentage entered in the Max Units field determines what will constitute an over-allocation for the resource.

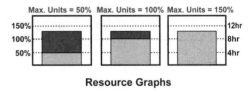

Resource Graphs

Note that the Max Units percentage is relative to the working hours entered on the Resource Calendar. The working hours can change from week to week. In other words, if you enter 50% as the maximum units, the person would be available 4 hours per day during full-time working hours. If the working hours are only a half day during certain days, the availability would be only 2 hours per day during those days.

Resource Availability

The availability of resources varies from one resource to another and from week to week. We'll discuss the different types of availability and how to enter them in Project 2010.

In many cases, you'll have to edit the Resource Calendar. If you are a project manager in the Project Server environment you may not have the proper access rights to add or change resource availability in the enterprise resource pool, but you still need to know how to do this for the resources that are private to your project, called local resources.

Temporary Availability

Example: Someone loaned to the project for a month.

Enter the temporary availability of a resource in the **Resource Information** 📇 dialog box:

1. Double-click a resource in the **Resource Sheet** view or Select the resource, click **Resource Information** 📇 on the **Resource** tab.

2. Click on the **General** tab and select **Change Working Time**; the dialog should now look like this:

You can mark days, entire weeks or months as Nonworking Time, leaving only temporary availability.

3. Select the **Work Week** tab and select the next blank cell under **Default**.

4. Type in a name for the temporary availability, like *April 2012* and press ⌨Tab.

5. Select the **Start/Finish** dates to define the period of temporary availability.

6. With the specific **Start/Finish** dates selected in the table, click on **Details** to open the **Details** dialog box for the selected temporary work weeks.

7. Select the days, (like Monday through Friday), in the **Select Day(s)** table and then either select ⊙ **Set days to nonworking times** or ⊙ **Set day(s) to these specific times**, (set specific times here).

8. Click [OK] in the **Change Working Time** dialog box.

Varying Availability   Example: Someone who's available full-time one month, but only half-time the next month.

In Project 2010 you can easily model varying availability. You can set up an entire profile of availability, such as 80% in April, 50% in May, 100% in June, etc. To enter the availability profile:

1. Double-click a resource in the **Resource Sheet** view or Select the resource, click **Resource Information** 📇 on the **Resource** tab.

2. Click on the **General** tab and select **Change Working Time**; the dialog should now look like this:

3. In the fields **Available from** and **Available to** enter the dates when the resource is available and the percentage of availability in the **Units** field.

4. If you have multiple periods to enter, after you enter the **Available to** date for the first period Project 2010 automatically fills in the next **Available from** date with the next day.

5. The Max Units field in the Resource Sheet can only display one percentage of all percentages entered in the availability profile. The one number displayed in the Max Units field will be the availability percentage as of the current date in the Project, Project Information dialog. As time goes by, the field Max Units will display all the different values from the availability profile.

Part-Time Availability

A part-time resource is someone who works fewer hours per day or fewer days per week than a full-time-equivalent resource as defined in the **File** tab, **Options**, **Schedule**, **Hours** per **Day** setting.

Part-time resources can be:

➤ People who work fewer than full-time hours each workday.

Set the working-time hours in the Resource Calendar to the appropriate number of hours per day. For example, the working hours could be set to 1:00 PM-5:00 PM for an afternoon job. We recommend this method.

OR

You can enter hours in the Resource Sheet with the Max Units set to 4h/8h * 100% = 50%. A problem with this method can be that all assignments will be at 50% involvement, and the person assigned to a meeting of 2 hours will be recorded as only spending 1 hour (2h * 50% = 1 hour) in that meeting, which may be unintended.

➤ People who work 4 out of 5 weekdays.

Enter this into the schedule by changing the appropriate weekday to a nonworking day in the person's Resource Calendar. (See "Entering Working Days and Hours for the Resource Calendar" above.)

➤ Someone who is working on multiple projects and only available part-time to your project.

Full-Time Availability

By default Project 2010 considers a full-time person to be someone who works 40 hours and 5 days a week. Microsoft has designated this as the default workweek, and any diversions from this are called exceptions.

People who work full-time need to have their Max Units set to 100% or 1.

The working hours set in the Resource Calendar should correspond with the number of Hours per Day and Hours per Week settings in the File tab, Options,

Schedule command. For example, if the hours per day in File tab, Options, Schedule command is set to 7.5 hours/day, the Calendar should show, for example, 8:00 AM-12:00 PM and 1:00 PM-4:30 PM (double-click on the resource and click on Change Working Time… to check this). If these two settings are out of sync, you will typically see decimals appear in durations, like 1.07 day.

Compressed Workweeks (Green Weeks)

One example of a compressed workweek is when a person works 10 hours per day, 4 days per week (called a 4-40 workweek). If there is more than one resource who will work a particular type of compressed workweek, we recommend you create a Base Calendar first. You can then base all resources who share the compressed workweek on this Base Calendar.

If you have only one resource working a compressed workweek change the Resource Calendar. For a 4-40 workweek you would typically enter it this way:

1. In the **Resource Sheet** select the resource, click **Resource Information** on the **Resource** tab, and the **Resource Information** dialog appears.

2. Click the tab **Working Time**; the dialog should now look like this:

3. Select **Default** on the **Work Weeks** tab in the **Change Working Time** dialog.

4. Click on Details, select Monday through Thursday, (hold down your ⌨Control key to select more than one day), and click on ⦿ **Set day(s) to these specific working times**:

5. In the first **From/To** table, enter in *7:00 AM* and *12:00 PM*; in the second **From/To** table, enter in *1:00 PM* and *6:00 PM*. Then click [OK].

6. Click on Details again, select Friday and click on ⦿ **Set days to non working times**. Then click [OK] and then [OK] again in the **Change Working Time** dialog.

The 4-40 Calendar is now created. Here, the resource is working 10 hours per day (40 hours per week), Monday through Thursday and off on Friday.

If you need to adjust a Resource Calendar for a special circumstance that occurs on a regular basis, find a way to model it rather than spending time adjusting it when it occurs. For example, if a resource gets every other Friday off, do not mark the Calendar that way, instead mark every Friday off and divide the total hours the resource works on Monday through Thursday. Although this is not perfect, it may be close enough to model your situation.

Overtime
Availability

Overtime work is work done outside the regular work hours as indicated in the Resource Calendar (or Project Calendar).

In the initial planning phase of a project, you wouldn't normally plan overtime unless the project is extremely time-constrained. Normally the overtime feature is only used during the execution phase, to try to compensate for slippages.

Overtime can be entered in different ways depending on whether you pay and what rate you pay for overtime:

➤ If the resource is not paid for overtime, but instead is compensated with extra time off, there are several ways to model this:

▸ You can enter the overtime by increasing the Max Units in the Resource Sheet to greater than 100%. This is the quick and easy way to enter overtime, and the resource will be working overtime during the entire project.
OR

▸ To be somewhat more precise you can create an availability profile in the Resource Information dialog 🔲 on the Resource tab. In Resource Availability you could specify overtime just for the period in which the resource works more than 100%.
OR

▸ Increase the working time in the Resource Calendar. For example, somebody works 10 hours overtime in one week, and in the second week the overtime is compensated with time off.
OR

▸ Enter the overtime by changing holidays or weekend days in the Resource Calendar to working days. Later, weekdays are set to nonworking days to compensate in time.

➤ If the resource is paid for overtime hours at the regular rate, you only need to check whether you kept the over-allocations reasonable. All regular and overtime hours worked are charged at the same standard rate.

➤ If the resource is paid for overtime hours at a higher rate, you have to enter all the hours worked in overtime separately. Refer to chapter 8 for an explanation of how to enter overtime hours.

Consolidated Resources

Consolidated resources are multiple resources who are entered into the schedule as one group instead of as individuals. For example, you can enter 5 Visual Basic programmers as 5 separate individuals, but you can also enter them as one team of 5 (a consolidated resource).

 Consider using a consolidated resource instead of a list of separate individual generic resources if skill sets are essentially equivalent. Depending on the situation, you may not need to replace the consolidated resource with actual names. This can be useful in modeling resources of third parties or consolidated resources who are not directly involved in your project.

You enter a consolidated resource as a single line item. The maximum units are set to the number of full-time equivalent individuals who are part of the consolidated resource. Full-time equivalency is defined in the **File** tab, **Options**, **Schedule** tab, **Hours per Day** setting. For example, if you have 2 full-timers and 2 half- timers on a team, the maximum units for that consolidated resource should be set to $(2 * 1) + (2 * 0.5) = 3$ or 300%.

 Consolidating resources can also be a wonderful way to keep the devilish details out of your schedule. For example, you can make an agreement with a team of 3 resources that you will not give them more work than 3 full-time equivalent resources. They will have to determine among themselves who will do which task, and because they know each other's expertise best, teams can be very good at that. As a project manager, you will spend a lot less time maintaining detailed resource data and keeping the individual workloads leveled.

Consolidating resources only makes sense if the resources can substitute for each other or if the resources are functioning as a small work group, a team. If you have experienced and novice resources, you can create two consolidated resources: junior and senior. For example, if you find that the experience level among your programmers varies widely, create a group of junior and a group of senior programmers. If that does not provide enough precision, you have to revert to modeling resources individually.

An Overview of Costs

Cost Situations

Economists distinguish between variable cost and fixed cost:

➤ Variable costs can vary with the amount of time needed, units consumed or number of times used. Labor cost is a time-related human resource cost. Facilities can also have time-related costs, like rent or lease expenses. Machines can have:

▸ Time-related cost such as rent

> ▶ Unit-related cost such as for paper used in a newspaper printing machine

> ▶ Use-related cost such as the setup cost of the printing machine. This can be entered in the **Cost/Use** field if the cost is incurred on every use of the resource.

➤ Fixed costs typically are associated with tasks.
Examples are expenses for licenses, patents and any fixed-price contracts given to subcontractors. Entering fixed costs using the resource type Cost and the Fixed Cost field will be covered in chapter 8.

The following table provides an overview and examples of the different types of costs as well as the way these costs are typically entered in Project 2010:

Cost Type	Example	Resource Type	Rate Field	Accrue at
Time related	3 days of work @ 300/d	Work	Std. Rate	Prorated
	2 months rent @ 400/mo	Material[3]	Std. Rate	Prorated
Unit related	3 doors @ 150/door	Material	Std. Rate	Start
Use related	$200 up front for bulldozer	Material	Cost/Use	Start (by default)
Varying rate	Work @ $300/d, after January 1st $350/d	Work	Cost Rate Table	Prorated
Fixed	Air Travel $1000 for a trip from San Antonio, TX to Atlanta, GA.	Cost	In the Assign Resources dialog box	
Fixed	Fixed-price contract painting the house: $8,500	—	Gantt Chart: Fixed Cost	Task Field: Fixed Cost Accrual[4]

The first thing to determine for the expense is the resource type: work, material, or cost.

Then the rate needs to be entered in the appropriate rate field; Project 2010 has many resource-related rate fields: Std. Rate, Ovt. Rate, Cost/Use and Cost rate tables.

---

3   If you make the facility a material resource, you have to enter the consumption rate in the assignment Units field in order to get a time-related cost. The consumption rate is the number of units used per time unit.

4   The task-related field Fixed Cost Accrual has the same options as the resource-related field Accrue At: Start, Prorated or End.

In the field Accrue At, you determine when the cost will take place:

➤ If you select Start, the cost will be scheduled on the start date of the assignment. Actual costs will be incurred on the Actual Start date.

➤ If you select Prorated during the planning phase, the cost is spread across the task duration proportional to the number of hours that are scheduled to be worked each day. During the execution phase, the actual costs accrue on the dates on which the actual hours were worked.

➤ If you select End the cost is accrued on the finish date of the task. Actual costs will be incurred on the Actual Finish date.

Material costs are often accrued at the start, whereas facility and machine costs are often accrued as prorated. For human resource costs, employees are typically prorated, whereas cost for consultants is often incurred at the end.

 The Cost/Use is always incurred at the start of the task and cannot be changed.

Project 2010 also has task-related cost fields: Fixed Cost and Fixed Cost Accrual. These are useful for entering firm fixed-price contracts and license costs. Fixed-price contracts often relate directly to a deliverable and license costs are often inputs to detail tasks. It makes sense to enter them in the task-related field Fixed Cost.

In practice, you will find more variations:

➤ A resource can have more than one type of cost associated with it. For example, a maintenance man can have a per-use fee of $50 for travel in addition to an hourly rate of $100. In this case, you would enter the per-use fee in the Cost/Use field and the hourly rate in the Std. Rate field.

➤ The cost rates themselves can change over time; this is known as varying cost rates or a rate profile. In Project 2010 you can capture a rate profile in the feature Cost Rate table. You can access the cost rate tables for a resource by double-clicking on the resource and clicking the tab Costs. Depending on when the effort is scheduled, Project 2010 will automatically take the appropriate rate to calculate the cost.

➤ You can have multiple cost rate tables per resource. Project 2010 provides up to five tables for each resource, so you can create five rate profiles per resource. For example, if you have a resource who does systems analysis, programming and testing, you could specify three different rate profiles (A, B and C) for each of these activities. When you assign the resource, you have to indicate per assignment which rate profile you want to use.

➤ Materials may have a consumption rate: how many units of the material are used per time unit? For example, you pour concrete that costs $1 per cubic foot and you know that you typically pour 2000 cubic feet a day with the crew you have. This consumption rate can be entered in the assignment-related Units field when you assign the resource to the task. In the Assign Resources dialog you would enter *2000/day* in the field Units. If the duration of the task is 3 days, the cost will be:

3 days * 2000/day * $1/cubic foot = $6000.

The duration of the task will determine the total cost for the task, and if the duration expands, more units of material will be consumed, which will increase the cost of the task. Essentially you have modeled a time-related cost for material resources.

➤ You may need to attribute a portion of a large capital cost expenditure to a project. For example, you may need to buy expensive test equipment that will be used in future projects as well. You only want part of this capital expense charged to your project, the part that your project should carry as an expense. If you know the amount, you can enter it in the task field Fixed Cost. Project 2010 does not have features to calculate the amount to charge to one project (project-related depreciation cost). You can use Excel to calculate the contribution per project.

➤ You may encounter discounts when purchasing large volumes of supplies or raw materials; you would need to enter a lookup table with all rate segments. This is something Project 2010 cannot easily handle. Again, you can use Excel.

➤ You may need to charge taxes or subtract refundable taxes to the cost amounts. Again, Project 2010 does not have features for this and Excel or your accounting system might help.

Entering Human Resource Costs

If, for example, you temporarily hire a programmer at $300/day, you can enter this in the **Resource Sheet** with the following steps:

1. Choose **View** tab, **Resource Sheet** .

2. Enter the name of the resource in the field **Resource Name**.

3. Leave the **Type** of the resource set to the default setting of **Work**.

4. Enter the rate in the field **Std. Rate**; for the programmer you would enter *$300/d*.

5. Enter the other cost rates **Ovt. Rate** and **Cost/Use**, if applicable.

6. Select an **Accrue At** option; choose **Start**, **Prorated** or **End**. The accrual determines when the cost will be incurred in the schedule and is important for cash-flow reports.

7. Assign the human resources to the tasks (we'll discuss this in the next chapter).

 Create an "average" or "blended" billable hourly rate for each resource instead of using their actual rate. This keeps their actual rates confidential. For example, some companies use an average rate for all resources. (E.g., all resources could be at $60 per hour or $75 per hour.) Some companies use a "blended" rate for resources. This rate is more specialized by the resource's role or responsibilities. (Project managers could be at $60 per hour, developers at $75 per hour.)

The time-related cost for facilities like rental and lease should be entered as material costs.

Entering Material Costs

The cost of material should be incorporated into the project model only if it will be paid from your project budget, and if it is significant enough to track.

If you expect many small expenses, don't track each expense separately. Project 2010 is not meant to be used as an accounting system. We recommend you create a petty cash or expense category and manage it as a separate budget line item. You can enter it as a Fixed Cost on the project summary task or on a separate detail task, like *manage petty cash*, forcing Project 2010 to include it in the total project budget.

If you decide a material expense should be tracked, enter it this way:

1. Choose **View** tab, **Resource Sheet**.

2. Enter the name of the resource in the field **Resource Name**.

3. Click in the field **Type** for the resource and a list button appears Work ; select **Material** Material from this list.

4. Enter a **Material Label**, which will show up in the Resource Graph View and other views to remind users that this is a material resource. Enter the label in plural, for example *bricks* instead of *brick*, because you typically assign more than one unit. You can even enter *thousand bricks* if you will enter the cost of 1000 bricks in the **Std. Rate** field instead of the cost of one brick. For bulk resources, you have to enter the unit of measurement; for example, for concrete this would be *cubic yards* or *cubic meters*.

5. In the **Std. Rate** field, enter the cost per unit for this resource. For bricks we could enter $2.00, for example. You can fill in a **Cost/Use** as well; for the bricks this could be the cost of transportation to the site, let's say *$400.00*. The overtime rate field is neither available nor needed for material resources. Notice that you cannot enter the time unit (*/h or /d*) for material resources; use consumption rates to model time-related cost for material resources.

6. Select the **Accrue At** method to determine on which date the cost will be scheduled in a time-phased view. You can choose **Start**, **Prorated** or **End**. Materials are often accrued at the start. Prorated is spread evenly with the number of hours that resources work on each day of the task duration. The Cost/Use is always incurred at the start of the task and cannot be changed.

The next screenshot of the Resource Usage view shows how the accrual for material costs works. The 1000 bricks cost $2 each and are accrued at the start of the task: 1,000 * 2 = $2,000. The mortar costs $5 per cubic foot and is accrued evenly with the hours worked on the task. The trowels at $20 each are accrued at the end of the task:

The prorated cost for mortar is evenly spread over time with the hours worked on the task. Notice that Alejandro only works mornings on Thursday and Friday.

The cost for bricks accrued at the start of the task.

		Resource Name	Accrue At	Work	Details	Aug 5,						
						S	M	T	W	T	F	S
1		bricks	Start	1,000 bricks	Cost		$2,000.00	$0.00	$0.00	$0.00	$0.00	
		lay bricks		1,000 bricks	Cost		$2,000.00	$0.00	$0.00	$0.00	$0.00	
2		Alejandro Acevedo	Prorated	32 hrs	Cost		$400.00	$400.00	$400.00	$200.00	$200.00	
		lay bricks		25.6 hrs	Cost		$400.00	$400.00	$400.00	$200.00	$200.00	
3		mortar	Prorated	100 cubic feet	Cost		$125.00	$125.00	$125.00	$62.50	$62.50	
		lay bricks		100 cubic feet	Cost		$125.00	$125.00	$125.00	$62.50	$62.50	
4		trowels	End	4 trowels	Cost		$0.00	$0.00	$0.00	$0.00	$80.00	
		lay bricks		4 trowels	Cost		$0.00	$0.00	$0.00	$0.00	$80.00	

The cost for 4 trowels at $20 each accrued at the end of the task.

We still need to learn how to assign the number of material resources to the tasks. We are going to learn this in chapter 8.

Entering Facility and Machine Costs

This is the most difficult resource situation to enter into Project 2010. The use of facilities and machines should not add to the Work (effort) of the project. This leads to the conclusion that they have to be entered as Material resources. But you cannot enter a time-related rate, like *$400/day*, in the Standard Rate field for material resources, though this is quite a common cost arrangement for facilities and machine rental. You can only enter unit- or use-related cost. For example, if you pay a fixed amount for every use of a training room, you can enter that cost in the Cost/Use field.

The best way to model time-related cost for facility and machine resources is to enter the resource as a material resource and use the consumption rate feature as a work-around to model its time-related cost for the task. The consumption rate is entered into the assignment-related Units field, which is found in the Assign Resources dialog or the Task Form.

For example, the training room costs your project *$600/day*. You enter the resource training room as a material resource in the Resource Sheet and you enter *600* as the Std. Rate. Then you create the task *training* and you assign the *training room* as the resource, and you enter the consumption rate of *1/d* as the Units for the assignment, which means that you will use one room per day (as the consumption rate)

This will appear in the Gantt Chart as follows:

	Task Mode	Task Name	Cost	Duration	Jul 22, '12	Jul 29, '12	Aug 5, '12
					S M T W T F S	S M T W T F S	S M T V
1		Training	$1,200.00	2 days			Training room[1/day]

Assign Resources

Task: Training

[+] Resource list options

Resources from Project1

Training room

Resource Name	R/D	Units	Cost		Assign
✓ Training room		1/d	$1,200.00		Remove
					Replace...
					Graph
					Close
					Help

The material resource training room costs $600/day and is assigned 1/d on the 2-day task which results in a cost of $1,200.

Hold down Ctrl and click to select multiple resources

You will learn more about making modifications to the Units field during resource assignments in chapter 8.

As you can see, we have used the consumption rate feature in Project 2010 to workaround the lack of a specific resource type for facilities. You can use the same workaround to model time-related cost for machines, e.g., when you rent equipment. Facility and machine costs are often accrued as prorated or at the end of a task.

Facility and machine costs are often accrued as prorated or at the end of a task.

When creating a resource that could be classified different ways, consider how you will pay for the resource. For example, if the resource *conference room* incurs a fee each time you use it, that may imply a cost per use situation. If *conference room* incurs an hourly rate, that may be a work resource.

Entering Varying Cost Rates

Varying cost rates can be entered in the Cost Rate table in the Resource Information dialog.

1. Select a resource and click ▊▤; the **Resource Information** dialog appears. Click the tab **Costs** and the dialog will look like this:

Resource Information

General | Costs | Notes | Custom Fields |

Resource Name: Andrew Caves

Cost rate tables

> In the Cost rate tables, rates can be entered and can vary over time (rate profile). Andrew is given a 10% raise each year. You can even enter 10% and Project 2010 will calculate the rate amount.

For rates, enter a value or a percentage increase or decrease from the previous rate. For instance, if a resource's Per Use Cost is reduced by 20%, type -20%.

A (Default) | B | C | D | E

$60.50/h

Effective Date	Standard Rate	Overtime Rate	Per Use Cost
--	$25.00/h	$50.00/h	$0.00
Sun 1/1/12	$27.50/h	$55.00/h	$0.00
Tue 1/1/13	$30.25/h	$60.50/h	$0.00

Cost accrual: Prorated ▾

Help   Details...   OK   Cancel

2. Enter the **Effective Date**, then enter the rates that will apply after that date.

OR

Enter the percentage with which you want the previous rate to change and Project 2010 will calculate the new rate for you.

3. Repeat the previous step as many times as the rate will change over time.

4. Click [OK]. Project 2010 will calculate using the appropriate rate, which depends on when the task is scheduled over time

In Project 2010, you can create rate profiles for all the different types of costs: Standard Rate, Overtime Rate and Per Use Cost (Cost/Use).

 Use the varying cost rate feature to incorporate rate changes for resources across time. This can be very useful in projects that have long durations where resource rates change. It allows you to reflect a pay raise or pay decrease for a resource.

Linking a Calculated Cost from Microsoft Office Excel

When you are dealing with capital costs, volume discounts or taxes, we recommend you calculate the cost to attribute to your project in Excel. Then copy the resulting cost value and paste it into the task-related Fixed Cost field or the resource-related Std. Rate field of your Project 2010 schedule. You can even create a dynamic link that will update the schedule automatically when the calculation changes.

The steps to do this for the Fixed Cost field are:

1. Create the calculation of the cost value in an Excel spreadsheet and save the Excel file (saving is essential if you paste link the number in step 3 instead of a regular paste without a dynamic link). Select the cell with the cost to be charged to the project in the Excel worksheet. Choose **Home** tab and click 📋 Copy ▾.

2. Switch to Project 2010 and apply the **Gantt Chart** view in which you display the field **Fixed Cost**. If needed, create the task and select the cell into which you want to paste the cost.

3. Click 📋.

   OR

If you expect the number to change several times, you may want to establish a dynamic link between your Excel 2010 spreadsheet and Project 2010 schedule. Do this by choosing on the **Home** tab, **Paste Special**, selecting ◉ **Paste Link,** selecting **Text Data** in the list and clicking [OK]. The number is now dynamically linked to the spreadsheet. Upon opening the schedule, Project 2010 will always either automatically update the number when you open the schedule or ask if you want to update the linked data (if the option in File, **Options**, **Advanced** tab, ☑ **Ask to update automatic links** is checked).

4. Cells with a dynamic link have a little triangle in the bottom right of the cell. To get rid of a dynamic link, simply select the cell and press [Delete] and a prompt will confirm that you want to remove the link.

Checks on the Resources

Perform the following checks to verify whether your resources have been modeled well:

➤ Are all resources identified in the Resource Sheet?
This is the case if all resources that could have a potential impact on the project are entered into the Resource Sheet. There can be impacts on scope, quality, duration or cost of the project. Resources and assignments should be entered for projects where:

- ▸ You expect that limited resource availability or heavy workloads may affect the end date of the project
- ▸ You have a cost budget for the project and are responsible for staying within that budget
- ▸ You have a budget expressed in person months and you have to stay within this effort budget
- ▸ You foresee a quality or scope impact on the project depending on which resources you will get

➤ Are all resources named completely and consistently using a naming convention like *<first name> <last name>* or *<last name>-<first name>*?

➤ Are there no overlaps between the resources or duplication of resources? If there are overlaps or duplications, Project 2010 will still aggregate the workloads of the resources, but these total numbers will be useless when you check on over-allocations. If Bill Tan is listed twice as a resource (as Bill Tan and William Tan), you would have to sum all time-phased workloads in order to determine if he is over-allocated. The workloads in the Resource Graph and in the Resource Usage can appear to be smaller than they really are when duplicate or overlapping resources exist.

➤ Is the availability of the resources appropriately modeled? This can be assessed by asking yourself the following questions:

   ▶ Does the availability of individuals not exceed 120% as captured in the resource field Max Units or the availability profile in the Resource Information dialog, General tab? You can set an arbitrary limit and choose the maximum to be 120%. It is unreasonable to ask resources for more than 120% availability for periods longer than one week. When you ask resources to work overtime for extended periods, their productivity decreases dramatically.

   ▶ If the Max Units are less than 100%, is there a valid reason for this? Valid reasons are that the project manager works with pure work time estimates, that the resources have other ongoing work (or other concurrent projects), or that the resource may be a part-time resource.

   ▶ Are the vacations of individual resources captured in their Resource Calendars? Vacations need to be entered, particularly when vacations are close to important deadlines. To check if vacations have been entered, choose **View**, **Reports**, **Assignments…**, **Who does what**. Click [Edit…], click tab **Details**, check ☑ **Calendar**, and click [OK]. In print preview, you will now see individual vacations listed under **Exceptions**, as well as the exceptions from the **Project Calendar**. You can copy this changed report back into your *Global.mpt* using **File, Info, Organizer** to have it ready for future schedule analysis.

➤ Are the costs of the resources appropriately modeled?

   ▶ Are human resources entered as Work resources in the resource field Type? Are facilities, machines and materials entered as Material resources?

   ▶ Do material resources have an appropriate Material Label to indicate their unit of measure? For bulk resources or consumable resources the Material Label should reflect the unit of measure, for example, the material label for cabling could be *yards* or *meters*.

- ▶ Are cost resources entered as Cost resources in the resource field Type?
- ▶ Are budget resources identified as Budget resources in the General tab on the Resource Information dialog box?
- ▶ Are the rates entered in the appropriate fields?
  - ▸ Time-related costs for work resources in the Std. Rate field
  - ▸ Unit-related cost for material resources in the Std. Rate field
  - ▸ Time-related cost for facilities and machines as material resources using two fields: the Std. Rate field where you enter the per-unit cost, and the assignment-related Units field where you indicate the number of units used per time unit (e.g., enter 2 rooms per day as *2/day*)
  - ▸ Use-related costs in the Cost/Use field
  - ▸ Overtime costs in the Ovt. Rate field (but only if the overtime is paid and paid at a higher rate than the standard rate).
  - ▸ Rates that vary over time in the Cost Rate Tables
  - ▸ Multiple rates per resource in the five Cost Rate Tables and the appropriate cost rate table (A, B, C, D or E) selected for each assignment
- ▶ Is the cost scheduled appropriately?
  This is important for managing the cash-flow of the project: Can bills be paid when they are supposed to be paid?
  - ▸ Does the resource-related Accrue At field reflect when the cost occurs: at the Start or at the End, or Prorated with the time-phased amount of work?

Review Questions

Review A

Is it possible to model the following cost situations in Project 2010? If so, how? If not, what would be a possible workaround?

1. Up-front fee of $500 for a bulldozer at a rate of $1,000/d for onsite work

2. A consultant who charges $400/d until January 1, then $450/d

3. Car rental with free mileage for the first 100 miles, then a fee of $0.45/mile

4. Penalty of $1,000/d for delivering late

5. Harry, who works as a business analyst at $500/d and as a systems analyst for $400/d

6. Volume discount for materials (for example, if you buy one door, it costs $150; if you buy 10 doors or more, they cost $90 each)

7. Pay an invoice within 30 days or pay a late charge of 10% of the invoice amount

8. Overtime hours accumulated throughout the year and paid at the end of the year

9. Courier costs for packages

10. Low and high season hotel room rates

Review B

Is it possible to model the following availability situations in Project 2010? If so, how?

1. Movers who only work on weekends

2. A server that needs to be tested for 48 continuous hours starting on a Friday

3. Somebody who works a compressed workweek of 10 hours per day and 4 days per week

4. An expert resource who will be available to your project for 10% in March, 20% in April and 50% in May; after that, she is unavailable

5. A part-time resource who only works mornings on Tuesdays and Thursdays

Review C   Which of the following resources should have its workload leveled in Project 2010? Enter **Yes** or **No** in the appropriate cell and explain your answer.

Resource	Level Workloads?
1. expert	
2. computer	
3. mortar	
4. boardroom	

Additional Practice   For experience working with the features you've learned about in this chapter, we strongly suggest that you review the Case Studies included in Appendix 1.

Chapter 8: Entering Assignments

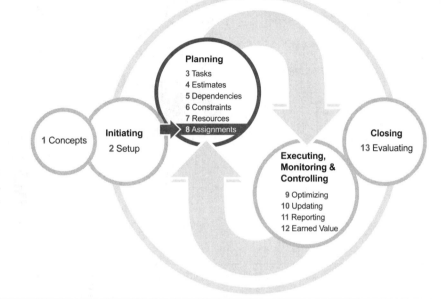

Assignments are the last type of data you need to enter into your project model. After you've finished, you'll have a complete model of your project.

After reading this chapter you will be able to:

> Explain what an assignment is and define assignment-specific fields
> Configure the Gantt Chart view to display assignment fields
> Assign resources using the Entry table, Task Information dialog box, Assign Resources dialog box, Task form view, and Team Planner view
> Assign costs for the following resource types: work, material, and cost
> Enter fixed costs on a task
> Create budget resources, enter budget values for each resource type, and compare budget values with planned values
> Modify assignment attributes to properly model resource availability
> Predict the impact of task type and effort-driven settings on assignments
> Select the most appropriate task type and effort-driven settings before making assignment changes
> Verify if assignments reflect scheduling best practices

Planning this schedule was so easy!

Great! Did you have any problem in assigning the resources?

Start
New finish!
(month 2)
Finish
(month 5)

Was I supposed to assign resources?

Vanna a

What Is an Assignment?

As discussed in chapter 7, resources refer to people, facilities, machinery, cost or materials needed to create the project product. Resources are assigned to tasks and significantly affect the quality, duration and cost of the project.

Earlier in this book we talked about populating task and resource fields. When a relationship exists between a task and a resource, you have an assignment. An assignment identifies which resource, in many cases person (or people), will work on a task. Assigning resources to tasks is also called resource loading, and when you're done you have a resource-loaded schedule. After resources are assigned, it is important to note that a new collection of assignment fields gets populated.

Assignment-Specific Fields

Each of the three data entities—tasks, resources and assignments—has its own specific fields. **Some fields may be called by the same name, but they contain different information depending on whether they belong to the task, resource or assignment.** Here are three examples:

➤ Start and Finish dates (task, resource and assignment-related)

➤ Max Units (resource-related) and Units (assignment-related)

➤ Work (task, resource and assignment-related)

Start and Finish

Tasks, resources and assignments all have Start and Finish dates. The start date of a task is not necessarily the same as the start date of its assignments. The start date of an assignment is when the resource starts working on the task. If Mary only works the last 2 days of the 5-day task, the start date of her assignment is different (3 days later) from the start date of the task.

Max Units and Units

In our second example the resource field Max Units represents availability and the assignment field Units (also called Assignment Units in some views) represents usage.

The Max Units field of a resource reflects the maximum availability of the resource to the project. For example, the Max Units would be 100% for a person who is entirely available to the project and 50% for a resource who is available half of her working hours. In the illustration, Mary is working half time on the project and has Max Units of 50%.

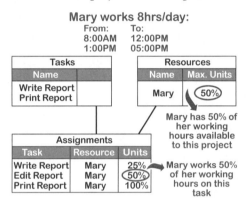

The assignment-related field Units is the percentage of her working hours that she is working on the task as set in her calendar. In the illustration, Mary works a regular work week, and a 50% assignment means for her 50% * 8 hours = 4 hours of effort per day on the task edit report (and not 50% * 50% = 25%). Four hours per day equals her maximum availability. If Mary worked a compressed workweek of 4 days a week and 10 hours per day, a 50% assignment would mean 5 hours of effort per day on the task. The percentage is always taken from the working hours on the calendar. The following table provides a summary:

Hours in Resource Calendar	Max Units on Resource Sheet	Assignment Units on a Task	Hours Calculated per Day
8	100%	100%	8
8	100%	50%	4
8	50%	50%	4
8	50%	100%	8

Note: The last row in the previous table creates an over-allocation for the resource. This situation will be addressed in the discussion about optimizing for limited resources in Chapter 9.

The assignment-related field Units reflects one of the following:

➤ Whether a person works full-time or part-time on the task

➤ How many individuals of a consolidated resource are needed on the task

➤ The amount of material resource that will be consumed on the task

If you want a resource to work all of her available working hours on a task, simply enter 100% in the field Units on the Task Form (or the Assign Resources window). If you enter less than 100%, you are asking the resource to work part of her available time on the task; you've created a part-time assignment.

 We recommend that you set an over-allocations standard for resources in your organization. For example, you may want a standard that resources are assigned no more than 150% of their time on each day and no more than 120% of their time on a weekly average. You may also decide that you won't address over-allocations unless they reach a certain threshold.

Work, Work and Work

The third and last example of how a field is different for tasks, resources and assignments is the field Work which is different on the Gantt table, the Resource Sheet, and the Task Form.

All are called by the same name (Work), but:

➤ In the Gantt Chart Work is the total effort of all resources working on the task.

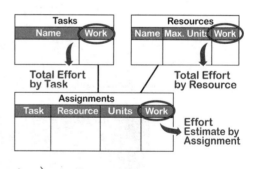

➤ In the Resource Sheet Work is the total effort for the resource in the entire project. (For material resources, it is the total number of units used in the project.)

➤ On the Task Form you can see the assignment-related Work field, which displays the effort of one resource on one particular task. This is a low level estimate and not an aggregate.

 Views in Project 2010 are created for a specific purpose and will restrict your ability to insert or display one or more of the following: task, resource or assignment fields. For example, the Resource Sheet view does not allow you to display Name from the Task fields.

Choosing the Options

The assignment-related options are shown in the following table. Before creating assignments, review them in the **Project Options**. On the **File** tab, in the **Backstage** view, click on ⊞ Options. The **Project Options** dialog box appears.

Project Options	Recommended Choices
Schedule	**Set the Options on the Schedule tab:** Show assignment units as a: `Percentage ▾` You can show assignment units in percentages or as decimals. **Percentage** is the best choice when you have part-time resources; if there are mostly consolidated resources, **Decimal** is better (e.g., 5 carpenters is easier to understand than 500% carpenters). This option is a global option; if you change it to decimal in one project, all your projects will use decimal numbers. If your schedule is e-mailed to someone else, it will follow the schedule properties of that person's machine. Duration is entered in: `Days ▾` Choose the default time unit. Changing this option after tasks are created will only affect new tasks and summary tasks. Work is entered in: `Hours ▾` Choose the default time unit display. This option can be changed at any time and all tasks already created plus any new tasks will update to the new time unit. Default task type: `Fixed Units ▾` Choose the type of task for any new tasks you create. This option is meant to be a time-saver. See the next section on Types of Detail Tasks for more information. ☐ New tasks are effort driven ⓘ This option works with the task type to model various resource scenarios. Our suggestion from chapter 4 still applies here. Leave this option off as the default setting.

Improving the Entry Table for Assigning Resources

Types of Detail Tasks

As covered in earlier chapters, there are three types of detail tasks (or simply Task Types): Fixed Duration, Fixed Units and Fixed Work. Each task has three variables:

> Duration is the amount of working time that passes between the start and end of a task. It is usually expressed in business days or business hours.

> Units reflect the number of resource units assigned, expressed as a percentage or a decimal.

> Work is the amount of effort applied directly to a task. It is usually expressed in person hours or person days. A person day represents one person working full-time for one day.

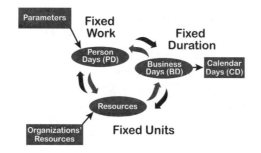

In chapter 4 we discussed the process of estimating, shown in the illustration. We recommended using Fixed Duration or Fixed Work tasks when first entering estimates.

It's important to be aware of the task type when you assign resources because Project 2010 performs calculations for each task type differently. It's a good idea, therefore, to insert the column Type in the Gantt table so you can see at any point what type of task you have.

You may also want to insert the field **Effort Driven**, because this field works with each task type and may affect the scheduling formula Duration x Units = Work. In chapter 4, we recommended keeping Effort Driven to *No* on Fixed Duration tasks because it works in a manner similar to the Fixed Work task type and it keeps the number of calculation scenarios down to a minimum.

Now that we have reached a point in this book where we are entering assignments, it is important to note that the Effort Driven field may need to be switched to *Yes* on some Fixed Duration or Fixed Unit tasks to model a specific scenario. We will discuss this in detail in this chapter.

If not already displayed, insert the field **Work** next to the **Duration** column. This will help you monitor changes as a result of the scheduling formula.

We recommend the following layout of columns when working with assignments:

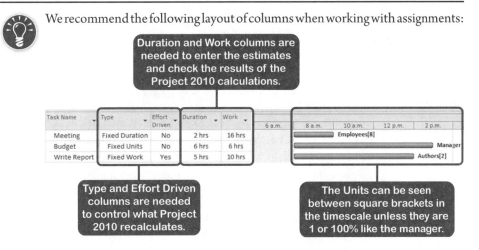

Duration and Work columns are needed to enter the estimates and check the results of the Project 2010 calculations.

Task Name	Type	Effort Driven	Duration	Work						
Meeting	Fixed Duration	No	2 hrs	16 hrs			Employees[8]			
Budget	Fixed Units	No	6 hrs	6 hrs						Manager
Write Report	Fixed Work	Yes	5 hrs	10 hrs						Authors[2]

Type and Effort Driven columns are needed to control what Project 2010 recalculates.

The Units can be seen between square brackets in the timescale unless they are 1 or 100% like the manager.

We can now see all three variables of the formula *Duration * Units = Work* with the *Units* visible between square brackets following the resource name (unless the units are 1 or 100%).

If there are multiple resources assigned to a task and you want to understand how the software applies the formula, you may need to consider each resource individually because resources may have different calendar hours per day.

You may also notice the column Resource Names. This field displays the same resource information that is located to the right of the Gantt bars but you may prefer to see it in the entry table.

Here's how to create the recommended layout.

1. On the **Task** tab, in the **View** group, click **Gantt Chart** .

2. Choose the **Entry Table** (if needed). On the **View** tab, in the **Data** group, click on the **Tables** down-arrow , **Entry**. The **Entry table** is displayed by default and has the columns: , Task Mode, Task Name, Duration, Start, Finish, Predecessors, Resource Names, and *Add New Column* (placeholder).

3. To insert the column **Work** after the column **Duration**, right-click on the column **Start** and choose **Insert Column** from the list; the list of available columns appears. Type or select **Work**.

Repeat step 3 for the fields **Type** and **Effort Driven**; we recommend you arrange the columns as indicated in the next screenshot:

	Task Mode	Task Name	Duration	Work	Type	Effort Driven	Resource Names

Reminder: you can hide columns by right-clicking on the column and choosing ⍤. A column can be moved by dragging the column heading.

We are now ready to make assignments.

Overview of Assigning Resources to Tasks

The following are the many different ways you can assign resources to tasks. The methods are organized for ease of explanation in this chapter starting with popular Gantt Chart view techniques. You will find some methods are simple (and quick) while other methods are sophisticated (and time consuming). The more sophisticated the method, the more detail it allows you to enter about the assignment:

> Spreadsheet/Table (left side)
> Task Information dialog box
> Assign Resources dialog box
> Task Form view (lower pane of a combination view)
> Team Planner view
> Task Usage view
> Resource Usage view

In most assignment methods, Project 2010 creates a flat workload, which means the work hours are evenly distributed across the life of the task. Generally, a flat workload is a good enough approximation of the true workload. If it isn't, you should consider breaking up the tasks into smaller tasks or use the work contour feature. Predefined work contours (discussed later) allow you to spread the work across the task duration in a certain pattern.

In general, we don't recommend the last two methods, Task Usage or Resource Usage views, for assigning resources because they require entering too much data and the data will need to be maintained for the life of the project. During project execution, you will have little time to maintain the schedule, but if you have an uneven resource contour, you'll need to use these two methods. It all depends on your specific project characteristics.

Be sure to assign a resource to every task where effort is required (every detail task).

We recommend and will discuss these methods in more detail: Spreadsheet/ Table, Task Information dialog box, Assign Resources dialog box, Task Form view and Team Planner view.

Collectively these methods will give you the speed and flexibility you need to properly model the efforts of your resources.

Assigning resources will trigger a recalculation: Project 2010 recalculates the work if it is a Fixed Duration task, or the duration if it is a Fixed Work task.

Information about adjusting task types to control the recalculation will be discussed later in this chapter.

As a general rule, the project manager will most likely know the duration estimate or the work estimate of a new task, and the task type should correspond to the estimate that you most want to control, either Fixed Duration or Fixed Work. The task type should **not** be Fixed Units when assigning resources because you may have problems when Project 2010 recalculates duration or work.

Assigning with the Spreadsheet/Table

One of the fast, easy ways to assign resources is to work with the popular Gantt Chart view and to use the default Entry table, located on the left-hand side of the view. If necessary, navigate here by clicking **Gantt Chart** in the **View** group on the **Task** tab. Additionally, verify you have the **Entry** table selected by clicking on the **Tables** down-arrow, **Entry**, in the **Data** group, on the **View** tab. If necessary, adjust the table to the recommended layout (discussed earlier).

Here's how to assign resources.

1. Verify you are in the **Entry** table of the **Gantt Chart** view.

2. Locate the row of the task to which you want to assign resources.

3. In the task's **Resource Names** field, click the down-arrow and then click the check box for each resource you want to assign to the task.

4. Click anywhere outside the resource list to accept the change.

5. Repeat for each task as needed.

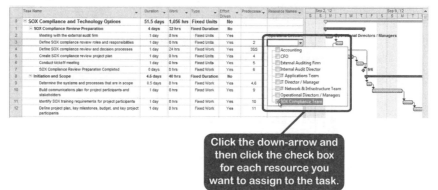

Click the down-arrow and then click the check box for each resource you want to assign to the task.

You will notice how very simple and fast this technique is and how the selected list of resource names automatically displays to the right of the Gantt bars. To change the assignment or remove a resource, simply repeat the same process and click again to select or deselect resources for the task.

To erase all resources for a task, select the **Resource Names** field and press the [Delete] key.

Selecting the Resource Names column and pressing the [Delete] key hides the column but does not remove any resource assignments.

Assigning with the Task Information Dialog

Another fast, easy way to assign resources is to continue to work with Gantt Chart view. If necessary, navigate here by clicking **Gantt Chart** in the **View group** on the **Task tab**. This option provides more choices over the last Spreadsheet/ Table selection because it provides the ability to adjust resource units and has a cost field used to enter amounts on cost type resources.

Here's how to assign resources.

1. Verify you are in the **Gantt Chart** view.

2. Locate the row of the task to which you want to assign resources.

3. Double-click the **Task Name** field to launch the **Task Information** dialog box.

4. On the **Resources** tab, in the first row, select the resource name from the down-arrow. If necessary fill in the **Units** and **Cost**. (Cost management will be discussed further below).

5. Repeat for each additional resource and then click OK.

6. Repeat for each task as needed.

Resource Name	Assignment Owner	Units	Cost
External Auditing Firm		1.00	$0.00
Internal Audit Director		1.00	$0.00
CFO		1	

Task Information — General | Predecessors | Resources | Advanced | Notes | Custom Fields

Name: Define SOX compliance review roles and responsibilities — Duration: 1 day — Estimated

Resources: CFO

Accounting
CFO
External Auditing Firm
Internal Audit Director
IT Applications Team
IT Director / Manager
IT Network & Infrastructure Team
Operational Directors / Managers
SOX Compliance Team

Help — OK — Cancel

Select the resource name from the down-arrow.

To remove a resource from a task select the name of the resource in the Resource Name field and press the ⌊Delete⌋ key. The selected list of resource names will automatically display to the right of the Gantt Chart bars.

The Assignment Owner field is used by Project Server to specify who is responsible for providing updates to the tasks in Project Web App. (Project Server and Project Web App are beyond the scope of this book.)

Assigning with the Assign Resources Dialog

The Assign Resources dialog box behaves differently than the Task Information dialog box in that it allows you to navigate between task and resource information without having to close and open the dialog box each time.

Some additional benefits of this option include:

➤ It provides filtering options to narrow down the resource list by specified criteria or by availability to work
➤ It provides the ability to display a resource graph for each resource
➤ It displays all available resources alphabetically, but shows the assigned resources at the top of the list for the selected task
➤ It offers the ability to assign resources with the Assign button or by dragging

 Using the Assign Resources Dialog box to assign several resources at once can yield different results than if the resources are added individually.

Assigning Resources by Dragging

1. On the **Resource** tab in the **Assignments** group, click **Assign Resources** ; the **Assign Resources** dialog box appears:

The Assign Resources dialog allows you to create assignments quickly.

The resources that are assigned have check marks. The dialog always lists them at the top of the list.

2. Click on the resource to assign.

3. Point to the resource selector ☐ in front of the resource name; the mouse pointer now has a person's (decapitated!) head attached:

4. Hold down the primary (typically left) mouse button, drag and drop the resource onto the task to which you want to assign it. The resource is now assigned; it has a check mark in front of its name. It appears in the field **Resource Names** and to the right of the task bar in the timescale.

5. If necessary, enter the **Cost** for any resource that has the type set to Cost. (Cost management will be discussed later).

6. Repeat for additional resources as needed.

Assign Multiple Resources to Multiple Tasks

To assign multiple resources to multiple tasks:

1. On the **Resource** tab in the **Assignments** group, click **Assign Resources** ; the **Assign Resources** dialog box appears:

2. Select the tasks to assign by dragging over them.

   OR

   Select them by holding down ⌞Control⌟ and clicking if the tasks are not adjacent.

3. In the Assign Resources dialog box, select the resource you want to assign or select multiple resources to assign by holding down ⌞Control⌟ and clicking on their names:

Multiple resources can be selected and assigned to one or more tasks at once.

Assign Resources			
Task: Unpack			
Resource list options			
Filter by:			
☐ All Resources			More Filters...
☐ Available to work 0h			
Add Resources ▼			
Resources from Relocation Chapter 8.5			

	Nancy Hilcrest			
Resource Name	R/D	Units	Cost	
✔ The Employees		35.00	$14,000.00	Assign
Boxes				Remove
Cablers				Replace...
Carpeteers				
John Falgon				Graph
Lunch for				Close
Moving Van				
Nancy Hilcrest				Help
Nelson Salin				
Pierre Roach				

Hold down Ctrl and click to select multiple resources

4. Click Assign ; a check mark appears in front of the name in the resource selector: ✔

When you use the Assign button instead of dragging resources to tasks, you can assign resources to multiple tasks all at once.

*Check Availability
Before Assigning*

You can check the availability of a resource while you are making assignments by selecting the resource in the **Assign Resources** dialog box. In order to view over-allocations across all projects that share resources, this function is best used in a consolidated master schedule (discussed in Appendix 2). We recommend you use this feature to prevent over-allocations from occurring in the first place, rather than sorting them out later, which can be a frustrating task.

Check resource availability before you assign a resource to each task.

1. Select the task to which you are about to assign resources. This is an important step because Project 2010 checks the availability of resources between the start and finish date of the task that is currently selected.

2. Insert the column **Work** by right-clicking on a column heading and choosing **Insert column**. Select **Work** from the list. In this field, you can see the total effort required on the task

3. On the **Resource** tab in the **Assignments** group, click **Assign Resources** ; the **Assign Resources** dialog box appears:

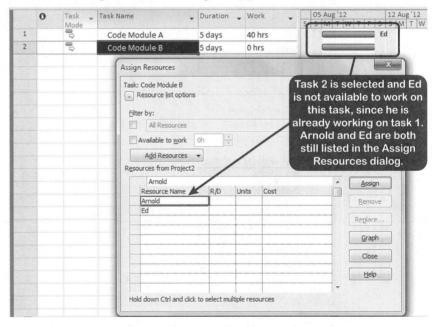

4. Check ☑ **Available to work** and enter the amount of effort that you need from the resource in the field to the right of it. Project 2010 will immediately list only the resources with enough availability (between the start and finish date of the selected task). This feature prevents you from having to switch to the Resource Usage view and back before you can make one assignment.

OR

In the **Assign Resources** dialog box, select the resource(s) in the list and click **Graph**; a **Resource Graph** will appear in the lower pane of **Gantt Chart** view. The graph allows you to verify within the duration of the task if the resource has enough availability.

5. The screen will look like this:

6. Select a resource from the resources that are available and click Assign .

 7. Make sure you clear ☐ **Available to work** again so that you see the entire list of resources for the next task.

8. You can quickly check the working hours of a resource by double-clicking on its name in the list.

Delete an Assignment

To delete an assignment:

1. On the **Resource** tab in the **Assignments** group, click **Assign Resources** 🏛; the **Assign Resources** dialog box appears.

2. Look at the check marks ✔ in front of the resource names that indicate which resources are assigned to the task(s) selected in the spreadsheet:

Assign Resources

Task: Meet to select

Resource list op

Filter by:

All Resource

Available to wor

The check marks indicate which resources are assigned to the selected task(s). Click one or more; the Remove button is now enabled.

Add Resources ▾

Resources from Relocation Chapter 8.5

John Falgon

Resource Name	R/D	Units	Cost
✓ John Falgon		1.00	$240.00
✓ Nancy Hilcrest		1.00	$280.00
✓ Nelson Salin		1.00	$1,200.00
✓ You		1.00	$600.00
Boxes			
Cablers			
Carpeteers			
Lunch for			
Moving Van			
Pierre Roach			

Assign

Remove

Replace...

Graph

Close

Help

Hold down Ctrl and click to select multiple resources

3. Select the resource to be removed.

4. Click [Remove].

Replace a Resource

To replace a resource:

1. Select the task(s) for which you want to replace the resource.

2. Display the **Assign Resources** 🏛 dialog box.

3. Select one of the assigned resources you want to replace.

4. Click [Replace...]; the **Replace Resource** dialog appears.

5. Select a resource and click [OK]; the resource will now be replaced without a recalculation.

If a task is in progress, only the remaining duration of the assignment will be reassigned to the new resource; all actual hours worked stay with the original resource. Assignments that are 100% complete will trigger an appropriate prompt:

Microsoft Office Project

The task is 100% complete.

Do you want to move the actual work to the new resource?

OK   Cancel

If you get this prompt, you may need to click Cancel.

Enter Assignment Units

When you assign resources using the Assign Resources dialog box, Project 2010 automatically assigns:

➤ The maximum availability (Max Units) of individual Work resources; if the Max Units of the resource is 1 or less

> ➤ Only 1 unit of the individual Work resource; if the Max Units is greater than 1
> ➤ Only 1 unit of consolidated Work resources
> ➤ Only 1 unit of a Material resource

 You cannot enter a value in the Units column for Cost Resources as you would for Work or Material Resources. The total amount for the Cost resource applied to the task is entered directly and not calculated using the Units assigned.

Units should be entered as a percentage (recommended for single resources) or as decimals (recommended for consolidated resources). You can work with either percentages or decimals by choosing **Show Assignment Units** as a (Decimal or Percentage). On the **File** tab, in the **Backstage** view, click on Options. The **Project Options** dialog box appears. Click the **Schedule** tab and look under the **Schedule** heading.

 Adjusting the Units may trigger a recalculation by Project 2010, so check the Task Type first. The task type should not be Fixed Units if you intend to change units. More about Task Types will be covered later in this chapter.

After resources are assigned, you can modify the assignment units. In the Assign Resources dialog box, select the name of the assigned resource (should have a check mark) and select the field Units. Enter the percentage of the resource's available working hours (or the number of resources you need from a consolidated resource) and then press the ⌅ Enter key. You don't need to click ⌐ Assign again after setting this attribute.

Assign Resources

Task: Evaluate the sites

Filter by:
☐ All Resources

☐ Available to work   0h

Add Resources ▾

> The units for John Falgon are entered as a percentage of his available working hours as specified in his resource calendar.

	Resource Name	R/D	Units	Cost
	John Falgon			
✔	John Falgon		100%	$240.00
✔	Nancy Hilcrest		100%	$280.00
✔	The Realtor		50%	$140.00
✔	You		100%	$600.00
	Boxes			
	Cablers			
	Carpeteers			
	Lunch for			
	Moving Van			
	Nelson Salin			

Assign
Remove
Replace...
Graph
Close
Help

Hold down Ctrl and click to select multiple resources

The field R/D indicates whether the assignment is a Request (requested to work on the task) or a Demand, (must work on the task for it to be completed successfully). Entering this is only important if you use the Resource Substitution Wizard feature in Project Server.

Even though the field Units asks for units to be entered, you can actually enter work in this field and Project 2010 will calculate the units required. If you do this, make sure you include the time unit, as in *20h*, to make it clear to Project 2010 that it should interpret your entry as person hours of work instead of as units.

Assigning with the Task Form View

The main advantage to this option is that you can see separate columns for units and work for each resource name. Using the lower pane is also an effective way to use your available screen space without having to move a dialog box around such as the Assign Resources dialog box. Note that you are limited to making resource assignments to one task at a time.

While there are numerous split screen configuration options in Project 2010, we will focus on the optimal settings for resource assignments.

To display the Task Form:

1. On the **Task** tab, in the **View** group, click **Gantt Chart** .

2. If necessary, select the **Entry** table, from the **Tables** down-arrow, in the **Data** group, on the **View** tab.

3. On the **View** tab in the **Split View** group, split the screen by selecting the **Details** checkbox and then in the down-arrow, click **Task Form**.

   OR

4. Double-click on the **sliding window** handle at the bottom right of the screen:

5. Click anywhere on the **Task Form** to display related options on the Ribbon, and then on the **Format** tab, click **Work** . Review your results with the following screen:

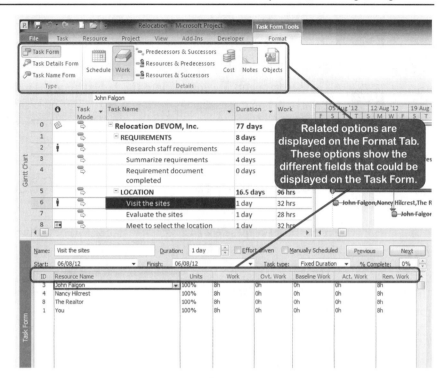

Assign Resources

1. On the **Gantt Chart** (upper pane), select the task to which you want to assign resources.

2. On the **Task Form**, click in the field **Resource Name**, and a list button will appear:

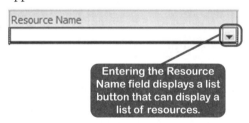

3. Click the list button and select a resource from the list that appears.

4. Optional: enter the **Units** (the percentage of the available working hours) or the **Work** (person hours of effort needed).

 Units and **Work** will be automatically filled in by Project 2010 after you click OK unless you decide to manually enter those values.

5. In the next blank **Resource Name** field, repeat steps 2-4 until you are done selecting resources.

6. Click ☐ OK ☐ once all resources are assigned.

If you prefer to use the keyboard to accept the assignments, you may need to press the ⌜Enter ↵⌟ key twice. The first time will accept the resource name selection and the second time will be equivalent to clicking OK.

 All new assignments are entered into the project model simultaneously, which triggers only one recalculation by Project 2010. This makes this method better for assigning multiple resources with specific **Units** or **Work** values; you are not triggering a recalculation with every assignment you add or remove, unlike in the **Assign Resources** dialog.

Delete an Assignment

On the **Task Form**, select an assigned resource, press ⌜Delete⌟ and click ⌜ OK ⌟.

Replace a Resource

On the **Task Form**, select an assigned resource, click the down arrow to choose an alternate resource and click ⌜ OK ⌟.

Assigning with Team Planner View

Team Planner view is new to Project 2010 and to take advantage of this view, you need the Professional version. The view is very easy to use and you can use drag and drop to create assignments. One of the unique aspects of Team Planner is you create an assignment by dragging a Task to a Resource versus prior techniques which focused on assigning a Resource to a Task. What makes this method different than prior methods discussed is you also have the ability to schedule the timeframe for the task based on effective resource usage.

1. On the **Task** tab, in the **View** group, click **Team Planner** 🗓.

2. Adjust the view as needed:

   a. Press ⌜Alt⌟ + ⌜Home⌟ to shift the timescale to the start of the project OR press ⌜F5⌟ to jump to the specific date you need.

   b. Zoom in or Zoom out using the ⊖ ▽ ⊕ **Zoom Slider** on the Status Bar until you display the desired level of detail.

   c. Move the dividing bar separating the list of resources with the list of tasks up or down to display the information you need. Refer to the following diagram:

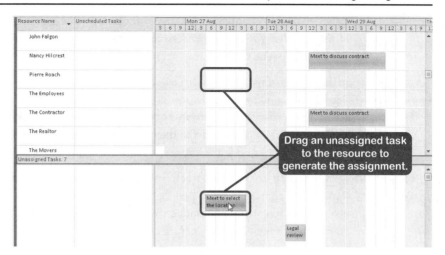

d. Make any other adjustments as desired.

3. Drag an unassigned task to the resource to generate the assignment.

Keep the following points in mind when working with this view:

➤ If tasks are unassigned, they appear on the lower section of the screen (below the horizontal dividing bar), regardless of the task mode.

➤ If they are unscheduled (no starting date set, as is the default with new, manually-scheduled tasks), they appear to the left of the vertical dividing bar. Only manually-scheduled tasks can be unscheduled.

➤ For templates and older files, even though the tasks are manually-scheduled, they may have a start date so they are not unscheduled. Thus they appear on the right of the vertical dividing bar.

➤ In summary, manually-scheduled tasks can appear anywhere, depending on whether they have a start date and/or resource; auto-scheduled can only appear on the top or bottom on the time phased portion of the Team Planner view, depending on whether or not they have a resource.

 Dragging an auto scheduled task in Team Planner view to a resource will add a Start no Earlier than constraint on the designated date. As discussed in chapter 6, we do not recommend setting unneccesary constraints for dynamic schedules.

 Use the Team Planner view only with manually scheduled tasks when making new assignments. This gives you the flexibility to schedule a task when a resource is available and avoid resource over-allocations. The task will start on the date you decide.

Cost Management

Earlier in this chapter we discussed techniques for assigning resources. Now we'll focus on where to enter resource costs and how Project 2010 computes the total cost for the task.

The total cost for a task is displayed in the field Cost in Gantt Chart view. This field is a summary of the variable costs associated with resource assignments and it includes cost per use amounts and fixed task costs. You may review your total estimate of the project Cost in the project summary task and compare it against your Budget Cost if you decide to create a budget.

Entering Costs on an Assignment

Project 2010 can help you track costs on your project when you assign work and material resources, such as people or equipment, or cost and budget resources, such as air travel or travel-budget. You can also assign a fixed cost to a task that is unrelated to people, equipment, or materials.

Variable Costs for Work Resources

People are the most popular work resources. When you enter the standard rate for a person and the person is assigned to a task, Project 2010 multiplies this rate by the amount of assigned work to estimate the cost of the assignment.

1. In the Resource Sheet, enter the name of the work resource for which you want to set the variable cost.

2. In the Std. Rate field for the selected work resource, enter the standard pay rate, for example, $50 per hour (*50/h*), or $400 per day (*400/d*).

3. If the resource has an overtime pay rate, enter this amount in the Ovt. Rate field, for example, $75 per hour (*75/h*). Project will apply this rate when you assign overtime hours. Refer to the section To Display the Task Form above for information on how to display the overtime hours.

> **This Ovt. Rate will be applied when you assign overtime hours to the resource.**

	ⓘ	Resource Name	Type	Max. Units	Std. Rate	Ovt. Rate	Cost/Use	Position	Accrue At	Function	Base Calendar
4		Nancy Hilcrest	Work	100%	$50.00/h	$75.00/hr	$0.00	Planner	Prorated	Employee	Standard
2		Nelson Salin	Work	100%	$150.00/hr	$0.00/hr	$0.00	CEO	Prorated	Manager	Standard
5		Pierre Roach	Work	100%	$75.00/hr	$0.00/hr	$0.00	Lawyer	Prorated	External	Standard
16		Students	Work	500%	$80.00/day	$0.00/hr	$0.00	Contractor	End	External	Standard

4. Optional: Specify the **Accrue At**, selecting either **Start** (beginning of task), **Prorated** (throughout the task duration), or **End** (end of task), from the drop-down. Prorated is the default setting.

Costs for Material Resources

Material resources are resources that are consumed or used up within a project. Examples of material resources are paper, cement, and lumber. Each material resource should have a specified unit of measurement in its Material Label field, for example, reams, pounds, or metric ton.

1. In the **Resource Sheet**, enter the name of the material resource for which you want to set the Standard Rate, for example, *cement*.

2. In the **Type** field, select **Material** from the type drop-down to specify this resource as a material resource.

3. Identify the specific unit of measurement for the resource in the **Material Label** field, for example, *Metric Ton*.

4. In the **Std. Rate** field, enter the cost per unit of the material resource. For example, if cement is measured by the metric ton and one metric ton costs $75, enter 75 in the **Std. Rate** field.

	ⓘ	Resource Name ▾	Type ▾	Material Label ▾	Initials ▾	Group ▾	Max. Units ▾	Std. Rate ▾	Ovt. Rate ▾	Cost/Use ▾	Accrue At ▾	Base Calendar ▾
13		Cement	Material	Metric Ton	C			$75.00		$0.00	Prorated	

When you assign a material resource to a task, you can change the number of Units and Project 2010 will multiply the Standard Rate by the Units to create the total material Cost for the task.

Optional: Specify the **Accrue At**, selecting either **Start** (beginning of task), **Prorated** (throughout the task duration), or **End** (end of task), from the drop-down. Prorated is the default setting.

Cost Per Use for Resources

Work resources like equipment sometimes have an additional cost for each time you use them. For example, a bulldozer might have a delivery charge along with its daily rate. Project adds this additional cost to the total variable costs each time the resource is used.

1. In the **Resource Sheet**, enter the name of the work resource for which you want to set the fixed cost.

2. In the **Cost/Use** field for the selected resource, enter the cost per use, for example, *250*.

> Project adds this additional cost to the total variable costs each time the resource is used.

	ⓘ	Resource Name ▾	Type ▾	Max. Units ▾	Std. Rate ▾	Ovt. Rate ▾	Cost/Use ▾	Accrue At ▾	Base Calendar ▾
13		Bull Dozer	Work	100%	$400.00/day	$0.00/h	$250.00	Prorated	Standard

Costs for Cost Resources

Cost resources are costs that help in completing a task but don't affect the scheduling of the task. Cost resources are something other than the people, equipment, or materials on a task. They can be items such as hotels, car rentals, and airfare.

Cost resources can be used to represent Fixed Costs on tasks. The value assigned may vary from one task to another, but on an individual task, the value does not vary with the number of resources or the duration of the task.

You cannot enter standard rate amounts for cost resources when they are created, as you do with work and material resources. The cost values are entered when the cost resource is assigned to the task. The amount for the cost resource can be different depending on the task to which it is assigned. For example, airfare costs for the *spring convention* task may be different than the airfare costs for the *summer convention* task, depending on airfare rates.

1. Make sure that the cost resource is entered and designated as **Cost** in the **Type** drop-down on the **Resource Sheet**.

2. In the **Gantt Chart**, double-click the task to which you want to assign the cost resource. The **Task Information** dialog box appears.

3. Click the **Resources** tab, click in the field **Resource Name**, and a list button will appear. Click the list button and select a resource name from the list.

Task Information				
General	Predecessors	Resources	Advanced	Notes	Custom Fields

Name: Conduct Kickoff meeting   Duration: 1 day? ☑ Estimated

Resources:

Airfare

Resource Name	Assignment Owner	Units	Cost
Airfare ▼			$500.00

Type the amount in the Cost field. You can only use this field for Cost type resources.

Help   OK   Cancel

4. Type the cost amount in the **Cost** field. For example, if airfare for the *Summer convention* task was $500, enter this amount in the Cost field.

5. Click OK .

Fixed Costs for Tasks

Sometimes you have a task cost that isn't dependent on any resource, for example, the cost of publishing an initial kick-off presentation for all stakeholders, or a fixed price contract with a law firm to review legal documents.

1. In the **Gantt Chart**, select the **Cost** table by going to the **View** tab, clicking on the **Tables** down-arrow ▦, and selecting **Cost**.

2. Select the task and in the **Fixed Cost** field, enter in the fixed cost for the task. For example, for *printing costs $500*.

	Task Name	Fixed Cost	Fixed Cost Accrual	Total Cost	Baseline	Variance	Actual	Remaining
25	Printing	$500.00	Prorated	$500.00	$0.00	$500.00	$0.00	$500.00

3. Specify the **Fixed Cost Accrual**, selecting either **Start** (beginning of task), **Prorated** (throughout the task duration), or **End** (end of task), from the drop-down. Prorated is the default setting.

In the default Cost table (displayed above), the **Cost** field is shown as **Total Cost**.

4. Project 2010 will then calculate the total cost for the task in the field **Cost** as: **Cost = Fixed Cost + All task related costs** (from material, cost, and work resource types)

The next screenshot shows the Task Usage view to illustrate this formula. The total cost of $3,800 for the task *lay bricks* consists of *$600 fixed cost, $2,000* material cost for the bricks and $1,200 labor cost for the bricklayers:

> The Cost for the task is the total of Fixed Cost, material cost and labor cost.

	ⓘ	Task Mode	Task Name	Fixed Cost	Cost	Duration	Work
1	▦	➡	⊟ lay bricks	$600.00	$3,800.00	5 days	40 hrs
			bricks		$2,000.00		1,000 bricks
			brick layer		$1,200.00		40 hrs

Notice that if you enter any cost directly into the **Cost** field for a task, the cost is immediately interpreted as **Fixed Cost** by Project 2010 and transferred into that field.

It is always a good idea to include a task note that identifies the fixed cost entered.

Assign a Cost resource instead of a Fixed Cost if you want a category of fixed costs that can be repeated across several different tasks and then aggregated by category.

Budget Costs for Budget Resources

Budget resources are special resources that are created specifically to list a budget category that needs to be tracked within a project on a high level (in the project summary task). Budget resources can be work, material, or cost resources.

Once the budget resource is created and assigned, the project work or project cost amounts can be rolled-up and compared to the budgeted amounts listed in the budget resource. (If you need to know how to create a budget resource, please see the section Entering Budget Resource in chapter 7.)

ⓘ	Resource Name	Type	Budget	Material Label	Initials	Group	Max. Units	Std. Rate	Ovt. Rate	Accrue At	Base Calendar
1	BUDGET Work	Work	Yes		BW					Prorated	Standard
2	BUDGET Material	Material	Yes	Metric Ton	BM					Prorated	
3	BUDGET Cost	Cost	Yes		BC					Prorated	

1. You can only assign the budget resource to the project summary task. This is because budget items are high-level and are rolled-up to the project summary task for easy comparison. Make sure that you have the project summary task visible. To do this: on the **Format** tab, in the **Show/Hide** group, choose ☑ **Project Summary Task**.

2. In the **Gantt Chart** view, select the project summary task (line 0) and on the **Resource** tab in the **Assignments** group, click **Assign Resources** 🖧; the **Assign Resources** dialog box appears.

3. Locate your budget resources. (If you include the uppercase word *BUDGET* in all your budget resources, they will be easy to identify).

4. In the **Assign Resource** window select the budget resource that you want to assign to the project summary task.

5. Click [Assign] and then click [Close].

Only resources identified as Budget resources can be assigned to the project summary task! The Budget column may be added to the Resource Sheet view or you can double-click a resource name to apply the budget attribute.

Budget Values for Work, Material, and Cost Budget Resources

After creating the budget resource and assigning it to the project summary task, you're ready to enter the budget work amounts for work and material resources, and the budget cost amounts for cost resources.

1. On the **View** tab, **Task Views** group, go to the **Task Usage** view 🖼 (illustrated below) or **Resource Usage** view 🖼.

2. Insert the **Budget Cost** column and the **Budget Work** column in the view.

3. In the **Assignment** row, enter the value for **Budget Cost** or **Budget Work** for the BUDGET resources:

   ▸ For *Work* **Type** Budget resources, enter the budgeted hours in the **Budget Work** column.

Be sure the resource BUDGET Work-Hours is listed on the **Resource Sheet** with **Type** *Work* and the **Budget** attribute *Yes*. Otherwise, you won't be able to enter the budgeted amount.

▶   For *Material* **Type** Budget resources (e.g. BUDGET Material-Cement), enter the budgeted amount as the total material units in the **Budget Work** column. For example, if 10000 metric tons of cement have been budgeted, enter *10000* in the **Budget Work** field.

Be sure the resource (e.g., BUDGET Material-Cement) is listed on the Resource Sheet with Type Material and the Budget attribute Yes. Otherwise, you won't be able to enter the budgeted amount.

▶   For *Cost* **Type** Budget resources (e.g. BUDGET Cost), enter the budgeted amount in the **Budget Cost** column, for example, *50000*.

Be sure the BUDGET Cost Resource is listed on the Resource Sheet with Type Cost and the Budget attribute Yes. Otherwise, you won't be able to enter the budgeted amount.

	ⓘ	Task Mode	Task Name	Budget Cost	Budget Work
0			⊟ **SOX Compliance and Technology Options**	**$50,000.00**	**5,000 hrs**
			BUDGET Work-Hours		5,000 hrs
			BUDGET Material-Cement		10,000 Metric Ton
			BUDGET Cost	$50,000.00	

You can only enter values in the Budget Work field for Budget resources where the Type is set to Material or Work. You can only enter values in the Budget Cost field for Budget resources where the Type is set to Cost.

The Budget Cost field totals all your Budget Resources in the Project Summary Task row, but the Budget Work field only includes the hours of your Budget Resources (if you use a Material resource, the amount of the material won't be added to the total hours).

Time-Phased Budget Resources

Sometimes you need to track a Budget Resource for a specific time period, like a specific month or week.

After you've created and assigned your budget resource to the project summary task, go to the **Task Usage** view [icon] (illustrated below) or **Resource Usage** view [icon] (notice that your screen is split into a left and right side).

1.   Continue with the **Task Usage** view as configured in the last section.

2.   Now you need to add **Budget Cost** and **Budget Work** to the timescale (right) portion of the view.

▶   Move your mouse to that area, right-click, and select **Detail Styles.** In the **Detail Styles** dialog box, select the **Usage Detail**s tab.

▶ Select **"Budget Cost"** from the available fields, then hold down your ⌘Control key and select "**Budget Work**" and then select **Show**.

▶ Click [OK] to insert these two columns into the timescale portion of the view. Adjust your columns as needed to see the added fields.

▶ You may hide the **Work** field on the timescale section of the view. To do this, right-click on the timescale section, then click **Work** in the shortcut menu.

 Use the Zoom Slider ⊖———◌———⊕ on the Status bar to Zoom In or Zoom out to set the specific time period for the budget values that you want to include. For example, you could show just months in the timescale.

In the Assignment view (on the right side of the screen), next to the budget resource for which you want to enter values, enter the budgeted work or budgeted cost values under the specific time scale, as shown in following screenshot.

> **Enter the budgeted work or budgeted costs values under the specific time scale.**

	Task Mode	Task Name	Budget Cost	Budget Work	Details	1st Quarter Jan	Feb	Mar	2nd Quarter Apr
0		⁼ SOX Compliance and Technology Options	$50,000.00	5,000 hrs	Budget Cost		$15,000.00	$25,000.00	$10,000.00
					Budget Work		2,000h	2,000h	1,000h
		BUDGET Work-Hours		5,000 hrs	Budget Cost				
					Budget Work		2,000h	2,000h	1,000h
		BUDGET Material-Cement		10,000 Metric Ton	Budget Cost				
					Budget Work (Metric Ton)	0	5,000	5,000
		BUDGET Cost	$50,000.00		Budget Cost		$15,000.00	$25,000.00	$10,000.00
					Budget Work				

Assignments on Summary Tasks

Project 2010 allows you to assign resources to summary tasks, but we discourage this: sooner or later you will end up with over-allocations that can't be resolved except by removing the resource from the summary task. Let's explain this.

If you assign a resource full-time to a summary task and also to one of its detail tasks, the workload of the resource will be twice its availability during that detail task.

In the illustration, you can see that Eduardo is assigned to the summary task *ST 1.1* and its detail task *DT 1.1.3*. You may think that you would never create a situation like this, but you inadvertently might because assignments on summary tasks don't show up in the default

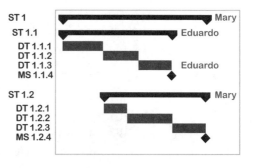

timescale in Project 2010 as they do in the illustration; only assignments on detail tasks are displayed. (You can change this: on the **Format** tab, in the **Bar Styles** group, click the down arrow on **Format** , click **Bar Styles**, **Text** tab.)

 An assignment on both a summary task and its own detail task causes an over-allocation that can't be solved by Project 2010. After all, if Project 2010 moves the detail task to a later date, the summary task will automatically extend as well and continue the over-allocation. You can't resolve the over-allocation yourself either, other than by removing the resource from the summary task (or from its detail task). So why bother assigning to summary tasks in the first place, if you normally assign resources to detail tasks?

A similar over-allocation can occur between the different levels of summary tasks. In the previous illustration you can see that Mary is assigned only to summary tasks *ST 1* and *ST 1.2*. Because *ST 1.2* is subordinate to *ST 1*, the over-allocation can't be solved unless you remove the resource from one of the summary tasks.

This situation can occur easily if you have several indentation levels. You could try to control this by only assigning resources to tasks that are on a certain outline level. You could insert the field Outline level and use that to prevent this type of over-allocation. But why did you add more levels of detail tasks, if you are not going to use them to delegate or model workloads? It looks like you could have saved yourself some time by not creating all those detail tasks in the first place!

Updating schedules with summary task assignments is also more cumbersome than when all assignments are on the lowest level. Again, we are back to one of our basic principles of modeling: leave things out that do not have added value.

 You may be tempted to assign to a summary task if all its detail tasks are scheduled in sequence without gaps and all are done by the same resource(s). But since it's almost as quick to select all the detail tasks and assign the resource(s) to them with one click, is it really worth the minimal time savings? We don't think so, and don't recommend that you assign to summary tasks even in this situation because of the substantial risk of encountering those stubborn over-allocations.

 In short, in our view, there are no situations in which you are better off assigning to summary tasks rather than to detail tasks. We recommend keeping the assignments on the lowest level, the detail level only.

 You can, however, assign resources to a **recurring** summary task with the **Assign Resources** tool on the **Resource** tab, because Project 2010 will automatically transfer these to the detail tasks and remove the assignment on the recurring summary task.

Assignments on Recurring Tasks

If you assign a resource to a recurring summary task with the **Assign Resources** tool , the assignments are immediately transferred to the detail tasks by Project 2010. In the illustration, the resources Mark and Brad are assigned to the recurring summary task *3 Status Meeting* and are automatically transferred by Project 2010 to the recurring detail tasks (that is where you want the assignments).

3 Status Meeting Mark, Brad
   3.1 Status meeting 1 Mark, Brad
   3.2 Status meeting 2 Mark, Brad
   3.3 Status meeting 3 Mark, Brad

 You can assign resources to the summary of recurring tasks if you want them all assigned to each recurrence, otherwise, assign separately to each recurrence.

You can assign to recurring tasks in situations such as:

➤ Long meetings: They can require considerable effort (work) from resources.

➤ Short meetings: You require attendance at short meetings, and want to show them as assignments in the to-do lists of team members.

 You should only assign to recurring tasks, such as status meetings, if the efforts for these meetings are not included in the work estimates that your team members provided to you.

Assigning to recurring detail tasks can easily result in over-allocations that Project 2010's leveling features will not resolve. The reason is that Project 2010 by default excludes recurring tasks from the leveling process by setting the field Level Assignments to *No* for the recurring detail tasks. You could switch it manually to *Yes*, but then your recurring tasks may be rescheduled, which is probably not what you want. We recommend you keep the meetings short, assign resources and ignore the over-allocations on recurring tasks.

Multiple, Uneven Assignments

If there are multiple assignments on a task, often one will drive the duration of the task: usually the assignment that takes the longest or starts the latest. The illustration shows that three engineers, *Joe*, *Frank* and *Mary*, are assigned to develop a prototype. Joe will work 10 days, Frank only the first 6 days and Mary only the last 5 days, so the duration will be 10 days. Joe and Mary determine or "drive" the duration of the job.

Joe: 10d
Frank: 6d at start
Mary: 5d at end

There are disadvantages to this practice:

➤ It is unclear who is supposed to take the lead on the task.

➤ Entering multiple uneven assignments can make it difficult to level workloads manually (as discussed in chapter 9). It is simpler if there is only one resource assigned per task. If you do this, however, you may end up with many more tasks in your schedule.

To create multiple, uneven assignments on a task you need to:

1. Split the screen in **Gantt Chart** view by selecting the Details checkbox and then in the down-arrow, click **Task Form**. These options can be found in the **Split View** group, on the **View** tab.

2. Change the details in the Task Form to show assignment start dates by clicking anywhere on the **Task Form** to activate it, and then on the **Format** tab, click **Schedule** ⊞.

3. Click in the field **Resource Name** and select a resource to assign from the list that appears . Repeat this for all resources you want to assign to the task. Enter a specific **Scheduled Start** date or **Delay** for each assignment.

4. Click ⟦ OK ⟧; you can see the result of the uneven assignments by choosing **Task Usage** on the **View** tab.

The result of the previous example would look like this:

Task Name	Work	Details	05 Aug '12							12 Aug '12					
			S	M	T	W	T	F	S	S	M	T	W	T	F
⊟ Research Requirements	168 hrs	Work		16h	16h	16h	16h	16h			24h	16h	16h	16h	16h
Joe	80 hrs	Work		8h	8h	8h	8h	8h			8h	8h	8h	8h	8h
Frank	48 hrs	Work		8h	8h	8h	8h	8h			8h				
Mary	40 hrs	Work		0h	0h	0h	0h	0h			8h	8h	8h	8h	8h

> **Joe and Mary determine the duration of the job.**

Typically, the resource with the least work finishes early, unless you change the start date of his or her assignment. In our example, Joe and Mary drive the task finish date.

Generally, we recommend that where possible, you split one task with multiple, uneven assignments into multiple tasks with a single assignment. There are two reasons:

⚠ The formula $D * U = W$ does not apply to a task with multiple, uneven assignments, but it does apply to the individual assignments.

 The project schedule will be simpler if you divide the task into multiple tasks, creating one task for each resource to avoid confusion about who is leading the task. This also simplifies the management of resource allocation. Where people need to get together to work as a group, you can create a short meeting task. (In the example shown in the screenshot, the meeting would take place on Monday, August 13.)

Changing Assignment Attributes

Another technique for adjusting assignments is to use the Assignment Information dialog box, for example, to change the default flat contour assignment pattern. This could be a useful technique to prevent over-allocations of resources.

1. Switch to a usage view, either the **Task Usage** or **Resource Usage**.

2. Double-click on an assignment. (Assignments have no ID number, and are in italics.) The **Assignment Information** dialog appears:

> The General Tab displays useful assignment-related fields:
> • Work: amount of effort (person days)
> • Work Contour to spread the effort
> • Cost Rate table to pick a rate profile

Assignment Information

General | Tracking | Notes

Task:	Research Requirements
Resource:	Nelson Salin
Work:	32h	Units:	1
Work contour:	Flat
Start:	Mon Aug 20, '12	Booking type:	Committed
Finish:	Thu Aug 23, '12	Cost:	$0.00
Cost rate table:	A	Assignment Owner:	

OK   Cancel

3. Make the changes to the assignment and click OK.

 Options available in the Assignment Information dialog box are limited when working with unassigned tasks or budget resources.

You can change many assignment-specific attributes; there are about 50 purely assignment-related fields. Some useful examples are:

➤ Start and Finish: These fields allow you to have one or more resources start later or finish earlier on a task than the rest.

➤ Delay: Instead of entering start or finish dates, you could enter a number of days delay for the assignment.

➤ Work contour: This allows you to spread the effort on a task in a pattern you choose. Refer to the next section for more information.

➤ Cost rate table: This allows you to select a specific rate profile for each assignment. This can be useful for small consulting firms that billed differently for each job.

 You can also document actual findings and lessons learned by assignment. This allows you to create a project archive as you proceed through the project.

Work Contours

Units = 1 means 100% of available hours (flat):

Units = 0.6 means 60% of available hours (flat):

Units vary from day-to-day: work contour "turtle":

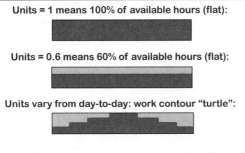

Work Contours determine how the work for a task is spread over time. By default, Project 2010 creates a flat contour on all resource assignments, meaning that work is distributed evenly across the duration of the task.

You can see three different assignments in the illustration. In the 100% and 60% assignments, the resource's work (effort) is spread evenly across the duration of the task in a flat pattern.

You can also spread the work over a task's duration in different, predefined patterns that Project 2010 calls work contours. There are eight predefined work contours, but you can also spread the work over the task duration yourself by entering the spread in the time-phased Work fields.

➤ You can apply one of the predefined work contours using the Assignment Information dialog. If you double-click on an assignment in either the **Task Usage** or **Resource Usage** view, the **Assignment Information** dialog will be displayed. You can then select a predefined contour from the list **Work contour**. Project 2010 will maintain the pattern of the contour when the duration or the work is changed during the planning phase.
➤ You can even fill in on a day-by-day basis how many hours you need from the resource over the duration of the task. You can enter the needed hours directly into the **Work** field in the timescale of the **Task Usage** view. (This level of detail is seldom needed in the planning of projects.)

 If you do decide to enter numbers in the timescale yourself, be aware that you'll spend a lot of time maintaining your schedule, since Project 2010 won't know how to make any needed adjustments to your spread. Particularly if you enter the required hours on a day-by-day basis, you will have a lot of data to maintain, and you're not likely to keep up with it during project execution.

 If you change the contour to anything other than "Flat", or enter work values manually into the timescale section of the usage views, Project 2010 will give you an icon in the indicators column.

Replacing Generic Resources with Individuals

We've mentioned before that if you initially don't know who your team members will be, you should simply assign generic resources. There are a couple ways in which you can replace generic resources with real individuals. One way is to type over the generic resource name with the name of the individual in the Resource Sheet.

Of course, this will replace the generic resource on **all** its assignments, so you only want to use it when you have a one-to-one correspondence between the generic resource and the individual. Otherwise, you are going to need one of the following methods which allows you to create just one generic resource for each role, function or position you need on your team, and do long-term resource planning where you accumulate workload far into the future onto generic resources:

➤ In the **Resource Usage** view, click on the cell on the extreme left of the assignment row (to select the entire row) and drag the assignment from the generic resource to a real person

OR

➤ You can use the [Replace...] button in the **Assign Resources** dialog. First, select the tasks with the generic resource to replace, then select the generic resource and click [Replace...] and select the substitute resource from the list presented.

Use the Replace feature to swap resources instead of deleting the resource and adding another resource.

Assignments and Task Types

In chapter 4 we entered data for the first time and explored the scenario where most of your tasks were either fixed duration or fixed work. However, we did not discuss the calculations that were occurring nor address various situations where either values or assignments may need to be changed. That will be the focus of this section.

As we learned in chapter 4, Project 2010 uses the following formula for these variables: Duration * Units = Work.

	Duration	* Units	= Work
Fixed Duration Meeting	2h	8	----
Fixed Units Inspect Site	----	1	6h
Fixed Work Translating	----	1	80h

As their names indicate, each of the three task types fixes (holds constant) one of the three variables in the formula. If you set a task to be fixed duration, Project

2010 will not change this duration. (This is a comforting thought, particularly if you have been haunted in the past by numbers being changed by Project 2010 that you didn't want changed.)

When you enter the second value (units or work), Project 2010 will calculate the third value for you.

➤ For example, if you have a task *meeting* with a fixed duration of 2 business hours, and you invite 8 people to the meeting, Project 2010 will calculate 2 * 8 = 16 person hours of work.

➤ Another example: a task to translate a small book may take one person 80 person hours to complete. The task would be set up as a fixed work task and would be completed over a 10-day duration. If a second person is assigned to assist with the task, Project 2010 will keep the work constant at 80 but recalculate the duration to 5 days.

You might ask yourself at this point: *Why is Project 2010 recalculating all these values constantly? It makes my life miserable!* The answer is that if it did not calculate them, you would definitely be working overtime with your calculator making those calculations yourself.

Project 2010 tries to help you, and it uses the broad assumption that every resource is equally effective and efficient, which is not true of course. However, in 90% of cases, this assumption is accurate enough for modeling purposes. Remember that we are deliberately simplifying the reality when we model projects. We try to approach reality as closely as possible, but with as little effort as possible. We are not trying to recreate reality in all its complexity in our schedule. Many project managers seem to forget this once they get going with Project 2010.

The following table suggests the best use for each task Type:

Type of task	Use for
Fixed Duration	➤ When the duration is the first thing you estimate ➤ If the duration does not decrease when human resources are added, such as when backing up a computer system ➤ Tasks that always have a group of resources assigned, such as meetings or training ➤ When the deadline is so tight that it's the primary driver for the duration of the task: you have to make it work within the available time frame ➤ When the workload is not your problem, e.g., you're using external resources, such as subcontractors and consultants

Type of task	Use for
Fixed Units (default)	➤ When the number of resources you have for the task is the first thing you know ➤ When you cannot get more resources to do the work ➤ When you want to change the duration or the work on a task while keeping the number of people working on the task the same (assignment units). We will discuss this later in the chapter ➤ When you want to keep the resource working on a task at a certain percentage of his available hours
Fixed Work	➤ When the effort required is the first thing you estimate ➤ When the effort required is the easiest thing to estimate. This is often the case. For example, you estimate that painting a home takes 60 person hours of effort. Estimating effort is often easier and more accurate than estimating duration: you don't need to take resource availability and holidays into account

The formula $D * U = W$ does **not** apply to:

➤ Tasks that have assignments with a work contour that is not flat.
➤ Tasks with multiple assignments where one assignment is longer than the others or starts later (called multiple or uneven assignments). The formula still applies for each individual assignment.

Three Rules for a Happy Life with Project 2010

Here are three rules we urge you to memorize and follow when you enter or change assignments. If you do, Project 2010 will become your obedient servant. If you don't, Project 2010 will inevitably recalculate values that you don't want changed. You can even end up in an endless loop, where you change a value, it changes a value, you change a value, etc.

Here are the rules:

1. Enter the first value as a duration estimate or work estimate and **fix** that number by setting the task Type accordingly. This will prevent Project 2010 from changing the number.
   ▸ If you enter a duration estimate, set the task Type to Fixed Duration (turn off Effort Driven).
   ▸ If you enter a work estimate, set the task Type to Fixed Work. (Effort Driven is always on with this task type).

2. Provide the second value in the formula Duration * Units = Work and let Project 2010 calculate the third value. Always provide only two of the three values!

▸ If you created a fixed duration task, assign the resources you need, and Project 2010 will calculate the work.

▸ If you created a fixed work task, assign the resources and Project 2010 will calculate the duration.

▸ If you estimate both duration and work, enter the duration as the first value and set the task Type to Fixed Duration with Effort Driven on. Enter work as the second value. When you assign the resource to the task, Project 2010 will apply the formula to calculate units.

 By providing both the duration and the work, Project 2010 only needs to know who will do the task and it will calculate the number of resources needed (units).

3. Before making a change to any of the three values in the formula, reconsider the task Type by asking yourself: *What Type of task do I need for this particular change?* More on this next.

 Enter the work estimate, duration estimate, or combined work/duration estimate; then set the task Type (select the Effort Driven choices, if needed), then assign the resource and let Project 2010 calculate the third variable.

The following examples will help you understand how entering an assignment calculates a value in Project 2010. All of these examples are on auto scheduled tasks.

 For manually scheduled tasks, you will NOT be able to change the Task Types or Effort Driven flag. Each resource added will add to the amount of work regardless of the Task type or Effort driven flag.

➤ **Planning a task where the duration needs to stay the same and the resources ARE NOT working together:**
1. Enter total duration for the task.
2. Set the Task as **Fixed Duration** with **Effort Driven** off.
3. Add one resource, click [OK].
4. Add a second resource, click [OK].
5. Work is calculated. Notice that the work hours are the same for each resource.

➤ **Planning a task where the duration needs to stay the same and the resources ARE working together:**
1. Enter total duration for the task.
2. Set the Task as **Fixed Duration** with **Effort Driven** on.
3. Add one resource, click [OK].
4. Add a second resource, click [OK].
5. Peak Units is calculated (discussed later). Notice that the total work hours stay the same but are divided across the resources.

If you are familiar with prior versions of Project (2007 or earlier), you will notice that the resource units stay at one (or 100%) instead of reducing to 0.5 (50%) each. New to this version is that the assignment units field no longer automatically changes during resource assignments. This is due to feedback from customers (including our own) that you do not want initial assignments to change. Refer to the next section on changing assignments for further information.

➤ **Planning a task where the work needs to stay the same (resources are working together):**
1. Enter total work for the task.
2. Set the Task as **Fixed Work** (**Effort Driven** is on automatically).
3. Add one resource, click [OK].
4. Add a second resource, click [OK].
5. Duration is calculated. Notice that the duration reduces by half.

➤ **Planning a task where you know the number of resources and the work hours, but you would like Project to calculate duration:**
1. Enter total work for the task.
2. Set the task as **Fixed Units**, **Effort Driven** on.
3. Add the resource name and enter the number of Units available, click [OK].
4. Duration is calculated. Notice the length of time is based on number of Units.

➤ **Planning a task where you know both duration and work, but you would like Project to calculate resource units:**
1. Enter total work and total duration for the task.
2. Set the task as **Fixed Duration, Effort Driven** on.
3. Add the resource name, click [OK].
4. Resource Units is calculated. Notice the number of Units reflects how many people you would need to complete the total hours within the length of time provided.

Changing an Assignment

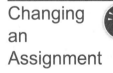

Before you make any changes to a task that could affect any of the three values in the formula D * U = W, you should always first think about the task type you need for that change. With every change, Project 2010 will recalculate one other value, and it may not recalculate the one you want.

The task **Type** and the **Effort Driven** attribute determine how Project 2010 will react. We suggest these steps when you change an assignment:

➤ Display and configure **Task Usage** view (explained below).
➤ Review or change the task **Type**.

➤ Determine the appropriate task Type by asking yourself: *I will be making a change to a value in the formula; which value do I want to keep the same?* The answer to this question will tell you which task Type you need. For example, if you want to keep the duration the same while you change the work, you should set the Type to Fixed Duration. If you want to keep the total amount of work on the task the same while you change the duration, you need Fixed Work.

 New to Project 2010, Units remains the same for existing resource assignments (refer to the examples below).

➤ Ensure Effort Driven is set to your desired option. For Fixed Work tasks, the effort driven is on by default.

➤ Then edit the value that you want to change on the assignment.

 Avoid changing the variable that is fixed if you want to predict what Project 2010 will do.

Before you change a variable, set or change the task Type and Effort driven choices, accept that change, and then change the variable.

When there are multiple, uneven assignments, one or more of the assignments can drive the duration of the task. Before you make a change, you should identify which assignment drives the duration of the task. Consider changing assignment fields instead of task fields.

 Notice that when you apply the task type Fixed Work the attribute Effort Driven is automatically turned on by Project 2010. When you change to a different task type again, the Effort Driven attribute stays on. Don't forget to turn it off if needed.

To replace one resource with another, Project 2010 provides a shortcut that doesn't trigger recalculations. Use the Assign Resources dialog 🐝, select the assigned resource and click [Replace...]. Select the new one and click [OK]. Unlike removing the resource and then reassigning someone else, replacing a resource doesn't cause recalculations.

Changing Assignment Examples

Before we provide specific examples, it's important to understand the difference between Assignment Units and Peak units (referred to as Peak in Project 2010):

➤ Assignment Units is the portion of a resource's time that you initially allocate to a given task (100% or 1 by default).

➤ Peak units show the maximum percentage of a resource's time that is needed at any point over the duration of the task. A resource will be considered over-allocated if the sum of their Peak Units—across all their tasks or

8

assignments—is greater than their Max Units entered on the Resource Sheet.

		Resource Name	Type	Material	Initials	Group	Max.	Std. Rate	Ovt. Rate	Cost/U
1		Cindy	Work		C		100%	$0.00/hr	$0.00/hr	
2	◈	Anson	Work		A		100%	$0.00/hr	$0.00/hr	

		Resource Name	Work	Assignment Units	Peak		Details	Aug 5, '12		
								S	M	T
2	◈	Anson	60 hrs		150%		Work		12h	12h
		Write Code	20 hrs	100%	50%		Work		4h	4h
		Prepare Documental	40 hrs	100%	100%		Work		8h	8h

In prior versions of Project, the role of these two fields was not clearly defined and in many cases Assignment Units would change in response to changes to other variables. Project 2010 no longer changes the Assignment Units. Instead, it changes Peak units so you can clearly see what is available versus what you are requesting for a specific task. In order to take advantage of these new features, we recommend that you change variables using Task Usage View, and that you insert both the Assignment Unit and Peak fields in the Usage Table.

Configure Task Usage View:

1. On the **Task** tab, in the **View** group, click the **Gantt Chart** down arrow and choose **Task Usage**.

2. On the **View** tab, in the **Data** group, click the **Tables** down arrow and choose **Usage**.

3. Right-click on **Start** and in the shortcut menu choose **Insert Column** and then click **Assignment Units**.

4. Right-click on **Start** and in the shortcut menu choose **Insert Column** and then click **Peak**.

		Task Mode	Task Name	Work	Duration	Assignment Units	Peak	Details	Aug 5, '12	
									S	M
1			⊟ Write Code	40 hrs	5 days			Work		8h
			Cindy	20 hrs		100%	50%	Work		4h
			Anson	20 hrs		100%	50%	Work		4h
2			⊟ Prepare Documental	40 hrs	5 days			Work		8h
			Anson	40 hrs		100%	100%	Work		8h

 When changing variables after resources have been assigned, use Task Usage View and display Assignment Units and Peak fields.

As a reminder of an earlier best practice, change the task Type and Effort Driven settings to isolate what variable you wish to freeze before changing another variable or modifying an assignment that would trigger a calculation. The instructions to change the task Type will apply to every situation below. Feel free to review the examples to help determine what task Type you need to set.

Change the task Type and Effort Driven Attribute before changing a variable:

1. In **Task Usage** view, double-click the name of the **Task** (the row with the ID number). The **Task Information** dialog box appears.

2. On the **Advanced** tab, in the **Task Type** list, choose the desired type.

3. On the **Effort Driven** check box, click the box either on (checked) or off (clear, not shaded).

4. Click [OK].

You are now ready to change your desired value.

To Change Work:

For Fixed Duration, Effort Driven Off task, or Fixed Duration, Effort Driven On task, change the Work value of the task (the row with the ID number) and watch the results:

	ⓘ	Task Mode	Task Name	Work	Duration	Assignment Units	Peak	S	Details	Jul 25, '10				
										S	M	T	W	T
1	⚑	🕑	⊟ a	120 hrs	5 days				Work	24h	24h	24h	24h
			Cindy	60 hrs		1	1.5		Work	12h	12h	12h	12h
			Anson	60 hrs		1	1.5		Work	12h	12h	12h	12h

	ⓘ	Task Mode	Task Name	Work	Duration	Assignment Units	Peak	S	Details	Jul 25, '10				
										S	M	T	W	T
1		🕑	⊟ a	40 hrs	5 days				Work	8h	8h	8h	8h
			Cindy	20 hrs		1	0.5		Work	4h	4h	4h	4h
			Anson	20 hrs		1	0.5		Work	4h	4h	4h	4h

To Change Duration:

For a Fixed Work task, change the Duration value of the task (the row with the ID number) and notice the Peak value changes:

	ⓘ	Task Mode	Task Name	Work	Duration	Assignment Units	Peak	S	Details	Jul 25, '10			
										S	M	T	W
1		🕑	⊟ a	80 hrs	10 days				Work	8h	8h	8h
			Cindy	40 hrs		1	0.5		Work	4h	4h	4h
			Anson	40 hrs		1	0.5		Work	4h	4h	4h

To Change Assignment Units:

For a **Fixed Work** task, change the Assignment Units value on each resource and notice the Peak value changes.

	ⓘ	Task Mode	Task Name	Work	Duration	Assignment Units	Peak	S	Details	Jul 25, '10				
										S	M	T	W	T
1		🕑	⊟ a	80 hrs	10 days				Work	8h	8h	8h	8h
			Cindy	40 hrs		0.5	0.5		Work	4h	4h	4h	4h
			Anson	40 hrs		0.5	0.5		Work	4h	4h	4h	4h

The task Type is not something you set once and never look at again. You continue to monitor it in order to control what Project 2010 calculates. If you reconsider the Type of task before every change, you will be able to predict and control Project 2010's recalculations.

Checks on Assignments

Here are some checks to help you verify whether you have applied best practices to the assignments in your schedule:

➤ Are you paying attention the task-related fields Type and Effort Driven for the detail tasks?
The available Types are: Fixed Duration, Fixed Units and Fixed Work. With this field, you can control what Project 2010 recalculates: duration, units or work. If you don't monitor the field Type, you are not controlling what Project 2010 does. If you don't use the field Type, you are using Project 2010 in a trial and error fashion: you change a field here, Project 2010 recalculates a value there, you don't like what you see and you change it back again ... and you start running after your own tail.

➤ Does each detail task have at least one human resource assigned?
If there are detail tasks without human resources assigned, you have not captured all the workloads in your project. If workloads are missing, the schedule may be too optimistic, since leveling workloads typically leads to longer schedules and later forecasts. An exception to this rule is that recurring detail tasks do not need resources assigned to them. You can check on this in one of two ways:

▶ In the Resource Usage view, there should be no detail tasks listed under the first category Unassigned.

▶ You can also apply filter *09a IIL Detail tasks without Resources Assigned*.[1]
The filter allows you to easily copy the tasks including their ID numbers into a schedule evaluation report.

Note that there may still be detail tasks with only material resources assigned if you check the Unassigned category or apply the filter, so neither check is bullet proof.

➤ Are there no assignments on the summary tasks?
As we discussed, if you assign resources to summary tasks you can easily end up with over-allocations that can't be resolved other than by removing the resource from the summary task. If you assign only to detail tasks, you will never end up with this stubborn type of over-allocation and will save yourself time when leveling workloads. Resolving over-allocations is challenging enough. You can check for assignments on summary tasks easily by applying the filter *09b IIL Summary Tasks with Resources Assigned*.[2]

---

1   This filter can be found in the file *IIL Project 2010 Tools.mpp* available for download at www.jrosspub.com. Click the link *WAV Download Resource Center* to enter the download site.
2   Ibid.

➤ Are all the costs appropriately modeled to include variable and fixed costs? Variable costs are driven by the number of units (percentage) of work or material resources assigned to a task. Task- or deliverable-related fixed costs are entered in the Fixed Cost field in the Gantt Chart or as a Cost resource from the Assign Resources dialog box.

➤ Is the cost scheduled appropriately?

▶ Does the task-related Fixed Cost Accrual field reflect when the fixed cost will be incurred?

▶ You can review the time-phased cost in the Task Usage or Resource Usage views.

➤ Have you utilized Budget resources to help you identify variances between your planned and projected costs?

Budget variables—created by setting the Budget flag in the Resource Information window—can be assigned only to the Project Summary task. The values for these resources are entered in the Budget Cost or Budget Work fields of the Task Usage or Resource Usage views.

Review Questions

1. What is the definition of an assignment?

2. In your own words, describe what the following fields represent:
   a. Units field in the Task Form
   b. Units field in the Resource Information dialog, tab General
   c. Max Units field in the Resource Sheet
   d. Work field in the Gantt Chart
   e. Work field in the Task Form
   f. Work field in the Resource Sheet
   g. Task-related Work field in the Task Usage view
   h. Assignment-related Work field in the Task Usage view

3. In your own words, what is a Work Contour?

4. A project manager realizes that she wants to model her project on a high level. She will only enter consolidated resources (pooled resources) in her Resource Sheet. What setting would you recommend she use in the "Show assignment units as" choice in the Project Options?

5. What are the three task types? How does each task type function? How would you use this feature of Project 2010?

6. In your own words, what are the three rules that will help you control what Project 2010 does when creating and changing assignments?

7. Before you make a change to an assignment, what question should you ask yourself and what field(s) should you check?

8. Describe two different ways of assigning resources to tasks in Project 2010. Describe them in detail in terms of mouse clicks or menu items to choose. What are the differences between these two methods in terms of the options you have?

9. Would you recommend making multiple, uneven assignments to many tasks in your schedule? Justify your answer in terms of pros and cons.

10. Would you recommend assigning resources to summary tasks? Justify your answer in terms of pros and cons.

11. When you assign a resource to a recurring summary task with the Assign Resources dialog, what will Project 2010 automatically do?

12. A resource is writing two different documents concurrently and you cannot plan or predict when he will be working on one or the other. How would you model this situation in Project 2010? In particular, what tasks and assignments would you create and what number of resource units would you assign?

Review B

Read the following situations and determine if you will likely make your first estimate in person days work (PD), business days duration (BD) or elapsed days duration (ED) and explain why. Indicate which type of task you recommend: Fixed Duration (FD), Fixed Units (FU) or Fixed Work (FW), and explain why.

	PD, BD or ED? Why?	FD, FU or FW? Why?
1. Writing a 10 page report that normally takes a person 4 hours per page to produce		
2. One load to be transported over a distance of 4,000 miles with one driver		
3. One package that has to be flown a distance of over 4,000 miles and has to arrive in 2 working days		
4. A house painter who is asked for a fixed price quote and the earliest end date for painting a family home		
5. A contractor gives a painter a maximum of 2 weeks to finish painting a building		
6. Backing up a computer system before the conversion to a new operating system, where the backing up requires little supervision once started		
7. A meeting with a presentation to all team members		

Additional Practice

For experience working with the features you've learned about in this chapter, we strongly suggest that you do the additional exercises for this chapter that are included in Appendix 1.

Chapter 9: Optimizing the Schedule

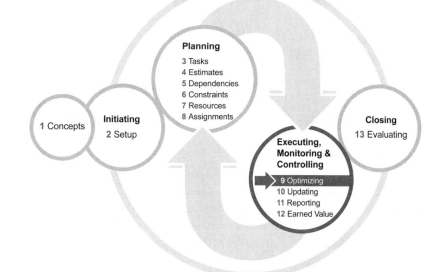

The good news is that you now have a dynamic model of your project. The worrisome news is that it's likely to reveal any or all of the following: the duration is too long, the cost is too high, and/or the workloads are unreasonable. Fortunately, with a dynamic model you can easily develop and explore different scenarios to find the best solution. You can optimize for time; for time and cost; or for time, cost and resource availability.

After reading this chapter you will be able to:

➤ Choose the appropriate approach for optimizing
➤ Optimize a project for time; for time and cost; or for time, cost and resources
➤ Solve a fragmented critical path
➤ Describe the difference between free slack and total slack
➤ Explain the assumptions and shortcomings of the Critical Path Method (CPM)
➤ Make workloads and over-allocations visible in Project 2010
➤ Solve problems with the workloads of your resources
➤ Determine and use the Resource-Critical Path for optimizing

Hey! Follow me! This way is shorter!

The Pulling Forces

During the project life-cycle, the project may be pulled by many forces that compete against one another and can make strong demands upon it. These are commonly referred to as the competing demands and include: scope, time, cost, quality, resources and risk.

These **competing demands** are initially client- and sponsor-driven. Then, through negotiation, they are turned into a realistic plan, and need to be maintained in balance through the project life cycle to produce the specified product, service, or result. A change in one demand will impact change in the others.

Optimizing the schedule is the process of making sure that the various factors that drive the schedule are in the best possible balance to minimize time and cost while meeting quality and scope requirements, while using the limited resources in the best way, and of course, keeping the risk at acceptable thresholds.

Optimizing is the true art of scheduling and requires you to consider all aspects of the project.

You typically optimize during planning in order to model or refine your project schedule to hit specified deadlines or constraints. Then, once you start execution, the monitoring and controlling processes will require further optimizations when you are moving away from your baseline and need to modify the remainder of the schedule. Managing the baseline is a topic we'll discuss when we talk about preparing for accepting updates..

Where Project 2010 Helps in Managing the Schedule

Optimizing the schedule means managing all the competing demands of the project with regard to one another. It begins by managing each dimension individually. Project 2010 provides sufficient features to manage many, but not all, demands of the project:

➤ **Quality**
The quality of deliverables must correspond to the specifications and expectations of the client. While you can schedule quality activities in Project 2010, the tool doesn't provide a full-fledged quality management system. Such a system typically contains the requirements, specifications or acceptance criteria for the deliverables, test scenarios and cases, etc. For software development and engineering projects, we recommend you complement Project 2010 with a requirements tracking system. However, even without a quality tracking system, quality impacts can and should always be considered while optimizing.

➤ **Scope**
The scope of a project is represented by the work breakdown structure. It contains the deliverables to be produced and the activities to be performed to produce them. Project 2010 is an excellent tool for managing **project** scope ("the work that must be performed to deliver a product, service, or result with the specified features and functions"[1]). However, it is not made for managing the **product** scope ("the features and functions that characterize a product, service or result"[2]). The product scope as it is described in requirements and specifications must be managed externally. The results of scope management (in particular, changes) should be reflected in the Project 2010 schedule.

➤ **Time**
Project 2010 does a fine job of managing the schedule and deadlines. Since a project is a temporary endeavor, every project manager will monitor and manage the duration of his or her project by definition.

➤ **Cost**
You can create a budget and manage the expenses for labor, facilities, machines, materials and other expenses with Project 2010. Not all project managers are given a monetary budget and not all monitor their project costs. In recent years, however, more organizations are empowering their project managers with budgets—and challenging them to stay within

---

1 ———*PMBOK® Guide – Fourth Edition*, PMI, 2008, p. 444.
2 Ibid., p. 442.

them. Project 2010 permits project managers to compare planned budgets with financial budgets from 3rd party accounting and enterprise resource planning applications.

➤ **Resources**

Workloads must stay within the availability of the resources. You can do workload leveling with Project 2010. When you level resource workloads, the critical path can become fragmented. We'll introduce a new concept for dealing with this: the resource-critical path that is needed to optimize resource-constrained schedules.

It should be noted that leveling an individual project, in the absence of other projects that share the same resources, can be a waste of time. More than that, attempting to level an individual project can actually create resource allocation issues that did not exist prior to leveling. For this reason, we'll introduce the subject of consolidated schedules in Appendix 2.

In Project 2010, a new feature called the Team Planner helps you see over-allocations and correct them by reallocating assignments. This feature allows project managers to see and graphically adjust assignments that way the Gantt Chart view does for tasks. The project manager also has the ability to assign tasks to resources using the Team Planner.

➤ **Risk**

When we define a schedule, we use estimates and assumptions that may change, so we need to consider risk dimension in our planning and forecasting. In previous versions, we could use three point estimates for durations and some probability approach with PERT analysis, but in Project 2010 these features were deactivated. If you want to develop qualitative risk analysis like Monte Carlo simulations, you will need to acquire some add-on tool that complements Project 2010.

If you use Project Server 2010 and/or SharePoint 2010, you may perform qualitative risk analysis to identify risks, evaluate their probabilities and impacts, prioritize, assign owners and develop the risk response planning strategies, and to monitor and control the risk processes during execution.

Consider impacts on quality, scope, time, cost, resources and risk, with every optimization change.

Improving one dimension of the project often impacts others. When the impact is negative, you are trading off among the dimensions. For example, if you hire more resources to meet a tight deadline, the impact may be positive on time, but negative on cost. Sometimes, you can find methods that are positive in more than one respect and neutral in others.

Three Approaches for Optimizing

Individually managing the six competing demands that influence the project is not enough (or even possible). They are all interrelated. For example, duration (time) is driven by scope, but scope may be influenced by time, as when project scope is reduced in order to hit an important deadline. Resources influence time, cost and scope, etc. Optimizing the schedule requires integration of the dimensions that affect the project schedule.

We'll present three different approaches for optimizing schedules. In all three we consider quality, scope and risk but because these dimensions don't differentiate the approaches, we haven't included the words scope, quality or risk in the approach names.

The three approaches we'll present are: Optimizing for Time; Optimizing for Time and Cost; and Optimizing for Time, Cost and Resources.

> **Optimizing for Time**
> This is also known as optimizing under the assumption of unlimited resources (the capacity to hire and release any resources you need when you need to). The other approaches will not assume that you have access to unlimited resources.
>
> Having unlimited resources also assumes that cost is not your primary concern and that you only need to consider the forces of quality, scope, risk and time. The common technique used in this situation is the Critical Path Method (CPM). Many industries have used CPM for decades; typically, the construction and consulting industries apply CPM. These industries tend to hire and release resources on an as-needed basis, often working with temporary or free-lance resources. Other industries find this optimization too narrow, particularly when cost is a concern or resources are not readily available.

> **Optimizing for Time & Cost**
> If you have a limited budget and cost is your primary concern, you should apply this approach. It is also applicable if you can find more money to solve quality, scope or time problems. For example, you could use additional money to buy better raw materials, rent better equipment or pay penalties for late delivery. However, if you use the extra money to increase resource availability, you should use the next approach instead of just focusing on time and cost, since you are now affecting the resources. You increase availability when you hire more people, subcontract to free-lancers or rent more facilities or equipment.

> **Optimizing for Time, Cost & Resources**
> If you must also consider the availability and capacity of resources in order to derive a feasible schedule for your project, use this approach. You make

trade-off decisions among quality, scope, time, cost and resource availability. An example of optimizing for time, cost and resources is when you consider paying extra to get more overtime from your team. If your resources are scarce, you will have to level the resource workloads

As you can see, we are adding one dimension with each optimization approach, and the optimizations become more complex as we add more dimensions. Including five out of the eight dimensions is the most complex optimization we will discuss in this book. It also is the most complex configuration Project 2010 can assist you with as a standalone tool.

Choosing the Options

On the **File** tab, in the **Backstage** view, click **Options**, **Advanced** tab in order to access the following options that are relevant for all optimizing approaches (use the scroll bar to find the sections):

Project Options	Recommended Choices
Advanced	**Set the Display Options on the Advanced Tab:**
★	☑ **Show project summary task** The project summary task (ID number zero) is inserted at the top of the task list. This is useful when optimizing because it displays the total duration, effort and cost of the project. You can choose to have this option only for the current project or to establish it as a default for all new projects, just choose <All new projects> in the drop down.
Advanced	**Set the Calculation Options on the Advanced Tab:**
★	☐ **Calculate multiple critical paths** We recommend you keep this option turned off, since a single project should only have one ending point in the network logic. If there are multiple ending points, there are multiple critical paths. This option is stored in the project schedule.
★	**Tasks are critical if slack is less than or equal to** `0 days` **days.** This field creates a threshold for marking tasks that are critical. Normally, this option is set to zero, which means critical tasks are those with zero or negative total slack, shown in red in the Tracking Gantt view. This option is stored in the project schedule.

Optimizing for Time - Techniques

The dimensions that we consider in this approach to optimization are quality, scope, time, and risk as indicated by the solid arrows in the illustration. When you try to decrease the duration of the project and trade-off against quality, risk

or scope, you are essentially doing an optimization on the dimension of time. The technique for this type of optimization is the CPM. Many project managers make a habit of keeping their eye on the cost and resources while crashing the critical path (shortening duration by adding resources), but we won't do that. We will discuss the CPM here in its original form, using time optimization only.

There are three principle techniques used in optimizing time: CPM, PERT and simulation.

➤ **The Critical Path Method**

CPM helps project managers meet deadlines by finding and highlighting the series of tasks that are most likely to affect those deadlines. The logical network is the basis for CPM. Using task durations, the longest (critical) path is determined and float on other paths' tasks are determined. Happily this is all done automatically by Project 2010.

Float or slack is the amount of time a task can be delayed before it affects the project end date. A critical task does not have float or slack, and any delay experienced on a critical task means your project end date will slip. CPM uses a single duration estimate for each task. We'll discuss CPM in more detail after we describe the other two techniques, PERT and simulation.

➤ **The PERT Method**

The **P**rogram **E**valuation and **R**eview **T**echnique (**PERT**) is a more sophisticated application of CPM. CPM uses one duration estimate for each task, while PERT uses three: optimistic (O), most likely (ML) and pessimistic (P). These durations are converted to an expected duration with the following formula: Expected Duration = (O + [4*ML] + P) / 6. This multipoint estimating introduces some adjustment for risk and probability. Project 2010 no longer has a PERT analysis feature, however, this can still be done in Excel and the results copied into the duration column in Project, or you can use customized fields with formulas to create your PERT calculations.

> ➤ **Simulation of the Schedule**
>
> Another way to make probability visible is by subjecting the schedule to Monte Carlo simulation. This type of simulation creates many versions of the same schedule based on the probability ranges you provide for certain estimates. The simulation software then averages over all the versions of the schedule to arrive at the probability for each possible finish date. Simulation is more powerful than PERT, because it quantifies the compounding effect of parallel paths as well. Due to the complexity of the calculations, Monte Carlo simulation is typically done with computer software which may be integrated into Microsoft Project.

We will further elaborate on CPM and Monte Carlo simulation in this book.

The Critical Path Method

The critical path determines how long your project will take. The concept is fairly simple. The illustration depicts a simple authoring project: outline the document, write the text, and edit the text, while somebody else makes graphics. When the text and the graphics are ready, the format can be created and the project is finished. All arrows are finish-to-start

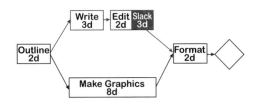

dependencies and durations are shown below the task names. Before we explain the critical path theory, you should ask yourself: What is the minimum duration for this project?

If you came up with the correct answer, 12 days, you understand the critical path concept intuitively. If you came up with a different answer, find the critical path by comparing the two parallel paths. Add the durations and any lags on each path and compare the totals. The longest one is the critical path: it determines the minimum duration of the project.

In the illustration, the two parallel alternatives for the critical path are the path *write* (3d) and *edit* (2d) which is 5 days long in total versus the path *make graphics* (8d). It is clear that the make graphics path is the longest and determines the project end date. To find the critical path, continue comparing parallel paths until you have checked them all and found the longest path in the whole network: this is the critical path. Sometimes a few chains are equally critical and you have multiple critical paths.

Parallel chains of tasks or paths make up a network, of which all but the critical path(s) have slack. Slack exists on a chain of tasks when it is performed in parallel with another chain that takes more time.

The critical path determines the minimum duration of the project. We call it the minimum duration, because the real duration may be longer when some resources are over-allocated. Over-allocations may force tasks to be delayed past the minimum duration.

Finding the critical path is challenging:

➤ When there are many parallel paths
➤ When different types of dependencies are used (Finish-to-Start, Start-to-Start, Finish-to-Finish, Start-to-Finish)
➤ When there are lags or leads on the dependencies

In these cases, it is nice to have a tool like Project 2010 that will identify the critical path for you.

To find the critical path, Project 2010 starts with all tasks stacked up at the project start date, as shown in the illustration. Then, based on task dependencies and durations, it schedules them out to the earliest possible dates (As Soon As Possible scheduling). Project 2010 performs this forward pass calculation to determine the earliest possible dates (early dates). Then it

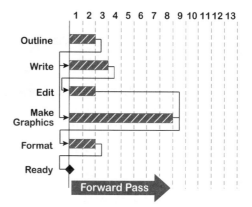

schedules all tasks As Late As Possible in the backward pass and calculates the latest allowable dates (late dates) to meet the earliest possible project finish date. The difference between early and late dates for a task is the task's slack.

Forward Pass

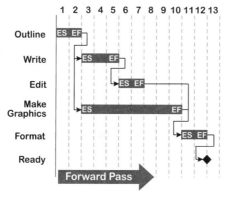

On the forward pass, Project 2010 calculates two dates for each task: the Early Start (ES) and the Early Finish (EF) date. The result of this forward pass is shown in the illustration. Project 2010 starts with the first task (*outline*), looks at its duration (2 days) and calculates the earliest date it can be ready. This is the Early Finish date. The outline will be ready at the end of day 2.

Project 2010 will then determine the date of the successor(s). *Write* and *make graphics* are the successors; they can start on day 3. The Early Start date of the successors will be the same as the Early Finish date of outline, unless other dependencies on the successors cause them to start later.

Project 2010 continues to calculate the Early Finish for *write* and *make graphics*. Format cannot start until both *edit* and *make graphics* are finished, and the earliest start date for *format* is therefore day 11 even though format could start on day 8, if it depended solely on *edit*. Project 2010 continues through the last task in the chain. The software now knows what the earliest finish date is for the project—day 12 in our example.

Backward Pass

Project 2010 then goes backward through the network starting at the project end date of day 12, to calculate the Late Finish dates for the tasks, as shown in

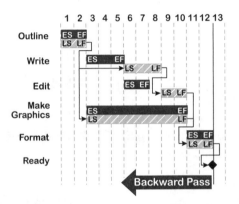

the illustration. The Late Finish date is the latest date a task should be finished in order to meet the project end date. By subtracting the duration of the task from the finish date, Project 2010 then calculates the Late Start date. The Late Start date is the latest date you can start working on the task to finish by its Late Finish date. For *format*, this is day 11, the same as its Early Finish date. You then continue with the Late Finish dates of the predecessors. *Edit* can finish on day 10 at the latest and the project will still end on day 12. *Edit* has a Late Finish date (day 10) that is 3 days later than its Early Finish date (day 7); therefore, *edit* has a time buffer called slack and is not a critical task.

If a task has more than one successor, like *outline*, Project 2010 has to take all successors into consideration to determine the late date. The start date of the earliest successor determines the Late Finish date of the task, in this case day 2 (*make graphics*), not day 5 (*write*). So, the latest finish for creating the *outline* is determined by the Late Start date of *make graphics*, and not the Late Start date of *write*. As a result, the early and the late dates for *outline* are the same; *outline* does not have slack and is another critical task.

There are two kinds of slack: Total Slack and Free Slack.

Calculating Total Slack

Total slack (TS) is the amount of time you can delay a task without affecting the project end date. The total slack is the Late Finish (LF) date minus the Early Finish (EF) date of a task: $TS = LF - EF$.[3]

It tells you how much a task can slip before delaying the whole project or other hard constraint dates in the schedule.

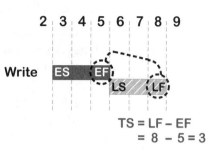

For example, the illustration shows that the task *Write* has 3 days of total slack ($TS = 8 - 5 = 3$). If the author calls you and tells you he fell ill, you would ask, "When do you think you might be better?" If the answer is more than 3 days, you know you should find somebody else if you can't permit the project to slip. (If the answer is less than 3 days, you may still have a problem, because the editor will now receive the text later, which might cause conflicts in her schedule. You need to communicate!)

The total slack of tasks can be:

➤ **Greater than zero: positive slack**
These tasks have slack and can be delayed for a period equal to their total slack. If you delay them more than that, the project as a whole will slip. You can often level some workloads by using the total slack of a task.

➤ **Equal to zero: zero slack**
Where the Late Finish date is equal to the Early Finish date, there is no slack. Tasks without slack are by definition on the critical path.

➤ **Less than zero: negative slack**
Tasks with a negative slack are tasks that don't meet the project deadline or hard constraint dates set in the schedule. Slack can only be negative if there are constraints, deadlines or other forces in the schedule that inhibit Project 2010 from finding and displaying a schedule that meets all those constraints.

Calculating Free Slack

The free slack (FS) of a task is the Early Start date of the task's successor minus the Early Finish date of the task itself. If there is more than one successor, you should take the Early Start date of the earliest successor: $FS = ES_{(earliest\ successor)} - EF$. The free slack of a task is always less than or equal to its total slack.

---

3   In fact, Project 2010 also calculates total slack on the start dates: $TS = LS - ES$; the lesser of the two total slacks will be the total slack displayed on the task.

In the illustration, the earliest successor of task Write is Edit, not Task x. The free slack tells you how much you can let the task slip before it affects any of its successors. *Write* does not have free slack, since the successor *Edit* starts immediately after *Write* finishes.

The difference between total slack and free slack manifests itself in the task *Write*; it has no free slack but 3 days of total slack. It can use the free slack of its successor *Edit* and slip without delaying the project end date. That is the beauty of the concept of total slack: it immediately tells you for each task when the project finish date or other constraint dates are in jeopardy.

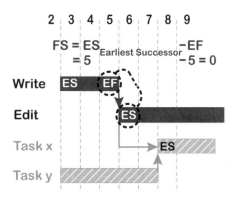

Project 2010 generates all the dates we discussed in the task fields Early Start, Early Finish, Late Start and Late Finish. The two slack fields are Total Slack and Free Slack.

The Critical Path

The critical path is the path with the tasks that have zero total slack. In our example, the tasks *Outline, Make Graphics* and *Format* are the tasks on the critical path. They are the dark task bars in the illustration.

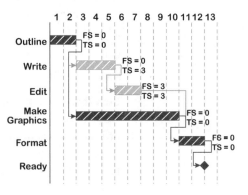

In the Tracking Gantt view the critical path is shown in red. You can also see the critical path in the Gantt Chart view: on the **Format** tab, in the **Bar Styles** group, select ☑ **Critical Tasks**. It's important to keep your eye on the critical path in order to bring your project in on time.

Find critical tasks and optimize them to shorten your schedule and finish on time.

*Constraints and
Negative Slack*

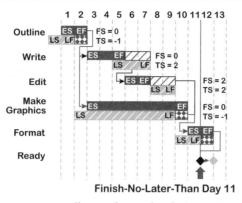

Finish-No-Later-Than Day 11

When you enter constraints into the schedule, all slack amounts change. The backward pass is calculated from the Finish No Later Than constraint date instead of the earliest possible project finish date. As a result, the late dates and total slack numbers change when you insert such a constraint. In our sample project, we will introduce a hard constraint that is one day before the earliest possible finish date of the project. The illustration shows how this constraint changes the total slack numbers of all tasks.

The forward pass determines the early dates, regardless of constraints. The backward pass takes constraints like Finish No Later Than into account.

You can see that the slack turns negative when the latest allowable dates (LF) are before the earliest possible dates (EF). The critical tasks now have –1 day total slack. Project 2010 identifies this as a scheduling conflict and warns you with a dialog:

This dialog alerts you to not meeting important constraint dates.

As you can see, Project 2010 gives you suggestions about how to resolve the conflict. The constraints that can cause scheduling conflicts, or negative slack, under forward scheduling are:

➤ Must Finish On
➤ Must Start On
➤ Finish No Later Than
➤ Start No Later Than

In backward scheduling, the following constraints can cause negative slack:

➤ Must Finish On
➤ Must Start On
➤ Start No Earlier Than
➤ Finish No Earlier Than

9

Because constraints affect the calculation of slack, you should use them as sparingly as possible, without compromising the quality of the project model. We recommend entering constraints for very hard deadlines only — the do-or-die dates. If the deadline dates are soft deadlines or target dates, use the deadline feature instead. Also, if you have constraints in the middle of your schedule, you will not see by how much the project end date is missed overall because constraints prevent tasks from floating past them. See chapter 6 for more information regarding constraints and deadlines.

If you do use the deadline feature, you won't get warning dialogs that alert you to conflicts in your schedule. Instead, a red flag will be raised in the Indicators column. Deadlines also allow you to see what the total slippage is on the project end date.

You can display a line in the timescale for the amount of negative slack a task has. In the **Gantt Chart** view, on the **Format** tab, in the **Bar Styles** group, click on the **Format** down-arrow, **Bar Styles**. There is an item called **Negative Slack** in the list under **From** and **To**. It allows you to display a line in front of the task bars that represents the amount of time a task slipped past its latest allowable finish date (Late Finish). To use this, choose the following settings:

The result would look like this screenshot:

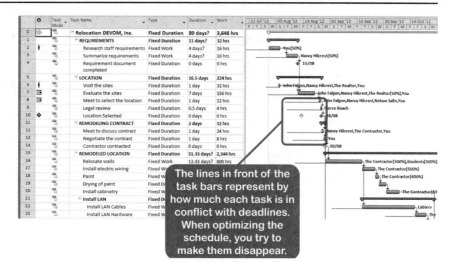

The lines in front of the task bars represent by how much each task is in conflict with deadlines. When optimizing the schedule, you try to make them disappear.

 Project 2010 will make all CPM calculations for manually scheduled tasks and for auto scheduled tasks, but be careful: when you change something in a manually scheduled task, CPM calculations will not be updated. In addition, Constraints are deactivated for manually scheduled tasks.

Steps to Optimize for Time

1. Show or highlight the critical path and slacks
2. Identify which tasks have potential time savings
3. Make a change to those tasks
4. Consider impacts on quality, scope and risk
5. Decide whether you want to keep the change
6. Repeat steps 3 – 6

In step 1 you identify the critical tasks since they drive the project duration. Do this by having Project 2010 show the critical path in red or highlight the cells with yellow. If the critical path switches to another parallel path while you are optimizing, Project 2010 will immediately show the new critical path, so that you always know which tasks are critical. Also, obtain the information about total slack and free slack, so that you know the flexibility of a task's scheduling when optimizing for time.

In step 2 you identify the critical task(s) with the greatest opportunity for saving time, so you should focus on those first. (In other words: Don't sweat the small stuff!)

In step 3 for each task you've selected, you come up with a way to do the work faster or with more overlap with other tasks. We will identify and explain crashing and fast tracking approaches for reducing overall duration. You also need to evaluate whether the trade-offs (step 4 and 5) on quality, scope, or risk are too high a price to pay for the time saved (we'll address cost and resources in the following optimizing approaches).

The explanation of these steps will take quite a few pages. We'll repeat the list of steps as we go.

Showing or Highlighting the Critical Path

Before you optimize, show or highlight the critical path on the Gantt Chart view.

There are many ways to do this in Project 2010; here are a few:

➤ Switch to the **Tracking Gantt** view that shows the critical tasks in red by default. On the **View** tab, in the **Task Views** group, click the **Gantt Chart** down-arrow and click **Tracking Gantt**.

➤ Use the new one-click critical path option. In any **Gantt Chart** view, on the **Format** tab, in the **Bar Styles** group, check ☑ **Critical Tasks**.

➤ Use the right click enhanced feature for displaying the Critical Tasks.

1. In any **Gantt Chart** view, if you **right click** on any blank part in Gantt Chart section, you will get a mini-menu with some options. Put the cursor over **Show/Hide Bar Styles** and a second mini-menu will appear:

⊞	Gridlines...
◷	Bar Styles
▤	Layout
	Nonworking Time...
◷	Progress Lines
	Show/Hide Bar Styles ▸
✓	Show Timeline
	Show Split

	Critical Tasks
	Slack
	Late Tasks
≣	Baseline ▸
≣	Slippage ▸
◷	Bar Styles

2. On the second mini-menu, click **Critical Tasks**.

➤ Use the new Highlight tool

1. In the **Gantt Chart** view (any task view), on the **View** tab, in the **Data** group, click the **Highlight** down arrow [No Highlight] ▾ to display the option list:

[No Highlight] | Timescale:

Built-In

[No Highlight]
Active Tasks
Completed Tasks
Critical
Date Range...
Incomplete Tasks
Late Tasks
Milestones
Summary Tasks
Task Range...
Tasks With Estimated Durations
Using Resource...

Clear Highlight
New Highlight Filter...
More Highlight Filters...

2. Select **Critical**. All critical task cells in the table now appear with yellow highlighting.

If you have schedules developed with previous versions of Project, in some cases, when you apply the highlighting feature, you will get a change in the color of the fonts instead a change in the color of the background.

➤ Use **Text Styles** to change the color of the critical task names or the color of the background:

1. In the **Gantt Chart** view (any task view), on the **Format** tab, in the **Format** group, click on **Text Styles** 𝐀. The **Text Styles** dialog box will appear:

2. Select from the list **Item to Change** [All ▼] the item **Critical Tasks**.

3. From the list **Color**, select the color you want, for example red.

4. From the list **Background Color**, select the color you want, for example yellow.

5. Click [OK]. All critical task information in the table (except critical milestones) are now in red and their cells are in yellow.

Displaying the Total Slack

Before we continue our discussion on optimizing for time, it is useful to note that the **Total Slack** field can be inserted or the total slack bar can be shown to troubleshoot issues in your schedule or to complement the one-click critical path.

Any tasks with a very large positive total slack number may have been accidentally left off the critical path because they are missing one or more dependencies to other tasks in the schedule.

➤ To insert the **Total Slack** column in any task table:

1. Right-click on the column heading just after where you want to insert it.

2. From the list of field names select the item **Total Slack**; you can do this quickly by typing the first few characters of the field name; then click [OK].

3. The field will now be displayed in the table. You can drag the dividing bar (between the table and the timescale) to the right to accommodate the new field in the view. To position the dividing bar on the edge of the nearest column, double-click on the divider.

You can also follow these steps to insert the Free Slack column to help you analyze the flexibility of your tasks related to their successor tasks.

➤ Show the **Total Slack** bar using the new one-click critical path option. In any **Gantt Chart** view, on the **Format** tab, in the **Bar Styles** group, check ☑ Slack.

➤ Show the **Total Slack** bar using the right click enhanced feature. In any **Gantt Chart** view, right-click on any blank part in Gantt chart section; a mini-menu will be displayed. Put the cursor over Show/Hide Bar Styles and a second mini-menu will appear. Click **Slack**.

The total slack identifies which tasks are critical (total slack less than or equal to zero) and which ones are not (total slack greater than zero). If the total slack is negative, you are missing the project deadline or one or more hard constraint dates in your schedule.

By default, Project 2010 shows tasks as critical if their total slack is less than or equal to zero. You can change this threshold: on the **File** tab, in the **Backstage** view, click **Options**, **Advanced** tab. Under the **Calculation options for this project:**, increase the field **Tasks are Critical if Slack is less than or equal to**: [0 days] **days** to the value you prefer. For example, you may want to identify tasks with 1 or 2 days of slack in order to keep an eye on the "near" critical tasks. With this you are raising the threshold for criticality in the CPM calculation.

What you will often see when you display the critical path for the first time in a schedule is that it is **not** a complete chain of tasks that stretches from the project start date to the project end date. Instead you'll see a fragmented critical path. We'll explore the possible causes of fragmentation. Project managers need to understand all paths that explains the entire project duration.

A Fragmented Critical Path: Possible Causes

Normally, the critical path provides a complete explanation of what happens between the project start and finish dates. However, the critical path often looks fragmented and may not provide this complete explanation.

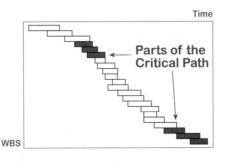

Only if you shorten the duration of a task on the critical path will the project duration shorten. If you cannot see the complete critical path, optimizing becomes a painful process of trial and error. Therefore, we recommend you analyze the causes of fragmentation first to find the complete critical path.

The critical path can become fragmented for various reasons:

➤ Unavailability of resources
➤ Schedule constraints and deadlines
➤ Elapsed durations
➤ Task calendars
➤ External predecessors
➤ Workload leveling

We'll discuss each of these.

Unavailability of Resources

In the illustration, the *Implement* task could take place on a week when Cindy has her vacation. The result is that Project 2010 will schedule *Implement* on the first next workable day when the resource is available, as shown in the illustration. Depending on when the predecessors of *Implement*

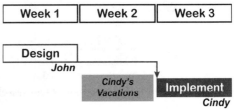

are done, this could create slack. When slack is created before the task *Implement*, the critical path will only start with the task *Implement* and therefore, only partially explain the project duration.

Is this real slack? Real slack is time that can be used as a buffer to compensate for slippages. In this case, the slack is real, because if the task *Design* slips one week, this will not impact the project end date.

In some situations, slippage is desirable. For example, you may want to finish the design and then start the implementation without a week in the middle (set to allow John to deliver the design to Cindy in the best possible way). This could be accomplished by making the schedule constraint As Late As Possible for the task *Design* (in the Task Information dialog box on the **Task** tab, in the **Properties** group). If you were to do this, the slack just moves over to the predecessors of *Design*, and the critical path will start with this task.

Because slack now exists on tasks earlier in the project, we consider them critical tasks because if we can compress them, they will impact the total duration of the project. To analyze this you need to be aware of the total slack and consider that any task with total slack equal or less than the slack produced for the unavailability of resources could be considered as a task where you can optimize its time and then optimize the total duration of the project. One option for showing these tasks as critical tasks is to raise the threshold for criticality by the same amount as the slack produced by the unavailability of resources. This will adjust the display of critical tasks and you will see a complete critical path. (You can adjust the criticality threshold explained earlier in this chapter).

If you adjust the critical threshold, this will be used to define critical tasks in the whole project, not just the period where you've detected the problem of a fragmented critical path. You may want to use the new threshold to analyze part of the schedule, detect the tasks that drive the total duration, and then return to the normal threshold equal to zero to continue with your project.

Schedule Constraints and Deadlines

We have already seen that constraints can cause negative slack when they are tight, but they can also cause positive slack when they are far out. Positive slack is essentially a buffer. Deadlines also affect the slack calculation in a fashion similar to constraints.

The illustration has two tasks: *Prepare Agenda* and *Meeting*. Typically, a formal meeting occurs on a specific date and should be entered with a Must Start On constraint. When you enter a fixed date, slack can be created on the predecessors of that task, and the critical path starts to look disjointed. Only the task *Meeting* will be indicated as critical, because *Prepare Agenda* now has slack.

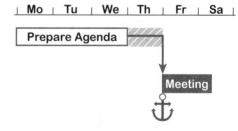

 This is another reason why we recommend using as few schedule constraints as possible without compromising the validity of the model of your project. In this situation, constraints make it more difficult to find the critical path because they tend to break it.

The constraints that can cause positive slack in forward and backward scheduling are listed in the Constraints and Negative Slack section earlier in this chapter. Other types of constraints won't fragment your critical path.

Again, you have to ask yourself: Is this real slack? In this case, the slack is real, because slippage on the predecessor *Prepare Agenda* doesn't impact the end date unless it slips more than a day. You have to solve this again by raising the threshold for critical tasks.

 Under certain circumstances, deadlines can also fragment the critical path, for example when there is a tight deadline halfway through the project and a time buffer at the end. In this case, you'll only see a partial critical path that runs to the deadline date. While this may be a reason to not use many deadline dates in your project schedule, if you must set either a constraint or a deadline, we recommend using a deadline. Deadlines let you see the compounded effect on the project end date that hard constraints obscure.

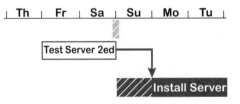

An elapsed duration is expressed in calendar days (as opposed to business days). A task with an elapsed duration can end during nonworking time, whereas its non-elapsed successor cannot start during non-working time; it can only start on the next business day. This creates slack on the elapsed duration task. In the illustration, we are installing a server, which is scheduled to start on Monday, because it has a regular duration. Before we can install the server, we want to test the server for 2 days continuously to make sure it does not fail under the testing conditions. Since the test is automated, we can have it end on a non-working day, like a weekend, then start the next task on the next business day. The task *Test Server* can slip until 8:00 AM Monday morning without affecting *Install Server*. This creates 1 day of slack on Test Server, which has a duration of 2 elapsed days (2ed).

Once more you have to ask yourself: Is this real slack? The slack is real here, because the *Test Server* task could continue for another day without impacting the project. Again, you can resolve this by raising the threshold for critical tasks.

Task Calendars

Task calendars can fragment the critical path. If the task *Design* can be ready long before the weather is good enough to start construction, it will have slack, and therefore will not be seen as critical. The task *Construct* and its successors will be critical, as shown in the illustration. The slack is real, and *Design* could take all slack without impacting the start date of *Construct*. The only way to find a complete path of the critical tasks before *Construct* is by raising the threshold for criticality.

External
Predecessors

An external predecessor is a task from another project schedule that drives a task in your schedule (see the illustration). If a task has an external predecessor, this predecessor could very well drive the task farther out than the other internal predecessors inside your schedule. If it does, it creates slack on these predecessors. This slack is real slack, because it can be used to compensate for slippages in your schedule. Again, it can be addressed by raising the threshold for criticality.

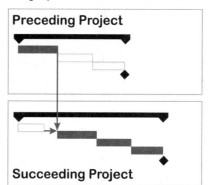

Workload Leveling

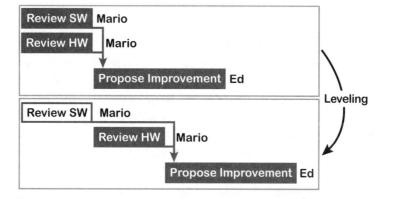

This illustration shows two tasks with one successor task. *Review SW* and *Review HW* could be done in parallel. They are independent of each other and can be done in any order; there is no logical dependency between them. After they are completed, the successor task *Propose Improvement* can be done. You have one resource, Mario, assigned full time to both predecessor tasks. Mario is overloaded and you decide to level his workload.

In this instance, no other resource is available and you've determined that the only way to solve the over-allocation is by delaying one of the tasks. As you delay one task, you create slack on the other task that competes for the same resource. As a result, the slack makes critical tasks noncritical, and part of the critical path evaporates before your eyes.

One last time, you have to ask yourself: Is this slack real? In this case, the answer is no. The slack is not real slack, because any delay in either task does impact the next task, and because they are in the critical path, does impact the project end date. If Mario needs more time for *Review SW*, his other task, *Review HW*, will slip. How are you going to solve this?

If the task *Review SW* slips, it will drive the task *Review HW* farther out, because the same resource does both, and there is a resource dependency between the two tasks. Both tasks are resource-critical, even though the current critical path algorithm suggests that only the task *Review HW* is critical. The CPM algorithm only looks at dependencies when it calculates the early and late dates: it doesn't take resource workloads into account. Remember that CPM assumes that resources are available in unlimited quantities. We will address the issue of limited resources later in this chapter.

Should You Add Logical Dependencies?

When we discussed dependencies we advised against using logical dependencies to show a resource dependency. Some people suggest that you should add dependencies to level out the workloads of the resources. Of course, you could model resource dependencies as logical dependencies that would

be soft dependencies. This works well until you start changing the assignments. In the illustration, if you substitute Mario on one of the two tasks, your schedule could be shorter than it is, because of a soft dependency that has now become obsolete! Adding logic to level workloads in order to keep your critical path intact is a static solution for a dynamic problem. As a consequence, the solution will have a short life. That's why we added question marks to the dependency in the illustration.

We recommend keeping your schedule dynamic. We'll explain a different method for resolving the over-allocations and optimizing in this situation in the section below on Optimizing for Time, Cost and Resources.

Many schedulers keep the resource workloads reasonable by creating extra logical dependencies. They know the schedule would not be feasible if they didn't use these extra dependencies that really do not reflect a mandatory sequence of tasks. If you are in this category, we invite you to consider a new method instead: the Resource-Critical Path method.

Identify Tasks with Potential Time Savings

1. Show or highlight the critical path and slacks
2. Identify which tasks have potential time savings
3. Make a change to those tasks
4. Consider impacts on quality, scope and risk
5. Decide whether you want to keep the change
6. Repeat steps 3 – 6

Now that you've highlighted the critical path and total slack, and done your best to make it continuous from start to end, the next step is find those tasks where you can gain the most time.

To do this, you need to analyze the logic of your whole schedule, critical path and total slack. Here are some filters and views that may help you do this:

➤ If your schedule is long, obtain a complete view of it: on the **View** tab, in the **Zoom** group, select **Entire Project** zoom ![icon].

➤ If you have a lot of tasks, you can also filter your schedule by critical path to obtain a more manageable view for your analysis.

➤ Long critical tasks may offer a better opportunity for applying actions to save time, so you might want to apply a sort by duration to help focus your view on long critical tasks. If you're applying rolling wave planning, some phases of your project life-cycle may be at the first levels with long durations; of course, you'll be limited in optimizing these phases until you have more information.

For more information about how to apply filters and sorts, see chapter 11.

The most important objectives are to understand the network of your schedule, determine if any parallel critical paths have appeared, decide if you need further breakdown or integration, and understand how your resources are participating. We'll present different approaches to reducing your schedule's time in the following section; each can be applied in different situations.

Schedule Compression

Shortening the Critical Path

1. Show or highlight the critical path and slacks
2. Identify which tasks have potential time savings
3. **Make a change to those tasks**
4. Consider impacts on quality, scope and risk
5. Decide whether you want to keep the change
6. Repeat steps 3 – 6

You want to optimize by analyzing the critical tasks and shortening them to shorten the project duration.

At this point you will be changing the schedule (time). Any change has to be evaluated in terms of the impact on the other competing demands: quality, scope and risk. (We could consider cost and resources, but in order to explain the actions to optimize time, for the moment we assume that unlimited resources are available to us. We will consider cost and resources later.)

The best solutions are those that reduce time without affecting quality, scope and risk. There are rarely, if ever, such ideal solutions and most solutions will require trade-offs.

The list below provides ideas on how to improve the schedule with the most effective ideas first. The first two actions involve fast-tracking, or overlapping activities. Fast-tracking follows the principle of working smarter instead of harder. If you choose to add resources instead, you will be working harder. Adding resources is called crashing.

We recommend you start by exploring whether the first two fast-tracking actions can be applied to your critical tasks. After exhausting the fast-tracking possibilities on critical tasks, go to the next action in the list. This is the quickest way to find the most time in your project schedule.

All actions are for tasks in the critical path. When you apply a change, you need to verify whether the critical path has changed as a result. It's also possible that you'll create parallel critical paths, so you'll need to apply actions in those parallel paths to get total schedule compression.

Checklist for Finding Potential Time Savings:

	Action
1.	Change sequential dependencies into partial dependencies (fast-tracking)
2.	Create parallel paths from a sequential path (fast-tracking)
3.	Split long tasks into shorter ones
4.	Change schedule constraints
5.	Shorten lags (waiting periods)
6.	Split task bars around Must Start On tasks
7.	Decrease duration estimates
8.	Add resources (crashing)
9.	Reduce the scope or delete tasks

Before making any change, check the current total duration of the project so you can see how the changes you make affect it. In the **Gantt Chart** view, on the **Format** tab, in the **Show/Hide** group, select ☑ **Project Summary Task.**

Change from Sequential to Partial Dependencies (Fast-Tracking)

There are four types of dependencies that can be combined with a positive lag time (waiting time/gap) or negative lag time (overlap/lead). The illustration on the right shows a Finish-to-Start dependency that is changed into an overlap of 3 weeks (lead or negative lag of –3w): FS – 3w. The overlap can be entered as an absolute lag in a number of days or weeks, like -3w.

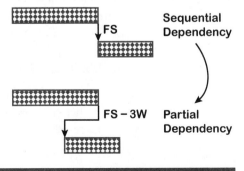

It can also be entered as a percentage of the duration of the predecessor (relative lag), like *-40%*. Since the start of the successor is dependent upon the partial completion of the predecessor, one could also speak of a partial dependency.

1. In the timescale of the Gantt Chart view, point the tip of the mouse pointer on the arrow of the dependency. Wait until the screen tip appears. Check to see if you are pointing to the dependency between the right tasks, because the dependency arrows can overlap one another.

2. Double-click if you have the right one; the **Task Dependency** dialog box appears:

You can easily change a sequential into a partial dependency by making the lag negative, like -4d or -50%.

You can keep the **Finish-to-Start** and make the lag negative (lead).

OR

You can select from the list **Type**: Finish-to-Start (FS) ▾ the **Start-to-Start** or **Finish-to-Finish** to overlap tasks.

3. Type in the **Lag** with absolute time units, like *-2d*, or in a percentage of the duration of the predecessor, like *-30%*. In a Finish-to-Start dependency, you will overlap the predecessor for the lag you specify. For Start-to-Start or Finish-to-Finish dependencies, enter zero or a positive lag to create partial dependencies.

4. Click OK ; you should now see the overlap you want between the two task bars in the timescale.

 If you can't select the right dependency with the mouse, you can use the Task Details Form to create the overlap. Click on the successor task in the **Gantt table**. On the **Task** tab, in the **Properties** group, click on **Details**, **Display Task Details** to display the **Task Details Form**, and you can make the lag negative in the **Lag** field of the predecessor.

Creating Parallel Paths

You can cut soft dependencies. Hard, mandatory dependencies should not be cut; it's just not realistic.

Cutting soft dependencies on critical tasks can result in large time gains, as shown in the illustration. However, you need to look at all the potential impacts. In the top scenario in the illustration, there is no risk of damaging the new carpet,

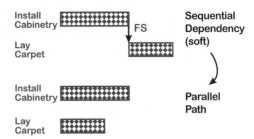

because it is laid after the cabinets have been installed (sequential dependency). In the bottom scenario, the carpet layers will have to protect the new carpet, because the two tasks are scheduled concurrently (parallel path). Of course the risk of damage will be higher and more effort may be required. Resource dependencies must be considered as well.

 We recommend you set a new dependency to the soft successor first before cutting the dependency, because otherwise the successor task bar might disappear off the screen to the start date of the project.

1. In the **Gantt Chart** view, point the tip of the mouse pointer to the arrow of the dependency and double-click on it; the **Task Dependency** dialog box appears:

> **Task Dependency**
>
> From: select the realtor
> To: visit the sites
> Type: Finish-to-Start (FS) ▼   Lag: 0d ▲▼
>
> [Delete]   [OK]   [Cancel]
>
> Delete the dependency by clicking Delete.

2. Verify whether the correct dependency is shown and click [Delete].

3. Click [OK]; the dependency is now removed.

When you apply fast-tracking consider these factors:

➤ You do not want scope and quality to change: consider techniques to meet all initial requirements and standards because there aren't any change in deliverables and task durations.

➤ Total duration of your project will be reduced.

> ➤ Fast-tracking may change the critical path. The reduction in critical path duration may be greater than total slack or some other parallel path, so you need to review your whole schedule every time you apply this technique.

> ➤ When you create overlaps or parallel paths, you change your resource requirements; you need to review their real availability before you accept the change.

> ➤ If the total duration of the project is reduced, overhead costs may also be reduced (facilities, supervision tasks, etc.).

> ➤ The cost may be increased if you require new resources (for parallel tasks) with higher rates, or if you need to increase supervision or facilities.

> ➤ Fast-tracking definitely increases risk on your project. For instance, if you have quality issues in some activity with fast-tracking considerations, and need to rework it, you must also rework the parallel or overlap activity. You must analyze the trade-off between time and risk (less time means more risk) before you accept the change.

Break Long Tasks into Shorter Ones

Breaking a long task into smaller tasks gives you more possibilities to optimize, as depicted in the illustration. The benefit is immediate if you can assign portions

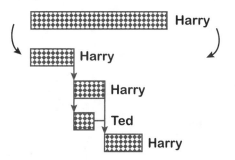

of the task to other non-critical, and perhaps even less expensive resources. The easiest way to break up a long task is by changing it to a summary task and adding detail tasks below it. You'll have to take the assignments and dependencies off the summary task. One advantage of this approach is that only the lowest level of detail of your schedule will change, which isn't very visible in reports. The possible disadvantage is that you are increasing the number of tasks and you will need more effort to keep your schedule updated during monitoring and controlling.

For a refresher on task management and linking, see chapters 4 and 5.

Change Schedule Constraints

Look for creative ways to remove constraints from your schedule. For example, if your project needs approvals from an executive board that meets only monthly, lobby hard for a faster, alternative route for approvals. This could take some "anchors" out of your schedule.

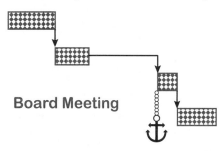

Board Meeting

1. Select the task with the constraint.

2. On the **Task** tab, in the **Properties** group, click **Task Information** ▣▤ , and the dialog box appears.

3. Click on the **Advanced** tab.

Task Information ☒

| General | Predecessors | Resources | Advanced | Notes | Custom Fields |

Name: Visit the Sites   Duration: 1d ⌃⌄ ☐ Estimated

Constrain task

Deadline: NA ▾

Constraint type: As Soon As Possible ▾   Constraint date: NA ▾

Task type: Fixed Duration ▾   ☐ Effort driven

Calendar: None ▾   ☐ Scheduling ignores resource calendars

WBS code: 2

Earned value method: % Complete ▾

The As Soon as Possible constraint is not a constraint under forward scheduling.

☐ Mark task as milestone

Help   OK   Cancel

4. Under **Constrain task**, change the **Constraint type** to **As Soon As Possible**.

    OR

    Change the **Constraint date** to an earlier date.

5. Click [OK].

Shorten Lags

If you find any lag between critical tasks, you might be able to reduce it now that you are armed with the argument that the lag is on the critical path. In the

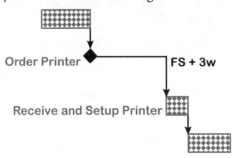

Order Printer ◆ FS + 3w

Receive and Setup Printer ▦

illustration example, you have to wait for the board's decision, and you typically have to wait 3 weeks before the board convenes. You might be able to lobby for an executive decision instead of a full board decision, which would save a few weeks and be a significant gain.

If the wait is for receiving supplies from a vendor, you can often work miracles by offering your supplier extra money for faster delivery.

To decrease lag:

1. In the **Gantt Chart** view, point the tip of the mouse pointer to the arrow of the dependency. Double-click on the arrow. The **Task Dependency** dialog box appears:

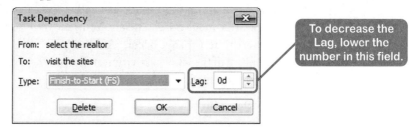

To decrease the Lag, lower the number in this field.

2. Verify whether the right dependency is shown and decrease the amount of **Lag**, then click OK.

Split Task Bars around Must Start On Tasks

If a team member has a meeting or training to attend, she has to drop her regular work on the agreed upon, fixed date for the meeting or training. You can model this by using schedule constraints like Must Start On. In the illustration on the right, your ongoing task cannot be completed before the meeting, and could be scheduled entirely after the meeting, but splitting it around the meeting gives the tightest schedule.

Before Optimization

After Optimization

To split a task bar:

1. Click on a task, choose the **Task** tab, and in the **Schedule** group, click **Split Task** ᐃ on the **Standard** toolbar. A yellow pop-up window appears, and the mouse pointer now looks like: |▶

2. Point to a task bar, and click to split it, then drag it to where you want the split to occur. A part of the task bar is split off and in the pop-up, you are shown what the new start and finish dates of the part will be when you release the mouse:

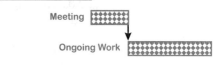

3. You can drag the split bar to any date you want and release the mouse button; the task bar will be split into two parts connected by dots:

Even though this feature appears to work well at first glance, we do not recommend using it during the planning phase of the project. The predecessors may reschedule the ongoing task, and its split should be moved accordingly to keep it scheduled around the short task with a fixed date. The problem is that the split does not move automatically. You may have to adjust your schedule manually every time a change occurs. Another problem is that you can only link the start or finish of the whole activity, not the middle parts. That's why we don't recommend using this feature.

There are better approaches:

> You can break down the task into multiple subtasks. For example, electricians wire a building, but after the inspection, they have to come back to install the switch plates. You could show this as one task with a split task bar, but it would be better to break it down into two tasks: pull cables and install switch plates. Now you can set dependencies between these tasks and keep your model entirely dynamic. If you have a choice between task breakdown and bar splitting, we recommend you break down the task rather than split its bar.

> Create a task calendar for those tasks that might be affected. In the task calendar, you indicate nonworking time for the duration of the Must Start On task. As long as the Must Start On date does not change, the calendar will do a fine job.

> Alternatively, you could allow the over-allocation of the resource to occur and then level the workloads. On the **Resource** tab, in the **Level** group, click **Leveling Options** and select ☑ **Leveling can create splits in remaining work**. In this case, the leveling will create a split, and when you level again, it will move the split as needed.

> Lastly, you could ignore the over-allocation, assuming that the resources will manage both tasks or maybe work overtime.

Decrease Duration Estimates

Often when you get closer to the tasks at hand you can provide more precise duration estimates. Sometimes you'll find that a task duration has been  overestimated. And sometimes you can find a better and quicker way to accomplish the task. In both cases, you can cut some of the duration. In many cases, however, decreasing the estimate is at the expense of quality or scope, and you should examine the trade-offs closely.

Add Resources (Crashing)

Often, managers ask for more resources when they start to feel the heat of their deadlines. In the illustrated example, the project manager asked for and got Ed

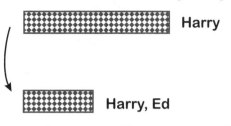

to help out with Harry's work. Adding resources may cost you more money, and may not reduce the duration. We have often observed that when new resources arrive, the best resources are taken off their jobs to train the new ones. This causes an initial increase in the slippage instead of a decrease.

How many people can you add to tasks? When optimizing for time only, you could in theory add an unlimited number, but in practice, there are limits. If you add too many people, they will get in each other's way and keep each other from being productive. The law of diminishing returns is applicable when adding resources. How many carpenters can work in one 10-by-15-foot room? Does adding more people to a meeting shorten the meeting duration? The degree to which additional resources will reduce duration depends on the nature of the work. If a task can be discretely divided into multiple subtasks that can be nicely divided among workers, then duration reduction is possible (but do consider supervision and training time).

There are also simple practical limits. Even though we have assumed we have access to unlimited resources, it doesn't seem reasonable to add more than the maximum units available in the resource sheet.

Crashing is defined by the *PMBOK* as "a schedule compression technique in which cost and schedule tradeoffs are analyzed to determine how to obtain the greatest amount of compression for the least incremental cost"[4]. So, once you have decided which tasks you want to crash, you need to analyze the extra resources needed for each task along with their cost implications to select the order or priority for crashing. Of course, you need to also analyze the risk implications.

Make sure you change the task type to Fixed Work before adding resources. This will ensure that the duration decreases when you add them.

---

4 ———*PMBOK® Guide – Fourth Edition*, PMI, 2008, p. 156.

Reduce Scope or Delete Tasks

Reducing scope is a matter of deleting deliverables. If you delete deliverables that are on the critical path, you will reduce the duration of the project. Just because a deliverable is on the critical path doesn't necessarily mean it is an important deliverable. The word critical in project management simply means that it is driving the project end date. If there were deliverables in critical tasks qualified as nice-to-have, these would be good candidates to delete. For example, in a course manual the deliverables index and glossary may be left out of an early version to save time. Of course, not delivering on what you promised may be dangerous from a contractual point of view; you must manage any change in deliverable with your client and sponsor.

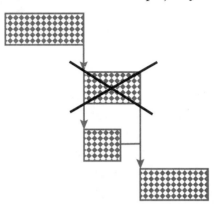

Alternatively, you could focus on the level below deliverables and find critical tasks to delete, as shown in the illustration. Sometimes you can find nice-if-we-get-around-to-it activities to cut. This may happen at the expense of the quality of the deliverables. If the quality requirement is a nice-to-have, you could cut the task. Deleting a task is as easy as clicking its row heading (ID number) and pressing ⌈Delete⌋. Note that testing and quality control tasks are easy to delete, but we strongly recommend that you restrain (or retrain) yourself from doing so.

 If you delete a task, you will lose all dependencies (predecessors and successors). First redefine the new dependencies that explain the logic of our network, then delete the task.

 Instead of deleting a task, you may decide to use the new Project 2010 feature to make the task Inactive, and preserve the original task information.

Consider Impacts on Quality, Scope, and Risk

1. Show or highlight the critical path and slacks
2. Identify which tasks have potential time savings
3. Make a change to those tasks
4. **Consider impacts on quality, scope and risk**
5. **Decide whether you want to keep the change**
6. Repeat steps 3 – 6

Next you have to evaluate the impact on quality, scope, and risk of the change in time you've made. You also need to consider cost and resources implications.

From the new project duration, you can see how much time you have gained, and whether it is worth the sacrifices you made on the scope of the project, the quality of the deliverables, and/or the addition of risk. Realize that if you have used constraint dates or odd resource calendars in the back end of your schedule, the project end date may be held captive. Only if you have an entirely dynamic model will you see that changes immediately pull the project end date back.

If you find that the change did not yield the expected result, simply click undo ↺ the correct number of times to get rid of it.

Then repeat steps 3 to 6 in the optimizing process until you have solved the scheduling conflict.

Project Statistics Dialog Box

You can check the impact of your optimization changes in the Project Statistics dialog box. To view it:

1. On the **Project** tab, in **Properties** group, click on **Project Information**. In the **Project Information** dialog box, click on **Statistics** [Statistics...] at the bottom to open the **Project Statistics** dialog window:

Project Statistics for '09 Optimizing - Time Cost Resources 4'		

	Start	Finish
Current	Aug 1 '12	Dec 4 '12
Baseline	Aug 1 '12	Nov 20 '12
Actual	Aug 1 '12	NA
Variance	0d	10d

	Duration	Work	Cost
Current	90d?	3,840h	$138,210.00
Baseline	80d	3,840h	$138,210.00
Actual	26.16d	376h	$12,960.00
Remaining	63.84d?	3,464h	$125,250.00

Percent c...
Duration:

Keep your eye on this field when optimizing for time.

[Close]

2. In the intersection of the **Current** row and the **Duration** column, you can see the new duration of the project.

 Modifying the **Quick Access Toolbar**, you can add the **Project Statistics** icon to your commands 📊. This way you can view it from wherever you are in your project without having to jump to the top of the project.

Monte Carlo Simulation

Earlier we introduced schedule simulation as one of the techniques used in optimizing the schedule. One thing is certain: unforeseen events will happen and you will need a time buffer to compensate for those events. This is a generally accepted project management best practice.

Once you have optimized the critical path, you should ask yourself: How much buffer should I reserve in my schedule in order to protect the project deadline? A time buffer is also known as a time contingency or time reserve. The harder your project deadline is, the more carefully you need to assess your buffer needs. Simulation can help you determine your buffer needs. Note that while the PERT method also addresses uncertainty, it is not as effective as simulation.

Project 2010 does not have simulation capabilities, but there are good add-ons available with which you can simulate Project 2010 schedules.

What Is Monte Carlo Simulation?

Monte Carlo simulation is the best known simulation technique. For tasks that are hard to predict, you specify the lower and upper limits of an estimate and choose a probability curve between those limits.

The simulating software generates estimates for all the tasks using these parameters. It uses number generators that produce estimates that comply with

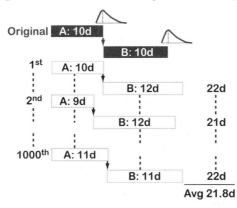

the range and the distribution curve you have chosen for the estimate. It creates the first version of the entire schedule and calculates the critical path. In the illustration on the left, the original schedule is shown as well as the 1st, the 2nd and 1000th version created by the simulation software.

Simulation will create as many versions as you want, but after a certain number of versions, every next one has less and less added value (the concept of diminishing returns). Simulations often create up to a thousand versions of the schedule. In each version, the critical path of the schedule is calculated. The simulation software will then calculate average project duration and probabilities for a range of finish dates.

Output of Monte Carlo Simulation

Simulation software creates an s-curve from the many versions of the schedule. An s-curve shows projected finish dates charted against the probability of

meeting those dates. The illustration shows such an s-curve. The benefit of the s-curve is that you can see the chance of completing your project by the date that Project 2010 indicates as the project finish date in your schedule (see current finish date in the illustration and its current probability).

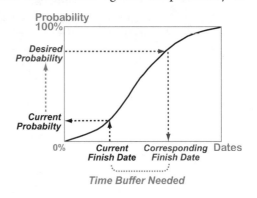

Alternatively, you can choose the level of probability you feel comfortable with, and derive the project finish date, or you can let executives choose it for you (see desired probability in the illustration). With the desired probability, you can find the corresponding finish date. You can quote this date to the client with a known degree of confidence that it can be met. There may still be other risks that you do not know about (unknown risks), but at least you have quantified known risks.

You can also calculate the size of the time buffer you need in your project. If you read from the s-curve that you need to add 3 weeks as a buffer to your current Project 2010 schedule to have 90% probability, you should insert this as a buffer "task" just before the project finish milestone and have it push out the milestone. Alternatively, you could include the buffer in your schedule as increased durations if you need to, but this is not the preferred way.

Why Do You Need Simulation?

Monte Carlo Simulation is often crucial, particularly in large complex projects, for two reasons:

➤ **Forecasts from one-point estimates tend to be too optimistic**
Experience has shown that schedules made with single estimates per task are optimistic in nature. The PERT technique, which uses multipoint estimates, addresses this problem, but doesn't address the next problem, that of converging paths.

➤ **Converging paths compound the time risk**
Converging paths decrease the probability of meeting a milestone date. The chance that the milestone will be accomplished on time decreases with every path that is added leading into the milestone. In the illustration, each path has an admirable chance for on time delivery of 90%, but the chance of delivering the milestone on time is exactly 81%. If one path is early, the other may be late and vice versa. When two paths both have to be finished for

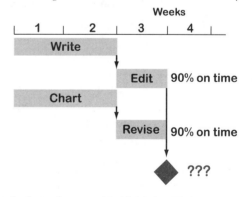

a milestone, you have to multiply their chances: 90% * 90% = 81%.

The more parallel paths you have in your schedule, the greater the schedule risk. In addition, the more equal the durations of the paths are, the greater the schedule risk.

This phenomenon is known as path convergence or merge bias. The aggregated effect of many merging paths of different lengths is very difficult to predict. While there may be rules of thumb and algorithms based on past experience to assess the need for contingency, simulation is the only way to statistically find out. The more parallel paths you see in your schedule, the more you will need to simulate the schedule. This need is even greater if those paths have similar durations.

The paths make it unlikely that your end date, as shown by your Project 2010 schedule, will be met. That is why project managers developed the habit of padding their schedules. Padding, as we define it, is inflating tasks to take risk and uncertainty into account. For example, a task that is most likely to get done in a week is estimated at two weeks because under adverse conditions, that's how long it might take. Alternatively, contingency reserves or buffers are allowances for slippage which are explicitly set aside. Tasks are estimated realistically and therefore the project can be controlled more tightly, while the targeted finish date or key milestone dates have realistically high probabilities of being met.

Simulation will help you to find the compounded effect of the parallel paths. You can use simulation to quantify how much of a contingency reserve or buffer you will need in your schedule. As you see, we recommend using simulation in combination with the Critical Path Method as an alternative to padding estimates for risk.

Assumptions of the Critical Path Method

In summary, critical path theory is based on three assumptions:
➤ Assumption 1: Task estimates are considered as one-point and deterministic data.
➤ Assumption 2: There is no merge bias or path convergence.
➤ Assumption 3: You have unlimited resources available.

We saw that assumption 1 does not hold true, but we can determine the magnitude of its effect by applying PERT or simulation.

As for assumption 2, merge bias (the effect of path convergence) does exist. This effect often causes the largest slippages in projects. Simulation is the only technique that can make the compounded effect of converging paths visible. Applying the CPM is useful, as long as you simulate as well. Many overruns can actually be foreseen and quantified when simulation is applied to schedules.

Assumption 3 is more difficult to deal with. Both the CPM and the PERT techniques assume that resources are available in unlimited quantities. If this is the case, the assumption can stand and the CPM is the technique to use. However, it is rare to have access to unlimited resources.

If you are managing the workload of your own scarce internal resources, CPM and the PERT techniques must be augmented by resource leveling.

Extra resources can be bought with money. We will therefore first introduce cost into the optimization (optimizing for time and cost), and then we will add the limited availability of resources (optimizing for time, cost and resources).

Optimizing for Time & Cost

When you optimize for time and cost, you should also consider scope, quality and risk. We will discuss the cost dimension before the resource dimension, because most resource decisions impact the cost side of our model. So the logical progression in our view is optimizing for time, then time and cost, then time, cost and resources.

Risk   Scope

Resources ⇐ Project ⇒ Time

Quality   Cost

Steps to Optimize for Time and Cost

1. Show or highlight the critical path and slacks
2. Identify which tasks have potential time savings
3. Make a change to those tasks
4. Consider impacts on quality, scope and risk
5. Decide whether you want to keep the change
6. Repeat steps 3 – 6

Any project manager who has a budget in money or in person hours should apply this type of optimization. The steps for optimizing for time and cost are very similar to the steps for optimizing for time. The differences are highlighted in bold in the illustration. Because you should not lose sight of the time dimension of the project, you still have to find the critical path. If you want to bring the duration of the project down, you should also apply the optimizing for time methods discussed in the previous section. Keeping the duration of a project as short as possible will also keep the cost of overhead expenses down. To keep the discussion on the process for time and cost optimizing simple, we will focus mainly on cost in the text that follows.

If you find that the restricted availability of resources is driving your finish date out, you will need to optimize for time, cost and resources, which is the third approach for optimizing. In that case, you should read this section as well, because in the next approach we will not discuss any methods to reduce cost.

Sort the tasks on cost to find the most expensive tasks. Develop ideas for how you might bring down the cost with no or minimal compromise on time, scope, quality or risk. Enter the change and check the results to see whether you want to keep the change. We will discuss how to accomplish some of these steps in Project 2010.

Display the Critical Path

You can show or highlight the critical path following the steps from the Optimizing for Time section above. Identifying the critical tasks and the slacks for normal tasks will allow you to consider the time impact when you apply some of the cost optimizing recommendations we present in the following steps.

Identify Tasks with Potential Cost Savings

To find the tasks which offer significant savings, you should analyze the whole project on all WBS levels. As with time, higher cost tasks may offer greater opportunity for savings, so you may want to sort the tasks on cost. You can use the table Cost in any task view, and then apply the sort (see chapter 11 to review sorting).

Use sorting for a temporary view, document your results and sort back by ID number.

Make Changes

The best measurements are those that improve cost and don't impact the other competing demands of quality, scope, risk, resources and time. Good luck finding these! However, here are ideas about what you can do.

Checklist for Finding Cost Saving Opportunities:

The actions are listed in order of overall perceived effectiveness; start at the top of the table and work your way down.

	Action	For
1	Find lower cost contracts	External contractors, consultants
2	Reassign to lower cost resources	Expensive resources
3	Break down a long task and reassign portions to lower cost resources	Long (critical) tasks
4	Shorten the project duration to decrease overhead cost	Critical tasks
5	Prevent paid overtime work	Resources with a higher overtime rate
6	Smooth the workloads	Resources with erratic workloads
7	Decrease the cost estimate	Any tasks with costs involved
8	Reduce the scope or delete tasks	Any tasks with costs involved

If you need to bring down the duration of your project as well, use the optimizing for time methods. Make sure you select those methods that do not increase the cost again. If you shorten the project duration, the overhead costs will also decrease (see method 4). You will save on expenses for project management, facilities, support staff and other overhead costs. Usually there is a stronger constraint, cost or time. Start with the stronger one and then work with the other. Of course, review trade-offs between competing demands.

If you are to manage the cash flow of your project as well as the overall cost, another measurement might be to renegotiate when the costs accrue and change the resource field Accrue at accordingly. Delaying the accrual of expenses will improve your cash flow.

Find Lower Cost Contracts

If you don't solicit multiple bids or proposals, doing so may create significant savings. Suppliers of materials, contractors and consultants are quick to determine whether or not they are in a competitive situation and will often quote accordingly. Another option is to research whether there are specialized firms that are quicker or better at their trade than other suppliers. If a specialized firm is using better technology, techniques, equipment or resources, it may be less expensive, even though the hourly rate may be higher. Remember to analyze risk aspects or any contract considerations: you may appear to have reduced cost, but if you've increased risk, your cost savings may not be realized.

Reassign to Lower Cost Resources

Use the Resource Usage view to find less expensive resources within your resource pool that you can substitute for expensive resources. Insert the columns with the total costs (Cost) and rates (Standard Rate) and find which assignments you can move to less expensive resources. You can reassign by simply dragging the assignment to another resource in the Team Planner view (**Resource** tab, **View** group) or using the Replace function on the Assign Resources icon (**Resource** tab, **Assignments** group). To analyze the possible impact on the total duration of the project, you also may need to level the resources.

Keep in mind that using a less expensive resource sometimes mean using a less effective resource (e.g., a junior resource with less experience). For other kinds of resources (machines, materials, software products), less expensive may mean lower quality, which may result in more effort and higher risk. Be careful not to be overly simplistic and optimistic in your thinking. And always consider risk impacts.

Reassign Portions of a Long Task

If you decide to break up a long task, perhaps the best way is to insert subtasks below it, thereby promoting it to a summary task. Then you assign less expensive resources to those subtasks to which they are suited and remove or reduce the use of the expensive resource. Don't forget to set appropriate dependencies, so as not to leave any loose ends in the network logic. If you can hook up some portions to much earlier tasks, you could save time as well. Also remember to factor in time and effort for supervision, communication and coordination.

Shorten the Project Duration

If you decrease the project duration, the overhead costs will decrease; you'll have less expense for the project manager, team leaders, facilities, equipment, etc.

9

Prevent Overtime Work	Preventing overtime work will only bring down the cost if you are actually paying a higher rate for overtime. For the how-to steps for decreasing overtime, refer to chapter 7. Of course, if you reduce overtime, you may be extending your project duration, which is a simple trade-off against the time dimension. You should only do that if saving cost is more important than finishing as early as possible.

Smooth Workloads   Workloads can be smoothed to reduce irregularities over time. In the illustration, the total workload before and after smoothing is the same 100 person days,

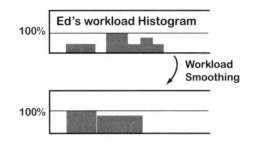

which would cost the same. However, if you're carrying the cost of the resource with the erratic workload during the times when the resource isn't working on your project, the actual cost is higher. The project budget doesn't show this cost, because it only shows the cost of the planned assignments. The extra cost of an erratic workload is a hidden cost in the plan; if you smooth the workload, you will decrease it. This hidden cost is difficult to quantify during the planning phase, but in general, you can say that the more erratic the workload, the higher the hidden cost in the project plan.

In addition, during the valleys, the resource with an erratic workload may lose momentum and have to re-ramp up. This cost is also hard to see unless the estimate for the tasks includes ramp up time.

 An intriguing paradox is that the scarcer a resource is, the more the resource should be shared between projects from the organization's point of view, but the less likely that project managers actually will share this scarce resource, particularly if they don't have cost responsibility.

Decrease Cost Estimates   Often when you get closer to the tasks at hand you can provide more precise cost estimates. Sometimes you'll find that a task has been overestimated in duration, in resources or in costs. And sometimes you can find a better way to accomplish the task. In both cases, you can cut some of the associated costs. In many cases, however, decreasing the estimate is at the expense of increasing the risk for not meeting quality or scope objectives, and you should examine the trade-offs closely.

Reducing the Scope or Deleting Tasks   As with time optimization, reducing scope means eliminating or changing deliverables and activity estimates. Remember that scope changes should be approved in advance.

When optimizing for time and cost, keep in mind the potential for impact on scope, quality, and risk (resources will be addressed in the next section). The competing demands are interrelated and the relationship between them must remain realistic and rational.

Cost Simulation   We discussed the advantages of applying simulation techniques to your critical path. You can also do cost simulations to analyze the impact of variables such as rates or fixed costs.

The output variable of the simulation could be the total cost of the project (Cost field) or the total cost at any level of the WBS. The s-curve output from the simulation will indicate the costs of the project against their probability, and will allow you to establish the cost reserve for your project.

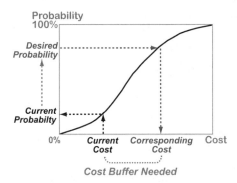

This concludes the second approach of optimizing for time and cost. We will now add the next dimension: resources.

Optimizing for Time, Cost & Resources

The next blue arrow we'll add to the illustration is resources. We add it to the dimensions we already monitor: quality, scope, risk, time and cost. Inclusion of resources means that you will monitor the workload of the resources relative to their availability. If you find that the limited availability (or unavailability) of resources affects the forecast dates, you are in a resource-constrained or resource-limited situation. In this case, you need to include resources in your optimization, otherwise your schedule will be too optimistic.

The resource dimension may involve trade-offs with:
➤ Cost, when you have to pay for extra resources or pay more for overtime
➤ Time, when you cannot solve over-allocations in any other way than by delaying tasks

In this section, to keep the discussion simple, we will only discuss how to trade off between time and resources. If you also need to bring down the cost of your project, you should consider the methods discussed above for optimizing for time and cost.

The optimization with resources becomes more complex, but if you handle this complexity, you can have confidence that the project is feasible as far as resources are concerned. This will increase the validity of your forecasts. A dynamic schedule should be able to change, or at least flag the need for change, as resources and their assignments change or as task durations change and affect resource dependent tasks.

Steps to Optimize for Time, Cost and Resources

1. **Check the workloads and level them**
2. Show the resource-critical path (RCP)
3. Find the critical resources
4. Make a change to those tasks
5. Consider impacts on quality, scope and risk
6. Decide whether you want to keep the change
7. Repeat steps 3 – 7

As the steps in the process chart show, the first thing you have to do is resource workload leveling (also called workload leveling or resource leveling). You have to check whether:

➤ The workloads are within the availability of the human resources
➤ The demand for facilities is within the availability of the facilities
➤ The work is within the capacity of the equipment

When resources are scarce, you will often find that the schedule extends when you level the workloads. This fragments the critical path, and you will need to find the resource-critical path (RCP). Once you have found the RCP, optimization is very similar to the methods used with the Critical Path Method.

Workload Leveling

The first step in optimizing for time, cost and resources is checking the workloads. If there are over-allocations, the workloads need to be leveled, that is, they have to be adjusted to eliminate overloads or accepted by authorizing overtime.

Ideally, you will have prevented over-allocations in the first place, since they are always painful to solve, particularly when you share resources with other project managers. You should consider using a master schedule to level resources that are shared among several projects. Within a single project, each project manager has the responsibility to make sure that the workloads are reasonable. Of thousands of schedules we have evaluated, we've found that this is often neglected: about 50% of the schedules we've evaluated had over-allocations.

We'll discuss how to level workloads in two different ways: by making manual changes to the schedule, or by letting Project 2010 automatically solve all over-allocations for you.

Checking the Workloads: Resource Graph

On the **View** tab, in **Resource Views** group, click on **Other Views** down-arrow, **Resource Graph**.

1. Hold down [Control] and press [Home] to make the timescale jump to the start of the project.

2. While still on the **View** tab, in the **Zoom** group, click on the **Zoom** down-arrow, then **Zoom Out** 🔍 and **Zoom In** 🔍 to adjust the timescale.

3. Press [Page Dn] to go to the next resource OR press [Page Up] to go to a previous resource.

The Resource Graph is also known as the resource histogram.[5]

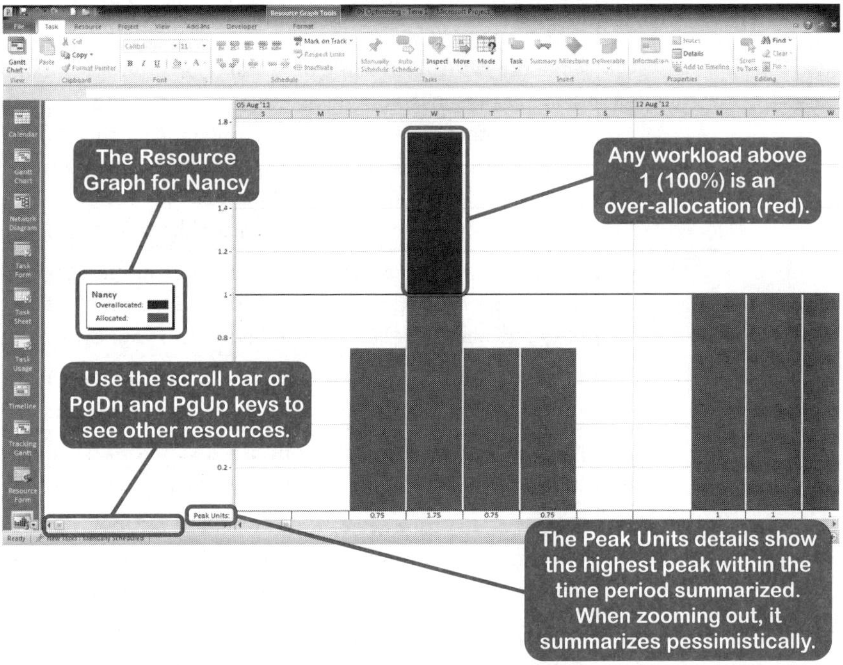

By default the Resource Graph shows the Peak Units. Peak Units allow you to find over-allocations very easily by zooming out; if you see any red bar appear, you have found an over-allocation. On the other hand, Peak Units presents an inflated picture of the real work when zoomed out, because it shows the highest bar during the time period summarized. In the **Resource Graph**

---

5 ———*PMBOK® Guide – Fourth Edition*, PMI, 2008.

view, on the **Format** tab, in the **Data** group, click on the **Graph** down-arrow
Peak Units ▾ to select a more realistic view of the workloads.

Manually Resolve the Workloads

There are many ways to resolve the workloads by hand without using the Automatic Leveling or Level Now features of Project 2010. The methods are listed in order of perceived effectiveness, with the first being the most effective in our view.

1.	**Reassign the best resources to critical tasks first and only to critical tasks.** Take non-critical tasks away from the best resources to reduce their workloads. Matching people to tasks so that the best person does the task also results in time gained, and is one of the rare methods for improving time and workloads at the same time.
2.	**Reassign tasks from critical resources to noncritical resources.** Critical resources are resources that force critical tasks to be delayed in order to keep their workloads sane. Critical resources extend the project duration and if you take some of their tasks away, you level their workloads and perhaps shorten the project duration
3.	**Take the critical resource off a task.** Sometimes you can do this when more than one person is working on the task, or as soon as you know who can handle the task other than the critical resource. Remember that the word "critical" doesn't mean the resource is an important resource; it just means the resource is driving the task and project duration. That sometimes makes it possible to simply remove the critical resource from the task to bring the workload down.
4.	**Hire extra resources.** If you hire extra resources, you can reassign the tasks from your critical resources to the new resources. This works well if the new resources have skills similar to or better than your existing resources.
5.	**Contract work out to subcontractors.** One definition of a subcontractor is someone who solves your workload problems in exchange for money.
6.	**Negotiate more resources from subcontractors.** If you can get more resources from subcontractors, the workload of existing resources can be reduced.
7.	**Fine-tune the number of units assigned to the tasks involved in the over-allocation.** For example, you could keep two tasks scheduled in parallel if you decrease the involvement of the resource to 50%, but make sure you keep the resource working with 100% focus on a critical task.
8.	**Break down long tasks into many shorter ones and reassign the short tasks to noncritical resources.** Breaking down tasks increases the number of scheduling possibilities dramatically.
9.	**Delay vacations until after the deadline.** This is where you start to trade-off against resources and require a lot of goodwill from your resources. Be careful to not put unreasonable demands on your resources because they will either burn out or leave.

10.	**Work during the weekend**. If an over-allocation occurs on a Friday, you can easily solve such a situation by asking the resource to work some hours over the weekend. Again you are trading off against the resource dimension.
11.	**Assign overtime**. Even though this does not solve the over-allocation, it shows that it has been dealt with. Again you are trading off against the resource dimension.
12.	**Change dependencies**. Decrease overlaps between tasks that are done by the same resource. Or, in the special case in which you have a team of people going from one city to another to install a system, consider setting extra, soft dependencies to prevent the team from being in two spots at the same time. This solidifies the order in which locations are rolled out and keeps the workloads reasonable.
13.	**Review quality standards and work estimates, which may decrease the workload**. You can often cut corners in the category of nice-to-have requirements without jeopardizing the project product.
14.	**Split task bars when multiple resources are assigned to move the workloads of the individual resources to where the workloads fit into their availability.**
15.	**Delay tasks**. Slip one of the tasks that compete for the same resource. If you decide to delay one task, choose the task that has the most slack and the least number of resources assigned. If you delay a task with other resources assigned, you may cause many new over-allocations. The less other resources are assigned, the less checking on workloads you need to do. Through the dependencies, successors may cause new over-allocations; you can never really tell what will happen when you start delaying tasks. You have to do it week by week.

 Project 2010 can't replace you as a manager in making these decisions:

➤ Adjust the units on assignments—how can software determine what a reasonable level of involvement is for all assigned resources?

➤ Adjust an effort estimate based on the overhead required for multiple resources and for different levels of resource expertise or quality

➤ Find qualified, external resources

➤ Ask resources what non-working time they are willing to sacrifice for the betterment of the project

➤ Determine which quality standards can be lowered without jeopardizing commitments or contracts

➤ Determine who the best resource is

➤ Determine who the most critical resource is

➤ Reassign tasks to less critical resources. (Project 2010 can't do this by itself; only with access to the enterprise resource pool from Project Server can it now find substitutes if all of the skills of the resources and skill requirements on the assignments are coded.)

What Project 2010 can do for you is:

➤ Split task bars where multiple resources are assigned (method 14), or

➤ Delay task bars (method 15).

Therefore, you have to level the workloads by hand if you want the tightest schedule possible. Let's explore the steps to do this in the easiest way possible.

The Steps to Level Workloads Yourself

Optimize resources first by using the **Resource Allocation** view or the new **Team Planner** view to evaluate over-allocations and then apply manual leveling techniques to resolve them.

To work with the Resource Allocation view, on the **View** tab, in the **Resource Views**, click the **Other Views** down-arrow. Click **More Views**, **Resource Allocation** and click on **Apply**.

The Resource Allocation view is most helpful for resolving over-allocations by hand.

1. A combination view appears with the **Resource Usage** view in the top pane and the **Leveling Gantt** in the bottom pane. The top view shows the over-allocated resources and the bottom view shows the conflicting tasks.

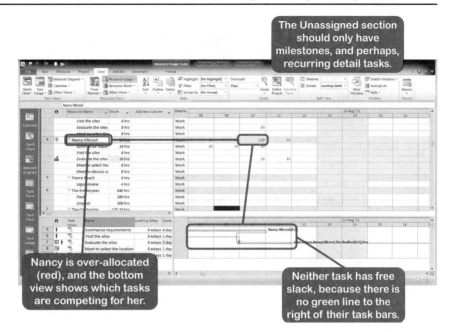

The Unassigned section should only have milestones, and perhaps, recurring detail tasks.

Nancy is over-allocated (red), and the bottom view shows which tasks are competing for her.

Neither task has free slack, because there is no green line to the right of their task bars.

2. Check to see if you forgot any assignments; if you did, there is no use starting the workload leveling. The heading **+ Unassigned** at the top contains the unassigned tasks. Click on the button **+** to expand them, and click **−** to hide them again. Typically, only the milestones and perhaps the recurring detail tasks should be listed in the **Unassigned** category. If you have not assigned resources to all detail tasks, you have not captured all the workloads, and you should not start the manual leveling process. Before you level, you want to be sure you have all of the players in the schedule. Hide all assignments in the top view by clicking on any column heading and then on the **View** tab, in the **Data** group, click on the **Outline** down-arrow. Select **Hide Subtasks**.

3. The over-allocated resources are shown in red. Position your mouse pointer over the icon ◈ in the **Indicators** ⓘ column. This is one indication of the need to level. Another is to look at the Indicators ⓘ column in the lower part of the window (the Leveling Gantt) and position your mouse over the red "person" symbol ⫯.

4. Scroll to the start of the project by dragging the scroll box on the horizontal scrollbar of the timescale to the far left. This step is important, since the tool will only look for over-allocations forward in time. Unfortunately, $\boxed{\text{Control}}$ + $\boxed{\text{Home}}$ does not work in the Resource Usage view.

5. Go to the first over-allocation by choosing the **Resource** tab, in the **Level** group, and clicking on **Next Over-allocation** 📊. Project 2010 starts at the date you have in view and searches forward day by day to find the next over-allocation. It does not stick to the selected resource.

6. Determine if the over-allocation is serious enough that it needs resolution. In our curriculum, we require project managers to resolve over-allocations when they exceeded 150% of a person's availability on a day-to-day basis and 120% on a week-by-week basis. Thresholds like these should be established within your organization. Resolve the serious over-allocations one by one.

Please note that the tool **Next Over-allocation** 📊:

➤ Often finds trivial over-allocations that you should ignore, for example two 1 hour tasks overlap

➤ Skips over-allocations that happened in the past, which is fine

➤ Sometimes does not find over-allocations that are serious

Nevertheless, we recommend this tool as the best tool available in Project 2010.

In the next illustration, you can see how the over-allocation is solved by delaying one of the tasks that was competing for the same resource:

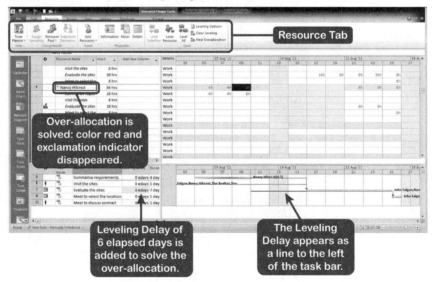

The bottom view can be improved by displaying a line for the total slack as well. If the free slack is not large enough, the total slack may provide possibilities to resolve the over-allocation. You will have to add a colored line for total slack to each task bar.

Click in the timescale portion of the bottom view, right click and choose **Bar Styles**. Scroll down until you see the **Slack** line item which depicts free slack.

Cut the **Slack** line and paste it back in twice. Change the **Name** of the first one to **Total Slack** and under **To** select **Total Slack** from the list. Change the name of the second one to **Free Slack** and change the **Shape** to the second to last item in the list (bar in middle) and change the color to **Lime** (light green) as shown in the following screenshot:

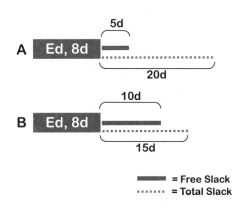

The Total Slack row is inserted above the Free Slack row.

 If you keep the same Shape, the lines will fall on top of one another. If you insert the total slack item above the free slack item, the shorter free slack line will be superimposed on the total slack line. Project 2010 creates the bars in the order they are listed. Now you can see how far you can delay tasks without affecting the next constraint date or the project end date.

If a task does not have enough free slack to solve over-allocations, you can use its total slack to solve the work overload. In the illustration, task A doesn't have enough free slack to solve the over-allocation, but it does have enough total slack. If you go beyond the total slack, you are slipping a constraint date or increasing the project duration. In the illustrated example, we would prefer to delay task B, since it resolves the over-allocation within the free slack, even though task B has less total slack. This assures us that no other successor is affected, which keeps the rest of the schedule the same. That is why we suggested the bright green for free slack and darker green for total slack. If we delay task A, successors will be affected. The art of project management is often to minimize the turbulence.

 A new feature in Project 2010 is the Team Planner View. This view displays the assignments for each resource in a time-phased, horizontal bar chart. The over-allocated portion of each assignment is indicated with a red bar above the assignment and a red bar below. Where previous versions of Project required you to assign resources to tasks, the Team Planner lets you assign tasks to resources. You may find this more intuitive to use.

To view the **Team Planner**, on the **Resource** tab, in the **View** group, click on **Team Planner**.

This new view allows you to manually level workloads visually. Tasks can be:

➤ Dragged into another resource's "swim lane" to reallocate the work
➤ Dragged to a new date (not recommended because you'll add a constraint date)
➤ Redistributed between different resources using defined assignment units

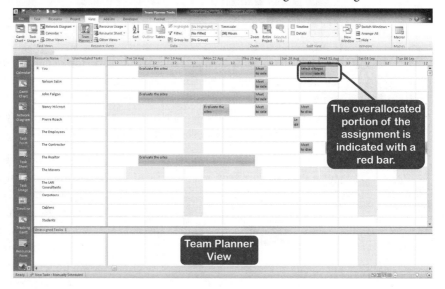

The overallocated portion of the assignment is indicated with a red bar.

Team Planner View

Have Project 2010 Level the Workloads

Level Facility and Machine Resources

To level human resources, you fill workloads up to the limit of their availability. If someone is only used 80% of his time, another small, part-time task could be added without causing over-allocation. We call this percentage leveling, since you try to fill availability up to 100%. This is what Project 2010 does.

In general, facilities and machines are either occupied or not and need yes/no leveling. Unfortunately, Project 2010 doesn't consider facilities and machines as separate types of resources. If you only assign facilities and machines at 100%, you can emulate yes/no leveling. Many people create a reservation system for boardrooms and training rooms outside of Project 2010 to keep their "workload" reasonable. You want planned availability to affect the forecasts in your project model. This assumes that you treat machines and facilities as work resources for the purpose of leveling.

Materials are consumable and don't need leveling. Materials are excluded from leveling and Project 2010 automatically sets the resource field **Can Level** to No.

Choose the Leveling Options

On the **Resource** tab, in the **Level** group, click on **Leveling Options** 📄 to access the **Resource Leveling** dialog box. We will discuss this dialog box section by section:

Leveling calculations

> ➤ We recommend you select ◉ **Manual**. If you select manual leveling, you can still have Project 2010 level the workloads whenever you want by clicking [Level Now] at the bottom of the same dialog. You can also delete any traces of leveling by clicking [Clear Leveling...] in this dialog; this will change all values in the task field **Leveling Delay** to zero.

Automatic leveling continuously levels the workloads and makes the task bars jump all over the place with every change you make in the schedule. Project 2010 levels mostly by delaying tasks. This option is a global option that takes effect in all your project schedules. Also, because you can often find better schedules by hand, we don't recommend using automatic leveling.

> ➤ In the list, **Look for over-allocations on a ... basis**, you can choose the granularity with which Project 2010 combs through the data to find over-allocations. A double workload on Monday, but a total workload of 16 hours in a week, constitutes an overload on a day-by-day basis, but not on a week-by-week basis. The setting is about the granularity of leveling. We recommend using **Day by Day** or **Week by Week** for most projects.

➤ Select ☑ **Clear Leveling values before leveling** if you want to clear the field Leveling delay of values left by previous leveling. Clear it if you want Project 2010 to add to the leveling delays incrementally; this often leads to unnecessarily long project durations. You may want to check this box if you are leveling one resource at a time. With this box checked, Project 2010 will not erase the previous resource you leveled.

Leveling range for <name of project>

➤ Select ◉ **Level entire project**. You normally level the entire project, but you can also indicate a date range.

Resolving over-allocations

➤ Select or clear **Level only within available Slack**.
You can check this option to develop a scenario when you want to know how many of the over-allocations Project 2010 can resolve within a certain time frame. Clear it if you want Project 2010 to resolve all your over-allocations; if you have kept the schedule dynamic, it will solve them all.

➤ ☑ **Leveling can adjust individual assignments on a task**
Check this option if you want to find the shortest, leveled schedule. If you have more than one person assigned to a task, this option will reschedule the individual assignments rather than all assignments as a group. The result is that task bars are often split into multiple parts, because each assignment on the task will be scheduled separately. This option is not applicable to tasks on which people are supposed to collaborate live in real time. If you use this option, you can still override it for certain tasks by entering **No** in the task field **Level Assignments**. Notice that Project 2010 sets this field by default to *No* for fixed duration and recurring detail tasks; for all other tasks it is set to *Yes*. If you clear it, Project 2010 will schedule the task only when the whole group is available.

➤ ☑ **Leveling can create splits in remaining work**
Select this option if you want to allow Project 2010 to split task bars. Splitting may generate a tighter schedule, because if you allow splitting, Project 2010 can schedule around tasks that have fixed dates. The drawback is that task bars become fragmented. If you want to exclude certain tasks from being split, clear their task field **Leveling can split**. Fixed duration tasks have this field set to *No* and will not be split by Project 2010, because it would increase their duration.

Three Automatic Leveling Scenarios

Again, make sure you have assigned resources to detail tasks before you start automatic leveling. If you haven't assigned resources to all detail tasks, you have not captured all the workloads, and the forecasts after leveling will be too optimistic. In the **Resource Usage** view, click on the heading **Unassigned** to view unassigned tasks. Typically, only the milestones and perhaps the recurring detail tasks should be listed in the **Unassigned** category. You can also use the Team Planner view to review unassigned tasks.

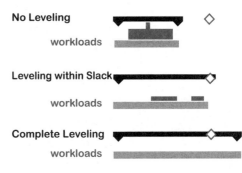

There are three scenarios you can develop with Project 2010, and you can switch back and forth among them as many times as you need to. Each scenario provides some useful information. The illustration shows all three, with the over-allocations shown in blue.

> **No leveling**
> If you look at the timescale in the Gantt Chart view, you often see several tasks scheduled concurrently. Where two concurrent tasks have the same resource assigned, the workloads can exceed the availability of the resource. If there are no over-allocations, you will not need to level. In that case, only the task durations and dependencies drive the duration of the project. This scenario answers the question: What is the project duration when the workloads are not leveled? This scenario tells us the minimum duration for the project.

> **Leveling within the slack of the project**
> If you create a milestone with a Must Finish On constraint on the proposed target date, you can level within the slack this hard date creates. This scenario answers the question: What workload will critical resources have while meeting the project target date? This scenario tells you how many extra resources you should hire in order to meet the target date.

> **Complete leveling**
> This answers: What is the end date of the project if the workloads of all resources are entirely leveled? This shows a comfortable deadline for the project and the team.

All three scenarios provide useful information when negotiating deadlines with upper management or clients:

➤ The no-leveling date from the first scenario is your resistance point in negotiations; you should not commit to an earlier date. You will still have to resolve all over-allocations if you commit to this date without delaying the project finish date which can be challenging depending on how many over-allocations you have.

➤ The remaining over-allocations from the second scenario may provide the common ground in your negotiations with the client. You can ask Project 2010 to resolve as many over-allocations as it can while staying within a certain time frame. You can then easily find out how many extra resources you need to hire to meet the target date and calculate the cost. If the client is willing to pay for the extra resources, you may have a date that meets your mutual needs.

➤ The finish date of the third scenario of complete leveling is the date we recommend you first quote to your client. It is a date that is nice to have, and that you will likely not get. It could be your starting position in negotiations.

Use the Leveling Gantt view to review the results of the leveling feature.

On the **Task** tab, in the **View** group, click on the **Gantt Chart** down-arrow. Select **More Views**, select **Leveling Gantt** from the list and click Apply.

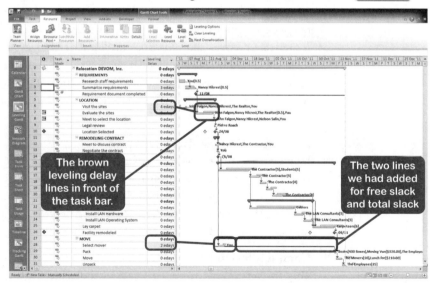

This view includes the field **Leveling Delay** as one of the columns, and also shows the delay graphically with a brown colored line to the left of any task bars that were delayed.

You can even make the three scenarios show up side by side in one Gantt Chart, which we will explain in detail.

No Leveling or
Clearing the
Leveling

You can only clear the leveling if you are in one of the task views. Change to a task view first, if necessary.

1. If you have leveled workloads before, the field **Leveling Delay** will have entries. To check if this is the case, make sure you see the **Leveling Delay** column.

2. To remove the leveling delay, on the **Resource** tab, in the **Level** group, click on **Leveling Options** . The **Resource Leveling** dialog box appears:

> Resource Leveling
>
> Leveling calculations
> ○ Automatic   ◉ Manual
> Look for overallocations on a   Day by Day ▼ basis
> ☑ Clear leveling values before leveling
>
> Leveling range for 'Relocation Chapter 8.5'
> ◉ Level entire project
> ○ Level   From: 01/08/12 ▼
>   To: 20/11/12 ▼
>
> Resolving overallocations
> Leveling order: Standard ▼
> ☐ Level only within available slack
> ☑ Leveling can adjust individual assignments on a task
> ☑ Leveling can create splits in remaining work
> ☐ Level resources with the proposed booking type
> ☑ Level manually scheduled tasks   **Level manually check box.**
>
> Help | Clear Leveling... | Level All | OK | Cancel

Project 2010 can level all the workloads in the schedule and remove all Leveling Delay. The Clear Leveling button is only enabled if a task view is active.

3. Select ◉ **Manual** and click [Clear Leveling...]; the **Clear Leveling** dialog appears:

> Clear Leveling   X
> ◉ Entire project   OK
> ○ Selected tasks   Cancel

4. Select ◉ **Entire Project** and click [OK]; you are now back in the task view. The numbers in the field **Leveling Delay** should all be zero.

5. If you want to compare all three scenarios in one Gantt Chart, you should at this point save the dates of this version. On the **Project** tab, in the **Schedule**

group, click on **Set Baseline** down-arrow 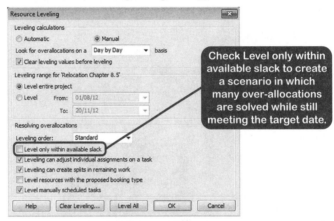, **Set Baseline** and select ◉ **Save interim plan** and **Copy Start/Finish into Start1/Finish1**.

You now know the minimum duration for your project; there can still be over-allocations in the schedule that need to be taken care of.

Leveling within the Slack of the Project

1. Make sure you have a project finish milestone where all dependencies come together. The project milestone should have a Must Finish On constraint on the proposed target date; a Finish No Later Than constraint does not work here. Make sure you have a minimum of other constraint dates, since they hinder the automatic leveling.

2. On the **Resource** tab, in the **Level** group, click **Leveling Options** and the **Resource Leveling** dialog box appears:

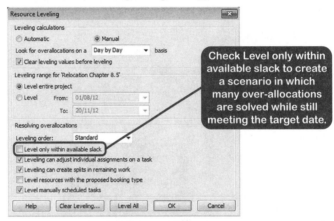

> Check Level only within available slack to create a scenario in which many over-allocations are solved while still meeting the target date.

3. Choose the granularity of the leveling by selecting from the list **Look for over-allocations on a …** basis the time unit in which Project 2010 should find over-allocations. We recommend **Day by Day** or **Week by Week** for most projects.

4. Check ☑ **Clear leveling values before leveling** to clear the field **Leveling delay** of old leveling values; Project 2010 will make a fresh start with the leveling.

5. Check ☑ **Level only within available slack**.

6. Clear ☐ **Level resources with the proposed booking type** unless you want the workloads of resources that are proposed but not committed on potential projects to be leveled as well.

7. Click [Level Now]. Project 2010 may alert you that it cannot resolve certain over-allocations, which is what we expected, since we gave it a fixed time frame.

8. Click [OK].

9. Check the workloads of the resources; there are often some over-allocations left.

10. If you want to compare all three scenarios in one Gantt Chart, you should at this point save the dates of this version. On the **Project** tab, in the **Schedule** group, click the **Set Baseline** down-arrow, **Set Baseline** and select ◉ **Set interim plan** and **Copy Start/Finish into Start2/Finish2**.

The workloads of the resources are likely still too high to meet the deadline, and you can analyze how much extra expense you would have to solve the over-allocations by hiring temporary workers. Or you can explore other methods to make the workloads reasonable.

Complete Leveling

1. Check if you have many hard scheduling constraints, because they will hinder this process of complete leveling.

2. If needed, insert the column **Leveling Delay** by right-clicking on the column heading **Duration**, choosing **Insert Column** and selecting the field **Leveling Delay** from the list. This field allows us to see the result of the leveling.

3. On the **Resource** tab, in the **Level** group, click **Leveling Options** within the **Level grouping ...**; the **Resource Leveling** dialog appears:

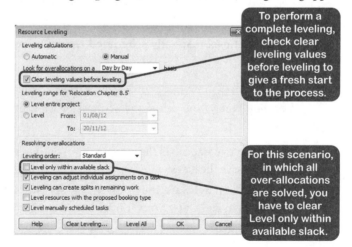

4. Choose the precision of the leveling by selecting from the list **Look for over-allocations on a** granularity with which Project 2010 should find over-allocations. We recommend **Day by Day** or **Week by Week** for most projects.

5. Select ☑ **Clear leveling values before leveling** if you want to clear the field **Leveling delay** of old leveling values, which we recommend.

6. Select ◉ **Level entire project**.

7. Clear ☐ **Level only within available slack**; otherwise Project 2010 may not solve all over-allocations.

8. Select ☑ **Leveling can adjust individual assignments on a task** if you want to find the shortest leveled schedule. Project 2010 schedules the assignments individually instead of as a group. You may end up with split task bars, but you can redo the leveling and clear the option to prevent bar splits, or you can set the task field **Level assignments** to *No* for task bars you don't want to be split.

9. Select ☑ **Leveling can create splits in remaining work** if you want to allow Project 2010 to split task bars. The drawback is that the task bars become fragmented. If you want to exclude certain tasks from being split, set their task field **Leveling can split** to *No*. Fixed duration tasks have this field already set to *No*.

10. Clear ☐ **Level resources with the proposed booking type**, unless you want resource workloads that are proposed but not committed on potential projects to be leveled as well. This is only relevant when using Project Server 2010.

11. Select ☑ **Level manually scheduled tasks** (unless there is a reason not to).

12. Click ⬚ Level Now . Project 2010 will delay certain tasks. In the column **Leveling Delay**, you can see which tasks have been delayed and by how long.

13. If you want to compare all three scenarios in one Gantt Chart, you should at this point save the dates of this version. On the **Project** tab, in the **Schedule** group, click on **Set Baseline** down-arrow, **Set Baseline** and select ◉ **Set interim plan** and **Copy Start/Finish into Start3/Finish3**.

The schedule is now realistic in the sense that the resources can finish the work assigned to them without the project end date slipping further. Check the end date in the **Finish** column of the project summary task; it has likely been delayed. Project 2010 will only be able to solve over-allocations without delaying the project finish when they are small.

Comparing the Three Scenarios in One Gantt Chart

To compare the three scenarios in terms of dates on the different milestones, you should create a new view and select separate bar styles for the Start1/Start2/Start3 data sets. These steps assume that you have already captured the three scenarios as shown in previous procedures.

1. On the **Task** tab, in the **View** group, click on **Gantt Chart** down-arrow, **More View**s and the **More Views** dialog box appears:

    > More Views
    >
    > Views:
    > Bar Rollup
    > Calendar
    > Descriptive Network Diagram
    > Detail Gantt
    > Gantt Chart
    > Gantt with Timeline
    > Leveling Gantt
    > Milestone Date Rollup
    > Milestone Rollup
    > Multiple Baselines Gantt
    > Network Diagram
    >
    > New... Edit... Copy... Organizer..
    >
    > Apply Cancel

    To show 3 scenarios in one Gantt, use the Multiple Baseline Gantt and Copy it.

2. Select **Multiple Baselines Gantt** and click Copy... .

3. The **View Definition** dialog box appears:

    > View Definition in '09 Optimizing - Time Cost 1'
    >
    > Name: Copy of Multiple Baselines Gantt
    > Screen: Gantt Chart
    > Table: Entry
    > Group: No Group
    > Filter: All Tasks
    > ☐ Highlight filter
    > ☐ Show in menu
    >
    > Help OK Cancel

4. Change the name of the new view to a descriptive title such as *Leveling Scenarios*. You can keep the rest of the settings.

5. Select ☑ **Show in menu**; the view will be available with only three mouse-clicks.

6. Click OK ; you are now back in the **More Views** dialog.

7. Click Apply .

8. In the **Gantt Chart** view, on the **Format** tab, in the **Bar Styles** group, click on the **Format** down-arrow 🖌, **Bar Styles** and change the settings so that

instead of the baseline dates the Start1/Finish1- Start3/Finish3 dates are shown. The changes you need to make are shown in the following dialog:

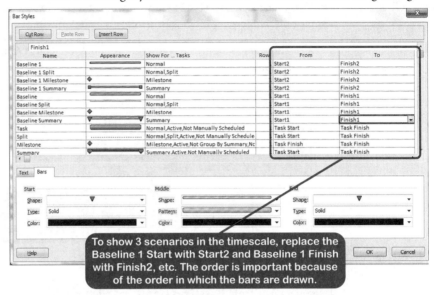

To show 3 scenarios in the timescale, replace the Baseline 1 Start with Start2 and Baseline 1 Finish with Finish2, etc. The order is important because of the order in which the bars are drawn.

9. Notice the order in which the dates are entered into the dialog. This order is a deliberate choice, since items listed higher are overlaid by lower items. Click OK.

10. You should now see the three task bars for each task and have the three scenarios next to each other in the timescale:

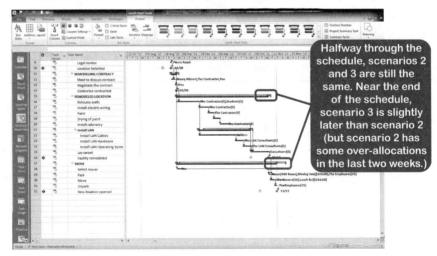

Halfway through the schedule, scenarios 2 and 3 are still the same. Near the end of the schedule, scenario 3 is slightly later than scenario 2 (but scenario 2 has some over-allocations in the last two weeks.)

Influencing Project 2010's Leveling

How can you predict which tasks will be postponed when resources are over-allocated? When you ask Project 2010 to level your schedule, it will try to intelligently choose which tasks to delay. It looks at the amount of slack on both tasks that compete for the same resource. It will delay the task that has most slack. This is smart, because the tasks with most slack are least likely to affect your project end date. However, it does not always delay the task you would prefer. Project 2010 offers you three choices to influence which tasks are delayed. You will find these on the **Resources** tab: in the **Level** group, click **Leveling Options** , **Leveling order** list down-arrow.

Here are some suggestions on when to use each:

> **ID Only**
> Project 2010 will level tasks based upon their ID numbers. It will give priority to tasks higher up in the list of tasks. Use this setting to prioritize projects in a consolidated schedule. Put your highest priority projects at the top of the list and then level your consolidated schedule using this option. Dragging projects up and down the list is less effort than maintaining priority numbers. (See Appendix 2 for information on how to consolidate schedules.)

> **Standard**
> This is the default setting and is used for regular leveling. Under standard leveling, the task with the most slack will be delayed.

> **Priority, Standard**
> When you aren't entirely happy with Project 2010's leveling, you can enter a priority number for certain tasks in the field Priority. In this way, you can influence which task is delayed in the leveling. This involves a fair bit of work if you do it on a task-by-task basis; it's quicker if you fill down a priority number for all tasks of a deliverable. Priority numbers can range from 0 to 1000. The higher the number, the higher the priority, and the more likely it will be that the task keeps its current dates.

Another way to influence leveling is to exclude certain tasks or resources as candidates for leveling.

Excluding Tasks from Project 2010 Leveling

If the priority number is set to 1000, Project 2010 will not delay the task, and will effectively exclude it from the leveling process. This is even the case if you use the ID or Standard setting in the Leveling order list.

Excluding Resources from Project 2010 Leveling

Typically, you would exclude subcontractor resources from leveling, because the workload of people external to your organization is normally not your problem.

You can exclude human resources by entering *No* in the resource field **Can Level**, or you can select which resources want to level:

1. In the **Resource Sheet** view select the resources you want to include.

2. In the **Resource** tab, in **Level Group,** click **Level Resource** 🐾, the **Level Resource** dialog box appears:

3. You can change the resources selected in the dialog box, and then click [Level Now]. Project 2010 will only level the workloads for those resources you selected. This allows you to quickly develops several scenarios.

Should I Level Myself or Have Project 2010 Level?

We've now discussed both ways of leveling workloads: doing it yourself or having Project 2010 do it for you. If you struggle with which to choose, here are some guidelines:

➤ If you have just a few over-allocations in your schedule, you could probably resolve them all yourself without puzzling for hours. If this is the case, we recommend you do it yourself by hand and don't use Project 2010's leveling features. You can think of ways to resolve these over-allocations that Project 2010 is not capable of doing. Project 2010 can only resolve over-allocations by delaying tasks, which may delay your project end date.

➤ If there are many over-allocations in your schedule, resolving them all by hand is a lot of work, and in that case, it may be easier to perform a complete leveling. This will likely push your project end date far out. You can then improve that date by finding the resource-critical path in your schedule and focusing on the resource-critical tasks. We will explain the concept of the resource-critical path in the next section.

How Leveling Affects the Critical Path

In the illustration below, there are two tasks: *write* a report and *read* another unrelated document. The tasks are not dependent upon each other; Harry can

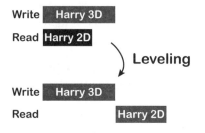

choose to do them in any order. Before leveling, the critical path is the task *write*. After leveling, *read* is the only critical task. Try this out in Project 2010! Don't worry, there is nothing wrong with your software; this is how the critical path algorithm is supposed to work and works in other scheduling software as well. The critical path theory assumes that you have access to unlimited resources.

In Project 2010, the leveled mini-schedule looks as follows:

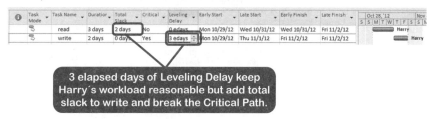

3 elapsed days of Leveling Delay keep Harry's workload reasonable but add total slack to write and break the Critical Path.

Here are the mathematics of the algorithm:

➤ On the forward pass, the Early Start for write is day 1 and the Early Finish is day 3 given the duration of 3 days. For *read* the Early Start is day 1; remember that there is no dependency between the tasks, and the Early Finish is at the end of day 5, given the delayed start date of day 4.

➤ On the backward pass, the Late Finish for read is also day 5; the Late Start, therefore, is day 4. *Write* has to be finished on the project finish date; the Late Finish date is day 5, since there is no dependency between the two. It has to start, at the latest, on day 3 to meet this date.

The total slack (Early Finish date subtracted from Late Finish date) of the task *read* is 5 − 5 = 0 days; the task is critical and highlighted in red. The total slack for *write* is 5 − 3 = 2 days; the task is not seen as critical by the algorithm. However, common sense dictates that there really is no slack on the task *write*, because it competes for the same resource, Harry. And if the task *write* takes longer, the task *read* will be moved out.

This example demonstrates the weakness of the critical path algorithm. The algorithm doesn't take resource dependencies into account, because it is built on the assumption that you have access to unlimited resources.

Access to unlimited resources is seldom the current reality in the global marketplace. Many organizations find themselves having to level the workloads of their resources, and in doing so, the critical path often becomes fragmented. The leveling of tasks can make the calculated total slack value of tasks meaningless and therefore the critical path as well. In fact, tasks with total slack may be driving the project end date, as is the case with the task *write* in the previous example. If *write* slips, it will move *read*, because of the resource dependency of Harry assigned to both tasks. The slack is false slack.

Critical Path or Resource-Critical Path?

We need a smarter critical path that takes resource dependencies as well as logical dependencies into account. We call this the resource-critical path (RCP).

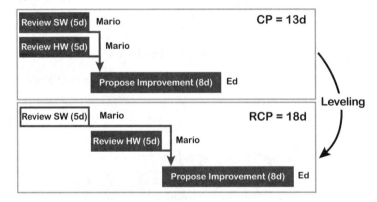

Given the example in the illustration, what should a project manager monitor, the critical path (CP) or the RCP? The answer is obvious. One should try to find the RCP in resource-constrained projects, rather than the critical path. Only the RCP provides a complete explanation of the project duration. It shows what drives the project end date at any time during the project duration, just as the critical path does in logic-constrained projects. The RCP is more helpful in a leveled schedule.

The Resource-Critical Path

The RCP describes a condition when tasks compete for the same resource at any point in time; those tasks have a resource dependency. An RCP looks at the logical dependencies **and** resource dependencies in the series of tasks and then determines the project duration based on this.

A task can be resource-critical because of a logical dependency or a resource dependency with another task. Notice the definition of an RCP is not very different from the critical path definition. However, other common descriptions of the critical path, like the sequence of tasks without slack, do not apply to the RCP, because resource-critical tasks can have slack. In the example we just discussed, the task *write* has slack, but still drives the project end date and is therefore as critical as *read*. Both are resource-critical tasks, however, because the same resource works on them. The RCP, in other words, is the chain of tasks that drives the project end date while taking into account that resources have limited availability. When you have relatively few resources, you should focus on the RCP instead of on the critical path.

An easy way to find out if you're in a resource-constrained situation is by leveling the workloads completely: if your project end date slips and the over-allocations are gone, you are in a resource-constrained project. If the end date did not slip, you are in a logic-constrained project.

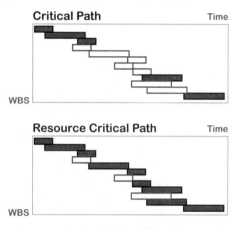

You can see in the illustration above that the RCP often includes some early critical tasks and then resource-critical tasks that are delayed, because of leveling. All those tasks drive the project end date. Resource-critical tasks are tasks that, when delayed, make the project end date slip. In a leveled schedule, any resource can be so limited in availability, or needed so much, that it could drive the project finish date.

Finding the Resource-Critical Path

1. Check the workloads and level them
2. **Show the resource-critical path (RCP)**
3. **Find the critical resources**
4. Make a change to those tasks
5. Consider impacts on quality, scope and risk
6. Decide whether you want to keep the change
7. Repeat steps 3 – 7

The next step is to find and highlight the RCP. There is no feature in Project 2010 that highlights the RCP for you. Therefore, it will involve some effort from you to implement the concept of the RCP. In order to optimize the schedule, it is imperative that you do identify the RCP.

We will discuss two methods to find the RCP: a manual process and an automatic process. IIL provides a macro that will automate finding your RCP.[6] If you manage resource-constrained projects, it will make your life much simpler.

> **Manual process**
> We recommend this process for small projects. Also, this process will help you truly understand the concept of an RCP and for that reason, we recommend you try this process first to enhance your understanding of RCPs.

> **Automatic process**
> After you understand the concept of the RCP, use our macro that identifies the RCP in your schedule very quickly. This macro is included in the files available for download that come with this book.[7]

Manual Process

It's easiest to identify resource-critical tasks by starting at the project end milestone and tracking backward. Look for driving predecessors or resources that are shared between the tasks. Tasks that are resource-critical have either a logical dependency or a resource dependency with earlier tasks. A logical dependency is shown as an arrow between the task bars in the Gantt timescale. A resource dependency occurs when two tasks are competing for the same resource. We recommend that you use the Gantt chart to identify the RCP: you can see in the timescale to the right of the task bars which resources are assigned.

Once you understand the process, you can find the RCP manually in a small schedule of up to one hundred tasks within minutes. In larger schedules, we recommend you use the automatic process.

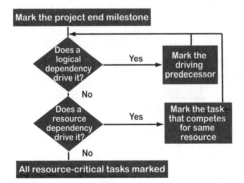

The flowchart gives an overview of the process. You will work backwards starting with the project finish milestone. This milestone is by definition resource-critical, so you mark it using the Marked field right away. You then ask yourself for this milestone: Does a logical dependency drive it? You check all the predecessors of the project milestone and determine which one is driving it to the date on which it starts. You will find a predecessor that has a finish date that is just before the start date of the finish milestone. Once you have found the

---

6   The RCP macro only works properly with the English version of Project 2010. IIL owns the copyright of this macro that was developed by Ken Jamison and adapted by Rafael Ruiz. This macro is provided for personal use only. If you would like to use this macro for business purposes, please contact our USA sales staff (212-758-0177) to purchase a corporate license.

7   See www.jrosspub.com.

driving task, you mark it as a resource-critical task. Then you go back to the top of the list of steps and start all over again with the marked task as the next task to analyze.

You start with the first question again: Does a logical dependency drive it? You check all its predecessors and check which predecessor finishes just before the detail task starts; this is most likely the driving predecessor. You may have to check for lags on dependencies to determine if the link is driving. If you find a driving predecessor, you mark it and go back to the top of the chart and continue with that task.

If you did not find a driving predecessor (which is often the case for detail tasks in a resource-constrained, leveled schedule), ask yourself the second question in the list of steps: Does a resource dependency drive it? Now you look at each resource assigned to the task, and you look for another task that finishes just before it that uses the same resource. Once you have found the driving task, you use the **Marked** field to mark the task that competes for the same resource and go back to the top of the step list and continue with that task. You continue until you have arrived at the project start date, at which point all resource-critical tasks are marked.

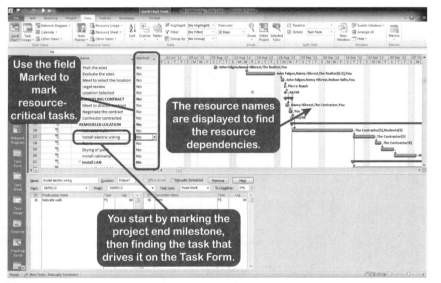

Use the field **Marked** to mark resource-critical tasks.

The resource names are displayed to find the resource dependencies.

You start by marking the project end milestone, then finding the task that drives it on the Task Form.

 As you can see in the screenshot, we recommend using the **Gantt Chart** with the **Task Detail Form** displayed at the bottom of the view to find the RCP. Make sure you insert the task field **Marked** to tag the tasks that you find to be resource-critical.

The steps to identify the RCP in your schedule are:

1. On the **Task** tab, in the **View** group, click on **Gantt Chart** down-arrow, **Gantt Chart**. Format the bars so that the resource name is shown to the right of the bars. Also, on the **Task** tab, in the **Properties** group, click on **Details** Details to display the **Task Details Form** (right click in the large grey blank area and select **Resources & Predecessors**) with the dependencies and their lags. Insert the field **Marked** and enter **Yes** for those tasks that you identified as resource-critical tasks. Mark all resource-critical tasks using the process explained above.

2. On the **Task** tab, in the **View** group, click the **Gantt Chart** down-arrow, **Tracking Gantt**, because it already has **Format**, **Bar Styles** settings that color the critical tasks red. Notice that the critical path is entirely fragmented: it does not explain the entire project duration, but the RCP does.

3. We will now make changes to the bar styles of the view, but you probably want to preserve the original Tracking Gantt view as well. Therefore, you should copy the Tracking Gantt view first. On the **View** tab, in the **Task Views** group, click on **Gantt Chart** down-arrow, **More Views**. The **More Views** dialog appears and **Tracking Gantt** is selected in the list. Click Copy... and enter a new name for the view, for exam *Resource-Critical Path*. Click OK and Apply. You are now back in the main screen with the new view displayed.

4. We will make the RCP look the same as the critical path. In the **Gantt Chart** view, choose the **Format** tab, and in the **Bar Styles** group, click **Format** down-arrow. Select **Bar Styles** and make changes to the bars so that all normal tasks have a blue task bar, except for tasks that are marked; they will appear in red. These changes are circled in the following screenshot:

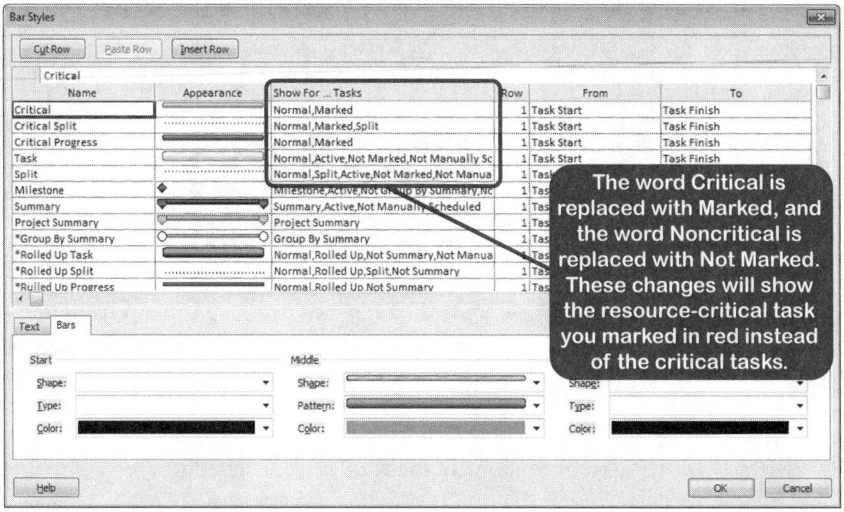

5. Click [OK]. You can now color task bars red if you change their field **Marked** to **Yes**, or you can change them back to blue by entering **No** in the **Marked** field. This is useful if you need to make corrections to your RCP.

6. Click ▼ in the column heading **Marked** and choose **Yes**. This filters and displays the resource-critical tasks only. To turn off the AutoFilter, on the **View** tab, in the **Data** group, click on the **Filter** down-arrow, **Display AutoFilter** ▽ selection to toggle on/off the AutoFilter.

7. Replace the % Complete to the right of the task bars with the resource names. On the **Format** tab, in **Bar Styles** group, click on **Format** down-arrow, **Bar Styles** and select the item **Critical**. Click tab **Text** and replace **% Complete** with **Resource Names**. You may want to get rid of the **% Complete** on the **Summary** tasks as well.

8. Make the dependency arrows disappear by starting with a **Gantt Chart** view and choosing the **Format** tab in the **Format** group. Click on **Layout** and under **Links**, select the first option.

If you follow these steps with the file *09 Optimizing - Time Cost Resources 5 – Intranet Project.mpp*[8], the schedule should now look like this:

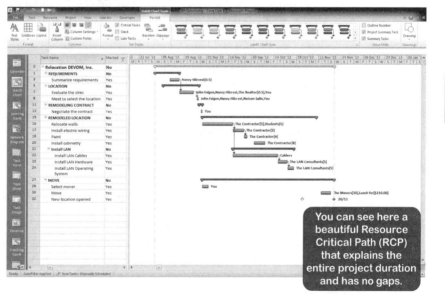

> You can see here a beautiful Resource Critical Path (RCP) that explains the entire project duration and has no gaps.

 To the uninitiated, the schedule now looks as if the regular red critical path is shown, except that it really is the RCP. The RCP drives the project end date, just like the critical path. The RCP provides a complete explanation for the project duration, just like the critical path would in a logic-constrained project. You

---

8   This file is available for download at www.jrosspub.com. Click the link *WAV Download Resource Center* to enter the download site.

could present this as your critical path to people who are not familiar with the concept of the RCP. They will not argue about the correctness of it, because you can easily prove that all red tasks drive the project end date. After all, if any of the tasks on the RCP slips, the project will take longer.

Automatic Process

Identifying the RCP should be done in an automated fashion, because when you are making changes to the schedule during optimization, you need to find the new RCP over and over again (just as you do with the critical path).

IIL now provides a macro that can identify the RCP in your schedule. You can run this macro by opening the file *IIL Project 2010 Tools.mpp* available for download at www.jrosspub.com. Click the link *WAV Download Resource Center* to enter the download site.

For the Project 2010 version, the RCP macro now identifies inactive and manual tasks and treats them as follows:

➤ Inactive tasks:
The schedule may contain inactive tasks. The macro simply does not consider them in the process to find the RCP.

➤ Manual tasks:
If the schedule contains a manual task that has a valid start date, a valid finish date and a valid duration, then the macro will include the task during the process to find the RCP.

If the schedule contains a manual task that has an invalid start date, finish date or duration, then the macro will inform you about it before the process begins.

RCP Macro - Verifing conditions

There are 5 invalid tasks that may affect the RCP.
(Manual tasks with invalid start, invalid finish or invalid duration)

Continue?

Yes   No

You still may go on with the RCP process but the results will be incomplete if the invalid manual task happened to be in the RCP.

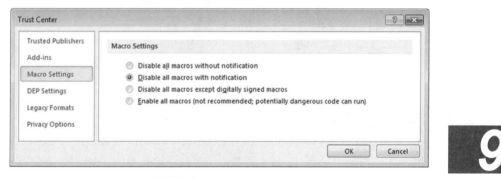

Here are the steps to run the RCP macro successfully:

1. Make a backup copy of the file you want to work with.

2. Open the file you want to work with.

3. On the **View** tab, in the **Macros** group, click the **Macros** down-arrow, **Macro Security**, **Macro Settings**. Select the **Disable all macros with notification** radio button.

4. Resolve all over-allocations in your .mpp file BEFORE you run the RCP macro.

5. Open a second file that contains the Macro *IIL Project 2010 Tools.mpp*. Enable macros when you open the file.

6. Switch to the .mpp file that you will run the RCP macro on, (**View** tab, **Switch** group, select the **Switch Windows** icon).

7. On the **View** tab, in the **Macros** group, click the **Macros** down-arrow, **View Macros**. Select the **RCP_2010** macro and click on **Run** to run the Macro.

8. Click on **Yes** to acknowledge the author and the copyrights of the macro.

9. The macro uses the **Marked** field. So, if your schedule has one or more tasks with a *Yes* value in the **Marked** field, a dialog box will give you an opportunity to copy the values of the **Marked** field to another **Flag** field.

10. When the macro finishes the RCP process, you will see a view called **RCP auto** that has been created by the macro. This view shows the Resource Critical Path.

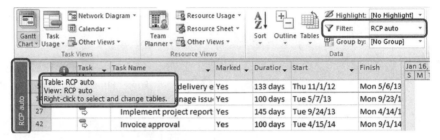

	Task	Task Name	Marked	Duration	Start	Finish	Jan 16,
		delivery e	Yes	133 days	Thu 11/1/12	Mon 5/6/13	
1		nage issu	Yes	100 days	Tue 5/7/13	Mon 9/23/1	
27		Implement project report	Yes	145 days	Tue 9/24/13	Mon 4/14/1	
42		Invoice approval	Yes	100 days	Tue 4/15/14	Mon 9/1/14	

Table: RCP auto / View: RCP auto / Right-click to select and change tables.

11. Before saving your schedule, make sure it is still intact, since IIL does not provide any warranties and cannot be held liable for damage to your schedule.

Why Should I Care About the Resource-Critical Path?

Since understanding the RCP approach requires some effort, we feel compelled to raise your motivation. Here are five reasons why applying the RCP approach is worthwhile in any resource-constrained schedule: the RCP drives the project end date, reveals the critical resource(s), uncovers potential domino effects, allows workload smoothing and allows smarter fast-tracking.

➤ **The RCP Drives the Project End Date**

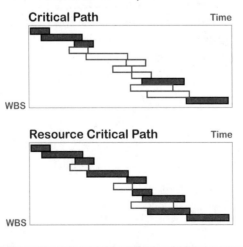

Typically, somewhere along the critical path, the resources start to constrain the schedule more than the logic, and the RCP overtakes the critical path, driving the project end date. As you can see in the illustration, the white tasks constitute the regular critical path, but leveling has delayed many of them. The result of leveling is shown as blue tasks. The

RCP is the combination of the critical tasks early in the schedule and all the resource-dependent tasks later on. If any of these tasks slip, the project will finish later; the resource-critical tasks drive the project end date.

Needing to review the RCP doesn't mean you can ignore CPM. There are many situations that are not resource-constrained, as well as situations in which organizations decide not to allow (lack of) resources to drive the schedule out. In those situations, the RCP is not needed and CPM will do.

➤ **The RCP Reveals the Critical Resource(s)**

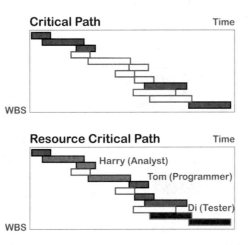

The RCP shows who the critical resources are and when they are critical. It's important to know at any time which resource determines the speed of progress in your project. Only when you know who is critical can you pay special attention to facilitating their work (e.g., provide a work environment that is free of interruptions, respond to issues promptly, and announce each week to the team who the critical resources are and ask the team to respect their time and provide whatever cooperation they need).

Managers get things done through others and the RCP allows project managers to focus on people instead of on tasks.

➤ **The RCP Uncovers Potential Domino Effects**

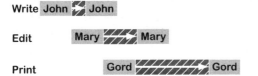

Have you ever experienced an avalanche of changes after you made one small change? If you make one change to a schedule, you may trigger a disastrous domino effect.

The illustration above shows that when John became sick, his task slipped. Mary had planned to finish her part just before her holiday. When John finished late, Mary had left for her holiday, so her part slipped even more. When she returned, finished her part and handed off to Gord, he was temporarily reassigned to another project and would return in 3 weeks. You decide not to wait for Gord and assign a new person. The new person will need 1 week of introduction and training, and so forth and so on… One little slip that seems innocuous can cause big delays because of resource dependencies. As we've said, project management is often the art of minimizing the turbulence.

The RCP makes the most important resource dependencies visible. If you make the relationships between the resources visible, you can make changes to the schedule in a more educated fashion. If you monitor only the conventional critical path, you may not realize that you are creating an avalanche of changes.

> ### The RCP Allows Workload Smoothing

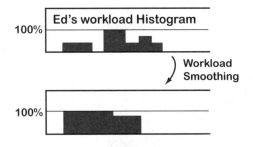

Often there is a huge cost involved with erratic workloads, as shown in the illustration.

How much does Ed's workload cost before and after smoothing? He has periods when he can twiddle his thumbs and other periods when he is overloaded (and may be wishing he had another job). We often see companies burn out their critical resources, especially in time-to-market organizations. If a critical resource burns out, the individual and the organization are severely hurt. For organizations, this often has expensive consequences in terms of dissatisfied employees, demoralized work culture, sick leave, attrition, as well as the cost of finding new, highly specialized people. It also costs money when deadlines are missed or contracts are lost.

The RCP keeps an eye on the workloads continuously, because workloads drive the RCP. Therefore, it allows you to monitor and manage workloads better. The eventual cost of a smooth workload is often less than the cost of an erratic one.

➤ **The RCP Helps to Fast-Track Smarter**

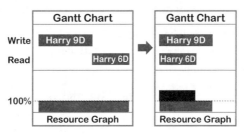

When fast-tracking your schedule, you may create workload problems if you only focus on the critical path.

You may work a long time to find a shorter schedule, and just when you think you have a better schedule, you may find you have only replaced time problems with workload problems. In the illustration, the dependency between *write* and *read* was cut, and this created an over-allocation for Harry. The schedule is no longer feasible. If you ignore the resource dependencies and just focus on logical dependencies, you may create short schedules. However, because of new over-allocations, these schedules may not be feasible.

What Is the Nature of the Beast?

Now that you understand why it's important, we'll explore the nature of the RCP a bit further.

First, it's important to realize that each resource has its own RCP. In the illustration, the schedule is leveled every time for only one of the resources. This creates as many RCPs as there are resources. Harry, Ed and Di are all critical resources, but when leveled, Di pushes the end date out farther than Harry or Ed does. Di is the most critical resource. When shortening Di's RCP, you will arrive at a point after which Ed is more critical than Di. At that point, you have to shift your focus to Ed's workload instead of Di's.

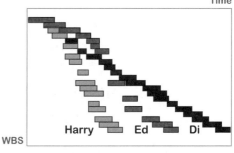

What we left out of this picture is that there are hand-off points between resources. The RCP may be pushed out farther than you would expect simply based on the RCPs of individuals. These hand-off points always run over a logical dependency. The logical dependencies link the chains of the resource dependencies together. The RCP has tasks that may be resource dependent on each other or logically dependent. The RCP typically reveals that multiple resources are on the RCP.

We'll present three different specific situations in which finding the correct RCP can be challenging:

➤ The RCP with multiple critical resources

> When multiple resources are assigned
> Both logical dependencies and resource dependencies exist

Scheduling software will have to find the right RCP in all three situations before one can reasonably state that a solid RCP algorithm has been found and this challenge has been met.

> **The RCP with Multiple Critical Resources**

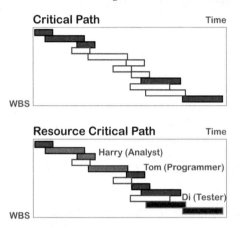

Different resources typically work on tasks on the RCP. In the typical software development project, the analysts drive the front end of the schedule, the programmers the middle and the testers the back end. Every time there's a hand-off to the next resource, there is a logical dependency. Again, logical dependencies connect the chains of resource-dependent tasks. The RCP clearly shows who is driving the project duration and when they are driving it.

> **When Multiple Resources are Assigned**

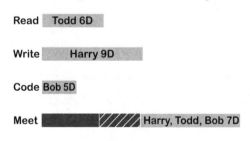

Multiple resources on a task pose a challenge for the algorithm that finds the RCP. The illustrated example has resources assigned full-time to the tasks shown and multiple resources assigned to the last task, Meet. The algorithm has to pick the right resource as the critical one. In this case, Harry is the critical resource. In the traditional Critical Path Method, this is similar to a task that has multiple predecessors and the algorithm has to identify the driving predecessor.

➤ **Logical Dependencies and Resource Dependencies**

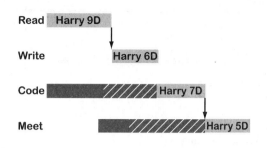

In the illustration, leveling has delayed the tasks *Code* and *Meet*. The difficulty in this situation is that there is no hard dependency between *Write* and *Code*, only a resource dependency. An algorithm that identifies the RCP has to be able to handle a combination of logical dependencies and resource dependencies. In the Manual Process flowchart, you therefore ask both questions. First, does a logical dependency drive the schedule? If not, does a resource dependency drive the schedule?

Methods to Optimize for Time, Cost and Resources

1. Check the workloads and level them
2. Show the resource-critical path (RCP)
3. Find the critical resources
4. **Make a change to those tasks**
5. Consider impacts on quality, scope and risk
6. Decide whether you want to keep the change
7. Repeat steps 3 – 7

We're now ready to make changes to the resource-critical tasks. When the project has to finish earlier than the current schedule, it has to be shortened. The best measurements are those that improve time, cost and resources and meet quality and scope requirements without increasing risk. Unfortunately, there are no such ideal measurements. What you choose will depend on your project's environment and context. The next table provides indications as to what the effect of each action could be in a typical project, but you have to ask yourself what the possible impacts in your own project might be. You need to consider actions previously explained in the sections on optimizing for time and optimizing for time and cost, and use them in combination with the following.

The actions are ranked in order of overall effectiveness. We recommend starting at the top of the table with the two fast-tracking methods. After exhausting the fast-tracking, go to the next action in the table.

9

	Action	For
1.	Change sequential dependencies into partial dependencies (fast-tracking)	resource-critical tasks
2.	Create parallel paths from a sequential path (fast-tracking)	resource-critical tasks
3.	Break down long tasks into many shorter ones	resource-critical tasks
4.	Change schedule constraints	resource-critical tasks
5.	Shorten lags (waiting periods)	resource-critical tasks
6.	Split task bars around a Must Start On task	resource-critical tasks
7.	Decrease duration estimates	resource-critical tasks
8.	Reduce the scope or delete tasks	resource-critical tasks
9.	Reallocate the best resources to the resource critical tasks	resource-critical tasks
10.	Increase assignment units to full-time assignments for critical resources	resource-critical, fixed work tasks
11.	Assign overtime hours to critical resources	resource-critical, fixed work tasks
12.	Add noncritical resources	resource-critical, fixed work tasks
13.	Replace critical resources with noncritical resources	resource-critical, fixed work tasks
14.	Remove a critical resource when multiple resources are assigned	resource-critical tasks
15.	Postpone vacation of critical resources to after the deadline	resource-critical tasks

Some remarks about optimizing an RCP:

➤ The methods are repeated in this table, because they are also valid in situations with limited resources. The difference is that these methods will now only work on resource-critical tasks instead of critical tasks. The actions are ranked by overall effectiveness.

➤ Fast-tracking on the RCP is not as effective as on the critical path. However, it still is the preferred method to start with because it is quality, scope and cost neutral. Fast-tracking is less effective on the RCP, because:

▶ There are fewer dependencies on a RCP, since it consists of logical dependencies and resource dependencies.

▶ You can't fast-track two tasks if the same resource is working on both tasks and they are linked. Fast-tracking is changing the dependencies in such a way that more tasks take place concurrently. When you overlap tasks, workloads are moved as well, and you may create over-allocations. Fast-tracking has to be applied with greater care. The RCP will show you which tasks have the same resources assigned that will cause new over-allocations when you overlap them. You should focus your fast-tracking efforts on tasks that are done by different resources. For example, when you remodel an office, the tasks of carpenters and electricians can overlap each other, as long as the carpenters start a few days ahead and finish a few days earlier. Fast-tracking is typically effective at hand-off points between critical resources.

➤ Actions 10 through 13 can shorten the durations of resource-critical tasks. These methods will work for all task types except Fixed Duration tasks. Before using one of these methods, you have to change the task Type to Fixed Work, assuming the amount of effort required stays the same.

➤ Overhead or support tasks should not be on the RCP. Overhead tasks support the real work and should not drive the project end date. If you see the project manager, team leaders, or technical support or administrative support people on resource-critical tasks, you may have found an easy way to shorten your project. In most cases, these people can and should be taken off the RCP. After all, they are managing or supporting the real critical resources (or at least that is what they are supposed to do).

We discussed the first eight methods; we will discuss the remainder of them next.

➤ Reallocate the Best Resources to the Resource Critical Tasks

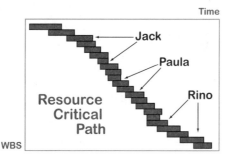

This is the best and most basic principle to apply when trying to find the shortest schedule possible while keeping quality up and cost down. After you have created the detailed schedule and leveled the workloads, you have a better idea about which tasks are driving your project duration: these are the resource-critical tasks. Ask yourself: Have I assigned my best resources to my most critical tasks? If not, you have an opportunity to shorten your project duration by moving your best resources to these tasks.

➤ Increase Assignment Units

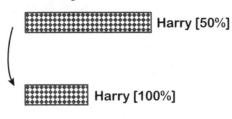

Harry [50%]

Harry [100%]

If a resource is working half-time on a critical task, you can finish the task earlier if you can get the resource to temporarily work full-time on it. Again, the right task type—fixed work—has to be applied if you want to see the duration decrease. You may have to negotiate for Harry with another project manager. (But remember to remind the other project manager that if you can have him full-time, you'll be able to release him sooner.)

To change a resource to full time, in the Gantt Chart, select a resource-critical task.

1. On the **Task** tab, in the **Properties** group, click on **Details** [icon] Details to display the **Task Details** Form at the bottom of the screen:

		Task Mode	Task Name	Type	Duration	Work	ul '12	22 Jul '12	05 Aug '12	19 Aug '12	02 Sep '12	16 Se
0			⊟ Relocation DEVOM, Inc.	Fixed Duration	80 days?	3,648 hrs						
1			⊟ REQUIREMENTS	Fixed Duration	11 days?	32 hrs						
2			Research staff requirements	Fixed Work	4 days?	16 hrs		You[0.5]				
3			Summarize requirements	Fixed Work	4 days?	16 hrs			Nancy Hilcrest[0.5]			
4			Requirement document completed	Fixed Duration	0 days	0 hrs			15/08			
5			⊟ LOCATION	Fixed Duration	16.5 days	224 hrs						
6			Visit the sites	Fixed Duration	1 day	32 hrs			John Falcon,Nancy Hilcrest,The Realtor,You			
7			Evaluate the sites	Fixed Duration	7 days	156 hrs				John Falcon,Nancy Hilcrest		

Name: Research staff requirements   Duration: 4 days?   ☑Effort driven ☐Manually Scheduled   Previous   Next

Dates   Constraint
Start: 01/08/12 ▾   As Soon As Possible ▾   Task type: Fixed Work ▾
Finish: 06/08/12 ▾   Date: 01/08/12 ▾   WBS code: 1.1
◉ Current ○ Baseline ○ Actual   Priority: 500 ⬍   % Complete: 0% ⬍

ID	Resource Name	Units	Work	Predecessor Name	Type	Lag
1	You	0.5	16h			

If you increase the units to 1(100%), the task duration will decrease and the RCP will be shorter.

2. Determine which assignment drives the duration of the task if more than one resource is assigned.

3. Select from the list **Task type** [Fixed Units] ▾ and click [OK]. This assures that Project 2010 will shorten the duration when you increase the resource units.

4. Increase the resource units on the task so that the resource works full-time on the critical task. Click [OK]. The duration should be decreased.

➤ Assign Overtime Hours

If you can get resources to work overtime, critical tasks can often be finished earlier. In the illustration, the second bar shows a shorter duration. Two situations can arise:

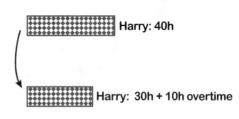

Harry: 40h

Harry: 30h + 10h overtime

▶ If overtime will not be charged to the project, then change the resource calendar of that particular resource. You can increase the working hours or change holidays to working days. You can compensate by giving the resource time off later.

▶ If overtime will be charged to the project at a higher overtime rate, then overtime should be entered in the overtime field (Ovt. Work) in the Task Details Form. The cost of the project will increase.

The detailed steps are:

1. Select a resource-critical task.

2. Pull up the **Task Details Form** in the bottom pane and right click in the large gray area to the right. Select **Work** to display the **Ovt. Work** field. The screen should now look like this:

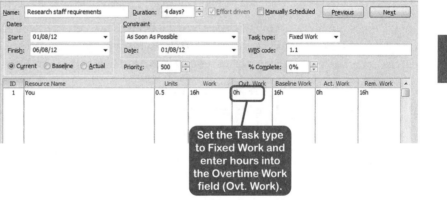

Set the Task type to Fixed Work and enter hours into the Overtime Work field (Ovt. Work).

3. Set the **Task type** to **Fixed Work** and click [OK].

4. Determine which resource drives the duration of the task, and enter the overtime hours to be worked in the field **Ovt. Work**.

5. Click [OK]; Project 2010 schedules the hours worked in overtime outside the regular working time and automatically calculates a shorter duration.

Do not lower the original work estimate; Project 2010 subtracts overtime from the original estimate before calculating the new duration.

➤ Add Noncritical Resources

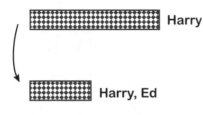

Two resources can normally finish a task faster than one (assuming it is easily divided). When you add a resource, the duration will decrease, but it will only decrease if you have the right task type applied to the task before adding the resource. When you add a resource to a fixed work task, the same amount of work is now performed by two resources and can be done twice as fast. Project 2010 will calculate this for you.

Let's think about what happens in practice. When you hire new resources, you have to train them. You would typically take your best resources off their crunching to train the new ones. At first, you will see a short-term decrease in the rate of progress. If all works well, you hope that in the longer term the progress accelerates. For this reason we have marked this method with a "?" for the Time dimension in the table. Look carefully at your situation to judge whether adding resources would actually help.

1. Select a resource-critical task.

2. On the **Task** tab, in the **Properties** group, click on **Details** ▦ Details to display the **Task Details Form** in the bottom of the screen. Determine which resource drives the duration of the task.

3. Select from the list **Task type** | Fixed Units ▼ | the type **Fixed Work** to ensure that Project 2010 will shorten the duration when a resource is added. Click | OK |.

4. Assign another resource and click | OK |; the duration should decrease.

➤ Replace Critical Resources

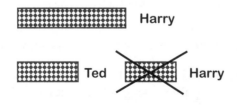

If you replace a critical resource with a noncritical resource, you may able to schedule more tasks in parallel. In the illustration, Ted replaces critical Harry on the second task, which can now be done in parallel with the first one. The gain in time equals the duration of the second task.

Some people argue that you cannot substitute critical resources; otherwise they would not be critical (as in "important"). Remember that the word critical has a different meaning in project management: it doesn't mean that the resource is important to the task, it simply means that the resource is driving the project duration. In fact, the resource could be a second-choice resource, and it is not a good idea to have your project duration be driven by second-choice resources if you are working against time. That's why we started by having you check if you applied your best resources to your most critical tasks.

1. In the **Gantt Chart**, select a resource-critical task on which you can replace a critical resource.

2. On the **Task** tab, in the **Properties** group, click on **Details** ⊞ Details to display the **Task Details Form** on the bottom of the screen. Determine which resource drives the duration of the task.

3. Click on the name of the critical resource in the **Task Details** Form and use the list [⠀⠀⠀⠀⠀⠀⠀⠀⠀⠀▼] to select the substitute resource.

4. Click [OK].

If you prefer to use the **Assign Resources** dialog instead:

1. On the **Resource** tab, in the **Assignments** group, select **Assign Resources** 🐾 and the dialog box appears:

Select the critical resource from the resources that are assigned. This enables the Replace button, which you can use to replace the resource.

443

2. Click on the critical resource in the **Assign Resources** dialog.

3. Click Replace.... The **Replace Resource** dialog overlays the **Assign Resources** dialog.

4. Click on the replacement resource, and click OK. Level your schedule again and keep the change if the duration of the project decreased; otherwise, return to the previous version by closing the schedule without saving.

➤ Remove a critical resource when multiple resources are assigned

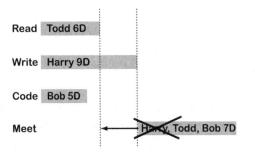

If there are multiple people working on a task, and one of them is a critical resource who has a lot of other work at the same time, you should ask yourself how important the involvement of the critical resource is on this task. If the other people could do without the critical resource, you should consider removing the critical resource from the task. (Again, a critical resource does not mean that the resource is important for the successful completion of the task.) In the illustration, Harry is removed from the task, which shortens the RCP.

➤ Postpone vacations

If you can convince your resource to postpone a vacation until after a critical deadline, you may be able to meet the deadline. In the illustration, the deadline is depicted as a diamond.

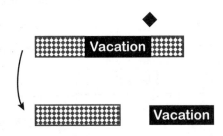

To move a vacation:

1. On the **Project** tab, in the **Properties** group, click **Change Working Time** and the **Change Working Time** dialog box appears:

The resources are in this list. When you select a resource, its resource calendar will be shown.

2. Under **For calendar:** `Standard (Project Calendar) ▾` select the specific resource calendar (previously created) with the vacation you want to postpone.

3. On the **Exceptions** tab in the **Change Working Time** dialog box, select the vacation exception that you want to edit under the **Name** column.

4. Move the vacation for this resource to later dates after the deadline in the **Start** and **Finish** columns. Move and edit these new vacation dates by clicking on the **Start** and **Finish** columns.

5. Next, select **Details** and in the **Details** dialog box make sure that **Nonworking** is selected for the new vacation exception time frame, then click `OK`.

6. Click `OK`. The schedule should now be shorter.

Consider the Impacts

> 1. Check the workloads and level them
> 2. Show the resource-critical path (RCP)
> 3. Find the critical resources
> 4. Make a change to those tasks
> **5. Consider impacts on quality, scope and risk**
> **6. Decide whether you want to keep the change**
> 7. Repeat steps 3 – 7

After making changes to time, cost and resources, you have to consider the impacts on quality, scope, and risk (the six competing demands).

You can now see how much time you have gained, and whether it is worth any sacrifices you may have made on the scope of the project or the quality of the deliverables.

Whenever you make a change to a resource-critical task, the workloads may move or change. You can check to see if this created new over-allocations by displaying the Resource Usage view. You may have to level the schedule again and determine the new RCP once more. You could make several changes before identifying the new RCP. At this point it may very well be an entirely different series of tasks.

Before identifying the RCP tasks again, we recommend that you unmark all resource-critical tasks first. To unmark all, click on the column heading **Marked** and on the **Task** tab, in the **Editing** group, **Clear** within the **Editing** grouping, click the **Clear** down-arrow , **Clear All**.

Optimizing for time, cost and resources is challenging and practitioners are greatly helped now that the RCP can be found automatically.

Simulation of the Resource-Critical Path

We discussed simulation of the critical path. You can also simulate resource-critical paths in resource-constrained schedules. You do need to change the leveling to automatic leveling so that the simulation software does not forget to keep the workloads reasonable.

On the **Resource** tab, in the **Level** group, click **Leveling Options** select **Automatic** and clear **Level only within available slack**.

This ensures that for each scenario of the schedule the workloads are entirely leveled before the project duration is calculated.

As you can imagine, simulating RCPs requires major computing power, so make sure you run this on the fastest computer in your office.

The reasons why you should consider simulating RCPs are the same reasons you'd simulate the critical path:

➤ Durations are more likely to extend than shrink. Estimates do not follow a normal distribution, but have a distribution that is typically skewed to the pessimistic side.

➤ The more parallel paths you have, the more delays will compound at the merge points (path convergence or merge bias).

If you simulate the RCP, you have taken care of all three assumptions that cripple the utility of the traditional critical path: the previous two reasons and the fact that the critical path assumes access to unlimited resources. This is what we recommend for resource-constrained projects.

Apart from that, there are extra factors that are quantified when you simulate resource-constrained schedules. We referred to these factors previously as domino effects:

➤ The average effect of fixed date personal vacations on the project duration. It is hard to predict how much the project end date will change when some tasks are moved a little bit. The simulation software will run many scenarios and will eventually average the impact of the hard-date vacations.

➤ The average effect on the project duration of asynchronous working hours of resources: What overall delay will you experience from some resources working a regular workweek and some a compressed workweek? This effect is also hard to predict other than through simulation.

➤ When you identify activities that have time risk, you should also identify those activities where exact resource availability is not entirely certain. When you decide what distribution curve you need on those tasks, you can incorporate the likelihood of resource availability in the range of estimates and the curve you choose for these tasks.

 The s-curve output from the simulation will indicate the probability by date for a range of project finish dates. Our experience is that most people tend to underestimate the overall effect of all the factors discussed. We see this over and over again in classes where we ask participants to estimate the outcome of a simulation on a tiny project while showing them the exact inputs of the simulation. We therefore recommend you quantify the factors we discussed that can throw your schedule off its baseline by simulating your schedules. After all, as a project manager, it is prudent to minimize so-called known risks. You will still have to deal with enough unknown unknowns.

Checks on the Optimized Schedule

Here are checks to verify if you have applied best practices when optimizing your schedule.

Optimizing Workloads

➤ Is the total effort within the person hour budget of the project (if a budget is available)?
To find the total effort of the project on the **Project** tab, in the **Properties** group, click **Project Information**, **Statistics...** Statistics... and look in row **Current**, column **Work**.

➤ Are the workloads for the resources reasonable?
  ▸ We work with these limits: the workload for individuals should not exceed 150% of their regular availability within any week and should not exceed 120% for periods longer than a week. The parameters may

differ for your organization. Be sure to check with your PMO (project management office) or the authority that sets these guidelines.

▶ The workload of consolidated resources (groups) should not exceed their availability.

▶ The workloads should be fairly smooth, since there are hidden costs involved with erratic workloads.

Note that it is not enough to just check if there is any red in the Resource Usage view. Project 2010 often highlights more resources in red than are truly over-allocated. If there is an over-allocation during only one business hour, the resource will be shown in red. On the **Resource** tab, in the **Level** group, click on **Next Over-allocation** 🔢 to check the over-allocations. This tool is more selective and more reliable. However, even this tool does not always find all over-allocations, and it also highlights trivial over-allocations (e.g., 1 hour).

Optimizing Costs

➤ Is the cost modeled using the right fields and in the appropriate way? The following fields are available in Project 2010:

▶ Resource Sheet fields: **Type**, **Material Label**, **Standard Rate**, **Overtime Rate**, **Cost Per Use** and **Accrue At**. A resource can also have a **Cost Rate Table**.

▶ Gantt Chart fields: **Fixed cost** and **Fixed cost accrual**.

➤ Is the total cost within the budget of the project (if a cost budget is available)? You can find the total cost of the project by checking **Project Statistics** and looking in row **Current**, column **Cost**.

Optimizing Time

➤ Are there as many parallel paths as logically possible in the network of dependencies?
Novice schedulers tend to schedule all tasks in one long sequential chain. This creates many soft dependencies that make the duration of the project unnecessarily long. When optimizing for time, it is important to schedule in parallel what logically can happen simultaneously.

➤ Are there any unresolved conflicts between the task calendars and resource calendars?
If there are conflicts, the forecasts may be too optimistic. You can find the conflicts by looking in the **Indicators** ℹ️ column for the icon 📇.

➤ Are the deadline dates and other constraints met in the schedule?
You can check this by applying filter **10 IIL Deadlines or Constraints not met**.[9] It displays tasks with deadlines or constraints that have negative slack. When deadline or constraint dates are not met, the schedule may forecast a project end date that is too optimistic.

---

9   This filter can be found in the file *IIL Project 2010 Tools.mpp* available for download at www.jrosspub.com. Click the link *WAV Download Resource Center* to enter the download site.

➤ Does the schedule have a critical path or a resource-critical path?
You can check the critical path by applying the Tracking Gantt view. This view highlights the critical path in red by default.

▶ If a schedule is extended when the workloads are leveled, a resource-critical path needs to be identified. Resource-critical tasks need to be marked manually.

▶ The (Resource) critical path can only consist of detail tasks and milestones. It should not contain level of effort tasks (overhead tasks or recurring tasks) or summary tasks (since the logic and the resources should be kept on the detail tasks).

➤ Does the (resource) critical path provide a complete explanation for the project duration?
You can check the completeness by displaying the (resource) critical path and checking for gaps. Normally, there should be no gaps and every business day should have at least one critical task (unless there are lags on critical dependencies). If you find gaps, the (resource) critical path is fragmented, and the tasks that are most critical need to be identified in the schedule.

Tools to Assist with Analyzing the Impact of Changes

In each of the optimization techniques, there is a need to analyze the impact of changes each time you attempt to compress the schedule. In presenting this material, we have suggested that you insert the project summary line (line 0) or use the Project Statistics tool to see the overall impact on the project. Project 2010 also offers three tools to assist you with viewing impacts at the task level.

Multiple Levels of Undo

Out of the box, Project 2010 comes with 20 levels of undo. You can increased this up to 99 levels: on the **File** tab, click on ⚙ Options , **Advanced**. Under the **General** section, change the **Undo** levels: to the desired number.

Having the ability to perform multiple levels of undo permits you to try out several different scenarios and "back out" of each one. You can try one set of changes and see the impact. If the impact is not what you were looking for, simply back out using the **Undo** toolbar button ↩ or use the drop-down arrow to the right of the button to select the point you want to roll back to.

Change Highlighting

When you make a change to a cell within Project 2010's tables, for example the Entry Table, Project 2010 will highlight all of the cells impacted by this change. This provides you with a great way to measure all of the impact to your schedule, not just the high-level overview. This feature can be customized through the **Gantt Chart** view, on the **Format** tab, in the **Format** group, click **Text Styles** 𝔸 . Under **Item to Change** select **Changed Cells**. Pick a background color to indicate the cells that have changed.

Task Inspector

During the discussion of Optimizing for Resources, we emphasized the importance of being able to determine the true driver of a task when identifying the resource critical path. We focused our discussion on logical dependencies and resource dependencies. Project 2010 provides a tool for helping identify the drivers of a particular task. On the **Task** tab, in the **Tasks** group, Click on the **Inspect down-arrow** ✎, **Inspect Task** to display the **Task Inspector** side pane on the left of the screen. (In Project 2007, this was called the Task Driver Pane.)

The **Task Inspector** side pane will indicate what is driving a particular task to start on a given date. Factors affecting the start of tasks include:

➤ Over-allocations and Repair Options
➤ Manual or Auto Scheduling Options
➤ Predecessor tasks
➤ Project, task and resource calendars
➤ Lags and leads
➤ Constraints
➤ Leveling delays

Since the driving force on any task could be a combination of these items, you will need to analyze the information to determine which of these is the primary driving force.

Create an RCP to focus on both critical tasks and resource limits by marking the appropriate tasks and, if desired, formatting the chart to display the resource critical tasks.

Review Questions

1. We described three optimization approaches in this chapter: optimizing for time; optimizing for time and cost; and optimizing for time, cost and resources.
   a. What are the main differences between these approaches?
   b. Describe the situations in which you should apply each.
   c. What are the common techniques used in each approach?

2. Total slack is:
   a. The amount of time a task can move freely without affecting its successors.
   b. The difference between the Late Finish date and Early Finish date of the task.
   c. The amount of time in which the resource has to complete the task.
   d. The difference between the Early Start of the earliest successor and the Early Finish date of the task.

3. You receive a schedule and notice that the project finish milestone has a negative Total Slack of 10 days. In your own words, what does this mean?

4. There are six possible causes for fragmentation of the critical path; list four of them.

5. When optimizing for time:
   a. What are the seven process steps for shortening the critical path?
   b. What are at least six of the nine possible methods to shorten the critical path?

6. One of your team leaders suggests that the duration of one of her critical tasks could be decreased if you provide her with more people to do the work. What factors should you consider?

7. What methods are available to decrease the cost of a project? Give at least four of the eight methods discussed.

8. If you have Project 2010 level the workloads in your schedule, would the project duration be longer or shorter than if you leveled the workloads yourself? Why?

9. There are many ways to level workloads manually. Name at least eight.

10. In your own words, how does Project 2010 leveling affect the calculation and the display of the critical path?

11. We discussed five reasons why finding the resource-critical path might be a good idea. Name three.

12. There are 15 methods with which you can shorten the resource-critical path. Name as many as you can.

13. A project is experiencing a lack of progress during execution.

    a. How would you determine which resources you should ask to work overtime in order to make up the slippage? They will not be paid a higher rate for overtime.

    b. What Ribbon items do you need to choose and what mouse-clicks do you need to make to enter overtime into Project 2010?

14. One way a project manager can identify task drivers is to "walk" backwards through the schedule identifying the logical dependencies or the resource dependencies. Project 2010 provides what tool that can assist with this? What are the advantages and disadvantages of this tool.

Additional Practice   For experience working with the features you've learned about in this chapter, we strongly suggest that you do the additional exercises for this chapter that are included in Appendix 1.

Chapter 10: Updating the Schedule

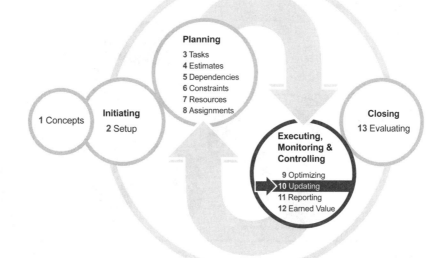

In the previous chapter on Optimizing, we compressed our schedule to make sure it was on track to meet project deadlines. In this chapter, we'll explore what you need to do after you have the go-ahead and can start executing the work on the project.

After reading this chapter you will be able to:

- ➤ Prepare your schedule for updating
- ➤ Set and maintain the baseline
- ➤ Determine whether to update your schedule by updating tasks or by updating assignments
- ➤ Update on the task level using actual start and finish, or actual and remaining duration
- ➤ Update on the assignment level using Outlook time sheets
- ➤ Handle the wide variety of update situations that occur in practice
- ➤ Communicate the status and the forecasts of your project
- ➤ Check whether your schedule is updated properly using scheduling best practices

I guess he didn't get the update
about this year's party.

Overview of Updating

You update a project schedule to record both what has happened in the past (the actuals) and what you forecast for the future of the project.

Executing a project is often a more chaotic experience than anticipated in the project plan:

➤ Progress can run behind on some tasks and ahead on others

➤ When a critical task slips, corrections to the schedule have to be made in order to meet the deadline

➤ Unexpected expenses or sudden budget cuts may have to be compensated for

➤ Tasks are completed out of sequence (e.g., team members work on tasks in the order they prefer)

➤ Deliverables or external dependencies may become delayed

➤ People fall sick

The basic process steps for updating a schedule are:

➤ Baseline the schedule: set it once for the entire schedule and maintain its integrity.

➤ Choose the client reporting period.

➤ Choose the update method.

▸ Tasks update: collect progress information on the task level. This requires less effort than updating assignments.

▶ Assignments update: collect actual hours worked, by day, by resource. When you update assignments, you work with time sheets.

➤ Update the schedule: enter the actual values and remaining estimates. This is discussed separately for each update strategy.

➤ Check to make sure the schedule has been updated correctly.

➤ Prepare status and forecast reports. You may need to re-optimize your schedule before reporting.

The Baseline

The baseline is a frozen copy of the final approved schedule. It is the target to aim for. As much as possible, the baseline should remain the same throughout the project.

Make sure you set the baseline <u>after</u> you have replaced any generic resources with real people. From a workload point of view you can't perform a feasibility check on your schedule until you have real people assigned.

In the illustration, you can see that each task bar is split into two parts. The top part is the current schedule—the dynamic model of the project. The bottom part is the static baseline you compare to the current schedule. If you display the status date as a line in the timescale, you have all you need to visually assess the status of a project.

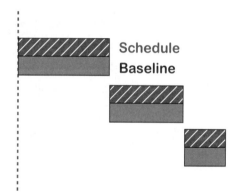

Viewing the Baseline

1. On the **View** tab, in the **Task Views** group, click on the **Gantt Chart** down-arrow and select **Tracking Gantt**. The Tracking Gantt displays two task bars for each task: the current schedule at the top and the baseline schedule (if present) at the bottom.

2. On the **View** tab, in the **Data** group, click on **Tables** 📑, and then select **More Tables**.

3. Make sure the **Task** radio button is selected at the top of the dialog box, then choose the table **Baseline** in the list.

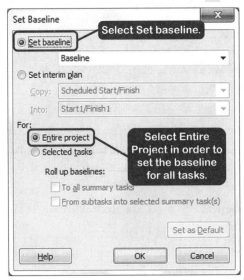

4. Click Apply.

The fields in the baseline date columns show NA when the baseline has not yet been set for the tasks.

Setting the First Baseline

1. On the **Project** tab, in the **Schedule** group, click **Set Baseline**, then select **Set Baseline**.

2. Select **Set Baseline from the drop-down**.

3. To set the baseline for all tasks, select ⊙ **Entire Project**.

4. Click OK; the original schedule is copied to the **Baseline** fields for comparison

	Task Name	Baseline Duration	Baseline Start	Baseline Finish
0	⊟ **Relocation DEVOM, Inc.**	**80 days?**	**Aug 1 '12**	**Nov 20 '12**
1	⊟ **REQUIREMENTS**	**11 days?**	**Aug 1 '12**	**Aug 15 '12**
2	Research staff requirements	4 days?	Aug 1 '12	Aug 6 '12
3	Summarize requirements	4 days?	Aug 10 '12	Aug 15 '12
4	Requirement document completed	0 days	Aug 15 '12	Aug 15 '12
5	⊟ **LOCATION**	**16.5 days**	**Aug 6 '12**	**Aug 28 '12**
6	Visit the sites	1 day	Aug 6 '12	Aug 6 '12
7	Evaluate the sites	7 days	Aug 16 '12	Aug 24 '12
8	Meet to select the location	1 day	Aug 27 '12	Aug 27 '12
9	Legal review	0.5 days	Aug 28 '12	Aug 28 '12
10	Location Selected	0 days	Aug 28 '12	Aug 28 '12

> The original schedule is copied to the Baseline fields for comparison.

> ➤ **Baseline Fields**

When you save a baseline, you save fourteen specific fields for tasks as we show in the following table below. This is done each time a new baseline is set.

Field	Copy to Baseline Field
Budget Cost	Baseline Budget Cost
Budget Work	Baseline Budget Work
Cost	Baseline Cost
Deliverable Finish	Baseline Deliverable Finish (Project Server 2010)
Deliverable Start	Baseline Deliverable Start (Project Server 2010)
Duration	Baseline Duration
Scheduled Duration	Baseline Estimated Duration
Scheduled Finish	Baseline Estimated Finish
Scheduled Start	Baseline Estimated Start
Finish	Baseline Finish
Fixed Cost	Baseline Fixed Cost
Fixed Cost Accrual	Baseline Fixed Cost Accrual
Start	Baseline Start
Work	Baseline Work

The resource and assignment fields also have baseline fields that are copied when you set the baseline.

Resource Baseline Fields:

Field	Copy to Baseline Field
Budget Cost	Baseline Budget Cost
Budget Work	Baseline Budget Work
Cost	Baseline Cost
Finish	Baseline Finish
Start	Baseline Start
Work	Baseline Work

Assignment Baseline Fields:

Field	Copy to Baseline Field
Budget Cost	Baseline Budget Cost
Budget Work	Baseline Budget Work
Cost	Baseline Cost
Finish	Baseline Finish
Start	Baseline Start
Work	Baseline Cost

As you see, a baseline is not a complete version of the schedule; many task-related fields are not captured in baseline fields. Don't use baselines if what you really need is a complete version of the schedule.

After you have final approval of the schedule and before you begin work, set the baseline. Even if it is only a temporary baseline and you plan to set a final baseline later, this gives you the option to compare plan against actuals early in the project.

After you baseline, check to see if your baseline is complete and includes values for all the baseline fields. You can check this by using the IIL filter called "**11 IIL Tasks with missing baseline info**".[1]

➤ **Additional Baselines**

Sometimes you want to save additional baselines, for example, after specific phases, time frames, or major scope changes. As we'll see later in this chapter, you can save up to eleven different baselines in Project 2010, which can be helpful in comparing variances between baselines and the schedule at different points in time.

---

1   This filter can be found in the file *IIL Project 2010 Tools.mpp* available for download at www.jrosspub.com. Click the link *WAV Download Resource Center* to enter the download site.

Project 2010 captures the date of each baseline in the name of the baseline. To see the date on which you set the baseline, on the **Project** tab, in the **Schedule** group, click **Set Baseline** .

Save a duplicate copy of your baseline in an empty additional baseline field. Immediately after you baseline, baseline again into one of the numbered baseline fields. This will set the correct date in both baselines. Record information on baselines in Notes on the project summary task.

Now in Project 2010 you can instantly view specific baselines that you captured in your schedule. On the **Format** tab, **Bar Styles** group, click on **Baseline**, and select the captured baseline in the drop-down menu that you would like to view.

> **Interim Plans**

There are also ten interim plans (Start1/Finish1 through Start10/Finish10), which are extra sets of the Scheduled Start and Finish date fields. In each of these you can store a set of start and finish dates you would like to keep.

Interim plans in Project 2010 now use the Scheduled Start and Finish fields and these fields will be copied into Start 1 and Finish 1. For more info on these fields, please see chapter 5.

You can copy a set into any other set at any time, even back into the current schedule (Scheduled Start/Finish). However, we don't recommend this because it affects the Duration and Work numbers. Be aware that unlike the baselines, the interim plans only contain the start and finish dates, and hold no duration, work or cost data. The interim plans are useful for a quick comparison before and after a series of changes.

Use interim plans to see the effects of a series of changes, focusing on Start 1 and Finish 1. Make sure you are not using these fields for other functions.

Maintaining the Baseline

The baseline is essentially a contract between the project manager and the sponsor or client of the project. You normally set the baseline only once, unless one of the following occurs.

➤ There are formal changes approved after the baseline has been set. These changes could be:
  ▶ Scope changes that entail adding or removing deliverables
  ▶ Substantial additions or deletions of tasks
  ▶ Substantial additions or losses of resources
  ▶ Substantial changes in resource rates or fixed cost
  ▶ Substantial changes in cost resources
  ▶ Substantial changes in budget cost and/or budget work
  ▶ Substantial changes in fixed cost accruals
  ▶ Substantial changes in the duration, start, or finish

➤ Other changes are approved or imposed that force you to re-think and re-baseline your schedule, like budget increases, changes of deadline, or availability of crucial resources.

➤ If errors in the schedule turn up unexpectedly, you would need to get formal approval to re-baseline the affected tasks.

➤ There might be exceptional circumstances such as a fire, strike or sudden economic recession.

➤ Acts of nature (e.g., a hurricane) may also affect your schedule. Even if these happen elsewhere, shipments for your project could be affected.

Only change or re-save the baseline when you receive formally approved changes. This is subject to each company's policies, so it is important to establish an approved baseline procedure for projects within your company.

If you acquire approval, you should re-baseline only those tasks that are affected. These are, of course, the tasks that are new and inserted, but don't forget their dependent successor tasks. You should initially be able to use the Change Highlighting feature to see which tasks may need to be re-baselined as a result of a previous change.

It's **not** a good idea to reset the baseline often, because comparing to a baseline that moves constantly is not meaningful. Your project becomes a target-seeking missile trying to catch up with a constantly moving target. Treat the baseline as a contractual agreement, even if it wasn't formalized with signatures. Insist that changes are brought forward through formal change requests. Incorporate changes only after they are formally approved. Pay attention to creating a clear and smooth change request process and communicating it to your stakeholders.

Changing the Baseline in Project 2010

If you baseline the entire schedule for a second time in the same way you did originally, you overwrite all the values in the baseline fields shown in the preceeding tables and the date on which the baseline was set. You may lose valuable (contractual) information if you do this inadvertently.

There is a way to preserve baselines. Project 2010 has fields for ten extra baselines (Baseline1 through Baseline10), and you can copy any of these baselines back into the active Baseline fields and between each other. This allows you to compare against any of your ten 'steady states'. Before you copy another baseline back into the baseline fields, make sure you save your most current baseline in the next available set of baseline fields and you document what each baseline set is for.

If you plan on using Earned Value this may be of particular importance. The Earned Value calculations can be based on any of these 11 baselines. On the **File** tab, in the **Backstage** view, click on **Options**, **Advanced**. In the **Earned Value Options for this Project** section, choose the current project or **All New Projects** in the drop-down, and then select the baseline that you want Project 2010 to point to from the list **Baseline for Earned Value calculation**. By default, Project 2010 points to **Baseline**, without any number after it. Please see chapter 12 for more information on Earned Value Management (EVM).

Here are the steps for changing the baseline:

1. To set the current baseline first, on the **Project** tab, in the **Schedule** group, click **Set Baseline**, and then select **Set Baseline** from the drop-down. The **Set Baseline** dialog appears.

    It's a good idea to set a baseline into baseline (#) each time you baseline and re-baseline your schedule. This means you save two baselines each time you baseline (or re-baseline), but the advantage is that you will have the proper data stored and available for analysis and rollbacks. All of the baseline fields without a number (1 through 10) reflect the current baseline and are used in default variance calculations.

2. Select ◉ **Set interim plan.**

3. Under **Copy** select the current Baseline and under **Into** select the next available set of baseline fields.

    The first time you revise your baseline this would be **Baseline1**. In that case, the dialog should now look like this:

Set Baseline

○ Set baseline

    Baseline (last saved on Aug 1 '12)   ▼

◉ Set interim plan

    Copy: Baseline   ▼

    Into: Baseline 1   ▼

For:

    ◉ Entire project

    ○ Selected tasks

        Roll up baselines:

            ☐ To all summary tasks

            ☐ From subtasks into selected summary task(s)

                                    Set as Default

    Help   OK   Cancel

> Set interim plan allows you to save the current baseline into one of the 10 baseline fields.

4. Click [OK]; the date on which you copied the baseline is captured in the name of the baseline in the list. This will help you manage multiple baselines.

5. Now you can revise the current baseline. Select the tasks affected by the change request in the Gantt spreadsheet. These can be:

   ▶ Newly inserted deliverables or tasks and any other tasks that are dependent on the new ones that may have shifted

   ▶ Successor tasks affected by canceled deliverables or tasks

6. On the **Project** tab, in the **Schedule** group, click **Set Baseline**, and then select **Set Baseline** from the drop-down. The **Set Baseline** dialog appears again.

7. Select the option For: ◉ **Selected tasks**.

8. Under **Roll up baselines**, check:

   ☑ **To all summary tasks** to update baseline information on all the higher-level summary tasks of the detail tasks selected.

   ☑ **From subtasks into selected summary task(s)** to update only the summary tasks that you selected. If you had not selected the specific summary tasks in step 1 and want to use this option, cancel the dialog, include those summary tasks in your selection as well, and start at step 5 again.

Set Baseline

○ Set baseline:

    Baseline (last saved on Aug 1 '12)   ▼

○ Set interim plan

    Copy: Baseline   ▼

    Into: Baseline 1

For:

    ○ Entire project

    ● Selected tasks

    Roll up baselines:

        ☑ To all summary tasks

        ☑ From subtasks into selected summary task(s)

                            Set as Default

    Help   OK   Cancel

Select this option in order to save changes in the current baseline for the selected tasks.

Check in order to update baseline information on all the higher-level summary tasks.

Check in order to update only the summary tasks that you selected.

9.   Click [OK].

Inactive Tasks

In Project Professional 2010, you can inactivate a task but still keep a record of it in the project schedule. When you inactivate a task, the inactive task does not affect resource availability, how the project is scheduled, or the timing and/or sequence of how the other tasks are scheduled, but it still remains in the project plan. You can also reactivate the task if you need to.

 Inactivating a task is only available with Project Professional 2010.

Why would you want to inactivate a task? You may have tasks in your project plan that are no longer used or one that no one devotes time to anymore. Or you may want to analyze the effects of a constraint on a project without deleting the task permanently.

 Project Professional 2010 now lets you inactivate a task but still keep a record of that task in the project plan.

 We recommend that you inactivate tasks that are not used anymore rather than deleting them. Once you baseline your schedule, you should not delete a task. Deleting tasks after baselining affects baseline integrity and destroys project history.

Inactivating a task is not a good way to archive completed tasks in your project schedule and this technique could have negative effects on the remaining schedule. We recommend that you leave these tasks as completed, instead of inactivating them.

To make a task inactive, select it and then on the **Task** tab, in the **Schedule** group, select **Inactivate** ⬭.

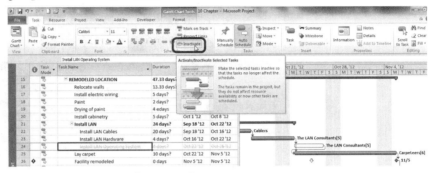

Choosing the Inactivate button will:
➤ Change the font color of the task text
➤ Change the appearance of the bar style
➤ Change the remaining work to 0h
➤ Add a strike-through line through the task name

In addition:
➤ Predecessor and successor dependencies will still be present but will not be taken into account for the calculation of dates, slacks, etc.
➤ If you re-activate a task, all dependencies will again be considered in the calculations.

If an inactivated task has dependent successor task(s), the dependency may appear to be intact, but it is not. Inactivating a task will remove the dependency from the schedule logic. It is important to reconnect the predecessor of the inactivated task to other successors in your schedule.

If you are using the Project Standard 2010 version, you do not have the inactivate tasks feature. As a work-around, we suggest using the cancelled tasks techniques described below.

Instead of deleting a task, add 'CANCEL' or 'DELETE' in capital letters to the task name. You should keep the work because when you re-baseline you need these numbers.

We don't recommend using this technique with Project Professional 2010. Also adding "CANCEL" or "DELETE" to task names in Project Server 2010 may impact resources' timesheets.

Set the task Type to Fixed Work. You need the cost for the same reason and should copy it into the field Fixed Cost. You can remove the assigned resources, since they will not do this task any longer and you don't want to keep false workloads for them in your schedule. You can mark the task as 100% complete; otherwise it would create an eternal cost and schedule variance in your Earned Value report.

You should consider submitting change requests to re-baseline your changes.

If there is no formal change request, you have to be careful with deleting tasks that you don't need any longer, particularly when you do Earned Value performance reporting. If you simply delete these tasks, you compromise the integrity of the baseline, because it decreases the total baseline work and baseline cost on the summary tasks the next time you change the baseline and roll up to the summary tasks.

Establish an approved clearing or deleting baseline procedure within your company.

The Client Reporting Period

Updates of your schedule should be synchronized with your client reporting period. As we discussed in chapter 3, ten reporting periods can be used as a guideline for providing your client with enough information to allow for corrective action. Of course your sponsor, client or project management office (PMO) may request a specific reporting cycle.

You don't want more reporting periods than you need, because each progress report takes time and effort to prepare, and adds to the overhead cost of managing the project. Overhead can run up to 25% of the total cost of projects, which can be a lot of money.

What does this mean for our projects? Here are guidelines you can use for projects of different durations.

Project Duration	Minimum Client Reporting Frequency	Maximum Client Reporting Frequency
1 month	every other business day	every business day
3 months	weekly	twice a week
1 year	monthly	every week
2 years	every two months	every month
5 years	every half year	every two months

As the project manager you should ask your team to report status back to you at least as frequently as the client needs reports. Sometimes, team members can report more frequently to you as the project manager than you report to the client.

Showing Progress

Graphically –
Tracking Gantt
View

Project progress can be seen best in the Tracking Gantt view. This view displays the task bars as shown in the illustration. The scheduled task will fill in with solid dark blue in Project 2010 to indicate how much progress has been made (*Actual*). Notice that the actual duration represents the number of days a team member has worked on the task to date, even though people tend to think of it only as the number of days the task took when completed.

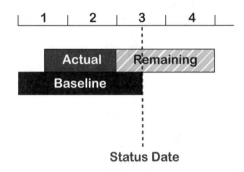

Ideally, the actual duration runs up to the status date, indicating that the task is progressing as scheduled. In the illustration, you can see that the progress has fallen behind. The rest of the bar, Remaining (in light blue in Project 2010), represents the Remaining Duration—the time remaining before the task will be completed.

Project 2010 uses the following formula:
Actual Duration + Remaining Duration = Duration

You can see that the duration is often recalculated through this formula when you update the schedule, which causes deviations from the baseline duration.

The Baseline allows us to analyze slippages. In the illustration, where the timescale indicates weeks, you can see that:

➤ The task started 0.5 week later (Actual Start) than scheduled (Baseline Start).

➤ The task duration was already revised from 2.5 (Baseline Duration) to 3.5 weeks (current Duration); this is a 1-week difference.

➤ The progress is still behind; the task is also progressing 0.5 week slower, because the Actual Duration (progress) is 0.5 week behind the status date. This 0.5 week of work to be done should be rescheduled to the future. It is likely the slippage will further increase, since progress was slower than expected in the last update period, and the remaining duration may need to be increased again.

Mathematically

You can express progress in terms of the duration progress at the task level. As long as you keep revising the Remaining Duration with your latest estimates, the total Duration will be recalculated, and Project 2010 will calculate the % Complete.

The % Complete in the illustrated formula is a calculated indicator of progress on tasks. If you want, you can even have Project 2010 calculate and enter time sheet information based on Actual Durations entered.

$$\% \text{ Complete} = \frac{\text{Actual Duration}}{\text{Duration}}$$

$$\% \text{ Work Complete} = \frac{\text{Actual Work}}{\text{Work}}$$

Alternatively, you can collect time sheets and enter the actual hours worked on the level of assignments from the time sheets. If you revise the Remaining Work, the total work will be recalculated. The formula is similar to the one for durations: Actual Work + Remaining Work = Work. Project 2010 will then calculate the % Work Complete, which will also be a useful progress indicator. With this information, Project 2010 can also calculate the Actual Duration and Remaining Duration on the task level, and update the tasks accordingly.

Updating Strategies

There are two different strategies for updating your schedule: you can update tasks or update assignments. An assignment is always a combination of a task and a resource, as discussed in chapter 8. Assignments are on a more detailed level than tasks, since one task can have multiple assignments if there are multiple resources assigned.

➤ Updating tasks means updating these fields for each task in the following order:
  ▶ Actual Start
  ▶ Actual Duration
  ▶ Remaining Duration (if the task is in progress)
  ▶ Actual Finish (if the task is already finished)

➤ When you update assignments with time sheet information, you typically update for every assignment of a resource:
  ▶ Actual hours by day or by week in the timescale field Actual Work (Note that there is also an assignment-related field Actual Work in the spreadsheet that is the total of all the timescale entries; we are not referring to that field here.)
  ▶ Remaining hours by assignment in the field Remaining Work in the spreadsheet.

The illustration summarizes the two ways of updating the schedule. If you update tasks, Project 2010 can update the assignments for you. If you update the

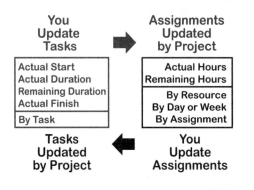

assignments from the time sheets, Project 2010 can update the tasks. Project 2010 will do this for you if you select this option on the **File** tab, in the **Backstage View**, click on **Options**, **Schedule**. Under the **Calculation options for this project:** section, check ✓ **Updating task status updates resource status**.

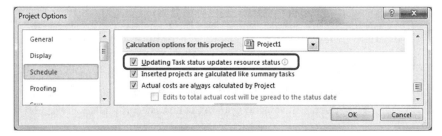

Updating tasks is quick and easy: you only have to enter actual dates and durations, and in most cases, you can do that with the mouse. Since you only specify the Actual Start date and not all the dates on which the work took place, Project 2010 proportionally spreads the actual hours in the timescale. This makes this method less precise than entering actual hours worked from time sheets when you update assignments, but in many situations it is precise enough.

Updating assignments requires more numbers to process and therefore more work during project execution. For example, if you have a schedule with 300 tasks and 10 weekly reporting periods, every week you may have to update an average of 30 tasks, 20 of which may have been completed in that week.

In the previous example, if you do a task update:

➤ For the 20 completed tasks, you'd collect actual start and actual finish, but if you are not interested in exact dates, you would only have 20 actual durations.

➤ For the 10 tasks in progress, you'd collect actual start, actual duration, and remaining duration. If you are not interested in exact dates, you could make do with 20 pieces of information (10 actual durations, 10 remaining durations).

The grand total for updating tasks therefore is 20 + 20 = 40 pieces of data (recommended).

For an assignment update, we'll have to make more assumptions. Let's assume that the average task duration is 4 days and the average number of resources per task is 1.5:

➤ For the 20 completed tasks: 20 tasks * 4 days * 1.5 resources = 120 pieces of data

➤ For the 10 tasks in progress: 10 tasks * 4 days * 1.5 resources = 60 pieces of data

The grand total for updating assignments is: 120 + 60 = 180 pieces of data.

 As you can see, if you update assignments instead of tasks, you'll be processing roughly two to four times as much data during the project execution phase when you are very busy. If you don't have an electronic time sheet system in place, we recommend you do task updates instead of assignment updates.

 We've seen too many project managers stop updating their schedules during project execution because they either fail to get needed the information from team members or they drown in the flood of data and/or errors. If you abandon updating your schedule, you lose the model that provides you with up-to-date forecasts and allows you to do what-if scenarios to determine the best course of action. You lose your grip on the project. It is better to have a less precise grip than no grip. We recommend that you consider carefully which update strategy best fits your situation.

Let's move on to a detailed discussion of updating tasks.

Updating Tasks

Here are the things you need to do when updating tasks:

➤ Collect the update information by task
➤ Choose the Options. On the **File** tab, in the **Backstage View**, click on **Options**. Prepare the view:
  ▶ Change the view to **Tracking Gantt**
  ▶ Apply the **Tracking** table
  ▶ On the **Task** tab, **Schedule** group, you will find icons for Tracking.
➤ Set the **Status Date** for updating
➤ Set the task **Type** of the tasks you will update to **Fixed Units** (we recommend this, but it's up to you which variable you want to control)
➤ Enter the update information
➤ Check whether the schedule is updated correctly
➤ Prepare the status and forecast report. You may need to re-optimize your schedule before reporting on it

10

What Data to Collect?

When you update tasks, it's helpful to be aware of the formulas shown in the illustration. They explain the values that Project 2010 calculates when we enter actuals. Notice that Actual Duration is not only the number of days that you worked on a task after it is done. While the task is in progress, Actual

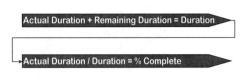

Duration is the number of days that you have worked on it up until the status date. Remaining Duration is the forecast of how many additional days a task will take from the status date forward to completion.

When you update tasks, you enter the Actual Duration and can allow Project 2010 to calculate the Remaining Duration and the % Complete using the formulas shown in the illustration.

Once resources start working on a task, they can often make much better estimates about how long it will take. If you find that the remaining duration calculated by Project 2010 is too short or too long, you should update the Remaining Duration field with a more precise estimate. Project 2010 will then recalculate the total Duration (Actual plus Remaining) and decrease or increase the % Complete accordingly.

If you want to enter % Complete instead of the Actual Duration, it will be a longer, two-step process that follows the formulas in the illustration on the left.

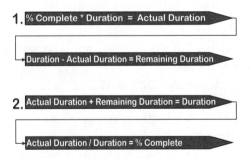

You can see that it is more complicated. First you enter the % Complete (step 1 in illustration), but when you revise the Remaining Duration (step 2), Project 2010 recalculates the % Complete you first entered. You may not like that. Why enter a number that will change in most cases?

More importantly, you have to ask yourself what it means if a team member tells you "I am at 90% complete." Does it mean:

➤ *I'm almost finished!* (this is what we would like it to mean, of course)
➤ *I have spent 90% of the time I was supposed to spend on this task*
➤ *I have just figured out how to do this, and now I will do it*
➤ *I did all the easy stuff, now I will start the difficult stuff!*
➤ *Last week it was 80% complete, so this week it must be 90%*

> ➤ *I want the project manager to think that I am at 90% complete!*
> ➤ *Leave me alone, so I can do my work; I am busy enough!*
> ➤ *I have started to work on the task!*

We ask groups of project managers what they have found *90% complete* means, and inevitably they indicate that *90% complete* can mean any of the above! We therefore recommend you ask for Actual Start, Actual Duration and Remaining Duration instead of % Complete when collecting update information; ask for facts rather than fiction. Using % Complete is less objective than entering the actual number of business days that people worked on a task (Actual Duration). The number of days somebody really worked on a task can easily be counted and is factual information.

If you choose to enter % Complete instead of having it calculated by Project 2010, we recommend that you:

➤ Still ask for Remaining Duration updates, since they will keep your forecasts accurate. If you only enter % Complete your forecasts will be inaccurate.

➤ Allow fairly rough increments in % Complete only. We suggest increments such as 0%, 25%, 50%, 75%, 100% as shown on the Tracking tool icons on the Ribbon. To use these, go to the **Task** tab, **Schedule** group, and view the **Tracking tool icons**. You may want to only allow 0% and 100%. In this case, you can simply ask: *are you finished or not?* This question does not leave much room for wishful thinking (or outright manipulation). However, you need to have a fairly detailed schedule in order to get good results with rough percentages. The durations of the detail tasks should be nearer to 1% than 10% in the 1% – 10% rule. If you create tasks that are small enough, you can get to the facts more easily.

➤ Consider the options that will influence how Project 2010 will spread the actual hours worked when entering **% Complete**.

On the **File** tab, in the **Backstage** view, click on **Options**, **Advanced**; the main options are:

☑ **Move end of completed parts after status date back to status date** which moves the actual hours worked to before the status date.

☑ **Move start of remaining parts before status date forward to status date** which moves the remaining durations to after the status date.

☑ **Edits to total task % complete will be spread to the status date**. If you change a % complete, Project 2010 can calculate the actual hours and spread them out to the status date when this option is on. When it is off, the actual hours will be entered where they were scheduled or from the Actual Start date onward and splits will often appear in the task bars.

Since we don't recommend it, we won't discuss updating with % Complete any further and will instead explain how to update with Actual Duration and Remaining Duration in more detail.

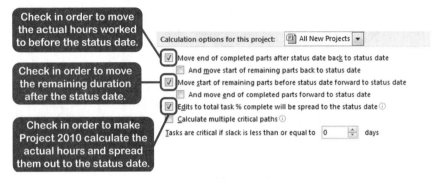

Check in order to move the actual hours worked to before the status date.

Check in order to move the remaining duration after the status date.

Check in order to make Project 2010 calculate the actual hours and spread them out to the status date.

Collecting Data
You need to collect the following information for task updates from your team members. We recommend that you use the following questions:

➤ *On what date did you start working on the task?* (Actual Start)
This question is only needed if accuracy of actual dates is important.

➤ *How many business days have you worked on the task as of the status date?* (Actual Duration)

➤ *How many business days will you still need to finish the task after the status date?* (Remaining Duration) You need to ask this question only for tasks that are currently in progress.

➤ *On what date was the task finished?* (Actual Finish)
This question is often not needed if you kept the remaining durations up to date in previous updates.

 If you don't want to collect and enter this much information, we recommend you choose Remaining Duration as the absolute minimum. If you only keep the remaining duration estimates up-to-date and schedule them after the status date, the forecasts will be valid. The next thing to add to the mix would be the Actual Duration.

 Instead of collecting Actual Duration and Remaining Duration, you can also collect Actual Work and Remaining Work on the task level. If most of your tasks are based on effort (Work), this may make even more sense. You enter your data into the fields Actual Work and Remaining Work, of course.

There are two common ways to collect data for task updates:

➤ Regular status meetings:
In a short meeting (one hour at most), you can quickly ask each team member for this information. You then enter it, or have it entered. Some

project managers have it entered immediately during the status meeting and display the schedule on a large screen to reveal new schedule conflicts that can be discussed and resolved right away.

➤ To-do list turn-around reports:
You can distribute to each team member to-do lists that also contain empty fill-in fields for the status information. Ask the team members to enter the status information and return it to you by the end of the week, at which time they get the next to-do list. If you report weekly, create a to-do list that covers two weeks ahead to show what is coming up, and to allow the resource to make progress ahead of schedule. Note that such a list is not as detailed as a time sheet.

Choosing the Options for Updating Tasks

On the **File** tab, in the **Backstage** view, click on **Options**. Here are the options we recommend for updating tasks using Actual and Remaining Duration:

For each option, you'll need to select either the name of the project you want the changes applied to or **All New Projects** for any new schedules you want to create. If you choose **All New Projects**, the existing schedules are not affected, because these options are stored in the project schedule.

Project Options	Recommended Choices
Advanced	**Set the Calculation Options on the Advanced tab:**
	In the **Calculation options for this project**, select either **<schedule name of the project>** in the drop-down or **All New Projects**.
	Calculation options for this project: ☐ Project1 ▼ ☑ Move end of completed parts after status date back to status date ☐ And move start of remaining parts back to status date ☑ Move start of remaining parts before status date forward to status date ☐ And move end of completed parts forward to status date ☐ Edits to total task % complete will be spread to the status date ⓘ
	☑ **Move end of completed parts after status date back to status date** This moves the actual duration bar to before the status date. Actual work done is moved into the past. We recommend you turn this on. ☐ **And move start of remaining parts back to status date** The remaining duration bar will cuddle up to the status date (unless there are dependencies that keep it where it is). You can turn this off.
	☑ **Move start of remaining parts before status date forward to status date** This moves the remaining duration bar to after the status date. Work still to be completed is moved to the future. We recommend you turn this on. ☐ **And move end of completed parts forward to status date** This moves the actual duration bar to cuddle up to the status date. You can turn this off.

10

Project Options	Recommended Choices
	☐ **Edits to total task % complete will be spread to the status date** If a task is falling behind, the progress entered will be evenly spread to the status date. This option is only relevant if you enter % Complete.
Advanced	**Set the General Options on the Advanced tab:**
	In the **General options for this project**, select either <**schedule name of the project**> in the drop-down or **All New Projects**.
	☐ **Automatically add new resources and tasks** Clear checkmark to prevent a typo in a resource name from accidentally adding a new resource. Works similarly for tasks.
	☐ **Allow cell drag and drop** Clear checkmark to prevent accidentally dragging data on top of other data in your baselined schedule.
Schedule	**Set the Scheduling Options on the Schedule tab:**
	In the **Scheduling options for this project**, select either <**schedule name of the project**> in the drop-down or **All New Projects**.
	☑ **Split in-progress tasks** **Allows** moving the uncompleted portion of a task to after the **Status** Date by splitting the task bar. With this option cleared, the options on the **Calculation** tab cannot split any task bars and will behave quite differently as a result.

Project Options	Recommended Choices
Schedule	**Set the Calculation Options on the Schedule tab:** In the **Calculation options for this project**, select either <**schedule name of the project**> in the drop-down or **All New Projects**. Calculation options for this project: ▣ All New Projects ▾ ☑ Updating Task status updates resource status ⓘ ☑ Inserted projects are calculated like summary tasks ☑ Actual costs are always calculated by Project ☑ **Updating task status updates resource status** Updating the tasks will update the actual work of the assignments. We recommend you keep this option checked for task updates. Only clear it if you want to update the tasks and the assignments separately. ☑ **Actual costs are always calculated by Project** Updating the tasks will update the **Actual Cost**. It is up to you whether you want Project 2010 to do that.

 Notice that the **Advanced** and **Schedule** tabs options, (on the **File** tab, in the **Backstage** view, click on **Options**, then select **Advanced** or **Schedule** tabs), help to reschedule in-progress tasks, but they have no effect on tasks that have not started yet, but should have started per the status date. These tasks may have to be rescheduled to after the status date to put them into the future where they belong, since work can only be done in the future. As you can see, these options help when updating the schedule, but do not guarantee that your schedule will be entirely up to date.

Prepare the View

1. On the **View** tab, in the **Task Views** group, click on the **Gantt Chart** down-arrow Gantt Chart ▾ and select **Tracking Gantt**.
   The current schedule is shown in the top half of the task bars (colored blue or red). The baseline is shown as the gray bottom half of the task bars (there is no gray bottom task bar if the project has not been baselined).

2. The **Tracking table** has all the fields in which to enter data for task updates. To apply it, on the **View** tab, in the **Data** group, click on **Tables** and select **Tracking** from the drop-down. The **Tracking table** looks like the following screenshot:

Task Name	Act. Start	Act. Finish	% Comp.	Phys. % Comp.	Act. Dur.	Rem. Dur.	Act. Cost	Act. Work
0 Relocation DEVOM, Inc.	NA	NA	0%	0%	0 days	80 days?	$0.00	0 hrs
1 REQUIREMENTS	NA	NA	0%	0%	0 days	11 days?	$0.00	0 hrs
2 Research staff requirements	NA	NA	0%	0%	0 days	4 days?	$0.00	0 hrs
3 Summarize requirements	NA	NA	0%	0%	0			
4 Requirement document completed	NA	NA	0%	0%	0			
5 LOCATION	NA	NA	0%	0%	0 d			
6 Visit the sites	NA	NA	0%	0%	0 days	1 day	$0.00	0 hrs
7 Evaluate the sites	NA	NA	0%	0%	0 days	7 days	$0.00	0 hrs
8 Meet to select the location	NA	NA	0%	0%	0 days	1 day	$0.00	0 hrs
9 Legal review	NA	NA	0%	0%	0 days	0.5 days	$0.00	0 hrs
10 Location Selected	NA	NA	0%	0%	0 days	0 days	$0.00	0 hrs
11 REMODELING CONTRACT	NA	NA	0%	0%	0 days	2 days	$0.00	0 hrs
12 Meet to discuss contract	NA	NA	0%	0%	0 days	1 day	$0.00	0 hrs
13 Negotiate the contract	NA	NA	0%	0%	0 days	1 day	$0.00	0 hrs
14 Contractor contracted	NA	NA	0%	0%	0 days	0 days	$0.00	0 hrs

Enter actual progress into the Tracking Table.

3. To select the **Tracking** tool icons, go to the **Task** tab, **Schedule** group.

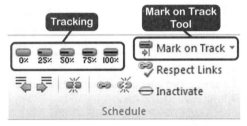

The Tracking tool icons are the handy tools you'll need for updating.

*Set the
Status Date*

Always set the Status Date before each update, as Project 2010 uses this date in some key calculations.

1. On the **Project** tab, **Properties** group, click on **Project Information** , and set the **Status Date**. Or on the **Project** tab, **Status** group, click on **Status Date** and set the **Status Date**.

2. Change the **Status Date** to the date through which you want to update tasks and compare the schedule against the baseline.

3. The **Status Date** does not yet appear as a vertical line in the timescale. While in the **Gantt Chart** view, on the **Format** tab, **Format** group, select the **Gridlines** drop-down arrow, **select Gridlines** and select **Status Date** in the list as the line to change. Choose a dashed line in a bright color.

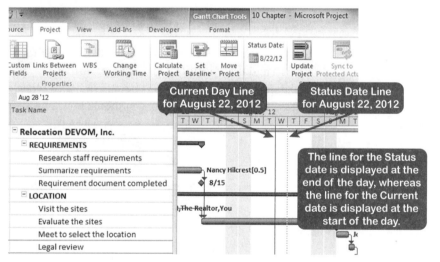

4. Click [OK]; the Status Date line is now visible in the timescale, similar to this:

 Project 2010 uses the system date of your computer to continuously update the current date. When you open your schedule again tomorrow, you will find tomorrow's date as the current date. The status date stays the same, since you last entered it, and will refresh your memory about when your last update took place. The line for the status date is displayed at the end of the day, whereas the line for the current date is displayed at the start of the day.

Set the Task Type for Tasks to Update

When you enter update information into Project 2010, you trigger recalculations in the formula D * U = W (Duration * Units of resources assigned = Work). The task Type has to be set so that it triggers the recalculations you want from Project 2010.

When we update tasks, we change the durations. Fixed duration is therefore not the right Type of task, because we are not controlling what Project 2010 recalculates. When you extend task durations, you typically want to keep the resources that work on the task the same (units), and see the total work (effort) increase. The type Fixed Units is appropriate for that purpose. If you want the number of resource units to be recalculated when the duration changes, you could choose Fixed Work.

1. Click on any column heading in the **Tracking Gantt** spreadsheet to select all tasks.

   OR

   Select just those tasks that need to be updated.

2. On the **Task** tab, **Properties** group, click **Task Information** 🖳 on the Ribbon and the **Multiple Task Information** dialog appears (the Multiple Task Information dialog appears because more than one task was selected). Click the **Advanced** tab; the dialog should now look like this:

The Advanced tab allows you to do global changes to the Task Type.

The Multiple Task Information dialog allows you to make global changes to the schedule.

3. Select from the list **Task type** the item **Fixed Units**. Changing the task type does not trigger a recalculation. Only a change in one variable in the formula: *Duration * Units = Work* will do that.

4. Clear ☐ **Effort driven** and click [OK]. Note that summary tasks continue to be **Fixed Duration**.

Task Updating Situations

The following six situations are the basic ones you will come across (or combinations thereof) when updating tasks:

➤ Tasks that Ran as Scheduled
➤ Tasks that are Running as Scheduled
➤ Tasks that are Running Behind
➤ Tasks that Will Take Longer (or Shorter)
➤ Tasks that Started Late (or Early)
➤ Tasks that Finished Late (or Early)

You will encounter all of these situations, and there is a best way to update information for each of them. We will detail how-to steps for each situation.

If you know that your project is almost on schedule, a quick way of updating most of your schedule is by clicking on a column heading to select all the tasks and then clicking 🖶 the **Mark On Track** icon on the **Task** tab, **Schedule** group on the Ribbon. This updates your entire project as if it is running exactly according to schedule. Now you can tweak the status of some tasks that are off schedule with the next steps.

Tasks that Ran as Scheduled

You simply need to mark these tasks as 100% complete.

1. In the Tracking Gantt view, select the tasks that were completed as scheduled by dragging or holding down [Control] and clicking on the tasks.

2. Click **100% Complete** 🔳 on the **Task** tab, **Schedule** group

OR

Enter *100%* in the **% Complete** field of the tracking table.

OR

Click **Mark On Track** 🖶

Tasks that are Running as Scheduled

In this case, you want to show actual progress up to the status date.

1. Select the tasks that are on schedule by dragging or by holding down ⌷Control⌷ and clicking on them.

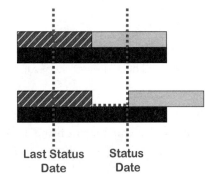

75%

Status Date

2. Click **Mark On Track** 🛒 on the **Task** tab, **Tracking** group; this updates all selected tasks as if they are exactly on schedule as of the status date.

Tasks That are Running Behind

Last Status Date   Status Date

This situation requires more updating effort. You will need to capture the actual progress, but because the task is behind, you will also have to bring the incomplete portion of the task bar forward to after the status date. Lastly, you will have to review the forecast of the remaining duration. If the task is progressing slower than planned, it was underestimated and you may have to increase the remaining duration.

In the illustration, you can see that progress is falling behind, because the solid color of the actual progress does not run up to the status date in the task bar at the top. The bottom task bar has a split showing the incomplete portion of work rescheduled to after the status date

1. Enter the **Actual Duration** of the task (the number of days you have worked on the task); Project 2010 will calculate the new remaining duration and % Complete. If you need, you can enter a new **Remaining Duration** (the number of business days still to go) and Project 2010 will calculate the new **% Complete**.

2. If there is remaining duration scheduled in the past, reschedule it in the future, after the status date. You can do this by dragging that part of the task bar.

   OR

   Select the task and click the **Update Project** icon 📄 (located on the **Project** tab, **Status** group, select **Update Project**.) Then select the radio button **Reschedule uncompleted work to start after**: and select the **date** to reschedule the uncompleted work from the calendar drop-down. Then select for the **Entire project** or for **Selected tasks**. This will split the task bar if the option ☑ **Split in-progress tasks** is in effect (found on the **File** tab, in the **Backstage** view. Click on **Options**, and select the **Schedule** tab).

OR

You don't need to do a thing if you checked ☑ **Move start of remaining parts before status date forward to status date** (on the **File** tab, in the **Backstage** view, **Options**, **Advanced**).

You have to move the remaining duration out to the future, so that the dependent successors will be rescheduled. If you forget this, you end up with a status report instead of a forecast report. A status report is like a report on yesterday's weather instead of a forecast report on tomorrow's.

 You still have to ask yourself if the forecasted finish date is accurate. If you look at the rate of progress in the illustration, you will notice that it is more or less half of what it should be. Half of the work that should have been completed since the last status has been accomplished. If the interruptions or slow progress continue, the eventual duration will be double the baseline duration. You can see that currently the forecasted duration is less than double the baseline duration. The remaining duration should be increased even more if you expect the progress to continue at the same pace. Running behind now goes hand in hand with taking longer in the future.

 To check whether your schedule is updated correctly, make sure all completed work is before the status date and uncompleted work is after the status date. Reschedule uncompleted work into the future.

Add a note to any task where progress is not going as planned to record the reasons why, as this provides good project documentation.

*Tasks That
Will Take Longer
or Shorter*

In this situation, good progress was made, but the realization sinks in that the remaining duration will not suffice. We need to increase the remaining estimate, or we may need to shorten it. (Hey, it happens!)

Since we are going to change the duration, you'll trigger a recalculation through the formula $D * U = W$. You should not leave the task type set to Fixed Duration, since Project 2010 might recalculate the units or the work. If you choose Fixed Units, the work will change. If you choose Fixed Work, the number of resources (units) working on the task will change.

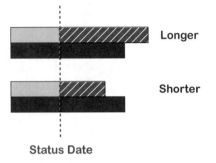

1. If needed, set the **Type** of task to Fixed Units tasks (or Fixed Work).

2. Enter the **Actual Duration** of the task.

3. Revise the **Remaining Duration**.

    OR

    Change the remaining duration with the mouse by pointing to the right side of its task bar. When you see the single-headed arrow mouse pointer ▶, drag to change the remaining duration to compensate for the slippage. If you cannot get it on the right date, click **Zoom In** 🔍 (on the **View** tab, **Zoom** group, click **Zoom**, and select **Zoom In** from the drop-down first).

4. You may have to use optimization methods to shorten your schedule to compensate for the slipped finish date.

*Tasks That Started
Late or Early*

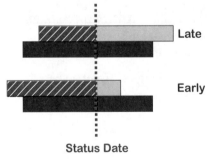

In this situation, the task did not start when planned. The illustration shows that the top task started late, and the bottom task started early. If you updated your schedule regularly and if you had a dynamic schedule (with all dependencies and few constraints), the start date may have moved already to the right date. If that is not the case, you have to enter it.

1. Point to the middle of the blue task bar, and when you see a four-headed arrow mouse pointer ✥, drag the task bar to its new start date. If you cannot get it on the date you want, click **Zoom In** 🔍 (on the **View** tab, **Zoom** group, click **Zoom**, and select **Zoom In** from the drop-down first).

OR

Enter the date in the field **Act. Start** of the **Tracking table**.

OR

Select the task with a delayed start. Click **Update Tasks** 📝, located on the **Task** tab, **Schedule** group, select the drop-down arrow on the **Mark On Track** icon, **Update Tasks**, then fill in the **Actual Start** date and click OK .

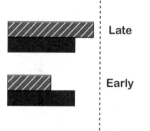

Fill in these fields in order to Update the Task.

2. You may have to use optimization methods to shorten your schedule to compensate for the slipped finish date

Tasks That Finished Late or Early

In this situation, you need to enter the finish dates. In the illustration, you can see that the top task finished late relative to the black baseline bar. The bottom task finished early. If you update your schedule regularly, however, you often don't need to enter finish dates. When you revise the remaining duration, Project 2010 changes the finish date to the right date, or close to it. If it still isn't the right date, you can enter that date into the project schedule.

Late

Early

Status Date

The steps are:

1. Point to the right side of the task's blue task bar, and when you see a single-headed arrow mouse pointer ▶, drag the finish to its new date. Set the task to 100% complete.

OR

Enter the date in **Act. Finish** of the **Tracking table**.

OR

Select the task with a slipped finish date, and on the **Task** tab, **Schedule** group, select the **Mark On Track** icon down-arrow, and choose **Update**

Tasks In the **Update Tasks** window, enter the **Actual Finish** date and click [OK].

2. You may have to use optimization methods to shorten your schedule to compensate for the slipped finish date.

"My Reality Is More Complex..."

There are certain situations that seem more difficult to update than those we've discussed:

➤ Combination of situations
For example, what to do with a task that started late, runs behind and will take longer?

➤ Updating out of sequence
What if tasks have been done out of sequence? For example, a task is already in progress that is scheduled to start in the future.

➤ New activities on the fly
What if you realize while working on a task that it actually consists of more tasks, or what if you decide to reassign resources?

We will discuss each situation in more detail.

Combination of Situations

No matter how complex your situation is, it is always a combination of the six situations we've already discussed.

For example, let's say the situation on a two-day task on May 2nd at 5PM is:
➤ The Actual Start date is May 2nd with a Baseline Start of May 1st (Task started late)
➤ The Remaining Duration is revised from 1 day to 2 days (Task running behind)

In a situation like this, we recommend you start with updating the Actual Start, then the Actual Duration, and the Remaining Duration last. Graphically speaking, you enter data going from left to right over the task bar. If you keep this in mind, you will never see unexpected results in Project 2010. It will help you if you put the columns in the right order.

The resource worked only May 2nd on the task; the Actual Duration is one day. The % Complete will be calculated at 50%. Before entering the Remaining Duration, the schedule will look like this:

	Task Name	Actual Start	Actual Duration	Remaining Duration	% Complete	Apr 29, '12 S S M T W T F S
1	Evaluate the Sites	May 2 '12	1 day	1 day	50%	50%

When you enter the Remaining Duration, you trigger a recalculation of the % Complete and it will be 33%; you have completed one day of a three-day task that was a two-day task. See the next schedule:

	Task Name	Actual Start	Actual Duration	Remaining Duration	% Complete	Apr 29, '12 S S M T W T F	May 6 S S M
1	Evaluate the Sites	May 2 '12	1 day	2 days	33%		33%

Updating Out of Sequence

Occasionally, you may need to show progress on a task that is scheduled in the future. But since normally a task can only start when its predecessors are finished the predecessors of the task may logically prevent you from moving the task earlier. If work has started on a future task, you need to show progress on it, regardless of the logic of the dependencies. This is known as out-of-sequence updating..

Updating out of sequence is simple, because actuals are stronger than any other scheduling feature in Project 2010. Entering actuals overrides the logic of the dependencies and even schedule constraints, so you can go ahead and update in the same way.

The option **Split in-progress tasks** (on the **File** tab, in the **Backstage** view, click on **Options**, **Schedule**) will affect the result in out-of-sequence situations assuming you've selected ☑ **Move end of completed parts after status date back to status date** (on the **File** tab, in the **Backstage** view, click on **Options**, **Advanced**):

➤ If selected, the remaining duration stays where its dependencies hold the task. This is called retained logic.

➤ If cleared, the remaining duration is scheduled to start on the status date, which pulls the successors back to the status date. This is called a logic override, or a progress override.

 Make sure you check the final result, because in some cases you want to retain the logic and in other cases you want to override it.

New Activities on the Fly

During project execution, you often realize you omitted some tasks, or you may find better approaches for creating deliverables. Generally it is better to add new activities to show changes rather than to attempt to modify existing activities.

This is particularly true if you have already reported any progress on the activities. For example, if progress is lagging, you could decide to reassign a portion of a task to somebody else. In that case, you can make this clearer if you leave the baselined activities as they are and create a new activity for this extra resource. The new activities end up without a baseline and are clearly marked as new activities that are inserted on the fly to capture how the project really unfolded. In the case of contract disputes, you need to communicate clearly what the plan was and what happened in reality. Some experts go as far as capturing all impacts by creating new tasks. This technique is particularly useful for litigation when a contract dispute erupts, but it also allows you to learn from your project experience.

Updating Manually Scheduled Tasks

You may need to manually schedule a task because you don't have all the information about the task or you are using the rolling wave planning approach.

If you have created a manually scheduled task, it will not be automatically adjusted from changes made to task dependencies or to the project calendar: a manually scheduled task will stay right where you put it in the schedule. You will need to keep it manually updated in your schedule. You will also need to review any direct dependencies to the manually scheduled task for accuracy in your logic.

As you can see in the screenshot below, the manually scheduled task has a different look in the Gantt Chart, shown with a teal Gantt bar color. If the auto-scheduled tasks are updated and move out, the manually scheduled task stays put, but the teal Gantt bar now will contain a dotted line surrounding it. This signals that a scheduling conflict may be present.

If you hover over this bar, the **Manual Task Warning** dialog appears as shown below. If you right-click on this dotted bar, a mini-menu appears, giving you choices on how to resolve this possible conflict. You can **Respect Links**, **Fix in Task Inspector**, or **Ignore Problems For This Task**.

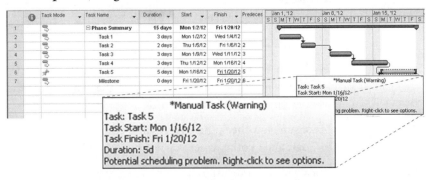

Updating Assignments

Here are the things you need to do when updating assignments using time sheets:

➤ Choose the options: on the **File** tab, in the **Backstage** view, click on **Options**.

➤ Prepare the view:
   ▸ Change the view to **Resource Usage**, and customize it
   ▸ Apply the table **Work**, and customize it

➤ Set the **Status Date** for this update

➤ Set the task **Type** to **Fixed Units** for all tasks to be updated

 When updating assignments, set **ALL** task types to **Fixed Units**.

➤ Collect the data using time sheets.

For electronic time sheets, you can use the Project Web Apps or Outlook time sheets if your organization installs and deploys Project Server or third party time sheets that integrate well with Project 2010. You could also work with paper time sheets, but such a system is laborious and often abandoned during project execution. We'll focus on electronic time sheets only. If you don't have an electronic time sheet system, we recommend updating tasks instead.

➤ Transfer the time sheet information into the schedule.
This is where the Project Web Apps time sheet system sets itself apart from many other time sheet systems. Once you've reviewed the time sheet numbers, you simply click one button to transfer the accepted numbers from Project Web Apps into the Project 2010 schedule. Other time sheet systems may not transfer the time sheet information into the Project 2010 schedule.

➤ Check whether the schedule is updated correctly.

➤ Prepare the status and forecast report.
You may need to re-optimize your schedule before reporting on it.

What Data to Collect?

You need to make choices about what data to collect from your team members and enter into the Resource Usage or Task Usage view:

➤ **Percentage of work complete**
Because percentage of work complete is such a weak metric, we don't recommend using this type of time sheet.

➤ **Actual Work completed**
Collapse or expand the timescale to reflect the frequency with which you collect data. For example, you can collect daily data, weekly data or even bimonthly data, depending on your project's needs.

➤ **Remaining Work**
Insert a column for Remaining Work and enter estimates of what remains to be done.

➤ **Actual Start and Actual Finish**
Entering Actual Start and Actual Finish is not necessary when updating by assignment and using the Resource Usage view, because these are entered automatically when you fill in your timesheet. However, it may be necessary to enter this if you use a timescale other than daily.

Choosing the Options for an Assignments Update

On the **File** tab, in the **Backstage** view, choose **Options** to set the following options:

For each option, you'll need to select either the name of the project you want the changes applied to or All New Projects for any new schedules you want to create.

If you choose All New Projects, the existing schedules are not affected, because these options are stored in the project schedule.

Project Options	Recommended Choices
Schedule	**Set the Calculation Options on the Schedule tab:** In the **Calculation options for this project**, select either **\<schedule name of the project\>** in the drop-down or **All New Projects**. Calculation options for this project: 🅿️ All New Projects ▾ ☑ Updating Task status updates resource status ⓘ ☑ Inserted projects are calculated like summary tasks ☑ Actual costs are always calculated by Project ☑ **Updating task Status updates Resource Status** We recommend you check this option so that Project 2010 calculates the % Complete on the task level. However, if you turn this off, you will not see % Complete on tasks which allows you to enter them. This is useful if you want to update both tasks and assignments simultaneously. (Doing both types of updates is a lot of work.) ☑ **Actual costs are always calculated by Project**. Project 2010 will calculate the actual cost if you keep this turned on. If you want to enter actual cost numbers yourself, you should turn it off. **Set the Scheduling Options on the Schedule tab:** In the **Scheduling options for this project**, select either **\<schedule name of the project\>** in the drop-down or **All New Projects**. Scheduling options for this project: 🅿️ All New Projects ▾ ☑ **Autolink inserted or moved tasks** Disabling **Autolink** will prevent accidental changes to the network logic in the baselined schedule. ☑ **Split in-progress tasks** Allows you to split the task bar and move the remaining duration after the status date. We recommend keeping this option on.

Advanced	**Set the Calculation Options on the Advanced tab:**
	
	In the **Calculation options for this project**, select either \<schedule name of the project\> in the drop-down or All New Projects.
	
	Calculation options for this project: 🅿️ All New Projects ▾
	☑ Move end of completed parts after status date back to status date
	  ☑ And move start of remaining parts back to status date
	☑ Move start of remaining parts before status date forward to status date
	  ☑ And move end of completed parts forward to status date

Project Options	Recommended Choices
	Selecting or clearing the four options shown on this screen has no effect when you work with traditional time sheets. (See also explanations after this table.)
Advanced	**Set the General Options on the Advanced tab:**
	☐ Automatically add new resources and tasks This prevents accidentally adding resources during updating and re-optimizing.
	In the **General options for this project**, set the **General options for this project:** for the current open project <**schedule name of the project**> in the drop-down or select **All New Projects** for any new schedules you want to create.
	If you choose **All New Projects**, the existing schedules are not affected, because these options are stored in the project schedule.
	General options for this project: 📄 All New Projects ▾ ☐ Automatically add new resources and tasks
	☐ **Allow cell drag and drop** Prevents accidentally dragging data on top of other data in your baselined schedule. We recommend turning it off at this point.
	Edit ☐ Allow cell drag and drop

Prepare the View   We will first explain how to create a timesheet using the Resource Usage view in Project 2010.

In case you receive updates from each resource individually, you should probably use the Resource Usage view. Unfortunately, the view cannot display the status date line. Instead, click on the timescale on that date; it stays selected and can act as a status date.

1. On the **View** tab, in the **Task Views** group, click on the **Gantt Chart** down-arrow and select **Resource Usage** from the drop-down.

2. Create a new table. On the **View** tab, **Data** group, click **Tables**, **More Tables**; the **More Tables** dialog appears:

10

The Resource related tables are listed here.

3. Select the table **Work**, and click [Copy...]; the **Table Definition** dialog appears:

4. Give the table a name, for example *Update Assignments*. After the field **Name**, insert the fields **Baseline Work, Work, Actual Work, Remaining Work** and % **Work Complete**. Abbreviate their column titles in the field **Title** to save space, (e.g., *Bas.Work, Work, Act.Work*). Click [OK] and [Apply].

The field names listed here will appear as columns in the spreadsheet. You can insert and delete fields.

5. Change the time to a one-character time unit label to save character space: on the **File** tab, in the **Backstage** view, click on **Options, Advanced**. Under the **Display Options for this Project** section, make the change, then click [OK].

6. Make sure you are back in the **Resource Usage** view. On the timescale, notice that only the field **Work** is shown. Right-click anywhere on the right-side below the timescale and select **Detail Styles ...** from the pop-up menu; the **Detail Styles** dialog appears:

The Detail Styles dialog lists all the fields available in the timescale.

Selected Field

Select a field in the list on the left to Show in the Resource Usage timescale or a field in the list on the right to Hide.

7. In the list **Available Fields**, select **Baseline Work** and click on `Show >>`. Do the same for the field **Actual Work**, which will be the input field. Perhaps you should even give this field a different background color. Rearrange the fields so that the **Baseline Work** field is at the top. Click `OK`.

The view should now look like:

View ready for checking assignment updates.

Time sheet information can be entered or changed in the Act. Work fields of the assignments in the timescale.

*The Formulas
Behind the
Screens*

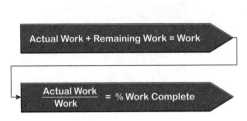

The illustration shows the formulas that Project 2010 will use when updating the assignments in your project. You should keep these formulas in the back of your mind, because they explain the values that Project 2010 calculates and displays. The formulas define the relationships between the four variables: Actual Work, Remaining Work, Work and % Work Complete. If you enter only two of the four, Project 2010 will use the formulas to calculate the other two.

*Set the Task Type
for All Tasks*

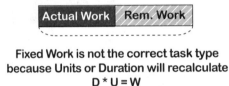

**Fixed Work is not the correct task type
because Units or Duration will recalculate
D * U = W**

The task field Type has to be set in such a way that it triggers the right recalculations. When working with time sheets, we will be entering Actual Work and Remaining Work values that cause the Work value to be recalculated as shown in the illustration: Actual Work + Remaining Work = Work. Fixed work is therefore not the right type of task, because we will not control what Project 2010 recalculates; will it recalculate the units or the duration? Remember you change one, fix another and have Project 2010 calculate the third one. When updating assignments, you typically want to see the effect on the Duration of the task (forecast), while keeping the same resources on the task (Fixed Units). Again, Fixed Units seems the most appropriate type of task for updating assignments as it was for updating tasks. If the task duration cannot be extended, you can consider adding resources.

1. Switch to the Tracking Gantt view. On the **View** tab, in the **Task Views** group, click on the **Gantt Chart** down-arrow and select **Tracking Gantt** from the drop-down.

2. Click on a column heading in the table area of the Gantt chart view to select all the tasks.

3. On the **Task** tab, **Properties** group, click the **Information** icon on the Ribbon and the **Multiple Task Information** dialog appears (because more than one task was selected):

Multiple Task Information

General | Predecessors | Resources | **Advanced** | Notes | Custom Fields

Name: _____   Duration: _____ ⬍ ☐ Estimated

Constrain task

Deadline: _____

> Use the Advanced tab for changing the Type and Effort driven attributes of tasks.

Constraint type: _____ ▼   Constraint date: _____ ▼

Task type: _____ ▼   ☑ Effort driven

Calendar: _____ ▼   ☑ Scheduling ignores resource calendars

WBS code: _____

> The Task type and Effort driven attributes.

Earned value method: _____ ▼

☐ Mark task as milestone

Some of the fields above are not editable because the task is Manually Scheduled.

[Help]   [OK]   [Cancel]

4. Click the **Advanced** tab and select **Fixed Units** from the list **Task** type
   [Fixed Units ▼].

5. Clear ☐ **Effort Driven** and click [OK]. We recommended earlier that you keep **Effort Driven** turned off. Note that summary tasks continue to be **Fixed Duration**.

Updating the Costs

Cost Updating Strategies

You Update Tasks ➡ Assignments Updated by Project

Actual Cost Remaining Cost	Actual Cost Cost (there is no remaining cost field)
	By Resource By Day or Week By Assignment
By Task	

Tasks Updated by Project ⬅ You Update Assignments

Updating costs is similar to updating the schedule:

➤ You can update the tasks and have the assignment details automatically updated by Project 2010.

➤ You can update the assignments and have the tasks automatically updated by Project 2010.

Project 2010 uses information about your task and assignment progress and actual work data to update actual costs, but depending on your project considerations, you may need to update your cost manually if:

➤ Rates of your real resources are different from what you defined in your baseline

➤ Fixed Costs change

> ➤ Some other actual cost considerations cause you to need to update them manually

Updates in Resource Rates

If a resource rate changes and the tasks where this resource is assigned haven't started yet, you just need to change the rate in the resource information, and Project will use the new rate to calculate the new cost.

 If the resource with the new rate is assigned to a task with some previous progress, the new rate will be updated for past actual cost records and for remaining costs. You need to decide if this is what you want. If your change in the resource rate needs to be applied as of a specific date, you will need to update the new rate using the Cost Rate Tables for the resource and establish the date where the new rate should be used (see chapter 7 for more information about Cost Rate Tables).

Updates in Fixed Costs

If you need to update tasks with fixed costs, do it in the same form where you enter the initial fixed cost information. As soon you enter progress in the tasks, Project 2010 will calculate the actual costs with the updated fixed costs. Of course you can compare your new costs against your baseline records.

Manual Updates in Actual Costs

You can manually enter actual costs in the time-phased Actual Cost fields on the task level or on the assignment level. This can be a useful way to keep the cost of your project up–to-date on a daily or weekly basis.

Setting the Options for Assignment Cost Updates

 By default, Project 2010 calculates actual costs automatically, based on the accrual method you set and the actual time progress you enter. If you want to enter actual costs yourself, you must first turn off the automatic updating of actual costs.

1. To turn off automatic updating of actual costs, on the **File** tab, in the **Backstage** view, click on **Options**, then select the **Schedule** tab.

2. In the **Calculation options for this project** section in the lower portion, clear ☐ **Actual costs are always calculated by Project**.

3. Click OK .

Preparing the View for Updating Costs

1. On the **View** tab, in the **Task Views** group, click on the **Gantt Chart** down-arrow. Select **More Views** and choose the **Task Usage** view from the drop-down, then click on **Apply**.

2. On the **View** tab, **Data** group, click **Tables**, and choose **Tracking**; the fields for updating tasks are displayed.

3. Right-click anywhere on the right-side of the **Task Usage** view below the timescale and select **Detail Styles...** from the pop-up menu; the **Detail Styles** dialog appears.

4. In the list **Available Fields** (left-side) of the **Detail Styles** dialog, select **Cost** and click [Show >>] to add it to the **Show These Fields** window area on the right-hand side. Do the same for **Actual Cost**. Click [OK]. The **Cost** and **Act. Cost** fields are now also displayed in the timescale:

	Task Name	Act. Start	Act. Finish	Act. Cost	Details	Wed 01 Aug		Sat 0
						12	3	6
0	Relocation DEVOM, Inc.	01/08/12	NA	$1,760.00	Work	4h	4h	4h
					Cost	$300.00	$300.00	$300.00
					Act. Cost	$300.00	$300.00	$300.00
1	REQUIREMENTS	01/08/12	NA	$1,760.00	Work	4h	4h	4h
					Cost	$300.00	$300.00	$300.00
					Act. Cost	$300.00	$300.00	$300.00
2	Research staff requirements	01/08/12	06/08/12	$1,200.00	Work	4h	4h	4h
					Cost	$300.00	$300.00	$300.00
					Act. Cost	$300.00	$300.00	$300.00
	You	01/08/12	06/08/12	$1,200.00	Work	4h	4h	4h
					Cost	$300.00	$300.00	$300.00
					Act. Cost	$300.00	$300.00	$300.00

Update the running totals in the spreadsheet.

Or enter the cost day by day, week by week, in the timescale.

5. Update running totals on the task or assignment level: add the new cost to the running total displayed in the spreadsheet column **Act. Cost**, and enter the new running total of actual cost.

OR

Update in the timescale on a week-by-week basis on the task or assignment level: enter expenditures in the **Act. Cost** row in the week you incurred those costs.

Checks on an Updated Schedule

The following checks reflect best practices for updating schedules. A schedule has to be updated if today's date is later than the project start date. If the project should have started, the schedule needs to show actuals and revised forecasts.

The following questions will help you determine if the best practices for updating schedules were applied:

➢ The schedule needs a good baseline, because it will be the standard for comparing the progress. What is the quality of the baseline in the schedule?

▸ Is a baseline present?
Keep in mind that projects planned far into the future that haven't been approved yet don't necessarily need a baseline.

▸ Is the baseline complete?
You can verify the presence and completeness by applying the filter **11 IIL Tasks with missing baseline info**.[2] The filter displays any tasks

---

2   This filter can be found in the file *IIL Project 2010 Tools.mpp* available for download at www.jrosspub.com. Click the link *WAV Download Resource Center* to enter the download site.

without entries in Baseline Start, Baseline Finish, Baseline Duration or Baseline Work. (When assignments are created after the baseline is set, the Baseline Work field is still empty. Note that the filter does not check on the field Baseline Cost.)

▸ Is the baseline the approved baseline?
The baseline cannot be reset without formal approval of the appropriate project stakeholders.

▸ Is the baseline relevant?
If the project has deviated too far from the baseline, a new baseline needs to be negotiated, since the baseline should provide a meaningful standard of comparison for the current schedule. You can check this by looking at how far the current schedule is removed from the baseline. Does the project have a fighting chance to catch up with the baseline again, or is it a lost cause? If it is a lost cause, you should submit a change request to change the baseline.

➤ Are the appropriate options selected (on the **File** tab, in the **Backstage** view, **Options**) for the chosen updating strategy?

▸ For task updating (revising the task-related **Actual Duration** and **Remaining Duration** fields), the options should be set as follows:
Tab **Schedule**: ☑ **Split in-progress tasks**
Tab **Schedule**: ☑ **Updating task status updates resource status**

▸ For assignment updating (entering numbers from the time sheets into the assignment-related **Actual Work** and **Remaining Work** fields), the options should be set as follows:
Tab **Schedule**: ☑ **Split in-progress tasks**
Tab **Schedule**: ☑ **Updating task status updates resource status**
If you keep this option selected, you should not enter **% Complete** on tasks, because this may override time sheet data.

▸ For updating both the tasks and the assignments, the options should be set as follows:
Tab **Schedule**: ☑ **Split in-progress tasks**
Tab **Schedule**: ☐ **Updating task status updates resource status**
You cannot enter both types of information unless you clear this option.

➤ Is the **Status Date** set to an appropriate date?
The **Status Date**, (on the **Project** tab, in the **Properties** group, click on **Project Information**), should be set to a date that is close to today's date. If it is too far in the past, the schedule may be out-of-date. If it is too far in the future, the project manager is guessing the progress instead of entering factual progress.

➤ Is the task type of soon-to-be-updated tasks set to **Fixed Units** and non **Effort-driven**?

When you update the schedule, you change the durations (task updates) or the work (assignment updates). We recommended Fixed Units and non Effort-Driven, because you typically first would like to see what the schedule looks like when the same resources continue to work on the task. You can always re-optimize the schedule.

➤ Is the schedule up to date per the **Status date**?

▶ Are all actual durations (actual work/actual hours worked) scheduled in the past?

The actuals are scheduled in the past if they are earlier than the status date. Otherwise, the schedule does not have up-to-date forecasts. When you bring actual durations to the past, all their dependent tasks may be rescheduled earlier as well, which improves the forecasts. This is why rescheduling is important. You can verify this by applying the filter **12 IIL Reschedule Actual Durations…**[3]

▶ Are all remaining durations (remaining work) scheduled in the future? The remaining estimates are scheduled in the future if they are later than the status date. You cannot leave unfinished work scheduled in the past. The work should be moved to the future to update the forecast dates of all dependent tasks. Otherwise, the schedule does not reflect up-to-date forecasts and you have created a status report, instead of a forecast report. You can verify this by applying the filter **13 IIL Reschedule Remaining Durations…**[4]

▶ Are the remaining durations (remaining work) revised?

If not, the schedule may not reflect up-to-date forecasts. If the project manager has been revising the durations of detail tasks, these will be displayed. This filter is different from the other filters in the sense that if it displays tasks, it is good. If the filter does not display any tasks, it is an indication that the project manager is not revising his (remaining) durations while updating. If remaining durations are not revised, the forecasts are not very accurate, and may not even be reliable. You can display the tasks with a revised duration by applying the filter **14 IIL Remaining Durations revised.**[5]

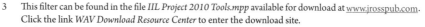

3 This filter can be found in the file *IIL Project 2010 Tools.mpp* available for download at www.jrosspub.com. Click the link *WAV Download Resource Center* to enter the download site.

4 Ibid.

5 Ibid.

Prepare the Status and Forecast Report

Whether you update tasks or assignments, the Tracking Gantt chart is good for reporting progress and new forecasts. On the **View** tab, in the **Task Views** group, click on **Gantt Chart** arrow _{Chart ▾}, and select **Tracking Gantt** from the drop-down to apply this view.

On the **View** tab, **Data** group, click **Tables**, **More Tables** and select **Variance**. Click **Apply** to see the current schedule and baseline dates. The screen should look similar to this:

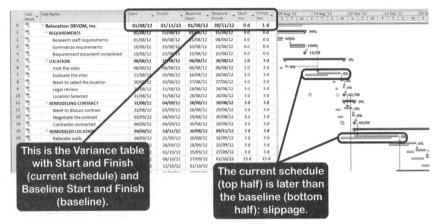

This is the Variance table with Start and Finish (current schedule) and Baseline Start and Finish (baseline).

The current schedule (top half) is later than the baseline (bottom half): slippage.

The Tracking Gantt view depicts progress using the calculated date field Complete Through. To see this field on the **Format** tab, **Bar Styles** group, click **Format** and choose **Bar styles**. Look under **To**.

The **Complete Through** field:

➤ Follows closely the Actual Duration that you enter when you update tasks
➤ Is the number of days for which actual hours are entered when you update assignments

Notice that the Tracking Gantt does not show progress on the tasks (% Complete and Actual Durations) if you work with time sheets and you cleared the option

■ **Updating Task Status updates Resource Status** on the **File** tab, **Options**, **Schedule** tab. With the option off, the **% Complete** and **Actual Duration** are not calculated for tasks.

Review Questions

1. What are the process steps for updating schedules?

2. a. What benefit can you gain from a baseline in your schedule?
   b. How do you set a baseline in Project 2010?
   c. How often do you set it?

3. What are legitimate reasons for changing your baseline?

4. How do the following indicators relate to each other? Please describe their relationship using formulas.
   ▸ Actual Duration
   ▸ Remaining Duration
   ▸ Duration
   ▸ % Complete

5. There are two main strategies for updating schedules. What are they and what are the main differences between them?

6. When collecting update data, you could ask for % complete. What are the weaknesses of this metric?

7. a. What Tab on the Ribbon do you need to choose to set the status date?
   b. Why do you need a status date?

8. a. What task type do you recommend when updating tasks?
   b. How can you change multiple tasks to this task type?

9. What are the pieces of data that you will need to collect when you want to update assignments?

10. When checking whether your schedule is properly updated, what do you look at?

Additional Practice For experience working with the features you've learned about in this chapter, we strongly suggest that you do the additional exercises for this chapter that are included in Appendix 1.

Chapter 11: Reporting

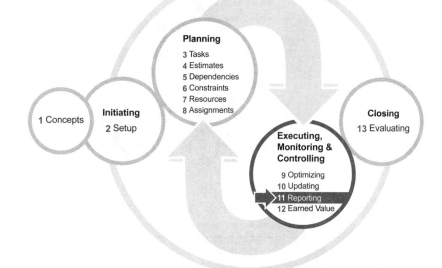

Now that you've learned how to create and update your project schedule, we'll move on to methods for reporting on the schedule and budget, and enabling stakeholders to monitor project progress against the plan.

After reading this chapter you will be able to:

> Use and customize the standard reports provided by the Report feature in Project 2010
> Customize views for reporting with custom tables, filters and groupings
> Create Visual Reports by using Excel 2010 and Visio 2010
> Create some useful and hard-to-get-at reports, as well as one page performance reports
> Use the **Organizer** to copy custom objects between projects
> Format and print standard reports and other outputs
> Format and print outputs from views: Gantt Chart, Network Diagram, Calendar, Resource Sheet, Assignment, Team Planner and Timeline
> Export information to other Office applications for a quick report or presentation
> Create a Macro to automate a complex or frequently used function that's performed frequently

Do you suppose they know that we were coming
to bring food and supplies?

Vanna a.

Project Communications Management

Project communications management is about making sure that project stakeholders get the information they need to effectively carry out their roles to perform, manage and direct the project. The reporting capabilities available in Project 2010 can be of tremendous value in achieving this goal.

Choosing the Options

There are some options you'll want to be aware of when reporting. To review the options, on the **File** tab, in the **Backstage** view, click on **Options**.

Project Options	Recommended Choices
Schedule	**Set the Schedule Options on the Schedule Tab:**
	Week starts on: [▾]
	By default the selection is *Week starts on Sunday* but some companies prefer to use the first day as Monday to avoid confusion in a timescale view like a **Gantt Chart**

Project Options	Recommended Choices
	Show that scheduled tasks have estimated durations
	Project 2010 considers auto scheduled task durations to be estimated durations. For tasks that are auto scheduled (rather than manually scheduled) it will show a question mark (?) in the duration column. This might be confusing to stakeholders. To suppress the question marks, clear the check box.
	New scheduled tasks have estimated durations
	Clear this if you don't want to see question marks for any new tasks you create.
	Show assignment units as a: Decimal ▾
	You'll want to choose which will best represent your resource needs for reporting: a **Percentage** or **Decimal** format.
Advanced	**Set the Advanced Options on the Advanced Tab:**
	You may need to change the time units for **Minutes**, **Hours**, **Days**, **Weeks**, **Months**, and **Years** to a shorter abbreviation for written reports.

For manually scheduled tasks, you can enter a status comment as a placeholder in the Duration field or in the Start and Finish date fields. See more on manually scheduled tasks in chapter 3.

Communication Features in Project 2010

In this chapter, we will use the words printout, output and performance reports to refer to what people normally call a report.

You can print a report or a view to communicate information.

➤ **Reports**
   Several different standard reports are available in Project 2010 in the **Reports** command by choosing the **Project** tab, **Reports** group. All reports are table-like with precise, numeric information. Only the standard reports allow you to print the project calendar and resource calendars. For a more detailed discussion on this, see the section "Using Reports" later in this chapter.

➤ **Views**
   A view is what you see on the screen; Project 2010 always has a view applied. A printout of a view shows on paper whatever you created on the

screen. Project 2010 is very user-friendly in this respect: rarely will you see differences between the screen and paper views.

- ▶ You can print any view from the menu except for any of the form views (Task Form, Resource Form and Relationships Diagram).
- ▶ Graphical charts, like the Gantt Chart, Network Diagram and Resource Graph can only be printed through views.
- ▶ Only in views can you apply the feature of grouping (**View** tab, **Data** group, then select **Group** by).
- ▶ Most of the views can be copied as pictures to other Office programs. (On the **Task** tab, **Clipboard** group, select **Copy Picture** from the **Copy** icon drop-down list.)
- ▶ The enhanced copy and paste functions allow you to move project content defined in a view to and from Office programs more easily, retaining the formatting, outline levels and column headers.

> **Visual Reports**
Visual Reports utilize the power of a desktop OLAP cube to create PivotTables, PivotCharts and PivotDiagrams by integrating with Excel 2010 and Visio 2010. This expands the reporting ability of Project 2010 to a level that was previously limited to Project Server.

Using this new capability you can rapidly "slice and dice" project data to create more meaningful reports. Once these reports are created, you can dynamically change them by altering their dimensions and measures to answer any question that may arise during an executive or management briefing. To create and view these reports, see "Visual Reports" later in the chapter.

> **SharePoint 2010 and Project Server 2010**
SharePoint 2010 is an excellent collaboration tool that allows project managers to communicate with stakeholders either by exporting project files to a SharePoint site or by synchronizing to a task list with Project Professional. This is a quick and easy way to collaborate and share project status where you don't need Project Server as a foundation.

For more information about SharePoint 2010 and the synchronization of task lists, refer to chapter 3.

Project Server 2010 is a full Project, Program and Portfolio Management solution that can scale to meet enterprise requirements and allow you to communicate with stakeholders via a website—the way of the future. Project Server 2010 is not only a communication tool; it facilitates team collaboration and delegation during the entire life cycle of the projects.

Since the scope of this book is limited to Project Standard and Professional 2010, we will mention Project Server 2010 as a reference of functionality but won't go into detail.

➤ **Comparison of Reporting Options**

The following table provides a comparison of your reporting options. This may help you determine which option is best suited for a particular situation:

Reports	Views	Visual Reports	SharePoint 2010	Project Server 2010
Paper based	Paper & view based	Paper & view based	Online	Online
One-way communication	One-way communication	One-way communication with an ability to meet the needs of a broad audience	Two-way collaboration	Two-way collaboration
No edits (Print Preview)	Edits possible	Edits possible	Some edits possible	Some edits possible
Somewhat customizable	Highly customizable	Highly customizable	Somewhat customizable	Highly customizable
Quick and easy	More effort	May require some effort to learn about PivotTables, but quick and easy after that	Most effort to create new reports, but quick and easy after they are defined	Most effort to create new reports, but quick and easy after they are defined
Tables only	Tables & timescale charts	PivotTables, PivotCharts and PivotDiagrams	Tables & Calendar and Gantt views	PivotTables & all charts

In this chapter, we will discuss printing reports and views on paper and how to create meaningful Visual Reports.

Using Reports

Several different standard reports are available in Project 2010 in the Project tab, Reports group.

On the **Project** tab, **Reports** group, choose the ▦ **Reports** icon. The **Reports** dialog appears:

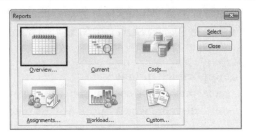

To print a report, first select the report category you want and then select a specific report to view in the print preview window. You can choose a standard report from these categories:

➤ **Overview**
Overview reports show information for the entire project duration, including summary tasks, critical tasks, project milestones, cost and schedule information.

➤ **Current Activities**
Current activity reports show a variety of task information, such as tasks that are not started, in progress, completed or behind schedule (slipping).

➤ **Costs**
Cost reports show budgets by task for the entire project duration, time-phased budget (cash-flow), tasks and resources that are over budget, and earned value information for all tasks.

➤ **Assignments**
Assignment reports show assignments by resource for the entire project duration, assignments for only the resources you specify, assignments displayed by week or resources that are over-allocated.

➤ **Workload**
Workload reports show task usage or resource usage information.

There is also a **Custom** category, which allows you to create a new report, customize an existing report or copy any of the reports just discussed.

Certain outputs can only be created if you use the standard Reports feature in Project 2010:

➤ **Project Summary**: Gives statistics on the entire project. You can find it in the section **Overview** (**Project** tab, **Reports** group, **Reports**, **Overview**). It provides project health indicators like current Finish date versus Baseline Finish date and current Cost versus Baseline Cost. It is similar to the Project Statistics dialog (on the **Project** tab, **Properties** group, choose the **Project Information** icon, then select Statistics...).

> ➤ **Project Calendar**: Prints the holidays and working hours. You can find it in the section **Overview** listed as **Working Days**.

> ➤ **Resource Calendars**: Print the resource-specific calendars that can be included in any resource report. To include the resource calendar information, double-click on **Custom...** (**Project** tab, **Reports** group, **Reports**, **Custom**) and select any of the resource-related reports (e.g. **Resource**). Click <kbd>Edit...</kbd>, and on the **Details** tab check ☑ **Calendar**.

This is a good way to check if the vacations of team members were captured in the schedule.

Preview Reports

To preview reports in Project 2010:

1. On the **Project** tab, **Reports** group, choose the 🔢 **Reports** icon. The **Reports** dialog appears:

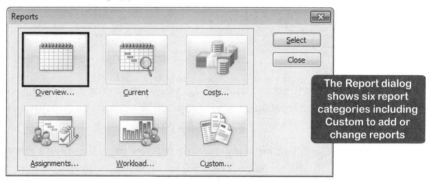

> The Report dialog shows six report categories including Custom to add or change reports

2. If you double-click on **Overview** reports, the **Overview Reports** dialog appears:

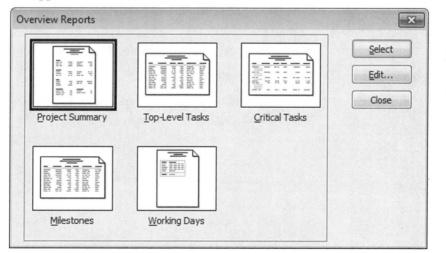

11

3. Some performance reports, like the **Project Summary** report, can also be produced in Visual Reports. If you double-click on it, you will see the report preview in the **Backstage Print** view :

> The Project Summary report shows total Duration, Work and Cost, as well as dates relative to the baselines.

International Institute for Learning Inc.
Julio Diaz, PMP
as of Sep 17 '12

Dates			
Start:	Aug 1 '12	Finish:	Nov 8 '12
Baseline Start:	Aug 1 '12	Baseline Finish:	Nov 8 '12
Actual Start:	Aug 1 '12	Actual Finish:	NA
Start Variance:	0 days	Finish Variance:	0 days

Duration			
Scheduled:	71.26 days	Remaining:	53.67 days
Baseline:	71.26 days	Actual:	17.59 days
Variance:	0 days	Percent Complete:	25%

Work			
Scheduled:	490.59 days	Remaining:	447.09 days
Baseline:	490.5 days	Actual:	43.5 days
Variance:	0.09 days	Percent Complete:	9%

Costs			
Scheduled:	$152,950.40	Remaining:	$142,170.40
Baseline:	$152,930.00	Actual:	$10,780.00
Variance:	$20.40		

Task Status		Resource Status	
Tasks not yet started:	14	Work Resources:	11
Tasks in progress:	3	Overallocated Work Resources:	1
Tasks completed:	15	Material Resources:	1
Total Tasks:	32	Total Resources:	13

1 of 1

> You will get an error message when proceeding to print preview if you don't have a printer set up on your computer. You can set one up through Windows, even if it is only for print preview purposes.

4. When hovering over the preview page, the mouse pointer looks like this: . If you click on an area of the page, you can zoom in on the details, and with another click you will zoom out again.

5. To change the margins, header or footer, click the **Page Setup** link at the bottom of the **Settings** area.

6. To print the report, click .
To return without printing, click any of the menu tabs, e.g., **Project** tab.

Customize a Report

To customize a report:

1. On the **Project** tab, **Reports** group, choose the Reports icon and the **Reports** dialog appears:

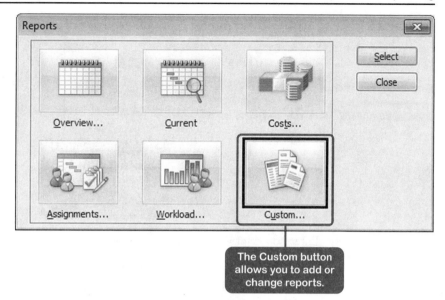

> The Custom button allows you to add or change reports.

2. Double-click on **Custom…** ; the **Custom Reports** dialog appears:

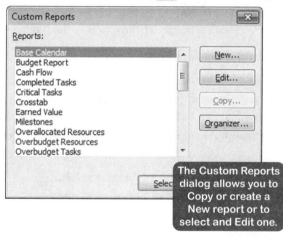

> The Custom Reports dialog allows you to Copy or create a New report or to select and Edit one.

3. Select from the list a report that is closest to what you want and click Copy… to copy the report while leaving the original intact.

You can also click Edit… to edit the report itself, but it is better to use the copy button and leave the original reports intact.

Some reports can't be copied, for example the Base Calendar and the Project Summary report. You can only edit the font and style in these reports.

4. If you select a task-related report, the **Task Report** dialog appears:

Task Report

Definition | Details | Sort

Name: Copy of Task

Period: Entire Project

Count: 1

Table: Entry

Filter: All Tasks ☐ Highlight

☐ Show summary tasks
☐ Gray bands

There are separate dialogs for task (shown in screenshot) resource, assignment, and cross tab reports. Each has different options.

5. Enter a descriptive name for your report in the field **Name**.

    Depending on the type of report you choose, the dialog provides the appropriate choices. For an explanation of your choices, see the next section on Report Customization Options or click [Help] (if available).

6. Click [OK] when done.

7. Click [Select] to display the report in the **Backstage Print** view.

8. If it looks good, click **Print** 🖨 .

Report Customization Options

Four types of basic customizable reports exist: Task, Resource, Monthly Calendar and Crosstab (combines tasks and resources). To open these reports, refer to step 2 above and click on ▯. Here are the most common options for customizing reports:

> **Definition** tab
> Choose the **Period**, the **Table** and the **Filter**.
> Check ☑ **Gray bands** to print gray bands separating individual tasks or resources. This improves readability.

> **Details** tab
> Choose the data to include in the report. If you are editing a task-related report, you can include certain task fields. In resource reports, you can include resource fields. In both resource and task reports you can include assignments. In crosstab reports, you can decide to include totals, gridlines and the date format you want to use.
> Check ☑ **Border around details** to print borders around the details you include in the report.
> Check ☑ **Show totals** for any fields that should be added up; the totals are shown at the bottom of the report.

> **Sort** tab
> Specify a sort order for the records in the report.

On all tabs you can click | Text... | to open the **Text Styles** dialog, where you can choose the font and type styles for the report.

Use Views to Create Reports

Views can be customized in many ways. The steps for customizing views may seem elaborate, but we think you'll find that the time you invest in customizing views is worth it:

> You have far more flexibility in designing your reports than you have with the Report feature
> Once you've customized a view you can access it with only two mouse-clicks
> You may be able to re-use customized views in other projects

As seen in chapter 2, a view applies a screen (e.g., Gantt, Form, Calendar), a table (which may contain custom fields), a filter and a group. Because the definition of the view asks what screen, table, filter and group to use, it is best to create those first. A view contains many other settings:

> The sorting order (**View** tab, **Data** group, **Sort** arrow)
> Any formats applied or objects created through the Format tab
> All page setup settings from the **Print Backstage** view. (Go to the **File** tab, in the **Backstage** view, click on **Print** and then select **Page Setup**).

Some views may apply only the screen as it appears in the Timeline view, or a combination of those objects, for example, the Calendar view which contains only the screen and filter.

Here's the sequence of steps for customizing a View:

1. Define the fields you want to show. Fields can be either existing fields or fields that you can customize. In the extra fields in Project 2010 (like Text1, Number1, Flag1, among others) you can enter Excel-like formulas. You can even add graphical indicators like red/yellow/green to indicate status.

   Customized Fields will be explained in detail later in this chapter.

2. Select existing or create new **Table**: which fields do you want?

3. Select existing or create new **Filter**: which tasks or resources do you want to show?

4. Select existing or create new **Group** to categorize the tasks or resources.

5. Select existing or create new **View** that also applies the newly created **Table**, **Filter** and **Group**.

6. Sort the records.

7. Apply any formats you want, such as text styles or bar styles.

8. Choose the **Page Setup** settings.

9. Draw using the **Drawing** dropdown list. (On the **Format** tab, **Drawings** group, choose the **Drawing** icon and select a form from the drop-down list.)

10. If you are using a pre-existing view, save the view as a new view.

In previous versions we recommended that you create new views before doing the table selection, sort, format, page setup and drawing in order to keep the integrity of the pre-existing views and tables. You can now work on any pre-existing view and save the changes as a new view with the Save View command (On the **View** tab, click any view button down-arrow and click **Save View**). This way you can always return to the pre-existing view by using the Reset to Default command. This new feature is also available for Tables.

The table, filter and group also exist as separate objects in the Organizer (Go to **File** tab, in the **Backstage** view, click on **Info** tab, select the **Organizer** button). If you want to create a new customized view, for example a one page *Executive Overview* view, you can create a table called *Executive Overview*, a filter called *Executive Overview* and a group called *Executive Overview*. When you create this new *Executive Overview* view, make sure you specify the newly created table, filter, and group in the dialog box. Now when you apply the view, it will apply all its *Executive Overview* components. If you name them all the same, it is clear that they belong together. This helps when you want to share the view with the Organizer; you can easily see which objects belong together.

You can start the name of certain objects with an * (asterisk) or a number to shuffle them to the top of the list. Or you can use an acronym to indicate they are customized for your organization (for example, at the International Institute for Learning, we use IIL).

New views can be created using a single view or a combination view. A combination view applies two other views, one in the top and one in the bottom pane. Combination views are useful for analyzing projects, because what you select in the top view is always shown in more detail in the bottom view.

You can print the row and column totals in the timescale of the Usage views by choosing:

☑ **Print row totals for values within print date range** and

☑ **Print column totals** from the **Page Setup** options.

On the **File** tab, in the **Backstage** view, click the **Print** tab; the **Print Backstage** view will be displayed. At the bottom of the **Settings** area, click on the **Page**

Setup link; the **Page Setup** dialog box appears. Click on the **View** tab and select the **Print** options. Click **OK**. The **Print Range** can be set in the **Settings** area of the **Print Backstage** view.

Now that we've seen the sequence of steps for customizing a view, let's examine each step in detail.

Customize Fields

Field: Number 1

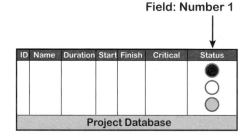

Project 2010 has many extra fields in the project database that are called Text1-Text30, Flag1-Flag20, or Number1-Number20. You can claim and rename these extra fields. You can even enter Excel-like formulas in them so that they calculate performance measurement metrics specific to your organization. You can also go one step further and choose graphical indicators for the metrics (red/yellow/green) to reveal the health of the project quickly. In the illustration, the Number1 field was changed to traffic light indicators. Executives tend to like traffic lights; they can quickly find the problem areas.

The steps to customize fields are:

1. On the **Project** tab, in the **Properties** group, click ⬛; the **Custom Fields** dialog appears:

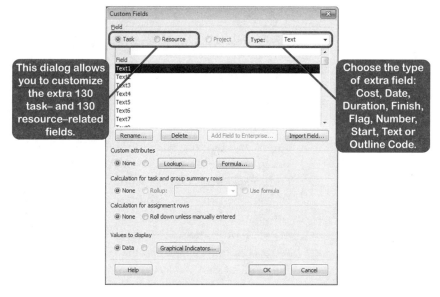

2. First decide if you want to customize a ◉ **Task** or a ◉ **Resource** field. Notice that the ◉ **Project** radio button is not available unless you are working with Project Server.

3. Then select the **Type** of field from the list `Cost ▼`. There are a total of 130 task-related fields and 130 resource-related fields, in addition to the Lookup fields that can also be customized.

   ▶ **Cost1** - **Cost10** fields can capture extra dollar information like committed cost, which is useful if you have a budget from which to commit dollars. You could use another cost field to calculate the amount of available budget, which is the total budget minus the committed amount. (The accounting system typically does not help here because it only becomes aware of expenditures when invoices are received.)

   ▶ **Date1** - **Date10** fields can store dates used to find the Resource-Critical Path.

   ▶ **Duration1** - **Duration10** fields can be used to store durations of interim plans. You have to either calculate or copy them yourself, since saving an interim plan (**Project** tab, **Set Baseline**, ◉ **Set interim plan**) only saves the start and finish dates.

   ▶ **Finish1** - **Finish10** fields are used to store finish dates in interim plans.

   ▶ **Flag1** - **Flag20** fields are used to save yes/no information, for example to indicate if a resource is willing to travel.

   ▶ **Number1** - **Number20** fields are often used to enter formulas that calculate with other numeric fields. For example, you create a formula that calculates the time performance with an under/over percentage; this formula could look like: **Duration Variance / Baseline Duration** * 100%.

   ▶ **Start1** - **Start10** fields are used to store start dates in interim plans.

   ▶ **Text1** - **Text30** fields are used to store extra textual information, like the name of the performing organization for tasks or the position or department for resources. Text fields can be enriched with a pick list, known as a **Lookup** table in Project 2010. The **Lookup** table allows you to restrict users to select only predefined values.

   ▶ **Outline Code1** – **Outline Code10** fields are customizable codes that let you categorize tasks and resources. With custom **Outline Codes** you can create breakdown structures other than the deliverable-oriented work breakdown structure (WBS). You will need to first establish a **Code Mask** and then set a **Lookup** table compatible with the defined **Code Mask** so that users can choose structured values from a list. You can then sort, group, or filter your tasks or resources using this structure, e.g., group all employees on an organization breakdown structure (OBS), or sort by cost code.

4. Select an available field in the list. The **Field** list is refreshed when you choose the Type.

5. Click [Rename...] to give the field a more descriptive name that reveals its purpose in the **Rename Field** dialog. Click [OK].

   Eventually you will see that the field is now listed under both names in the database. For example, if you changed the name *Cost1* to *Committed Budget*, you will see that the field is listed as *Cost1 (Committed Budget)* and *Committed Budget (Cost1)*.

6. Set **Custom attributes**:
   ▸ You can create a pick list for the field. Click [Lookup...].
   ▸ If you are creating an Outline Code you will need to define the Code Mask. In the **Edit Lookup Table for <Outline Code1>**, click the ✚ Code Mask and click the [Edit Mask...]. The **Code Mask Definition for <Outline Code1>** dialog appears. Define the characteristics to code every level of your Outline and click [OK].
   ▸ You can enter an Excel-like formula in the field. Click [Formula...].

7. Decide if you want Project 2010 to calculate values on summary tasks or on group headings by selecting your preferences under **Calculation for task and group summary rows**. You can select the ◉ **Rollup** if you want the result to be calculated by **Sum**, **Average**, **Maximum** or **Minimum** value or select the ◉ **Use formula** to apply the same formula. These options can vary depending on the Type of field used.

8. Under **Values to display** you can create [Graphical Indicators...] by specifying a **Test** and choosing an Image for the range of **Value(s)**. You can add tests and images for each different range of values. By default, summary and detail tasks will use the same tests, but you can create separate tests, values and images for:
   ▸ ◉ **Nonsummary rows**
   ▸ ◉ **Summary rows**, if you clear the option:
     ☑ **summary rows inherit criteria from nonsummary rows**
   ▸ ◉ Project summary, if you clear the option:
     ☑ **project summary inherits criteria from summary rows**

 Project 2010 has some unique functions that can be very useful when creating formulas. For example, the ProjDateDiff function can give you the number of business days between two dates and even base it on a base calendar of your choice. These functions are often better than using your own, like [*Baseline Finish*] – [*Finish*], since the function will give you the number of calendar days instead of business days. Most data in Project 2010 is expressed in business days.

When you develop formulas, you can only enter the type of data that corresponds to the Type of field you are customizing (e.g., you can't put letters in number fields or numbers in flag fields).

 When defining the Test for Graphical Indicators, it is important to know the order of the tests, excluding the results of the previous tests. For example, if you test for a value that is greater than 1, you can't then test whether the value is within 1 and 2 because the first test already excluded any value greater than 1. In other words, make sure your test is set up in logical order using the stated criteria values.

 You can also rename columns by selecting the column and then on the **Format** tab, in the **Columns group**, click ![icon] **Column Settings**, then select **Field Settings**. The **Field Settings** dialog appears so you can edit the field **Title**. If you do this, the field will only be renamed in the active table, since the column titles are stored in the table object.

Tables

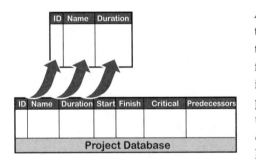

A table is a selection of fields from the project database, including their order of display. You can use fields you may have customized in a table. A table doesn't contain project data; it is only a layout. In this respect Project 2010 is different from other applications like Word or Excel where tables do contain data. In the illustration above, the table at the top displays only the fields ID, Name and Duration out of all the fields present in the Project 2010 database.

Use an Existing Table

1. Make sure you are in one of the table views—a spreadsheet with columns and rows. The Network Diagram, Resource Graph, Team Planner, Timeline or Calendar views don't use tables, nor do views that are fill-in forms.

2. On the **View** tab, in the **Data** group, click ![icon], and choose the table you want to apply. The currently displayed table (if listed) has a check mark in front of it.
   OR
   Right-click on the **Select All** area ![icon] where the column headings intersect with the row headings in the spreadsheet. A pop-up menu appears from which you can choose the table to apply.

3. The layout of columns is now replaced by a new layout which follows the definition of the table object you applied.

4. You can rearrange the columns very quickly by clicking on a column heading, releasing the mouse and dragging the column when you see the mouse pointer.

5. Insert or remove columns manually. Right-click over the column heading and click either **Insert Column** or **Hide Column**.

6. Decide if you want to keep this table as a new table. To save the table as a new one, on the **View** tab, in the **Data** group, click , **Save Fields as a New Table**. The **Save Table** dialog appears. Type the name of the table and click OK .

7. Return to the original table. To reset the table to the default, on the **View** tab, in the **Data** group, click , **Reset to Default**.

Some worthwhile tables to be aware of are:

➤ **Cost** table contains the Fixed Cost fields that are handy when you have subcontracts

➤ **Schedule** table contains all the fields related to the Critical Path Method

➤ **Summary** table which brings date, duration, cost and effort data together in one table. Most other tables have either cost or schedule data

➤ **Tracking** table which is used for updating as shown in the previous chapter

➤ **Work** table is useful when you track the work (effort) completed rather than the task completion

➤ **Variance** table which is used to track variances between the baseline dates and real or forecast dates

There are more tables available. On the **View** tab, in the **Data** group, click , **More Tables…** Some of the additional tables are:

➤ **Baseline** table that shows all baseline fields

➤ **Constraints** table shows the fields **Constraint Type** and **Constraint Date** that allow you to view any constraints you might have in your schedule

➤ **Earned Value** table for Earned Value progress reporting

Design a New Table   Instead of constantly changing the Entry table for reports you want to create, you can create and save a new table object for each report you need with options in addition to move, add or hide columns.

1. On the **View** tab, in the **Data** group, click **More Tables…**; the **More Tables** dialog appears:

11

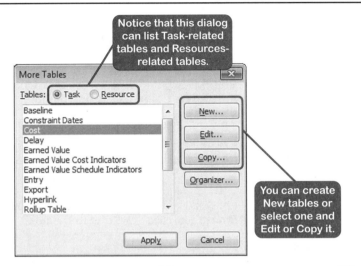

Notice that this dialog can list Task-related tables and Resources-related tables.

You can create New tables or select one and Edit or Copy it.

2. To list the task tables, select ⦿ **Task**; for resource tables select ⦿ **Resource**.

3. In the **Tables** box select the table that is closest to what you want, and click [Copy...] to create a duplicate with which to work. The **Table Definition** dialog appears:

The cost table is copied and can be customized to suit your needs in terms of fields columns.

The fields that will appear as columns in the spreadsheet

4. In the **Name** box, type a new name for the table.

5. Now you're ready to customize it:

   ▸ To delete a field in the table, click the row to delete and click [Delete Row].

   ▸ To insert a new field in the table, click the row before which you want the new field to appear and click [Insert Row].

▶ To replace a field, click on its **Field Name** and select the new field from the list that appears.

6. In Project 2010, you can choose to wrap the text in each column heading by setting **Header Wrapping** to **Yes**.

 You can also wrap the text in the field by selecting this option. The row height will be affected with this option. For more detail on this topic go to Wrap Task Names later in this chapter.

7. If you want to list the new table in the menu, check ☑ **Show in menu**.

8. If you want to lock the first field, check ☑ **Lock first column**. This allows you to select an entire task or resource record in the database without the locked title scrolling off the screen. The data can't be edited in the locked column, which is just fine for ID numbers which are maintained by Project 2010 anyway.

9. In Project 2010, you can choose to ☑ **Auto-adjust header row heights**.

10. You are able also to choose to ☑ **Show 'Add New Column' interface**. This option will show a blank column at the end of the table where adding a new column is very easy.

11. If you are showing Dates in the table, you can select a different format specific for this view by selecting the Date format: Default ▾

12. When you're done, click [OK]. You are now back in the **More Tables** dialog.

13. To apply the table and return to your project, click [Apply].

14. You can now adjust the column width of a column by pointing anywhere on the right-hand side of the column heading.

 When you want to establish shortcut keys for the tables, you can add the "&" symbol before the specific letter you want to use as the shortcut. For example, the Entry table has the shortcut key using the "E" and it is indicated in the Name as: "&Entry". In the Table dropdown button, it is showed as Entry.

Filters

A filter selects and displays records from the project database based on criteria that you set. You can filter tasks or resources. Project 2010 allows you to create criteria that look in any field in the database. The filter does not contain the project data; it is just the screen applied to the project database. In the illustration, the tasks with a duration greater than 5 days have been filtered from the database, which renders only 2 records from the database.

ID	Name	Duration
1	write	7d
2	edit	6d

Duration > 5d

ID	Name	tion	Start	Finish	Critical	Predecessors
1	write	7d				
2	edit	6d				
3	read	2d				

Project Database

 A filter doesn't display any detail tasks that are collapsed under their summary task, even if they meet the criteria. To display detail tasks, expand all summary tasks, using the ⊞ tool, before you apply a filter.

 When applying a filter, the summary task's information includes both the detail tasks that are included in the filter and the detail tasks that are not. So if you want your summary task to reflect only a subset of detail tasks it is better to apply a grouping than a filter.

 The filter [**No Filter**] is the default filter in task views so that you see all tasks or all resources. As their names suggest, these are not real filters, because they display every record present in the project database. To get rid of a filter in a view, reapply the [**No Filter**] "filter" or select ✕ **Clear Filter** or press F3

Apply an Existing Filter

1. On the **View** tab, in the **Data** group, click the list ▼ **Filter:** [No Filter] ▼ .

2. Select a filter from the list. Only the records that meet the criteria in the filter definition are now displayed. If you want to see a filter's definition, select from the list ▼ **Filter:** [No Filter] ▼ , **More Filters …** and click [Edit…].

Some useful filters included in Project 2010 are:

➤ **Critical** displays all tasks that drive your project end date. Note that the word *critical* doesn't mean important, it simply means that there is a *Yes* in the calculated field **Critical**.

➤ **Cost Overbudget** displays the tasks that cost more than their baseline cost.

➤ **Date Range …** displays tasks that fall in whole or in part within the period you indicate. This allows you to focus on the tasks in the coming weeks.

➤ **Milestones** displays all important events in your schedule such as the delivery dates for deliverables. It looks for *Yes* in the calculated field **Milestone**.

➤ **Slipping Tasks** displays all tasks that are forecasted to finish later than their baseline.

➤ **Summary Tasks** displays all summary tasks and gives you a high-level view of the project. It looks for *Yes* in the calculated field **Summary**.

➤ **Using Resource…** displays tasks assigned to a resource of your choice. This allows you to create simple to-do lists. It looks for tasks that contain the name of the resource in the **Resource Names** field.

➤ **Active Tasks** displays tasks that are still part of the scope of the project. It looks for *Yes* in the calculated field Active.

➤ **Late Tasks** displays tasks that are running behind baseline.

➤ **Manually Scheduled Tasks** displays tasks that are manually scheduled.

➤ **Tasks Without Dates** displays tasks that don't have a Start or Finish date.

Some useful resource filters to be aware of are:

➤ **Overallocated Resources** displays resources with too much work at certain times. Realize though, that it will display resources that may only have an over-allocation during a single hour in the entire project. It looks for resources with *Yes* in the calculated field **Overallocated**.

➤ **Slipping Assignments**, when applied in the **Resource Usage** view, displays those resources with assignments that are late.

Just as with tables, there are advantages to creating a new filter object for each reporting need, so you will not have to change or recreate your filter every time.

Design a New Filter 1. On the **View** tab, in the **Data** group, select from the list ▾ **Filter**: [No Filter] ▾ **More Filters…**; the **More Filters** dialog appears:

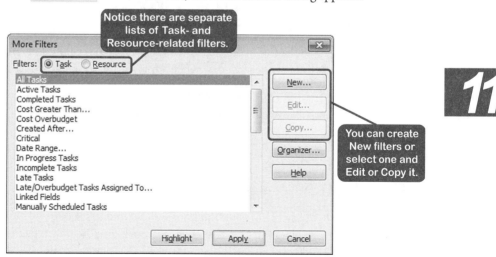

2. Select ◉ **Task** to see a list of task-related filters or ◉ **Resource** for resource-related filters.

3. Click on a filter that is close to what you want and click [Copy...]; this will keep the original intact. The **Filter Definition** dialog appears:

The Milestone filter is copied here and can now be customized.

Filter Definition in 'Project1'

Name: Copy of Mil&estones   ☑ Show in menu

Filter:

[Cut Row] [Copy Row] [Paste Row] [Insert Row] [Delete Row]

And/Or	Field Name	Test	Value(s)
	Milestone	equals	Yes

This filter looks in the task field Milestone and displays all tasks with Yes for this attribute.

☑ Show related summary rows

[Help]   [Save] [Cancel]

4. Enter a name for the filter; keep it the same as the table you created.

5. To list the new filter in the menu, check ☑ Show in menu.

6. Change the filter definition:

   Select the field to filter on from the list under **Field Name**.

   Select the comparison from the list under **Test**.

   Enter the **Value(s)**; for an explanation of your many options in this field, see the discussion that follows these steps.

7. You can add more conditions by adding **And** or **Or** in the **And/Or** field and entering the second condition on the second line. **And** results in fewer records displayed, whereas **Or** results in more records displayed.

8. Check ☑ **Show related summary rows**, if you want to see the summary rows related to the tasks that are compliant with the filter definition.

9. Click [Save].

10. Click [Apply].

The **Value** field in the **Filter Definition** dialog can contain:

➤ Other field names that you select from the list
   This allows you to make comparisons between fields. For example, to display all tasks that have slipped, the filter definition would be: *Finish is greater than [Baseline Finish]*. Notice that in the field **Value** field names are enclosed in square brackets.

> ➤ Literal values that you type in, for example:
>   - ▸ *Yes* to filter on a flag field
>   - ▸ *$10,000* to filter on a cost field
>   - ▸ *5 days* to filter on duration or work
>   - ▸ *Jan 15, 2012* to filter on dates

> ➤ Prompts for the user to enter a value
>   This creates a totally customized, interactive filter. You have to enter the prompt in a format similar to: "<text of the prompt>"? where <text of the prompt> is the question to display. An example is *"Enter the minimum duration"*?. Notice that you need to include the quotation marks and the question mark at the end. As a result, the following dialog appears when you apply the filter, and after clicking [OK] the desired records are displayed:

Example of a totally customized, interactive filter.

Groups

Groups allow you to categorize the tasks (or resources) on certain attributes. When you apply a grouping to the task list, the original structure of the WBS will be temporarily hidden and the new grouping will be displayed.

In the illustration, you can see that the tasks are categorized on the attribute Critical in two groups of Yes and No. The task-related field Critical is a calculated yes/no field that indicates whether or not a task is critical. When you apply *No* Group again, the grouping will disappear, and the work breakdown structure will reappear.

Grouping can be done on multiple levels. You can create alternative breakdown structures by grouping on a field. You can even create multi-level breakdown structures that are an alternative to the WBS. You can do so using an outline field (e.g., Outline Code1) in which you code the levels of the new breakdown.

For example, your finance department may request a breakdown of tasks by accounting codes for Team member, Manager and Subcontractors:

523

Task Name	Accountin Code	Baseline	Total Cost	Variance	Actual	Remaining
⊟ Labor Cost	LC	$138,350.00	$152,930.00	$14,580.00	$10,780.00	$142,150.00
⊟ Internal Employee	LC.1	$35,380.00	$35,380.00	$0.00	$3,860.00	$31,520.00
2 research staff requirements	LC.1	$1,200.00			$0.00	$1,200.00
3 summarize requirements	LC.1				$560.00	$0.00
4 requirements document completed	LC.1				$0.00	$0.00
6 select the realtor	LC.1				$1,200.00	$0.00
10 legal review	LC.1	$300.00	$300.00	$0.00	$300.00	$0.00
11 location selected	LC.1	$0.00	$0.00	$0.00	$0.00	$0.00
13 select the contractor	LC.1	$1,200.00	$1,200.00	$0.00	$1,200.00	$0.00
16 negotiate the contract	LC.1	$600.00	$600.00	$0.00	$600.00	$0.00
17 contractor contracted	LC.1	$0.00	$0.00			
22 drying of paint	LC.1	$0.00	$0.00			
26 facility remodeled	LC.1	$0.00	$0.00			
28 select mover	LC.1	$1,200.00	$1,200.00			
29 pack	LC.1	$15,120.00	$15,120.00	$0.00	$0.00	$15,120.00
31 unpack	LC.1	$14,000.00	$14,000.00	$0.00	$0.00	$14,000.00
32 new location opened	LC.1	$0.00	$0.00	$0.00	$0.00	$0.00
⊟ Overhead (Management)	LC.2	$6,840.00	$6,920.00	$80.00	$6,920.00	$0.00
7 visit the sites	LC.2	$1,400.00	$1,400.00	$0.00	$1,400.00	$0.00
8 evaluate the sites	LC.2	$1,400.00	$1,400.00	$0.00	$1,400.00	$0.00
9 meet to select the location	LC.2	$2,320.00	$2,320.00	$0.00	$2,320.00	$0.00

Field used for the new grouping of task records.

The grouping even displays sub totals on each group level.

As you can see in the screenshot, the original WBS is entirely hidden and all task records follow a new breakdown structure. The grouping feature even calculates totals on the group headings.

This grouping feature ability gives Project 2010 the features of a relational database.

An example of a grouping of resources is shown in the following screenshot.

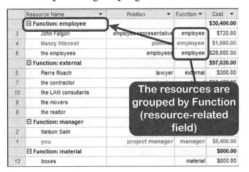

Resource Name	Position	Function	Cost
⊟ Function: employee			$30,400.00
3 John Falgon	employee representative	employee	$720.00
4 Nancy Hilcrest	planner	employee	$1,680.00
6 the employees	employees	employee	$28,000.00
⊟ Function: external			$97,020.00
5 Pierre Roach	lawyer	external	$300.00
7 the contractor			
10 the LAN consultants			
9 the movers			
8 the realtor			
⊟ Function: manager			
2 Nelson Sain			
1 you	project manager	manager	$8,400.00
⊟ Function: material			$800.00
13 boxes		material	$800.00

The resources are grouped by Function (resource-related field)

Notice that if an item falls in more than one group, the item is repeated. For example, if you assigned two resources to a task and then grouped the tasks by resource, the task name will show up under both resources. In this case, the subtotals would be meaningless.

Apply an Existing Grouping

1. On the **View** tab, in the **Data** group, click the list ⊞ **Group by:** [No Group] ▾ ; the list with different groupings appears.

2. Select a group from the list; the task or resource records are sorted and displayed within their groups.

Some worthwhile standard groups that are available are:

➤ **Complete and Incomplete Tasks** which separates past tasks from future tasks.

➤ **Milestones** which allow you to display milestones at the top of your list in two clicks. If you need more sophistication, for example only hand-picked milestones, you will have to mark them in one of the extra Flag fields and develop a custom filter.

➤ **Priority Keeping Outline Structure** which allows you to recreate the WBS original outline code with an additional grouping by priority. This group is a very good example of nesting by several characteristics.

➤ **Active vs Inactive** which allows you to organize tasks into active and inactive groups.

➤ **Auto vs Manual** which organizes tasks by Task Mode, Auto or Manually Scheduled.

➤ **Resource** which organizes tasks by assigned resource.

➤ **Status** which organizes tasks into the groups Future Task, On Schedule, Late and Complete.

Design a New Grouping

Just as with tables and filters, there are advantages to creating a new group object for each reporting need, so you won't have to recreate your group every time.

1. On the **View** tab, in the **Data** group, select from the list ⊞ **Group by:** [No Group] ▾ **More Groups...**; the **More Groups** dialog appears:

Notice there are separate lists for Task- and Resource-related groups.

More Groups

Groups: ◉ Task ○ Resource

No Group
Active v. Inactive
Auto Filter Group
Auto Scheduled v. Manually Scheduled
Complete and Incomplete Tasks
Constraint Type
Critical
Duration
Duration then Priority
Milestones
Priority
Priority Keeping Outline Structure
Resource
Status

New...
Edit...
Copy...
Organizer...

You can create New groups or select one and Edit or Copy it.

Apply   Cancel

2. Select ◉ **Task** to see a list of task-related groupings or ◉ **Resource** for resource-related groupings.

3. Click on a group that is close to what you want and click [Copy...]; this will keep the original intact. The **Group Definition** dialog appears:

Group Definition in 'Project1'

Name: Copy of Mi&lestones   ☑ Show in menu

Milestone

	Field Name	Field Type	Order
Group By	Milestone	Task	Descending
Then By			
Then By			

☐ Group assignments, not tasks

Group by setting for Milestone

Font: Calibri 10 pt, Bold   Font...

Cell background:

Pattern:

Define Group Intervals...

You can group the Milestones at the top of your task list. Executives will be able to quickly establish the status of your project by looking at the group of milestones.

☐ Show summary tasks
☐ Maintain hierarchy

Help   Save   Cancel

4. Enter a name for the group; keep it the same as the name of the table you created.

5. To list the new group in the menu, check ☑ **Show in menu**.

6. Change the group definition:
    Select the field to **Group** by or **Then** by from the list under **Field Name**.

Select **Descending** or **Ascending** from the list under **Order**.

If you choose a numeric field, it is important to select the intervals as well by clicking [Define Group Intervals...]. If you skip this, Project 2010 will group on each value, which is rarely useful.

7. Click [Save]; you are now back in the **More Groups** dialog.

8. Click [Apply].

Notice that you can group on assignment fields in the Task Usage view instead of on tasks; if you do so, the tasks will disappear temporarily. Instead of grouping on the task-related **Cost** field, for example, you can group the assignments instead. In the **Group Definition** dialog, check ☑ **Group assignments, not tasks**; this enables the list under **Field Type**. From this list, select **Assignment**. The grouping will now hide the task-related rows and use the assignment-related rows instead. In the **Resource Usage** view, you can group the assignments instead of resources.

Select a View

A view contains:

➤ A reference to the screen name that reflects the graphic area (Gantt Chart, Calendar, Resource Form, Task Form, etc.)
➤ A reference to the table it uses, which can contain custom fields
➤ A reference to the filter it applies
➤ A reference to the group by which it categorizes the records
➤ Any formats applied through the Format tab
➤ The sorting order applied via **View** tab, **Data** group, select **Sort**
➤ The Page Setup settings (on the **File** tab, on the **Backstage** view, select the **Print** tab and choose **Page Setup**)
➤ Any drawing objects created with the Drawing dropdown list (on the **Format** tab, **Drawings** group, select the **Drawing** icon)

The following illustration depicts this:

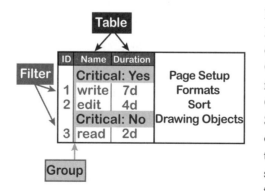

Perhaps you've noticed that the Format tab looks different in each view. For example, the Calendar view provides different format menu items than the Gantt Chart view. Also, the Page Setup dialog contains different options for each view. The fact that the menus change when you switch views can be confusing to the occasional user of Project 2010. The reason for the changes is that the settings are specific to each view and are stored in the view object. Thanks to it, the view provides a steady display and printout of the project information.

 The **Format** tab contains "specialized tools" for the specific view that you are currently in. Notice these specific tools, represented in the highlighted area over the Format tab, are available in the Calendar, Gantt, Network Diagram, Resource Sheet, Resource Usage, Task Form, Task Sheet, Task Usage, Team Planner, and Timeline views.

It's a good idea to create a new view for each of your reporting needs. The view can also be added to the **Built-in** menu: on the **Task** tab, in the **View** group, click on the **Gantt Chart** down-arrow. If you do this, the view can then be accessed with two simple mouse-clicks. The appearance of views can be fine-tuned using the sorting and format menus.

Create a New View

1. On the **Task** tab, in the **View** group, click on the **Gantt Chart** down-arrow, **More Views**; the **More Views** dialog appears:

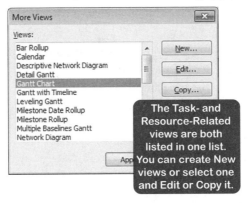

2. Choose the view that is closest to what you want and click Copy....
   OR
   Click New...; the **Define New View** dialog appears, which allows you to choose between creating a ⦿ **Single view** or a ⦿ **Combination view**. We will focus on a single view in the rest of the steps. Click OK.

3. The **View Definition** dialog appears:

A copy of the Gantt Chart view is created here and the custom-made Table, Group and Filter objects can now be referred to in the lists.

4. Fill in the **Name** of the new view and select the **Table**, the **Group** and the **Filter** from the lists. If you've given all the components of the view the same name, it's obvious they belong together. If you haven't, you can still return to the definition dialogs for table, group and filter to rename them.

5. If you want this view to show the filtered criteria instead of applying the filter, check ☑ **Highlight filter**; the view will highlight the tasks that are compatible with the filter criteria.

6. If you want this view to show in the menu, check ☑ **Show in menu**; the view will be available with only two mouse-clicks.

7. Click [OK]; you are now back in the **More Views** dialog.

8. Click [Apply].

When creating a New view from scratch, you will also be able to select the Screen you want to have (for example, Gantt Chart, Task Usage, Resource Form, Network Diagram).

Sort the Records

On the **View** tab, in the **Data** group, click on the **Sort** down-arrow and pick one of the listed sort orders. Note that the records won't be sorted on individual line items, but first by the summary task families and then by individual line items.

If you want to customize the sort order:

1. Make sure you are in a **Task** view to sort tasks and in a Resource view to sort resources. On the **View** tab, in the **Data** group, click on the ⁀ **Sort** down-arrow, **Sort by**; the **Sort** dialog appears:

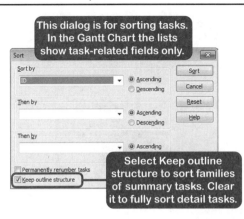

This dialog is for sorting tasks. In the Gantt Chart the lists show task-related fields only.

Select Keep outline structure to sort families of summary tasks. Clear it to fully sort detail tasks.

2. Select the first sort order key from the Sort by list; if you think you'll need a second sort key to break any ties, select it from the list **Then by**.

3. An important choice is whether you want to ☑ **Keep outline structure**. If you do, Project 2010 will only sort the families of summary tasks. If you don't keep the outline structure, Project 2010 will do a complete and continuous sort of all line items, ignoring the breakdown structure.

 Be careful to **never** ☑ **Permanently renumber tasks** in any task view; this is the quickest way to wreck the structure of your WBS completely.

4. Click ⌸ **Sort** and the sort will be applied.

5. To reset the sort order (if you did not renumber), simply resort by ID number by choosing **Task** tab, in the **Data** group, click on the **Sort** down-arrow, by **ID**.
OR
Click **Undo** ↩ to set it straight.
OR
Close your schedule without saving. This one is very effective if you did accidentally renumber.

 The sort order is stored in the view object in which you applied the sort. Each view can have a different sort order.

Copy Views Between Projects

Once you have created a view object, you can use it in other projects or share it with other people. You can even put it in your *Global.mpt* file and use it in all your other project schedules.

1. Open the schedule that contains the object, and open the schedule to which you want to copy the object.

2. On the **File** tab, in the **Backstage** view, click **Info**, **Organizer** button; the **Organizer** dialog appears:

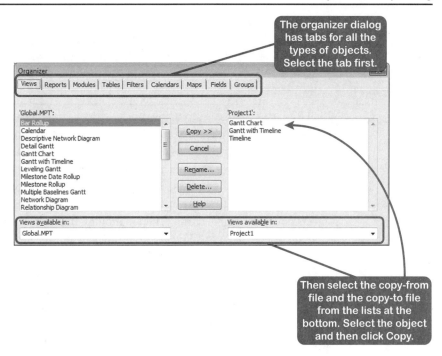

The organizer dialog has tabs for all the types of objects. Select the tab first.

Then select the copy-from file and the copy-to file from the lists at the bottom. Select the object and then click Copy.

3. Click on the **View** tab as the type of object to copy.

4. In the list on the left at the bottom of the dialog, under **Views available in**, select the schedule from which to copy the object and in the list on the right, select the schedule to copy to.

5. Select the view object to copy and click Copy >> .

 The arrows pointing direction in the **Copy** button will modify themselves in order to indicate where to copy, left-right or right-left.

6. Click the tab **Fields** and copy the fields the view uses in its table.

7. Click the tab **Tables** and copy the table that the view uses.

8. Click the tab **Filters** and copy the filter object that the view uses.

9. Click the tab **Groups** and copy the group object that the view uses.

10. Click Close when done.

 Before copying a view object to other projects, make sure you know all the related objects of this view (table, filter, group, and any custom fields) in order to copy them with the view. Otherwise the view will not perform as you expect.

 As you can see, it's a lot easier to see which objects are the components of one view if you've given them all the same name.

The Organizer allows you to copy objects into the Global.mpt file. Any objects you put into this global template are visible in all your projects, unless there is already an object in the project schedule that has the same name. Give objects unique names if you want to see them in any schedule to which you copy them.

Visual Reports

Visual Reports extend the reporting capability by using Microsoft Excel to create PivotTables and PivotCharts, and Microsoft Visio to create PivotDiagrams. Those PivotTables, PivotCharts and PivotDiagrams allow you to automatically sort, count, break down and total the data stored in a database in order to change the summary's structure by dragging and dropping fields graphically. The Visual Reports enable you to make informed decisions about critical data in your projects and your organization. The technology that permits this capability is found in Project 2010's local OLAP (On-line Analytical Processing) Cube.

OLAP Cubes

There are two basic types of databases. One stores transactional data (similar to your bank account) and the other is a data warehouse that stores static data. OLAP cubes mine data from static databases to provide information needed to make decisions. If data in the static database changes, the OLAP cube must be refreshed in order to be current. Since the OLAP cube is dealing with predefined static data structures, it is a very fast way to deliver data to the end user.

Pre-Defined Visual Reports

Project 2010 includes 16 out-of-the-box reports that can be used immediately for any project. To utilize them, on the **Project** tab, in the **Reports** group, click on **Visual Reports**. The **Visual Reports – Create Report** dialog appears.

The top section displays all of the predefined reports. These are filtered by the applications that were used to create them. You can check ☑ **Microsoft Excel** to view only the Excel reports, or ☑ **Microsoft Visio** to view the Visio reports, or both to see all available reports.

The predefined reports are grouped on tabs that represent each of the 6 available cubes and we can classify them as follows:

Category	Description
All	All 16 available reports are shown combining Summary and Usage.
Summary (Task, Resource or Assignment)	The summary reports do not include timephased data, (duration data distributed over time as in weeks, months, or years) so you are able to review totals of the available fields.
Usage (Task, Resource or Assignment)	The usage reports are based on timephased data, so you can establish reports of fields performing over time.

Information may vary depending of the cube that is being created (Task, Resource or Assignment).

Also note that some of the reports are created using the metric scale and others use the U.S. conventions.

Follow these steps to generate a predefined Visual Report:

1. On the **Project** tab, in the **Reports** group, click .

2. In the **Visual Reports – Create Report** dialog, select the tab for the report category you want.

3. Select the report you want and notice that a Sample report appears to the right in the sample box.

If you want to open a different report located in a specific folder, check ☑ **Include report templates from:** and click [Modify...]. The Modify Location dialog appears so you can navigate your libraries to locate the <folder> where the additional templates are located and click [OK].

4. In the **Select Level Of Usage Data To Include In The Report** box, select years, quarters, months, weeks, or days. This will be the lowest level to which you want to drill down. Give this some thought because the lower the level, the more data has to be stored in the cube and the slower your response time will be.

5. Once you have defined the cube, click the **View** button.

Project will compile the information required by the selected report and will build the OLAP cube and display the visual report in either Excel or Visio. This will take you to a graphic of your data. If the graphic was created with Excel, you are looking at a PivotChart; if the graphic was created with Visio, you are looking at a PivotDiagram. A PivotDiagram is a hierarchical layout of the data, much like a WBS or an OBS. The data is aggregated from the lower levels up to the higher levels. This gives you a great breakdown of the composition of the summary data.

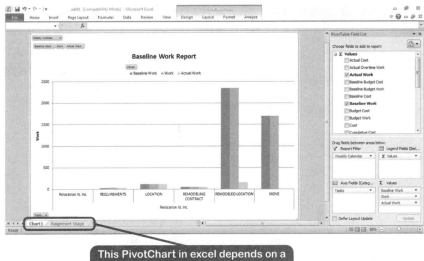

This PivotChart in excel depends on a PivotTable that can be seen by clicking the Assignment Usage Worksheet.

 In the Excel Visual Report, you can view or change the PivotTable data (the data that the report is based on) by going to the second tab (called either **Assignment Usage** or **Task Summary** or similar) below the worksheet. See the screen shot below:

If you change the data, variables or depth of detail, the chart will immediately change to reflect the data.

6. You can print and/or save the report in Excel 2010. On the **File** tab, in the **Backstage** view, click either **Print** to send it to a printer or **Save & Send** to save it as a file (PDF, XPS, XLSX).

Some worthwhile Visual Reports to be aware of are:

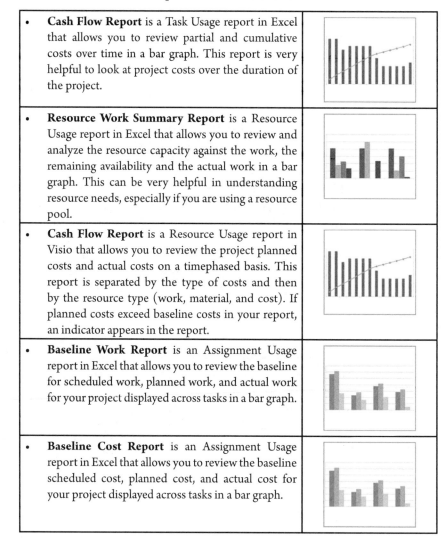

• **Cash Flow Report** is a Task Usage report in Excel that allows you to review partial and cumulative costs over time in a bar graph. This report is very helpful to look at project costs over the duration of the project.	
• **Resource Work Summary Report** is a Resource Usage report in Excel that allows you to review and analyze the resource capacity against the work, the remaining availability and the actual work in a bar graph. This can be very helpful in understanding resource needs, especially if you are using a resource pool.	
• **Cash Flow Report** is a Resource Usage report in Visio that allows you to review the project planned costs and actual costs on a timephased basis. This report is separated by the type of costs and then by the resource type (work, material, and cost). If planned costs exceed baseline costs in your report, an indicator appears in the report.	
• **Baseline Work Report** is an Assignment Usage report in Excel that allows you to review the baseline for scheduled work, planned work, and actual work for your project displayed across tasks in a bar graph.	
• **Baseline Cost Report** is an Assignment Usage report in Excel that allows you to review the baseline scheduled cost, planned cost, and actual cost for your project displayed across tasks in a bar graph.	

• **Earned Value Over Time Report** is an Assignment Usage report in Excel that allows you to review a line chart report that plots AC (actual cost of work performed), planned value (budgeted cost of work scheduled), and earned value (budgeted cost of work performed) over a timephased duration.	
• **Task Status Report** is an Assignment Summary report in Visio that allows you to review a diagram of the work and percent of work complete for project tasks, containing indicators showing when baseline work exceeds work, when baseline work equals work, and when work exceeds baseline work. Percent of work complete is represented by the data bar.	
• **Resource Remaining Work Report** is a Resource Summary report in Excel that allows you to review a bar graph, displaying remaining work and actual work for each work resource, represented in assignment units. This report is very easy to understand because the columns with actual work look like they are being filled and the ones with no actual work look empty.	

Modifying Visual Reports

The PivotTable data for any of the reports is shown in a split window. On the left is the PivotTable with rows, columns, and the body of the table.

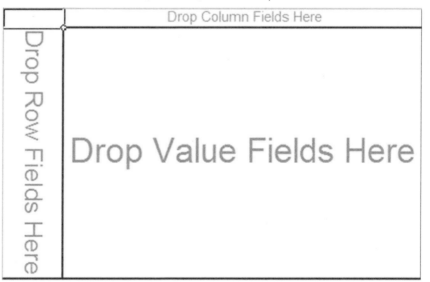

On the right side of the screen is the PivotTable field list. The top portion of this window is a list of the fields that are included in the cube. To select or change the data presented on the chart, drag fields into the appropriate areas below referred to as row labels, column labels, filters, and the values summation. Alternatively, you can drag the fields directly onto the PivotTable.

To do this, drag the column data (often timescale information) into the column area on the table. Then drag the fields that you want to see in the rows (perhaps organizational data, such as resources or departments) to the row area. Finally, whatever data you want to look at "sliced and diced" by (in our example, it would be organizational information by time), you drag to the body of the table. When you are finished, you have a multi-dimensional table — a PivotTable.

Because the cube is saved once it's created, you can change or "pivot" the data to look at different aspects. This could help you when you're meeting with a stakeholder who asks to see the data from a different perspective or asks you to drill down further.

Define a New Visual Report

If the fields that you want to include in your table are not present in the PivotTable field list, you will need to create a new template (cube) or modify an existing template. To do this, open up the Visual Reporting feature, choose **New Template** or **Edit Template** and you will be presented with a field picker. Choose the fields you want to include in your PivotTable. Once the new cube is complete, you need to save the cube before proceeding.

Most of the time, the predefined report templates will serve you well enough. If they don't meet your needs, you can edit the templates or create new ones by following these steps:

1. On the **Project** tab, in the **Reports** group, click.

2. In the **Visual Reports** dialog, click [New Template...]. The **Visual Reports-New Template** dialog appears.

Visual Reports - New Template

Complete the following steps to create a new template:

1. Select Application

Choose the application that you want to use for this report templa

- ◉ Excel

- ○ Visio (Metric)   ○ Visio (US Units)

> Visual Reports creates 6 cubes available as Data Type: Task Usage, Resource Usage, Assignment Usage, Task Summary, Resource Summary and Assignment Summary.

2. Select Data Type

Choose the data on which you want to report.

Task Usage ▾

> The Field Picker will show what fields are available for the Data Type selected.

3. Select Fields

Choose the fields you want included in the report.

Field Picker...

Click OK to create the new report template.

Help   OK   Cancel

3. In the **Select Application** section, choose between ◉ Excel to create an Excel template, or ◉ **Visio** (**Metric**) to create a Visio template.

 If you install Project 2010 in English, you will be able to select Visio with US units.

4. In the **Select Data Type** section, select the type of data that you want to use in the report (**Task Usage**, **Resource Usage**, **Assignments Usage**, **Task Summary**, **Resource Summary** or **Assignment Summary**).

5. To verify the fields available for the **Data Type** selected, click Field Picker... . The **Visual Reports-Field Picker** dialog appears.

6. Add or remove fields and click OK .

7. In the **Visual Reports-New Template**, click OK . The program chosen to create the template is opened. Now you are able to define your PivotTable, PivotChart or PivotDiagram.

8. When the report is ready, go to the **File** tab, in the **Backstage** view and click **Save as**.

9. In the **Save As** dialog, in the **File** name box, give a name to your template and click Save .

 As in views and tables, Visual Reports also allows you create a new template from an existing one. You just have to select the report that is similar to what you want to create and click **Edit Template**. **The Field Picker** dialog will be shown so you can add or remove fields and then click **Edit Template**. Save the report with a different name than the original template.

 While standard text reports are managed in the Organizer (**File** tab, select the **Info** tab in the **Backstage** view, choose **Organizer**, then the **Reports** tab); Visual Reports are managed here under **Manage Template**. To do this, select the existing or customized Visual Report and then click **Manage Template**. The following location, which can vary according to the language of your installation, will be open: **<C:\Users\IIL*username*\Roaming\Microsoft\Templates\1033>**. Any new template dropped in this location will be available for your Visual Reports.

 If you are completely new to PivotTables, PivotCharts or PivotDiagrams, a good reference manual on Excel, Visio or even PivotTables will serve you well here.

Saving a Cube or Database

As an alternative way to share the Project OLAP reporting cube database to do more advanced data analysis in either Excel or Access, you can export the OLAP database as a .cub or .mdb file. Once saved in a specific format, you can open the cube (.cub) in Excel and create a PivotTable with the imported fields or you can open the data in Access (.mdb), to create any kind of report in this platform.

To save a cube or database follow these steps:

1. On the **Project** tab, in the **Reports** group, click ▮▮.

2. In the **Visual Reports** dialog, click Save Data... . The **Visual Reports-Save Reporting Data** dialog appears.

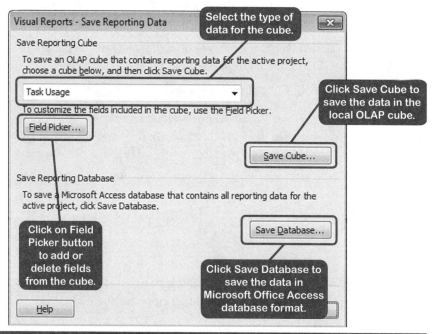

3. You can either **Save Cube** or **Save Database** data in Access. To save the cube select the kind of data you are saving (e.g. **Task Usage**, **Resource Usage**, **Assignment Usage** or **Task Summary**, **Resource Summary**, **Assignment Summary**). If you need additional data not currently included, use the **Field Picker** button to select additional fields that you would like to include in your cube.

4. Click [Save Cube...] to save the cube or click [Save Data...] to save the data in Access.

5. Browse to the location where you want to save the cube data, and then click [Save]. The process to save will end with a message indicating the save was successful.

6. Click [Close] in the dialog boxes and now you are able to manipulate the exported file.

One Page Performance Reports

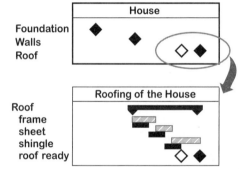

This heading may seem pretentious if you are juggling a schedule with thousands of tasks. Regardless of the size of the project, you can always surprise your executives and clients with one page performance reports. There is a simple technique to do this, and it will make your stakeholders happy as they often prefer concise information, such as a one page report.

The first one page report should only show the major milestones. That is all you need if all the milestones are on schedule and the budgets are feasible. Where a milestone is off its baseline, you provide a second one page report that gives an explanation for the discrepancy.

In the illustration, the milestone chart at the top shows slippage on the *Roof* milestone. In the bottom one page report, the detailed cause of the slippage is shown. With a few one page reports, you can give an adequate status and forecast report for a project of any size.

In a similar fashion, you can create a one page high-level cost report. If there are discrepancies, you can create another one page report with the explanation for the differences.

You will have to master the filters feature of Project 2010 to accomplish this.

An additional option for this kind of reporting is the new Timeline view, which allows you to summarize the main milestones or tasks in a single continuous timeline.

Although the Timeline view is an easy way to summarize several tasks, it can show only current or forecast information, not the baseline. If you need to include the baseline, the traditional milestones report is a better option.

Checks on Reporting

Use the following checks to verify whether you used best practices for project reporting. The checks pertain to what custom view objects you developed in your schedule.

➤ Is there a one page status report available as a separate view object in your project schedule that displays the major milestones relative to the baseline?

▶ Are the milestones filtered in this view instead of listed together in the WBS?

Many project managers put the major milestones at the top of their schedule to create a one page overview of the project. This makes the network of dependencies very complex in the Gantt Chart, because the dependencies run up and down with long arrows. Instead, we recommend using a separate view that displays all milestones using the Milestones filter.

▶ Are the appropriate milestones chosen to represent the status and to forecast a large project?

▶ If you have many milestones, you may end up with multiple pages. Instead of reporting on all milestones, you can mark certain milestones as major milestones using a flag field (Flag1 - Flag20). The filter of the view should display these major milestones. If you use the **Flag1** field, the filter definition would be: *Flag1 equals Yes*. You then make this filter part of the view: on the **View** tab, in the **Task Views** group, click **Gantt Chart** down-arrow, **More views**, select the view in the list and click Edit... . Select your newly created filter to replace the default filter in this view and click OK . When you switch to the view, the filter will automatically be applied. Identifying the right milestones can be a challenge here; you could print all milestones the first time and ask the executive to highlight the 30 most important milestones once (about 30 lines fit within one page).

▶ If you are using the Timeline view, you can just select the milestones or tasks you want to show and Add or Remove them from the **Timeline**. On the **Task** tab, in the **Properties** group, click 🖫 **Add to Timeline**. Click 🖫 **Add to Timeline** again if you want to remove it.

▶ Does the one page view report give an appropriate impression of the health of the project?

➤ If your schedule has a Resource-Critical Path, is there a separate view object that displays it?

The view should have the resource-critical tasks flagged in the field Marked or in a Flag field.

Examples of Useful or Hard-to-Get-At Reports

We will discuss the following special reports in more detail. Some are very useful, others are just hard to get at:

➤ Responsibilities by department
➤ Workload histogram for individuals and groups
➤ To-do lists in the Calendar view
➤ Reports that include the notes
➤ The time-phased budget

Responsibilities by Department

With the Group feature, it is easy to communicate lists of responsibilities by department, or resources by type. The next screenshot shows a resource by type grouping:

	ⓘ	Resource Name ▾	Work ▾	Details	Jul	Aug	Sep	Oct	Nov	Dec
		⊟ Function: No Value	0 days	Work						
		⊞ Unassigned	0 days	Work						
		⊟ Function: cost		Work						
11		⊞ Moving Van		Work						
12		⊞ Lunch for Team during Move		Work						
		⊟ Function: employee	149 days	Work		8d	1d			
3		⊟ John Falgon	3 days	Work		3d				
		visit the sites	1 day	Work		1d				
		evaluate the sites	1 day	Work		1d				
		meet to select the location	1 day	Work		1d				
4	◈	⊟ Nancy Hilcrest	6 days	Work		5d	1d			
		summarize requirements	2 days	Work		2d				
		visit the sites	1 day	Work		1d				
		evaluate the sites	1 day	Work		1d				
		meet to select the location	1 day	Work		1d				
		meet t...		Work			1d			
6		⊟ the employees	140 days	Work					140d	
		pack	70 days	Work					70d	
		unpack	70 days	Work					70d	
		⊟ Function: external	316.5 days	Work		2.5d	118.5d	148.5d	47d	
5		⊞ Pierre Roach	0.5 days	Work		0.5d				
7		⊞ the contractor	234 days	Work			118.5d	88.5d	27d	
8		⊞ the realtor		Work		2d				
9		⊞ the movers	20 days	Work					20d	
10		⊞ the LAN consultants	60 days	Work				60d		
		⊟ Function: manager	15 days	Work		12d	3d			
1	◈	⊞ you	14 days	Work		11d	3d			
2		⊞ ...	... day	Work		1d				

Effort needed by department, by resource and by assignment.

Third level: assignments

Second level: resources

First level: departments

1. On the **View** tab, in the **Resource Views** group, click **Resource** sheet.

2. Enter the department in which each person works in the field **Group**.

3. On the **View** tab, in the **Resource Views** group, click **Resource Usage**.

4. Select from the list [No Group] ▾ on the **Ribbon** in the **Data** group, the item **Resource Group**; the result will show three outline levels:
  ▸ The first level shows the resource groups, e.g., departments
  ▸ The second level shows all resources working in each department
  ▸ The third level shows all the assignments for each resource

Workload Histograms

Workload histogram is synonymous with *Resource Graph* in Project 2010. When you enter the group or department the resource works in, you can create interesting workload histograms. For example, you can create a graph that compares the workload of an individual with the total work for that group (department).

The next screenshot shows the total work of *Nancy Hilcrest* relative to the total workload of all internal resources (as characterized in the field **Group**) displayed using the **Group...** filter.

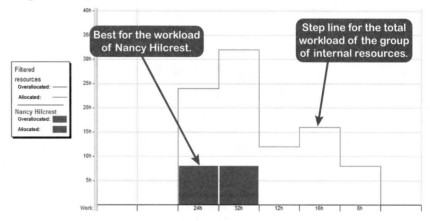

1. Choose **View** tab, in the **Resource Views** group, click **Resource** sheet.

2. Enter the department in the **Group** field for each resource.

3. On the **View** tab, in the **Resource Views** group, click **Other Views** down-arrow, **Resource Graph**.

4. Press [Page Dn], until you see the graph of the individual for whom you want to compare the workload to the total workload of the department or group.

5. Notice that the Resource graph displays Peak Units by default. The Peak Units format always displays the highest over-allocation in red, even if it is just one 200% over-allocation during one hour in an entire year. On the **Format** tab, in the **Data** group, select from the list **Graph:** [Peak Units ▾], **Work**, which exchanges the **Peak Units** for **Work** numbers. Work provides a more accurate picture than Peak Units. The format Work displays the total number of person days of effort per time unit.

6. While still in the **Resource** graph view, on the **Format** tab, **Format** group, select the **Bar Styles** icon and the **Bar Styles** dialog appears:

Bar Styles

Filtered resources
Overallocated resources

Show as: Step Line

Color:

Pattern:

Allocated resources

Show as: Step Line

Color (K):

Pattern:

Proposed Bookings

Show as: Don't Show

Color:

Pattern:

Resource
Overallocated resources

Show as: Bar

Color:

Pattern:

> Select under Filtered Resources to show a Step Line for Over-allocated work and for Allocated work. You will see the resource versus the total for the group if you filter on the group it belongs to.

Allocated resources

Show as: Bar

Color:

Pattern:

Proposed Bookings

Show as: Don't Show

Color:

Pattern:

☑ Show values
☐ Show availability line

Bar overlap: 0 %

Help   OK   Cancel

7. In the **Filtered Resources** section (left) select from the list **Show as**: `Don't Show` ▾ **Step Line** for both **Overallocated** work and **Allocated** work as shown in the previous screenshot, and click `OK`. The view now shows stepped bars for the workload of the resource and a red line for the total work in the project (filter is still **All Resources**).

8. Make sure you have filled in the resource-related field **Group** in the **Resource Sheet**. Then go to the **View** tab, on the **Data** group, select from the list ▼ Filter: [No Filter] ▾ **Group…** the **Group** dialog appears:

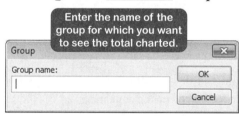

> Enter the name of the group for which you want to see the total charted.

Group

Group name:

OK   Cancel

9. Enter the name of the group to which the resource belongs in the field **Group name** and click `OK`. Now you see the workload of the resource relative to the total workload of the department the person belongs to.

10. Create the header and footer by choosing **File** tab, in the **Backstage** view, click on the **Print** tab, then select **Page Setup**.

For further explanations on Page Setup settings, refer to the section Adjust the Page Setup later in this chapter.

11. Print the report by clicking **Print** 🖨.

Note that unfortunately, you cannot change the y-axis; Project 2010 often creates a y-axis that is too long.

To-Do Lists in Calendar View

The Calendar view doesn't show many tasks within a one day view. When we first discussed this view (review chapter 2), we stated that the Calendar view is particularly suited for creating to-do lists by resource. There are several reasons for this:

➤ Typically, a resource has only one or two tasks on any given day. Two tasks, but not more, can easily be displayed in the Calendar view.

➤ Not all people understand Gantt Charts, but most people can read calendars. To-do lists in the Calendar view are generally easier to understand than in the Gantt Chart.

➤ You can show the resource-specific holidays and vacation days in this view.

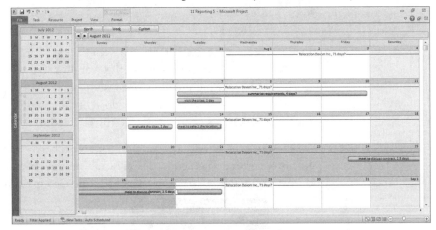

Create a To-Do List for a Resource

1. On the **View** tab, in the **Task Views** group, click ▦ **Calendar**.

2. Select from the list ▽ **Filter:** [No Filter] ▾, the **Using Resource…** filter. The **Using Resource** dialog appears:

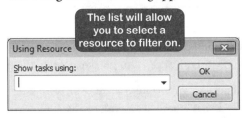

3. Select from the list **Show tasks using** the resource for which to create the to-do list. Click OK .

4. To create the shading for vacation time, right-click over the gray area next to Custom , click Timescale...; the Timescale dialog appears. Click the tab **Date Shading**:

Timescale

| Week Headings | Date Boxes | Date Shading |

Show working time for: Nancy Hilcrest

Sample:

Aug 1

Exception shading

Exception type:

Base Calendar Nonworking Days
Base Calendar Nondefault Working Days
Resource Calendar Working Days
Resource Calendar Nonworking Days

Select a resource and then a pattern for the Resource Calendar Nonworking Days.

Pattern:

Color:

OK   Cancel

5. Under **Show working time for**, select the resource of this to-do list and choose the appropriate pattern and color settings. Click OK . The view now colors or shades the nonworking days for the resource.

6. Create the header and footer by choosing the **File** tab in the **Backstage** view. Click on **Print**, **Page Setup**.

7. Print the report by clicking **Print** .

Formatting & Printing Reports

Now that you've created your view, it's time to format and print that report that you want to distribute to various stakeholders. No matter how interesting and to the point the data is, very few will scan through pages and pages of small, mono-font reports to get to the substance of the report. Your reports need to be formatted in a way that makes the data easy to find, read and interpret.

General Formatting Considerations

The Format tab offers many options to improve the appearance of the output. Any change you make through the Format tab will be stored in the view object that you have on the screen when you make the change.

The Format tab changes when you apply another view. For example, when you are in the Gantt Chart view, the Format tab has a legend at the top indicating Gantt Chart Tools; this is the way that you know that clicking the Format tab, you will access specific options available to format this view. When you realize that each view has its own format menu, you understand that Project 2010 is a much bigger application than it first appears to be.

Following a discussion of general formatting and printing considerations, we will examine the different formatting and printing options for the following specific views:

> Gantt Chart view
> Network Diagram view
> Calendar view
> Resource Sheet view
> Assignment views (Resource Usage and Task Usage)

Choices that are available to you include:

> What text and bar formats do you want?

You can customize the text for an individual task using the **Tasks** tab, and apply any option in the **Font** group or format an individual bar by double-clicking the bar and applying any format in the **Format Bar** dialog box. You can do it faster by applying a style to each type of task by choosing **Format** tab, and in the **Format** group, click **Text Styles** or in the **Bar Styles** group, click **Format** down-arrow and choose **Bar Styles**. We recommend you use the styles first before overriding the styles for single tasks.

You will also find very helpful the new predefined menu of Gantt Chart Styles which can be accessed by choosing **Format** tab, and in the **Gantt Chart Style** group, click the down-arrow. The available styles are in two groups: **Scheduling Styles** and **Presentation Styles**. The first group uses the colors of the bars to distinguish between manually or auto scheduled tasks and the second group will format all the tasks with the same format. You can verify this by applying any available format and then accessing the **Bar Styles** dialog box, by choosing **Format** tab, in the **Bar Styles** group, click **Format** down-arrow and choose **Bar Styles**.

> Which date formats do you want in the spreadsheet and in the timescale?

First choose the default date format for all date fields. On the **File** tab, in the **Backstage** view, click **Options**. In the **Project Options** dialog, in the **Project View** section, select from the **Date Format** list, the format you want to keep for your file. If you want to change the date order (e.g., from mmddyy to ddmmyy), you have to go to the **Control Panel**, **Clock**, **Language**, and **Region**, **Region and Language** (for Windows Vista and Windows XP the root is **Control Panel**, **Regional and Language Options**).

To override the default date format in a specific table, on the **View** tab, in the **Data** group, click ▦, **More Tables…**, click Edit… and select the format you want from the **Date Format** list at the bottom.

To override the default date format in the timescale when you display dates next to the task bars, on the **Format** tab, in the **Format** group, click **Layout** and select the date format from the list **Date Format**.

➤ Do you want to show dependencies in the **Gantt Chart** or **Tracking Gantt?**

On the **Format** tab, in the **Format** group, click . The **Layout** dialog appears; in the **Links** section select the ◉ the option without links or with straight or hooked arrows.

➤ Do you want to roll up detail task bars into their summary task bars in the **Gantt Chart?**

A regular summary task bar looks like this: . A rolled-up summary task bar looks like this with detail task bars rolled up onto it, or like this with milestones rolled up. You can choose between:

- No rolling up (default)
- Rolling up certain hand-picked detail task bars
  Choose the task bars by selecting them: choose the **Task** tab, **Properties** group, and click the **Task Information** button. On the **Task Information** dialog, check ✓ **Roll up** and click OK . Take similar steps for the summary task.
- Rolling up all detail task bars onto their summary task bars
  On the **Format** tab, in the **Format** group, click . On the **Layout** dialog, check ✓ **Always roll up Gantt bars**. To make the rollup appear only when summary tasks are collapsed, you can then also check ✓ **Hide roll up bars when summary expanded**. Click OK .

➤ What fields do you want to show in the timescale of the Task Usage and Resource Usage views?

You can select fields other than the default Work field. On the **Format** tab, in the **Details** group check any ✓ of the available fields for a quick pick. Better yet, click for a complete list. The **Detail Styles** dialog will pop up allowing you to quickly pick a field listed in the Available fields: list and send it to the **Show these fields:** list by clicking Show >> (or << Hide to do the opposite).

➤ What graph details do you want on the Resource Graph view?

You can graph details other than the default Peak Units. On the **Format** tab, in the **Data** group, select from the **Graph:** list the details you want to graph (Work, Cost, Percent Allocation, Remaining Availability, etc.).

Notice that the peak units allow you to find over-allocations quickly, but give an inflated impression of the workloads when you zoom out from days to weeks to months in the timescale. Workloads seem to inflate, because Project 2010 takes the highest bar (the peak unit) of the 4 weeks in a month to summarize the entire month. You should consider changing to the details Work for a more realistic depiction of the expected workload over time.

General Printing Considerations

The Backstage Print Preview

Use the Backstage Print preview to check the header, footer, legend, margins and the timescale before printing or to check the position of the boxes on a Network Diagram.

1. Apply the view you want to print.

2. On the **File** tab, in the **Backstage** view, click **Print**:

Select the printer, the printer properties, the number of copies and Print.

Navigation buttons to browse pages of the printout and Multiple Page Buttons to zoom out the entire pages

Define the Settings for the printing, if you want the entire project or just Specific Dates or Pages, the Landscape Orientation and the size of paper. Additional settings can be set up in the Page Setup Link.

3. Use the multi-page button to zoom out and get an overview of all the printed pages, and then click on one of the pages to zoom into that page.

4. On the **Backstage Print** preview, click where you would like to zoom in to see part of a page in more detail. Click again to zoom out.

5. To change the options available for your printer, click **Printer Properties**.

6. To change the margins, header, footer or legend text, click **Page Setup**.

7. To print the view, click **Print**.

8. To exit print preview without printing, click any tab on the Ribbon.

Print the Current View

To print the current view:

1. Ensure you are at the **Backstage Print Preview.** On the **File** tab, in the **Backstage** view, click **Print** .

> Select the printer from the list and click on the Properties button to set specific printer settings.

2. Select a printer in the **Printer** list.

3. Click **Printer Properties** to select the options available for the printer, such as paper source and orientation. Note that the choices you make here apply to all applications. Click ☐ OK ☐ when when finished to go back to the **Backstage Print** Preview.

4. Specify the Settings explained below.

 Colors you may have used are automatically replaced by hatch patterns on a black-and-white printer.

Print Settings

To print the current view, select from the following settings:

➤ **Print range** of **Pages** and **Dates**
Under **Settings**, select from the ▦ down-arrow list the range you want to print. You can select the **Entire Project**, **Specific Dates** and/or **Pages**.

➤ **Paper Orientation**
Use the second down-arrow list of the **Settings** to choose **Portrait** or **Landscape Orientation**.

➤ **Paper size**
Use the last down-arrow list of the Settings to define your paper size.

Page Setup Settings   The page setup settings are stored in the view object.

To see them on the **File** tab, in the **Backstage** view, click **Print**. Under **Settings**, click the **Page Setup** link.

> The Page Setup dialog allows you to change the layout of data. The settings you choose are stored in the current view.

➤ **Page** tab
  ▸ **Orientation**: When you print the timescale, it is often best to change from ⦿ **Portrait** to ⦿ **Landscape**. This may allow you to keep the entire timescale on one page.
  ▸ The **Scaling** option will shrink or enlarge the print image from 10% to 500%, but is only available if your printer can handle scaling.

➤ **Header**, **Footer**, **Legend** tab
Choose the position first: **Left**, **Center** or **Right**. You can type in any header text, or better, use the lists **General** or **Project Fields** at the bottom of the dialog to select standard phrases. Select the item from the list and then click [Add]; this will add a cryptic code for it in the header, footer or legend. These codes refer to entries you made in the **Advanced Properties**. If you make changes in that dialog, all headers of all views will be updated automatically.

To access the **Advanced Properties** information of the **Project** file, on the **File** tab, in the **Backstage** view, click **Info**, and then click the `Project Information ▾`, **Advanced Properties**.

By default, the header font size is small. To increase it, select the text by dragging over it and clicking $\boxed{\text{A}}$; the **Font** dialog appears, where you can choose the font, style and size.

➤ **View** tab
The important options for task views (except the Calendar view) are:

▸ ☐ **Print all sheet columns** will print all columns, even if they are hidden behind the timescale.

▸ ☐ **Print first** $\boxed{3}$ **columns on all pages**: You should not have to use this option if your report is only one page wide.

▸ ☑ **Print Notes**: This will create a separate page with notes by task. The task IDs are used to relate the notes to the tasks.

▸ ☑ **Print blank pages** will print a page even if it does not show any task bars (timescale) or nodes (Network Diagram).

▸ ☑ **Fit timescale** to end of page is only useful when your timescale does not reach the right-hand side of the page. This option will stretch it, filling the page. Note that it does not shrink the timescale; it only stretches it.

▸ Available in Task Usage or Resource Usage views only:
☑ **Print row totals for values within print date range**
☑ **Print column totals**
These options allow you to add the row totals to the timescale of the usage views on the right-hand side and column totals at the bottom by day, by week or by month, depending on the current time unit.

More detailed information on the Page Setup settings can be found in this chapter under the subject Formatting & Printing the Gantt Chart View.

Insert the Project Logo into the Header or Footer

1. On the **File** tab, in the **Backstage** view, click **Print**.

2. Under **Settings**, click the **Page Setup** link.

3. Click the tab **Header** or **Footer**.

4. Choose the position: **Left**, **Center** or **Right**

5. Click **Insert picture** 🖾; the **Insert Picture** dialog appears:

This dialog lets you insert the logo of the project into the header or footer.

6. Navigate through your directory system and select the image file with the logo of your project.

7. Click [Insert]; the logo is now displayed in the header.

8. If the logo image is too big, you can click on it and selection handles will appear around the image. Point to a corner selection handle and drag it to resize the picture.

Any object you insert in the file increases the file size, so it is useful to determine an appropriate size and resolution for the logo before inserting it. This way you will be able to handle it in another application before moving it into Project to control the resolution and file size.

Check the Spelling

Before you start the spell checker, you should prevent Project 2010 from highlighting abbreviations or codes you use:

1. On the **File** tab, in the **Backstage** view, click **Options**, **Proofing** in order to access the spelling options that are relevant.

2. In the **When correcting spelling in Microsoft Office programs**, check the following options:
   ☑ **Ignore words in UPPERCASE**
   ☑ **Ignore words that contain numbers** to eliminate stopping on abbreviations or codes

3. Under the **When correcting spelling in Project**, keep checked ☑ those columns you want the spell-checker to check; uncheck ☐ the rest.

4. Click [OK].

5. To perform the spell checking, on the **Project** tab, in the **Proofing** group, click ✓.

6. When the spell checker displays a misspelled word in the **Not In Dictionary** field, you can:

   ▶ Click [**Ignore**] or [**Ignore All**] to ignore one or all occurrences of the misspelled word
   OR

   ▶ Type the correction in the **Change To** field and click [**Change**] or click [**Change All**].

   ▶ Click [**Add**] to add the word to the user dictionary.

Insert Manual Page Breaks

You can insert a page break to control exactly what information prints on which page. Although this functionality is not by default in the ribbon, you can customize the Ribbon or the Quick Access Toolbar to make it available.

1. On the **File** tab, in the **Backstage** view, click **Options**, **Quick Access Toolbar**.

2. In the **Project Options** dialog, in the **Choose commands from**: drop-down list, click **All Commands**.

3. Scroll down the commands box until you find the **Insert Page Break** command, click [**Add ->**] and click [**OK**]. The ⬤ **Insert Page Break** button is now available in the **Quick Access Toolbar**.

4. Select the task or resource where you want to begin the next page.

5. Click the ⬤ **Insert Page Break** button. A line that represents the page break will appear above the task or resource you selected.

6. On the **File** tab, in the **Backstage** view, click **Print** and verify the page break in the **Backstage** Preview.

 The page breaks set in the table also insert breaks in other reports that are based on the same table. Therefore, use them only when really needed.

To remove page breaks, position your cursor in any cell below the line of the page break (e.g. same cell when you inserted it) and click ⬤ **Insert Page Break** button.

Adjust Column Width

When you see a cell with hidden or incomplete information, the column isn't wide enough to display the value in the cell. To expand the column width point to the right-hand divider in the column heading. When you see the mouse pointer ↔, double-click. This expands the column width to fit all rows in the schedule, not just the visible rows. Please note that the Predecessor and Successor columns can cause the column to become very wide.

Note that with the Wrap Text function you can accommodate the hidden information by affecting the row height. To apply the Wrap Text, select the cell or the column title, choose **Format** tab, in the **Columns** group, click 📑.

Shorten or Stretch The Timescale

The timescale often has to be adjusted either because it spills over onto the second page and you want to shorten it, or because it occupies only a small part of the page and you want to stretch it.

> **Shorten the Timescale**
> 1. On the **View** tab, in the **Zoom** group, select from the list **Timescale**: `Days ▾`, 🔍 **Timescale…** or double-click on the timescale; the **Timescale** dialog appears.
>
> 2. On any of the tier tabs (**Top Tier**, **Middle Tier**, **Bottom Tier**), decrease the Size percentage which will shorten the timescale. Check the **Preview** box at the bottom to see how far you can go.
> Or
> Modify the units by modifying the **Units** drop-down and the **Count** field. It is a good practice to start with the **Bottom Tier**, then the **Middle Tier** and if shown, the **Top Tier**.

In the task and resource usage views, you can drag the width of the time unit columns to the size you want.

> **Stretch the Timescale to One Page**
> 1. On the **File** tab, in the **Backstage** view, click **Print**. Under **Settings**, click the **Page Setup** link. The **Page Setup** dialog appears.
>
> 2. Click the **View** tab and check ☑ **Fit timescale to end of page**. This will stretch the timescale to fill the page.

Send a Schedule to Colleagues

To send a schedule to colleagues:

1. On the **File** tab, in the **Backstage** view, click **Save & Send**, **Send as Attachment**.

2. Click the **Send as Attachment**. The schedule will be attached to the e-mail. The **Choose Profile** dialog may appear: select a user profile, and click `OK`. The new e-mail message dialog appears:

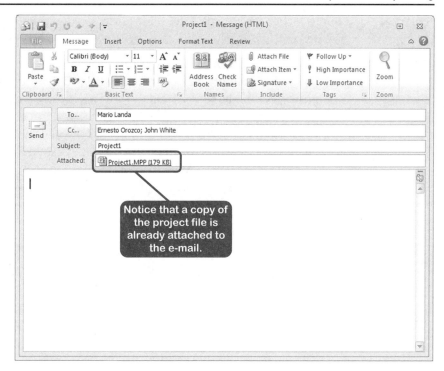

Notice that a copy of the project file is already attached to the e-mail.

3. Fill in the **To** and the **CC** fields, and send the message.

 Notice that you don't even need to save your schedule before sending it; the system always sends the schedule as it appears on your screen

If you don't want your colleagues to be able to change your project schedule, you should create a Portable Document File (PDF) or a XML Paper Specification (XPS) using the new support of Project 2010 to export in those formats. On the **File** tab, in the **Backstage** view, click **Save & Send**, **Create PDF/XPS Document** and then click . The **Browse** dialog will appear. Indicate the name of the file and the place to drop it and click OK.

Sometimes when printing or viewing your document, it is important to retain it's data and formatting. Using the PDF and XPS formats in the Create PDF/XPS Document feature helps with this. Note that the PDF format is more frequently used for sharing documents than for printing documents.

11

Formatting & Printing the Gantt Chart View

In this section we'll prepare the Gantt Chart view for printing. There are two wizards available to help you:

➤ **Copy Picture to Office Wizard** on the **Task** tab.
This wizard has potential, but requires trial and error to adjust the copied picture, as it can be so small that you can't read it. This is because the wizard doesn't allow you to adjust the timescale (time units, skip factor for time units, zoom factor/size). We recommend that you first make it look good on the screen and then use this wizard to quickly export what you see on the screen to Word, PowerPoint or Visio. To access the **Copy Picture** wizard, on the **Task** tab, in the **Clipboard** group, click the **Copy** down-arrow, **Copy Picture**.

➤ **Gantt Chart Wizard**
With the Gantt Chart Wizard you can choose format options for the Gantt Chart by answering prompts. This wizard allows you to enjoy some of the gems hidden in the **Format** tab, **Bar Styles** group. Some of the things you can accomplish with this wizard are:

▶ Display the critical path by coloring the critical task bars red. (This can also be done through the menu items on the **Format** tab, **Bar Styles** group, check ✔ **Critical Tasks**.)

▶ Display text of your choice to the left of, to the right of, or inside the task bars for summary tasks, detail tasks and milestones. (This can also be done through the menu items on the **Format** tab, **Bar Styles** group, , **Bar Styles**, **Text** tab.)

▶ Change the shape and color of the task bars for summary tasks, detail tasks and milestones. (This can also be done through the menu items on the **Format** tab, **Bar Styles** group, **Bar Styles**, **Bars** tab.)

 The **Gantt Chart Wizard** is available in Project 2010, but not in the default Ribbon. You must customize either the **Ribbon** or the **Quick Access Toolbar** to have this feature available.

 To customize the ribbon, choose **File** tab, in the **Backstage** view, click **Project Options**, **Customize Ribbon**. For more detail about customizing the ribbon, please refer to chapter 2.

Adjust Text Styles

Text styles can be applied to certain task types. The dialog is similar to the **Format**, **Font** dialog except that the font dialog is used for formatting only those tasks that are selected, whereas the **Text Styles** dialog allows you to format based on the type of task.

1. On the **Format** tab, in the **Format** group, click **Text Styles**; the **Text Styles** dialog appears:

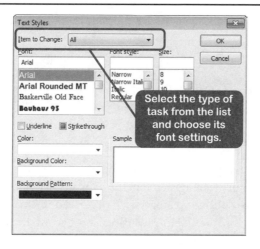

2. From the list **Item to Change:** All ▾ at the top, select the type of task to change. Then select the format using **Font, Font style, Size** and **Color**. Check the **Sample** box at the bottom to see your selections.

3. Click [OK].

 If you select the item **All**, all the text will be affected, even the text styles you previously set.

The **Bar Styles** group, on the **Format** Ribbon allows you to color the critical task bars red. With the **Text Styles** dialog you can color the text of the task names of the critical tasks red as well to make them appear uniform and stand out whether you look in the spreadsheet or in the timescale.

Wrap Task Names   You can double the row height of only the tasks with long names (skip the first step if you want to do this) or you can double the height of all rows. The task names will wrap around automatically.

1. Select the tasks to adjust the row height by holding down [Control] and clicking the row headers of the tasks to adjust.

   OR

   Select the entire spreadsheet by clicking on the table selector at the intersection of the row and column headings in the top left corner of the spreadsheet: [ ].

2. Point to one of the selected row dividers in the row headings (normally the ID column); make sure you see the double-headed arrow mouse pointer ‡.

3. Drag the divider down to at least double the row height. Project 2010 will automatically wrap the text onto the second line, but only wrap the words

in the text fields, like Task Name, Notes and the extra fields (Text1, Text2, etc.).

OR

 On the **Format** tab, in the **Columns** group, click

 You will double the number of pages in your printout if you double the row height for all rows.

Adjust Column Width

➤ You can wrap the text in the column headings as well. Right click on the column heading and on the pop up list select **Field Settings**; in the **Field Settings** dialog check ☑ **Header Text Wrapping** and click ⬜ OK . If the column width is too narrow for the title, it will start wrapping automatically.

➤ Right click on the column heading and on the pop up list select **Field Settings**; the **Field Settings** dialog appears. Click ⬜ Best Fit ; the column width automatically takes the appropriate width for all tasks in the project, even the ones not currently visible on the screen.

OR

Point to the divider in the column heading, and make sure you see a double-headed mouse pointer: | Duration ⇄ Work |

Double-click. The width of the column is now wide enough to accommodate the widest text in the field for the entire project (up to a maximum of about 150 characters).

Position the Pane Divider on a Column Split

You can put the divider between the spreadsheet and the Gantt chart exactly on the border of a column.

1. Point with the mouse pointer anywhere on the vertical divider that separates the spreadsheet from the timescale; you should now see the mouse pointer ◀▐▶.

2. Drag it close to the column split where you want it.

3. While you continue to see the mouse pointer ◀▐▶, double-click and the divider now jumps to the column split that is closest to it.

View the Whole Project Timescale

This option will change the timescale so that you can see the entire project within one screen width.

On the **View** tab, in the **Zoom** group, click 🔍 Entire Project;

Format the Timescale

In the Status bar, you are able to zoom in or zoom out by directly clicking on the zoom slider ⊖———∇————⊕ or on the **View** tab, in the **Zoom** group, click 🔍, 🔍 **Zoom Out** or **Zoom In** 🔍.

➤ To customize the timescale to your exact preference:

1. Double-click on the timescale itself [Sep 9, '12 | S M T W T F S].

   OR

   On the **View** tab, in the **Zoom** group, select from the list **Timescale**: [Days ▾], 🔍. The **Timescale** dialog appears:

   ![Timescale dialog box showing Top Tier, Middle Tier, Bottom Tier, and Non-working time tabs. Middle tier formatting with Units: Months, Label: Jan '09, Count: 1, Align: Left, Tick lines checked, Use fiscal year checked. Timescale options Show: Two tiers (Middle, Bottom), Size: 100%, Scale separator checked. Preview showing Jun '10, Jul '10, Aug '10, Sep '10, Oct '10, Nov '10 with weekly numbers. Labels point to Middle tier and Bottom tier.]

2. If you want to display the third tier, select **Three tiers** in the **Show** list. Choose the settings for the **Top Tier** (top of the timescale), the **Middle Tier** and the **Bottom Tier** by clicking on the appropriate tabs. The **Count** is an increment: if it is set to 2 in a day-by-day timescale, it will go from the 1st to the 3rd and so forth. As a result, only every other day will be displayed.

3. Click [OK].

Having three tiers in the timescale allows you to show the fiscal year and calendar year timescales next to each other so that there can be no misunderstanding about dates. (You can set the start month of the fiscal year in **File** tab, **Options**, **Schedule**. Select from the list **Fiscal year starts in**.)

By using the Timescale drop-down menu, you are able to set the bottom tier and project automatically assigns the middle or upper tier a logical timescale that is larger than the previous. On the **View** tab, in the **Zoom** group, select from the list **Timescale:** Days ▾ the scale-unit for the bottom tier.

Format the Task Bars

1. Double-click anywhere in the background of the timescale area.

   OR

   On the **Format** tab, in the **Bar Styles** group, click **Format** down-arrow and choose **Bar Styles**. The **Bar Styles** dialog appears:

> The task bars can be customized in this dialog. Select an item in the top and then choose its Text and Bar setting in the bottom.

Name	Appearance	Show For ... Tasks	Row	From	To
Task		Normal,Active,Not Manually Scheduled	1	Task Start	Task Finish
Split	....	Normal,Split,Active,Not Manually Schedul	1	Task Start	Task Finish
Milestone	◆	Milestone,Active,Not Group By Summary,Nc	1	Task Finish	Task Finish
Summary		Summary,Active,Not Manually Scheduled	1	Task Start	Task Finish
Project Summary		Project Summary	1	Task Start	Task Finish
*Group By Summary		Group By Summary	1	Task Start	Task Finish
*Rolled Up Task		Normal,Rolled Up,Not Summary,Not Manua	1	Task Start	Task Finish
*Rolled Up Split	....	Normal,Rolled Up,Split,Not Summary	1	Task Start	Task Finish
*Rolled Up Progress		Normal,Rolled Up,Not Summary	1	Task Start	CompleteThrough
*Rolled Up Milestone	◇	Milestone,Rolled Up,Not Milestone			ish
External Tasks		External Tasks,Not Milestone			ish
External Milestone	◇	Milestone External Tasks			ish

> Selected item and its bar settings

Text | **Bars**

Start
Shape: ▾
Type: ▾
Color: ▾

Middle
Shape: ▾
Pattern: ▾
Color: ▾

End
Shape: ▾
Type: ▾
Color: ▾

Help   OK   Cancel

2. In the list in the top half (see next screenshot), select the type of task for which you want to change the appearance:

Name	Appearance	Show For ... Tasks
Task		Normal,Active,Not Manually Scheduled
Split	....	Normal,Split,Active,Not Manually Schedule
Milestone	◆	Milestone,Active,Not Group By Summary,Nc
Summary		Summary,Active,Not Manually Scheduled
Project Summary		Project Summary

3. Choose your settings for the selected task type at the bottom of the dialog on the **Text** and **Bars** tabs.

4. Click OK .

Some remarks about this powerful, but not so intuitive dialog box:

➤ Project 2010 first creates in the Gantt chart the task bar listed at the top, and then draws the second task bar on top of the first one. If they overlap, only the second bar can be seen fully. Therefore, the order in which the items are listed is important. Lower ones can cover higher ones in the list.

➤ Under Show For … Tasks:

▸ The word *Normal* is used as a default for any task that is not a summary task, not a milestone, not a flagged and not any of the other task types shown in the pull-down list.

▸ You can use the listed items. You can also type in the word *Not* in front of each item to create an exception for that type of task. *Not Summary* means format the task bars as specified for any task type except for summary tasks.

▸ You can specify multiple criteria separated by a comma. The comma functions as a "logical and", i.e., if you request *Normal, Split* the comma between *Normal* and *Split* means that it will apply this bar style only to tasks that are normal and have a split. No other tasks are affected.

➤ The lists you can display in the fields *From* and *To* have all the regular task fields in them, but also some additional ones specifically for the timescale, like the CompleteThrough date and Negative Slack. Neither one is a regular task field you can display in the spreadsheet. The CompleteThrough is used in the Tracking Gantt to display progress bars.

➤ On the **Text** tab in the bottom half of the dialog, you can add text to the left of, the right of, or even inside the task bars. You will find the following default settings in the Gantt Chart:

▸ Resource Names are shown to the right of detail task bars.

▸ The Start dates are shown to the right of milestone diamonds.

Show Milestone Diamonds on Summary Task Bars

1. Select the milestones by holding down ⌗Control and clicking on each milestone in the **Task Name** column.

2. On the **Task** tab, in the **Properties** group, click **Task Information** ▣ and the **Task Information** dialog appears. Click the tab **General**; the dialog now looks like this:

3. Check ✓ **Roll up**.

4. Click [OK].

5. Select the summary task, click **Task Information** 🖽 again and make sure that the option ✓ **Roll up** is selected:

6. Click [OK].

Adjust the Page Setup

Setting the Page Orientation

The Page Setup settings are view specific. For each view listed in the View menu, you can set different settings that are stored in the view object itself.

The Gantt Chart usually fits better when printed in Landscape. To change the orientation:

1. On the **File** tab, in the **Backstage** view, click **Print**. Under **Settings**, click the **Page Setup** link; the **Page Setup – Gantt Chart** dialog appears. Any changes you make in this dialog are stored in the current view, in our case the **Gantt Chart** view.

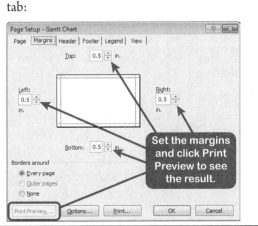

2. On the **Page** tab you can change:
   ▸ The page orientation from **Portrait** to **Landscape**
   ▸ The **Scaling** option to fit the report on a certain number of pages

3. Click [OK] to see the results on screen or on paper.

Set the Margins

To set the margins:

1. On the **File** tab, in the **Backstage** view, click **Print**. Under **Settings**, click the **Page Setup** link and the **Page Setup** dialog appears. Click the **Margins** tab:

2. Set he margins you need. Click [OK] to check if the settings are right.

Create a Header, Footer or Legend

To create a header, footer or legend:

1. On the **File** tab, in the **Backstage** view, click **Print** 🖶 . Under **Settings**, click the **Page Setup** link, and the **Page Setup** dialog appears. Click the tab **Header**, **Footer** or **Legend**:

Header is currently selected.

If you added specific values (see below), the references appear inside square brackets preceded by an ampersand. The font size was increased for this view.

There are several buttons to add general information and two lists to Add value from specific fields.

2. Click the tab Left, Center or Right and position the cursor inside the text box where you want to add a reference to project data. You can even press [Enter ↵] to create extra lines.

3. Select a reference from the **General** list at the bottom and click [Add]. The reference is inserted at your cursor position. Add as many text references as needed; most refer to data entered in **Advanced Properties** (on the **File** tab, **Backstage** view, **Info** tab, [Project Information ▾]) and the **Project Information** [Project Information ▾] (on **Project** tab, **Properties** group) dialogs and all start with an ampersand (&). You can also type literal text such as: *Page &[Page] of &[Pages]*, which will print as *Page 1 of 9*.

4. Using the **Project fields** list at the bottom, you can insert project-level information, like the **Baseline Finish** and forecast **Finish** date, or the **Baseline Cost** and forecast **Cost**, or calculated values, like the **% Complete** and **Remaining Duration** for the project.

5. Click one of the buttons to add information quickly:

Button	For
A	Format Text Font: font, size and style To format the text in the header, select the text first and then click **A**.
🔢	Insert Page Count: page number
📑	Insert Total Page Count: total number of pages
🗓	Insert Current Date: the system date
🕐	Insert Current Time: the system time
📄	Insert File Name: the schedule name
🖼	Insert Picture: Takes you into a dialog for inserting a graphic image into the header, footer or legend; often used to insert the project logo

Click **OK**.

Reports That Include the Notes

The **Notes** field can hold a lot of text; there is virtually no limit to it. You may need to capture a lot of text when creating a WBS dictionary or capturing checklist items or reminders to yourself. To include the notes in a report, you have two options:

➤ Print all the notes together on a separate notes page using a view
➤ Print the notes in between the tasks they relate to using a Report

Print a View with a Separate Notes Page

The following is an example of a separate notes page using views:

WBS Dictionary International Institute For Learning

1   **REQUIREMENTS**
     The requirements deliverable includes:
     • researching the wishes of all the staff thought a questionaire by email
     • the results should be sumarized in order to achieve an 80% satisfaction rate by the personnel it is important to find out
       about the requirements.
5   **LOCATION**
     The location deliverable is the new location with the following requirements.
     • the location should have a capacity of up to 150 work spaces.
     • the location should be accesible for disabled people.
     • the location should have parking facilities for at least 50 cars.
     • the location should modern work cubicles and an open workspace.
     Tht deliverable is the physical location and the contract with the landlord or lease holder. The corporate lawyer should review
     contract.
12   **REMODELING CONTRACT**
     The deliverable Remodeling Contract is the contract with the general contractor to renovate the office space to meet the needs
     and requirements of the work force. At least two different contractors should be asked for bid.
18   **REMODELED LOCATION**
     The deliverable Remodeled Location is the finished new location ready to be moved into. All the activities of the general
     contractor should be included in this deliverable.
27   **MOVE**
     The deliverable Move is the physical transfer of equipment, materials and archives to the new location. The employees will
     have to pack their own files and materials.
     The move will have to take place on a weekend to minimize the interruption of normal operations and to minimize the cost of
     unproductiveemployees.

Page 7

7 of 7

To create it, follow these steps:

1. In the **Gantt Chart**, on the **File** tab, in the **Backstage** view, click the **Print** tab. Under **Settings**, select from the down-arrow list, **Notes**

   OR

   Click the **Page Setup** link. The **Page Setup** dialog appears.

   The View tab has an option to include the notes.

2. Click the **View** tab.

3. Check ☑ **Print notes**.

4. Click ⟨ OK ⟩.

Print a Report with Notes in Between Tasks

The following report shows the notes inserted in between tasks:

Notes in between tasks.

1. On the **Project** tab, in the **Reports** group, click the ▦ **Reports** icon, the **Reports** dialog appears:

Under Custom you can customize the report.

2. Double-click on **Custom** 📄; the **Custom Report** dialog appears.

3. Scroll down the list and select **Task**; the dialog should now look like:

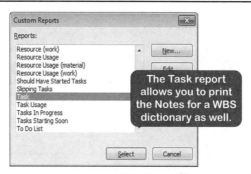

4. Click [Edit...]; the **Task Report** dialog appears.

5. Click the **Definition** tab, if needed, and check ☑ **Show summary tasks** to include the deliverables.

6. Click the **Details** tab and check ☑ **Notes**, as in the following screenshot:

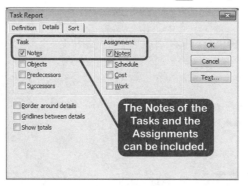

7. The notes will now appear in between the tasks in the printout. Click [OK] and click [Select].

Formatting & Printing the Network Diagram View

Printing the Network Diagram can be helpful in communicating the flow of the logic to team members and other stakeholders. Prior to printing, you can change the appearance of the view to suit your needs.

The Layout of the Nodes

You can customize which fields are shown, the border of the nodes and the font.

Display Only the Task Name

Change the layout of the fields on the task nodes in such a way that only task names will show. This will allow you to see many more nodes within one screen.

1. Ensure you are in the **Network Diagram** view. On the **Task** tab, in the **View** group, click 🔳 **Network Diagram**.

2. On the **Format** tab, in the **Format** group, click ⬗ **Box Styles** and the **Box Styles** dialog appears:

3. Click [More Templates…], and the **Data Templates** dialog opens:

Data Templates

Templates in "Network Diagram":

Standard
Cost
Earned Value
External
Inserted Project
Milestone
Summary
Tracking
WBS
Work

New...

Copy...

Edit...

Import...

Delete...

> Click on each template and in the Preview pane, you can see what its layout is.

Preview

Show data from task ID:

[Name]	
Start: [Start]	ID: [ID]
Finish: [Finish]	Dur: [Duration]
Res: [Resource Names]	

Close

4. Here you can define a **New** template or **Copy** an existing one to use as the base to create a custom one.

5. Click New... , and the **Data Template Definition** dialog opens:

Data Template Definition

Template name: Data Template 1

Format cells

Show data from task ID: 0

Cell Layout...

Choose cell(s):

> You can choose the fields you want to display on each node in the Network Diagram.

Font...   Calibri ...

Horizontal alignment: Left

Vertical alignment: Center

Limit cell text to: 1 line

Show label in cell:

Date format:

Help   OK   Cancel

6. Enter a name for this template in the field **Template Name**, for example *Task Names Only*.

7. In the table-like area below **Choose cell(s)**, click on a cell in the grid; a list button appears:

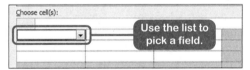

Choose cell(s):

> Use the list to pick a field.

8. Select from this list the field to display. If you want task names only, select the field **Name**. You have now created a new layout template.

9. If you have long task names, set **Limit cell text** to more than one line.

10. Click [OK], and you are now back in the **Data Templates** dialog; you can see the newly created template listed:

11

```
Standard
Cost
Earned Value
External
Inserted Project
Milestone
Summary
Task Names Only
Tracking
WBS
Work
```

11. Click [Close], and you are now back in the **Box Styles** dialog.

12. Now we have to apply this template to the different types of tasks. Notice that within one Network Diagram view you can apply several templates to different types of tasks to make them look exactly the way you want. Select under **Style Settings For** all the different types of tasks by dragging over them, or select them more specifically by holding down [Control] and clicking.

13. Under **Data Template** display the list and select the data template you just created.

14. Click [OK], and the **Network Diagram** view now shows nodes with only the task names, which fits many more nodes within one screen.

 This allows you to create fancy Network Diagrams with dates on the milestones, but durations on the detail tasks, costs on the summary deliverables, etc., all within one view.

Change the Border of the Nodes

You can use different border formats for different types of tasks.

1. Ensure you are in the **Network Diagram** view. On the **Task** tab, in the **View** group, click ▦ **Network Diagram**.

2. On the **Format** tab, in the **Format** group, click 🖫 **Box Styles** and the **Box Styles** dialog appears:

3. In the list **Style Settings for** select the type of task for which to change the border.

4. In the bottom section, **Border**, you can choose the **Shape**, **Color** and **Width**. The **Preview** area in the top right shows what it will look like when done. You can also choose a fill **Background Color** and a **Pattern**.

5. If you have more than one data field inside the nodes, you can choose to:
   ☑ **Show horizontal gridlines** and/or
   ☑ **Show vertical gridlines.**

6. Click [OK].

Change the Font

To change the font in a report:

1. Ensure you are in the **Network Diagram** view. On the **Task** tab, in the **View** group, click 🖼 **Network Diagram**.

2. On the **Format** tab, in the **Format** group, click 🖌 **Box Styles** and the **Box Styles** dialog appears:

3. Click [More Templates...], and the **Data Templates** dialog opens:

4. In the list **Templates in <schedule name>** select the data template for which to change the font.

5. Click [Edit...], and the **Data Template Definition** dialog opens.

6. Click [Font...], and select the font type and size you need.

7. Click [OK], and you are back in the **Data Template Definition** dialog.

8. Click [OK], and you are back in the **Data Template** dialog.

9. Click [Close], and you are back in the **Box Styles** dialog.

10. Click [OK], and you should see the new font applied.

The Layout of the Diagram

Show Dependency Type on Arrows

It's often helpful to see the type of dependency displayed for each task relationship, as in the following screenshots:

➤ Without lag: [FS] ▸

➤ With lag: ⊣ FS+5d ▸

This makes it easier to verify the network logic.

1. Ensure you are in the **Network Diagram** view. On the **Task** tab, in the **View** group, click 🖼 **Network Diagram**.

2. On the **Format** tab, in the **Show/Hide** group, check the ☑ **Link Labels**

   OR

   On the **Format** tab, in the **Format** group, click 📊 **Layout**, and the **Layout** dialog appears:

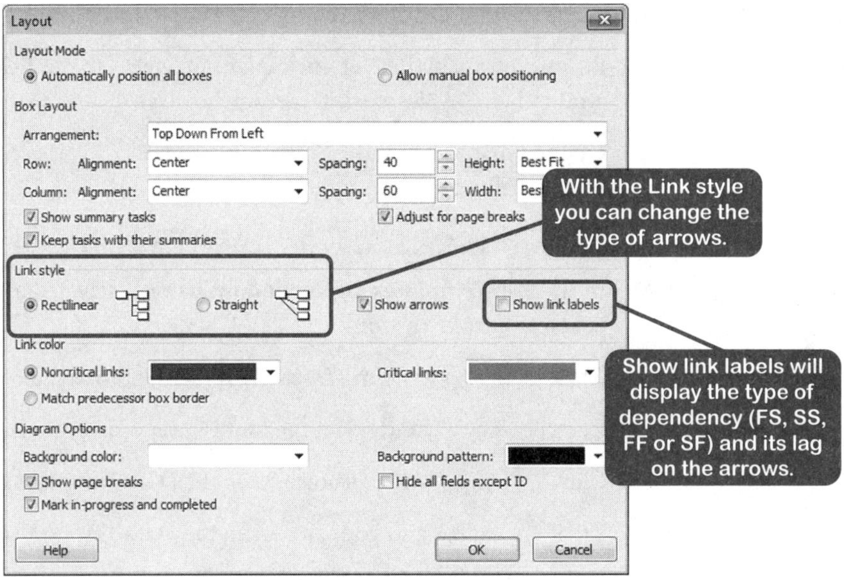

With the Link style you can change the type of arrows.

Show link labels will display the type of dependency (FS, SS, FF or SF) and its lag on the arrows.

3. Under **Link style** check ✓ **Show link labels**.

4. Click [OK], and you will now see **FS** attached to each Finish-to-Start arrow, as well as **SS**, **FF** and **SF** attached to their respective arrows. You will also see any **Lag** (lead) displayed.

Change Arrow Type   To change the arrow type:

1. Ensure you are in the **Network Diagram** view. On the **Task** tab, in the **View** group, click 🔲 **Network Diagram**.

2. On the **Format** tab, in the **Show/Hide** group, check the ✓ **Straight** to set the arrow type to straight or uncheck ☐ **Straight** to set it as Rectilinear.

    OR

    On the **Format** tab, in the **Format** group, click 🔲 **Layout**, and in the **Layout** dialog, in the **Link style** section, select the type of arrow: ⦿ **Rectilinear** or ⦿ **Straight**. Click [OK].

Display Progress Marks   You can indicate the status of a task with diagonal lines in the nodes:

➤ not started: [visit the sites]

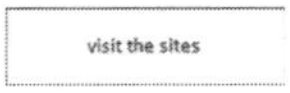

➤ in progress: [summarize requirements]

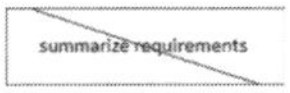

➤ completed: [research staff requirements]

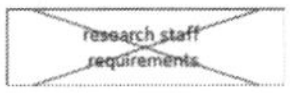

You can toggle these on and off by choosing the **Format** tab, in the **Show/Hide** group, checking or clearing the ✓ **Progress Marks**.

Hide Summary Tasks

Summary tasks look like parallelograms in the Network Diagram view:

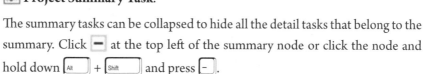

Summary tasks have a collapse/expand button that will hide/display all their detail tasks.

Write	
Start: Thu 8/2/12	ID: 1
Finish: Fri 8/3/12	Dur: 2 days?
Comp: 0%	

If you set all the logic between detail tasks, as we recommend, you can remove the summary tasks from the screen to remove clutter.

On the **Format** tab, in the **Show/Hide** group, check or clear the ☑ **Summary Tasks** to show or hide the summary tasks.

You can do the same for the Project Summary Task by checking or clearing the ☑ **Project Summary Task**.

Collapse or Expand Summary Tasks

The summary tasks can be collapsed to hide all the detail tasks that belong to the summary. Click ▬ at the top left of the summary node or click the node and hold down [Alt] + [Shift] and press [-].

They can be expanded again by clicking ✚ or holding down [Alt] + [Shift] and pressing [+].

Notice that if you collapse a summary task, you hide the detail tasks and also their dependencies. The network may now appear to have loose ends that may not really be loose ends. All real loose ends need to be tied up. Before checking the logic in the Network Diagram, we recommend you expand all summary tasks, by going to the **View** tab, in the **Data** group and clicking ⊞ **Outline** down-arrow, **All Subtasks**.

Improve the Node Layout

Project 2010 attempts to arrange the nodes as well as it can. By default, the nodes are laid out from the top left to the bottom right, but Project 2010 has several layout arrangements to choose from. You can improve the layout by choosing a different arrangement, or you can move nodes manually.

➤ **Select a Layout Arrangement**
 1. On the **Format** tab, in the **Format** group, click ▦ **Layout**, and the **Layout** dialog appears:

For automatic positioning, you can select an arrangement from the list.

2. Make sure that under **Layout Mode**, ◉ **Automatically position all boxes** is selected.

3. Under **Arrangement** use the list:

   Top Down From Left ▾ to change the layout of the nodes.

4. Click [OK], and the layout of the nodes changes. If the layout isn't satisfactory, try another layout arrangement.

There are also time-phased arrangements available by day, week or month; these are also known as Time-Scaled Network Diagrams. Unfortunately, Project 2010 does not show a timescale. The time-scaled view is useful when optimizing the network.

In addition to selecting a layout arrangement for all of the nodes, you can make adjustments to the layout of selected nodes.

➤ **Improve the Layout of Selected Nodes**
   If you are manually arranging the nodes, you may still want to position groups of nodes within the selected arrangement.

   1. On the **Format** tab, in the **Format** group, click 🖫 **Layout** and select ◉ **Allow manual box positioning**. Select an **Arrangement** from the list and click [OK].

   2. Select the nodes by dragging a lasso around them.

OR

Hold down [Control] and click on them.

3. On the **Format** tab, in the **Layout** group, click 🖭 **Layout Now**. Project 2010 rearranges the nodes as best it can according to the arrangement that is currently selected in the **Layout** dialog.

➤ **Lay Out Single Nodes Manually**

1. On the **Format** tab, in the **Format** group, click 🖭 **Layout**, and the **Layout** dialog appears:

Layout	☒

Layout Mode

○ Automatically position all boxes   ◉ Allow manual box positioning

Box Layout

Arrangement: Top Down From Left

Row:	Alignment:	Center ▼	Spacing:	40 ▲▼	Height: Best Fit
Column:	Alignment:	Center ▼	Spacing:	60 ▲▼	Width: Best Fit

☑ Show summary tasks   ☑ Adjust for page breaks
☑ Keep tasks with their summaries

> If you want to drag boxes around, select Allow manual box positioning.

Link style

◉ Rectilinear   ○ Straight   ☑ Show arrows   ☐ Show link labels

Link color

◉ Noncritical links: ▬▬▬ ▼   Critical links: ▬▬▬ ▼
○ Match predecessor box border

Diagram Options

Background color: _____ ▼   Background pattern: ▬▬▬ ▼
☑ Show page breaks   ☑ Hide all fields except ID
☑ Mark in-progress and completed

Help		OK	Cancel

2. Select ◉ **Allow manual box positioning**.

3. Click [OK].

4. Point to the border of the node you want to move, and make sure that the mouse pointer changes to 🔆.

5. Click and hold down, then drag the node to its new location.

➤ **Lay Out Groups of Nodes Manually**

1. First you have to select all nodes to move as a group. Click on the first node and hold down [Control]; then click on the other nodes. The nodes are highlighted to show they have been selected

OR

Click and hold down to drag a lasso around all the task nodes to select

OR

Hold down [Control] and click on the border of a summary task to select it and all its detail tasks

OR

Hold down [Shift] and click on the border of a detail task to select its entire chain of successors.

2. Click and hold down on the border of one of the selected nodes. Make sure you see the mouse pointer 🖟.

3. Click and hold down to drag the group to its new location.

Don't choose the **Format** tab, Layout group, 🖼 **Layout Now** after moving nodes manually; it rearranges the entire Network Diagram and undoes all your laborious manual moving. If it happens by accident, you can undo the mess by choosing **Undo Entry** 🔄 from the **Quick access toolbar** (before doing anything else).

Formatting & Printing the Calendar View

Adjust Row Height and Column Width

While in the Calendar view, click [Custom] and select the number of weeks to display within one screen to adjust the row heights of the days.

OR

Point to the horizontal divider that separates the weeks; the mouse pointer changes to ✚. Click and drag the divider up to decrease the height of all rows. Drag it down to increase the height.

You can always use the Month and Week buttons which return default sizes. The [Month] **Month** button returns a 4-week view and the [Week] **Week** button returns a 7-day view.

Double-click the right-hand side of the column dividers between the days to adjust the column widths so they best fit in the entire screen. You can also drag them, but this usually takes several trial and error attempts.

Change the Timescale

While in the **Calendar** view, double-click on the timescale; the **Timescale** dialog appears. Click tab **Week Headings**:

On the page **Week Headings** you can:

➤ Change the titles shown for the months, weeks and days.

➤ Select **Show week with** ◉ **5 days** as opposed to the default **7 days** if your team never works weekend days.

Format the Calendar View

In the **Calendar** view, choose **Format** tab, and in the **Format** group, click 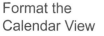 **Bar Styles**. You can:

➤ Choose the appearance of the different types of tasks.

> ➤ Add text labels inside the task bars by selecting the labels in the **Field(s)** dropdown list. You can even add multiple labels, like **Name** and **Resource Name**, but you will find that in short task bars, the text is often cut off to fit inside the bar.

> ➤ When task names are too long for the task bars, which is common for one-day tasks, use ☑ **Wrap text in bars**.

Improve the Layout of Task Bars

1. In the **Calendar** view, choose the **Format** tab. In the **Layout** group, click the ⬛ launcher to the right; the **Layout** dialog appears

2. Under **Method** you can select different layout arrangements for the task bars:

   ◉ **Use current sort order** will list the task bars based upon the active sorting.

   ◉ **Attempt to fit as many tasks as possible** tries to optimize the use of space by displaying more than one bar horizontally.

3. If you check ☑ **Automatic layout**, the task bars will be rearranged every time the sort order changes or tasks are inserted or deleted.

Formatting & Printing the Resource Sheet View

The **Project Guide** toolbar has a link on the **Report** side pane, called **Print current view as a report**. Unfortunately, the wizard mostly helps you with the **File, Page Setup** and **File, Print** choices and little with the choices in the **Format** menu. Next we will discuss additional features not covered by the wizard.

Customize the Table

1. On the **View** tab, in the **Data** group, click ▥, **More Tables…**; the **More Tables** dialog appears:

> **More Tables**
>
> Tables: ◉ Task ○ Resource
>
> Baseline
> Constraint Dates
> Cost
> Delay
> Earned Value
> Earned Value Cost Indicators
> Earned Value Schedule Indic
> Entry
> Export
> Hyperlink
> Rollup Table
>
> New...
> Edit...
> Copy...
>
> Notice that this dialog can list Task-related tables and Resource-related tables.
>
> Apply   Cancel

2. Select ◉ **Resource** to display the list of resource-related tables. Select a table that is close to what you need and click [Copy...]; the **Table Definition** dialog appears:

> **Table Definition in 'Project1'**
>
> Name: Copy of &Cost   ☐ Show in menu
> Table
>
> [Cut Row] [Copy Row] [Paste Row] [Insert Row] [Delete Row]
>
> ID

Field Name	Align Data	Width	Title	Align Title	Header Wrapping	Text Wrapping
ID	Center	6		Left	Yes	No
Name	Left	20	Resource Name	Left	Yes	Yes
Cost	Right	14		Left	Yes	No
Baseline Cost	Right	14		Left	Yes	No
Cost Variance	Right	14	Variance	Left	Yes	No
Actual Cost	Right	14		Left	Yes	No
Remaining Cost	Right	14	Remaining	Left	Yes	No

> Date format: Default   Row height: 1
>
> ☑ Lock first column
> ☑ Auto-adjust header row heights
> ☑ Show 'Add New Column' interface
>
> These fields will end up as columns in the spreadsheet.
>
> Help   OK   Cancel

3. Change the **Name** for the new table to a more descriptive name.

4. To add this table to the menu, check ☑ **Show in Menu**.

5. To delete a field from the table, click the row to delete and click [Delete Row] or press [Delete].

6. To insert a new field in the table, click the row before which you want the new field to appear and click [Insert Row] or press [Ins] on its **Field Name** and select the new field from the list that appears. Select the field from the list.

7. Click [OK] and [Apply].

Extra columns you may have used (**Text1, Text2, ... Number1, ... Flag1**) can be permanently renamed. On the Project tab, in the Properties group, click **Custom Fields** icon. This feature allows you to create new fields for resources like *Position* or *Telephone Number*. You can permanently rename these fields in the project database by clicking [Rename...]. This is a better way than simply changing the Title in the Table Definition dialog which will only be visible in that particular table.

Sort Resources Alphabetically

On the **Task** tab, in the **Data** group, click on the **Sort** down-arrow and pick one of the predefined sorting orders, such as **By Cost, By Name** or **By ID**.

OR

To sort on other fields:

1. On the **Task** tab, in the **Data** group, click on the **Sort** down-arrow, **Sort by...**; the **Sort** dialog appears:

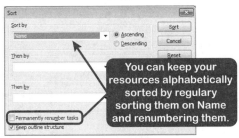

2. Then choose the first sort key in the **Sort by** list and the sorting order ⦿ **Ascending** or ⦿ **Descending**. If necessary, set a second key under **Then by** to break ties that may occur in the sorted list.

3. You can check the ☑ **Permanently renumber resources option** to keep the resources sorted in the chosen order. This will ensure that the resources are listed alphabetically in all lists where resource names are shown.

4. Click [Sort] to effect the sorting.

Format the Text

To make formatting changes to your text:

1. In the **Resource Sheet** view, choose **Format** tab, and in the **Format** group, click **Text Styles**; the **Text Styles** dialog appears:

Text Styles allow for quick changes to the font of certain types of resources.

2. Select from the list **Item to Change** the **Over-allocated resources** and notice that by default these critical resources are displayed in red.

3. Choose a font, style, size and color for the item and click [OK].

Format the Gridlines

You can add or remove gridlines in your report:

1. While in the **Resource Sheet** view, choose **Format** tab, and in the **Format** group, click ▦ **Gridlines**. The **Gridlines** dialog appears:

Gridlines can be added or removed.

2. Select an item in the list **Line to change** first, then select the **Type** of line for this item, its **Color** and **At Interval**. Click [OK].

Choose the Page Setup

To make changes in the page setup of your report:

1. On the **File** tab, in the **Backstage** view, click **Print**. Under **Settings**, click the **Page Setup** link; the **Page Setup – Resource Sheet** dialog appears. Any changes you make in this dialog are stored in the current view, in our case the Resource Sheet view.

2. On the tab **Page** you can change:
    ▶ The page orientation from **Portrait** to **Landscape**
    ▶ The **Scaling** option to fit the report on a certain number of pages

3. Click the **Margins** tab if you want to adjust the width of the page margin.

4. To insert **Headers, Footers** or a **Legend**, review the instructions.

5. Select other options you need.

6. Click [OK] to see the results on screen or on paper.

7. You can preview the view on the right area of the **Backstage** Print view.

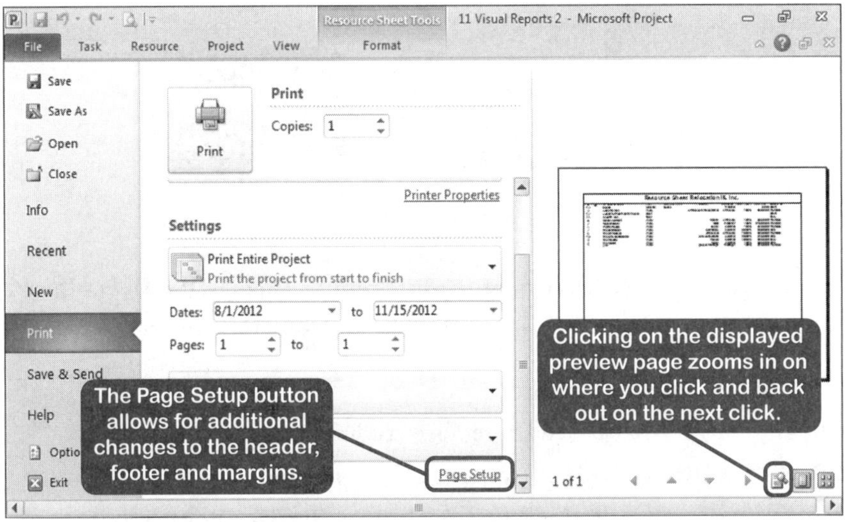

8. Print the report by clicking **Print** .

Formatting & Printing Assignment Views

The Time-Phased Budget

If your financial department asks you as the project manager to predict how much money your project needs each month, you can print a time-phased budget. You have two options:

➤ Time-phased budget by resource: Use the Resource Usage view
➤ Time-phased budget by task or deliverable: Use the Task Usage view

The following sample report shows expenses by deliverable by month:

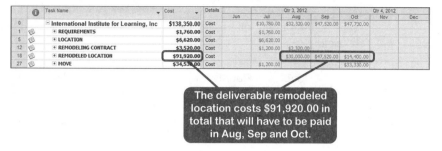

The deliverable remodeled location costs $91,920.00 in total that will have to be paid in Aug, Sep and Oct.

To create this view:

1. On the **View** tab, look in the **Task Views** group for the **Task Usage** (or in the **Resource Views** group for the **Resource Usage** if you want the report by resource).

2. On the **Task** tab, in the **Editing** group, click **Scroll to Task** to scroll the numbers into view; you will see the details **Work** displayed by default, which is the required effort spread over time.

3. On the **Format** tab, in the **Details** group, check the ☑ **Cost** box. Notice the check mark of ☑ **Work**; the work details are currently shown in the chart.

   OR

   Right-click in the blue area of the timescale, and choose from the menu **Cost**.

4. On the **Format** tab, in the **Details** group, clear ☐ **Work** to turn this field off;

   OR

   Right-click in the blue area of the timescale, and choose from the menu **Work**.

5. Adjust the level of detail of the outline structure you want to show. In the **Task Usage** view, on the **View** tab, in the **Data** group, click **Outline** down-arrow and choose the appropriate level of detail. In the example, only deliverables are shown. In the **Resource Usage** view, click on any column heading and click **Hide Subtasks**.

6. Adjust the timescale to show the time unit your financial department would like to see. By using the Status bar, you can zoom in or out by directly clicking on the zoom slider .

7. Make sure you can read all the numbers in the timescale; if the columns are too narrow, you will see ####. You can adjust the column width of the bottom tier timescale units by dragging their right-hand borders.

OR

Double-click on the timescale itself and in the **Timescale** dialog, adjust the **Size %**.

8. Create the header and footer in the **File** tab, **Backstage** view, **Print**, **Page Setup** dialog.

9. Print the report by clicking **Print** .

Print the Assignments

On the **View** tab, in the **Task Views** group, click **Task Usage** to apply the **Task Usage** view, which shows all assignments in detail. The assignments appear in this view as resource names, since the task names are indented below their tasks:

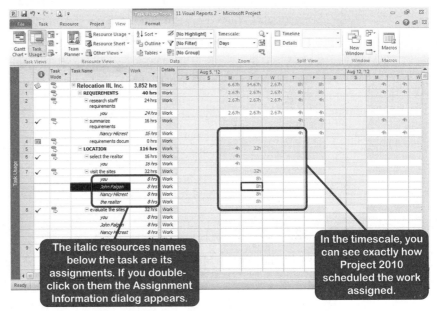

The italic resources names below the task are its assignments. If you double-click on them the Assignment Information dialog appears.

In the timescale, you can see exactly how Project 2010 scheduled the work assigned.

To display the assignments below each resource, on the **View** tab, in the **Resource Views** group, click **Resource Usage**. Assignments appear in this view as task names, since the resource names are already listed.

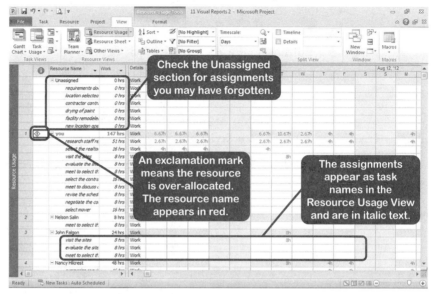

If you don't see the numbers in the timescale, select a resource and click **Scroll to Task** . On the **Task** tab, in the **Editing** group, click **Scroll to Task** .

Adjust the timescale to show the time unit you would like to see. By using the Status bar, you can zoom in or out by directly clicking on the zoom slider , or on the **View** tab, in the **Zoom** group, select from the list **Timescale:** Days , to get it exactly right.

You can now print row totals and column totals in the timescale of the usage views. In the **Task Usage** or **Resource Usage** view, you can select these totals by choosing the **File** tab, **Backstage** view, **Print**, **Page Setup** link, **View** tab and checking ☑ **Print row totals for values within print date range** and ☑ **Print column totals**.

Print the Assignments with the Team Planner

2010

In addition to the **Resource Usage** and **Task Usage** views, you have the new view **Team Planner** which is a more intuitive way to display the assignments and easily see overallocations of your resources.

1. On the **View** tab, in the **Resource Views** group, click **Team Planner** to apply the **Team Planner** view.

2. Adjust the level of detail of the outline structure you want to show. In the **Team Planner** view, on the **Format** tab, in the **Format** group, click **Roll -up** down-arrow and choose the appropriate level of detail.

The level you select in this option will show the level of detail of the assignment. If you select a summary task level of detail, only the summary tasks will be shown. It's usually better to show all the detail tasks by selecting the **All tasks** option.

3. Select a resource and click **Scroll to Task** . On the **Task** tab, in the **Editing** group, click **Scroll to Task** .

4. Adjust the timescale you would like to see. In the Status bar, you can zoom in or out by directly clicking on the zoom slider .

5. Modify the format for the different bars by using any of the options available in **Format** tab, **Styles** group.

6. Create the header and footer in the **File** tab, **Backstage** view, **Print**, **Page Setup** dialog.

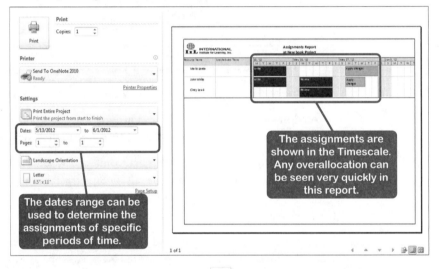

The dates range can be used to determine the assignments of specific periods of time.

The assignments are shown in the Timescale. Any overallocation can be seen very quickly in this report.

7. Print the report by clicking **Print** .

Create a Timeline Report

While in any view, you can activate the **Timeline** view as a split by choosing **View** tab, and in the **Split** view group, checking the ☑ **Timeline** box.

1. Select the tasks, summary tasks or milestones you want to show in the **Timeline**.

2. On the **Task** tab, in the **Properties** group, click **Add to Timeline** .

3. Adjust the timescale you would like to see. In the Status bar, you can zoom in or out by directly clicking on the zoom slider .

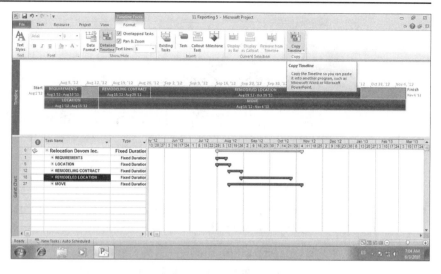

4. Modify the format for the different bars by using any of the options available in Format tab.

▶ **Text Styles**: lets you set the font type, style, size and color for specific items of the timeline, for instance you can change the Timescale text style

▶ **Date Format**: lets you change the displayed date format as an exception to the default format.

▶ **Detailed Timeline**: when activated, shows the name and dates of each task inside the boxes of tasks; when deactivated, it shows just the boxes.

▶ **Overlapped Tasks**: separates the overlapping tasks in different rows.

▶ **Pan & Zoom**: this option works with a combination view, for instance the Gantt Chart and the Timeline. When checked, it will show a shadow box in the timeline with the dates included where you can pan to the right or left to focus on a specific window of time. The Gantt view will also move to that specific window of time.

▶ **Display as Bar**: this button will only activate after you select a task in the timeline. Then clicking on it will change the format of the task from a callout to a bar or vice versa.

▶ **Display as Callout**: this button will only activate after you select a task in the timeline. Then clicking on it will change the format of the task from a callout to a bar or vice versa. Callout display will help you to represent summary tasks or to save space in the timeline.

▶ **Remove from Timeline**: this button will remove the task from the Timeline view but not from the database.

5. To print the view:

   ▶ Create the header and footer in the **File** tab, **Backstage** view, **Print**, **Page Setup** dialog.
   ▶ Print the report by clicking **Print**.

6. To copy it, on the **Format** tab, in the **Copy** group, click ▦ **Copy Timeline** and select the option where to copy (**For E-mail**, **For Presentation or Full Size**).

7. Paste in the desired application. For instance, in PowerPoint, select the slide and in the **Home** tab, click 📋 **Paste**.

 When copying for presentation, in PowerPoint click the **Paste** down-arrow (this activates the **Paste Options** menu) to select among 3 options:

➤ **Use Destination Theme**: If you want the image to take the theme of the destination presentation that you are pasting to. This option will also paste the image as different components that will be editable from PowerPoint. For instance, you can change the font size and color, etc.

➤ **Keep Source Formatting**: If you want the image to keep the original theme from the origin. This option will also keep the image as different components that will be editable from PowerPoint.

➤ **Picture**: This will paste the image as a picture with limited possibilities to edit the elements.

Common Printing Problems and Their Fixes

Some of the more common printing issues, their symptoms, and fixes are listed in the following table.

Printing Issue	Symptom	Fix
Timescale cropped	The last unit of time on the time line is truncated at the edge of the page.	Choose **Page Setup**, **View.** Select **Fit timescale to end of page**. Check results in Print Preview.
Wrong print range	The printout contains too many or too few rows or columns from the selected table.	Pre-select the desired number of rows in the table. Also, in **Page Setup**, **View**, select **Print first [x] columns on all pages** to pre-set the desired number of columns from the table. Check results in Print Preview.

Printing Issue	Symptom	Fix
Wrong page breaks	The page break occurs at an inappropriate place in the selected list of rows from the table.	Select the row in the data table just below where you want the page break to appear. Choose **Insert, Page Break** to force the page break at that location. Check results first in Print Preview.
Wrong zoom factor	The printout of the chart portion of the Gantt Chart view has either too narrow or too wide a time line.	In the Standard toolbar, click either **Zoom In** or **Zoom Out** to adjust the timescale before printing. Check results in Print Preview.
Wrong legend data	The data displayed in the legend area is either incorrect or missing.	Choose **Page Setup**, **Legend**. Fill in the Legend with the desired text or field names. Check results in Print Preview.

How to Build a Macro

What is a macro?

A macro is a piece of programming code. You can insert a macro into a Project file to add new functionality or to simplify the use of Project 2010.

Using macros, you can customize your project so it fits almost every requirement you or your user may have. For example, you can:

➤ Insert predefined tasks in your project, including their names, duration, etc., with a single click.

➤ Add a new capture form to register customized fields values, simplifying the capture process if your project has a large number of customized task fields.

➤ Transfer the data from your project to Excel or another system in a specific required format.

➤ Transfer data from another system to your project, validating the data in the process. The macro can also generate a log file to show you the changes in your project and any external data that was not accepted.

➤ Do an automatic review of the quality of your project, considering the criteria and rules defined in your organization. For example, the macro can check that all the task names in the first level of the WBS start with a 3 digit code.

Some of these examples require programming skills, but you can make very interesting macros with not too much effort.

In order to use the macro options, you must configure the Macro Settings in the Trust Center so the macros are enabled. On the **View** tab, in the **Macros** group, click **Macros** down-arrow, ⚠ **Macro Security**. There you can select ⦿ **Enable all macros** and click [OK].

You can create a macro in two ways:
- ➤ Use the Record Macro menu option (no programming)
- ➤ Write the programming code directly in the Visual Basic for Applications (VBA) editor

Create a macro using the Record Macro menu option

Lets create a simple macro that changes the font color of a selected cell to red:

1. Select a task in the **Task Name** field.

2. On the **View** tab, in the **Macros** group, click **Macros** down-arrow, **Record Macro**.

   OR

   On the **Developer** tab, in the **Code** group, click **Record Macro**.

If you don't have the **Developer** tab displayed, you will need to activate it. On the **File** tab, in the **Backstage** view, click **Options**, **Customize the Ribbon**. On the right box under **Main Tabs**, check the box ☑ **Developer** and click [OK].

3. Fill the Record Macro dialog box:
   a. **Macro Name**: *<ChangeCellToRed>* (the macro name cannot have spaces nor special characters).
   b. Enter the **Shortcut Key** (*E*, for example) that you want to use to execute the macro. Most of the letters cannot be used here because they are already associated with another action. Usually *A, E, J, L, M, Q*, are available. (If, when you finish this procedure, your macro does not run, try changing the shortcut key).
   c. Select **Store macro** in: *<This Project>*.
   d. Capture **any description** you like.
   e. Under **Row References**: keep selected ⦿ **Relative** (the default value).
   f. Under **Column references**: keep selected ⦿ **Absolute** (the default value).

Record Macro

Macro name: ChangeCellToRed

Shortcut key: Ctrl + E

Store macro in: This Project

Description:

Macro ChangeCellToRed
Macro Recorded 29 Jul '10

Row references
- ⦿ Relative
- ○ Absolute (ID)

Column references
- ⦿ Absolute (Field)
- ○ Relative

[OK]   [Cancel]

4. Click [OK].

 After you click [OK], Project 2010 records every action you perform, so be careful to perform only the actions you want the macro to capture. Since Project 2010 is recording, the **Record Option** in the **Developer Menu** has changed to **Stop Recording**.

5. On the **Task** tab, in the **Font** group, click **A** ▾ **Font Color** down-arrow, **Dark Red**. You just changed the selected cell font color to red.

6. On the **Developer** tab, in the **Code** group, click ■ **Stop Recording**.

Your macro is generated. You can now simply click **Ctrl+E** (or whatever key you selected as shortcut key) on any cell to change the font color to red. Or you can select multiple cells in the usual way (with Ctrl or with Shift keys) and run the macro. All the selected cells will be in red.

You can undo the macro's actions with **Undo (Ctrl+Z)**.

Create a macro writing VBA code

All macros, including the ones created with the Record Macro option, are generated with VBA code.

 For this example, we will use the previous macro. To follow the example we recommend that you first use the Record Macro option described in the previous steps to record the macro.

To see the code generated by the Record Macro option with the VBA Editor:

1. 1. Do one of the following:

   On the **Developer** tab, in the **Code** group, click 📖 Visual Basic.

   OR

Key [Alt] + [F11]

In the **Visual Basic for Application Editor**, the left side of the screen shows a **Project Explorer** window, the right side shows the code window.

2. In the **Project Explorer** (left) window, in the **VBA Project** branch, select the Project you are using under the folder **Microsoft Project Objects**.

3. In the **Modules** folder double-click to open **Module1**. You can now see something like this:

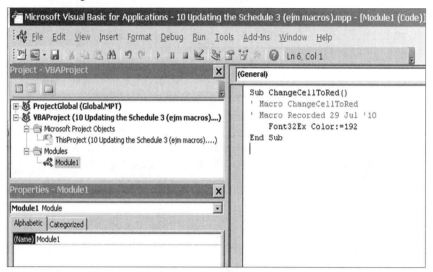

The VBA code of the macro you created is displayed in the Code Window. The **Sub** <*ChangeCellToRed*> is the subroutine that performs the color change on the selected cell.

It is beyond the scope of this book to explain Visual Basic structures and programming techniques, but here is a piece of code that performs the following actions:

1. Verifies that the current project has a status date, otherwise the program ends.

2. For each detail task in the project: If the task started before the status date and the task's % Complete field equals 0, informs the user that the task must be updated.

The macro's name is <**CheckTasksNotUpdated**>.

Here's the code. Notes after an apostrophe are simply comments to clarify the code.

```
Sub CheckTasksNotUpdated()
'100729 Rafael Ruiz - IIL México
Dim t As Task

'verify that the project Status Date exists
If ActiveProject.StatusDate = "NA" Then
    MsgBox "There is not Status Date", vbExclamation, "macro Check Tasks Not Updated"
    Exit Sub 'the macro ends
End If

For Each t In ActiveProject.Tasks
'this is the cycle to review every task in the project
    If Not t Is Nothing Then 'do not check blank lines
        If Not t.Summary Then  'do not check summary tasks
            If DateDiff("d", t.Start, ActiveProject.StatusDate) >= 0 Then
                'the task started before the status date
                If t.PercentComplete = 0 Then
                    'there is not progress in the task
                    MsgBox "Task " & t.ID & ". " & t.Name & vbCr & "should be updated", _
                        vbExclamation, "macro Check Tasks Not Updated"
                End If
            End If
        End If
    End If
Next t
'finish the ckecking
MsgBox "macro Check Tasks Not Updated is finished", vbOKOnly, "macro Check Tasks Not Updated"
End Sub
```

After you've created the macro, here's how you run it:

On the **Developer** tab, **ViewMacros**, select the macro **CheckTasksNotUpdated** and click on **Run**.

When the macro finds a task with a start earlier than the **Status Date** and % **Complete** of 0, it displays a message like the following:

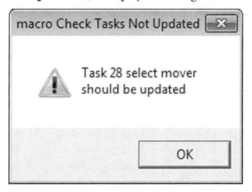

At the end of execution, the message is:

597

If the macro found that the Status Date is not established then it shows a message like this:

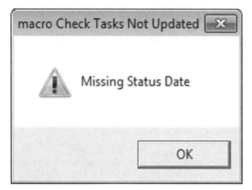

The code in this example is self documented, so you can follow it easily. If you have any doubts, you can copy the code to your project or download the project file *IIL Project 2010 Tools.mpp* from the J. Ross Publishing website (click the *WAV Download Resource Center* to enter the download site) and use the VBA help which is very complete and clear. Simply put the cursor on the word you want to know about and press [F1].

For example, selecting the word **DateDiff** and pressing [F1], opens the help window with the following information:

Macros are a very powerful tool in Project. We think you'll find it worthwhile to study and use them.

Review Questions

1. Is it possible to create a one page report for a 1,000-task schedule that reflects the performance of the project? Would you recommend doing this?

2. What are the different reporting options in Project 2010? What are their main differences?

3. What objects, elements and settings are stored in a view?

4. How can you transfer an object to another project schedule?

5. Can you print the following items?
   Would you do this through a report or through a view?
   Please indicate the exact name of the report or view.

Can you print?	Yes/No	Through which Report or View?
a. Gantt Chart		
b. Project Calendar		
c. Resource Calendar		
d. Project statistics (as shown in the dialog)		
e. Cash outflow report		
f. Notes		

6. How would you quickly format all the milestone task names and milestone Gantt bars?

7. How would you create a Visual Report in Excel for a Resource Work Summary Report?

8. What information should be included in your header, footer, or legend on every printout? Why?

9. We discussed several ways to display the critical path on the Gantt chart. Name one of those ways.

10. Is there a way in which you can easily display the entire project duration in the timescale on your screen? If so, what are the steps in Project 2010 to accomplish this?

11. Discuss ways in which you might modify versions of a status report to better address the needs of two target audiences: executives and team members.

Additional Practice   For experience working with the features you've learned about in this chapter, we strongly suggest that you do the additional exercises for this chapter that are included in Appendix 1.

Chapter 12: Earned Value Management

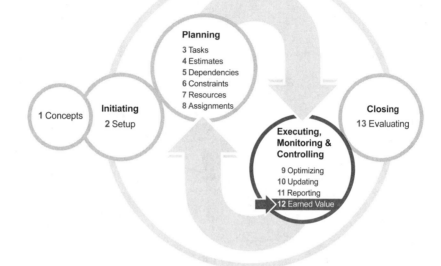

In previous chapters, we've reviewed how to effectively use Project 2010 to plan and control a project. In this chapter, we'll explain what Earned Value Management (EVM) is, and how it can be applied using Project 2010.

After reading this chapter you will be able to:

> Explain EVM elements
> Integrate scope, schedule and cost into a planned performance measurement baseline for applying EVM
> Identify the different Earned Value Measurement techniques and how to apply them with Project 2010
> Explain the different settings and options that control EVM calculations in Project 2010
> Measure the value you have earned on your project by comparing the planned to actual work
> Evaluate schedule, cost and work performance on a project
> Identify variances between actual and baseline information
> Get forecasts for your projects
> Update and maintain the project performance baseline
> Print EVM reports

Didn't you say you were **90%** done?

Yes, we have **90%** of the materials and we have used **90%** of the time.

Vanna a.

Overview of Earned Value Management

A key success factor in any project is the project manager's ability to make the right decisions on a timely basis. You can only do this if you have information on your project's progress that is clear, reliable and up-to-date. Equally important is the ability to give stakeholders like customers and sponsors clear and concise information about the project's progress and probable outcome.

EVM is an approach to measuring project performance that is based on comparing planned and actual progress related to scope, time and cost.

If you have a good EVM system in place, you'll get the feedback you need, and this will enable you to identify problems and issues early, report them and help you keep your project on time and on budget.

EVM is a controversial topic. Some people believe it's impossible to manage a project successfully without EVM and that it is fundamental to making correct decisions on their projects. Others think that EVM is a complex technique that isn't worth the effort necessary to implement it.

At IIL, we are in the first group: we think EVM is important. We believe that those who are not convinced about the advantages of EVM may not know how to simplify its application with a tool like Project 2010. In some countries like the US, there are government agencies and other organizations that mandate the use of EVM in managing projects.

EVM gives you objective answers to the most common questions asked in a project environment:

➤ How is the project going?
➤ Are we ahead of or behind schedule?
➤ Are we running under or over budget?

EVM also helps you answer questions about the future of your project such as:

➤ What is the remaining work going to cost?
➤ When is the project going to finish?
➤ What will the total cost be?

Because EVM helps you analyze performance patterns and trends, you can make forecasts and based on them, implement needed corrective actions.

In order to implement EVM in a project, it's critical to integrate the approach in the initial planning of the project. EVM must be used to define, in an integrative way, what work is to be done in the project (scope), when the work should be done (schedule), and the needed resources and their rates to perform the work (cost). With these three key parts—scope, schedule and cost—you can define a Performance Measurement Baseline (PMB) and get commitments from the key stakeholders. A PMB is an approved and integrated scope-schedule-cost plan for the work against which project execution is compared to measure project performance, as shown in the following graphic.

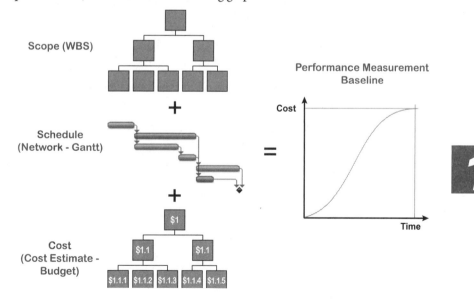

During project execution EVM is used to monitor and control the planned work by providing information on progress in a clear and accurate way. EVM is a critical assist in helping you keep the project performance within tolerance limits you determine for variances against the PMB, and in allowing you to make reliable forecasts related to project completion.

The Basic Elements

There are three key values (and other calculated values) which are used to measure all progress. The three key values are:

➤ Planned Value (PV)
PV is the value of the performance measurement baseline at the status date. It represents what you should have done according to the plan. It is also known as the Budgeted Cost of Work Scheduled (BCWS).

➤ Earned Value (EV)
EV is what you have accomplished at the status date, valued with the costs used to define the performance measurement baseline. EV is also known as Budgeted Cost of Work Performed (BCWP).

➤ Actual Cost (AC)
AC is the cost you have incurred for the accomplished work at the status date. AC is also known as Actual Cost of Work Performed (ACWP).

The three key elements described above can also be expressed in percentages, dividing the values by the final project planned cost in the original performance measurement baseline, which is known as Budget at Completion (BAC).

➤ Planned Value Percentage (PV%): PV% = PV / BAC
➤ Earned Value Percentage (EV%): EV% = EV / BAC
➤ Actual Cost Percentage (AC%): AC% = AC / BAC

Based on these three key values, you can calculate variances, indices and forecasts as follows.

Variances

➤ Schedule Variance (SV). SV = EV − PV
SV represents the deviation against the baseline schedule at the status date.

➤ Cost Variance (CV). CV = EV − AC
CV represents the deviation against the baseline cost at the status date.

➤ Schedule Variance Percentage (SV%). SV% = SV / PV
SV in percentage

➤ Cost Variance Percentage (CV%). CV% = CV / EV
CV in percentage

A positive variance means performance is better than planned, zero variance means performance is as planned, and a negative variance means performance is worse than planned.

Indices

➤ Schedule Performance Index (SPI). SPI = EV / PV
SPI is the efficiency rate for measuring schedule performance: it tells you whether you are ahead of, on or behind schedule.

If the status date is later than the finish baseline date and the project or task is not finished, the SPI will only improve as work progresses. In this case, SPI will always be equal to one when work is finished independently of the actual finish date; thus, SPI does not provide any schedule performance information after a project or task is finished.

➤ Cost Performance Index (CPI). CPI = EV / AC
CPI is the efficiency rate to measure cost performance: it tells you whether you are under or over budget.

Indices greater than one mean performance is better than planned, indices equal to one mean performance is as planned, and indices less than one mean performance is worse than planned.

➤ To Complete Performance Index (TCPI). TCPI = (BAC – EV) / (BAC – AC)
TCPI is the efficiency rate required for the remaining work needed to finish the project within budget.

A TCPI of greater than one means cost performance for the remaining work must be better than planned to finish on budget, a TCPI equal to one means cost performance for the remaining work must be as planned to finish on budget, and a TCPI less than one means cost performance for the remaining work could be less than planned and still finish on budget.

Forecasts

➤ Estimate at Completion (EAC).
The forecasted final project cost. EAC can be calculated in different ways, depending on historical performance data and trends.

▸ EAC = BAC – CV
Future costs would be the same as in the baseline because variances to date were atypical.

▸ EAC = BAC / CPI
Future costs are calculated based on the cost performance efficiency rate to date.

▸ EAC = BAC / (CPI * SPI)
Future costs are calculated based on the cost and schedule performance efficiency rates to date.

12

    ▶   EAC = AC + New estimate for remaining work
Future costs are calculated based on a new cost estimate.

➤ Estimate to Complete (ETC). ETC = EAC – AC
Forecasted cost of remaining work

➤ Variance at Completion (VAC). VAC = BAC – EAC
Forecasted cost deviation at project completion

➤ Variance at Completion Percentage (VAC%). VAC% = VAC / BAC
VAC in percentage

➤ Cost Performance Index at Completion (CPIAC). CPIAC = BAC / EAC
The forecasted cost performance efficiency rate at project completion

Forecasts with Time-Based Schedule Measures in EVM

There is an emerging approach in EVM that takes time-based schedule measures instead of cost measures to calculate the schedule performance, using the time axis (x) instead of a cost axis (y) in calculations.[1] The idea is to have schedule performance using durations instead of cost values.

The previous forecasts, variances and indices are all cost related. Using EVM you can also calculate time-based forecasts, variances and indices as follows:

➤ Time Estimate at Completion (EACt). The forecasted duration of the project.
EACt = (BAC / SPI) / (BAC / Baseline Duration) = Baseline Duration / SPI

SPI is used to generate a rough estimate of when you will complete a project if the trends continue. It's a good estimate, but doesn't take into account the critical path and slacks. For example, you may have delays in non-critical tasks that cause an SPI less than one, that will cause an EACt greater than the baseline duration. Analyzing the critical path in your schedule will enable you to see if you will deliver on time.

Our recommendation is to use a dynamic schedule and update remaining work that will allow you to update the whole schedule. The updated duration of your dynamic schedule will be your best EACt.

➤ Time Variance at Completion (VACt). VACt = Baseline Duration – EACt
Forecasted schedule deviation at project completion

➤ Time Variance at Completion Percentage (VACt%). VACt% = VACt / Baseline Duration VACt in percentage

---

1   ——*Practice Standard for Earned Value Management*, PMI, 2005, p.18.

> Time Schedule Performance Index at Completion (SPIACt).
SPIACt = Baseline Duration / EACt
Forecasted schedule performance efficiency rate at project completion.

SPIACt in conjunction with SPI provides adequate schedule performance data, when the status date is later than the finish date and after the project or task is finished.

The EVM key elements, variances, indices and forecasts previously explained are shown in the following graphic.

Earned Value Management

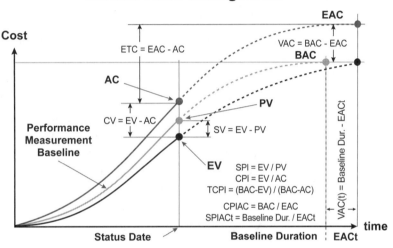

In summary, EVM gives you a better and more complete picture of project performance and helps you to make forecasts, but more importantly, it gives you the feedback you need to make the right decisions about the remaining work and to propose corrective actions that enable you to finish on time and on budget.

Applying Earned Value Management with Project 2010	We are going to present how to apply EVM using Project 2010. You need to enter certain elements correctly in your project to obtain correct EVM information.
	There are many EVM tables, views and fields that come with Project 2010 that will help you to manage your projects. You can also customize fields in Project 2010 in order to cover all of the calculations mentioned above. We'll cover these as they arise in the chapter.
EVM and Planning	As stated above, EVM relies on having a well laid out plan that addresses scope, schedule and cost. Let's look more deeply at that requirement.
Scope	During project scoping, you need to decompose the project work into manageable elements that will be the control cells of your project; these

elements are commonly called control accounts. Control accounts are where scope, schedule and budget (planned cost) all come together at a level of detail in the WBS. Control accounts are made up of one or more work packages. Each work package must be in one and only one control account. If you develop a good WBS, you will have an excellent foundation for applying EVM.

As we'll discuss later in this chapter, you need to define the detail level you want to manage in the control accounts because this will allow you to implement EVM in a practical way with Project 2010.

 We recommend that you establish the control accounts at the lowest level of the WBS (detailed tasks) in Project 2010 because it is where the duration, resources and costs are defined.

Once you've defined the WBS, we recommend that you assign a unique management responsibility for each control account. You can do this easily using a Responsibility Assignment Matrix.

Schedule

EVM relies on a schedule for the accomplishment of the work. In terms of schedule, EVM can be applied with the static information we get from a Gantt diagram, but we highly recommend that you have a dynamic schedule that will enable you to respond to change and keep the schedule up to date. The schedule enables you to see what accomplishments were planned for what points in time, and then determine the degree to which the project is both on schedule and on budget.

Resources and Cost

To use EVM you must provide resource effort and cost estimates for tasks. As you've learned, Project 2010 allows you to manage different types of resources and rates to model all project costs.

If for some reason you won't be performing detailed resource control, you can manage fixed cost to the control accounts. This is useful in large projects where you need to control costs on a higher level, or when you have subcontractors who do their own detailed resource control.

Time Phased Budget and Earned Value Measurement Techniques

EVM requires a time-phased budget: this is the key to effective implementation of EVM. A time-phased budget is a project budget that identifies how much money or labor is to be expended on each task for each time period in the project schedule. Project 2010 will automatically generate the time-phased budget if you have created a schedule and entered effort and cost data for your control accounts. But it may not be exactly what you need for monitoring and controlling with EVM. You need to address a fundamental question, which is how you are going to measure the progress of task completion, and reflect this in your planning information in Project 2010.

PMI's *Practice Standard for Earned Value Management*[2] describes Earned Value measurement techniques. The following table is an adaptation of the techniques established in the PMI standard. The techniques primarily refer to the way you account for task progress.

Planning and Progress Earned Value Measurement Techniques

Deliverables or Work Product Characteristics	Duration of Work Effort	Recommended EV Measurement Technique	
Tangible	1 or 2 Measurement Periods	Fixed Formula	
	More than 2 Measurement Periods	Weighted Milestones	
		Percent Complete	% Duration Complete
			% Work complete
			% Physical Units Complete
			% Physical Complete
Intangible	Any	Apportioned Effort	
		Level of effort	

As we can see from the table, the recommended technique for measuring progress on task completion depends on two factors: the tangibility of the deliverable being produced and the task duration.

The following discussion of various EV measurement techniques includes recommendations for how to model each technique in Project 2010 based on the results we've obtained in real projects. You may find, though, that there are other modeling techniques that provide good results as well.

Fixed Formula

This is a simplified technique for assessing task progress quickly and easily. The most common fixed formulas are 0/100 and 50/50. With the 0/100 formula, no progress is credited until 100% of a task or deliverable is done. With 50/50, you credit a task or deliverable as 50% complete when the task is started, and the other 50% when it's finished. Any other percentage combination can be used, e.g., 30/70, 25/75.

We recommend this technique when you have short duration tasks (one or two reporting periods) and when you don't want to have bother with the evaluation of partial task progress during the project.

➤ Fixed Formula 0/100 in Project 2010
To model tasks with a 0/100 formula in Project 2010, the simplest method is to select **End in field Accrue At** in the resource you are assigning to the task. If you are not assigning resources, just directly a fixed cost, then select **End in tasks field Fixed Cost Accrual**.

If you modify the field **Accrue At** for a resource, costs will be accrued at the end of the task for all tasks to which this resource is assigned. You

---

2 ———*Practice Standard for Earned Value Management*, PMI, 2005

should review whether the resource is used in other tasks where other EV measurement techniques would be more suitable.

➤ Fixed Formula 50/50 in Project 2010
There is no direct way to apply the 50/50 formula technique in Project 2010. You need to break down the task into two subtasks: one for the first 50% with resources or fixed costs accrued at the start, and other for the remaining 50% with resources or costs accrued at the end. (You can take the same approach with other splits, e.g., 30/70, 25/75.)

We've seen schedules with costs prorated to generate the baseline, and then progress managed with the 50/50 formula, crediting 50% of progress at the actual start, and 100% at the finish. This is a mistake: for the correct application of EVM, the baseline must be generated with the same approach that you will use to track progress.

The following picture presents examples of tasks planned with Fixed Formulas. It includes a **Gantt Chart** view and a Task Usage view. The tasks included have the following characteristics:

➤ Task 1. Normal Task. 10 days duration, Resource 1 assigned with rate $100/hr, accrued prorated.

➤ Task 3. 0/100 with Resource. 10 days duration, Resource 0/100 assigned with rate $100/hr, accrued at end.

➤ Task 4. 0/100 with Fixed Costs. 10 days duration, $8,000 fixed cost accrued at end.

➤ Task 6. 50/50 with Resource, broken down into two tasks:
  ▸ Task 7. 50% at the beginning. 5 days duration, Resource 50/50 B assigned with rate $100/hr, accrued at start.
  ▸ Task 8. 50% at the end. 5 days duration, Resource 50/50 E assigned with rate $100/hr, accrued at end.

➤ Task 10. 50/50 with Fixed Costs, broken down into two tasks:
  ▸ Task 11. 50% at the beginning. 5 days duration, $4,000 fixed cost accrued at start.
  ▸ Task 12. 50% at the end. 5 days duration, $4,000 fixed cost accrued at end.

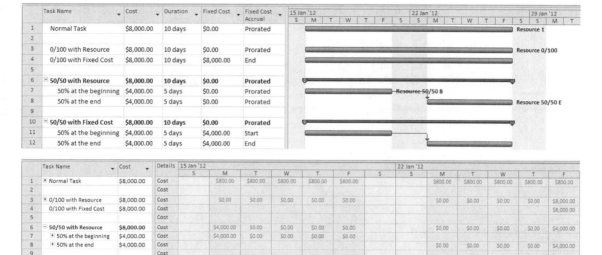

#	Task Name	Cost	Duration	Fixed Cost	Fixed Cost Accrual
1	Normal Task	$8,000.00	10 days	$0.00	Prorated
2					
3	0/100 with Resource	$8,000.00	10 days	$0.00	Prorated
4	0/100 with Fixed Cost	$8,000.00	10 days	$8,000.00	End
5					
6	50/50 with Resource	$8,000.00	10 days	$0.00	Prorated
7	50% at the beginning	$4,000.00	5 days	$0.00	Prorated
8	50% at the end	$4,000.00	5 days	$0.00	Prorated
9					
10	50/50 with Fixed Cost	$8,000.00	10 days	$0.00	Prorated
11	50% at the beginning	$4,000.00	5 days	$4,000.00	Start
12	50% at the end	$4,000.00	5 days	$4,000.00	End

Gantt resource labels: Resource 1; Resource 0/100; Resource 50/50 B; Resource 50/50 E.

#	Task Name	Cost	Details	S	M	T	W	T	F	S	S	M	T	W	T	F
1	+ Normal Task	$8,000.00	Cost		$800.00	$800.00	$800.00	$800.00	$800.00			$800.00	$800.00	$800.00	$800.00	$800.00
2			Cost													
3	+ 0/100 with Resource	$8,000.00	Cost		$0.00	$0.00	$0.00	$0.00	$0.00			$0.00	$0.00	$0.00	$0.00	$8,000.00
4	0/100 with Fixed Cost	$8,000.00	Cost													$8,000.00
5			Cost													
6	− 50/50 with Resource	$8,000.00	Cost		$4,000.00	$0.00	$0.00	$0.00	$0.00			$0.00	$0.00	$0.00	$0.00	$4,000.00
7	+ 50% at the beginning	$4,000.00	Cost		$4,000.00	$0.00	$0.00	$0.00	$0.00							
8	+ 50% at the end	$4,000.00	Cost									$0.00	$0.00	$0.00	$0.00	$4,000.00
9			Cost													
10	− 50/50 with Fixed Cost	$8,000.00	Cost	$4,000.00												$4,000.00
11	50% at the beginning	$4,000.00	Cost	$4,000.00												
12	50% at the end	$4,000.00	Cost													$4,000.00

As you can see, the 0/100 formula is easy to apply, but the 50/50 formula triples your number of tasks (the summary original task and two subtasks.) This could complicate your planning, but also simplify your monitoring and controlling.

Weighted Milestones

The weighted milestones technique is recommended for tasks with relatively long durations (more than 2 reporting periods), where it could be difficult to evaluate partial progress, but where you have specific milestones with verifiable deliverables to which you can assign weighted values in relation to the total cost of the task.

➤ Weighted Milestones in Project 2010

The easiest way to apply weighted milestones is to break the task into the different required milestones, and assign to each new task fixed costs according to its specific weighted value. To model the durations, you can link the milestones and define lag times.

If you need to manage resources for a task, do not assign resources as milestones if you are going to use EVM. A milestone has zero duration, so the work will always be zero, and all EVM will also be zero.

If you need to manage resources, we recommend that you break down the task into subtasks with material resources, with rates according to the weighted values, accrued at the end. These subtasks will have the duration needed to reflect the delivery times, and if you want, they can be marked as milestones so they are represented with the milestone symbol in the Gantt diagram.

The following screen shows two tasks with weighted milestones. One has milestones and fixed costs, and lag times in the links to establish the durations.

The other has subtasks with the durations shown and marked as milestones, with material resources with costs accrued at the end. They are shown in the **Gantt Chart** view and Task Usage view.

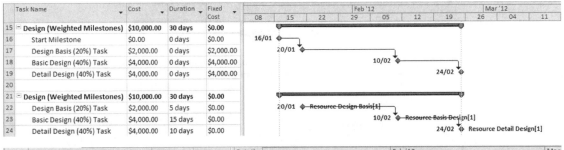

	Task Name	Cost	Duration	Details	08	15	22	29	05	12	19	26
15	Design (Weighted Milestones)	$10,000.00	30 days	Cost		$2,000.00			$4,000.00		$4,000.00	
16	Start Milestone	$0.00	0 days	Cost								
17	Design Basis (20%) Task	$2,000.00	0 days	Cost		$2,000.00						
18	Basic Design (40%) Task	$4,000.00	0 days	Cost					$4,000.00			
19	Detail Design (40%) Task	$4,000.00	0 days	Cost							$4,000.00	
20				Cost								
21	Design (Weighted Milestones)	$10,000.00	30 days	Cost		$2,000.00	$0.00	$0.00	$4,000.00	$0.00	$4,000.00	
22	Design Basis (20%) Task	$2,000.00	5 days	Cost		$2,000.00						
23	Basic Design (40%) Task	$4,000.00	15 days	Cost			$0.00	$0.00	$4,000.00			
24	Detail Design (40%) Task	$4,000.00	10 days	Cost						$0.00	$4,000.00	

Percent Complete

The most generally used EV measurement technique is percent complete, where progress is credited according to the percentage completed at the status date. The main problem with this approach is establishing an objective way to decide the percentages of progress. We'll cover this later.

You can calculate the percent complete using any of four methods that are suitable for different situations:

> % Duration Complete = Actual Duration/Total Duration
> This can be used for almost any task; the only condition is that you use the actual duration to date to establish the amount of progress. This means that the task will have a continuous linear performance through its duration. % Duration Complete can be misleading for many, if not most tasks. A task estimated for two weeks is not necessarily 50% complete because 50% of the duration has passed.

> % Work Complete = Actual Work/Total Work
> This is recommended for tasks where the progress on work is uneven, for example where the assigned resources work different hours per day, or where you have split tasks. (If the progress on the task is uniform, we recommend that you use % Duration Complete because it's easier to apply in Project 2010.) Note that total work is actual work + remaining work. Estimated remaining work to completion should be assessed regularly.

➤ % Physical Units Complete = Actual Units/Total Units
Use this measure when the task has material outcomes or deliverables that you can measure in physical units (e.g., number of items produced, tons, cubic meters, etc.) that are relatively equal in effort applied and proportion of time used.

➤ % Physical Complete
Use when the partial progress of the task is determined based on the subjective evaluation of physical progress made toward producing its deliverables, and this physical progress can't be evaluated with an objective measurement like one of the three described above.

➤ % Complete in Project 2010
You don't need to do anything special to establish the plan and the Performance Measurement Baseline in Project 2010 using any of % Complete EV measurement techniques. You just need to develop your schedule and assign the corresponding resources in the normal manner.

Apportioned Effort

This technique is recommended when a task has a direct relation with another task that has its own EV measurement technique. The first task could have a tangible and verifiable deliverable, but it is difficult to evaluate its partial progress. Instead we can define its partial progress according to the partial progress of the related task. An example of this kind of task could be the quality assurance of a design task.

➤ Apportioned Effort with Project 2010
To apply this technique in Project 2010, the only thing you need to do during planning is to make sure both tasks use the same EV measurement technique. For instance, if you have a quality assurance task that is related to a design task that was defined with weighted milestones, the QA task should also be planned with similar weighted milestones.

Level of Effort

There are tasks that do not produce tangible and verifiable deliverables, or that produce a lot of them and you do not want to control them individually, for instance, in a project management task where you produce a lot of products like analysis, plans, updates, reports, meetings results, etc. For these tasks, we recommend you use the technique called Level of Effort (LOE), which means to assign a certain level of resources during task duration, without specific criteria to evaluate partial progress on the task.

➤ Level of Effort with Project 2010
To plan a task with LOE technique, just assign the resources needed to the corresponding tasks; no special adjustment is needed.

12

Performance Measurement Baseline

To get the PMB in Project 2010, you need to set the baseline of your project (see chapter 10).

The total cost of the project that you have defined in your baseline is known as Budget at Completion (BAC). In Project 2010 the name of the field is **Baseline Cost**, although it is shown as **BAC** in the different views.

EVM Performance Analysis and Forecasting

The Basic Elements with Project 2010

Project 2010 has integrated all that you need to manage the three EVM basic elements, with some considerations we'll explain.

Planned Value (PV)

In Project 2010, PV is calculated automatically based on your status date and your previously established baseline. The name of the field is **BCWS**, although in the different views it appears as **Planned Value – PV (BCWS)**, but this is just the label for the column title.

If you manage different baselines in your project, you can select which baseline you want your calculations to report against.

1. On the **File** tab, in the **Backstage** view, click on ⬚ Options . In the **Project Options** dialog box, click **Advanced**.

2. Use the scroll bar to see the **Earned Value options for this project**, and on **Baseline for Earned Value calculation**, select which Baseline you want to use to make earned value comparisons in your project, then click ⬚ OK ⬚.

Project Options
General
Display
Schedule
Proofing
Save
Language
Advanced
Customize Ribbon
Quick Access Toolbar
Add-Ins
Trust Center
Automatically add new views, tables, filters, and groups to the global
Display options for this project: 12 Earn Value Management
Minutes: min
Hours: hr
Days: day
Weeks: wk
Months: mon
Years: yr
Add space before label
Show project summary task
Underline hyperlinks
Hyperlink color:
Followed hyperlink color:
Cross project linking options for this project: 12 Earn Value Management
Show external successors
Show external predecessors
Show 'Links Between Projects' dialog box on open
Automatically accept new external data
Earned Value options for this project: 12 Earn Value Management
Default task Earned Value method: % Complete
Baseline for Earned Value calculation: Baseline
Calculation options for this project: 12 Earn Value Management
Move end of completed parts after status date back to status date
And move start of remaining parts back to status date
Move start of remaining parts before status date forward to status date
And move end of completed parts forward to status date
Edits to total task % complete will be spread to the status date
Calculate multiple critical paths
Tasks are critical if slack is less than or equal to 0 days
Earned Value options
OK
Cancel

Project Options
General
Display
Schedule
Proofing
Save
Language
Advanced
Customize Ribbon
Quick Access Toolbar
Add-Ins
Trust Center
Automatically add new views, tables, filters, and groups to the global
Display options for this project: 12 Earn Value Management
Minutes: min
Hours: hr
Days: day
Weeks: wk
Months: mon
Years: yr
Add space before label
Show project summary task
Underline hyperlinks
Hyperlink color:
Followed hyperlink color:
Cross project linking options for this project: 12 Earn Value Management
Show external successors
Show external predecessors
Show 'Links Between Projects' dialog box on open
Automatically accept new external data
Earned Value options for this project: 12 Earn Value Management
Default task Earned Value method: % Complete
Baseline for Earned Value calculation: Baseline
Baseline
Baseline 1
Baseline 2
Baseline 3
Baseline 4
Baseline 5
Baseline 6
Baseline 7
Baseline 8
Baseline 9
Baseline 10
Calculation options for this project:
OK
Cancel

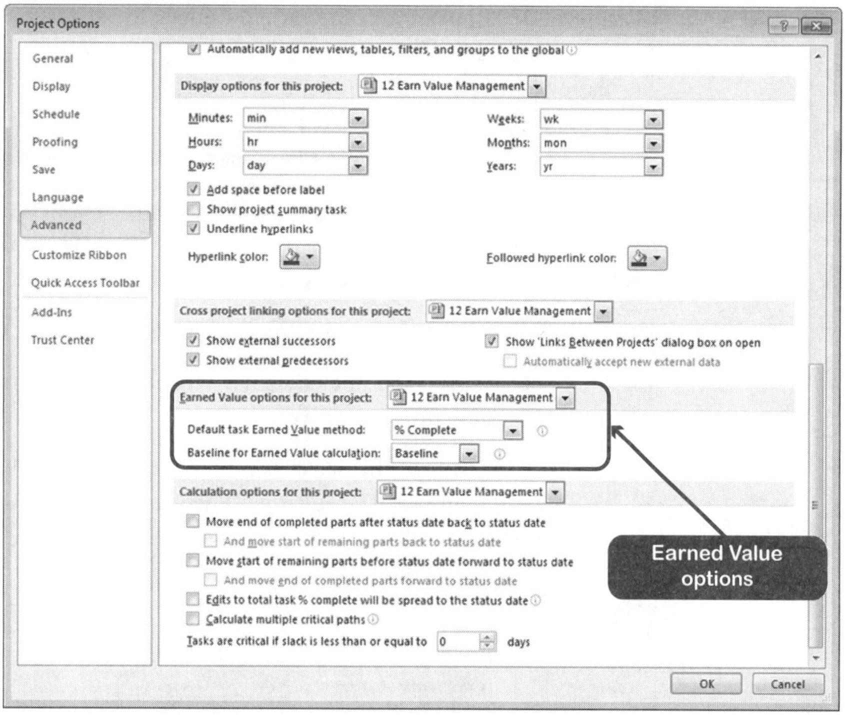

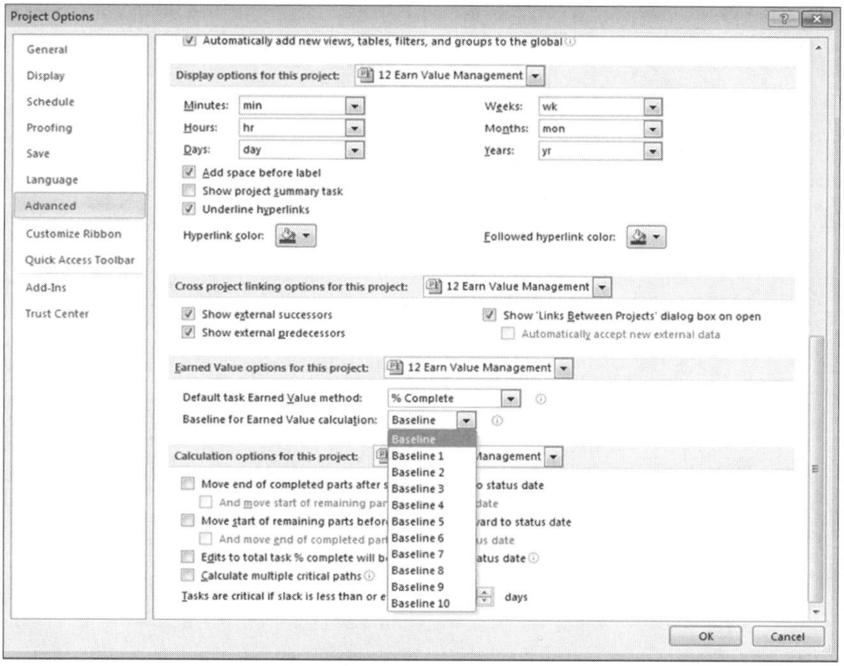

Earned Value (EV)

In Project 2010, the name of the earned value field is **BCWP**, and it is shown as **Earned Value - EV (BCWP)** in different views. Project 2010 uses one of two calculations for EV, depending on which you have previously selected:

➤ EV = % Complete ∗ Baseline Cost

➤ EV = Physical % Complete ∗ Baseline Cost

As you see, these two methods of calculation don't cover all the EV measurement techniques described above, but we'll see how you can apply the others, and what advantages and limitations you will encounter.

You can select **% Complete** or **% Physical Complete** for the whole project.

1. On the **File** tab, in the **Backstage** view, click on ⊟ Options. In the **Project Options** dialog box, click **Advanced**.

2. On **Advanced**, use the scroll bar to see the **Earned Value options for this project**, and on **Default task Earned Value method** select whether **% Complete** or **Physical % Complete** should be used for earned value analysis in your project, then click [OK].

If you want to change the method for a specific task(s) rather than all tasks, in the **task dialog** box, **Advanced** tab, in **Earned value method**, select **% Complete** or **Physical % Complete**, as you see in the screen below.

Task Information					
General	Predecessors	Resources	Advanced	Notes	Custom Fields

Name: _____   Duration: ____ ☐ Estimated

Constrain task

Deadline: _____ ▼

Constraint type: _____ ▼   Constraint date: _____ ▼

Task type: _____ ▼   ☑ Effort driven

Calendar: _____ ▼   ☑ Scheduling ignores resource calendars

WBS code: _____

Earned value method: _____ ▼

% Complete

Physical % Complete

☐ Mark task as milestone

Some of the fields above are not editable because the task is Manually Scheduled.

Help   OK   Cancel

Actual Cost (AC)

In Project 2010 the name of the actual cost field is **ACWP**, and it is shown as **Actual Cost – AC (ACWP)** in the different views. Project 2010 by default calculates AC as you enter your progress, but you can choose to enter the AC.

1. On the **File** tab, in the **Backstage** view, click on ▤ Options . In the **Project Options** dialog box, click **Schedule**.

2. On **Schedule**, use the scroll bar to see the **Calculation options for this project** and then uncheck ▦ **Actual costs are always calculated by Project**.

The Basic Elements in Percentages

If you want the three basic EVM elements in percentages, you will need to define customized fields in Project 2010. You need to divide the values by Budget at Completion (BAC). Remember that in Project 2010, BAC is in the **Baseline Cost** field.

As an example, here are the steps for defining PV%:

1. On the **Format** tab, in the **Columns** group, click **Custom Fields** . The **Custom Fields** dialog box appears:

2. In the **Custom Fields** dialog box, in **Type**, select **Text**. (The text type will allow you to manage the formulas and format of the field.)

3. In the **Field** portion of the screen, select a Text field that is free (we'll use **Text1**).

4. Click the **Rename** button and in the **Rename Field** dialog box, type "*PV%*".

5. Under **Custom attributes**, click the **Formula** button.

6. In the **Formula for 'PV%'** dialog box, type:

    IIf([Baseline Cost]=0,"NA",Format([BCWS]/[Baseline Cost],"0.00%"))

Instead of typing the entire formula, you can use the buttons: Insert Field, Insert Function, Import Function and mathematic and logical operations. Note that we include a conditional verification, *If Baseline Cost = 0 then "NA"*, to avoid a division by zero error. We also include a percent format for the field. When you finish click [OK].

7. You will see a warning message:

Microsoft Project

Existing data in the "PV%" field will be deleted because all values will now be calculated by the formula.

To replace all data in the "PV%" field with the new calculated values, click OK.

To return to the Formula dialog box, click Cancel.

[OK] [Cancel]

Click [OK].

8. Under **Calculation for task and group summary rows**, choose **Use formula.**

9. Under **Values to display**, choose **Data**.

10. Click [OK].

Now, you just need to insert the new customized field in the view you want.

Variances, Indices and Forecasts with Project 2010

As we have said, a major benefit of EVM is the ability to assess variance and make forecasts based on the performance to date. In Project 2010 there are default fields for many of the variances, indices and forecasts. In the following table we have included EVM names, formulas and their corresponding fields and formulas in Project 2010.

Note: All Project 2010 fields included in the following table are referred to as Task Fields. There could be some differences between these and the equivalent fields used for resource, assignment, task-assignment, resource-assignment, resource time-phased, and assignment time-phased fields. You can consult Project 2010 Help to review considerations and formulas used in each field.

Note: Where *customized field* is shown in the table, it means that there is not a default field in Project 2010, but you can use a customized field using the indicated formulas.

EVM		Project 2010	
Name	**Formula**	**Field Name**	**Formula**
DATA			
Planned Value (PV)		BCWS	Calculated as cumulative time-phased baseline costs up to the status date or today's date
Earned Value (EV)		BCWP	BCWP = % Complete * Baseline Cost Or BCWP = Physical % Complete * Baseline Cost
Actual Cost (AC)		ACWP	Calculated as cost of work performed or Manual
Budget at Completion (BAC)		Baseline Cost	Copy Cost field information when Baseline set
Planned Value % (PV%)	PV% = PV / BAC	*Customized Field*	PV% = BCWS / Baseline Cost
Earned Value % (EV%)	EV% = EV / BAC	*Customized Field*	EV% = BCWP / Baseline Cost
Actual Cost % (AC%)	AC% = AC / BAC	*Customized Field*	AC% = ACWP / Baseline Cost
VARIANCES			
Schedule Variance (SV)	SV = EV – PV	SV	SV = BCWP – BCWS
Cost Variance (CV)	CV = EV – AC	CV	CV = BCWP – ACWP
Schedule Var. % (SV%)	SV% = SV / PV	SV%	SV% = (SV / BCWS) * 100
Cost variance % (CV%)	CV% = CV / EV	CV%	CV% = [(BCWP – ACWP) / BCWP] * 100 (*Same formula as CV% =CV / BCWP*)
INDICES			
Schedule Performance Index (SPI)	SPI = EV / PV	SPI	SPI = BCWP / BCWS
Cost Performance Index (CPI)	CPI = EV / AC	CPI	CPI = BCWP / ACWP
To Complete Performance Index (TCPI)	TCPI = (BAC – EV) / (BAC – AC)	TCPI	TCPI = (Baseline Cost – BCWP) / (Baseline Cost – ACWP)
FORECASTS			
Estimate at Completion (EAC) (*Depending on your project situation, you may choose between different options*)	EAC = BAC – CV	*Customized Field*	EAC1 = Baseline Cost - CV
	EAC = BAC / CPI	EAC	EAC = ACWP + (Baseline Cost – BCWP) / CPI (*Same formula as EAC = BAC / CPI*)
	EAC = BAC / (CPI * SPI)	*Customized Field*	EAC3 = Baseline Cost / (CPI * SPI)
	EAC = AC + New Estimate to Complete	Cost	Calculated as costs already incurred for work performed by resources assigned to the tasks, in addition to the costs planned for the remaining work
Estimate to Complete (ETC)	ETC = EAC – AC	*Customized Field*	ETC = EAC – AC (*If you chose a different formula for EAC, you should use the customized field for the EAC you selected*)
Variance at Completion (VAC)	VAC = BAC – EAC	VAC	VAC = Baseline Cost – EAC (*If you chose a different formula for EAC, you would need to calculate a new VAC with a customized field*)

EVM		Project 2010	
Name	**Formula**	**Field Name**	**Formula**
Variance at Completion % (VAC%)	VAC% = VAC / BAC	*Customized Field*	VAC% = VAC / Baseline Cost
Cost Performance Index at Completion (CPIAC)	CPIAC = BAC / EAC	*Customized Field*	CPIAC = Baseline Cost / EAC *(If you chose a different formula for EAC, you would need to calculate a new VAC with a customized field)*
(*) Time Estimate at Completion (EACt)	EACt = Baseline Duration / SPI	*Customized Field*	EACt = Baseline Duration / SPI
	New duration based on network and critical path analysis	Duration *(If you have a dynamic schedule and you are updating remaining work information)*	
(*) Time Variance at Completion (VACt)	VACt = Baseline Duration - EACt	Finish Variance	Finish variance = Finish Date – Baseline Finish Date *(Project 2010 differs from the EVM approach here: negative days means ahead of schedule and positive days means behind schedule. If you want to follow the same approach as other variances, you should use a customized field: VACt = - Finish Variance)*
(*) Time Variance at Completion % (VACt%)	VACt% = VACt / Baseline Duration	*Customized Field*	VACt% = VACt / Baseline Duration
(*) Time Schedule Performance Index at Completion (SPIACt)	SPIACt = Baseline Duration / Duration	*Customized Field*	SPIACt = Baseline Duration / Duration

(*) If your Actual Start date is different than your Baseline Start date, EACt, VACt, VACt% and SPIACt could be biased. For instance, take a 10-day baseline duration task that has an actual start date 5 work days ahead of the baseline start date, and the estimated duration at completion (EACt) for the task is the same 10 days already planned. Applying the formulas presented in the table, you would have:

➤ Baseline Duration = 10 days

➤ EACt = 10 days (using the updated duration that is the same as planned)

➤ VACt = 10 – 10 = 0 days

➤ VACt% = 0 / 10 = 0%

➤ SPIt = 10 / 10 = 1.00

Analyzing the results you can conclude that the task will be delivered as planned, when in fact it's obvious that there will be a 5-day delay in task delivery (the Finish Variance field will show 5 days, which is correct).

To correct this problem, you may create a new EACt field calculated as the Baseline Duration plus Finish Variance: EACt = Baseline Duration + Finish Variance

With this adjustment, your results will be:

> ➤ Baseline Duration = 10 days
> ➤ EACt = 10 + 5 = 15 days
> ➤ VACt = 10 – 15 = -5 days. (5 days delayed)
> ➤ VACt% = -5 / 10 = -50%. (50% delayed)
> ➤ SPIt = 10 / 15 = 0.67 (index below one, performance worse than planned)

Now, we have a better representation of schedule performance. Of course you can combine the formulas to obtain the analysis you prefer.

Applying EVM Performance Analysis & Forecasting with Project 2010

Now let's look at some examples of how to manage progress and EVM in Project 2010, based on the EV measurement techniques just covered.

Note that all examples in this section will use the international date convention: dd/month/yy. If you have set a different date format in your computer, you should enter your dates according to that convention (they will of course appear different from the format of the dates in this chapter).

Fixed Formula

The following screen shows tasks with fixed formulas 0/100 and 50/50, according to the baselined plan.

	Task Name	Baseline Duration	Baseline Cost	
3	0/100 with Resource	10 days	$8,000.00	
4	0/100 with Fixed Cost	10 days	$8,000.00	
5				
6	50/50 with Resource	10 days	$8,000.00	
7	50% at the beginning	5 days	$4,000.00	
8	50% at the end	5 days	$4,000.00	
9				
10	50/50 with Fixed Cost	10 days	$8,000.00	
11	50% at the beginning	5 days	$4,000.00	
12	50% at the end	5 days	$4,000.00	

You now need to update your schedule with the following progress information for status date Fri 20/Jan/12:

> ➤ Task 3. 0/100 with Resource: Started three days late, but the responsible team member assures you it will be delivered on time, working normal hours.

> ➤ Task 4. 0/100 with Fixed Costs: Started on time and the responsible person says the task will be delivered next Wednesday, but with a final cost of $10,000.

> ➤ Task 6. 50/50 with Resource: Started three days late and the responsible person says the task will have the same duration and resources as planned.

> ➤ Task 10. 50/50 with Fixed Costs: Started on time and will be delivered next Wednesday with a final estimated cost of $10,000.

Steps in Project 2010:

First define the Status Date:

1. On the **Project tab**, in **Status** group, click **Status Date** 🗓. The **Status Date** dialog box appears:

```
┌─────────────────────────────────────┐
│ Status Date                    ⟨⟩    │
│  ┌───────────────────────────────┐   │
│  │ Select Date:  20 Jan '12    ▼ │   │
│  │                               │   │
│  │     [  OK  ]    [ Cancel ]    │   │
│  └───────────────────────────────┘   │
└─────────────────────────────────────┘
```

2. In the **Status Date** dialog box, select or type *Fri 20/Jan/12*.

3. Click [OK].

Update Task 3. 0/100 with Resources:

1. On the **View** tab, in **Data** group, click **Tables** 📇 and select **Tracking**.

2. For task 3 in the **Act. Start** column enter or select Thu *19/Jan/12*. Notice that the bar moves on the **Gantt Chart**.

3. In the **Act. Dur.** column enter or select *2 days*. **Rem. Dur.** will change automatically to *8 days*.

4. In the **Rem. Dur.** column enter or select *5 days*. (The task is to finish on time according to the person responsible.)

Update Task 4. 0/100 with Fixed Costs:

1. For task 4, in the **Act. Start** column enter or select Mon *16/Jan/12*.

2. In the **Act. Dur**. column enter or select *2 days*. **Rem. Dur.** will change automatically to *5 days*.

3. In the **Rem. Dur.** column enter or select *3 days* (to finish next Wednesday).

4. After the **Act. Cost** column insert the **Fixed Cost** column.

5. For task 4, in the **Fixed Cost** column, enter *10000*.

Update Task 6. 50/50 with Resource:

1. For task 7, in the **Act. Start** column enter or select Thu *19/Jan/12*.

2. Select task 7 and enter or select *2 days* in the **Act. Dur.** Column.

Update Task 10. 50/50 with Fixed Costs:

1. Select task 11 and click **Update as Scheduled** in the **Tracking** toolbar.

12

2. For task 11 in the **Fixed Cost** column, enter *5000*.

3. For task 12 in the **Rem. Dur.** column, enter or select 3 *days*.

4. For task 12 in the **Fixed Cost** column, enter *5000*.

We have updated the progress and the remaining work. Your **Tracking Gantt** should look like this:

	Task Name	Act. Start	Act. Finish	% Comp.	Phys. % Comp.	Act. Dur.	Rem. Dur.	Act. Cost	Fixed Cost	15 Jan '12	22 Jan '12	29 Jan '12
3	0/100 with Resource	19 Jan '12	NA	29%	0%	2 days	5 days	$0.00	$0.00			29%
4	0/100 with Fixed Cost	16 Jan '12	NA	63%	0%	5 days	3 days	$0.00	$10,000.00		63%	
5												
6	⊟ 50/50 with Resource	19 Jan '12	NA	20%	0%	2 days	8 days	$4,000.00	$0.00			20%
7	50% at the beginning	19 Jan '12	NA	40%	0%	2 days	3 days	$4,000.00	$0.00		40%	
8	50% at the end	NA	NA	0%	0%	0 days	5 days	$0.00	$0.00		0%	
9												
10	⊟ 50/50 with Fixed Cost	16 Jan '12	NA	63%	0%	5 days	3 days	$5,000.00	$0.00		63%	
11	50% at the beginning	16 Jan '12	20 Jan '12	100%	0%	5 days	0 days	$5,000.00	$5,000.00	100%		
12	50% at the end	NA	NA	0%	0%	0 days	3 days	$0.00	$5,000.00	0%		

Note that our schedule reflects not only all progress information to date, but because we updated the remaining work, the result is a dynamic schedule. If the tasks had successors, they would be affected, as well.

Note also that the % Complete information does not correspond to our techniques; remember that we've been calculating costs and the % Complete formula depends on task duration (% Complete = Actual Duration / Duration).

Let's see the EVM information. The following screen shot is the default Earned Value table, with some extra columns: PV%, EV%, AC%, SPI, CPI, Cost, and VACt. (PV%, EV%, AC%, and VACt are customized fields calculated as we previously explained).

	Task Name	Planned Value - PV (BCWS)	Earned Value - EV (BCWP)	AC (ACWP)	PV%	EV%	AC%	SV	CV	SPI	CPI	BAC	EAC	Cost	VAC	VACt
3	0/100 with Resource	$0.00	$0.00	$0.00	0.00%	0.00%	0.00%	$0.00	$0.00	0	0	$8,000.00	$5,600.00	$5,600.00	$2,400.00	0 days
4	0/100 with Fixed Cost	$0.00	$0.00	$0.00	0.00%	0.00%	0.00%	$0.00	$0.00	0	0	$8,000.00	$10,000.00	$10,000.00	-$2,000.00	2 days
5																
6	⊟ 50/50 with Resource	$4,000.00	$4,000.00	$4,000.00	50.00%	50.00%	50.00%	$0.00	$0.00	1	1	$8,000.00	$8,000.00	$8,000.00	$0.00	-3 days
7	50% at the beginning	$4,000.00	$4,000.00	$4,000.00	100.00%	100.00%	100.00%	$0.00	$0.00	1	1	$4,000.00	$4,000.00	$4,000.00	$0.00	-3 days
8	50% at the end	$0.00	$0.00	$0.00	0.00%	0.00%	0.00%	$0.00	$0.00	0	0	$4,000.00	$4,000.00	$4,000.00	$0.00	-3 days
9																
10	⊟ 50/50 with Fixed Cost	$4,000.00	$4,000.00	$5,000.00	50.00%	50.00%	62.50%	$0.00	-$1,000.00	1	0.8	$8,000.00	$10,000.00	$10,000.00	-$2,000.00	2 days
11	50% at the beginning	$4,000.00	$4,000.00	$5,000.00	100.00%	100.00%	125.00%	$0.00	-$1,000.00	1	0.8	$4,000.00	$5,000.00	$5,000.00	-$1,000.00	0 days
12	50% at the end	$0.00	$0.00	$0.00	0.00%	0.00%	0.00%	$0.00	$0.00	0	0	$4,000.00	$5,000.00	$5,000.00	-$1,000.00	2 days

Note that all values are based on progress and the EV measurement techniques selected. Note also that the EV% values reflect a better percent of progress of tasks, so we recommend you display EV% in **Gantt Charts** instead of % Complete.

Weighted Milestones

The following screen shows tasks with weighted milestones:

	Task Name	Baseline Duration	Baseline Cost				
15	⊟ Design (Weighted Milestones)	30 days	$10,000.00				
16	Start Milestone	0 days	$0.00	16/01			
17	Design Basis (20%) Task	0 days	$2,000.00	20/01			
18	Basic Design (40%) Task	0 days	$4,000.00		10/02		
19	Detail Design (40%) Task	0 days	$4,000.00			24/02	
20							
21	⊟ Design (Weighted Milestones)	30 days	$10,000.00				
22	Design Basis (20%) Task	5 days	$2,000.00	20/01 Resource Design Basis[1]			
23	Basic Design (40%) Task	15 days	$4,000.00		10/02 Resource Basis Design[1]		
24	Detail Design (40%) Task	10 days	$4,000.00			24/02 Resource Detail Design[1]	

Now, consider the following progress information for a status date of Fri 10/Feb/12:

➤ Task 15. *Design* (Weighted Milestones): Started as scheduled, *Design Basis* milestone was accomplished on Tue *24/Jan/12, Basic Design* milestone was rescheduled for Fri 17/Feb/12, and *Detail Design* milestone was rescheduled for Fri 2/Mar/12.

➤ Task 21. *Design* (Weighted Milestones): Started as scheduled, *Design Basis* milestone was accomplished as scheduled, *Basic Design* milestone was accomplished on 03/Feb/12, and *Detail Design* milestone was rescheduled for Fri 17/Feb/12.

Steps in Project 2010:

Define the Status Date:

1. On the **Project** tab, in **Status** group, click **Status Date** ▦. The **Status Date** dialog box appears:.

> Status Date ☒
>
> Select Date: 10 Feb '12 ▼
>
> OK Cancel

2. In the **Status Date** dialog box, type or select Fri 24/Feb/12 .

3. Click OK .

Update Task 15. Design (Weighted Milestones):

1. In **Tracking Gantt** view, select **Tracking table** (on the **View** tab, in **Data** group, click **Tables** ▤ and select **Tracking**).

2. Select task 16, then on the **Task** tab, in the **Schedule** group, click **Mark on Track** ⤳ in order to establish the actual start of the task.

3. Double-click on task 17, and in the **Task Information** dialog box, click the **Predecessors** tab.

4. For the **Start Milestone** Predecessor task, type or select 7 in the **Lag** column. This reschedules the second milestone; notice how the **Gantt** chart is updated.

5. Click [OK].

6. Select task 17, then on the **Task** tab, in the **Schedule** group, click **Mark on Track** in order to establish 100% completion of the milestone.

7. Double-click on task 18 and in the **Task Information** dialog box, click the **Predecessors** tab.

8. For the **Design Basis Milestone** Predecessor row, type or select *18* in the **Lag** column. This reschedules the third milestone. Note that the **Gantt** chart is updated.

Update Task 21. Design (Weighted Milestones):

1. Select task 22 then on the **Task** tab, in the **Schedule** group, click **Mark on Track**.

2. For task 23, in the **Act. Start** column, type or select *Fri 20/Jan/12* to establish the actual start date of the task marked as milestone.

3. For task 23, in the **Act. Dur.** column, type or select *10* days, and in the **Rem. Dur.** column, type or select *0* days. With this we have marked the task as 100% complete on the status date. Note that task 24 *Detail design* was also rescheduled.

4. Select task 24, then on the **Task** tab, in the **Schedule** group, click **Mark on Track**.

We have updated the progress and the remaining work. Your **Tracking Gantt** view should show:

	Task Name	Act. Start	Act. Finish	% Comp	Phys. % Comp.	Act. Dur.	Rem. Dur.	Act. Cost	Fixed Cost	
15	Design (Weighted Milestones)	16 Jan '12	NA	0%	0%	0 days	35 days	$2,000.00	$0.00	0%
16	Start Milestone	16 Jan '12	16 Jan '12	100%	0%	0 days	0 days	$0.00	$0.00	16/01
17	Design Basis (20%) Task	24 Jan '12	24 Jan '12	100%	0%	0 days	0 days	$2,000.00	$2,000.00	24/01
18	Basic Design (40%) Task	NA	NA	0%	0%	0 days	0 days	$0.00	$4,000.00	17/02
19	Detail Design (40%) Task	NA	NA	0%	0%	0 days	0 days	$0.00	$4,000.00	02/03
20										
21	Design (Weighted Milestones)	16 Jan '12	NA	80%	0%	20 days	5 days	$6,000.00	$0.00	80%
22	Design Basis (20%) Task	16 Jan '12	20 Jan '12	100%	0%	5 days	0 days	$2,000.00	$0.00	20/01
23	Basic Design (40%) Task	20 Jan '12	03 Feb '12	100%	0%	10 days	0 days	$4,000.00	$0.00	03/02
24	Detail Design (40%) Task	06 Feb '12	NA	50%	0%	5 days	5 days	$0.00	$0.00	17/02

As with the previous example, our schedule reflects all progress and remaining work information in a dynamic way. Note also that the % of progress displayed in the **Gantt** chart is correct because in this view we displayed EV% instead of % Complete.

The following screen shot shows EVM information.

	Task Name	Planned Value - PV (BCWS)	Earned Value - EV (BCWP)	AC (ACWP)	PV%	EV%	AC%	SV	CV	SPI	CPI	BAC	EAC	Cost	VAC	VACt
15	⊟ Design (Weighted Milestones)	$2,000.00	$2,000.00	$2,000.00	20.00%	20.00%	20.00%	$0.00	$0.00	1	1	$10,000.00	$10,000.00	$10,000.00	$0.00	-5 days
16	Start Milestone	$0.00	$0.00	$0.00	NA	NA	NA	$0.00	$0.00	0	0	$0.00	$0.00	$0.00	$0.00	0 days
17	Design Basis (20%) Task	$2,000.00	$2,000.00	$2,000.00	100.00%	100.00%	100.00%	$0.00	$0.00	1	1	$2,000.00	$2,000.00	$2,000.00	$0.00	-2 days
18	Basic Design (40%) Task	$0.00	$0.00	$0.00	0.00%	0.00%	0.00%	$0.00	$0.00	0	0	$4,000.00	$4,000.00	$4,000.00	$0.00	-5 days
19	Detail Design (40%) Task	$0.00	$0.00	$0.00	0.00%	0.00%	0.00%	$0.00	$0.00	0	0	$4,000.00	$4,000.00	$4,000.00	$0.00	-5 days
20																
21	⊟ Design (Weighted Milestones)	$6,000.00	$6,000.00	$6,000.00	60.00%	60.00%	60.00%	$0.00	$0.00	1	1	$10,000.00	$10,000.00	$10,000.00	$0.00	5 days
22	Design Basis (20%) Task	$2,000.00	$2,000.00	$2,000.00	100.00%	100.00%	100.00%	$0.00	$0.00	1	1	$2,000.00	$2,000.00	$2,000.00	$0.00	0 days
23	Basic Design (40%) Task	$4,000.00	$4,000.00	$4,000.00	100.00%	100.00%	100.00%	$0.00	$0.00	1	1	$4,000.00	$4,000.00	$4,000.00	$0.00	5 days
24	Detail Design (40%) Task	$0.00	$0.00	$0.00	0.00%	0.00%	0.00%	$0.00	$0.00	0	0	$4,000.00	$4,000.00	$4,000.00	$0.00	5 days

Note that all values reflect current progress and the EV measurement techniques selected. If you review the EVM information of both main tasks, it seems that everything is progressing according to the baseline, and this is true according to the EV measurement technique selected. But if you review VACt you will notice a variance in the final delivery: 5 days behind schedule in the first main task, and 5 days ahead of schedule in the second main task. You'll also note this in the Gantt chart. It is very important to always analyze the information at the status date and the forecasts at completion.

Note also that in task *16 Start Milestone*, NA appears in the PV%, EV%, and AC% columns. This is because this is just a milestone to mark the start of the main task, and is without resources or costs, thus its **Baseline Cost** is zero. When you apply the formulas to obtain EV data as a percentage, you divide it by the **Baseline Cost**. When we defined the customized fields, we included an "if then" verification that sends "NA" in case of a **Baseline Cost** equal to zero, to avoid an error message. It is very important that you identify any possible errors in your formulas to define the right algorithms.

Percent Complete

To demonstrate this technique, let's assume the following planned tasks, shown in the screen below:

> ➤ % Complete (Duration) tasks
> > ▸ Case a. Duration 20 days. 1 work Resource W1 (std. rate = $100/hr) assigned
> > ▸ Case b. Same as case a
> > ▸ Case c. Same as case a
> > ▸ Case d. Same as case a
> > ▸ Case e. Duration 20 days. 1 work Resource W2 (std. rate = $100/hr) assigned

> ➤ % Complete (Work) task. Duration 20 days. 1 work Resource W1 (std. rate = $100/hr) assigned

> ➤ % Complete (Units) task. Duration 20 days. 20 units of material Resource M1 (std. rate = $800/unit) assigned

> ➤ % Complete (Physical) task. Duration 20 days. 1 cost Resource C1 ($16,000) assigned

	Task Name	Baseline Duration	Baseline Cost	Gantt
26	− % Complete (Duration) tasks	20 days	$80,000.00	
27	Case a	20 days	$16,000.00	Resource W1
28	Case b	20 days	$16,000.00	Resource W1
29	Case c	20 days	$16,000.00	Resource W1
30	Case d	20 days	$16,000.00	Resource W1
31	Case e	20 days	$16,000.00	Resource W2
32				
33	% complete (Work) task	20 days	$16,000.00	Resource W1
34	% complete (Units) task	20 days	$16,000.00	Resource M1[20 Units]
35	% complete (Physical) task	20 days	$16,000.00	Resource C1[$16,000.00]

Now, consider the following progress information for a status date of Fri 24/ Feb/12:

> ➤ Task 26. % Complete (Duration) tasks
>   ▶ Task 27. Case a. Task progress is 30% in duration
>   ▶ Task 28. Case b. Task progress is 60% in duration
>   ▶ Task 29. Case c. Actual start on Mon 23/Jan/12, there have been 5 days of work, and the remaining duration is estimated at 15 days
>   ▶ Task 30. Case d. Started as scheduled, there have been 10 days of work, and the remaining duration is estimated at 5 days
>   ▶ Task 31. Case e. Started as scheduled, there have been 10 days of work, and the remaining duration is estimated at 5 days. The actual rate of the resource assigned is $110/hr

> ➤ Task 33. % Complete (Work) task. The resource assigned presented his actual work report:

	15 Jan '12							22 Jan '12					
	S	M	T	W	T	F	S	S	M	T	W	T	F
Actual Work (hrs)		8	6	2	10	2			8	8	8	4	4

> ➤ Task 34. % Complete (Units) task. There have been ten days of work, 12 units have been produced, and the remaining units will be produced in the following 8 days

> ➤ Task 35. % Complete (Physical) task. The percent of physical progress is 40%

Steps in Project 2010:

Define the Status Date:

1. On the **Project** tab, in **Status** group, click **Status Date** 🏭. The **Status Date** dialog box appears:

Status Date ⊠

Select Date: 27 Jan '12 ▼

OK   Cancel

2. In the **Project Information** dialog box, in **Status Date**, type or select *Fri 27/Jan/12*.

3. Click   OK .

Task 26. % Complete (Duration) tasks.

We'll look at a number of different options for updating here, each of which has slightly different results.

Update Task 27. Case a:

1. In the **Tracking Gantt** view, select **Tracking table** (on the **View** tab, in **Data** group, click **Tables** 🔲 and click **Tracking**).

2. In the **% Comp.** column for task 27, type or select *30%*.

If you just enter the % Complete, you may have the correct current progress information, but you are not using a dynamic schedule approach: you are not reflecting the delay in the remaining work. You can see this in EVM forecasts. The **Tracking Gantt** view and EVM table you should get are shown below:

	Task Name	Act. Start	Act. Finish	% Comp.	Phys. % Comp.	Act. Dur.	Rem. Dur.	15 Jan '12	22 Jan '12	29 Jan '12	05 Feb '12	12 Feb '12
27	Case a	16 Jan '12	NA	30%	0%	6 days	14 days					30%

	Task Name	Planned Value - PV (BCWS)	Earned Value - EV (BCWP)	AC (ACWP)	PV%	EV%	AC%	SV	CV	SPI	CPI	BAC	EAC	Cost	VAC	VACt
27	Case a	$8,000.00	$4,800.00	$4,800.00	50.00%	30.00%	30.00%	($3,200.00)	$0.00	0.6	1	$16,000.00	$16,000.00	$16,000.00	$0.00	0 days

3. Select task 27, then on **Project** tab, in **Status** group, click **Update Project** 🗐. The Update Project dialog box appears:

Update Project

○ Update work as complete through: 27 Jan '12 ▼

    ◉ Set 0% - 100% complete

    ○ Set 0% or 100% complete only

◉ Reschedule uncompleted work to start after: 27 Jan '12 ▼

For: ○ Entire project   ◉ Selected tasks

Help   OK   Cancel

4. Select **Reschedule uncompleted work to start after** (you will see the status date previously selected in the date field), and select **For: Selected tasks**, then click [OK].

With this, you will reschedule the remaining work starting the next work day. This is fine: now you have reflected the delay in finish date, but you are creating a split inside the bar, and this will cause problems in the EVM calculations for the next period. The **Tracking Gantt** view and EVM table you should get are shown below:

Task Name	Act. Start	Act. Finish	% Comp.	Phys. % Comp.	Act. Dur.	Rem. Dur.								
27	Case a	16 Jan '12	NA	30%	0%	6 days	14 days							30%

Task Name	Planned Value - PV (BCWS)	Earned Value - EV (BCWP)	AC (ACWP)	PV%	EV%	AC%	SV	CV	SPI	CPI	BAC	EAC	Cost	VAC	VACt
27	Case a	$8,000.00	$4,800.00	$4,800.00	50.00%	30.00%	30.00%	($3,200.00)	$0.00	0.6	1	$16,000.00	$16,000.00	$16,000.00	$0.00	-4 days

Now we'll look at another way to update the progress of this task.

1. Select task 27 and on **Task** tab, in **Schedule** group, click **0% Complete** 0% to return progress to 0%.

2. On the **File** tab, in the **Backstage** view, click on **Options**. The **Project Options** dialog box appears. Click on **Advanced**:

3. On **Advanced**, use the scroll bar to see the **Calculations options for this project**, and check the option **Move start of remaining parts before status date forward to status date**. Click OK .

4. In the % Comp. column for task 27, type or select 30%.

This gives you the same result as the previous method in one step. But you still have the split.

Finally, here's an option that eliminates the split.

1. Select task 27 and on the **Task** tab, in the **Schedule** group, click **0% Complete** to return progress to the original 0%.

2. On the **File** tab, in the **Backstage** view, click on **Options**. The **Project Options** dialog box appears; click on **Advanced**. On **Advanced**, use the scroll bar to see the **Calculations options for this project**, and check the option **Move end of completed parts forward to status date**. Click OK .

3. In the % Comp. column for task 27, type or select 30%.

Notice that you get the same progress, but have moved the actual start of the task to eliminate the split. The current progress now coincides with the status date. This is much better for further EVM calculations and you are applying the dynamic schedule approach. Your screen should look like this:

	Task Name	Act. Start	Act. Finish	% Comp.	Phys. % Comp.	Act. Dur.	Rem. Dur.	15 Jan '12 ... 19
27	Case a	20 Jan '12	NA	30%	0%	6 days	14 days	30%

	Task Name	Planned Value - PV (BCWS)	Earned Value - EV (BCWP)	AC (ACWP)	PV%	EV%	AC%	SV	CV	SPI	CPI	BAC	EAC	Cost	VAC	VACt
27	Case a	$8,000.00	$4,800.00	$4,800.00	50.00%	30.00%	30.00%	($3,200.00)	$0.00	0.6	1	$16,000.00	$16,000.00	$16,000.00	$0.00	-4 days

Task 28. Case b.

1. In the **Tracking Gantt** view, select **Tracking table** (on the **View** tab, in **Data** group, click **Tables** and click **Tracking**).

2. For task 28, in the **% Comp.** column, type or select *60%*.

We have a situation similar to Case a, but with more progress than planned. If you just enter the **% Complete**, you may have the correct current progress information in the **Tracking Gantt** view, but you'll create big problems in your EVM calculations. The progress after the status date is not reflected in EVM calculations: PV, EV, AC are shown as scheduled, without the additional progress. In addition, you aren't using the dynamic approach. Here's what you'd get:

	Task Name	Act. Start	Act. Finish	% Comp.	Phys. % Comp.	Act. Dur.	Rem. Dur.	15 Jan '12 ... 12
28	Case b	16 Jan '12	NA	60%	0%	12 days	8 days	60%

	Task Name	Planned Value - PV (BCWS)	Earned Value - EV (BCWP)	AC (ACWP)	PV%	EV%	AC%	SV	CV	SPI	CPI	BAC	EAC	Cost	VAC	VACt
28	Case b	$8,000.00	$8,000.00	$8,000.00	50.00%	50.00%	50.00%	$0.00	$0.00	1	1	$16,000.00	$16,000.00	$16,000.00	$0.00	0 days

3. Select task 28 and on **Task** tab, in **Schedule** group, click **0% Complete** to return progress to the original 0%.

4. On the **File** tab, in the **Backstage** view, click on **Options**. The **Project Options** dialog box appears; click on **Advanced** (same screen shot shown before). On **Advanced**, use the scroll bar to see the **Calculations options for this project**, and check the option **Edits to total task % complete will be spread to the status date**.

5. For task 28, in the **% Comp.** column, type or select *60%*.

Now it is a little better: the current status line now shows the whole progress, and the EV is now right. But the AC is still just considering the work up to the status date, so the EVM calculations are wrong, and the **Gantt** chart and forecasts are still not reflecting the dynamic schedule approach. The results are:

	Task Name	Act. Start	Act. Finish	% Comp.	Phys. % Comp.	Act. Dur.	Rem. Dur.	15 Jan '12 ... 12 Feb '12
28	Case b	16 Jan '12	NA	60%	0%	12 days	8 days	60%

	Task Name	Planned Value - PV (BCWS)	Earned Value - EV (BCWP)	AC (ACWP)	PV%	EV%	AC%	SV	CV	SPI	CPI	BAC	EAC	Cost	VAC	VACt
28	Case b	$8,000.00	$9,600.00	$8,000.00	50.00%	60.00%	50.00%	$1,600.00	$1,600.00	1.2	1.2	$16,000.00	$13,333.33	$16,000.00	$2,666.67	0 days

Now, let's look at other ways to update the progress of this task.

1. Select task 28 and on the **Task** tab, in the **Schedule** group, click **0% Complete** 0% to return progress to the original 0%.

2. On the **File** tab, in the **Backstage** view, click on **Options**. The **Project Options** dialog box appears, then click on **Advanced**. On **Advanced**, use the scroll bar to see the **Calculations options for this project**, and check the option **Move end of completed parts after status date back to the status date**.

3. For task 28, in the **% Comp**. column, type or select *60%*.

The actual start date is adjusted and the progress coincides with the status bar. The EV is now correct, but you've created a split with the problems mentioned before, you are still missing the dynamic schedule approach, and the forecasts don't reflect the extra progress that's been made. The results look like this:

	Task Name	Act. Start	Act. Finish	% Comp.	Phys. % Comp.	Act. Dur.	Rem. Dur.	
28	Case b	12 Jan '12	NA	60%	0%	12 days	8 days	

	Task Name	Planned Value - PV (BCWS)	Earned Value - EV (BCWP)	AC (ACWP)	PV%	EV%	AC%	SV	CV	SPI	CPI	BAC	EAC	Cost	VAC	VAC1
28	Case b	$8,000.00	$9,600.00	$9,600.00	50.00%	60.00%	60.00%	$1,600.00	$0.00	1.2	1	$16,000.00	$16,000.00	$16,000.00	$0.00	0 days

Now here's a final way to enter the same progress for the Case b task.

1. Select task 28 and on the **Task** tab, in the **Schedule** group, click **0% Complete** 0% to return to the original 0%.

2. On the **File** tab, in the **Backstage** view, click on **Options**. The **Project Options** dialog box appears; click on **Advanced**. On **Advanced**, use the scroll bar to see the **Calculations options for this project**, and check the option **And Move start of remaining parts back to status date**.

3. For task 28, in the **% Comp**. column, type or select *60%*.

Now, you will get both the correct EVM calculations and the dynamic schedule approach. The results are:

	Task Name	Act. Start	Act. Finish	% Comp.	Phys. % Comp.	Act. Dur.	Rem. Dur.	
28	Case b	12 Jan '12	NA	60%	0%	12 days	8 days	

	Task Name	Planned Value - PV (BCWS)	Earned Value - EV (BCWP)	AC (ACWP)	PV%	EV%	AC%	SV	CV	SPI	CPI	BAC	EAC	Cost	VAC	VAC1
28	Case b	$8,000.00	$9,600.00	$9,600.00	50.00%	60.00%	60.00%	$1,600.00	$0.00	1.2	1	$16,000.00	$16,000.00	$16,000.00	$0.00	2 days

Task 29. Case c.

1. In the **Tracking Gantt** view, select **Tracking table** (on the **View** tab, in the **Data** group, click **Tables** and click **Tracking**).

2. For task 29, in the **Act. Start** column, type or select Mon *23/Jan/12*. Note how the bar is updated.

12

3. For task 29, in the **Act. Dur.** column, type or select *5 days*. Note that the Remaining Duration is updated to *15* days, and the % Complete is calculated to *25%*.

 We highly recommend that you update task progress as we did for the Case c task. It is simple, easy, and you can forget all of the switches and conditions explained for Cases a and b. The EVM calculations are right, and the dynamic schedule approach is applied.

Task 30. Case d.

1. In the **Tracking Gantt** view, select **Tracking table** (on the **View** tab, in the **Data** group, click **Tables** and click **Tracking**).

2. For task 30, in the **Act. Start** column, type or select Mon *16/Jan/12* . Note how the bar is updated.

3. For task 30, in the **Act. Dur**. column, type or select *10* days, and in the **Rem. Dur.** column, type or select *5* days. Note the % Complete is calculated to *67%*.

Again, this is an easy way to update a task and all the calculations are correct.

Task 31. Case e.

1. In the **Tracking Gantt** view, select **Tracking table** (on the **View** tab, in the **Data** group, click **Tables** and click **Tracking**).

2. For task 31, in the **Act. Start** column, type or select Mon *16/Jan/12*. Note how the bar is updated.

3. For task 31, in the **Act. Dur.** column type or select *10* days, and in the **Rem. Dur.** column, type or select *5* days. Note the % Complete is calculated to *67%*.

4. On the **View** tab, in **Resource Views** group, click on **Resource Sheet** .

5. In the **Resource W2** row, in the **Std. Rate** column, type *110* to update the resource rate.

As you can see, this is the best way to update tasks which use a percent of duration completed EV measurement technique. The results for cases c, d and e are shown below. We recommend that you analyze the results obtained and practice the different options with the tool.

	Task Name	Act. Start	Act. Finish	% Comp.	Phys. % Comp.	Act. Dur.	Rem. Dur.						
29	Case c	23 Jan '12	NA	25%	0%	5 days	15 days						25%
30	Case d	16 Jan '12	NA	67%	0%	10 days	5 days				67%		
31	Case e	16 Jan '12	NA	67%	0%	10 days	5 days				67%		

	Task Name	Planned Value - PV (BCWS)	Earned Value - EV (BCWP)	AC (ACWP)	PV%	EV%	AC%	SV	CV	SPI	CPI	BAC	EAC	Cost	VAC	VACt
29	Case c	$8,000.00	$4,000.00	$4,000.00	50.00%	25.00%	25.00%	-$4,000.00	$0.00	0.5	1	$16,000.00	$16,000.00	$16,000.00	$0.00	-5 days
30	Case d	$8,000.00	$10,666.67	$8,000.00	50.00%	66.67%	50.00%	$2,666.67	$2,666.67	1.33	1.33	$16,000.00	$12,000.00	$12,000.00	$4,000.00	5 days
31	Case e	$8,000.00	$10,666.67	$8,800.00	50.00%	66.67%	55.00%	$2,666.67	$1,866.67	1.33	1.21	$16,000.00	$13,200.00	$13,200.00	$2,800.00	5 days

Task 33. % Complete (Work) task

1. On the **View** tab, in **Task Views** group, click on **Task Usage** .

2. On the **View** tab, in **Data** group, click on **Tables** and select **Tracking**.

3. Right click on any part of the time-phase data section, and check **Baseline Work**, **Work**, and **Actual Work** to display these rows:

⬥	Detail Styles...
√	Work
√	Actual Work
	Cumulative Work
√	Baseline Work
	Cost
	Actual Cost
	Show Timeline
	Show Split

4. For Resource W1 (task 33), in the **Actual Work** row, type the hours reported:

	15 Jan '12							22 Jan '12					
	S	M	T	W	T	F	S	S	M	T	W	T	F
Actual Work (hrs)		8	6	2	10	2			8	8	8	4	4

The Task Usage will look like this:

Task Name	% Comp.	% Work Complete	Phys. % Comp.	Details	15 Jan '12							22 Jan '12					
					S	M	T	W	T	F	S	S	M	T	W	T	F
33 ⊟ % complete (Work) task	44%	38%	38%	Base. Work		8h	8h	8h	8h	8h			8h	8h	8h	8h	8h
				Work		8h	6h	2h	10h	2h			8h	8h	8h	4h	4h
				Act. Work		8h	6h	2h	10h	2h			8h	8h	8h	4h	4h
Resource W1			38%	Base. Work		8h	8h	8h	8h	8h			8h	8h	8h	8h	8h
				Work		8h	6h	2h	10h	2h			8h	8h	8h	4h	4h
				Act. Work		8h	6h	2h	10h	2h			8h	8h	8h	4h	4h

Note that when you update the assignment, the task is also updated. The hours that the resource didn't work were passed to the end of the task in the following work days, as you can see below:

Task Name	% Comp.	% Work Complete	Phys. % Comp.	Details	05 Feb '12							12 Feb '12					
					S	M	T	W	T	F	S	S	M	T	W	T	F
33 ⊟ % complete (Work) task	44%	38%	38%	Base. Work		8h	8h	8h	8h	8h							
				Work		8h	8h	8h	8h	8h			8h	8h	4h		
				Act. Work													
Resource W1			38%	Base. Work		8h	8h	8h	8h	8h							
				Work		8h	8h	8h	8h	8h			8h	8h	4h		
				Act. Work													

The hours were passed to the next work days because the task is a fixed units type. If the task were fixed duration, the hours would have been prorated in the original 10 remaining days. Of course the EVM calculations would be different.

Now let's review the percent of progress.

In the screen below you can see the columns **% Comp.**, **% Work Complete**, and **Phys. % Comp**. The calculations of these fields are:

➤ % Complete = Actual Duration/Duration = 10 days / 22.5 days = 44%
➤ % Work Complete = Actual Work/Work = 60 hrs / 160 hrs = 38%
➤ Physical % Complete = You need to enter this percentage

To review the EVM calculations, we inserted columns BCWS (PV), BCWP (EV) and ACWP (AC) in the same **Task Usage** view:

	Task Name	% Comp.	% Work Complete	Phys. % Comp.	BCWS	BCWP	ACWP
33	⊟ % complete (Work) task	44%	38%	0%	$8,000.00	$7,152.83	$6,000.00
	Resource W1		*38%*		*$8,000.00*	*$6,000.00*	*$6,000.00*

As you can see, Planned Value (BCWS) is the same in the task and in the assignment, because it is calculated with the baseline information and the status date. Actual Cost (ACWP) is the same also, because it is calculated considering the actual work and the rate of the resource.

The problem is the Earned Value (BCWP): in the assignment it's calculated with the % Work Complete, but in the task it's calculated with % Complete (duration). Because we don't have a uniform distribution of work, the percentages are different.

We consider the EV of the assignment to be correct here , because as of the status date we are behind in (EV<PV), although in cost, we are as planned (EV=AC). If you analyze the task information, while it seems that you have savings, this is not true. (Note: In the previous screen, PV, EV and AC are shown as BCWS, BCWP and ACWP.)

In Project 2010, you can select **% Complete** or **Physical % Complete** to calculate the Earned Value in tasks; we hope that in a future version we can also select **% Work Complete**. To solve the problem, we recommend selecting **Physical % Complete** as the Earned Value Method for the task, and copying the **% Work Complete** of the assignment into the **Physical % Complete** of the task. The result is:

	Task Name	% Comp.	% Work Complete	Phys. % Comp.	BCWS	BCWP	ACWP
33	⊟ % complete (Work) task	44%	38%	38%	$8,000.00	$6,080.00	$6,000.00
	Resource W1		38%		*$8,000.00*	*$6,080.00*	*$6,000.00*

This is better. The only little problem is that in this case the correct percentage is 37.5%, but Project 2010 first rounds the decimals and then makes the calculation, so we have $6,080 as EV, instead of $6,000. While this will have some effect on the rest of the calculation, remember that you need information to help you make the right decisions: this is not an accounting system where you need last decimal precision.

Task 34. % Complete (Work) task.

1. On the **View** tab, in the **Task Views** group, click on **Task Usage**.

2. On the **View** tab, in the **Data** group, click on **Tables** and select **Tracking**.

3. Right-click on any part of the time-phase data section and check **Baseline Work**, **Work**, and **Actual Work** to display these rows.

4. For Resource M1 (task 34), in the **Actual Work** column type 12 (the units reported as received). Note that in the time-phased data section, the Actual Work of the first two weeks was updated, and also the Work for the remaining two weeks. The results are:

Task Name	% Comp.	% Work Complete	Phys. % Comp.	Act. Work	Details	15 Jan '12							22 Jan '12					
						S	M	T	W	T	F	S	S	M	T	W	T	F
34 ⊟ % complete (Units) task	56%	56%	0%	0 hrs	Base. Work		0h											
					Work													
					Act. Work													
Resource M1		60%		*12 Units*	Base. Work (Units)		1	1	1	1	1			1	1	1	1	1
					Work (Units)		1.2	1.2	1.2	1.2	1.2			1.2	1.2	1.2	1.2	1.2
					Act. Work (Units)		1.2	1.2	1.2	1.2	1.2			1.2	1.2	1.2	1.2	1.2

Task Name	% Comp.	% Work Complete	Phys. % Comp.	Act. Work	Details	29 Jan '12							05 Feb '12					
						S	M	T	W	T	F	S	S	M	T	W	T	F
34 ⊟ % complete (Units) task	56%	56%	0%	0 hrs	Base. Work													
					Work													
					Act. Work													
Resource M1		60%		*12 Units*	Base. Work (Units)		1	1	1	1	1			1	1	1	1	1
					Work (Units)		1	1	1	1	1			1	1	1			
					Act. Work (Units)													

Note that the 12 units entered as Actual Work were divided in the ten first days, reflecting 1.2 units per day in the Actual Work row in the time-phased data. Because there are 8 remaining units, the Work row reflects 1 unit per day in the next 8 days. It is also important to note that because we have a material resource, there is no work reflected in the task row, and the % **Work Complete** for the task cannot be calculated. So Project 2010 copies the % complete value to the % **Work Complete** of the task; in this case it is 56%.

For EVM calculations, we have the same problem as with the previous task we analyzed: the % Complete is different from the % **Units Complete** (that is the % **Work Complete** of the assignment). The solution again is to select **Physical % Complete** as the Earned Value Method in the task and copy the % **Work Complete** of the assignment into the **Physical % Complete** of the task. If you do this, the **Tracking Gantt** view and EV table obtained are as follows. We've included the % **Complete (Work)** task and % **Complete (Units)** task:

	Task Name	% Comp.	% Work Complete	Phys. % Comp.		15 Jan '12	22 Jan '12	29 Jan '12	05 Feb '12	12 Feb '12
33	% complete (Work) task	44%	38%	38%						38%
34	% complete (Units) task	56%	56%	60%						

	Task Name	Planned Value - PV (BCWS)	Earned Value - EV (BCWP)	AC (ACWP)	PV%	EV%	AC%	SV	CV	SPI	CPI	BAC	EAC	Cost	VAC	VACt
33	% complete (Work) task	$8,000.00	$6,080.00	$6,000.00	50.00%	38.00%	37.50%	-$1,920.00	$80.00	0.76	1.01	$16,000.00	$15,789.47	$16,000.00	$210.53	-2.5 days
34	% complete (Units) task	$8,000.00	$9,600.00	$9,600.00	50.00%	60.00%	60.00%	$1,600.00	$0.00	1.2	1	$16,000.00	$16,000.00	$16,000.00	$0.00	2 days

Task 35. % Complete (Physical) task.

1. Go to **Tracking Gantt** view. Double-click on task 35.

2. In the **Task Information** dialog box, click the **Advanced** tab.

3. For **Earned Value Method**, select **Phys. % Comp.**, and click [OK].

4. For task 35, in the **Phys. % Comp**. column, type *40%*. This updates the EVM information.

5. For task 35, in the **% Comp.** column, type **40%.** This updates the schedule information.

If you select **Phys. % Comp.** as the EV method for a task and you decide to update the task just with this percentage, we recommend entering the same percentage in the **% Complete** field to update the schedule.

Now, reviewing the EVM information you will find this:

	Task Name	Planned Value - PV (BCWS)	Earned Value - EV (BCWP)	AC (ACWP)	PV%	EV%	AC%	SV	CV	SPI	CPI	BAC	EAC	Cost	VAC	VACt
35	% complete (Physical) task	$0.00	$0.00	$0.00	0.00%	0.00%	0.00%	$0.00	$0.00	0	0	$16,000.00	$16,000.00	$16,000.00	$0.00	-2 days

Note that the information in BAC, EAC and Cost are correct, but there is no information in the rest of the fields. Remember we assigned a Cost Resource Type to this task, and in Project 2010, Cost Resources are not included in EVM calculations. This is a big issue for us, so we are forced to recommend that you avoid using Cost Resources in your project if you want to manage it with EVM. We hope that a future version of the software will include Cost Resources for EVM calculations.

To solve the problem in our task, we should reassign a new material resource, or assign a fixed cost to manage the % Complete (Physical) EV measurement technique.

Apportioned Effort	In Project 2010 it's not possible to directly relate the progress of one task to another in an automated way. It is possible to do something with the dynamic links described in chapter 5, but we don't recommend this. To apply an apportioned effort measurement in Project 2010, just follow the same steps in defining EV for both tasks.
Level of Effort (LOE)	LOE tasks do not have a progress measurement method, so we recommend that you update the actual start date, the duration, and the resources assigned, and then use the **Update as Scheduled** icon in the Tracking toolbar. This will cause your EV to always equal your PV, which is exactly what you want (your AC may be different). In LOE we just need to track the cost variances.

EVM and Quality Thresholds

In every company there are acceptable tolerances of performance, and EVM allows you to establish quality thresholds so you'll know if the project is within the control limits or is out of control. This will also allow you to practice management by exception, directing your attention to projects and tasks with problems.

The indices and variances calculated in EVM are perfect for this. You can define tolerable zones (green) for a specific range of an index, then a warning zone (yellow) to attract attention, and a trouble zone (red) that indicates a major correction is needed. The following graphic illustrates this:

Quality Thresholds and Performance Indices

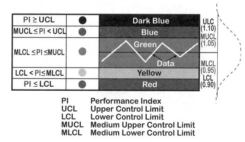

PI	Performance Index	
UCL	Upper Control Limit	
LCL	Lower Control Limit	
MUCL	Medium Upper Control Limit	
MLCL	Medium Lower Control Limit	

The graphic shows the results of control limits with traffic light indicators. We have included the blue zone if the performance indices are "too good", because this is not really good. If you are performing far better than your baseline, you may have, for example, excess resources who could be used on other projects or excessive padding in your schedule. In the graphic, you can substitute any performance index you're using (SPI, CPI, CPIAC, SPIACt, etc.) for the "PI" in the graphic.

Control limits can be determined according to your quality system (six sigma or other), or your own best criteria. Once you have defined your control limits, you can use customized fields and use whatever graphics you prefer. The following picture is an example of a view with traffic signals for SPI, CPI, SPIACt, and CPIAC. (The signals are in red, yellow, green and blue depending on status.)

Performance Measurement Baseline Updating

It is fundamental to maintain the integrity of the performance measurement baseline throughout the project lifecycle. The integrity of scope, schedule and cost should all be maintained. There are two common situations where we need to change and update our baseline. If the scope of the work changes, then the estimated cost and schedule could also change and these changes should be reflected in a revised baseline. Or if we have had such poor performance that the original baseline is worthless as a tool for measuring the current performance, then a revised baseline may be needed. Of course all changes to the baseline must be done according to your integrated change control plan.

In Project 2010 we can create a new baseline, update the existing baseline or set multiple baselines.

> **Create a Complete New Baseline**
> You should only rebaseline your project if the degree of change dictates that you need a new baseline and/or a complete new baseline is approved for some other reason.
>
> 1. On the **Project** tab, in the **Schedule** group, click **Set Baseline** 🖹. The **Set Baseline** dialog box appears.
>
> 2. In the **Set Baseline** dialog box, choose **Set baseline**, choose **Entire project**, and click [OK].
>
> 3. A message asking if you're sure want to overwrite the data in the existing baseline will be displayed. Click **Yes**, and you will have the new baseline.

When you set a new baseline, it is possible that your EVM calculations will show discrepancies between your previous and new report. We recommend that you document the new baseline and explain that you are reporting against a new baseline.

➤ **Update the Existing Baseline**

If you have authorized changes that need to be incorporated in the baseline but you don't want to lose all baseline information for unchanged tasks, you should update the existing deadline.

Select the new tasks and set the baseline choosing **For Selected** tasks options. We also recommend you choose the **Roll up baselines to all summary tasks** option. With this, you will have a new baseline that will include the new tasks while maintaining the rest of the tasks with the original baseline. Of course, you will need to document the baseline change to understand your new EVM calculations.

In case of changes meant to decrease the scope and delete tasks, if you just delete the tasks, the baseline will keep their rolled up values, and you will not have any way to decrease them from the baseline. We recommend that you just delete the assignments and/or fixed cost, establish the durations as zero, and then follow the steps in the previous paragraph.

➤ **Set Multiple Baselines**

Another option is to set and manage multiple baselines. Every time you need to rebaseline your project, you can set a new baseline. You just need to choose the corresponding baseline number when you are setting the baseline instead of overwriting the original.

If you set a new baseline, you will need to change the baseline for earned value calculations:

1. On the **File** tab, in the **Backstage** view, click on **Advanced**.

2. Use the scroll bar to see the **Calculations options for this project**, and on **Earned Value options for this project**, on **Baseline for Earned Value calculation**, select the baseline you already defined.

Again, you should document this to avoid confusion in EVM reports and data analysis.

 If you change the baseline, Project 2010 will take this new baseline for all EVM calculations, but the views where the baseline is displayed in the **Gantt** chart (like **Tracking Gantt**) will show the original baseline (the baseline without number in Project 2010). To change the baseline graphic, on the **Format** tab, in the **Bar Styles** group, click **Baseline** , and select the baseline previously set that you want to show in your chart. You can also use the **Multiple Baselines Gantt** default view. Another option is to always use the baseline without a number as the active baseline, copying the current baseline always into the baseline without number, as explained in chapter 10.

EVM Special Cases

In our professional experience, we've found some special cases where the use of EVM has some issues or roadblocks. Here is a summary of those situations with our recommendations for managing them.

Manually Scheduled Tasks

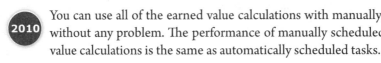

You can use all of the earned value calculations with manually scheduled tasks without any problem. The performance of manually scheduled tasks in earned value calculations is the same as automatically scheduled tasks.

Inactive Tasks

If you inactivate a task before you set the baseline, the task won't be considered in baseline values and won't affect any future earned value calculation.

If you set the baseline and later you inactivate a task, the task is in the original baseline considerations, so the Planned Value will be calculated as you define the status date. Of course, if you inactivate the task, you won't update it and you won't have Earned Value or Actual Cost. This means you will have variances against the baseline because of the inactivated task. That may be correct, but if you don't want these variances, you will need to re-baseline the project. (See the **Performance Measurement Baseline Updating** section earlier in this chapter.)

No Cost Management

We have found some organizations (more than we imagined) where cost control in projects is not used. In these organizations projects developed by internal resources do not need to control cost management, they only control hours. Actually the hours control is indeed a form of cost control; they just need to multiply the hours by the rates and they will have a cost management system. But, some organizations are not likely to manage actual costs in internal projects and we need to find a solution.

Project 2010 bases EVM on cost fields, but if you don't track costs, you can use one of following recommendations:

➤ **$ 1.00 / hour Rate**
   If you have resources assigned to your project tasks, and these resources do not have rates, just use a general rate of $1.00/hour. With this, you will have your EVM calculations using the common unit "Hour" instead of "$". Of course your views and tables will show the currency symbol, but you will know that the numbers represent hours. Some organizations evolve in this way: they start with the $1.00/hour rate, then the Finance Department provides a prorated general cost per hour, until finally they arrive at a cost management system with actual rates by resource.

➤ **Weighted Factors**
   We've also found organizations that manage projects without resource assignments. This is not recommended. If you have one of these projects, we recommend you establish a weighted factors system. You simply assign a weighted factor to each task, based on your experience as a project

manager (greater weights are given to the most important tasks). You can use the **Fixed Cost** field to assign the weighted factors, and when you set the baseline, you will have enough data to use EVM. Of course, all the cost indicators will be meaningless because your EV will be always equal to the AC, but all of the schedule indicators should help you to improve your project results.

➤ **Days as Cost**

If you don't have costs and don't want to use weighted factors, you can just copy the Duration of the tasks in the Fixed Cost field and set the baseline. With this you will have the durations as weighted factors that allow you to have all schedule indicators in your project. This could be good for projects that have short tasks with one resource assigned to each one. We don't really like this approach, but in some small projects, it is better than having just the Gantt bars.

Some Tasks with Costs and Some Tasks without Costs

We have often found projects where some tasks have associated costs (e.g., external contractors) while others don't (e.g., internal resources). This is a big issue if you want to apply EVM, because the tasks without costs will not have a cost baseline (BAC), and without a cost baseline your PV, EV and AC will be zero. This means that whether or not you accomplish these tasks, you will not have any indication in your variances and indexes. The solution should be assigning the right costs to all tasks, but we know that in some environments that isn't easy.

To address this you can do one of the following:

➤ **Master Project with Two Sub-Projects**

One solution is to set up one project for your tasks with associated costs and another project for your tasks without costs, and then consolidate both projects in a Master Project (see Appendix 2 for information about Master Projects). For the project without costs we recommend that you follow the weighted factors approach described above. Try to use weighted factors that represent a total cost that can be compared against the other project with costs, in a proportion that you consider a reasonable split between the two.

With this approach, you'll have a total EVM for your project with costs, and an EVM with schedule indicators for your project without costs and for your master project. This has functioned well in some environments: if you want to analyze your cost performance, you just go to your project with costs; if you want to look at schedule performance, you can use your master project indicators.

> ➤ **Project with Flags and Filters**
>
> If you don't want to manage a master project and two different projects, or your project has the tasks assigned so that you can't easily separate them into two projects (e.g., a lot of interactions between internal resources and external resources), you will need to combine tasks with and without costs in the same project. Our recommendation is to assign costs as weighted factors in internal tasks and use a customized flag field to mark which tasks have real costs and which tasks have costs as weighted factors. Then you can use filters and specific views to show real cost indicators and schedule indicators.

Uneven Resource Assignment and Multiple Resources

As we've seen throughout the chapter, EVM in Project 2010 functions better with uniform assignments. If you have uneven resource assignments we saw that it is better to change to physical % complete as your EV method for the task and copy the **% Work Complete** into the **Physical % Complete** field. This could be laborious but simple.

A bigger problem is when you have multiple resources with different rates assigned to the same task, and for any reason those resources do not work uniformly. The problem now is that neither **% Complete** nor **% Work Complete** will represent task progress because the rates are not the same. In these instances you'll need to make some manual computations to arrive at the correct % of progress. To avoid this, try to assign one resource per task. If that is not possible, try to manage uniform distributions in order to use **% Complete**. If that is not possible, you may need to accept some approximations in your EVM calculations.

Information at the Middle Level of the WBS

The general recommendation is to have your control accounts at the lowest level of your WBS, where you normally assign resources and costs in Project 2010. But in some large projects you may need to define your control accounts at some middle level of your WBS, and then continue your breakdown until you have tasks that you can integrate in your network. This could be a problem, because you also need to break down your costs and resources through the lowest level of the WBS, and you may not have the elements to do this.

We have said that you should not assign resources or costs to summary tasks, but this could be the only solution to this problem. Keep in mind that assigning resources at the summary level may cause some problems with progress information, because the progress of a summary task depends on its detailed tasks, and if you have parallel paths you may have some percentages that may not represent the real status.

Reporting EVM with Project 2010

Text Report: Earned Value

The report **Earned Value** calculates the values for BCWS, BCWP, ACWP, SV, CV, EAC, BAC, and VAC for project tasks and displays the results in a text report.

Follow these steps to run this report:

1. On the **Project** tab, in the **Reports** group, click **Reports** ▦. The **Reports** dialog box appears:

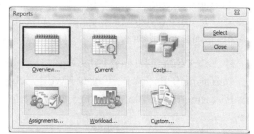

2. In the **Reports** dialog box, click **Cost** and then click **Select**.

3. In the **Cost Report** dialog box, select **Earned Value** and then click **Select**; the **Backstage** view appears in the **Print** section with Earned Value report information:

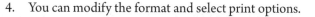

4. You can modify the format and select print options.

Using Views as EVM Reports

Remember you can always use your views as reports.

The default EVM tables and fields that you can use in task views are:

➤ **Earned Value:** Task Name, Planned Value – PV (BCWS), Earned Value – EV (BCWP), AC (ACWP), SV, CV, EAC, BAC, VAC

> **Earned Value Cost Indicators**: Task Name, Planned Value – PV (BCWS), Earned Value – EV (BCWP), CV, CV%, CPI, BAC, EAC, VAC, TCPI. (Note that AC is missed in this Cost Indicators table, but you can insert it.)

> **Earned Value Schedule Indicators**: Task Name, Planned Value – PV (BCWS), Earned Value – EV (BCWP), SV, SV%, SPI

The default EVM tables and fields you can use in Resource views are:

> **Earned Value**: Resource Name, Planned Value – PV (BCWS), Earned Value – EV (BCWP), SV, CV, EAC, BAC, VAC

We recommend using customized views to support your EVM reporting needs; you can include customized fields and graphic indicators that help with the interpretation and analysis of data.

Visual Report: Earned Value Over Time

The Excel visual report called *Earned Value Over Time Report* takes the Actual Cost of Work Performed, Budgeted Cost of Work Scheduled, and Budgeted Cost of Work Performed, and plots this task information over time on a line chart for the project.

Follow these steps to run this report:

1. On the **Project** tab, in the **Reports** group, click **Visual Reports** ; the **Visual Reports – Create Report** dialog box appears:

2. In the **Visual Reports – Create Report** dialog box, click the **All** tab or the **Assignment Usage** tab, then select the **Earned Value Over Time Report**.

3. On the bottom of the Visual Reports dialog box, select **View**, and your Earned Value Over Time Report will now be created in Excel. (See chapter 11 for more information about Visual Reports.)

EVM and Project 2010 Conclusions

EVM is a great technique when you have the right information and Project 2010 is a powerful tool to facilitate your application of EVM.

The key to effective implementation of EVM is to keep your model as simple as you can. You need to balance the necessity of accurate detailed information with the need for easy handling of your model.

To enhance EVM with Project 2010 there are add-ons in the market which offer improved features and graphical reporting. These add-ons work very well with Project 2010 in a standalone environment, but most of them have problems when you are working connected to Project Server 2010 because of incompatibilities with the Enterprise Global Template.

We have reviewed different ways to apply EVM with 2010; each has advantages, disadvantages and limitations.

Try to analyze your project and define what will work best for you. Don't force your project to fit some specific approach.

Always remember the main objective of EVM is to give you the right feedback to facilitate your decision making; EVM itself will not make successful projects. That requires a project manager willing to do the required analysis and take corrective actions when needed.

Here's a summary of our recommendations for applying EVM with Project 2010:

Setting Up

➤ Define the customized fields you want to use for EVM. (These could be in a Template defined by your PMO)

➤ Define customized views and reports for EVM. (These could be a Template defined by your PMO)

➤ Define a default task Earned Value method (% Complete or Physical % Complete) for all projects (choose the method you think will be used the most)

➤ Define different options that affect EVM calculations

➤ Define quality thresholds for EVM variances and indices

Planning (all steps need to include previous step review in an iterative way)

➤ Define the WBS and the Control Accounts

➤ Define the Earned Value measurement technique to be used in each task

➤ Define your dynamic schedule

> Assign resources and/or fixed costs to all tasks

> Establish your time phased budget (Project 2010 will do this automatically)

> Set your performance measurement baseline

Executing, Monitoring and Controlling (for each report period)

> Set the status date

> Record progress for each task according to the EV measurement technique defined in planning (update actual work, rates, costs, etc.)

> Update remaining work, duration, rates, costs, etc., for each task

> Perform EVM data analysis

> Calculate or define forecasts

> Propose corrective actions as needed for the remaining work

> Deliver reports

> Maintain the integrity of the baseline

Review Questions

1. What are the benefits of EVM?

2. You have been preparing Earned Value reports for your sponsor each month. The partial results of your reports are reflected in the chart below. How would you describe the performance of your project to date? What, if any, actions should you be taking?

Status Date	SPI	CPI
1-September-2012	1.50	1.40
1-October-2012	1.35	1.40
1-November-2012	1.20	1.28
1- December-2012	?	?

3. Stoplight charts have become an increasingly popular way to implement Management By Exception (MBE). Describe how you would implement this in your organization and how you might calculate tolerance levels for your graphical dashboard.

4. What are the differences between % Complete and Physical % Complete? When is it appropriate to use one versus the other? Where do you go in Project 2010 to select this option?

5. You find a problem in a project. The project has a defined baseline and task progress has been entered for all tasks for the first report period. The ACWP field show the right cost for the work reported, but the BCWP and BCWS fields are zero. What could be the problem here?

6. You realize that it is important to maintain the baseline on your project. You are in the practice of keeping the original baseline stored in the "Baseline without a number". As you receive approved scope changes you store a new baseline in Baseline##. What will be the impact of this practice in your earned value reporting? What are ways that you could prevent these impacts?

7. Describe and define the following acronyms:
   - PV
   - EV
   - AC
   - ETC
   - EAC
   - VAC
   - BAC

8. What is the common unit that earned value uses to report values in Project 2010?

9. What do the following indications mean:

Term	Indication	Meaning
VARIANCES		
Cost Variance (CV)	< 0	
Cost Variance (CV)	> 0	
Schedule Variance (SV)	< 0	
Schedule Variance (SV)	> 0	
INDICES		
Schedule Performance Index (SPI)	< 1	
Schedule Performance Index (SPI)	> 1	
Cost Performance Index (CPI)	> 1	
Cost Performance Index (CPI)	< 1	
To Complete Performance Index (TCPI)	< 1	
To Complete Performance Index (TCPI)	> 1	

10. Provide task examples where you can use each of the following EVM techniques, and a brief explanation of your recommendation:

EV Measurement Technique	Example	Explanation
0/100 Fixed Formula		
50/50 Fixed Formula		
Weighted Milestones		
% Duration Complete		
% Work Complete		
% Physical Units Complete		
% Physical Complete		
Apportioned Effort		
Level of Effort		

Additional Practice For experience working with the features you've learned about in this chapter, we strongly suggest that you do the additional exercises for this chapter that are included in Appendix 1.

Chapter 13: Evaluating the Project

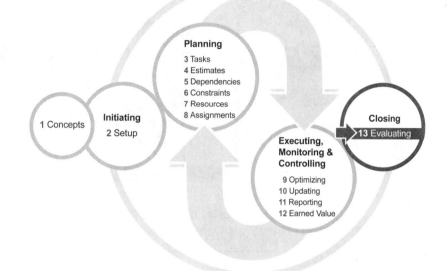

In this chapter, we'll explore how to analyze your experience on a completed project to become a better project manager on future projects.

The success of a project should be evaluated in terms of the accomplishment of the objectives and benefits that were defined when the project was approved, keeping in mind that these objectives may have changed during the project lifecycle, so you should review the impact of changes and variances in project objectives that may have affected project benefits.

After reading this chapter you will be able to:

> Explain why project evaluation is important
> Review the actual results against the baseline
> Review the history of baselines set
> Compare two versions of a schedule
> Prepare a list of questions that will help you evaluate a finished project
> Create templates for future projects
> Discuss what to capture in lessons learned

Dad when I asked for a lion for my birthday,
I wanted one I could play with!

Why Evaluate?

Project evaluations *can* be a waste of time: if you allow the focus of the evaluation to be on assigning blame for things that went wrong, you'll create an atmosphere loaded with animosity and finger pointing. Evaluations that focus only on finding fault with people for past mistakes are worse than a waste of time.

The purpose of project evaluation is to analyze both the successes and the failures of a completed project to help conduct better projects in the future. Only by learning from the past can we become better prepared for the future. But evaluation is useful only when the focus is on—and stays on—the future. Lessons learned can lead to improvements in all phases of future projects, e.g., the integrity of the WBS, the accuracy of estimates, the use of dependencies, the management of resources and the appropriateness of assignments.

It's important to include your team in the project evaluation process, both for their benefit as a learning experience and for the value of their contributions to lessons learned. If you decide to hold a team debriefing meeting, make sure you lead it in a way that encourages people to focus on gain for the future instead of on pain from the past. One way you can prevent finger pointing is to encourage self assessment by starting each question with: "*What could I have done to … ?*" It is equally important to analyze your successes, so that the things you and your team did well can be leveraged for future projects.

There is always room to deliver projects better. When you stop asking yourself the question *What could we have done better?*, you will stop learning from your experiences. In this age where the only constant seems to be rapid change, nobody can afford to stop learning. Life-long learning is the motto for success.

What to Evaluate: Project Results and Benefits

We need to remember that projects are authorized for the value they are expected to provide. For most projects, the value may not appear until sometime later—sometimes years after their completion. On others, the value may be evident as soon we deliver the results or even with some partial deliverables. In any case, the real evaluation of a project must include the analysis of the benefits achieved against the value originally defined in the business case.

Our book scope doesn't cover project benefits definition and analysis, so we are going to talk in this section about project performance evaluation based on variations against the baseline.

During project performance, the competing demands pull in different ways and may cause some tradeoffs between project objectives during the execution of the project. Therefore, we should review our results against both the original and any revised commitments. In order to do this, we compare our results against the baseline(s) set and we compare different versions of a schedule.

Comparing Baselines or Schedules

You can evaluate the performance of your project by comparing your actual results to your baseline(s). You may also find it useful to compare either different baseline versions or different schedule versions you've saved at different times. This will help to:

➤ Evaluate project results (the final baseline or schedule), against versions used at earlier phases of the project
➤ Learn from past projects by comparing successive versions of a baseline or schedule

Comparing Results against Baseline(s)

You can compare the actual data against the baseline you have defined. You can use different views and tables for this, and you may also include your customized fields or the EVM evaluation. For instance, here is an example of a finished project where you can easily review the actual against the baseline data:

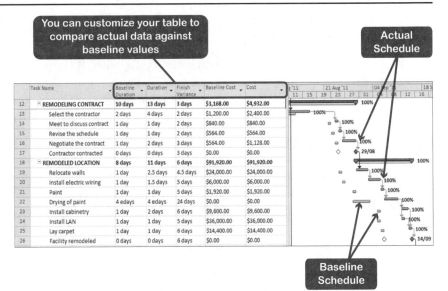

In some projects you may need to define multiple baselines to keep your schedule dynamic and to capture historical changes. For instance, you might have the following:

➤ Baseline 1: based on the original commitments with the client
➤ Baseline 2: based on the design developed by the contractors awarded the work
➤ Baseline 3: based on an approved major scope change

To analyze the different baselines used in your schedule, you can review the **Multiple Baselines Gantt View**:

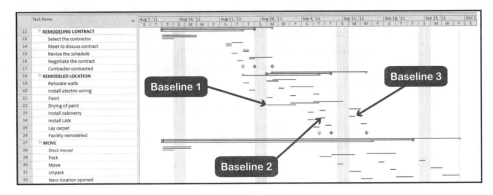

Comparing Two Versions of One Project Schedule

You can also evaluate the performance of your project by comparing two schedule versions that you may have saved at different times, depending on the information that was available. You can use this feature to:

➤ Evaluate project results (final schedule) against schedule versions used in earlier phases of the project

➤ Learn from past projects by comparing successive versions of a schedule

➤ Troubleshoot a schedule by comparing it to previous versions

➤ Check what changes collaborators or subcontractors made to their schedules after you sent a version for them to start working with

➤ Learn from exercises in this book. For example, to check your results in the Relocation Project exercises (Appendix 1), you can compare your files against the solution file available for download at www.jrosspub.com. Please click the link *WAV Download Resource Center* to enter the download site

2010

To create a report showing the differences between two versions of one schedule:

1. Open the most recent version of the schedule.

2. On the **Project** tab, click **Compare Projects** 📊, and the dialog **Compare Project Versions** appears:

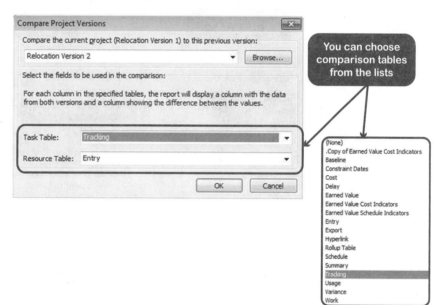

3. Enter or browse the previous version of the schedule and select **Task Table** and **Resource Table** to be included in the report.

 If the file you wish to compare with is already open, simply select it from the list.

4.   Click [OK]. Project 2010 will show the **Comparison Report**:

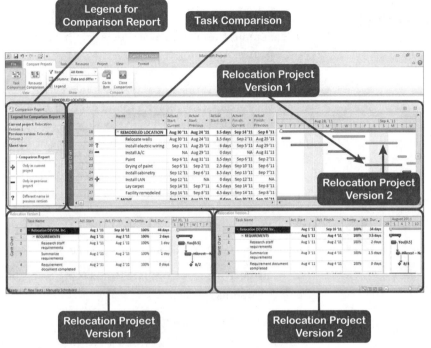

5.   You can also click the Resource Comparison button 👥👥 :

6. Once you have finished your analysis, select the **Close Comparison** icon on the **Compare Projects** tab, **Compare** group, to close the report or to save it for future reference. You save a comparison report the same way you save a project; be sure that you are in the **Comparison Report** side when you click on **File** tab. You will see in the **Info** section the information about the Comparison Report:

To proceed with saving, just use **Save** or **Save As** in the usual way.

 When saving a project comparison report, use a standard naming convention like Comparison_Report or Comp_Rpt in the file name for easy identification later.

Evaluation Questions

In addition to the objectives evaluations previously explained, you should complement your project analysis with some evaluation questions that really touch on all aspects of the project. There are many tools you can use for project evaluation: interviews with key stakeholders, questionnaires, review of your project results and change management forms.

Here are a few suggestions with respect to evaluating how you used your schedule as a tool to manage and control the project:

1. Was the schedule clear to all stakeholders? How can we make it clearer in future projects?

2. Was the WBS complete? Was it easy to understand? Did it function as a tool for delegation? Were the deliverables in it clearly formulated, or did some deliverables cause confusion? How can we improve the WBS for similar projects in the future?

3. Were the estimates optimistic or pessimistic? What factors caused the estimates to be optimistic or pessimistic? How can we better forecast these factors in future projects?

4. You may gain a rough insight into people's tendencies by studying their track records from previous projects. You can get a quick impression if you look in the **Actual Work** field and compare it to the **Baseline Work** field of a finished project. The more estimates a person has made, the more confidence you can have in this tendency to err. Was there enough of a time buffer in the schedule to compensate for unforeseen events? Which tasks consumed most of the buffer? Why? We discussed how up to three versions of the schedule can be shown next to each other in the timescale; a view like this would be very helpful for this analysis. What can we do in the future to prevent similar tasks from slipping?

5. Was the schedule easy enough to maintain during project execution? Was the network of dependencies complete, and did it update the forecasts automatically? Could accurate status and forecast reports be generated at each reporting period? How can we produce the reports more easily in future projects?

6. Were the right resources available at the right times? How can we better predict or ensure the availability of resources in future projects?

7. Did we apply the best practices to our schedule that were described throughout the book and summarized in chapter 14? How can we improve our skills in Project 2010? Are there features that were particularly helpful? Are there features that we did not take advantage of?

We recommend you capture these findings in lessons learned on the project.

To prevent painful lessons learned in the school of hard knocks, we recommend you use a checklist to evaluate the quality of your schedule during the planning phase of the project. In the next chapter, we will provide a checklist you can use to check the quality of the schedule as soon as it is created. This checklist will allow you to be more proactive in your future projects.

Creating Templates

Once you have evaluated the results of your project, it's a good practice to transfer your knowledge and the lessons learned about your project to other colleagues in your organization. You can prepare an evaluation summary to communicate your evaluation and you can also create a template to be used in futures projects, if you and your PMO support this.

To create a template you:

1. Open the schedule for which you want to create the template.

2. On the **Format** tab, in the **Drawings** group, click **Drawings**.

3. In the list, click **Text Box** and then when the black plus appears, click and drag within the Gantt Chart area until you draw a box.

4. Inside the box provide instructions on using the template. For example, can you add or delete tasks and summary tasks, describe the areas the template provides and the areas future users need to provide, and add reminders to check the start date and calendar, etc.

 Draw a large box so it is easily noticed. Be sure to remind people to delete the text box before saving or printing the schedule.

5. On **File** tab, click 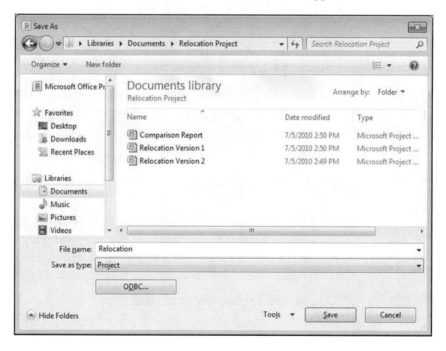 **Save As** . the **Save As** screen appears:

6. Enter the name of your template in **File name**:

7. On **Save as type** choose **Project Template**. The dialog box will change to:

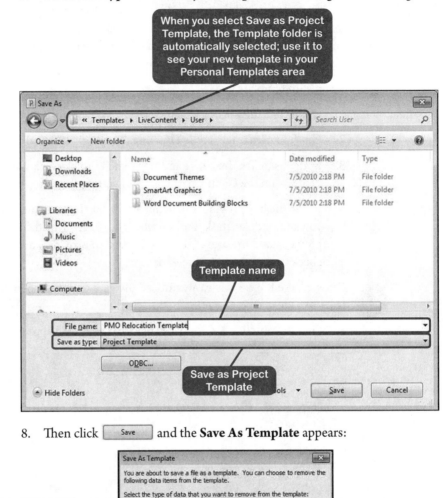

8. Then click [Save] and the **Save As Template** appears:

9. Choose which schedule information you don't want included with the template. Then click **Save** and your template is ready.

To open your template, refer to chapter 2.

Review Questions

1. You have been managing a new project for the last couple of months. As you enter into phase three of the project, you want to compare the different baselines, to see variances along the way. What view do you use in Project 2010 for this comparison and how did you capture these baselines along the way, assuming that you captured an original, phase 1 and phase 2 baseline?

2. You made a copy of the original project plan and are now optimizing duration on the copy and doing some "what-if" analysis to see if you can shorten the finish date. You like what you see, but want to compare your results to the original plan before making these changes to the original plan. How would you go about this comparison using Project 2010?

3. You are in the PMO and notice that most of the processes for departments follow the same project management methodologies. Your project managers create new projects from scratch, which takes a lot of extra development time in the planning phase. How could you help your project managers using Project 2010 to cut down their development time for planning?

Additional Practice For experience working with the features you've learned about in this chapter, we strongly suggest that you do the additional exercises for this chapter that are included in Appendix 1.

13

Chapter 14: Summary

We've now discussed the use of Project 2010 throughout the entire life cycle of a project. As a summary, we'll bring together the many recommendations we've made regarding best scheduling practices, and provide you with checklists, instructions and tools for future use.

Here's what this chapter includes:

➤ A final discussion of the attributes of a dynamic project model
➤ Instructions for obtaining additional tools we've provided for checking schedules
➤ Our Best Practices Checklist
➤ A checklist for troubleshooting dates in Project 2010 schedules

It didn't take as long as you'd think:
I used Dynamic Scheduling with Microsoft Project 2010!

Attributes of a Dynamic Project Model	A good schedule:

A good schedule:

> Is a model of the project
> Provides valid forecasts
> Is dynamic and easy to maintain

A Model of the Project

> A model should be a deliberate simplification of the complex reality. If you can't explain the model to your stakeholders, the model is too complex.
> A model of the project provides forecasts

Provides Valid Forecasts

A schedule will only produce valid forecasts if:

> It contains all deliverables
> The basis for estimates is consistent with the working times on the project calendar
> The time estimates seem reasonable for the work to be done
> During the project, the schedule produces accurate forecasts. You should assess this throughout the project's life cycle by seeing how actual results compare to planned results, milestone by milestone.

Dynamic and Easy to Maintain

The ideal of a totally dynamic model is that if one thing changes in reality, you should have to change only one field in your Project 2010 model. Even though this ideal is hard to reach, you can get very close to it if you set your schedule up in the right way. A schedule is dynamic if it:

> Has as few constraints as possible
> Has a complete network of dependencies

> Has resource dependencies clearly and accurately stated
> Is easy to maintain so that it can be kept alive during project execution
> Is kept up to date in a timely manner
> Continuously provides forecasts
> Is in an electronic format and could be accessible online

Tools and Best Practices Checklist

Throughout the book, we've made many recommendations for making your schedule a valid and dynamic model of your project. These recommendations are compiled in the Best Practices checklist later in this chapter. You can use this list to evaluate the quality of your project schedule and to check on the use of best practices.

If your schedule meets these guidelines, you have created a valid, dynamic model of your project. You have positioned yourself to bring the project to a successful completion. From experience, we can say that managing a large schedule is a nearly impossible task if it does not meet the requirements of the checklist. Schedules that meet the requirements need the least maintenance during the execution of the project.

They are also the easiest schedules to work with when you are managing multiple projects.

You need the single schedules to meet all requirements on the checklist if:

> You need to create an integrated program schedule for a large endeavor from subschedules. You need to apply the checklist on the subschedules. See Appendix 2 for more information on subschedules and consolidated schedules.
> You want to monitor and level the workloads across multiple projects.
> You want to apply Monte Carlo simulation to your schedules.

We provide tools with the checklist to check your schedules in an efficient manner, and we will discuss these next.

Copyright of the Tools and Checklist

The tools and checklist are copyrighted material: © 2011 by International Institute for Learning, Inc. This checklist is provided to you for personal purposes only. If you would like to use this checklist for commercial purposes within your organization, please contact IIL and talk to one of our sales representatives about licensing these tools and the checklist. See www.iil.com or call 1.212.758.0177 (USA).

DISCLAIMER: "No rights to copy, decompile, reverse engineer, create derivative works or distribute are being granted or implied. By choosing to use the filters and macros, you understand and agree (1) that IIL cannot be held liable for any damage to your schedule or business as a result of using the filters and macros and (2) to indemnify IIL from all liability whatsoever for any damages that may occur resulting from the use of these tools".

Tools to Check Your Schedules

We provide several tools to make checking your schedules easier. You will find them in the file *IIL Project 2010 Tools.mpp* available for download at www.jrosspub.com. Click the link *WAV Download Resource Center* to enter the download site.

Here's what you'll find there.

RCP Macro

The **RCP** Macro will identify the resource-critical path in a resource-constrained schedule. Please note that the RCP Macro only works properly with the English version of Project 2010. Refer to chapter 9 for more detail about the resource critical path and for instructions on how to use the RCP Macro.

Three small macros provided in previous versions of this book have been eliminated, because you can perform the same functions with the following Ribbon options:

➤ To expand all summary tasks: On the **View** tab, in the **Data** group, click the **Outline** down-arrow, **All Subtasks**. Every time before you apply a filter, you have to expand all tasks.
➤ To display or hide the project summary task: On the **Format** tab, in the **Show/Hide** group, select or deselect **Project Summary Task**.
➤ To zoom the timescale so that you can see the entire project: On the **View** tab, in the **Zoom** group, click on **Entire Project**.

For simplicity of use, you can add the Ribbon buttons to the Quick Access Toolbar (right click on the button Add to Quick Access Toolbar).

Filters

You can copy the filters to specific projects or to your global.mpt by using the Organizer:

1. Open the file ***IIL Project 2010 Tools.mpp*** in Project 2010 that you downloaded from the *WAV Download Resource Center*.

2. On the **File** tab, choose **Info** and select **Organizer**.

3. In the **Organizer** window, select the **Filter** tab to copy all of the customized IIL filters into your schedule.

Now that you've copied the filters to your global.mpt, they will be available for your projects.

Open the project and apply the specific filter as described below. Make sure that all summary tasks are expanded before applying any of these filters, since filters never display detail tasks that are collapsed under their summary tasks.

On the **View** tab, in the **Data** group, click the **Outline** down-arrow, then select **All Subtasks** to expand all detail tasks. After you use a filter, press [F3] to stop the filter and display all tasks again.

➤ **01 IIL Level of Detail < 1% of Proj Dur…**: An interactive filter that prompts for the minimum duration for detail tasks to check the level of detail in the WBS using the 1% – 10% rule. The filter does not display summary tasks, recurring tasks or inactive tasks.

➤ **02 IIL Level of Detail > 10% of Proj Dur…**: An interactive filter that prompts for the maximum duration for detail tasks to check the level of detail in the WBS using the 1% – 10% rule. The filter does not display summary tasks, recurring tasks or inactive tasks.

➤ **03 IIL Inactive Tasks**: Allows you to display the inactive tasks. You can use this filter to help you determine if any of your inactive tasks can be activated or deleted.

➤ **04 IIL Summary Tasks with Dependencies**: Displays all active summary tasks with dependencies on them. If there are many summary tasks with dependencies, it makes checking the completeness of the network logic and tracing the critical path too difficult. We recommend keeping the logic on detail tasks as much as possible.

➤ **05 IIL Detail Tasks without Predecessors**: A filter that displays detail tasks without any predecessors to find the starting points of the network of dependencies. Detail tasks without predecessors may start on the project start date or will have a Start No Earlier Than constraint (SNET). The network of dependencies can have multiple starting points, but only one ending point. This filter displays all starting points of the network. You can then see if there are starting points in the network that should perhaps have a predecessor. This filter does not show recurring tasks and inactive tasks.

➤ **06 IIL Detail Tasks without Successors**: A filter that displays detail tasks without any successor to find tasks that are not incorporated in the network of dependencies (loose ends). There should be only one ending point in the network of dependencies, otherwise critical path and slack calculations are not likely to be correct. This filter does not show recurring and inactive tasks.

➤ **07 IIL Detail Tasks with SS or FF**: This filter displays all tasks involved in a Start-to-Start (SS) or Finish-to-Finish (FF) dependency. SS and FF dependencies can easily have loose ends in the network of dependencies and have to be checked separately and carefully. Inactive tasks are shown by this filter when they are part of an SS or FF dependency.

➤ **08 IIL Constraints other than ASAP**: A filter that displays any tasks with a constraint other than As Soon As Possible (ASAP). A dynamic model should have as few constraints as possible. Recurring tasks are not shown, because they should have constraints. This filter does not show inactive tasks.

➤ **09a IIL Detail Tasks without Resources Assigned**: This filter displays all detail tasks without any resources assigned. You can also check this by looking under Unassigned in the Resource Usage view, but this filter allows you to copy the task IDs and names into a report of what tasks do not have resources assigned. . With that information, you can find the tasks without assignments easily. If assignments haven't been made, workloads won't be accurate and forecasted dates may be too optimistic. This filter does not show milestones or inactive tasks.

➤ **09b IIL Summary Tasks with Resources Assigned**: This filter complements the 09a IIL Detail Tasks without Resource Assigned filter and displays all summary tasks with resources assigned. If summary tasks have assignments, you can easily end up with over-allocations. We recommend keeping the assignments on detail tasks as much as possible. This filter does not show inactive summary tasks.

➤ **10 IIL Deadlines or Constraints not met**: This filter displays items with deadlines or constraints that have negative slack. These deadlines or constraint dates are not met, and the schedule may forecast dates that are wrong. Special consideration is taken for manual tasks because their total slack is always zero and they have no constraint dates, so the filter shows manual tasks that have a deadline in which the finish date is greater than the deadline. This filter does not show inactive tasks.

➤ **11 IIL Tasks with missing baseline info**: A filter that displays any tasks that do not have baseline information in Baseline Start, Baseline Finish, Baseline Duration or Baseline Work. When assignments are created after the baseline is set, the Baseline Work field is often empty on these tasks. Notice that the filter does not check the field Baseline Cost. This filter does not show milestones or inactive tasks.

➤ **12 IIL Reschedule Actual Durations ...**: An interactive filter that prompts you for the status date twice and displays tasks with an Actual Start or Actual Finish date after the status date. All actual dates should be in the past, i.e., earlier than the status date. As the status date, enter the date on which the schedule was submitted. With this filter, you can determine if there are actuals in the future, which does not make sense. There should be no Actual Start or Actual Finish dates later than the status date. The filter shows if the schedule is updated properly and thus if the forecasted dates are accurate and reliable. This filter does not show inactive tasks.

➤ **13 IIL Reschedule Remaining Durations...**: An interactive filter that prompts you for the status date twice and displays tasks with remaining durations scheduled in the past (earlier than the status date). With this filter you can determine if the schedule is updated properly and if the forecasted dates are accurate and reliable. This filter does not show inactive tasks.

➤ **14 IIL Remaining Durations revised:** This filter displays all detail tasks for which the current duration is not equal to the baseline duration. If the filter displays any tasks, it would indicate that the project manager is revising the remaining durations. Regular revision of remaining durations is important to ensure that the forecasted dates are accurate and reliable. Provide feedback to the project manager only if the filter does not display any detail tasks. This filter does not show inactive tasks.

Best Practices Checklist for Schedules

In the checklist, we have used the words summary task and detail task very carefully. It is important that the words are interpreted correctly for the guidelines to make sense. A summary task is any task with indented subtasks listed beneath it on a lower level in the WBS. A detail task is any task without indented subtasks in the WBS.

The checklist is a succinct summary of this book. It has the following categories that correspond to chapters in this book:

➤ Background Information about the Project
➤ Setting up the Project
➤ Entering Tasks
➤ Entering Estimates
➤ Entering Dependencies
➤ Entering Deadlines, Constraints and Task Calendars
➤ Entering Resources
➤ Entering Assignments
➤ Optimizing the Schedule
➤ Updating the Schedule
➤ Reporting
➤ Earned Value Management
➤ Evaluating the Project

The filters mentioned in the checklist can be found in the file *IIL Project 2010 Tools.mpp* available for download at <u>www.jrosspub.com</u>. Please click the link *WAV Download Resource Center* to enter the download site.

Background Information About the Project

You need to know the answers to the following questions in order to make a thorough evaluation of the schedule:

➤ What is the benefit of the project?

➤ Which is the priority and risk of the project?

➤ Who are the key stakeholders of the project?

➤ Does the project need to address a specific methodology or process?

➤ What is the objective or final product of the project?

➤ What is the deadline date of the project? Is it shown as a deadline date in the schedule?

➤ Does the project have a cost budget? If yes, how much?

➤ Does the project have a person hour budget (effort)? If yes, how many person hours, person days, person weeks, person months or person years?

➤ Did the project manager gather pure work time estimates or gross work time estimates?

➤ Did the project manager apply the rolling wave approach in the schedule? If so, what is the duration of the detail planning window?

➤ Will the project manager do task updates (durations) or assignment updates (time sheets) or both?

Setting Up the Project

Here are some checks to verify that you used best practices when setting up your project:

➤ Does the Comments field in the Project Properties (**File**, **Info**, **Project Information**, **Advanced Properties**) contain a succinct description of the objective or final product of the project?

The description is visible as a Note on the project summary task. You need to have appropriate background information on the project to properly evaluate the schedule.

➤ Are the Exception days (holidays and other non-working time) entered in the Standard Calendar?

➤ Do the working hours as specified in the Project Calendar through Change Working Time correspond to the Hours per day conversion values set in the Project Options?

For example, working times of 8:00 AM-12:00 PM and 1:00 PM-5:00 PM are consistent with 8 hours per day and 40 hours per week. If the settings are inconsistent, your forecasts are either too optimistic or too pessimistic. Also, you might see decimals in the task durations.

The quickest way to check consistency is by launching the **Change Working Time** window from the **Project** tab of the Ribbon. The button Options... will take you directly to the **Project Options**.

➤ Do all of the project options match your organization's standards and your personal selections? Click the **File** tab to go to the **Backstage**, then click **Options** to review all the settings.

Entering Tasks

➤ Do you want the default for your new tasks to be auto-scheduled or manually-scheduled (on the **File** tab, **Backstage** view, **Options**, **Schedule** tab)?

➤ Are there deliverables in the WBS and are the deliverables complete, but lean?

➤ Does the WBS have a logical hierarchy?
  ▶ Is the WBS an indented list with multiple hierarchical levels instead of a long list without structure?
  ▶ Does each summary task have at least two subtasks?
  ▶ Is there any duplication or logical overlap between deliverables?
  ▶ Does each group of subtasks capture all the work of their summary task (top-down check)?
  ▶ Does each item logically relate to its summary tasks on all higher levels (bottom-up check)?
  ▶ Is the feature Project Summary Task used instead of a physical project summary task?   (On the **Format** tab, **Show/Hide** group, select the check box for **Project Summary Task.**) Project 2010's project summary task has ID number 0 (zero) in the first column.

➤ Are there enough milestones—roughly one for each summary task? You can check this by applying the standard filter **Milestones.**

➤ Does the WBS have the right level of detail?
  ▶ Is it clear how deliverables will be created and what the activities involved are?
  ▶ Is the WBS lean enough that you'll be able to update all detail tasks in the schedule during project execution?

➤ Is the WBS clear to all project stakeholders?

14

*Entering
Estimates*

Once you've gathered initial estimates, you'll want to perform some reasonability checks on them.

➤ Are the estimates reasonable given the work that needs to be performed? You will need some technical expertise and recorded past experience to verify if estimates are reasonable. If you don't have this technical expertise, you can:

▶ Review the schedules of previous, similar projects

▶ Ask team members with technical knowledge to peer review each others' estimates

▶ Ask a subject matter expert to review the estimates

➤ Did you include manually scheduled tasks for items where you are not able to provide a complete estimate?

➤ Was the rolling wave approach applied to activities in the future that you are only planning at a high-level?

➤ Did your estimate for each task include a work or duration estimate and did you set the appropriate task type and effort-driven settings?

➤ Are the estimates that you collected consistent with the working hours entered in the Standard Project Calendar? For example, if you collected pure estimates did you reduce the hours per day to reflect purely productive hours per day, such as 5.5 or 6. If they are not consistent, the schedule will be too long or too short.

➤ Do the durations of your estimates fall within the 1% – 10% Rule (as discussed in chapter 3 and reviewed below)?

➤ Are the completion of key deliverables of your project modeled as milestones with zero days duration?

➤ Did you include buffers to address schedule risk?

Once you have done your estimating and the other steps in the process (including assigning resources and setting dependencies), you can find the project duration easily by:

clicking **Project Information** 🔲 on the **Project tab** and clicking ❲ Statistics... ❳.

OR

viewing the **Duration** field of the project summary task. You can display the project summary task by choosing ☑ **Project Summary Task** on the **Format** tab. This task will appear at the top of the list as a task with ID number 0.

In chapter 3 we covered the 1% – 10% rule: the duration of any detail task should be between a minimum of 1% of the project duration (rounded) and a maximum of 10% of the project duration (rounded). (Note that this rule is a guideline.)

If you find a task that is longer than 10% of the project, you can split the task into multiple subtasks. Or if the assigned resources are working part-time on the task, you can increase their commitment to full-time, and the duration will decrease. This is more refinement to the WBS, discussed in chapter 3.

Notice that the 1% – 10% rule should only be applied to the durations and not to the work values (effort). If there are many part-time assignments or many multiple assignments per task, the boundaries for work estimates should be narrower or wider than for the duration. In general, the minimum and maximum values for work are harder to indicate, which is why we stayed away from that.

You can check the 1% – 10% rule in your project by applying the filter **01 IIL Level of Detail < 1% of Proj Dur** or filter **02 IIL Level of Detail > 10% Proj Dur**.

Entering
Dependencies

➤ Is the network of dependencies complete?
A complete network allows the schedule to update itself and displays the correct critical path. The network is complete if the task bars of all detail tasks and milestones are tied up at the end of the schedule. The network can have multiple starting points, but only one ending point. Only then will the critical path calculation be correct. The following questions will help determine if the network is complete:

▶ Is the logic only set on detail tasks and milestones?
If dependencies run over summary tasks and detail tasks in parallel, it is too hard to check if the network is complete and too hard to trace and understand the critical path. Therefore, we recommend that you keep the logic on the detail tasks and milestones only. You can check if there are dependencies on summary tasks by applying the filter **04 IIL Summary Tasks with Dependencies.**

▶ Are all the starts of the detail tasks and milestones linked to at least one other detail task or milestone? Exceptions are:
   ‣ Tasks that can start when the project starts or that are driven by external forces or deliveries rather than by hand-offs within the project
   ‣ External delivery milestones with a Start No Earlier Than constraint date
   ‣ Recurring tasks
   ‣ Overhead tasks
You can verify if all starts are linked by applying the filter **05 Detail Tasks without Predecessors**. Note that if the project manager used SS

or FF dependencies, the filter is not conclusive. You can check if there are tasks with SS or FF dependencies by applying filter **07 IIL Detail Tasks with SS or FF**.

▶ Are all ends of the detail tasks and milestones linked to at least one other detail task or milestone? Exceptions are:
  ▸ The project end milestone
  ▸ Recurring tasks
  ▸ Overhead tasks

A loose end, hanger or dangling task is a detail task that does not have its finish tied to any other task. In any project there should only be one loose end, the project finish milestone.

You can verify if all ends are linked up by applying the filter **06 IIL Detail Tasks without Successors**. Note that if the project manager used SS or FF dependencies, the filter is not conclusive. There will be another check on those.

▶ Do you have SS and FF dependencies properly linked up?
If you used SS or FF dependencies in your schedule, you should filter and display all those tasks with SS and FF dependencies and check on loose ends manually. You can do this by applying the filter **07 IIL Detail Tasks with SS or FF**. Since the filter will display both the predecessor and successor involved in the SS or FF dependency, you can check if they are hooked up properly to other tasks by revealing the Predecessors and Successors fields. What you should look for is:
  ▸ Does a task with SS in the Successor field also have an FS or FF successor that ties up its end?
  ▸ Does a task with FF in the Predecessor field also have an SS or FS predecessor that ties up its start?

▶ Are there tasks with an unreasonably large amount of Total Slack?
You can check this by doing a descending sort on Total Slack. On the **View** tab, choose **Data** group, **Sort**, **Sort by**, and in the **Sort** dialog box, select **Total Slack** from the **Sort by** list, then select **Descending** and click **Sort**. Check if the tasks with most slack were expected to have a lot of slack. If not, you have found missing logic. Even after you have given all detail tasks a successor, you should still apply this check because even if each task has a successor, it does not guarantee that you haven't forgotten important links. Checking the Total Slack will actually lead you to where you forgot to set important dependencies in your model of the project. This check is very effective in catching missing logic in schedules. Remember that if you miss just one essential dependency, your critical path is wrong, your forecasts are not valid and your model is not dynamic.

▶ When a change is entered into the schedule, does it update the rest of the schedule automatically and appropriately through dependencies? Is the entire schedule still valid? Where the schedule is not valid, an essential dependency might be missing. If you have to check the entire schedule after each change, you don't have a dynamic model. Remember, the logic should be helpful, especially during project execution when you update your schedule regularly.

➤ Is the Network Logic simple enough?
If you can't explain the network to your project team, it's too complex. Are there redundant dependencies that make the network too difficult to explain and maintain:

▶ Are there dependencies that leapfrog each other?
▶ Are there dependencies that run in parallel on detail tasks and their summary tasks? If that is the case, remove the summary task dependencies.

➤ Does the network have circular logic?
Circular logic does not make sense, because it is not clear which task should be scheduled first. Project 2010 warns you not to set circular logic within a single schedule.

➤ Does the logic of the network make sense?
After the previous checks on dependencies are done, you should perform one more high level check to see if the resulting schedule actually makes sense. You can best check this by showing only the first outline levels of the WBS and checking if the timing of the deliverables (or phases) makes sense on this high level. Use the ⊞ button on the **View** tab, and in the **Data** group click on the Outline down-arrow to display **Outline level 2** or **Outline level 3** depending on the size of your project. Even though you may not be an expert in the field of this project, you can pick up on common sense problems like *design* scheduled before *construction*, *write* before *print*, etc. Realize that if you followed our recommendations and minimized the number of constraints and entered all dependencies, the start and finish dates of the tasks are entirely driven by the network of dependencies. If the resulting schedule does not make sense, you probably overlooked an essential dependency.

Checks on Deadlines, Constraints and Task Calendars

Here are some checks you can use to verify whether you've applied best practices in your use of deadlines and constraints in your dynamic model of the project:

➤ Is the project deadline date captured in the schedule?
It can be set using the Deadline feature date or using the Constraint feature in Project 2010. The deadline or constraint date needs to be set on the project

finish milestone. Whether you use a deadline or a constraint depends on how hard the project target finish date is.

➤ Have you minimized Task Calendars in the schedule?
As we discussed, Task Calendars have a very specific purpose and should only be used in those situations where needed.

➤ Does the schedule have as few schedule constraints as possible?
Constraints make the schedule rigid and jeopardize a dynamic schedule. However, constraints are legitimate on:

▶ Recurring detail tasks (like *status meetings 1*, *status meetings 2*, etc.)

▶ External dependencies, such as delivery of supplies or arrival of materials

▶ Activities that have to take place on a certain agreed-upon date, like *deliver presentation* and *conduct training*. In general, these are activities in which a number of people are involved.

▶ Do-or-die-by dates, such as launches or opening dates of events for which marketing and advertising has already been done. Huge recurring sporting events which take place at set times in the calendar would also be good examples.

▶ Activities affected by weather conditions (e.g, in Canada asphalting streets starts no earlier than April 1st, because of the cold). You can also use the Task Calendars feature for these situations. Task Calendars would be a better way in the case of the multi-year planning of infrastructural works; unlike constraints, task calendars will push a job automatically out to the next year if it will no longer fit within the current year.

You can display all tasks that have constraints by applying the filter **08 IIL Constraints other than ASAP**. The filter will not display recurring detail tasks. Recurring detail tasks have SNET constraints. This is because they are usually dependent on an established time rather on than another task.

Entering Resources

Resources and assignments are particularly important in projects in which you expect that limited resource availability or huge workloads will influence the project end date. They are also important if there is a budget and the cost needs to be managed.

➤ Are all resources identified in the Resource Sheet?
Resources and assignments should be entered for projects where:

▶ You expect that limited resource availability or huge workloads will affect the end date of the project

▶ You have a cost budget for the project and you are responsible for staying within that budget

▶ You have a budget expressed in person months and you have to stay within this effort budget

▶ You foresee a quality or scope impact on the project depending on which resources you will get

➤ Are Budget resources identified and entered in on the project summary task?

➤ Are all resources named completely and consistently using a naming convention like *<first name> <last name>* or *<last name>-<first name>*?

➤ Are there no overlaps between the resources or duplication of resources?
If there are overlaps or duplications, Project 2010 will still aggregate the workloads of the resources, but these total numbers will be useless when you check on over- allocations. If Bill Tan is listed twice as a resource (as Bill Tan and William Tan), you would have to sum all time-phased workloads in order to determine if he is over-allocated. The workloads in the Resource Graph and in the Resource Usage can appear to be smaller than they really are when duplicate or overlapping resources exist.

➤ Is the availability of the resources appropriately modeled?
This can be assessed by asking yourself the following questions.

▶ Does the availability of individuals not exceed 120% as captured in the resource field **Max Units** or the availability profile in the **Resource Information** dialog box, tab **General**, in the **Resource Availability section**, in **Units** column?
At the International Institute for Learning, we set an arbitrary limit and choose the maximum to be 120%. We think it is unreasonable to ask resources for more than 120% availability for periods longer than one week. When you ask resources to work overtime for extended periods of time, their productivity goes down dramatically. So, apart from the fact that it is unreasonable to ask resources for much overtime over extended periods, it doesn't help your project. In your organization, the actual threshold may be different from 120%.

▶ If the Max. Units are less than 100%, is there a valid reason for this?
Valid reasons are that the project manager works with pure work time estimates, the resources have other ongoing work or concurrent projects, or the resource may be part-time.

▶ Are the vacations of individual resources captured in their resource calendars? Vacations need to be entered, particularly when there are important deadlines close to the vacations. To check if they are entered, on the **Project** tab, **Reports** group, click on **Reports**. Click on **Assignments** and on [Select], then **Who does what**, click [Edit...]. On the **Details** tab, check ✔ **Calendar**, and click [OK], then in **Assignment Reports** click [Select]. The **Backstage** view will appear and in print preview you will now see individual vacations listed under **Exceptions**, as well as the exceptions from the Project Calendar. Verify if the individuals' vacations are listed. You can copy this changed report back into your *Global.mpt* using the **Organizer**, on the **File** tab, on **Info**, to have it ready for future schedule analysis.

➤ Are the costs of the resources appropriately modeled?

▶ Are human resources entered as Work resources in the resource field Type? Are facilities, machines and materials entered as Material resources?

▶ Do material resources have an appropriate Material Label to indicate their unit of measure? For bulk resources or consumable resources the material label should reflect the unit of measure, for example, the material label for cabling could be *yards or meters*.

▶ Are cost resources entered as Cost resources in the resource field Type?

▶ Are budget resources identified as a Budget resource in the General tab on the Resource Information dialog box?

▶ Are the rates entered in the appropriate fields?

  ▸ Time-related costs for work resources in the Std. Rate field.

  ▸ Unit-related cost for material resources in the Std. Rate field.

  ▸ Time-related cost for facilities and machines as material resources using two fields: the Std. Rate field where you enter the per-unit cost, and the assignment-related Units field where you indicate the number of units used per time unit, for example, 2 rooms each day should be entered as *2/day*.

  ▸ Use-related costs in the Cost/Use field.

  ▸ Overtime costs in the Ovt. Rate field (but only if the overtime is paid and paid at a higher rate than the standard rate).

  ▸ Rates that vary over time in the Cost Rate Tables.

  ▸ Multiple rates per resource in the five Cost Rate Tables and the appropriate Cost Rate Table (A, B, C, D or E) selected for each assignment.

  ▸ Task- or deliverable-related fixed costs in the Fixed Cost field (or as a Cost resource in the Assign Resources dialog box) in the Gantt Chart.

▶ Is the cost scheduled appropriately?
This is important for managing the cash-flow of the project: *Can bills be paid when they are supposed to be paid?*

> ▸ Does the resource-related Accrue At field reflect when the cost occurs: at the Start or at the End, or Prorated with the time-phased amount of work?
> ▸ Does the task-related Fixed Cost Accrual field reflect when the fixed cost will be incurred?

Entering
Assignments

Here are some checks to help you verify whether you have applied best practices to the assignments in your schedule:

➤ Are you paying attention to the task-related fields Type and Effort Driven for the detail tasks?

The available types in the field Type are: Fixed Duration, Fixed Units or Fixed Work. With this field, you can control what Project 2010 recalculates: duration, units or work. If you don't monitor the field Type, you are not controlling what Project 2010 does. You are using a software tool, but you have no idea what the tool can do for you. This is similar to having a carpenter's stud finder, but not knowing how to use it. Instead you start drilling holes in the drywall hoping to find the studs by trial and error. If you don't use the field Type, you are using Project 2010 in a trial and error fashion; you change a field here, Project 2010 recalculates a value there, you don't like what you see and you change it back again … and you start running after your own tail.

➤ Does each detail task have at least one human resource assigned?

If there are detail tasks without human resources assigned, you have not captured all the workloads in your project. If workloads are missing, the schedule may be too optimistic, since leveling workloads typically leads to longer schedules and later forecasts. An exception to this rule is that recurring detail tasks do not need resources assigned to them. You can check on this in one of two ways:

> ▸ In the Resource Usage view, there should be no detail tasks listed under the first category Unassigned.
> ▸ You can check for detail tasks without resources assigned by applying the filter **09a IIL Detail Tasks without Resources Assigned**.

➤ Are there no assignments on the summary tasks?

As we discussed, if you assign resources to summary tasks you can easily end up with over-allocations that can't be resolved other than by removing the resource from the summary task. If you assign only to detail tasks, you will never end up with this stubborn type of over-allocation and will save yourself time when leveling workloads. Resolving over-allocations is challenging enough. You can check for assignments on summary tasks easily by applying the filter **09b IIL Summary Tasks with Resources Assigned**.

> ➤ Are all the costs appropriately modeled to include variable and fixed costs? Variable costs are driven by the number of units (percentage) of work or material resources assigned to a task. Task- or deliverable-related fixed costs are entered in the Fixed Cost field in the Gantt Chart or as a Cost resource in the Assign Resources dialog box.

> ➤ Is the cost scheduled appropriately?
>   ▶ Does the task-related Fixed Cost Accrual field reflect when the fixed cost will be incurred? You can review the time-phased cost in the Task Usage or Resource Usage views.
>   ▶ Have you utilized Budget resources to help you identify variances between your planned and projected costs?
>   ▶ Budget variables—created by setting the Budget flag in the Resource Information window—can be assigned only to the Project Summary task. The values for these resources are entered in the Budget Cost or Budget Work fields of the Task Usage or Resource Usage views.

Optimizing the Schedule

Optimizing Workloads

> ➤ Is the total effort within the person hour budget of the project (if a budget is available)?
> If you add the Project Statistics ⌁ button to the Quick Access Toolbar you can see the total final amount of work for the project by looking in the Current row and the Work column.

>   ▶ Are the workloads for the resources reasonable?
>   We work with these limits: the workload for individuals should not exceed 150% of their regular availability within any week and should not exceed 120% for periods longer than a week. We chose these levels to prevent burnout, attrition and dramatic loss of productivity. The parameters may differ for your organization. Be sure to check with your PMO (project management office) or the authority that sets these guidelines.
>   ▶ The workload of consolidated resources (groups) should not exceed their availability.
>   ▶ The workloads should be fairly smooth, since there are hidden costs involved with erratic workloads.

Note that it is not enough to just check if there is any red in the Resource Usage view. Project 2010 often highlights more resources in red than are truly over-allocated. If there is an over-allocation during only one business hour, the resource will be shown in red. Use the **Next Overallocation** tool on the **Resource** tab in the **Level** group to check the over-allocations. This tool is more selective and more reliable. However, even this tool does not always find all over-allocations, and it also highlights trivial over-allocations (e.g., 1 hour).

Optimizing Costs

➤ Is the cost modeled using the right fields and in the appropriate way?
The following fields are available in Project 2010:

▶ Resource fields: Type, Material Label, Standard Rate, Overtime Rate, Cost/Use, and Accrual At. A resource can also have cost rate tables.

▶ Task fields: Fixed Cost and Fixed Cost Accrual.

➤ Is the total cost within the budget of the project (if a cost budget is available)?
You can find the total cost of the project by clicking **Project Statistics** ⋎ on the Quick Access Toolbar and looking in the **Current** row and **Cost** column.

Optimizing Time

➤ Are there as many parallel paths as logically possible in the network of dependencies?
Novice schedulers tend to schedule all tasks in one long sequential chain. This creates many soft dependencies that make the duration of the project unnecessarily long. When optimizing for time, it is important to schedule in parallel what logically can happen simultaneously.

➤ Are there any unresolved conflicts between the task calendars and resource calendars?
If there are conflicts, the forecasts may be too optimistic. You can find the conflicts by looking in the **Indicators** ⓘ column for the icon 📵.

➤ Are the deadline dates and other constraints met in the schedule?
You can check this by applying filter **10 IIL Deadlines or Constraints not met**. It displays tasks with deadlines or constraints that have negative slack. When deadline or constraint dates are not met, the schedule may forecast a project end date that is too optimistic.

➤ Does the schedule have a critical path or a resource-critical path?
The (Resource) critical path tells you which tasks drive your project end date. You can check the critical path by applying the Tracking Gantt view. This view highlights the critical path in red by default.

▶ If a schedule is extended when the workloads are leveled, a resource-critical path needs to be identified. Resource-critical tasks need to be marked manually.

▶ The (resource) critical path can only consist of detail tasks and milestones. It should not contain level-of-effort tasks (overhead tasks or recurring tasks) or summary tasks (since the logic and the resources should be kept on the detail tasks).

➤ Does the (resource) critical path provide a complete explanation for the project duration?

You can check the completeness by displaying the (Resource) critical path and checking for gaps. Normally, there should be no gaps and every business day should have at least one critical task (unless there are lags on critical dependencies). If you find gaps, the (resource) critical path is fragmented, and the tasks that are most critical need to be identified in the schedule.

Updating the Schedule

The following checks reflect best practices for updating schedules. A schedule has to be updated if today's date is later than the project start date. If the project should have started, the schedule needs to show updated information with actuals and revised forecasts.

The following questions will help you determine if the best practices for updating schedules were applied:

➤ What is the quality of the baseline in the schedule?
The schedule needs a good baseline, because it will be the standard for comparing the progress.

➤ Is a baseline present?
Keep in mind that projects planned far into the future that haven't been approved yet don't necessarily need a baseline.

➤ Is the baseline complete?
You can verify the presence and completeness by applying the filter **11 IIL Tasks with missing baseline info**. The filter displays any tasks without entries in Baseline Start, Baseline Finish, Baseline Duration or Baseline Work. When assignments are created after the baseline is set, the Baseline Work field is still empty. Note that the filter does not check on the field Baseline Cost.

➤ Is the baseline the approved baseline?
The baseline cannot be reset without formal approval of the appropriate project stakeholders.

➤ Is the baseline relevant?
If the project deviated too far from the baseline, a new baseline needs to be negotiated, since the baseline should provide a meaningful standard of comparison for the current schedule. You can check this by looking at how far the current schedule is removed from the baseline. Does the project have a fighting chance to catch up with the baseline again, or is it a lost cause? If it is a lost cause, you should submit a change request to change the baseline.

➤ Are the appropriate options selected in **File** tab, on **Backstage** view, on **Options**, for the chosen updating strategy?
  ▸ For task updating (revising the task-related **Actual Duration** and **Remaining Duration** fields), the options should be set as follows:

Schedule, Scheduling options for this project: ☑ Split in-progress tasks

Schedule, Calculation options for this project: ☑ Updating task status updates resource status

▶ For assignment updating (entering numbers from the time sheets into the assignment-related **Actual Work** and **Remaining Work** fields), the options should be set as follows:

Schedule, Scheduling options for this project: ☑ Split in-progress tasks

Schedule, Calculation options for this project: ☑ Updating task status updates resource status. If you keep this option selected, you should not enter **% Complete** on tasks, because this may override time sheet data.

▶ For updating both the tasks and the assignments, the options should be set as follows:

Schedule, Scheduling options for this project: ☑ Split in-progress tasks

Schedule, Calculation options for this project: ☑ Updating task status updates resource status

You cannot enter both types of information unless you clear this option.

Reporting

➤ Is there a one-page status report available as a separate View object in your project schedule that displays the major milestones relative to the baseline?

▶ Are the milestones filtered in this view instead of listed together in the WBS?

▶ Many project managers put the major milestones at the top of their schedule to create a one-page overview of the project. This makes the network of dependencies very complex in the Gantt Chart, because the dependencies run up and down with long arrows. This makes it very difficult to check if the network of dependencies is complete. Instead, we advocate using a separate view that displays all milestones using the **Milestones** filter.

▶ Are the appropriate milestones chosen to represent the status and to forecast a large project?

▶ Does the one-page view report (often prized by executives) give an appropriate impression of the health of the project?

➤ If your schedule has a Resource-critical path, is there a separate view object that displays it?

The view should have the resource-critical tasks flagged in the field Marked or in a Flag field.

➤ Is every key stakeholder receiving the appropriate information?

▶ Is there a set of views with an appropriate selection of objects to deliver different information to different stakeholders?

▶ Are you aware of the format in which every stakeholder prefers to review the information? Some stakeholders prefer graphics (use Visual Reports), others like fast and understandable tables (use the textual Reports), while others analyze the information in other tools like Excel or other databases (save the database in an OLAP cube or Access format). If you want to analyze your project with your own views, you can define your own views and tables in project and make them available for all your projects.

▶ Is there a process when updating your project that you can automate? You can start your own macros to facilitate this process.

Earned Value Management (EVM)

➤ Setting Up

▶ Are you going to use default EVM fields? If not, have you defined customized fields you want to use for EVM?

▶ Are you going to use EVM default views and reports? If not, have you defined customized views and reports for EVM?

▶ Have you defined a default task Earned Value method (% Complete or Physical % Complete?)

▶ Have you defined the different options that affect EVM calculations?

▶ Have you defined quality thresholds for EVM variances and indices?

➤ Planning

▶ Have you defined your WBS and Control Accounts?

▶ Have you defined an earned value measurement technique for each task?

▶ Have you defined your dynamic schedule?

▶ Have you assigned resources (with rates) and/or fixed costs to all tasks?

▶ Have you established your time phased budget?

▶ Have you set your performance measurement baseline?

➤ Executing, Monitoring and Controlling (for each report period)

▶ Have you set the status date?

▶ Have you recorded progress for each task according to the EV measurement technique defined in planning (update actual work, rates, costs, etc.)?

▶ Have you updated remaining work, duration, rates, costs, etc. for each task?

▶ Have you performed EVM data analysis?

▶ Have you calculated or defined forecasts?

▶ Have you proposed corrective actions as needed for the remaining work?

▶ Have you delivered reports?

▶ Have you maintained the integrity of the baseline?

Evaluating the Project

➤ Project Evaluation
▶ Was the schedule clear to all stakeholders?
▶ How can you make it clearer in future projects?
▶ Was the WBS complete and easy to understand?
▶ Did the WBS function as a tool for delegation?
▶ Were the deliverables in the WBS clearly formulated or did some deliverables cause confusion?
▶ How can you improve the WBS for similar projects in the future?
▶ Were the estimates optimistic or pessimistic?
▶ What factors caused the estimates to be optimistic or pessimistic?
▶ How can you better forecast these factors in future projects?

➤ Baseline
▶ Did you capture an initial baseline?
▶ Did you update the baseline after approved changes?
▶ Did you compare baselines against your current schedule?
▶ Were you able to do forecasting on your project after you baselined?

➤ Compare two versions of a schedule
Did you compare different versions of the project?

➤ Capturing Lessons Learned
▶ Did you capture lessons learned and share them with stakeholders?
▶ Did you create project templates for future use based on lessons learned?
▶ How can you improve for the next project?

Checklist for Troubleshooting Dates in Project 2010 Schedules

Use this checklist of questions if you're having trouble figuring out why a task is scheduled on particular dates. The questions are ranked in terms of precedence: the higher on the list, the stronger the effect on the task dates. Start at the top of the list and continue down until you find the item that explains the task's date.

1. First, press $\boxed{\text{F9}}$ to force a recalculation. Even if you have automatic recalculation on, you may occasionally have to do this to refresh a calculation. Check to see if this solved the problem.

2. Does the task have an actual start date?
Does one of its predecessors or successors have an actual start date?
Insert the column **Actual Start** to check this.

3. Is there a hard constraint on the task or on its predecessors or successors?
Insert the column **Constraint Type** to check.

4. Is there a task calendar on the task or on its predecessors or successors?

Insert the column **Task calendar**. To see the task calendar's non-working days, on the **Project** tab, on **Properties** group, click **Change working time**, then on the **Change Working Time** dialog box, select the task calendar from the list at the top under **For Calendar:**.

5. Is there a leveling delay on the task (or on its predecessors)?
   Insert the column **Leveling Delay**. If the task is delayed for the purpose of leveling the workload of resources, there will be an entry in this field.

6. What predecessors does the task have?
   Insert the field **Predecessors**. Is there a lag on the dependency?
   If there is more than one predecessor, typically only one of them drives the start date of the task in question.

7. For Fixed Work/Fixed Units tasks: Are there vacation days set on the calendar of the resource who works on the task or on its predecessors or successors?

8. Are there splits in the task bars?
   Fixed Duration tasks can have weird splits in their task bars if one of the resources is not available when the task is scheduled. Fixed Duration task bars can also have leading dots before the task bar or trailing dots following the task bar that are leftover task bar splits. You can often get rid of these dots by changing the task type to Fixed Units or Fixed Work.

9. Task-specific constraint tendencies (ASAP or ALAP):
   If you have an ALAP task constraint in an ASAP schedule, it tends to move dependent ASAP tasks out to later dates.

10. Default constraint tendencies (ASAP or ALAP):
    You can check the default constraint in **Project** tab, on **Properties** group, click **Project Information**. If you **Schedule from Project Start Date**, the default is **ASAP**; if you **Schedule From Project Finish Date**, the default is **ALAP**. Under **ASAP** scheduling, tasks will tend to stay close to the project start date, unless one of the previous factors overrides this. Under **ALAP** scheduling, tasks will tend to stay close to the project finish date.

In Closing

If you have any further questions, don't hesitate to contact us.

We invite you to take on the challenge of becoming certified in Microsoft Project 2010. You can take advantage of IIL's Project 2010 Belt curriculum (White Belt, Orange Belt 2010, Blue Belt 2010, and Black Belt 2010) to do this through self-study, live virtual training or through traditional classes, public or onsite. Please visit our Web site, www.iil.com, to read up on our entire certification curriculum. We hope to personally welcome you into one of these courses.

And remember that the files below are available for download at www.jrosspub.com. Click the link *WAV Download Resource Center* to enter the download site.

➤ The solution files for the case study exercises included in Appendix 1
➤ Filters to check the quality of your own schedules
➤ The RCP macro for identifying the resource-critical path

We thank you for the time you spent reading this book; we hope you found it worthwhile.

14

Appendix 1: Case Studies

This appendix provides structured practice using Project 2010 to help you solidify what you've learned throughout this book. We've organized the material by chapter and recommend that you do each set of exercises immediately after reading the related chapter.

You'll find the following types of practice:

➤ **Hands-on exercise project: The Relocation Project**
Test yourself by creating a schedule with Project 2010 in the Relocation Project exercises. You'll be the project manager responsible for an office move of about 100 co-workers to a new location that you have yet to find.

The solutions to the Relocation Project exercises are available for download at www.jrosspub.com. Click the link *WAV Download Resource Center* to enter the download site.

➤ **Troubleshooting**
These exercises will help you understand some of the pitfalls people commonly encounter using Project 2010. All of the exercises are based on situations we've encountered over many years of reviewing and certifying Project schedules. The typical troubleshooting situation is one in which the schedule stubbornly refuses to do what the creator expects. The exercises can help you prepare for providing technical support to other Project 2010 users.

➤ **Case studies**
The case studies are provided to give you additional practice in the subject matter of Dynamic Scheduling. The files have been updated to reflect current dates and the new features of Project 2010.[1]

Enjoy!

---

1   The names in the case studies are fictitious. Any resemblance to names of existing people or organizations is purely coincidental.

Chapter 2: Getting Started with Project 2010

Chapter Objectives

Objective:

Prepare the project file to facilitate the beginning of a project plan

Project 2010 Objectives:

1. Create a new Project 2010 file
2. Set the Project Properties
3. Set the File Options
4. Set the Project Calendar
5. Set the Leveling Resources Settings

Exercise Deliverables:

Project 2010 file finished to continue with the next chapter exercise

Case Study Information:

Relocation Project — Scope Statement

You are put in charge of relocating your office. You have to find a new location and organize the move. The following is the scope statement for the project, signed by your CEO.

Scope Statement for the Relocation Project of DEVOM, Inc.

Project accounting code: MOVE001

The Business Need

DEVOM, Inc. is growing and needs larger facilities to accommodate the expanding workforce.

The Project Objectives

➤ To be moved and operational in the new location by November 1, 2012
➤ To stay within the available budget of $150,000
➤ To have an 80% satisfaction rate from the personnel for the new work environment

The Project Deliverables and Requirements

➤ A project plan (including WBS, Network Diagram, Gantt Chart, budget, resource list and assignments)
➤ A new rented or leased location that has a maximum capacity of 150 work spaces and should:
  ▸ Be accessible to disabled people
  ▸ Have parking facilities for at least 150 cars
  ▸ Have modern work cubicles and an open workspace
➤ Contracts with the landlord, the general contractor and the moving company
➤ The physical move of people and equipment

The Project Constraints

➤ The work on the project is to start no earlier than August 1, 2012

➤ The personnel have to be asked for input as to the location and facilities needed

➤ The disruption to the normal operations of DEVOM, Inc. should be minimized and may not exceed a loss of 200 person days caused by the project

➤ Clients will have to be able to contact DEVOM, Inc at any time by phone, fax and e-mail

➤ The purchase of new materials and equipment shall be budgeted and approved separately

➤ The new location will be within the boundaries of the city and its suburbs

➤ The need for expansion is so urgent that the project has priority over normal operations

➤ Any changes to the project objectives will require the approval of the CEO

The Project Assumptions

➤ The market will continue to grow at the same rate

➤ The current furniture can be reused

➤ The current workstations can be reused

➤ The current LAN and servers will be replaced

Date: ... ...

Your signature:..

Project Manager, Relocation Project   CEO, DEVOM, Inc.

Relocation Project — Create a new Project 2010 file and set the project properties

You decide to make a project plan and to put the schedule in Project 2010, so fill in the date and sign the scope statement above, to take charge of this project.

1. Create a new Project 2010 file.

2. Set the start date for the project to August 1, 2012.

   On the **File** tab, in the **Backstage** View, click on **Info**.

   Under **Project Information**, place the mouse over the **Start Date**, click ▼ and set the **Start Date**.

3. Click on **Project Information** `Project Information ▾`, **Advanced Properties,** and on the **Summary** tab enter the title of the project: Relocation *DEVOM, Inc.*

4. You are the responsible project manager; enter your own name under **Manager**.

5. Enter *DEVOM, Inc.* under **Company**.

6. Formulate one sentence that captures the essence of the relocation project and enter it in the field **Comments**.

7. Click [OK], to close the dialog.

8. Save the file as *Relocation.mpp*.

Relocation Project — Set the File Options

Continue to work in the file *Relocation.mpp* and enter only the following. On the **File** tab, in the **Backstage View**, on ⊟ Options :

Project Options	Set to
General	Date Format: Wed Jan 28 '09 User name: \<your name\>
Schedule	*Hours per day: 8*
	Hours per week: 40
	Days per month: 20
	☑ Show scheduling messages
	Show assignment units as a: *Decimal^2*
	New tasks created: *Manually Scheduled*
	Duration is entered in: *Days*
	Work is entered in: *Hours*
	Default task type: *Fixed Duration*
	☐ New tasks are effort driven
	☑ Tasks will always honor their constraint dates
	Calculate project after each edit: ◉ On
Advanced	☑ Automatically add new resources and tasks

Click [OK], to close the dialog.

Relocation Project — Set the Project Calendar

Continue to work with your file *Relocation.mpp* and enter the following:

1. On the **Project** tab, **Properties** group, click on **Change Working Time** 📅. Check that the working hours on the **Standard (Project Calendar)** are:
8:00AM to *12:00AM* and
1:00PM to *5:00PM*

If not, follow the instructions in chapter 2, **Setting The Project Calendar** section.

---

2   In this project we will use individual and group resources and will therefore use decimals rather than percentages.

2. Enter the following national holidays for the months September, October and November in the **Standard (Project Calendar)**. Since this project takes place in the US, enter the following national holidays of the United States:

   ▶ *Labor Day, September 3rd 2012*
   ▶ *Columbus Day, October 8th 2012*
   ▶ *Veterans Day, November 12th 2012*

Relocation Project – Leveling Resources Settings

1. Continue to work with your file *Relocation.mpp* and ensure that on the **Resource** tab, on **Level** group, on the Leveling Options, the calculation mode is set to **manual**.

Now that you've finished with the deliverables, you can compare your file with the solution file *03 Entering Tasks.mpp* available for download at www.jrosspub.com. Click the link *WAV Download Resource Center* to enter the download site.

Troubleshooting

Open the file *02 Wrong Hours per Day.mpp* available for download at www.jrosspub.com. Click the link *WAV Download Resource Center* to enter the download site.

Correct the Hours per day, setting the file to 8 hours per day without affecting the durations. On the **File** tab, in **Backstage** view, click on **Options**, and on the **Schedule tab** change the hours per day.

Chapter 3: Entering Tasks

Chapter Objectives

Objective:

Capture the work breakdown structure (WBS) with the help of the software to the level of detail tasks, which are the basis for the next planning processes.

Project 2010 Objectives:

1. Enter the WBS
2. Indent Tasks
3. Set the Task Mode

Exercise Deliverables:

Project WBS in Project 2010

Exercise and Case Study Information:

Relocation Project — Entering the WBS

Continue to work with your file *Relocation.mpp* or open the file *03 Entering Tasks. mpp* available for download at www.jrosspub.com. Click the link *WAV Download Resource Center* to enter the download site.

1. On the **File** tab, in the **Backstage View**, on ⊞ **Options**, click on **Schedule**. Check the following:
   ▸ The **Default task type** is set to **Fixed Duration**.
   ▸ The option ☐ **New tasks are effort-driven** is cleared.

2. On the **Gantt Chart** view, on the **Format** tab, in the **Show/Hide** group, verify that the option ☑ **Project Summary Task** is checked.

3. Enter the WBS for the Relocation Project into Project 2010 as shown in the next table.[3]

4. Indent the detail tasks under their summary tasks. The summary tasks are the tasks in capital letters.

ID	Task Name	ID	Task Name
1.	REQUIREMENTS	20.	*Install electric wiring*
2.	*Research staff requirements*	21.	*Paint*
3.	*Summarize requirements*	22.	*Drying of paint[4]*
4.	*Requirement document completed*	23.	*Install cabinetry*
5.	*LOCATION*	24.	*Install LAN*
6.	*Select the realtor*	25.	*Lay carpet*

---

3   Capital letters are used here to indicate which tasks will eventually become summary tasks. Project 2010 displays the summary tasks in bold type to make them stand out by default. This will happen when you indent tasks.

4   You might wonder if drying of paint should be entered as a task, because it happens by itself. We use it here only to illustrate the use of an elapsed duration. Alternatively, you could enter it as lag on the dependency between paint and its successor.

ID	Task Name	ID	Task Name
7.	*Visit the sites*	26.	*Facility remodeled*
8.	Evaluate the sites	27.	*MOVE*
9.	Meet to select the location	28	*Select mover*
10.	*Legal review*	29.	*Pack*
11.	*Location selected*	30.	*Move*
12.	*REMODELING CONTRACT*	31.	*Unpack*
13.	*Select the contractor*	32.	*New location opened*
14.	*Meet to discuss contract*	33.	*POST MOVE REVIEW*
15.	*Revise the schedule*	34.	*Inspect building and identify open issues*
16.	*Negotiate the contract*	35.	*Interview employees and identify open issues*
17.	*Contractor contracted*	36.	*Negotiate completion of open issues*
18.	*REMODELED LOCATION*	37.	*Complete contractor payments*
19.	*Relocate walls*	38.	*Complete lessons learned*

Relocation Project — Indent the tasks

1. Select all the detail tasks from the list above (tasks not in uppercase letters). Keep the selection and on the **Task** tab, **Schedule** group, click on ⇨. Now the detail tasks are indented and the summary tasks are displayed in **bold type** to make them stand out.

Relocation Project – Set Task Mode

1. Select all the indented tasks except the last 6 tasks that include the POST MOVE REVIEW summary task. Keep the selection and on the **Task** tab, **Tasks** group, click on **Auto Schedule**.

Save your Relocation.mpp file for future exercises.

Compare your file with the solution file *04 Entering Estimates.mpp* available for download at www.jrosspub.com. Click the link *WAV Download Resource Center* to enter the download site.

Case Study: "My First Time …"

Norm was feeling proud but tense as he drove home from work: he'd just received his first assignment as a project manager. Norm felt the assignment was recognition of his outstanding technical expertise, and he was eager to get to work.

In the evening, Norm started to break down the work. This project was different from other projects he'd worked on, and though he had some idea about what deliverables and activities would be needed, he was worried about whether he'd be able to identify all of them. He decided that as a leader, he wanted to stay ahead of his team and create a WBS so his team would be impressed. That night he worked very hard and lost some sleep over his WBS. The next day, he introduced it to the team with, "Here is what we are going to do..." His team was quick to point out that he'd forgotten to incorporate the logistics, documentation and training components in his WBS.

Questions:

1. What do you think about Norm's decision to create a WBS by himself?

2. What led him to do it by himself?

3. Would you have done it by yourself if you were in his shoes? Why or why not?

Troubleshooting

Open the file *03 My Outline.mpp* available for download at www.jrosspub.com. Click the link *WAV Download Resource Center* to enter the download site.

Explain why the outline does not function as an outline with summary tasks that can be collapsed and expanded.

Chapter 4: Entering Estimates

Chapter
Objectives

Objective:

Assign the duration estimates and/or work estimates for each task within the WBS.

Project 2010 Objectives:

1. Enter Work Estimates.
2. Enter Duration Estimates.
3. Set Task Type.
4. Set Effort Driven.

Exercise Deliverables:

Project Tasks with Work and Duration estimates in Project 2010

Relocation Project
— Entering
Estimates and
Task attributes

Continue to work with your file *Relocation.mpp* or open the file *04 Entering Estimates.mpp* available for download at www.jrosspub.com. Click the link *WAV Download Resource Center* to enter the download site.

1. Insert the fields **Type**, **Effort Driven**, **Duration** and **Work** in the Gantt table in the order they appear in the column headings of the next table.

2. On the **File** tab, in the **Backstage** view, on **Options**, click on **Schedule** and verify that the time unit for **Work is entered in** is set to Hours.

3. Enter the data from the table below into the Relocation project file. The tasks with a zero duration will become milestones. Where no data is provided you don't enter anything; Project 2010 will fill in the default duration of *1 day*? and the default work of *0 hrs*. Leave these as they are; you cannot blank them out.

ID	Task Name	Type	Effort Driven	Duration	Work
1.	**REQUIREMENTS**	**Fixed Duration**[5]	**No**		
2.	*Research staff requirements*	*Fixed Work*	*Yes*		*16h*
3.	*Summarize requirements*	*Fixed Work*	*Yes*		*16h*
4.	Requirement document completed	Fixed Duration	No	0	
5.	**LOCATION**	**Fixed Duration**	**No**		
6.	*Select the realtor*	*Fixed Duration*	*No*	*4 d*	
7.	*Visit the sites*	*Fixed Duration*	*No*	*1 d*	

5   Notice that you cannot change the **Type** of a summary task; it is set by Project 2010 to **Fixed Duration**. No **Durations** or **Work** numbers are provided for summary tasks because these are calculated by Project 2010 when the summary tasks are in Auto Schedule mode. In Manually Schedule mode you can change the summary task duration to create estimates.

ID	Task Name	Type	Effort Driven	Duration	Work
8.	*Evaluate the sites*	*Fixed Duration*	*No*	*1 d*	
9.	*Meet to select the location*	*Fixed Duration*	*No*	*1 d*	
10.	*Legal review*	*Fixed Duration*	*No*	*0.5 d*	
11.	*Location selected*	*Fixed Duration*	*No*	*0 d*	
12.	**REMODELING CONTRACT**	**Fixed Duration**	**No**		
13.	*Select the contractor*	*Fixed Duration*	*No*	*2 d*	
14.	*Meet to discuss contract*	*Fixed Duration*	*No*	*1 d*	
15.	*Revise the schedule*	*Fixed Duration*	*No*	*1 d*	
16.	*Negotiate the contract*	*Fixed Duration*	*No*	*1 d*	
17.	*Contractor contracted*	*Fixed Duration*	*No*	*0 d*	
18.	**REMODELED LOCATION**	**Fixed Duration**	**No**		
19.	*Relocate walls*	*Fixed Work*	*Yes*		*800h*
20.	*Install electric wiring*	*Fixed Work*	*Yes*		*200h*
21.	*Paint*	*Fixed Work*	*Yes*		*64h*
22.	*Drying of paint*	*Fixed Duration*	*No*	*4ed*[6]	
23.	*Install cabinetry*	*Fixed Work*	*Yes*		*320h*
24.	*Install LAN*	*Fixed Work*	*Yes*		*480h*
25.	*Lay carpet*	*Fixed Work*	*Yes*		*480h*
26.	*Facility remodeled*	*Fixed Duration*	*No*	*0 d*	
27.	**MOVE**	**Fixed Duration**	**No**		
28.	*Select mover*	*Fixed Duration*	*No*	*2 d*	
29.	*Pack*	*Fixed Duration*	*No*	*2 d*	
30.	*Move*	*Fixed Work*	*Yes*		*160h*
31.	*Unpack*	*Fixed Duration*	*No*	*2 d*	
32.	*New location opened*	*Fixed Duration*	*No*	*0 d*	
33.	**POST MOVE REVIEW**	***Fixed Duration***		*3 months approx.*	
34.	*Inspect building and identify open issues*	*Fixed Duration*		*tbd*	

---

6   Notice the "*e*" in "*4ed*"; this is an elapsed duration that continues through the night and weekend.

ID	Task Name	Type	Effort Driven	Duration	Work
35.	*Interview employees and identify open issues*	*Fixed Duration*		*tbd*	
36.	*Negotiate completion of open issues*	*Fixed Duration*		*tbd*	
37.	*Complete contractor payments*	*Fixed Duration*		*open issues*	
38.	*Complete lessons learned*	*Fixed Duration*		*tbd*	

Save your Relocation.mpp file for future exercises.

Compare your file with the solution file *05 Entering Dependencies.mpp* available for download at www.jrosspub.com. Click the link *WAV Download Resource Center* to enter the download site.

Case Study — Escalated Estimates

Mildevices, Inc. is a manufacturer of military products. The company makes navigation and intelligence products. LCD screens and consoles are some of its major products. Mildevices has engineering and manufacturing staff. There is a project control office with 25 project management staff members, and this office reports directly to the Vice President of Operations. The project control staff supports the engineers in delivering the projects.

Upper management typically initiates a new project. One executive becomes the project sponsor and finds an engineer that she will appoint as the project manager. The project manager puts the budget together with his team, and the budget is submitted for approval by the executives.

Executives typically cut the budget proposed by the engineers, because they are concerned with the bottom line of the company. The engineers find that the cuts are applied arbitrarily and often feel they end up with impossibly tight budgets. As a consequence, they start to increase their estimates in order to end up with reasonable budgets. In subsequent projects, the executives react to this in turn by cutting the proposed budgets even more. The new cuts are done in a way that makes even less sense to the engineers. As a result, the project managers now jack up their estimates even further and hide their padding in the estimates wherever they can. At this stage, the openness and the mutual trust are gone between the executives and project managers.

One of the schedulers in the project office, Debbie, says this about these developments: "The numbers the engineers receive back from senior management are so ridiculously low that they just laugh at them." Inevitably, she says, budget overruns take place.

Questions:

1. In your opinion, is the estimating done in a professional manner at Mildevices?

2. What type of problem is this? Is it predominantly an organizational problem, a cultural problem or a financial problem?

3. If a project manager asked you for advice, what would you recommend to break this escalating spiral?

4. If an executive asked you for advice, what would you recommend to break this escalating spiral?

Chapter 5: Entering Dependencies

Chapter Objectives

Objective:

Develop a network that represents a dynamic model of the project.

Microsoft Project 2010 Objectives:

1. Enter dependencies in a variety of ways to link tasks.

Exercise Deliverables:

Project network diagram in Project 2010.

Relocation Project — Entering Dependencies

Continue to work with your file *Relocation.mpp* or open the file *05 Entering Dependencies.mpp* available for download at www.jrosspub.com. Click the link *WAV Download Resource Center* to enter the download site.

Enter the following dependencies using the 🔗 **Link button**, on the **Task** tab, on **Schedule** group:

1. The tasks *research staff requirements, summarize requirements* and *requirements document completed* are sequentially dependent upon each other.

2. The tasks of the deliverable *LOCATION* are all sequentially dependent upon each other.

3. The tasks of the deliverable *REMODELING CONTRACT* are all sequentially dependent upon each other. The dependency between *select contractor* and *meet to discuss contract* has a lag of 5 days; it allows 5 days to get the participants together to meet.

4. The tasks *relocate walls* through *install cabinetry* of the deliverable *REMODELED LOCATION* are sequentially dependent upon each other.

5. The tasks of the deliverable *MOVE* are all sequentially dependent upon each other.

Enter the following dependencies by holding down [Control] and clicking to select the tasks, and then using the 🔗 **Link** tool:

6. In the deliverable *REMODELED LOCATION* the tasks *install cabinetry* and *install LAN* can take place concurrently after the paint dries. Drying of paint is the predecessor for both tasks.

7. After the tasks install cabinetry and *install LAN* are finished, the carpet can be put in place. *Lay carpet* is the successor for both tasks.

8. After the carpet is laid (*lay carpet*), the milestone *facility remodeled* is accomplished.

You forgot to set the dependencies between the deliverables (phases). Stay in the **Gantt Chart** or switch to the **Network Diagram** to enter these dependencies:

9. The task *evaluate the sites* can start after *summarize requirements* is finished.

10. The task *select the contractor* can start after the milestone *location selected* is accomplished.

11. The task *select mover* can start after *location selected*.

12. The task *relocate walls* can start after the milestone *contractor contracted*.

13. The task *pack* can start after the milestone *facility remodeled*.

Answer the following questions about the dependencies in the Relocation Project:

1. Using the Task Details ⊞ Details, what drives the task *Relocate Walls*?

2. How long is this project initially estimated to run?

3. Looking at the Network Diagram, is there a distinctive critical path (the red boxes)?

4. Are there any dependencies on summary tasks?

5. Although all of the summary tasks show row totals, the totals are calculated differently depending on the nature of the fields. How are the totals from the detail tasks reflected in the summary tasks for the fields Durations, Work and Cost?

6. If you are not managing resources with Project 2010, at this point do you have a valid schedule?

Save your *Relocation.mpp* file for future exercises.

Compare your file with the solution file *06 Entering Constraints and Deadlines. mpp* available for download at www.jrosspub.com. Click the link *WAV Download Resource Center* to enter the download site.

Case Study: CoalPower

CoalPower power station has approached you to do a 3-day introductory workshop on Project 2010. CoalPower is a first-time client and it seems this 3-day contract will be its only need for training and consulting for a while, even though the organization is large and has multiple plants. The key players at CoalPower are:

➤ Andy is the plant manager. You find out that you and he share a similar cultural heritage, and that this provides an easy basis for conversation with him. Andy sits in on the first part of the on-site workshop you're conducting. He is only interested in the big picture: what can Project 2010 do for the organization. Andy is concerned about the frequent delays in the engineering projects, as you found out when you talked one-on-one during a lunch break.

➤ <u>Norm</u> manages the engineers who manage repair, maintenance and construction projects in the power station. They also design the modifications that are needed. You have had difficulties negotiating with Norm. He told you, only after you had closed your consulting contract, that you would have to travel an extra 250 miles to get to the project site.

➤ <u>Dave and Harry</u> manage major maintenance projects like the replacement of the $2M turbine condensers. Replacing these condensers will stop operations in the entire plant. They have been planning their projects mostly off the tops of their heads. Norm is getting increasingly anxious about this and has told them, "If you get sick, nobody knows what to do or how to do it. I need to see a detailed plan of your projects!"

➤ <u>Art</u> is the technical drawing expert. He designs most of the small modifications and creates the technical drawings. Art is overworked and has, at any given time, 50 projects on his plate. Norm often criticizes Art for not delivering drawings when Norm wants them.

Questions

Dave and Harry are struggling with the whole concept of scheduling and what benefits it will provide to them:

1. Do you expect them to be motivated to use the tool? Why?

2. How will they benefit from scheduling their projects with Project 2010?

3. What do you think of Norm's approach of forcing them to schedule their projects?

4. How important are dependencies in their schedule?

Art approaches you during one of the breaks to talk one-on-one:

5. What is his main concern in scheduling his projects?

6. How should he model his many projects in Project 2010? Address in particular whether he should use dependencies in his schedule:
   a. Between the tasks within one project
   b. Between his projects

7. How will Art benefit from modeling his projects in Project 2010?

Chapter 6: Entering Deadlines, Constraints and Task Calendars

Chapter Objectives

Objective:
Include the constraints and deadlines of the dynamic model that represents the project.

Project 2010 Objectives:
1. Enter Constraints.
2. Enter Deadlines.
3. Enter Task Calendars.

Exercise Deliverables:
Project network diagram with deadlines and constraints in Project 2010.

Relocation Project — Entering Constraints and Deadlines

Continue to work with your file *Relocation.mpp* or open the file *06 Entering Constraints and Deadlines.mpp* available for download at www.jrosspub.com. Click the link *WAV Download Resource Center* to enter the download site.

1. Set deadlines on the following milestones:

ID	Milestone	Deadline Date
11	Location selected	August 20, 2012
17	Contractor contracted	August 29, 2012
26	Facility remodeled	October 24, 2012
32	New location opened	October 31, 2012

2. Enter the following constraints:

ID	Task	Constraint
9	Meet to select the location	Start No Earlier Than August 27, 2012
29	Pack	As Late As Possible

3. The CEO, *Mr. Salin*, is out of the country until *August 27, 2012*.
   Schedule the task *pack* As Late As Possible, otherwise the equipment may be packed days before the actual move takes place over the weekend. You want the employees to be packed as late as possible on the Friday before the weekend.

Relocation Project — Task Calendars

1. You realize that due to the project requirement that disruption to normal company operations be minimal, the move will have to take place over the weekend. For the task *Move*, set all the weekdays to nonworking days and the weekend days to working days, so the move will take place on a weekend.

2. Use the Change Working Time 🗓 to create a new calendar called *Weekends*. Establish a working time of 8 hours per day for Saturday and Sunday.

3. Assign this new calendar to the task *Move*.

Save your *Relocation.mpp* file for future exercises.

Compare your file with the solution file *07 Entering Resources.mpp* available for download at www.jrosspub.com. Click the link *WAV Download Resource Center* to enter the download site.

Chapter 7: Entering Resources

Chapter Objectives

Objective:

List all resources that will be involved in the execution of the project tasks.

Project 2010 Objectives:

1. Enter Resources and their details.
2. Enter Budget Resources.

Exercise Deliverables:

Resource sheet with all resources and their details in Project 2010.

Relocation Project — Entering Resources

Continue to work with your file *Relocation.mpp* or open the file *07 Entering Resources.mpp* available for download at www.jrosspub.com. Click the link *WAV Download Resource Center* to enter the download site.

This table shows the resources needed for the relocation project. Notice that there are generic resources in the list, like *movers*. You found their rates by telephoning around. There is no **Cost/Use** for these resources.

Resource Name	Type	Material Label	Position	Function	Max. Units	Std. Rate	Accrue at
you[7]	*Work*		*project manager*	*manager*	*1*	*$75/h*	*Pro-rated*
Nelson Salin	*Work*		*CEO*	*manager*	*1*	*$150/h*	*Pro-rated*
John Falgon	*Work*		*employee representative*	*employee*	*1*	*$30/h*	*Pro-rated*
Nancy Hilcrest	*Work*		*planner*	*employee*	*1*	*$35/h*	*Pro-rated*
Pierre Roach	*Work*		*lawyer*	*external*	*1*	*$75/h*	*Pro-rated*
the employees	*Work*		*employees*	*employee*	*75*	*$25/h*	*Pro rated*
the contractor	*Work*		*contractor*	*external*	*50*	*$30/h*	*End*
the realtor	*Work*		*realtor*	*external*	*1*	*$35/h*	*End*
the movers	*Work*		*movers*	*external*	*40*	*$25/h*	*End*
the LAN consultants	*Work*		*LAN consultants*	*external*	*20*	*$75/h*	*End*
Moving Van	*Cost*						*End*

---

7 Fill in your own name instead of *"you"*.

Resource Name	Type	Material Label	Position	Function	Max. Units	Std. Rate	Accrue at
Lunch for Team during Move	*Cost*						*Start*
boxes	*Material*	*Boxes*		*material*		*$2*	*Start*

1. Customize the table for the Resource Sheet view as shown in the table above. The fields Position and Function are not standard fields in Project 2010. You can use the fields **Text1** and **Text2** and permanently rename them Position and Function respectively using the **Field Settings** feature, on the **Column Settings** drop down list.

2. Enter the resources. Use the Fill Down feature for the columns *Function* and *Accrue* at.

3. Sort the list of resources with resource **Name** as the first sorting key. Select the option to permanently renumber the resources.

4. You've resisted pressure to work longer hours, and with the rest of the team will keep regular working hours.

5. *Nancy Hilcrest* will go on a 1-week holiday in the third full week of August 2012.

6. You realize that the task *Move* needs to be executed during the weekend (you have already created a specific calendar and assigned it to the task in chapter 6). But the resources *Movers* use the standard calendar, so they won't be able to work on weekends and you are creating a conflict. To solve this, just assign the right calendar to the *Movers*. Compare your file with the solution file *08 Entering Assignments.mpp* available for download at www.jrosspub.com. Click the link *WAV Download Resource Center* to enter the download site. Make sure you select to compare the resource information as well by selecting the **Resource Table** named **Entry**.

7. Save your Relocation.mpp file for future exercises.

Relocation Project — Budget Resources

1. Open the file *07 Budget Resources 1.mpp* available for download at www.jrosspub.com.

2. In the Resource Sheet view add the resource *Labor* and make it a cost type resource.

3. Double-click on the *Labor* resource and on the **General** tab of the **Resource Information** dialog box, select the **Budget box** and click on OK.

4. On the **Gantt Chart** view and using the **Assign Resources** Dialog box, assign the *Labor* resource to the **Project Summary Task**. Note that if you try to assign the *Labor* resource to any other summary or detail task you will not be able to.

5. Go to the **Resource Usage** view and insert the column **Budget Cost**.

6. Right-click on the right side of the screen and select **Detail Styles**. From the available fields show the **Budget Cost** field and click OK.

7. Using the Zoom icons in the toolbar, zoom in or out until the timescale is showing months on the middlescale. You can then enter the monthly budget into the proper months.

8. Enter a *Labor* budget of $30,000 for August, September, October, and November of 2012. You should be able to see the total budget of $120,000 in the **Budget Cost** column (field).

9. If you don't allocate cost to your resources you can set this up so that your *Labor* resource is a work type resource. How would you associate your labor resources to the *Labor* budget? Think about using a custom resource field for this purpose. For example in the Resource Sheet view you might choose to make the custom field *Text3* a field that contains Budget Type. For all the work resources and the Labor Budget resources you would select *Labor* as the Budget Type. In the Resource Usage or Task Usage View you could group by Budget Type. This would yield a comparison of budget costs on Labor to actual costs on Labor.

   Compare your file with the solution file *07 Budget Resources 2.mpp* available for download at www.jrosspub.com. Click the link *WAV Download Resource Center* to enter the download site.

Troubleshooting   Open the file *Last Name First Name.mpp* available for download at www.jrosspub.com. Click the link *WAV Download Resource Center* to enter the download site.

1. Enter your first name in the resource sheet, and then enter your last name. Questions:
   ▸ Why does the first name show up in two fields?
   ▸ Why does the second entry override the first one?

2. Create a new project file and try entering the resource *Smith, Harry*. Why does Project 2010 not allow you to do that?

Chapter 8: Entering Assignments

*Chapter
Objectives*

Objective:

Assign resources to project tasks.

Project 2010 Objectives:

1. Assign Resources.
2. Change Assignments.

Exercise Deliverables:

Resource-loaded project schedule in Project 2010.

*Relocation Project
— Entering
Assignments*

Continue to work with your file *Relocation.mpp* or open the file *08 Entering Assignments.mpp* available for download at www.jrosspub.com. Click the link *WAV Download Resource Center* to enter the download site.

> Enter the assignments as shown in the next table. First, add the fields **Type**, **Effort Driven**, **Duration** and **Work** to the **Gantt Chart** view in such a way that the view matches the *Task Fields* column headings in the next table. Note that you cannot add the *Assignment Fields* shown in the table; you have to enter the assignment information in the **Assign Resources** dialog or in the **Task Form**.

> Remember that Project 2010 uses the formula *Duration * Units = Work* and will calculate for each detail task the third value that is not provided in the next table.

> Think about the easiest way to enter each assignment; decide whether you should use the **Assign Resources** dialog or the **Task Form**. The **Task Form** is best when you want to assign multiple resources with specific numbers for units and/or work.

> Only the **Fixed Work** tasks are **Effort Driven**.

TASK FIELDS – Gantt Chart View					ASSIGNMENT FIELDS – Assign Resources Dialog Box	
Task Name	**Type**	**Effort Driven**	**Dur.**	**Work**	**Resource Names**	**Units**
REQUIRE-MENTS	*Fixed Duration*	*No*				
research staff requirements	*Fixed Work*	*Yes*		*16h*	*You*	*0.5*
summarize requirements	*Fixed Work*	*Yes*		*16h*	*Hilcrest*	*0.5*

TASK FIELDS – Gantt Chart View					ASSIGNMENT FIELDS – Assign Resources Dialog Box	
Task Name	Type	Effort Driven	Dur.	Work	Resource Names	Units
LOCATION	Fixed Duration	No				
select the realtor	Fixed Duration	No	4 d		You	0.5
visit the sites	Fixed Duration	No	1 d		Falgon Hilcrest the realtor You	1 1 1 1
evaluate the sites	Fixed Duration	No	1 d		Falgon Hilcrest the realtor You	1 1 0.5 1
meet to select the location	Fixed Duration	No	1 d		Falgon Hilcrest Salin you	1 1 1 1
legal review	Fixed Duration	No	0.5 d		Roach	1
REMODELING CONTRACT	Fixed Duration	No				
select the contractor	Fixed Duration	No	2 d		You	1
meet to discuss contract	Fixed Duration	No	1 d		the contractor Hilcrest You	1 1 1
revise the schedule	Fixed Duration	No	1 d		You	1
negotiate the contract	Fixed Duration	No	1 d		You	1
REMODELED LOCATION	Fixed Duration	No				
relocate walls	Fixed Work	Yes		800h	the contractor	10
install electric wiring	Fixed Work	Yes		200h	the contractor	5

					ASSIGNMENT FIELDS – Assign Resources Dialog Box	
TASK FIELDS – Gantt Chart View						
Task Name	Type	Effort Driven	Dur.	Work	Resource Names	Units
paint	Fixed Work	Yes		64h	the contractor	4
drying of paint	Fixed Duration	No	4 ed			
install cabinetry	Fixed Work	Yes		320h	the contractor	8
install LAN	Fixed Work	Yes		480h	the LAN consultants	5
lay carpet	Fixed Work	Yes		480h	the contractor	6
MOVE	Fixed Duration	No				
select mover	Fixed Duration	No	2 d		You	1
pack	Fixed Duration	No	2 d		the employees boxes, Moving Van[$320]	35 400
move	Fixed Work	Yes		160h	the movers, Lunch [$210]	10
unpack	Fixed Duration	No	2 d		the employees	35

Save your *Relocation.mpp* file for future exercises.

Compare your file with the solution file *09 Optimizing — Time 1.mpp* available for download at www.jrosspub.com. Click the link *WAV Download Resource Center* to enter the download site.

Notice that the project is missing its November 1 deadline. We will need to optimize the schedule in the next chapter.

Relocation Project — Changing Assignments

Continue to work with your file *Relocation.mpp* or open the file *09 Optimizing — Time 1.mpp* available for download at www.jrosspub.com. Click the link *WAV Download Resource Center* to enter the download site.

How should you go about making the following changes to the assignments? You may need to change the **Type** of the task first.

The task *install LAN* currently has a duration of 12 days, 5 consultants working on it and 60 days of work.

1. You would like to know how long the task *install LAN* would take if there were 10 *LAN consultants* instead of 5 while keeping the work the same. What task type do you need before you make this change?
   You should get a duration of 6 days. Keep this change.

2. You want to know how many consultants are needed if you want the task *install LAN* done in 3 days while keeping the work the same. What task type do you need before you make this change?
   You should find that 20 *LAN consultants* are needed. Keep this change.

3. You think you over-estimated the work; you will need only 30 days of work instead of 60 days of work and you want to keep the duration to 3 days. What is the number of consultants needed now? What task type do you need before you make this change?
   You should find that 10 consultants are needed. Keep this change.

4. You want to keep the number of consultants to 10, but you want to change the duration from 3 to 12 days. How much work is now on the task? What task type do you need before you make this change?
   You should end up with 120 days of work. Keep this change.

5. You want to bring the number of consultants down to 5 while keeping the 12-day duration. How much work is now on the task? What task type do you need before you make this change?

This brings us back to where we were at the start of this exercise after exploring several scenarios.

Chapter 9: Optimizing the Schedule

*Chapter
Objectives*

Objective:

Analyze the project and come up with proposals to optimize duration, costs and resources in order to fulfill the project objectives.

Project 2010 Objectives:

1. Understand the Gantt Chart.
2. Shorten the Duration.
3. Lower the Cost.
4. Solve over-allocation by assigning a task to a free resource, using Team Planner.
5. Solve over-allocation using resource leveling.

Exercise Deliverables:

Various project optimization proposals in Project 2010.

*Relocation Project
— Understanding
the Gantt Chart*

Open the file *09 Optimizing — Time 1.mpp* available for download at www.jrosspub.com. Click the link *WAV Download Resource Center* to enter the download site.

1. Display the field **Total Slack** in the spreadsheet of the **Gantt Chart**.

2. Is the total slack expressed in calendar days, business days or person days?

3. Why does the negative slack change from task 14 *meet to discuss contract* to task 15 *revise the schedule*?[8]

4. Why does the negative slack change in the middle of task 21 *paint* and task 24 *install LAN*?[9]

5. Why does the negative slack change from task 26 *facility remodeled* to task 30 *move*?[10]

6. Why does the negative slack change from task 30 *move* to task 31 *unpack*?[11]

*Relocation Project
— Shortening the
Duration*

In this exercise, you'll use the optimizing for time approach.

Open the file *09 Optimizing — Time 1.mpp* available for download at www.jrosspub.com. Click the link *WAV Download Resource Center* to enter the download site.

Currently, the forecasted finish date is November 20, but your CEO insists that the office be moved by November 14 .

---

8   Hint: Nancy is on holiday the third full week in August.
9   Hint: there is a task with an elapsed duration between them.
10   Hint: there is a deadline on task 26.
11   Hint: The movers only work on the weekend.

1. Display the critical path in your schedule. Make sure you understand all the total slack numbers on each task (described in the previous exercise, Relocation Project—Understanding the Gantt Chart).

2. The objective of this exercise is to bring down the duration (time) of the project as much as is reasonably possible. Use the methods discussed in chapter 9 to get ideas. Come up with your own ways to bring down the duration of the project as much as you can. Try them out and see how much time they save. Try to:

   ▶ Make the project end date as early as possible, or
   ▶ If you have a hard constraint on the project end milestone, make the **Total Slack** on the project end milestone *new location opened* positive and as large as possible.

3. Try your ideas out and see if they work. If you keep a change, make a note of it, in order to compare your measures against the solution.

Relocation Project — Ideas for Shortening the Duration

In this exercise you'll use the optimizing for time approach. To illustrate how a schedule can be optimized, we'll explain a complete optimization that will cut the project duration down to almost half the original duration. A similar reduction can be achieved in many projects by applying all of the techniques discussed in chapter 9.

Open the file *09 Optimizing — Time 2.mpp* available for download at www.jrosspub.com. Click the link *WAV Download Resource Center* to enter the download site.

The current duration of the project is 77 days.

When the tasks are sorted by duration, you can see that the tasks *drying of paint, install LAN, relocate walls* and *lay carpet* are some of the longest tasks. All of these tasks are critical and seem to be a good starting point for finding time in the schedule.

Enter the following changes to shorten the relocation project:

1. Create an overlap in the dependency on *relocate walls*, so that *install electric wiring* is done mostly in parallel with relocating the walls. Overlap *relocate walls* and *install electric wiring* with a Finish-to-Finish plus 1 day dependency. The electricians can start on a wall as soon as the carpenters have it up. What is the duration of the project now?

2. Cut the dependency between *lay carpet* and *install cabinetry* and cut the dependency between *lay carpet* and *install LAN*. Instead, make *lay carpet* dependent on *drying of paint*. Create new dependencies from *install cabinetry* and *install LAN* to *facility remodeled* to get rid of the loose ends

in the network. You can lay carpet in parallel with installing cabinets and installing the LAN. What is the duration of the project now?

3. Notice that the critical path is fragmented at this point. We have to make sure that we continue making changes to critical tasks only. Make the necessary changes to the schedule in such a way that you see most of the critical path in the schedule again. Change the type of dependency between *install electric wiring* and *paint* to Finish-to-Finish plus 1 day. The painters can start on a wall as soon as the electricians finish it. What is the duration of the project now?

4. Change the type of dependency between *paint* and *drying of paint* to Finish-to-Finish plus 1 day. The paint starts drying as soon as the first wall is painted. What is the duration of the project now?

5. Change the type of dependency between *facility remodeled* and *pack* to Finish-to-Finish. The packing should ideally be ready when the facility is ready. What is the duration of the project now?

6. Cut the dependency between *location selected* and *select the contractor*, and make *select the contractor* dependent on *evaluate the sites*. Create a new dependency between *location selected* and *meet to discuss contract*. You can select the contractor when you have an idea which location will be chosen. What is the duration of the project now?

7. Get rid of the Start No Earlier Than constraint on task 9 *meet to select the location* and arrange for a conference call or internet meeting with the CEO, who is abroad. What is the duration of the project now?

8. Overlap *summarize requirements* and *research staff requirements*, Finish-to-Finish plus 1 day. You can start summarizing as soon as you receive some completed questionnaires. What is the duration of the project now? Notice that the duration did not come down, because task 14 was split even further because of Nancy's holiday.

9. Get rid of the lag on the dependency between task 13 *select the contractor* and task 14 *meet to discuss contract*. Make sure that you give advance notice of 5 days to the participants you expect at the meeting, so the 5-day time frame for calling the meeting is not needed anymore. What is the duration of the project now?

10. Change the task *install LAN* into a summary task by adding the following subtasks: *install LAN cables (Auto Schedule Mode, 160h of Fixed Work, predecessor relocate walls)*, *install LAN hardware (Auto Schedule Mode, 160h of Fixed Work, predecessor install LAN cables)*, and *install LAN operating system (Auto Schedule Mode, 160h of Fixed Work, predecessor install LAN hardware, successor facility remodeled)*.

Cut the dependencies between *drying of paint* and *install LAN* and between *install LAN* and *facility remodeled*. Keep the resource units at 5 units for all subtasks; remove the *LAN consultants* from the summary task. The result is a more refined schedule. What is the duration of the project now?

11. Increase the resource units of the *contractor* for the task *lay carpet* from 6 to 12. This decreases the duration of *lay carpet* to 5 days, which is now done entirely in parallel with *install cabinetry*. What is the duration of the project now?

12. You decide to ask the *LAN consultants* to work with 8 consultants instead of 5. Change all assignments of the *LAN consultants* to 8 units on the subtasks of *install LAN*. This will reduce the duration of the subtasks to 2.5 days. What is the duration of the project now?

Please answer the following questions:

1. Check the duration of the project. We have reduced it from 77 to 39 days. This is almost **half** of the original duration and most changes are quite defensible. You have seen here an example of how you can find time in your project schedule if you create a dynamic model of your project in the first place. Could you apply similar methods to your own project schedule?

2. Were trade-offs made against the scope or quality of this project? What are they? Would you undo some proposed changes? Why?

3. If you arrived at a different final duration, find the differences between your file and the solution file *09 Optimizing — Time 3.mpp* available for download at www.jrosspub.com. Click the link *WAV Download Resource Center* to enter the download site.

Relocation Project — Lowering the Cost

In this exercise, you'll use the optimizing for time and cost approach. Open the file *09 Optimizing — Time Cost 1.mpp* available for download at www.jrosspub.com. Click the link *WAV Download Resource Center* to enter the download site.

1. The objective now is to bring down the cost of the project while maintaining or decreasing the duration. Use the methods that were discussed in chapter 9 to get ideas. Come up with your own ways to bring down the cost of the project as far as you can. Try them out and see how much money they save.

2. Log each change and the total cost of the project after each change you keep.

3. Compare your results against the ideas that we will discuss in the next exercise.

*Relocation Project
— Ideas for
Lowering the Cost*

In this exercise you'll use the optimizing for time and cost approach.

Open the file *09 Optimizing — Time Cost 2.mpp* available for download at www.jrosspub.com. Click the link *WAV Download Resource Center* to enter the download site.

You found some new resources:

Name	Type	Position	Function	Max. Units	Std. Rate	Accrue at
Carpeteers	*Work*	*Contractor*	*external*	*20*	*$140/d*	*End*
Cablers	*Work*	*Contractor*	*external*	*5*	*$40/h*	*End*
Students	*Work*	*Contractor*	*external*	*5*	*$80/d*	*End*

You find a specialized carpet company *Carpeteers* that is willing to do the job. Create this new resource. Carpeteers estimates the work will take 30 person days, and they will do it with 10 employees.

1. What is the current cost of the project?
    What is the current cost for the task *lay carpet*?
    What is the current duration of the project?

2. Reassign the task to Carpeteers.
    What is the new forecasted cost for *lay carpet*?
    How much did we save on this task?

3. What is the new total cost of the project?

4. What is the new total duration of the project? Why is it not lower?

5. What consequences does this change have for the scope and quality of the project? Why?

6. Would you keep the reassignment to *Carpeteers*?

Enter the following additional changes to lower the cost of the relocation project:

1. Delete the task *revise the schedule*; it is a nice-to-have task. Add a new dependency to keep the original logic. How much is the total cost now?

2. Delete the task *select the realtor* and hire the one you know. Is there a possible trade-off in doing this? How much is the total cost now?

3. Delete the task *select the contractor* and hire the one you know. Add a new dependency to keep the original logic. Is there a possible trade-off in doing this? How much is the total cost now?

4. Make the task *install LAN* a summary task by adding the following subtasks: *install LAN cables* (*Auto Schedule Mode, 160h of Fixed Work*, predecessor *relocate walls*), *install LAN hardware* (*Auto Schedule Mode, 160h of Fixed Work*, predecessor *install LAN cables*), and *install LAN operating system* (*Auto Schedule Mode, 160h of Fixed Work*, predecessor *install LAN hardware*, successor *lay carpet*).

   Keep the resource units at 5 units for all subtasks; remove the *LAN consultants* from the summary task. Cut the dependencies between *drying of paint* and *install LAN* as well as the dependency between *install LAN* and *Lay Carpet*. You ask the LAN consultants to use cheaper resources to do the cabling. They offer you specialized *cablers*, as shown in the table at the beginning of the question. Reassign the task *install LAN cables* to the cheaper resource *cablers*. How much is the total cost now?

5. You ask the contractor to come up with sharper estimates to save cost. He offers to provide students who can help the carpenters relocate walls. He proposes to replace half of the carpenters with *students* per the table. Are there possible trade-offs on time, scope or quality? How much is the total cost now?

6. In your search to reduce cost you decide that the 35 employees should pack all their stuff in 1 day instead of 2 days. Are there possible trade-offs on time, scope or quality? How much is the total cost now?

Please answer the following questions:

1. The cost should now be $108,610.00, down from $138,210.00. If you found a different answer, compare it with the solution file *09 Optimizing — Time Cost 3.mpp* available for download at www.jrosspub.com. Click the link *WAV Download Resource Center* to enter the download site. Make sure you insert the column Cost before comparing.

2. What is the forecasted duration for the project now?

3. Are there trade-offs in the scope or quality? What are they? Will you keep the proposed changes? Why?

Relocation Project — Solve Over-allocation by Assigning a Task to a Free Resource

In this exercise, you'll use the optimizing for time, cost and resources approach and solve over-allocation by assigning a task to a free resource. Open the file *09 Optimizing — Time Cost Resources 1.mpp* available for download at www.jrosspub.com. Click the link *WAV Download Resource Center* to enter the download site.

1. Which view do you recommend for checking the over-allocations? (You could use Resource Sheet, Resource Graph, Team Planner, and others.)

2. You find that Nancy Hilcrest and yourself are over-allocated. Try to solve the over-allocations by finding other resources who are available and can perform the work.

3. Using the **Team Planner** view, assign the tasks with over-allocation problems to other resources. You can reassign Visit the Sites task (assigned to *Nancy Hilcrest*) to *Nelson Salin*, and *Select the Contractor* task (assigned to *You*) to *Nelson Salin* also.

4. Note that previous changes do not affect the project duration, but they do affect the project cost. Because *Nelson Salin* is the CEO, his rate is higher than *Nancy Hilcrest's* and your rates. Somebody should authorize the trade-offs.

5. Compare your file with the solution file *09 Optimizing — Time Cost Resources 2.mpp* available for download at www.jrosspub.com. Click the link *WAV Download Resource Center* to enter the download site.

Relocation Project — Solve Over-allocation Using Resource Leveling

In this exercise you'll try the optimizing for time, cost and resources approach and level the workloads automatically. Open the file *09 Optimizing — Time Cost Resources 3.mpp* available for download at www.jrosspub.com. Click the link *WAV Download Resource Center* to enter the download site. What is the current duration of the project?

1. Use resource leveling to resolve all the over-allocations. Which view do you recommend for analyzing the results of workload leveling? Which field does Project 2010 change when leveling? Which tasks were delayed? By how much?

2. Has Project 2010 increased the duration and/or cost of the project? Why?

3. Are there any trade-offs in scope or quality? Would you keep the solution proposed by Project 2010? Why?

4. Compare your file with the solution file *09 Optimizing — Time Cost Resources 4.mpp* available for download at www.jrosspub.com. Click the link *WAV Download Resource Center* to enter the download site. Make sure you insert the column **Leveling Delay** before comparing.

Intranet Project — Shorten the Duration

In this exercise, you will use the optimizing for time, cost and resources approach using the resource-critical path (RCP). Open the file *09 Optimizing — Time Cost Resources 5 — Intranet Project.mpp* available for download at www.jrosspub.com. Click the link *WAV Download Resource Center* to enter the download site.[12]

1. How many resources do you need by month?

---

12 We will use a different project here, because we saw in the previous exercise that the workload leveling did not affect the project end date. In other words, the critical path was identical to the resource critical path.

2. Would you level this schedule manually? Why?

3. What is the current duration of the project?

4. Level the workloads automatically. What is the duration now?

5. Check the critical path in the schedule. Does it make sense?

6. Mark the RCP by entering **Yes** in the field **Marked** for each resource-critical task.

7. In the **Tracking Gantt** view, on the **Format** tab, **Bar Styles** group, choose **Format**, **Bar Styles** and change the settings to show a blue bar for all **Normal** tasks (critical and noncritical) and a red task bar for all **Normal**, **Marked** tasks (instead of for **Critical** tasks). You should now see red task bars for all tasks on the RCP in the schedule.

8. Compare your file against the file *09 Optimizing — Time Cost Resources 6 — Intranet Project.mpp* available for download at www.jrosspub.com. Click the link *WAV Download Resource Center* to enter the download site; the files should look the same.

9. The objective now is to bring down the duration of the project as much as possible (time), while maintaining or lowering the cost and keeping the workload reasonable (resources). Bring down the duration by shortening the RCP. Log each change and the resulting total duration of the project for each change you decide to keep. Try a few changes before you find the new RCP.

10. Compare your results against the ideas that we will discuss in the next exercise.

Intranet Project — Ideas for Shortening the Duration

In this exercise, you'll use the Optimizing for Time, Cost and Resources approach using the RCP.

Open the file *09 Optimizing — Time Cost Resources 6 — Intranet Project.mpp* available for download at www.jrosspub.com. Click the link *WAV Download Resource Center* to enter the download site.

1. What is the current duration and cost of this project schedule?
The challenge is to find methods to decrease the duration of the project that don't increase cost and don't cause new work overloads. You have to focus on the resource-critical tasks on the RCP. The following changes are examples of such measures. Enter these changes into the schedule:

2. We should be able to take the project manager off the RCP. In general, a project manager should never be on the critical path, except perhaps in very small projects where he does tasks as a resource as well. Cut the dependency between task 9 *Define specific functionality* and task 10 *Develop project plan*.

Give the task 10 *Develop project plan* a new predecessor: task 3 *Define user requirements*. Give task 9 *Define specific functionality* a new successor: task 11 *System designed*. Is task 10 still resource-critical? Are there new work overloads? Level the workloads again. Determine the new RCP. What are the duration and cost of the project now?

3. Notice that the *Roll-out manager* is working only 50% on task 50 *Communicate roll out plan to users*. Increase this to 100% while keeping the work on the task the same. Level the workloads in the schedule again. What is the duration and cost of the project now?

4. You see that the longest resource-critical tasks are tasks 36 *Develop web pages* and 37 *Develop any custom functionality*. They take 20 days in the current schedule. If you can find an extra web designer for task 37 *Develop any custom functionality*, you can schedule those two tasks in parallel. You ask the resource manager for an extra designer and you get one for that one task. Create a new resource *Web Designer 2*, with the same rate as the first designer and assign her to task 37 *Develop any custom functionality*. Set a new dependency between task 35 *Determine development tool* and 37 *Develop any custom functionality*. Are there new work overloads? Level the workloads again. Determine the new RCP. What are the duration and cost of the project now? Are tasks 36 and 37 still resource-critical?

Please answer the following questions:

1. We started with a schedule of 70 days that was not leveled. We then leveled and ended up with 114 days. We then shortened the schedule again to 90 days without increasing the cost and without (new) work overloads. Does the current RCP make sense? Why?

2. Compare your file with the solution file *09 Optimizing — Time Cost Resources 7 — Intranet Project.mpp* available for download at www.jrosspub.com. Click the link *WAV Download Resource Center* to enter the download site.

Case Study — Multinational IT

The client is the IT department of a large multinational company. Recently, the organization made the corporate decision to switch from using Project Workbench to using Project 2010 for all of its projects. The project managers still work very much as they did when they used Project Workbench; they like to enter actual hours worked and remaining hours. The organization has a separate time sheet system that reports actual hours worked by project or by category over many projects (e.g., "maintenance").

Managers in the IT department are using the Project 2010 schedules as checklists. Many of them become frustrated using the scheduling features of Project 2010 and revert to using Excel instead. When this was acknowledged, the client decided to organize basic training in Project 2010 using a local training provider. Since the training, one year ago, the situation has not improved much, and many people are still using Excel. The ones who use Project 2010 are not taking advantage of all the features of the application.

In interviews with several users you find that they experience the following problems:

➤ Double data entry of actual hours into the time sheet system and into the project scheduler.

➤ IT executives impose tight deadlines and use cost-payback arguments to successfully defend these challenging project deadlines. Your clients, the IT project managers, tell you, *"We have not been able to prove that these deadlines are not feasible."*

➤ The organization has a matrix structure; many resources are working part-time on the project and are shared across several projects. There are many over-allocations, so many in fact that the project managers were advised by Project Workbench consultants to use Auto Schedule (automatic workload leveling), after which they should try to shorten the schedule.

➤ The organization experiences ripple effects between projects; a change in one project can have impacts on other schedules.

➤ Most projects are independent and do not have cross-project dependencies.

➤ The training did not teach participants how to apply Project 2010 to their own real life projects.

There is a need for more guidance so that project managers begin using the more beneficial features of Project 2010.

Questions

1. Which feature of Project 2010 should be used to address the ripple effect across projects?

2. What optimization method do you recommend in this situation? Why?

3. Will they then be able to prove that the imposed deadlines are not feasible?

4. What would you recommend in order to:
   ▸ Get more project managers to use Project 2010?
   ▸ Get project managers to use more features of Project 2010?

Troubleshooting   1. Open the file *09 Sure Critical.mpp* available for download at www.jrosspub.com. Click the link *WAV Download Resource Center* to enter the download site.

Why are only tasks 3, 4, 5 and 6 shown as critical and not tasks 1 and 2?

2. Open the file *09 Why Overload.mpp* available for download at www.jrosspub.com. Click the link *WAV Download Resource Center* to enter the download site.

   Why is the resource *you* over-allocated in the week of September 2 to 9; this resource is only showing 1.5 days of work for the entire week?

3. Open the file *09 MSF Application Development.mpp* available for download at www.jrosspub.com. Click the link *WAV Download Resource Center* to enter the download site.

   Level the workloads completely. You may be prompted that Project 2010 cannot solve an over-allocation; choose **Skip All**. Why is the project duration now extended to the year 2049?

Chapter 10: Updating the Schedule

Chapter Objectives

Objective:

Update the project tasks and try out options for optimizing the entire project.

Project 2010 Objectives:
1. Update Tasks.
2. Optimize for Time and Cost.

Exercise Deliverables:

Project 2010 file with updated status and optimizations.

Relocation Project – Updating Tasks

Open the file *10 Updating the Schedule 1.mpp* available for download at www.jrosspub.com. Click the link *WAV Download Resource Center* to enter the download site.

1. In the **Tracking Gantt** view and **Tracking** table, hide the **Physical % Complete** field.

2. Set the baseline for the entire project.

3. Set the **Status Date** and the **Current Date** to *September 17, 2012* and create a gridline for the status date in the Gantt timescale. (Line to Change: Status Date, Type: Continuous Line, Color: Red)

4. Set the following options on the **File** tab, in the **Backstage** view, on
   📄 Options, on **Schedule**:
   ☑ **Updating Task status updates resource status**
   ☑ **Actual costs are always calculated by Project**

5. Switch the task type to **Fixed Units** and non **Effort-Driven** for all tasks.

6. Enter the status of the project by updating the tasks. As of *September 17, 2012* the situation is: All the tasks until *Remodeled Location* are done and ran as scheduled. (This update includes the *Select Mover* task.)

7. The contractor started late, because he finished his previous contract late. He supplied the following update:

Task	Started	Actual Duration	Remaining Duration
relocate walls	*12 Sept.*	*2d*	*15 d*

The rest of the tasks are not started yet.

8. Don't forget to check whether there are any remaining durations scheduled before the status date. Reschedule these after the status date. Also check if

there are actual durations after the status date and reschedule these before the status date.

9. Describe the status of the project in your own words.

10. Compare your file with the solution file *10 Updating the Schedule 2.mpp* available for download at www.jrosspub.com. Click the link WAV Download Resource Center to enter the download site.

Relocation Project – Optimizing for Time and Cost Again

Open the file *10 Updating the Schedule 2.mpp* available for download at www.jrosspub.com. Click the link *WAV Download Resource Center* to enter the download site.

1. You find this schedule too risky; you need to meet the new deadline date of November 13, 2012 and on top of that, you need a time buffer to meet the project deadline. You decide to explore whether working overtime offers solutions. The overtime rates are:

Name	Std. Rate	Overtime Rate
The employees	$ 25/h	$ 50/h
The contractor	$ 30/h	$ 50/h
The LAN consultants	$ 75/h	$ 100/h
The Realtor	$ 35/h	$ 45/h

2. What is the cost of the project now?

3. Which people would you ask to work overtime first in order to meet the November 13th deadline? Why?

4. You want to explore whether overtime by the contractor can solve the schedule conflict.
   How many overtime person days do you propose on which tasks to meet the deadline?

5. How much does your project cost if you pay the overtime rates?

6. Could you negotiate to pay regular rates instead?

7. How would you enter the overtime work if you pay the regular standard rate?

8. Compare your file with the solution file *10 Updating the Schedule 3.mpp* available for download at www.jrosspub.com. Click the link *WAV Download Resource Center* to enter the download site.

Chapter 11: Reporting

Chapter Objectives

Objective:

Use Project 2010 to generate reports designed to fulfill the various purposes, stakeholders and needs of the project.

Project 2010 Objectives:
1. Prepare Visual Reports.
2. Prepare an executive overview.
3. Report on cost by function.
4. Print the Gantt Chart.
5. Print the Resource Sheet

Exercise Deliverables:

Various report and print views in Project 2010 and Excel.

Relocation Project — Visual Reports

This exercise will introduce you to a type of Visual Report. If you would like additional practice creating Visual Reports we suggest that you locate a text on Excel or Pivot Tables.

Open the file *11 Reporting 1.mpp* available for download at www.jrosspub.com. Click the link *WAV Download Resource Center* to enter the download site.

1. In the **Visual Reports – Create Report** dialog box, select the *Excel Report… Resource Remaining Work Report*.

2. Set level of usage data to include to **Weeks**. Click on the **View** button. A report will be created in Excel.

3. In Excel, click on the **Resource Summary** tab at the bottom of the worksheet.

4. Select menu item **Pivot Table** on the **Options** tab.

5. Click in the middle of the data region in the pivot table to make the **PivotTable Field List** appear.

6. On the **PivotTable Field List**, check ☑ **Actual Cost** and **Remaining Cost** to add them to the report.

7. Click on the **Chart 1** tab at the bottom of the worksheet. Note that the chart was dynamically updated with the actual cost and remaining cost data.

Relocation Project — Preparing an Executive Overview

Open the file *11 Reporting 1.mpp* available for download at www.jrosspub.com. Click the link *WAV Download Resource Center* to enter the download site. We will create a custom view that provides executives with a high-level overview of the project.

1. Create a new task table named *Executive Overview*. Use the columns **ID**, **Name**, **Duration** and **Cost**.

2. Create a new filter, *Executive Overview*, to display milestones and their summary tasks.

3. Create a new view, *Executive Overview*, and show it in the menu. Make sure that when you apply the view *Executive Overview*, the corresponding table and filter are both applied.

4. Hide the question marks in the duration column: on the **File** tab, **Backstage** view choose ▣ **Options** on Schedule, clear the option ▢ **Show that scheduled tasks have estimated duration**.

5. Apply the following **Formatting**, on the **View** tab, on the **Zoom** group, in the Timescale dropdown list on the **Timescale**... 🔍 settings:

Timescale Settings	Middle Tier	Bottom Tier
Units	Months	Days
Label	Jan '09	1,2,3,4,...
Count	1	7
Align	Center	Center
Size	100%	100%

6. Format the **Header, Footer** and **Legend** of the Gantt Chart as follows:

Page Tab	Section	Set to	Font
Header	Center	&[View] &[Project Title]	Calibri, Bold, 20
Footer	Left	&[Manager] &[Company]	Calibri, Regular, 8
	Right	&[Date]	Calibri, Regular, 8
Legend	Legend on	◉ None	

7. Compare your file with the view *Executive Overview* in the solution file *11 Reporting 2.mpp* available for download at www.jrosspub.com. Click the link *WAV Download Resource Center* to enter the download site.

Relocation Project — Reporting Cost by Function

Open the file *11 Reporting 2.mpp* available for download at www.jrosspub.com. Click the link *WAV Download Resource Center* to enter the download site.

1. Switch to the **Resource Sheet** view.

2. Create a new resource table *Cost by Function* that shows the fields **ID**, **Name**, **Position**, **Function** and **Cost**. Remember that the Position and Function fields corresponds to Text 1 and Text 2 field.

3. Create a grouping *Cost by Function* so that you can easily read the total cost by function category of the project.

4. Create a new Resource Sheet view named *Cost by Function* that is shown in the menu. The view should apply the corresponding table and grouping.

5. Set the **Page Setup** settings to the following:

Tab	Section	Set to
Page	*Orientation*	*Portrait*
	Scaling	*Fit to: 1 page wide by 1 tall*
Margins	*top, bottom, left, right*	*1 inch or 2.5 cm*
	Borders Around	*every page*
Header	*Center* *Calibri, Bold, 16*	*&[View]*
Footer	*Left*	*&[Manager] &[Company]*
	Center	*none; delete the default entry*
	Right	*&[Date]*

6. Compare your file with the solution file *11 Reporting 3.mpp* available for download at www.jrosspub.com. Click the link *WAV Download Resource Center* to enter the download site.

Relocation Project — Printing the Gantt Chart

With the tasks, estimates, dependencies and constraints completed, we now have entered all the data needed to print a Gantt Chart. Open the file *11 Reporting 1.mpp* available for download at www.jrosspub.com. Click the link *WAV Download Resource Center* to enter the download site.

1. Format the timescale of the Gantt Chart in the following way:

	Middle Tier	Bottom Tier
Units	Months	Days
Label	Jan '09	1, 2,...
Count	1	7
Align	Center	Center

	Middle Tier	Bottom Tier
Size	100 %	100 %

2. Format the **header**, **footer** and **legend** of the Gantt Chart in the following way:

Page Tab	Section	Set to	Font
Header	Center	&[View] &[Project Title]	Calibri, Bold, 16
Footer	Left	&[Manager] &[Company]	Calibri, Regular, 8
	Right	&[Date]	Calibri, Regular, 8
Legend	Legend on	◉ None	

3. Do a print preview to see the report.

4. Compare your file with (a printout of) the solution file *11 Reporting 4.mpp* available for download at www.jrosspub.com. Click the link WAV *Download Resource Center* to enter the download site.

Relocation Project — Printing the Resource Sheet

Continue to work with the file from the previous exercise.

1. Apply the following on the **Format** tab, **Format** group, in **Text Styles** 𝔸:

Item to Change	Font	Font Style	Size
All	Calibri	Regular	10
Row & Column Titles	Calibri	Bold	10

2. Enter the following **Page Setup** settings:

Tab	Section	Set to	Font
Page	Orientation	Landscape	
	Scaling	Fit to: 1 pages wide by 1 tall	
Margins	Top, Bottom, Left, Right	1 Inch or 2.5 cm	
	Borders Around	Every page	
Header	Center	&[View] &[Project Title]	Calibri Bold 16
Footer	Left	&[Manager] &[Company]	Calibri Regular 8
	Right	&[Date]	

3. Apply the following on the **Format** tab, Format group, in **Gridlines** ⊞:

Line to Change	Normal – Type
Sheet Rows	blank (at top of list)
Sheet Columns	blank (at top of list)

Line to Change	Normal – Type
Title Vertical	*blank (at top of list)*
Title Horizontal	*blank (at top of list)*

4. Do a print preview to see the results.

5. Compare your file with a printout of the solution file *11 Reporting 5.mpp* available for download at www.jrosspub.com. Click the link *WAV Download Resource Center* to enter the download site.

Chapter 12: Earned Value Management

Chapter Objectives

Objective:

Demonstrate Earned Value relevance over the entire project.

Project 2010 Objectives:
1. Update the progress of tasks.
2. Apply Earned Value Management (EVM).
3. Analyze the performance of the project based on EVM methodology.

Exercise Deliverables:

Earned Value Visual Report in Project 2010 and Excel.

Relocation Project — Earned Value Management

Continue to work with your file *Relocation.mpp* or open the file *12 EVM 1.mpp* available for download at www.jrosspub.com. Click the link *WAV Download Resource Center* to enter the download site.

1. Set the current view so you are able to see the **Tracking Gantt View**, the **Tracking Table**, and locate all the Tracking tools.

2. Go to **Project Information** ▣ and set the **Current** and **Status Date** to *10/24/2012*. You should be able to see the Current and Status Date line in the Gantt Chart. If not go to **Format**, **Gridlines** and adjust both of these lines so they are visible.

3. Reschedule task 19 *Relocate Walls* to start after the Status Date.

4. On 11/13/2012 you want to report on status. Go to **Project Information** ▣ and set the **Current** and **Status Date** to *11/13/2012*.

5. On 11/13/2012, the status of the project is:
   ▸ Task 19 *Relocate Walls* is 100% complete with no more delays.
   ▸ The electrical wiring in the new location was not up to code as was originally thought. The effort to complete Task 20 *Install Electric Wiring* was severely underestimated. To complete this task within the original estimated duration, a total of 10 Contractors were required. This task is now 100% complete.
   ▸ Task 21 *Paint* has not started yet.

6. On the **View** tab, in the **Data** group, click on **Tables** ▤ and show the *Earned Value Table*.

7. How would you describe the performance of *Install Wiring*? *Paint*?

8. What is the overall status of the Relocation Project?

9. Take a look at the Earned Value Visual Report for this Project. It is an Excel Chart and Table called *Earned Value Over Time*. Does this reflect your conclusions from the previous EVM analysis you did with the Earned

Value Table? Does the Earned Value Over Time Visual Report add any new information?

10. Save this file as *12 EVM 2.mpp*.

Troubleshooting   Open the file *12 EVM 2.mpp* available for download at www.jrosspub.com. Click the link *WAV Download Resource Center* to enter the download site.

1. Are the values in the table correct?
2. Why not?
3. What should be done to provide correct values?

Chapter 13: Evaluating the Project

Chapter Objectives

Objective:

Analyze your experience on a completed project in terms of the accomplishment of the objectives and benefits that were defined when the project was approved.

Project 2010 Objectives:
1. Compare baselines.
2. Use the Compare Projects feature.
3. Create templates for future projects.

Exercise Deliverables:

Compared projects in Project 2010

Template in Project 2010

Compare Baselines

Open the file *13 Evaluating 1.mpp* available for download at www.jrosspub.com. Click the link *WAV Download Resource Center* to enter the download site.

1. Go to the **Tracking Gantt** view and **Tracking** table. You can now compare the actual information against the active baseline.

2. Set the **Status Date** to November 2, 2012 and create a gridline for the status date in the **Gantt timescale**. (Line to Change: **Status Date**, Type: **Continuous Line,** Color: **Red**).

3. Set the current view so you are able to see the **Tracking Gantt View** and the **Tracking Table**. Update progress as follows:

Task	Actual Start	Actual Finish	Actual Duration	Remaining Duration	Predecessor
Relocate walls	12 Sept.	05 Oct.	16 d	0 d	Stays the same
Install electric wiring	09 Oct.	12 Oct.	04 d	0 d	Stays the same
Paint	15 Oct.	16 Oct.	02 d	0 d	Stays the same
Drying of paint	16 Oct.	20 Oct.	04 ed	0 ed	Stays the same
Install cabinetry	26 Sept.	05 Oct.	08 d	0 d	Relocate walls (FF + 1 day)
Install LAN	17 Oct.		12 d	02 d	Paint
Lay carpet	22 Oct.		09 d	01 d	install LAN (FF + 1 day)

4. With this new information, you were authorized to set a new baseline for the entire project. Do it, without deleting any other baseline.

5. In this schedule baselines 2 and 3 had already been defined, so go to the **Multiple Baselines Gantt** view to compare the different baselines in order to evaluate the performance of your project.

6. Compare your file with the solution file *13 Evaluating 2.mpp* available for download at www.jrosspub.com. Click the link *WAV Download Resource Center* to enter the download site.

Compare Projects   Keep the *13 Evaluating 2.mpp* file open. Also open the file *13 Evaluating 3.mpp*, that is a previous version of the schedule, available for download at www.jrosspub.com. Click the link *WAV Download Resource Center* to enter the download site.

1. From *13 Evaluating 2.mpp* file, go to **Project** tab, **Reports** group, and select **Compare Projects**. Choose *13 Evaluating 3* file and select **Tracking**, for **Task Table**.

2. Take a look to the available windows and analyze your performance.

3. Save this file as *Relocation Analysis.mpp*.

4. Compare your file with the solution file *13 Evaluating 4.mpp* available for download at www.jrosspub.com. Click the link *WAV Download Resource Center* to enter the download site.

Create Templates   Open the file *13 Evaluating Template 1.mpp* available for download at at www.jrosspub.com. Click the link *WAV Download Resource Center* to enter the download site.

1. On the **Format** tab, **Drawings** group, select *Text* box from the **Drawing** drop down list.

2. Put the text box over the chart area and type: *This is a Template*.

3. Save the file as template, select *all* for type of data to remove from the template, and name it *Relocation*, so the file will be: *Relocation.mpt*

4. Compare your file with the solution file *13 Evaluating Template 2.mpt* available for download at www.jrosspub.com. Click the link *WAV Download Resource Center* to enter the download site.

Appendix 2: Consolidated Schedules

Chapter Objectives

Objective:

Manage consolidated schedules with Project 2010.

Project 2010 Objectives:

1. Create a central resource pool from scratch or from an existing schedule.
2. Insert subprojects into a consolidated schedule.
3. Explain what a cross-project link is and why it is used.
4. Level resources across projects.
5. Baseline a consolidated schedule.

Exercise Deliverables:

Resource pool in Project 2010

Consolidated Schedule in Project 2010

Case Study Information:

Resource Pool

You are the manager for a major event and have to organize the tasks and resource assignments.

Open the *A2 Consolidated Schedule Resources 01.mpp* file (blank project) available for download at www.jrosspub.com. Click the link *WAV Download Resource Center* to enter the download site.

1. Go to the **Resource** sheet view and type the following data:

Resource Name	Type	Std. Rate
Alejandro Acevedo		$75.00/hr
Francisco Ambriz		$50.00/hr
Julio Díaz	Work	$70.00/hr
Mario Landa		$30.00/hr
You (type your name)		$110.00/hr

2. Save your file and keep it opened.

You have identified the preliminary tasks of the event and now need to assign resources from the pool. In the **Gantt Chart** view type the following:

WBS	Task	Duration	Predecessor	Resource Names
1	Shipping Event Materials			
1.1	Ship materials	01 d		Alejandro Acevedo
1.2	Ship any necessary supporting equipment	02 d	1.1	Francisco Ambriz
2	Manage Day of Event	05 d	1.2	You

WBS	Task	Duration	Predecessor	Resource Names
3	*Market Event Success*	*02 d*	*2*	*Julio Diaz*
4	*Event Complete*	*0d*	*3*	

You realize that the tasks *Manage Day of Event* and *Market Event Success* require activities like manage vendors and speakers, select sites, and prepare contracts, etc., so you decide to turn both tasks into subprojects. Now you have a Program to manage.

As a program manager, you assign the project managers and tell them to use your resource list as a pool so they have to create their plans using your file.

Now you need to act as the project managers for the subprojects.

1. Download and save the *A2 Consolidated Schedule Resources 02.mpp* and *A2 Consolidated Schedule Resources 03.mpp* files. These two files have the schedules already entered without the resources assigned. They are available for download at www.jrosspub.com. Click the link *WAV Download Resource Center* to enter the download site.

2. In these two files you are going to use the *A2 Consolidated Schedule Resources 01.mpp* file resources, using the **Resource Pool** feature.

3. For the *A2 Consolidated Schedule Resources 02.mpp* make the following assignments:

Task Name	Resource Name
Review equipment	*Alejandro Acevedo*
Manage setup	*Francisco Ambriz*
Manage registration	*Julio Diaz*
Manage vendors	*Mario Landa*
Manage speakers	*Alejandro Acevedo*
Manage teardown	*Francisco Ambriz*
Route leads to sales	*Mario Landa*

4. Save the project baseline.

5. For the *A2 Consolidated Schedule Resources 03.mpp* make the following assignments:

Task Name	Resource Name
Finalize contracts	*Alejandro Acevedo, Francisco Ambriz, Julio Diaz*
Event debrief with speakers	*Alejandro Acevedo, Francisco Ambriz, Julio Diaz, Mario Landa*

Task Name	Resource Name
Event debrief with event team	*Julio Diaz*

6. Save the project baseline.

Consolidated Schedule

In the *A2 Consolidated Schedule Resources 01.mpp* file substitute the *A2 Consolidated Schedule Resources 02.mpp* and *A2 Consolidated Schedule Resources 03.mpp* files for the tasks named *Manage Day of Event* and *Market Event Success* respectively.

Cross-Project Links

In the *A2 Consolidated Schedule Resources 01.mpp* file where you now have inserted subprojects, link the following tasks across projects:

1. From *13 Evaluating 2.mpp* file, go to **Project** tab, **Reports** group, and select **Compare Projects**. Choose *13 Evaluating 3* file and select **Tracking**, for **Task Table**.

Task	To Task	Type
Ship any necessary supporting equipment	*Review equipment*	FS
Manage vendors	*Finalize contracts*	FS

2. You realize that the task *Manage speakers* will really take 1.5 days. You change it, and now you notice that an over-allocation has appeared.

Level Resources Across Projects

Continue to work in the *A2 Consolidated Schedule Resources 01.mpp* file.

On the **Resource** tab, **Level** group, select **Level Resource** feature for all the resources assigned. Note that there are no more over-allocations, but your finish date has changed.

Baseline a Consolidated Schedule

1. Set the baseline for your entire program file.

2. Save the master project and the subprojects.

3. Compare your file with the *A2 Consolidated Schedule Resources 04.mpp* solution file available for download at www.jrosspub.com. Click the link *WAV Download Resource Center* to enter the download site.

Appendix 2: Consolidated Schedules

A consolidated schedule can be used to bring separate subproject schedules together into a single schedule for managing, reporting, analyzing, and/or leveling shared resources.

Learning Objectives

After reading this appendix you will be able to:

➤ Describe the benefits of rolling up subproject schedules into a consolidated schedule
➤ Insert subprojects into a consolidated schedule
➤ Decide whether to insert subprojects with or without links and in read-only or read-write mode
➤ Refresh a consolidated schedule
➤ Explain what a cross-project link is and why it is used
➤ Set cross-project dependencies in a program to create an integrated program schedule
➤ Monitor, manage and maintain the links between projects
➤ List the advantages and disadvantages of cross-project links
➤ Follow the Dos and Don'ts when working with linked schedules
➤ Analyze integrated program schedules using gates
➤ Create a central resource pool from scratch or from an existing schedule
➤ Baseline a consolidated schedule

What is a Consolidated Schedule?

A consolidated schedule is assembled from:

➤ Independent subproject schedules that are brought together for reporting purposes
➤ Independent subproject schedules that share resources and are consolidated for analyzing and leveling purposes
➤ Interdependent subproject schedules that share resources and are consolidated for analyzing and leveling purposes
➤ Interdependent subproject schedules without shared resources that are consolidated for purposes of understanding the larger picture and reporting

We use the term consolidated schedule to mean bringing multiple subproject schedules together into one schedule, regardless of the purpose. Many texts differentiate between the types of consolidated schedules, for example:

➤ Master Project Schedule: A collection of smaller project schedules that are elements of the master (larger picture) project. An example might be a project where each department produces its own departmental schedule for the work.

➤ Program Schedule or Integrated Program Schedule: A collection of individual, but related, project or program schedules that are consolidated to facilitate the management of the program. An example might be a testing program, where each administration of a test rolls up into the testing program schedule.

➤ Consolidated Schedule: A more limited definition of consolidated schedules that includes schedules that have no relationship to each other, but are consolidated for purposes like leveling and reporting.

Many may view these as distinctions without a difference, but while the techniques are similar, the characteristics and use vary. For example, note that in each of the above definitions:

➤ Resources may or may not be from a common pool.
➤ The consolidated schedules may be temporary (brought together just for reporting or leveling) or may persist and be used to manage the program/project.

 Project 2010 refers to all of these instances as Master Projects and Subprojects in the help facility.

When to Consolidate Schedules

There are two common situations in which consolidated schedules are useful:

Large Schedules

Large schedules can quickly become unwieldy, and can benefit from being broken down into subprojects and then inserted into a consolidated schedule. There are two criteria you can use to determine if you have a large project that would benefit from this treatment:

➤ The number of hierarchical levels in your project team.
If you have more than two levels in your project team, you have a large project. In small or medium sized projects, the project manager interacts directly with the team members. If the project manager interacts with team leaders who supervise the team members, you have three levels in the project team hierarchy and your project is large.

> ➤ The number of tasks in the project schedule.
> You need to break a large schedule into multiple sub-schedules if the number of tasks gets difficult to handle in a single schedule. For example, finding the critical path in an extremely large schedule is a challenge, but in a smaller task schedule, the critical path may fit within one screen.

Multiple Schedules that Require Integration

The other situation where consolidated schedules are of use is when you have existing project schedules that you want to bring together. For example, you might want to bring a number of project schedules together into a consolidated program schedule.

PMI defines a program as "A group of related projects managed in a coordinated way to obtain benefits and control not available from managing them individually. Programs may include elements of related work outside of the scope of the discrete projects in the program".[1]

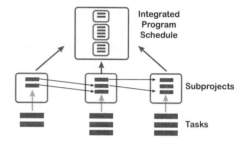

Managing a large project with many separate, non-integrated schedules can be cumbersome; Project 2010 allows you to place many projects into one "umbrella" or consolidated project. (You may also see this referred to as a program schedule, a master project or a roll-up project.) The project schedules you roll up into the consolidated project are often called subprojects or sub schedules.

Why Consolidate Schedules?

Consolidating schedules can be especially useful in the following situations.

> ➤ Subprojects share the same pool of resources
> Consolidating schedules is useful for analyzing and leveling resource use, particularly when there is competition for scarce resources.

> ➤ Subprojects have dependencies between them
> This is the case, for example, in a large software development program that is divided into the following subprojects: *Design, Development, Testing, Deployment, Documentation, Logistics* and *Training*. There are obviously many dependencies between these subprojects and benefits can be obtained from managing the subprojects in a coordinated fashion and treating them as an integrated program schedule.

> ➤ There are specific reporting needs on a group of projects
> Consolidating projects makes it easy to treat them as a program for reporting purposes.

---

1 ———*PMBOK® Guide — Fourth Edition*, PMI, 2008, p. 442.

> ➤ An organization runs many similar projects for one client
> The projects are often treated as an integrated program schedule.

Consolidated schedules can include either internal or external subprojects, or a combination of both. For example:

> ➤ Internal subprojects.
> All components are created by in-house departments. Examples:
>
> ▶ High-tech product development programs and pharmaceutical programs are often entirely internal, because of the confidential nature of these projects.
> ▶ Many IT-programs within multi-nationals are set up this way.

> ➤ External subprojects.
> The owner organization has subcontracted all components of the overall program. The project managers within the owner organization are managing the subcontractors using high-level schedules only, and are more like contract managers or outsourcing managers. The subcontractors maintain the detailed subschedules.

> ➤ Mix of internal and external subprojects.
> The owner creates some components, and has subcontracted some components to external performing organizations. This is a mixed program with some internal subproject and some external subprojects.

Checks to Perform before Consolidating

Each schedule that is to be consolidated should be checked first for the following characteristics, and any problems addressed before consolidating.

> ➤ Did the scheduler follow consistent scheduling guidelines?
> These guidelines are extremely important for large schedules. For example, if there are many constraints in the subprojects, you cannot analyze a large schedule easily, let alone optimize and/or change it.

> ➤ Is the baseline still what it should be?
> The baseline has to be the original baseline or a baseline that reflects only approved change requests.

> ➤ Are there errors?
> The scheduler could make accidental errors; to avoid them, ask:
>
> ▶ Are estimates reasonable?
> ▶ Are there inaccurate dependencies?
> ▶ Are there any over-allocations?
> ▶ Are there any scheduling conflicts?

> ➤ Are there omissions?
> The scheduler could have omitted the following things:
>
> ▶ Contractual deliverables/tasks

> ▸ Crucial dependencies
> ▸ Scarce expert resources
> ▸ Assignments of the scarce resources

If you receive a subproject schedule from a subcontractor, we recommend that you first analyze the schedule to see if any changes were made, particularly to the baseline. Subcontractors should not make changes to the baseline without your approval. You can use the project comparison feature for this by choosing **Project** tab, **Reports** group, select **Compare Projects** (see chapter 13).

Reviewing Options and Settings

When you create a consolidated schedule, it's important to remember that the subproject schedules will inherit many of the settings from the consolidated schedule. Several areas you should check include, but are not limited to:

> ➤ Calendars
> ➤ Fonts
> ➤ Default settings

To avoid confusion between the subprojects and the consolidated schedule, it is a good idea to standardize these before consolidating.

One setting that is often confused is the setting to calculate multiple critical paths or a single critical path.

1. On the **File** tab, in the **Backstage** view, click **Options**, **Schedule**. The **Project Options** dialog appears.

2. At the bottom, under **Calculation options for this project**, the setting ☑ **Inserted Projects are Calculated Like Summary Tasks** is used for Consolidated projects.
   > ▸ Check this box if you want a single critical path
   > ▸ Clear this box if you want to see a critical path for each subproject

3. In the **Project Options** dialog, click on **Advanced** tab.

4. The setting ☑ **Calculate Multiple Critical Paths** will be helpful if you want to review independent critical paths for subprojects that are not necessarily part of the consolidated critical path.

When working with projects that eventually will be consolidated as sub-projects, it is a good practice to create a project template that contains all the options, calendars, custom fields and defaults necessary for consolidation and deliver it to the stakeholders to use in their projects. This will make your consolidation process very fluent.

Creating a Consolidated Schedule

Consolidate with Automatic Linking of Files

There are two ways to create consolidated schedules. The first automatically links the files, while the second allows you to choose whether you want the files linked.

With this method you will consolidate all the projects that you select into a new master project. The files are automatically linked, which means that if any change takes place in the master or subproject file, the other file(s) will reflect the change.

1. Open all of the projects to be consolidated.

2. On the **View** tab, in the **Window** group click ⧉ **New Window**.

3. In the **New Window** dialog, select the projects that you want included and the **View** you want to display with the consolidated project and click
   [OK] .

If you use this method, you may not get certain warning messages, such as for circular dependencies.

To save the changes see the Saving section below.

Consolidate with Optional Linking of Files

Inserting a subproject into a master project and checking the **Link to Project** box creates a dynamic link between the two files. The subproject file will be visible in the master project. Any future changes applied to the subproject will be reflected in the master project, and vice-versa.

Inserting a subproject into a master project and clearing the **Link to Project** box actually creates a copy of the project in the master project. This is a static copy: future changes to the subproject won't be reflected in the master project, and vice-versa.

With this method you're able to choose whether or not you want the subproject files linked to the master.

1. Open a new, blank schedule. Save and name this file <XYZ Master Project> (follow your company's naming conventions for master projects).

2. Put your cursor on the first line in the **Task Name** column.

3. Choose **Project** tab and in the **Insert** group click 📌 **Subproject**.

4. In the **Insert Project** pane navigate to the name of the first project file you want to consolidate and select it.

5. Check or clear ✅ **Link to project**. You can insert a read-only copy of the file: click the down arrow on the right of the [Insert ▾] button and select **Insert Read-only**.

6. Click [Insert ▾] to insert the file,

   OR

   If you've checked ☑ **Link to project** , you can insert a read-only copy of the file: click the down arrow on the right of the [Insert ▾] button and select **Insert Read-only**.

7. Notice that the Project summary line is inserted with the project rolled up under it.

8. Continue to do this on each subsequent line for each additional project you want to add.

Options for Consolidating Subprojects

Read-write or Read-only Access

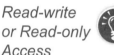

We recommend that you insert subprojects as read-only as a standard practice to prevent:

➤ Hogging the sub-schedules: if you insert a subproject read-write and you open the master project, while you're editing the master project, the subproject manager can't open his/her schedule in read-write mode and can't make changes to it.

➤ Accidental changes to the sub-schedules: you don't want to inadvertently change the schedules that are maintained by others.

You will, however, need read-write access to the subprojects when you want to do any of the following:

➤ Create cross subproject dependencies
➤ Resolve over-allocations
➤ Solve schedule conflicts in the master schedule

You can easily switch a read-only file to read-write and vice versa (see the section "Working with a Consolidated Schedule" below).

Saving

When you close out of the master file, you will be asked if you want to save the master file and individually you will be asked if you want to save each subproject file. You do not have to save the master file to maintain the changes and dependencies created in the master and affected on the subproject schedules. If you've consolidated subprojects for a temporary purpose such as for reporting, it's not recommended that you save the consolidated master file.

*Inserting
New Tasks*

Be careful when inserting new tasks under either a collapsed or expanded subproject:

➤ If you insert a task inside or just beneath an expanded subproject, the task will end up in the subproject.

➤ If you insert a new task just beneath a collapsed subproject, the task will end up in the program schedule.

➤ You can see in which schedule a task was inserted by looking at the ID-number. Note that the ID-numbering starts at 1 inside each subproject.

*Inserting
Subprojects on
Outline Levels*

You can insert a subproject on any indentation/outline level. This allows you to create a true breakdown structure for the program in which you insert the project schedules at the appropriate places to create the program breakdown structure the way you want it to be.

*Maximum Number
of Inserted
Projects*

The maximum number of schedules you can roll up in a master project using the Insert Sub-project feature (on the **Project** tab, in the **Insert** group, click **Subproject**) is about 998. The maximum number of tasks within one schedule is 400,000, so you can insert about 998 subproject schedules of 400 tasks each.[2]

Be aware that actual limits and performance speed depend on your computer's configuration.

*Multiple Levels of
Consolidation*

You can consolidate consolidated schedules. For example, if you have several subproject schedules, you can create a master schedule from them for the program. If your department has multiple program schedules, you can create a department schedule from the program schedules by inserting them into a consolidated department schedule.

Although Project 2010 lets you nest several levels of sub-projects, managing multiple levels of master projects can be cumbersome. A good practice before doing this is to establish the level of control that you really need and define a very good process of consolidation for updates. In general, the simpler your model is, the better.

*Modifying
the WBS to
Consolidate
Projects*

If you are creating a breakdown structure for the program in which you are inserting project schedules, you can establish a WBS-specific codification (coding scheme) that facilitates the localization of the subprojects into the consolidated project.

To modify the WBS code, you must define the codification in the Master Project as well as in the subprojects by following these simple steps:

---

2   These specifications are roughly the same as for Project 2007. To see any later updates please visit the site http://office.microsoft.com/en-us/project-help/CH010362739.aspx

1. On the **Project** tab, in the **Properties** group, click 📄 **WBS** icon, 🗂
   Define Code. The **WBS Code Definition** dialog appears.

2. In the WBS Code Definition dialog, you can set the following:

   a. **Code mask**: Use this to set the number of levels and the mask for every
      level. For the Master Project, you should establish at least the first level.
      You can choose a mask of numbers, uppercase or lowercase letters
      or special characters, depending on how you are modifying the WBS
      Code.

   b. **Project Code Prefix**: This field is very useful when consolidating
      projects. Every sub-project will have a specific **Code** that distinguishes
      it from others. For instance, if the subproject is the Phase II of a
      consolidated project, the prefix could be defined as *<PHII>*. With this
      option, all the tasks that belong to this sub-project will be identified
      with the prefix *<PHII>*.

   c. **Code preview**: This field allows you to preview the codification that is
      being established by the **Code** mask and **Project Code Prefix**.

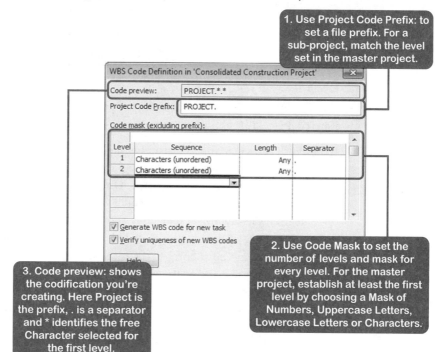

1. Use Project Code Prefix: to set a file prefix. For a sub-project, match the level set in the master project.

2. Use Code Mask to set the number of levels and mask for every level. For the master project, establish at least the first level by choosing a Mask of Numbers, Uppercase Letters, Lowercase Letters or Characters.

3. Code preview: shows the codification you're creating. Here Project is the prefix, . is a separator and * identifies the free Character selected for the first level.

When using characters (instead of numbers or letters) to define the code mask
of any level in the WBS, a placeholder asterisk "*" will be displayed in the code
so you can manually substitute the placeholder.

3. Click [OK].

4. If you are using a code mask other than **Characters**, go to step 7.

5. Right click the **Task Name** column, **Insert**, **WBS**.

6. Manually substitute the place holder asterisk "*" in the desired level.

7. Repeat this process for every Sub-project.

Sub-projects *Construction Phase I* and *Construction Phase II* are tasks of the master project.

The sub-project *Construction Phase II* was inserted as a subtask under the *Construction Project* Summary task. As a result, its codification is ruled by the codification of the master project. For the Master Project, the codification for level 1 and 2 was set as Characters and manually filled. Prefix is *PROJECT*, the first level for construction is identified by *CONS* and the second level by *PHII*.

The sub-project *Construction Phase II* was set with the Project Prefix *PHII*. The rest of the levels are numbers. All the tasks that belong to this sub-project contain this prefix.

Working with a Consolidated Schedule

The following discussion assumes that the projects you are working with are on a shared drive with appropriate access.

➤ Refresh takes place upon expanding the subproject schedules
If you open a program schedule and the subproject schedules are collapsed, you may not see the latest forecasts. Only when you expand the subproject schedules within the master schedule will Project 2010 retrieve the latest data from the subproject schedules or recalculate them.

▶ You have to make sure that when you open a master project, you first expand all subprojects. (In the master project select the project summary task and on the **View** tab, in the **Data** group, click ⊞ **Outline**, **All Subtasks**.)

▶ As an alternative, before you close the master project, if you expand all the subprojects, the next time you open the master, all subprojects will be refreshed.

➤ Ensure you have the latest version of the schedule
There are specific task-related fields for subprojects that can help you determine the latest version of your schedule:

▶ Inserted Project Indicator: In the **Gantt Chart** view, on the column ⓘ **Indicators**, an Inserted Project icon 🖳 will be shown for any inserted project summary task. Hovering the mouse over this icon will display a Smart Tag indicating the path of the sub-project.

▸ **Inserted Project Information** dialog: Double-click the subproject task and the **Inserted Project Information** dialog appears; click the **Advanced** tab. Under **Link to Project** you can read the path and the name of the subproject. Click <kbd>Browse...</kbd> to reroute to the latest version of the project

➤ Toggle a read-only file to read-write and vice versa
You need to toggle to read-write before you can make any changes to subprojects inside a master project. You need to do this when you try to resolve scheduling conflicts or over-allocations within the master project, or to set cross-project links in the master schedule.

Double-click the subproject task and the **Inserted Project Information** dialog appears; click the **Advanced** tab:

☑ **Read Only**: is checked if the subproject was inserted read-only. If you clear the checkbox to ☐ **Read-only** the schedule will switch to read-write, after you click <kbd>OK</kbd>, save the changes to the master project and re-open.

If you have the subprojects open in read-write mode in the master project, the subproject managers cannot make any changes to their subprojects! You need to minimize the time you keep the subprojects open in read-write mode. You should also establish processes and clearly communicate with the subproject managers who own the schedules about what times you will open their schedules read-write.

➤ Save changes to program/subproject schedules:
If you have made any changes to the master project schedule and you close it, first you will be asked if you want to save the changes for the master project and then for each of the subproject schedules. You must click an instruction for each project and you also have the option to say <kbd>Yes to All</kbd> or <kbd>No to All</kbd>.

Cross-Projects Dependencies

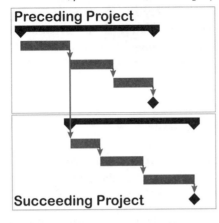

Preceding Project

Succeeding Project

Sometimes, you want schedulers or project managers to have their own schedules and work independently while there are dependencies between their projects. For example, the software development project may drive the software-testing project. These links are called cross-project links or interdependencies. Such projects are often subprojects in an integrated program schedule.

There are options to consider on **File** tab, **Backstage** view, **Options**, **Advanced**, section **Cross Project**

Linking options for this project:

➤ When ☑ **Show external successors** and ☑ **Show external predecessors** are checked, you can make sure you see the external tasks listed in the task list; they are shown in gray.

➤ When ☑ **Show 'Links Between Projects' dialog box on open** is checked, any subproject manager will be shown a report of the external cross-project links displaying the updates as explained in the following pages.

Setting Cross-Project Dependencies in the Master Schedule

If you create a cross-project dependency using the New Window method (on the **View** tab, in the **Window** group, click 🗗 **New Window**) and create a temporary merge of two sub-schedules for which you want to set cross project dependencies, you can easily create circular dependencies in the overall master schedule. A circular dependency will stop automatic recalculation, since Project 2010 cannot produce a schedule that meets the requirements of all dependencies. The master schedule is useless at that point.

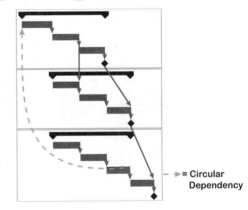

➤ = Circular Dependency

If you always create the cross project dependencies in the master schedule, Project 2010 will immediately warn you if you are creating a circular dependency.

We recommend you create cross project dependencies in the master schedule, because it will prevent you from accidentally creating a circular dependency.

You need to have read-write access to the subprojects in order to create cross subproject dependencies. If the subprojects are currently read-only, you have to toggle them to read-write, then close and re-open the master schedule.

In the master schedule, you can create cross project dependencies as you would set dependencies in single schedules. You can:

➤ Use the link tool 🔗 located on the **Task** tab in the **Schedule** group (recommended method).

➤ Drag between task bars to create the links by mouse. (If the tasks are far apart, this can be difficult.)

 The **Predecessors** tab in the **Task Information** dialog (double-click the task) will not be very helpful for setting cross project predecessors since it only shows the tasks available in the schedule to which the task belongs. Nevertheless, the **Task Information** dialog will be very helpful in reviewing the path of a cross project predecessor already set in the **ID** column (just click the row in the ID column for the predecessor and you will see the complete path of the predecessor schedule plus **ID**.)

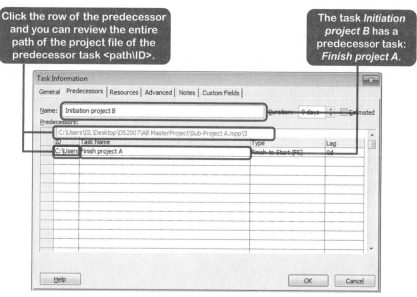

Establishing predecessors between projects is not as simple as entering the ID-numbers of the predecessor or successor as you can in a single schedule when setting dependencies. This is because the ID-numbers in a master schedule with linked sub-schedules will vary after you set cross project dependencies. The tasks of the subprojects keep their original ID-numbers except for the sub-schedule summary task which acquires an ID-number according to it's position in the master schedule.

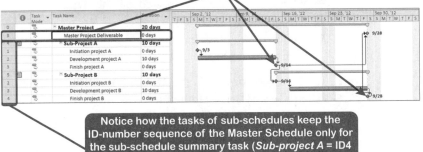

The ID-numbers of tasks in projects with cross-project dependencies will vary constantly depending on the number of the external predecessors or successors. For example, task *Master Project Deliverable* is a task of the Master Schedule and instead of having ID-number 1, it has ID-number 3. This is because there are 2 predecessors, *Finish project A* and *Finish project B*.

Notice how the tasks of sub-schedules keep the ID-number sequence of the Master Schedule only for the sub-schedule summary task (*Sub-project A* = ID4 and *Sub-project B* = ID5). The rest of the tasks of the sub-schedules keep their own sequences.

Although in master schedules the tasks of the sub-schedules keep their ID-numbers, when opened independently, if the **Show external predecessors** and Show external successors options are checked (**File** tab, **Backstage** view, **Options**, **Advanced**, **Cross Project Linking options for this project** section), cross project dependencies will be shown in a degraded gray color, acquiring an ID-number in the sub-schedule.

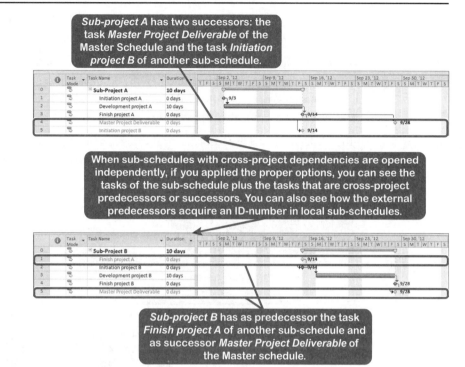

Sub-project A has two successors: the task Master Project Deliverable of the Master Schedule and the task Initiation project B of another sub-schedule.

When sub-schedules with cross-project dependencies are opened independently, if you applied the proper options, you can see the tasks of the sub-schedule plus the tasks that are cross-project predecessors or successors. You can also see how the external predecessors acquire an ID-number in local sub-schedules.

Sub-project B has as predecessor the task Finish project A of another sub-schedule and as successor Master Project Deliverable of the Master schedule.

 To quickly jump from the predecessor schedule to the successor schedule and back, Double-click on the gray ghost task (the external task).

Maintaining the Cross-Project Links

1. In Project 2010, open the successor project, and access the **Links Between Projects In** dialog. On the **Project** tab, in the **Properties** group, click 📄 **Links** between **Projects**.

 If the option **Show Links Between Projects dialog box on open** is activated (**File** tab, **Backstage** view, **Options**, **Advanced**, section **Cross Project Linking options for this project**), the dialog will pop up automatically when opening if changes were made to the related sub-schedules.

2. Click tab **External Predecessor**, and select one of the listed predecessor tasks in the list (these are the ones without an ID number); the buttons **Accept, All, Delete Link** and **Browse** are now enabled.

3. To update the selected link and accept the differences, click [Accept].
   To accept all differences listed in the dialog, click [All].
   To delete a link, select it and click [Delete Link].
   To indicate a new location or name of the schedule, click [Browse...].

4. View the **External Successors** and verify if the project manager who is dependent on your project has resolved all **Differences**. If you don't have read-write access to the successor project, you don't have authority to accept

or reject changes. Contact the project manager of the external successor project to resolve any differences that continue to appear.

 Notice that the **Accept** button is not disabled for external successors, even though you cannot make the decisions on behalf of the successor project manager. You cannot make the differences go away if you have read-only access.

The Links between Projects Dialog

The **Links Between Projects** dialog always has at least two lines for an external dependency. The first line (with ID number) contains the task in your project. The next line(s) contain information on the external task(s). The next screenshot shows that your task 2 has an external predecessor:

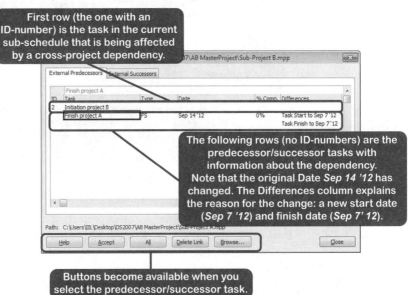

When you have an external predecessor or successor selected, you can see below the list the path and name of the schedule that contains the task.

The dialog has two columns that need more explanation: **Date and Differences**:

➤ **Date**:
The **Date** field here should be interpreted as the "old date". It is the old start date if it shows **Start** on the same line under **Differences** or the old finish date if it shows **Finish** on the same line under **Differences**.

➤ **Differences**: notes you can find in this field are:

Remark	Explanation	What to do?
None	The link is up-to-date.	Nothing.
File not Found	The linked schedule is deleted or renamed.	If moved, use the button to point to the new schedule. If the schedule is found the message will change to: **File Located**.
Delete External	The other scheduler deleted the anchor task for the external dependency (not the link!).	Select it and click **Accept** to remove your side of the dependency and remove the external task from your task list.
Create External	The link is partially set. One reason could be that the link was added by another scheduler who only had read-only access to your schedule and the link was saved in one schedule but not in the other.	Select it and click **Accept** to create a cross project dependency and add an external task to your schedule.
Task Start to <date>	The start date of your dependent task is changed, often driven out.	Accept the new date if you can manage it within the buffer of your project. If you can't accept it, ask the other project manager to resolve the slippage.
Task Finish to <date>	The finish date of your dependent task is changed, often driven out. This can happen with a Finish-to-Finish dependency.	Accept the new date if you can manage it within the buffer of your project. If you can't accept it, ask the other project manager to resolve the slippage.

If an external link itself is removed or a link is recorded partially (the link is visible in one sub-schedule but not the other), it does not cause the message **Delete External** to be displayed in the linked schedule. Instead, it shows up as no difference (**None**) or as a difference in start date (**Start To**) or finish date (**Finish to**) that makes it look like the link is still alive. If you double-click on such a ghost external task in the Gantt Table, the dependent schedule comes up and shows the you remark **Create External**. This allows you to re-establish the external link. The problem is that you cannot see if a link is still alive or not when the other person removed the external link.

 If the predecessor task is inactivated with the new feature to do so (**Task** tab, **Schedule** group, **Inactivate**), you will receive a notification that dates changed but until you accept it and close the dialog you will see on the screen the inactive task (task name with a line through the middle). Remember that this inactivate task option does not remove the task from the schedule. The inactivate task feature also does not affect any resource availability or how other tasks are scheduled, so your related tasks could be affected in an unexpected way. You will need to establish with the master schedule manager or the other sub-schedule manager how to establish a new reference.

*Advantages &
Disadvantages
of Cross Project
Links*

Cross project links have both strengths and limitations.

Advantages:

➤ Automatic, but controlled impacts between schedules
Links allow you to keep the schedule up-to-date automatically when other projects affect your schedule. The updating is controlled: upon opening the schedule, you are prompted as to which impacts you want to allow into your schedule.

➤ Ability to delegate ownership
Links allow you to delegate schedule ownership to the responsible people while maintaining program integrity.

Disadvantages:

➤ Requires one central repository (either a server or PC)
You need a central repository on a network server that is accessible to all project managers. If schedules are large, the connection needs to be fast.

➤ Takes full control (and ownership) away from the project manager
Some project managers feel that the ownership of their schedules is taken away from them because of the external links that impact their schedules. The fact of the matter is that you can review and control which impacts you accept. And even if you choose not to model the cross project impacts, you will still need to monitor and manage them.

➤ One project manager can break a dependency without the other project manager being notified
When you break a link, the other project manager will not see a specific notification in the **Links between Projects** dialog. The dialog just shows **None**, **Start to**, or **Finish to** which makes you think the link is still alive.

*Dos and Don'ts
for Cross Project
Links*

Because cross project links can be tricky to manage, we suggest you adhere to the following list of dos and don'ts.

Dos

➤ Document the cross project links by writing a **Note** on the external task. The **Notes** field is one of the few fields of external tasks that you can edit. The note is stored and visible in your schedule only.

➤ Set **Deadlines** in the dependent tasks so the driving project manager will be able to view these deadlines in the successor tasks and he also will be able to manage his own considerations or commitments.

➤ Create milestone tasks with the name <**External dependency**> to help the master-scheduler understand your dependencies with other projects and facilitate the management of tasks which connect to other projects.

➤ If you need to move an externally linked task, instead of cutting and pasting, you should drag and drop the task. Cut and paste is a temporary delete!

➤ Keep the **Show External Predecessor** and **Show External Successor** turned on (**File** tab, **Backstage** view, **Options**, **Advanced**, **Cross Project Linking options for this project** section). This will help prevent accidental deletion of tasks with external links.

➤ Keep the external task listed next to its internal task by dragging the pair of tasks with the mouse (do not use cut & paste, since this will remove links). Keep external predecessors above your task and external successors below it.

➤ Notice that the driving project manager can see if the dependent project manager has accepted the impacts or not. The driving project manager can call the dependent project manager to resolve issues if the **Differences** persist. The driving project manager cannot **Accept** the **Differences**, because (s)he does not own the driven schedule. The visibility creates peer review and peer pressure to resolve issues and keep the integrated program schedule valid.

Don'ts

➤ Don't delete an externally linked task.
If you delete an anchor task (task with an external dependency), you remove the external link as well.

➤ Don't cut and paste an externally linked task.
If you cut a task that has an external dependency using the clipboard tools, you will break the link. Instead, move it by dragging. Cutting a task is temporarily deleting it, and the link will be lost. The link may even be re-routed to another task in a best guess by Project 2010.

➤ Don't set the cross project links to your project summary tasks.
We don't recommend this because the external tasks will not be visible to the other project manager and may cause confusion. Don't allow other project managers to link to your project summary task. Nothing can be shown above project summary task with ID 0 (zero) in the task list in Project 2010. Those links will only be visible in the master schedule. In Chapter 5 you can find a more extended explanation.

> ➤ Don't open two schedules with **Differences** between them on one computer unless you are using a master-schedule.
>
> As soon as you open both schedules and edit them, all **Differences** between the two schedules are automatically accepted, even if you have just read-only rights to the other schedule. If you want to keep the **Differences**, save and close the one schedule first, and then open the second one. Make a quick screenshot if you want to compare the schedules. If you have read-write access to both schedules and save them, all differences will be automatically accepted without a prompt.

> ➤ Don't create long chains between many serial projects.
>
> If a project manager who is in the middle of the chain goes on vacation, the successor project managers will not see any impacts during his vacation. The chain will be only as strong as its weakest link.

 When dealing with cross-linked projects you should avoid not accepting those changes to your schedule made by another project manager without first talking to the original project manager who made the change. Not accepting changes (in the **Link Between Projects** dialog, click [Close]) certainly will not affect the tasks in your schedule, but it does not mean there is no dependency.

Analyzing the Critical Path by Gate

If you have a truly integrated program schedule with a series of subprojects that are all dependent upon one another, there should only be one critical path. All paths should come together in the program finish milestone.

But the critical path in a large schedule of 10,000 tasks can easily comprise a thousand tasks. This is too many to make sense of; we have to change the way we analyze the critical path in a large schedule.

In large program schedules, there are often several major milestones or gates with hard deadline dates. These constraints can cut the large network into independent sub networks. Now you can analyze each sub network and avoid having to deal with more data than you can analyze.

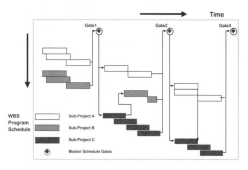

We recommend that you focus on one milestone at a time, and find the critical path on the milestone.

You can find the critical path on a gate milestone by looking at the amount of total slack of its predecessors and identifying the tasks that have the same (or smaller or more negative) amount of total slack. That predecessor is driving the gate milestone.

You can analyze a gate milestone by using various tools explained in previous chapters, mainly chapters 9 and 11. These tools range from very simple to more sophisticated:

➤ Task Inspect: Here you can trace back all the factors affecting a path of tasks. Select the task gate (milestone) and on the **Task** tab, in the **Tasks** group, click **Inspect**.

➤ The Tracking Gantt view differentiates the critical and non-critical tasks.

➤ The Schedule Table which allows you to review the Free Slack and Total Slack of tasks.

➤ You can apply a filter of Critical tasks or Date Range.

➤ You can create a custom field to classify tasks affecting a specific gate. Then create a filter or a group to see the specific gate tasks and create a view where you can differentiate critical and non critical tasks, and also see the total slack to perform the analysis.

➤ Create a Macro that helps you perform this analysis.

Creating a Central Resource Pool

A resource pool is a group of resources available for assignment to project tasks. It can be used by only one project or shared by multiple projects.

After you consolidate files into a master project file, the resources for the consolidated files remain separate. If you change resource information in the master project, the changes will be replicated in the subproject's source file. But you can't assign a resource to any project other than the subproject it came from.

If you insert several subproject schedules that have resources assigned to tasks, your master schedule Resource Sheet may contain duplicate resource names. This can be a real mess to try to straighten out. A single, central resource pool can be used to:

➤ Prevent duplications in the master schedule's resource sheet

➤ Facilitate the management of a large resource pool

➤ Standardize resource information within each schedule

In the Resource Sheet view, you can see to which projects the resources belong.

Repeated Resource Names from different projects can be listed in the master schedule.

	ⓘ	Project	Resource Name	Type	Material	Initials	Group	Max.	Std. Rate
1		Sub-Project A	Mario Landa	Work		ML	SME	100%	$50.00/hr
2		Sub-Project A	John White	Work			SME	100%	$50.00/hr
3		Sub-Project A	Cindy Lewis	Work		CL	SME	100%	$50.00/hr
4		Sub-Project A	Ed Lively	Work		EL	SME	100%	$50.00/hr
5		Sub-Project A	Anson Caliste	Work		AC	SME	100%	$50.00/hr
6		Sub-Project A	Rodolfo Ambriz	Work		RA	SME	100%	$50.00/hr
7		Sub-Project A	Rafael Ruiz	Work		RR	SME	100%	$50.00/hr
1		ABC Master Project	Mario Landa	Work		ML	SME	100%	$0.00/hr
2		ABC Master Project	Rafael Ruiz	Work		RR	SME	100%	$0.00/hr

If you create a centralized resource pool, you may also want to delegate a single individual or the project management office to maintain this file by keeping resource information current and making sure it's backed-up

	ⓘ	Project	Resource Name	Type	Material	Initials	Group	Max.	Std. Rate
1		ABC ResourcePool	Instructional Designer	Work		IDS		100%	$50.00/hr
2		ABC ResourcePool	Editor	Work		ED		100%	$50.00/hr
3		ABC ResourcePool	Graphic Designer	Work		GD		200%	$50.00/hr
4		ABC ResourcePool	Subject Matter Expert	Work		SME		700%	$50.00/hr
5		ABC ResourcePool	Support	Work		MXST		100%	$50.00/hr
6		ABC ResourcePool	Mario Landa	Work		ML	SME	100%	$50.00/hr
7		ABC ResourcePool	John White	Work		JK	SME	100%	$50.00/hr
8		ABC ResourcePool	Cindy Lewis				SME	100%	$50.00/hr
9		ABC ResourcePool	Ed Lively				SME	100%	$50.00/hr
10		ABC ResourcePool	Anson Caliste				SME	100%	$50.00/hr
11		ABC ResourcePool	Rodolfo Ambriz	Work		RA	SME	100%	$50.00/hr
12		ABC ResourcePool	Rafael Ruiz	Work		RR	SME	100%	$50.00/hr
13		ABC ResourcePool	John Winter	Work		JW	SME	100%	$50.00/hr
14		ABC ResourcePool	Jorge Fernández	Work		JF	MXST	100%	$50.00/hr
15		ABC ResourcePool	Alejandro Acevedo	Work		AA	MXST	100%	$50.00/hr
16		ABC ResourcePool	Heather Nolan	Work		HN	GD	100%	$50.00/hr
17		ABC ResourcePool	Alfonso Hernández	Work		AH	MXST	100%	$50.00/hr
18		ABC ResourcePool	Kristen Zekunde	Work		KZ	GD	100%	$50.00/hr
19		ABC ResourcePool	Luis M Arroyo	Work		LA	SME	100%	$50.00/hr
20		ABC ResourcePool	Francisco Ambriz	Work		FA	SME	100%	$50.00/hr
21		ABC ResourcePool	Guillermo Ambriz	Work		GA	MXST	100%	$50.00/hr
22		ABC ResourcePool	Andrés Cuevas	Work		AO	MXST	100%	$50.00/hr
23		ABC ResourcePool	Illeana Galipienzo	Work		IG	MXST	100%	$50.00/hr
24		ABC ResourcePool	Jane Davenport	Work		JD	ED	100%	$50.00/hr
25		ABC ResourcePool	Publisher	Material	FFP Contract	JROSS			$200,000.00

Only one resource pool with no duplicates

There are two approaches to creating a central resource pool. One is appropriate if you don't have any existing projects using resources. The second approach takes advantage of existing schedules with resources to quickly build the central resource pool, keeping rates, skills, and general information current.

Building a Resource Pool

Whenever you have schedules without resources, you can begin building your resource pool from scratch. To do this:

1. Open a new blank schedule. Save and name this file <*ABC Resource Pool*>, where **ABC** stands for your company's or division's name.

2. Go to the **Resource Sheet** view (**View** tab, **Resource Views** group, **Resource Sheet**) and enter each resource's name and information, just as you would for a single project. This time you will include all resources to be shared.

3. The Resource Pool file must be open to allow project schedules to use the pool.

4. Open the project that will be using these resources. On the **Resource** tab, in the **Assignments** group, click 📇 **Resource Pool, Share Resources**. The **Share Resources** dialog opens.

5. Under **Resources for** <ABCProject>, select the radio button that reads **Use Resources From** and click the box to select the resource pool <*ABC Resource Pool*>.

6. Under **On conflict with calendar or resource information**, chose either ◉ **Pool takes precedence** or ◉ **Sharer takes precedence** to resolve conflicts in a manner consistent with your organization's policies. (We suggest that in the event of a conflict, the resource pool should take precedence.)

If you go to the schedule's Resource Sheet view, you will now see all of the resources that were listed in the resource pool.

Building a Resource Pool from Existing Schedules

If you have schedules that already contain entries in the Resource Sheet view, you can capitalize on this to facilitate the building of the resource pool.

You can either clean the project with the Resource Sheet entries of all tasks, assignments, etc.; or migrate the resource database to a new project. (To migrate the resources click the **ID**-number of the rows you want to take, right-click, and in the floating list, select **Copy**. Then go to the Resource Sheet view of the new file, select the first available row, and on the **Task** tab, in the **Clipboard** group, click **Paste**.)

 You should standardize all of the resource names and information in the schedules before creating the resource pool. If any of the names are spelled differently or if nicknames are used, there will be an entry in the resource pool for every name variation.

 If your company intends to move to an enterprise project management solution such as Project Server, you may want to consider using a resource naming convention that is consistent with either your application in Outlook or Active Directory, depending on where you contemplate importing resources from.

Working with a Resource Pool

When you open the resource pool you will be prompted with an Open Resource Pool dialog. You will need to select from the following options:

➤ ◉ **Open resource pool read-only allowing others to work on projects connected to the pool**. This option will allow you to analyze all the assignments by using the **Team Planner** view or the **Resource Usage** view.

➤ ◉ **Open resource pool read-write so that you can make changes to resource information (like pay rates, etc.), although this will lock**

others out of updating the pool with new information. This option, will allow you to edit certain characteristics of the resources; it won't allow you to level any over-allocation of the resources.

> ◉ **Open resource pool read-write and all other sharer files into a new master project file. You can access this new master project file from the View tab, Switch Windows command**. This option will allow you to modify the resource characteristics (calendar, pay rates, etc.) and also will allow you to level any over-allocation by using the same methods discussed in chapter 9.

Adding more and more cross-linked projects to a centralized resource pool will degrade performance. If you start to see performance suffer, you may want to consider going to Project Server.

Baselining a Master Schedule

When you baseline a Master Schedule (consolidated schedule), keep in mind that you are working with a project file with its tasks; the project summary tasks of sub-schedules are the regular tasks for the Master schedule. When you set the baseline by following the standard process (**Project** tab, **Schedule** group, **Set Baseline**, **Set Baseline**, **Entire project**, **OK**), you are setting the baseline for the regular tasks of the master project. As the project summary tasks of the sub-schedules are in this category, they will have a baseline but it will not include the sub-tasks of those sub-schedules.

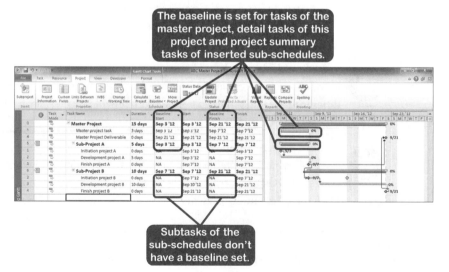

This approach can be very helpful when the master schedule manager wants to set a baseline to measure the performance of the master schedule, allowing the sub-schedule managers to set their own performance baselines. In the case of a program, the program manager will be able to measure against his commitments with the program board, while the project managers of sub-schedules will measure against their own commitments with the program manager.

The baseline of master schedules is easy to review in the **Tracking Gantt** view or by applying some simple commands on the **Format** tab. However, to review the baseline of the sub-projects summary, follow these steps:

1. On the **Format** tab, in the **Bar Styles** group, click **Format**, **Bar Styles**. The **Bar Styles** dialog appears.

2. Scroll down to the first available row, and on the **Name** column write <**Baseline Summary**>, in the **Show For ... Tasks** column, type **Project Summary**, **Summary.**

3. In the **From** column, select **Baseline Start** and in the **To** column, select **Baseline Finish.**

4. At the bottom of the dialog, click the **Bars** tab and in the zone **Middle**, in the **Shape** field select the option you prefer and in the **Color** field select a dark color.

For the **Shape** field, we suggest you use the 4th option which is a thin box aligned to the bottom of the Gantt.

Set the Sub-Schedules Baseline

If the master schedule manager and the sub-schedule managers agree on the same performance baseline, you can set the baseline for all the tasks by following the next steps:

1. In the master schedule, ensure all the tasks are displayed. Select all tasks and on the **View** tab, in the **Data** group, click **Outline**, **All Subtasks**.

2. On the **Project** tab, in the **Schedule** group, click ⬚ **Set Baseline**, **Set Baseline.** The **Set Baseline** dialog appears.

3. Under **For**, click the ◉ **Selected** tasks.

4. Under Roll up baselines check the ☑ **To all summary tasks**.

5. Click [OK].

An alternative approach to establish commitment is to set the baseline in the Master Schedule to the master project level, but do the actual baselining in each of the subproject schedules.

Using separate performance baselines between the master schedule and the sub-schedules can be very helpful to measure different levels of commitment, however it is important that the different stakeholders receive the appropriate information. The person in charge of coordinating the performance baselines should be very skilled at this, otherwise you run the risk of measuring lots and lots of information but losing control.

Final Thoughts on Consolidated Schedules

1. Leveling resources from individual schedules that are shared with other projects will not take into account the over-allocation in other projects.

2. Since not all dependencies can be complete until the subproject schedules are consolidated, optimization should wait until leveling and dependencies can be reviewed in the consolidated schedule.

3. Because of number 1 and 2 above, you can't gain agreement from stakeholders on finalized dates and costs.

4. Due to 1, 2, and 3 above, you should wait to baseline the schedule until after the consolidation has been accomplished (unless it is a "temporary/preliminary" baseline for impact analysis). In these cases you may want to use the rolling wave planning approach explained in chapters 3 and 4, where commitments to earlier phases can be established but later phases are set in a high-level plan.

Index

Q

R